The Jossey-Bass Nonprofit and Public Management Series also includes:

Hank Rosso's
Achieving Excellence
in Fund Raising

The Center on Philanthropy
at Indiana University
Indiana University–Purdue University Indianapolis

The Center on Philanthropy at Indiana University strives to increase the understanding of philanthropy and nonprofit management and improve their practice in the United States and internationally. The Center on Philanthropy also fosters relationships in the growing field of philanthropic and nonprofit studies. Through research, teaching, professional development and training, and public service and public affairs initiatives, the Center on Philanthropy is increasing knowledge about philanthropy and helping to develop the next generation of nonprofit professionals, scholars, volunteers, and philanthropists.

Founded in 1987, the Center on Philanthropy pioneered the field of Philanthropic Studies, a unique, interdisciplinary approach to studying philanthropy through the lens of the liberal arts that also incorporates the expertise of professional schools, including public affairs, business, law, education, social work, medicine and nursing. Today, more than sixty philanthropic studies faculty members in twenty-one disciplines conduct research and teach philanthropy and nonprofit management.

The Center on Philanthropy at Indiana University conducts basic and applied research, and seeks to build a closer relationship between research and professional practice in the nonprofit sector. The idea that university research and information on best practices informs and strengthens the work of nonprofit professionals and that the experience of professional practice informs research is one of the core principles that led to the creation of the Center on Philanthropy and remains a hallmark of its work today.

More than fifteen graduate, undergraduate, and doctoral-level academic program options available through the Center on Philanthropy, including online and executive courses, allow students to learn both the "how to" and the "why" of nonprofit management and philanthropy. The Center's programs encourage mid-career students and those new to the field to become reflective professionals who understand and consider the cultural, economic, historical, and social context and implications of the work they do and help them enhance their skills through critiquing, teaching, and reinforcing philanthropy's values.

Hank Rosso chose the Center on Philanthropy to be the home of The Fund Raising School, the only international, university, and curriculum-based fund raising education program. Since its founding in 1974, The Fund Raising School has taught successful, professional, ethical fund raising, volunteer board leadership, and nonprofit management practices to more than thirty thousand people from more than ten thousand organizations on six continents. Experienced fund raising professionals associated with the Center offer multiple sessions of nine different, regularly scheduled courses at The Fund Raising School in Indianapolis and in cities across the United States.

The Center on Philanthropy at Indiana University is headquartered at Indiana University–Purdue University Indianapolis (IUPUI) and offers programs on the IUPUI and Indiana University Bloomington campuses.

For more information, please contact:

The Center on Philanthropy at Indiana University
550 W. North Street, Suite 301
Indianapolis, IN 46202-3272
Telephone: 317-274-4200
Fax: 317-684-8900

Hank Rosso's Achieving Excellence in Fund Raising

2nd Edition

Henry A. Rosso and Associates
Eugene R. Tempel, editor

Foreword by Paulette Maehara

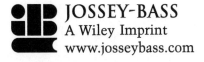

JOSSEY-BASS
A Wiley Imprint
www.josseybass.com

Published by Jossey-Bass
A Wiley Imprint
989 Market Street, San Francisco, CA 94103-1741   www.josseybass.com

Jossey-Bass books and products are available through most bookstores. To contact Jossey-Bass directly call our Customer Care Department within the U.S. at 800-956-7739, outside the U.S. at 317-572-3986 or fax 317-572-4002.

Jossey-Bass also publishes its books in a variety of electronic formats. Some content that appears in print may not be available in electronic books.

Credits are on page 532.

Library of Congress Cataloging-in-Publication Data

Rosso, Henry A., date.
[Achieving excellence in fund raising]
Hank Rosso's Achieving excellence in fund raising / Henry A. Rosso and associates ; Eugene R. Tempel, editor ; foreword by Paulette Maehara.—
2nd ed.
p. cm.—(The Jossey-Bass nonprofit and public management series)
Includes bibliographical references and index.
ISBN 0-7879-6256-2 (alk. paper)
1. Fund raising. I. Tempel, Eugene R., date. II. Title. III. Series.
HG177.R67 2003
658.15'224—dc21

2003001222

Printed in the United States of America
SECOND EDITION
HB Printing   10 9 8 7 6 5 4 3 2

The Jossey-Bass
Nonprofit and Public Management Series

*This book is dedicated
to continuing the legacy of Hank Rosso*

CONTENTS

TABLES, FIGURES,
AND EXHIBITS

EXHIBITS

FOREWORD

Has it really been twelve years since the release of *Achieving Excellence in Fund Raising*? In 1991, I was a fund raiser at the American Red Cross of the National Capital Chapter. In the intervening years, and especially during my tenure as President and CEO of the Association of Fundraising Professionals (AFP), I have observed firsthand the remarkable growth of philanthropic fund raising throughout the world, particularly in North America. The leadership and scholarship of Hank Rosso have influenced much of this growth.

Hank inspired by example. In his preface to this second edition, Gene Tempel tells us that Hank, in founding The Fund Raising School in San Francisco and in his teaching, writing, and leadership "found ways to help fund raisers substitute pride for apology in their work . . . [and] to recognize the importance of the public purposes supported by their work."

Through his pioneering work in professional development, Hank also left a legacy that continues in the extensive educational outreach of The Fund Raising School and the Center on Philanthropy.

AFP, then the National Society of Fundraising Executives (NSFRE), recognized Hank's contribution to the profession when it named him the Outstanding Fundraising Executive for 1985. The NSFRE recognized *Achieving Excellence in Fund Raising* with the Staley Robeson Prize in 1992. Given Hank's preeminence in the profession, it is fitting that this second edition of *Achieving Excellence* be released. This fine work will ensure that Hank's legacy will continue to inspire new generations of fund raisers. I commend Gene Tempel, The Center on Philanthropy, The Fund Raising School, and the authors who appear in this edition for their contribution to our literature.

PAULETTE MAEHARA
President and CEO
Association of Fundraising Professionals

A WORD ON
THE FIRST EDITION

The Center on Philanthropy and the editor and authors of *Hank Rosso's Achieving Excellence in Fund Raising,* second edition, acknowledge all the individuals who played a role in the first edition, *Achieving Excellence in Fund Raising.* First and foremost, we pay homage to Henry A. (Hank) Rosso, who conceived of the book and wrote eight of its twenty-three chapters. Hank created a structure for disseminating the wisdom of The Fund Raising School more broadly and recruited colleagues to share their knowledge along with his own.

Achieving Excellence was a major success. Over the past twelve years, more than seventeen thousand copies have been sold, enabling many to learn about the Rosso model and the Rosso philosophy.

This volume is dedicated to the contribution that Hank and his associates made in establishing fund raising as an ethical professional practice. That contribution earned *Achieving Excellence* the Association of Fundraising Professionals' Staley Robeson Prize in 1992.

FIRST EDITION AUTHORS AND THEIR CHAPTER TITLES

Phyllis A. Allen	"How to Research and Analyze Individual Donors"
Bonita M. Bergin	"Assessing Costs, Risks, and Results"
Phillip S. Brain Jr.	"Establishing a Planned Giving Program"

Roger M. Craver	"The Power of Mail to Acquire, Renew, and Upgrade the Gift"
Robert E. Fogal	"Standards and Ethics in Fund Raising"
Arthur C. Frantzreb	"Seeking the Big Gift"
Jane C. Geever	"How to Select and Use Fund Raising Consultants"
Kay Sprinkel Grace	"Leadership and Team Building"
	"Managing for Results"
	"Resources for Strengthening Fund Raising Skills"
Kim Klein	"Fund Raising at the Grass Roots Level"
Sheree Parris Nudd	"Thinking Strategically About Information"
Henry A. Rosso	"A Philosophy of Fund Raising"
	"Asset Building Through Capital Fund Raising"
	"Developing a Constituency: Where Fund Raising Begins"
	"Preparing a Case That Empowers Fund Raising"
	"Putting It All Together: The Integrated Development Plan"
	"The Annual Fund: A Building Block for Fund Raising"
	"The Trustee's Role in Fund Raising"
	"Understanding the Fund Raising Cycle"
K. Scott Sheldon	"Corporations as a Gift Market"
	"Foundations as a Source of Support"
Eugene R. Tempel	"Assessing Organizational Strengths and Vulnerabilities"

PREFACE

In the Foreword to *Achieving Excellence in Fund Raising,* Robert Payton predicted that Henry A. (Hank) Rosso's book would become a classic. It has. He predicted that readers would refer to the work as "Rosso." They do. Through "Rosso," tens of thousands of readers have been introduced to Hank's philosophy and to the principles of ethical philanthropic fund raising by which he lived. Through "Rosso," he expanded his audience far beyond the individuals he was able to reach directly through The Fund Raising School, which he founded. Fund raising, he taught, is the servant of philanthropy; it plays a quiet and dignified role. But we should not claim more than that. That is how Hank taught us to think about our roles as professionals. We could serve philanthropic interests by helping donors and organizations with common values and interests come together. But fund raising is not, he believed, about "getting gifts" or "making philanthropy happen." One of his basic goals was to substitute pride for apology in our work, to recognize the importance of the public purposes supported by our work, and to let the power of the case elicit the gift.

Hank created believers and disciples out of everyone he touched. Today fund raisers who call themselves disciples of Rosso carry out their work based on his teachings. The Center on Philanthropy at Indiana University owes its founding to Hank. And The Fund Raising School has continued to develop and expand thanks to the wisdom of the principles he espoused—the very principles that gave substance to *Achieving Excellence.*

When *Achieving Excellence* made its debut in 1991, it was one of the first texts to focus on philanthropy, fund raising, and nonprofit management. It was published just when U.S. colleges and universities began to take the study of these subjects seriously. Today we know much more about philanthropy, fund raising, and nonprofit organizations than we knew in 1991, and much in those areas has changed dramatically. Why, the World Wide Web did not even exist when Hank submitted his final text to Jossey-Bass!

Hank Rosso died on February 1, 1999. But his legacy lives among the practitioners whose work he inspired and at the Center on Philanthropy, especially The Fund Raising School, where the basic principles Hank espoused have been expanded and adapted and have become increasingly substantiated with research. The world of philanthropy and fund raising that Hank knew and the response to its needs may have changed dramatically since *Achieving Excellence* was published, but the principles Hank developed and articulated through both his school and his book are as relevant to the twenty-first century as they were to the last decade of the twentieth. The Center on Philanthropy and Jossey-Bass therefore agreed that a new edition of *Achieving Excellence* would be an appropriate way to demonstrate the relevance of Hank's work to the twenty-first century and to adapt the principles contained in *Achieving Excellence* to the contemporary context for philanthropy and fund raising in the years to come.

The Center on Philanthropy honors Hank as one of its founders and readily agreed to be the organizational sponsor for this edition. The original authors of *Achieving Excellence in Fund Raising* often taught for Hank and based their work on the curriculum of The Fund Raising School as it was in 1991. This new edition is written by authors who worked with Hank and who are carrying on in his spirit through our work with the Center on Philanthropy and The Fund Raising School.

This edition reflects the current curriculum of The Fund Raising School as it has evolved since the 1990s, based on the principles that Hank espoused. The school has developed special courses on the annual fund and capital campaign, and the Center on Philanthropy has set up international operations that have translated the courses into Spanish and Portuguese; German versions are currently under development. The faculty has been expanded nationally and internationally, new relationships and partnerships have been established, and faculty and staff at the Center on Philanthropy have embraced new knowledge to enhance the curriculum of The Fund Raising School. The authors of this edition have worked closely with The Fund Raising School and have contributed to its development.

Over the past twelve years, the nonprofit sector has grown dramatically and has become both more visible and more vulnerable. Hank's focus on stewardship and accountability as essential aspects of fund raising has given and continues to give us valuable guidance in this new environment.

In 1991, the *Giving USA* estimate of total philanthropic support was $105 billion; a decade later, it had doubled to $212 billion (AAFRC Trust for Philanthropy, 2002). In 1991, the country entered a recession, but the rest of the decade saw economic growth. The stock market went from 2,736.40 in January 1991 to 10,021.60 in January 2002 ("Historical Prices," 2002). New-technology companies created new wealth. Gifts to create new foundations became so significant that in 1996, *Giving USA* began reporting gifts to foundations to account for the philanthropy going to establish new foundations or donor-advised or donor-designated funds in community foundations. The core principles of an external orientation focusing on donors, connecting to donors based on common values and intersects, are helpful in dealing with the increased sophistication and complexity of donors and funders.

From 1991 to 2002, membership in the Association of Fundraising Professionals (AFP) grew from 12,644 members and 117 chapters to 25,563 members and 165 chapters. If AFP membership is reflective of growth in the fund raising profession generally, nonprofit organizations expanded their fund raising staffs dramatically to generate philanthropy from this growing wealth. The professional stance that Hank urged us to adopt has become even more important in dealing with this larger professional workforce.

GROWTH OF THE NONPROFIT SECTOR

Philanthropy and nonprofit organizations have always played a significant role in American society. But they play an even more significant role today. The nonprofit sector has grown to be a larger part of the U.S. economy. Between 1977 and 1997, the annual growth in income of the nonprofit (independent) sector was 3.2 percent, compared to 2.2 percent for business and 1.5 percent for government. The growth of employment in the nonprofit sector during that period outpaced both the public and for-profit sectors by a similar rate. Current operating expenditures for the nonprofit sector as a percentage of gross domestic product more than doubled from 3.8 percent in 1960 to 8.5 percent in 1999. Finally, the total number of 501(c)(3) organizations, not including religious congregations, more than doubled between 1982 and 1998, increasing from 322,000 to 734,000 (INDEPENDENT SECTOR, 2001b). This is the demand side of philanthropy. There are more opportunities for volunteer involvement and gift making. The focus on mission that Hank espoused is key for successful volunteer engagement and fund raising in this expanded array of opportunities for volunteers and donors.

SHIFTS IN INCOME SOURCES AND USES

Nonprofit organizations have become less dependent on philanthropy and more dependent on private sector payments or fees and government payments. According to INDEPENDENT SECTOR (2002), private contributions accounted for 23 percent of the income source in 1987 and 20 percent in 1997. Private sector payments or fees were 41 percent in 1987 and 38 percent in 1997. Government payments contributed 28 percent of nonprofit's income source in 1987 and 31 percent in 1997. The challenge for nonprofit organizations is to increase the share of income from philanthropy. Ethical philanthropic fund raising is essential to increasing the philanthropic share. The philanthropic share of nonprofit income is what distinguishes the sector: pluralistic response by individuals, protecting the minority from the tyranny of the majority represented by government funding, and making certain that services that are available for a fee to people who can pay market rates are also available to those who cannot pay.

As noted, overall giving reached $212 billion in 2001, twice the 1991 level. Individual contributions and bequests made up 83.5 percent of total giving in 2001, with individual giving accounting for 75.8 percent and bequests for 7.7 percent of all contributions. This is compared to a combined share of 87.6 percent in 1991, with individuals at 80.2 percent and bequests at 7.4 percent of total giving. Foundations and corporations comprise the remaining 16.5 percent of total giving for 2001 and 12.4 percent in 1991. Giving by foundations was 12.2 percent of the total in 2001 and 7.4 percent in 1991, and corporations contributed 4.3 percent of the total in 2001 and 4.9 percent in 1991.

The uses of philanthropic gifts also experienced drastic changes. Share of total gifts received in the sectors of education, human services, health, public and society benefit, environment, and unallocated gifts and gifts to foundations all increased. Giving to education was 10.6 percent of the total in 1991 and 15.0 percent in 2001, while the health sector's share grew from 7.8 percent in 1991 to 8.7 percent in 2001. In 1991, human services received 8.5 percent, public and society benefit received 4.0 percent, and the environment received 2.0 percent; ten years later, the figures were 9.8 percent, 3.0 percent, and 5.6 percent, respectively. Unallocated gifts and gifts to foundations grew from 3.8 percent to 12.1 percent. In three sectors—religion; art, culture, and the humanities; and international—percentage share decreased over the same period. Religion received 54.2 percent in 1991 and 38.2 percent in 2001; arts, culture, and the humanities dropped from 7.1 percent in 1991 to 5.6 percent in 2001; and gifts to the international sector were 2.1 percent of the total in 1991 and 2.0 percent in 2001 (AAFRC Trust for Philanthropy, 2002).

Total giving as a percentage of gross domestic product (GDP) in the United States has remained stable: around 2.1 percent of the total in the year 2001 and

2.2 percent ten years earlier (AAFRC Trust for Philanthropy, 2002). In many countries, particularly in Europe, philanthropy can reach 0.5 percent of GDP. Many countries engage in fund raising, often based on long-standing traditions. But there is global interest in adapting U.S. fund raising systems.

ORGANIZATION OF THIS BOOK

This new edition takes all these factors into account. All chapters from the original except Rosso's "A Philosophy of Fund Raising" have been rewritten and updated, and eleven new chapters have been added to deal with the changing environment, new fund raising opportunities, technological developments, and the continuing professional development of fund raising.

The thirty-four chapters in this new edition are grouped into seven parts. Part One contains two chapters that provide a contemporary context for philanthropy and Hank's classic original chapter, "A Philosophy of Fund Raising," with a commentary on its continuing relevance.

Part Two is about institutional readiness. Its chapters take us from planning for fund raising to the "total development plan." The material in these five chapters will help organizations take the initial steps in planning, environmental assessment, constituency identification, and mission and case development on which successful fund raising is built.

Part Three provides insights on the various programs organizations can develop as part of the total development plan. Hank challenged every student who came to The Fund Raising School to work toward the total development program. Not every organization can implement all aspects of the program immediately, but every organization should plan to implement each aspect as it can make the case for support and identify the potential donors for that program.

The first step in any fund raising endeavor is the development of a functioning annual fund program. Chapter Eight outlines the purposes of the annual fund, the roles it plays in a total development program, and steps to be taken to develop and maintain an annual fund program.

The four remaining chapters in Part Three deal with increasing donor involvement and increasing donor contributions to the organization. Chapter Nine outlines the essentials of establishing a major gifts program. Gifts of significance to both the donor and the organization are essential to meeting organizational needs and building the total development program. Many organizations have developed special initiatives to build endowment funds just as capital campaigns have traditionally helped organizations meet major capital needs for buildings, grounds, and equipment. Chapters Ten and Eleven provide information on these two initiatives. Chapter Twelve is an introduction to planned giving and outlines the steps necessary for organizing a planned giving program.

Large, complex campaigns often combine many of these programs—for example, including annual gifts, endowment gifts, and planned gifts in a single effort. Part Three will help readers understand the fundamentals for operating a total development program and the variations that are possible.

Part Four is dedicated to the various sources of philanthropic support that are available: individuals who make both lifetime and bequest gifts, corporations, and foundations. (We do not deal with government funding because it is not philanthropic support, although readers should realize that for many nonprofit organizations, government funding is the most significant source of support.)

This edition includes three new chapters focusing on individuals: "Women as Donors," "Contemporary Approaches to Philanthropy," and "Embracing Diversity in Fund Raising." Women are a significant force in philanthropy and often approach it differently from men, as explained in Chapter Sixteen. Much has been written and said about the "new donor"; Chapter Seventeen provides some useful perspectives for the fund raising professional. Part Four ends with a chapter on how different cultures approach philanthropy.

Part Five deals with special strategies for fund raising. Chapter Nineteen on direct mail is updated from the first edition. Direct mail continues to be a very successful fund raising strategy for many organizations. It is often the way small and relatively new nonprofit organizations begin their fund raising programs. Many nonprofits have also discovered the power of the Internet; Chapter Twenty provides background on how this new medium can be used at all levels of fund raising. Chapter Twenty-One illustrates the many uses of special events at different levels of the total development program and provides structures and forms for organizing them. The part closes with another chapter from the first edition, a special look at grassroots fund raising, reviewing how Rosso's total development plan can be adapted to small neighborhood or grassroots organizations.

Part Six is dedicated to the various aspects of managing a successful fund raising program. For Hank, fund raising was a management function to be integrated with other management functions, such as finance and administration. Chapter Twenty-Three deals with the various activities that have to be managed in a development program. Chapter Twenty-Four deals with exercising leadership through fund raising, involving volunteers, and building fund raising teams to carry out significant tasks. Chapter Twenty-Five looks at the board's engagement in the development of the mission and resources as well as its role in fund raising. Separate chapters deal with using information in the fund raising process and the role of technology, especially new technologies, in managing a fund raising program.

Part Six closes with two chapters that fund raisers must make part of their fund raising management skills. Hank used to say that it costs money to raise money. Chapter Twenty-Eight gives readers some guidance and presents budgeting as a management tool. The final chapter in this part is dedicated to helping successful fund raising executives learn how to use consultants as part of the fund raising team.

Part Seven deals with what Hank called "professional stance." Chapter Thirty is dedicated to ethical decision making in fund raising. It reminds us that Hank was committed to ethical philanthropic fund raising. Another of his maxims was that "fund raising begins with the board." Chapter Thirty-One is dedicated to stewardship. For Hank, stewardship was the most fundamental responsibility of nonprofit organizations serving the public good.

Fund raising is practiced internationally, and the lessons of The Fund Raising School have been taught on every continent except Antarctica. Chapter Thirty-Two provides an overview of how the Rosso principles have been successfully adapted in various cultures outside the United States. Chapter Thirty-Three, an essay on fund raising as a profession, is based on the principles and philosophy of Henry Russo. Chapter Thirty-Four ends the book with highlights of organizations, associations, programs, and Web sites where we can learn more about the ethical and technological aspects of fund raising, to enhance our professional stance.

REFLECTIONS ON THIS NEW EDITION

Hank Rosso's Achieving Excellence in Fund Raising, second edition, has integrity as a holistic work. It flows systematically from beginning to end. It is structured to introduce the aspects of a total development program, the internal and external environment for operating the program, and the professional management of the program integrated with the nonprofit organization's other management functions.

But the book does not have to be read from beginning to end. Readers interested in ethics will probably turn first to Chapter Thirty. Readers seeking to understand the operation of the annual fund and also its relationship to other fund raising vehicles and strategies will find Chapter Eight instructive. Individual chapters can be read in isolation because each chapter is cross-referenced to related information in other chapters.

This book provides a foundation for practitioners, volunteers, and others involved in the fund raising process. It provides a broad understanding of the process to all who take part in fund raising, as well as a rationale for various initiatives for chief financial officers, program directors, chief executives, and other officers who make organizational decisions related to fund raising.

Hank Rosso's Achieving Excellence in Fund Raising, second edition, will make an excellent textbook for college and university courses on fund raising and resource development. It will also serve as an excellent text for the novice or mid-level practitioner who has some experience with part of the total development program but who wants to develop a professional career requiring management of the entire program. Portions of the text, especially Parts One and Seven, will be useful to senior professionals who are interested in planning and other organizational renewal activities and developing their professional stance materials. Volunteers and board members will find their roles discussed in each chapter but may have special interest in Chapters Twenty-Four, Thirty, and Thirty-One. Institutional colleagues will find the first two parts and Chapter Twenty-Eight on budgeting particularly helpful in understanding how the fund raising process works, how the various aspects of fund raising relate, and the long-term organizational and financial commitments required to achieve success in fund raising.

Our colleague at the Indiana University Foundation, Kent Dove, has produced a series of books on fund raising with Jossey-Bass. His texts provide additional information on various fund raising programs and support services. Our colleague at the Center on Philanthropy, Tim Seiler, is editing a series of workbooks for Jossey-Bass to help practitioners apply the principles of The Fund Raising School to their organizations. *Hank Rosso's Achieving Excellence in Fund Raising,* second edition, provides a conceptual framework for those two series of publications. Practitioners using selections from either series or both of them will find in this text the contextual knowledge, rationale, and structure for incorporating the information from Dove, Seiler, and their colleagues. "Rosso II" provides a framework for developing a professional career in ethical philanthropic fund raising and an avenue for incorporating other resources as that career develops.

The contributors to this book had more in mind than writing another book on fund raising. The authors are committed to the integrity, the ethics, the professional stance for which Hank stood. It was that commitment that brought us together to create *Hank Rosso's Achieving Excellence in Fund Raising.* We are at once humbled by the possibility of working on texts that Hank had written or edited himself and privileged to extend his legacy into the twenty-first century.

Indianapolis, Indiana   EUGENE R. TEMPEL
December 2002

ACKNOWLEDGMENTS

*H*ank Rosso's *Achieving Excellence in Fund Raising,* second edition, would not have been possible without the first edition. So the primary acknowledgment for this book goes to Hank Rosso, who founded The Fund Raising School and in 1991 accepted the challenge to share his knowledge and experience with a larger audience. As you will see throughout this book, the authors of this volume have learned well from Hank. Their writing acknowledges the role that Hank played in shaping the thinking reflected in it. All of us are extremely grateful for the role he played in building ethical philanthropic fund raising.

Second, we wish to thank Hank's widow, Dottie Rosso, for her consultations as we planned the second edition, for the role she played in helping us think through the issues, and for the encouragement she gave us to continue Hank's legacy.

The Center on Philanthropy and Jossey-Bass have worked on many projects together. We appreciate the ongoing support of Dorothy Hearst and Johanna Vondeling, our editors at Jossey-Bass, who shared a vision for perpetuating Hank's legacy through this second edition.

Maggie Tittle, my graduate assistant during the 2001–2002 academic year, has made major contributions to this volume. Her management of the process, her search for missing data, and her interaction with the authors made this volume possible. Much of her work on this project was of a volunteer nature because her primary responsibilities during that year were to support the work of the Nonprofit Academic Centers Council. She continued her work on the volume past her graduate assistantship, and the authors and I owe her a debt of gratitude for her contributions. I thank Heidi Baker, my graduate assistant for 2002–2003, for her assistance in managing the final stages of the editorial work. I thank my administrative secretary, Anna Fender, for her editorial assistance, her communication with the authors, and her help in keeping track of the project. In her own quiet way, she has made a major contribution to this book. I also thank my colleagues at the Center on Philanthropy who filled in for me, helped me with other duties, and generally covered for me when I was occupied with editorial activities.

Finally, I want to thank my own family. I want to thank my son Zach for extensive assistance in entering two sets of editorial changes into the computer-based text. He relieved my staff and me of a huge burden. I thank my son Jonathan for his editing assistance, my son Jason, and my wife, Mary, for their support and encouragement in what became a yearlong effort.

—E.R.T.

THE EDITOR

EUGENE R. TEMPEL became executive director of the Center on Philanthropy at Indiana University on August 1, 1997. He has been closely involved with the center since its inception in 1987, first helping to develop the concept for the center and later chairing its organizing and policy committees. He serves on the center's board of governors and was the first elected president of the Nonprofit Academic Centers Council, a national organization of university centers dedicated to teaching, research, and service related to philanthropy and the nonprofit sector.

Tempel is a nationally recognized expert in the study and practice of philanthropy and nonprofit management. Since 1988, he has held numerous leadership positions in the Association of Fundraising Professionals, currently serving on its Ethics Committee. *The NonProfit Times* has named him to its list of the country's fifty most influential leaders in the nonprofit sector each year since the list was created.

A professor of philanthropic studies, higher education, and public administration, Tempel's career as a nonprofit professional also includes more than two decades of administration, fund raising, and teaching in higher education. He previously served as vice chancellor of Indiana University–Purdue University Indianapolis and as vice president of the Indiana University Foundation. His professional experience includes teaching, training, and consulting internationally. He is a member of several nonprofit and for-profit boards of directors and is a current member and the immediate past chair of the Indiana Commission on Community Service and Volunteerism.

Tempel is the author or coauthor of several works in the field, including *Fund Raisers: Their Careers, Stories, Concerns, and Accomplishments* (Jossey-Bass, 1996), written with Margaret A. Duronio. He earned a B.A. degree in English and philosophy from St. Benedict College, an M.A. in English and a doctoral degree in higher education administration from Indiana University, and holds the Certified Fund Raising Executive professional designation.

The Center on Philanthropy is headquartered on the campus of Indiana University–Purdue University Indianapolis (IUPUI) and operates programs on the IUPUI and Indiana University Bloomington campuses.

THE AUTHORS

DWIGHT F. BURLINGAME, Ph.D., CFRE, is associate executive director and director of academic programs at the Indiana University Center on Philanthropy and a professor in the Graduate School, Philanthropic Studies, and School of Public and Environmental Affairs. He is also a member of the faculty for The Fund Raising School of the Center on Philanthropy at Indiana University. He holds degrees from Moorhead State University, the University of Illinois, and Florida State. He is an active member of the Association of Fundraising Professionals' Research Council and of the Association for Research on Nonprofit Organizations and Voluntary Action (ARNOVA), where he served as treasurer for five years.

Burlingame has authored or coauthored eight books, more than forty articles, and over one hundred book reviews. He has recently agreed to serve as editor of a three-volume encyclopedia of philanthropy in the United States, to be published by Clio Press. He is active in the nonprofit community and is a frequent speaker, consultant, and writer on topics relating to philanthropy, nonprofit organizations, libraries, and development.

ALICE GREEN BURNETTE, principal of Advancement Solutions, has spent nearly four decades in the field of institutional advancement, finding solutions to the management, fund raising, marketing, and communications problems of nonprofit and quasi-public institutions. She recently completed a national research and leadership development project known as The Privilege to Ask, jointly funded by the Lilly Endowment, Inc., and the Ford Foundation.

Burnette was awarded an honorary doctor of humane letters degree from the Morehouse School of Medicine in April 2000, and in August 2000, the Center on Philanthropy presented her with the Henry A. Rosso Medal.

A graduate of Wheaton College in Massachusetts, Burnette retired in 1998 from the Smithsonian Institution as assistant secretary for institutional advancement. At the Smithsonian, she supervised a $65 million campaign to build the National Museum of the American Indian and provided oversight of fund raising and marketing activities associated with the Smithsonian's sesquicentennial in 1996.

She was director of development at Morehouse College and at Howard University and was the founding director of the Office of Private Sector Development at the United States Peace Corps.

DANIEL CONWAY is a writer, teacher, and consultant. He specializes in the integration of stewardship principles with the practice of professional fund raising. Since 1999, he has served as senior vice president for RSI-Ketchum, Inc., a nationally respected consulting firm with expertise in stewardship education and capital fund raising. He is also a member of the faculty of The Fund Raising School of the Center on Philanthropy at Indiana University.

Conway has published many articles on stewardship and philanthropy. In 1992, he was the principal writer and editor of *The Reluctant Steward*, published by the Christian Theological Seminary and Saint Meinrad School of Theology with funding from Lilly Endowment, Inc. In 1997, he coedited, with Cecelia Hart Price, *The Practice of Stewardship in Religious Fundraising*, Volume 17 of the New Directions in Philanthropic Fundraising series published by Jossey-Bass. Conway also served as an adviser to the U.S. Bishops' Ad Hoc Committee on Stewardship and contributed to their publication, *Stewardship and Development for Parishes and Dioceses: A Resource Manual*. A new publication edited by Dan Conway, *The Reluctant Steward Revisited*, was released by the Saint Meinrad School of Theology in 2002.

ELIZABETH A. ELKAS is assistant dean for development at the Indiana University School of Medicine. For fifteen years, she has helped build the program from a three-person shop focusing on annual gifts to a twenty-eight-person comprehensive development program engaged in its second capital campaign.

After working for a major U.S. pharmaceutical company, in 1985 she accepted a position with the Indiana University Foundation, where she focused on major gifts. During this time, she met Hank Rosso and Gene Tempel as the two men collaborated to bring The Fund Raising School to Indiana University. For the past decade, Elkas has relished the opportunity to pass on their principles as a faculty member of The Fund Raising School of the Indiana University Center on Philanthropy.

KAY SPRINKEL GRACE, CFRE, is a San Francisco–based organizational consultant, providing workshops and consultation to local, regional, national, and international organizations in campaign strategies, case and board development, staff development, and other issues related to leadership of the fund raising process. She has been a member of the faculty of The Fund Raising School since 1980 and serves on its advisory board.

She is the author of *Beyond Fund Raising: New Strategies for Nonprofit Innovation and Investment* (Wiley, 1997) and coauthor, with Alan L. Wendroff, of *High Impact Philanthropy: How Donors, Boards, and Nonprofit Organizations Can Transform Communities* (Wiley, 2000). She has published articles for *Fund Raising Management, Advancing Philanthropy,* and *Contributions.* She is the author of *The Board's Role in Strategic Planning.*

Her B.A. and M.A. are from Stanford University, where she served for two years as the first woman volunteer chair of the Stanford Fund, an annual fund. She served for three years as chair of the University of San Francisco Institute for Nonprofit Organization Management Advisory Board and is on the board of the Women's Philanthropy Institute and the Djerassi Resident Artist Program in Woodside, California.

JAMES M. GREENFIELD began his fund raising career in 1962 and has served three colleges and universities and five hospitals. In February 2001, he completed fourteen years as senior vice president for resource development at Hoag Memorial Hospital Presbyterian in Newport Beach, California, where he also was executive director of the Hoag Hospital Foundation. He is also a member of the faculty of The Fund Raising School of the Center on Philanthropy at Indiana University.

The author and editor of six books and more than thirty-five journal articles, Greenfield has pioneered assessment studies of fund raising practice. His *Fund-Raising Cost Effectiveness: A Self-Assessment Workbook* (Wiley, 1996) remains a seminal work in this field to assist fund raising professionals in formal evaluation of their results.

Greenfield was honored by the Association of Healthcare Philanthropy with its Harold J. (Si) Seymour Award as the AHP's 1993 Outstanding Fund Raising Professional. In 1994, the Association of Fundraising Professionals' Orange County, California, chapter named him the chapter's Outstanding Professional. He also received the AFP's Outstanding Fund Raising Executive award at its International Conference in New Orleans in March 2000.

THEODORE R. HART, ACFRE—an Internet and fund raising strategist with over sixteen years of experience in communications, fund raising, and nonprofit management—is founder and president of the international ePhilanthropy Foundation (http://ephilanthropy.org), created to foster the ethical and efficient use of the Internet for philanthropic purposes. He is also president of a fund raising consulting firm, Hart Philanthropic Services Group.

Throughout North America, Hart is frequently invited to lecture on fund raising, nonprofit management, ethics, and the Internet. He can be reached at ted-hart@ephilanthropy.org.

Skip Henderson, M.S.W., has management and fund raising experience in a variety of programmatic areas. In addition to teaching assignments, his current consulting clients include a national general aviation pilots' organization serving the transportation needs of low-income medical patients; a neighborhood development organization; a domestic violence counseling service; and miscellaneous counseling and board training assignments through affiliation with San Francisco's Management Center.

Henderson's consulting specialty is working with organizations that are in the early stages of their formation, or re-formation, looking toward financial stability with a diversified funding base.

As adjunct professor in the University of San Francisco's College of Professional Studies and Institute for Nonprofit Management, Henderson teaches in both the Master's of Nonprofit Administration Program and the institute's nonprofit management certification programs. He is also a member of the faculty of The Fund Raising School of the Center on Philanthropy at Indiana University.

James M. Hodge is a fund raising practitioner with extensive experience in both academic and health care settings. Specializing in major and planned gifts since 1979, he has also directed a comprehensive fund raising program at Bowling Green State University. He presently serves as assistant chair and director of principal gifts for the Mayo Clinic in Rochester, Minnesota. A member of the core teaching faculty for The Fund Raising School, he teaches the course "Developing Leadership for Major Gifts."

He serves on the editorial advisory board for the Jossey-Bass New Directions for Philanthropic Fundraising series of publications and edited (with Dwight F. Burlingame) Volume 16 in the series, *Developing Major Gifts,* published in 1997. In addition to frequent lectures at the Indiana University Center on Philanthropy, he teaches at other academic centers and conducts national and international workshops in development. For more than a decade he has served on alumni and foundation boards for his alma mater, Bowling Green State University, where he earned his B.S. and M.A. degrees. A member of numerous nonprofit boards, he has also served as consultant to several capital campaigns.

Ben Imdieke studied political science at Kalamazoo College, where he was student government president. Following a year helping to assemble the prospect pool for Kalamazoo College's $65 million "Enlightened Leadership" campaign, Imdieke was a Jane Addams–Andrew Carnegie Fellow at the Center on Philanthropy at Indiana University, a program he later coordinated while serving as research assistant to Robert L. Payton. He recently completed his M.A. in philanthropic studies, for which he was named Chancellor's Scholar. He now serves as assistant director of development for the Indiana University–Purdue University Indianapolis Library and is concerned with free exchange of information, community engagement, and continuing to build the excellence of the Philanthropic Studies Special Collection.

ANDREA R. KAMINSKI is vice president for research and programs at the Women's Philanthropy Institute, a nonprofit organization dedicated to inspiring women to fulfill their philanthropic potential. She created *WPINews,* a quarterly newsletter that profiles model programs and people in women's philanthropy, and coedited (with Anne I. Thompson) the book *Women and Philanthropy: A National Agenda.* She has written articles or chapters for *CASE Currents; The Nonprofit Handbook: Fund Raising* (third edition, edited by James M. Greenfield; Wiley, 2001); and other publications.

She is a member of the board of directors of the Urban League of Greater Madison and Wisconsin Women in Higher Education Leadership. She is also a member of the faculty of The Fund Raising School of the Center on Philanthropy at Indiana University and a member of the Madison chapter of the Association of Fundraising Professionals and the national AFP Research Council.

JANICE KERCHEVILLE is executive director of the Juvenile Diabetes Research Foundation, Rocky Mountain chapter, with overall responsibility for Colorado, Wyoming, and Montana. Prior to cofounding The JK Group/Colorado in January 2001, she was president and COO of DonorNet, LLC, an e-commerce service provider to 250 nonprofits in the United States and Canada. Previously, she served for ten years with Mile High United Way as both a vice president of the Campaign Division, raising nearly $35 million annually, and VP of the Major Gifts Division, creating and implementing its first-ever major gifts strategic plan and raising its first million-dollar gift.

Janice Kercheville serves on the faculty of The Fund Raising School and has published several articles and handouts on fund raising and the Internet. In addition, she serves on the board of directors of the Arthritis Foundation in Denver and the executive committee of the Alpha Gamma Delta Denver Alumni Club. She is a member of the Women's Foundation of Colorado and serves in a number of other volunteer capacities with organizations benefiting youth and seniors in the metropolitan Denver area. She can be reached at jkerch2@attbi.com.

JIM KERCHEVILLE is cofounder and principal of The JK Group/Colorado, a Denver-based public relations and organizational consulting firm, and senior consultant with Signature Resources of Denver, a consortium of companies and professionals providing strategic support to business and nonprofit organizations. Before founding The JK Group, he was director of editorial services for the Denver and Los Angeles offices of Alexander Ogilvy Public Relations World-wide, focusing on a wide range of high-tech clients.

Jim Kercheville also spent more than three years with Mile High United Way in Denver, principally as vice president of media relations and strategic planning. Previously, he had twenty-six years of experience with AT&T and US West (now Qwest) in public relations and human resources. As an independent consultant-writer, he has written scripts for marketing and training videos and has been a contributing writer to several publications, including *Network* magazine, for which he wrote in-depth, technical case studies. He is also an accomplished public speaker and conference facilitator-trainer. Jim Kercheville can be reached at jimkerch1@attbi.com.

KIM KLEIN is internationally known as a fund raising trainer and consultant. She is the series editor for the Chardon Press Series at Jossey-Bass, which publishes and distributes materials that help build a stronger nonprofit sector. She is the founder and copublisher of the bimonthly *Grassroots Fundraising Journal* and the author of *Fundraising for Social Change* (Chardon Press, 2000), now in its fourth edition; *Fundraising for the Long Haul* (Chardon Press, 2000), which explores the particular challenges of older grassroots organizations; and *Ask and You Shall Receive: A Fundraising Training Program for Religious Organizations and Projects* (Jossey-Bass, 2000), a teaching manual for lay leadership to teach each other grassroots fund raising. Her most recent book is an anthology of articles from the *Grassroots Fundraising Journal* called *Raise More Money* (Jossey-Bass, 2001), which she edited with her partner, Stephanie Roth.

Kim Klein has worked in all aspects of fund raising: as staff, as a volunteer, as a board member, and as a consultant. She is best known for adapting traditional fund raising techniques—particularly major donor campaigns—to the needs of organizations with small budgets that are working for social justice. She was named Outstanding Fund Raising Executive of the Year in 1998 by the Golden Gate Chapter of the National Society of Fund Raising Executives. She is also a member of the faculty of The Fund Raising School of the Center on Philanthropy at Indiana University.

MARGARET M. MAXWELL works with nonprofit organizations and boards throughout the country in the areas of strategic planning, governance, marketing, and fund development planning. Prior to her work as a consultant, she was vice president for the Children's Museum of Indianapolis, one of the nation's premier cultural institutions, as well as a newspaper reporter and editor. Her museum experience includes leadership roles in fund raising, marketing, strategic planning, and earned income program development.

Maxwell has been a faculty member of The Fund Raising School since 1991. In addition to her professional work, she serves as a board member for several

Indianapolis-area nonprofit organizations. She earned both a B.A. in journalism and an M.B.A. in marketing from Indiana University.

SHEREE PARRIS NUDD is vice president of Washington Adventist Hospital in Takoma Park, Maryland; a fellow in the Association for Healthcare Philanthropy; and founder of DesignsforGiving.com. In the mid-1980s, she was the youngest alum to establish a scholarship fund at Southwestern Adventist University in Texas.

A charter trustee of the Milton Murray Foundation for Philanthropy, Nudd wishes to acknowledge Milton Murray as a mentor and friend. Their search for meaningful quotes about giving and philanthropy led Murray and Nudd to create the *Giving Is Caring Quote-a-Day Calendar* (650,000 published to date). Charitable organizations use the calendar as a thoughtful and cost-effective way to recognize, cultivate, and delight their donors throughout the year.

GWENDOLYN PERRY, CFRE, is area director for the United Negro College Fund's Indianapolis office. She has worked in fund raising in Indiana for the past decade, supporting the missions of private institutions of higher education. She is past president of the Indiana chapter of the Association of Fundraising Professionals and serves as a faculty member at The Fund Raising School at Indiana University's Center on Philanthropy.

ROBERT PIERPONT, chairman of Pierpont & Wilkerson, began his career in fund raising management and consulting in 1958 when he returned to his alma mater, Widener University, to become its first full-time development officer. In 1972, he joined the consulting firm Brakeley, John Price Jones, where he served a wide variety of clients including colleges, universities, and the United States Olympic Committee. From the Brakeley firm, he went in 1979 to the Mount Sinai Medical Center, where as vice president of development he organized a $100 million capital campaign. During his six and one-half years there, giving increased from $13 million per year to $38 million.

In January 1986, he joined Pierpont Associates and in 1988 established Pierpont & Wilkerson.

Bob Pierpont has served as a national officer of both the National Society of Fund Raising Executives and its philanthropic foundation. He served for seven years as the first chairman of its Certification Board and chaired the NSFRE Ethics Committee. He is a frequent speaker at professional conferences as well as a member of the faculty of The Fund Raising School of the Center on Philanthropy at Indiana University.

DEAN REGENOVICH's clients include colleges and universities, and religious, cultural, health, and social service organizations. He provides his clients with a full range of campaign planning studies and ongoing campaign consultation, board development, and educational training.

Regenovich previously served as vice president for Grenzebach Giler & Associates, Inc., a philanthropic management consulting firm based in Chicago. He was the director of planned giving for the Indiana University Foundation from 1990 to 1997 and also served as the director of major gifts and planned giving for the Indianapolis Symphony Orchestra. He was also a senior consultant with Renaissance, Inc., where he provided technical charitable estate planning support to nonprofit organizations and professional financial advisers. He is also a member of the faculty of The Fund Raising School of the Center on Philanthropy at Indiana University.

Regenovich received a master's degree in taxation from the Georgetown School of Law in 1986, graduated magna cum laude from the John Marshall Law School in Chicago in 1983, and earned a B.S. degree from Indiana University in 1980. Before entering the development profession, he was in private law practice for five years, specializing in taxation and estate planning. He is licensed to practice law in Indiana, Illinois, and Florida.

JIM REID has accumulated a wide variety of administrative and instructional experience in most areas of institutional advancement and charitable organization fund raising thanks to almost thirty-five years in charitable resource development and nonprofit management in the Southwest. His assignments have included capital campaigns, foundation research and proposal writing, alumni affairs, annual giving, special gift clubs, telephone campaigning, and overall program motivation. He has served as chief development officer for small private colleges, two major state universities, and a statewide association of private colleges and has provided consulting services to a long list of clients. In addition, he has been instrumental in the development of training curricula for formal degree coursework in the preparation of college administrators and non-profit managers who seek a specialty in charitable resource development, fund raising, and advancement work. This interest in the preparation of fund raising professionals brought him to association with The Fund Raising School at the Indiana University Center on Philanthropy more than seventeen years ago.

Reid's eighteen-year-old fund raising consulting firm, Philanthropic Resource Associates (PRA), serves a wide variety of nonprofit organizations that depend on regular gift income to offer their programs to the public. As a member of the national board of the National Society of Fund Raising Executives (NSFRE) for nine years (1980–1989), Reid was a key member of the special task force for the development of the fund raising profession's first comprehensive certification program and examination, the NSFRE's CFRE Program.

MARCELLA ORVAÑANOS DE ROVZAR, a Mexican, studied architecture at Ibero-americana University and obtained the certificate in fund raising management for nonprofit organizations at the Indiana University Center of Philanthropy, as well as a degree in social responsibility at Navarra University's Science Institute for the Family. She graduated from the Rockefeller Foundation Philanthropy Workshop in 2001.

From 1989 to 1994, she was the development director, a board member, and vice-president for the Fundación Mexicana para el Desarrollo Rural (Mexican Rural Foundation), where she created the Women and Peasant Family program. She founded Modersa, S.A., a consulting firm for nonprofits. She created and contributed to the consulting board of UNICEF Mexico and later founded Procura A.C., a fund raising and institutional strengthening institute for nonprofit organizations and representative in Mexico and Latin America for The Fund Raising School of the Center on Philanthropy at Indiana University. To date, Procura has trained more than four thousand persons from more than fifteen hundred nonprofit organizations in Mexico and many more from other Latin American countries. Procura also performs consulting and research for the nonprofit sector in Mexico.

EDWARD C. SCHUMACHER is president of Third Sector, a Seattle-based consulting firm that provides workshops and consultation to local, regional, national, and international nonprofit organizations. Principal of his own firm since 1985, Schumacher had been an executive director, development director, and national staff member for twenty-five years before starting his own business. At the University of Washington, he helped found the Nonprofit Fund Raising Certificate Program and has been an instructor for fifteen years. He currently serves as lead instructor for The Fund Raising School at Indiana University's Center on Philanthropy. Ed has published two books on capital campaigns: *The Capital Campaign Survival Guide* (Elton-Wolf, 2000) and *Capital Campaigns: Conducting a Successful Fund-Raising Drive* (National Center for Nonprofit Boards, 2001). In the past decade, Schumacher has worked on three national pilot programs in endowment fund raising.

ROBERT SCHWARTZBERG is director of development for the University of Washington's Friday Harbor Laboratories on San Juan Island, in Washington State. He is also principal of SbergDev, a fund raising consulting firm that specializes in working with grassroots organizations. Schwartzberg has more than twenty-five years of leadership and professional experience in fund raising and has been directly involved in raising more than $35 million for nonprofit organizations. Since 1995, he has been a member of the faculty of The Fund Raising School at the Indiana University Center on Philanthropy, where he is a senior professional associate. He has also been an instructor in fund raising at George Washington University and on the faculty of the Social Action and Leadership School for Activists (SALSA) and the Support Center, both in Washington, D.C. In 1992, he received CFRE certification from the National Society of Fund Raising Executives

(NSFRE). Schwartzberg has a graduate certificate in public relations from American University and a bachelor's degree from the City University of New York at Queens College.

TIMOTHY L. SEILER is director of The Fund Raising School and its director for public service, as well as assistant professor of philanthropic studies at Indiana University's Center on Philanthropy. Formerly vice president of the Indiana University Foundation, Seiler was a major gifts officer for university development. As director of the foundation's Indianapolis office, he coordinated the constituency development program for the schools and programs of the Indianapolis campus. He also led the comprehensive fund raising program for the Indianapolis campus, which included staff for corporate and foundation relations, major gifts, planned giving, annual fund, prospect research, donor relations, and stewardship.

Seiler is an alumnus of The Fund Raising School and has been a faculty member since 1986. He teaches customized contract programs as well as core curriculum courses and frequently makes conference and seminar presentations nationally and internationally. He serves on the board of the Indiana Youth Institute and is a member of the Wallace Chair Advisory Committee of the American College.

Seiler has authored and edited numerous fund raising publications and is currently coeditor of New Directions for Philanthropic Fundraising, the quarterly series published by Jossey-Bass. He is editor in chief of the Jossey-Bass Excellence in Fundraising workbook series and author of the workbook *Developing Your Case for Support* (Jossey-Bass, 2001).

LILYA WAGNER has been associated with the Indiana University Center on Philanthropy since 1991. Her current position is associate director for public service. Among her assignments are several projects, including the Hispanic Stewardship Development Partnership. She is a faculty member of The Fund Raising School, works on curriculum preparation and revision, and is a frequent workshop presenter and speaker. Wagner also teaches graduate courses for Indiana University as a member of the Philanthropic Studies faculty. She has received several awards for her teaching and training, including the Indiana University School of Public and Environmental Affairs Award for Excellence in Graduate Education.

Her published writings include articles and book chapters on philanthropy, fund raising, and the nonprofit sector, along with books and numerous articles on a variety of general-interest and professional topics. *Careers in Fundraising* (Wiley, 2001), her most recent book, is a comprehensive volume on fund raising as a profession.

Prior to joining the Center on Philanthropy, she served as vice president for institutional advancement at Union College in Lincoln, Nebraska. She began her fund raising career in the health care field and has served as a volunteer and board member for human service, arts, and community organizations, assisting with fund raising and public relations. Wagner has done extensive international work, providing training and counsel for nongovernmental organizations is many countries.

Wagner holds a doctorate in education from the University of Florida in Gainesville and master's degrees in journalism and music.

MAL WARWICK, a noted consultant, author, and public speaker, has been involved in the nonprofit sector for nearly forty years. He is the founder and chairman of Mal Warwick & Associates, Inc., in Berkeley, California, a fund raising and marketing agency that has served nonprofit organizations since 1979, and of its sister company, Response Management Technologies, Inc., a data processing firm for nonprofit organizations. He is also cofounder (with Nick Allen) of donordigital.com LLC in San Francisco, California, which assists nonprofit organizations on-line, and is a cofounder of Share Group, Inc., in Somerville, Massachusetts. Collectively, Warwick and his associates are responsible for raising at least half a billion dollars—largely in the form of small gifts from individuals.

Warwick has written or edited fourteen books of interest to nonprofit managers, including *The Five Strategies for Fundraising Success* (Jossey-Bass, 1999), *Fundraising on the Internet* (second edition, Jossey-Bass, 2001), and the standard texts *Raising Money by Mail* (Strathmoor Press, 1996) and *How to Write Successful Fundraising Letters* (Strathmoor Press, 1994). He is editor of *Mal Warwick's Newsletter: Successful Direct Mail, Telephone & Online Fundraising* and is a popular speaker and workshop leader throughout the world.

Warwick is an active member of the Association of Fundraising Professionals and the U.S. representative of the Resource Alliance, based in London. He is one of the organizers of the annual International Fund Raising Congress and served for ten years on the board of the Association of Direct Response Fundraising Counsel, two of those years as president.

He was a cofounder of Business for Social Responsibility and served on its board during its inaugural year. He was recently elected to the board and the executive committee of the Social Venture Network. Since 1969, he has lived in Berkeley, California, where he is deeply involved in local community affairs. He was a cofounder of the Community Bank of the Bay, the nation's fifth community development bank, and serves on the boards of the Berkeley Community Fund and the Berkeley Symphony Orchestra.

ALAN L. WENDROFF, CFRE, a nonprofit executive for more than two decades, has been the principal of his own consulting firm since 1994. His practice is concentrated primarily on developing fund raising programs and counseling nonprofit agencies. His clients have ranged from arts organizations to health, human services, religious, and educational institutions. He teaches fund raising classes, face-to-face and on-line, at California State University in Hayward and conducts workshops at the Foundation Center and many other venues devoted to educating nonprofit professionals.

He is the author of *Special Events: Proven Strategies for Nonprofit Fund Raising* (Wiley, 1999) and the coauthor, with Kay Sprinkel Grace, of *High Impact Philanthropy: How Donors, Boards, and Nonprofit Organizations Can Transform Communities* (Wiley, 2000).

Wendroff is active with the Golden Gate chapter of the Association of Fundraising Professionals and is a member of the board of San Francisco's Lowell High School Alumni Association.

Hank Rosso's
Achieving Excellence
in Fund Raising

PART ONE

FUND RAISING:
CONTEXT AND PHILOSOPHY

H enry A. Rosso established The Fund Raising School to educate and train
fund raising practitioners and volunteers to secure the resources necessary for nonprofit organizations to carry out their work. The two chapters in Part One lay out the case for the nonprofit sector and philanthropy in the
United States (and in civil societies around the globe) and cover Hank Rosso's
philosophy of fund raising, a philosophy as valid for the twenty-first century as
it was in the twentieth.

Philanthropy plays a major role in American society. And the dynamics that
shape philanthropy are changing. Chapter One covers the important contribution to the public that philanthropy makes. Without a cause that contributes to
the public good, an organization does not have the ethical right to ask for funds.
The trust that undergirds philanthropy depends on this important foundation.
A mission dedicated to the public good was a key concept for Hank. This is the
context in which he developed his philosophy of fund raising. Chapter One also
deals with the changing world in which nonprofits carry out their work and the
challenges and opportunities they face in raising philanthropic funds.

Chapter Two is Hank's original chapter from the first edition of *Achieving
Excellence*, "A Philosophy of Fund Raising," with an added commentary on the
validity of the philosophy in the twenty-first century. The concept of fund raising as a servant to philanthropy sets the tone for the entire volume. The work of
fund raising flows from that concept. In this era of heightened accountability,

1

Hank's philosophy provides a useful perspective on the role of fund raising to support the acts of giving and volunteering.

CHAPTER ONE

Contemporary Dynamics
of Philanthropy

Eugene R. Tempel

Hank Rosso said that fund raising is the servant of philanthropy. He also said that the privilege to ask for philanthropic support depended on the public benefit, the social need being filled by the organization doing the asking. This chapter begins with an introduction to the critical roles that philanthropy plays in a civil society, discusses changes in the environment in which fund raisers do their work, and examines the tensions and challenges those changes present for philanthropic fund raising.

THE MULTIPLE ROLES OF PHILANTHROPY

Philanthropy plays a number of distinctive roles in U.S. society. Increasingly, other countries are turning to philanthropy to fill some of those roles as well. And while government and business also contribute to civil society, in the United States, philanthropy plays a larger role than anywhere else in the world. With three successive U.S. presidents from two different political parties emphasizing the importance of service to others, many observers believe that philanthropy and the nonprofit sector have taken their rightful place in U.S. society. Keeping the primacy of mission in mind, we can identify at least seven significant roles that nonprofit organizations and philanthropy play in a civil society: They reduce human suffering, enhance human potential, promote private equity

3

and justice, build community, provide human fulfillment, support experimentation and change, and foster pluralism.

Reduce Human Suffering

The first role is to reduce human suffering through such efforts as health care, human services, and international relief; to make life more comfortable for those who are injured or ill; to aid victims; and to assist those not able to sustain themselves. This is perhaps the oldest role of philanthropy, one that has existed throughout recorded history.

Enhance Human Potential

Enhancing human potential through religion, education, the arts, culture and the humanities, public and society benefit, the environment, and international efforts is the second role for nonprofit organizations in a civil society. The goal is to enable each person in society to go beyond his or her current state to reach his or her full potential.

Promote Private Equity and Justice

Philanthropy promotes equity and justice through human services and advocacy on behalf of those who cannot speak for themselves by promoting structures and programs in the public, private, and nonprofit sectors. Nonprofit organizations help build a more just society. Philanthropy also helps redistribute wealth in the economy.

Build Community

Another role of philanthropy is to build community. As Peter F. Drucker (1990, p. xvii) wrote:

> The major challenge for nonprofits is to give community a common purpose. Forty years ago, most Americans no longer lived in small towns, but they had still grown up in one. They had grown up in a local community. It was a compulsory community and could be quite stifling. Still, it was a community. . . . When I talk to volunteers in nonprofits, I ask, "Why are you willing to give all this time when you are already working hard in your paid job?" And again and again, I get the same answer: "Because here I know what I am doing. Here I contribute. Here I belong. Here I am a member of a community."

Community building is an important role of the nonprofit organizations for which we raise philanthropic funds.

Provide Human Fulfillment

Providing human fulfillment is a fifth role for philanthropy: the opportunity to become that best image we have of ourselves. Drucker (1990, p. xvii) notes that the task of nonprofits is much more than just getting extra money to do vital work. Giving is necessary above all, so that nonprofits can discharge the one mission they all have in common: to satisfy the need of the American people for self-realization, for living out of our ideals, our beliefs, our best opinions of ourselves. To make contributors out of donors means that the American people can see what they want to see—or should want to see—when each of us looks . . . in the mirror in the morning: someone who as a citizen takes responsibility. Someone who as a neighbor cares.

Support Experimentation and Change

Philanthropy also supports experimentation and stimulates change, improving our society, taking risks, exploring areas that the larger community or the market sector may be unwilling to enter, and looking for alternative or new solutions.

Foster Pluralism

Finally, philanthropy fosters pluralism. It challenges the status quo and goes beyond interests of the majority. It allows for multiple responses. Philanthropy, voluntary action, and voluntary association protect the minority from the tyranny of the majority. A democratic government, a civil society, allows parallel power structures to carry out what the government will not or cannot do.

A BRIEF HISTORY OF PHILANTHROPY IN THE UNITED STATES

Philanthropy is practiced in different ways and at different levels in cultures around the world. Sometimes it is primarily directed to religion. Informal philanthropy to friends, family, and neighbors, as in gathering goods and funds at a time of community crisis, is common to all cultures. Chapters Eighteen and Thirty-Two discuss philanthropy and fund raising in different cultures. Because this volume is primarily about fund raising in the United States, we note that philanthropy is present in all cultures, but nowhere is it such a structural part of society as in the United States. U.S. citizens give the largest percentage of personal income and have the largest percentage of the population volunteering.

We should also note that fund raising was not invented in the United States. The ancient Jewish code of *tzedaka* allows for the giver to be asked, although the gift of a giver who must be asked is not valued as highly as a gift spontaneously offered. Mullen (2002) notes that in the fourth century B.C., the Greeks used subscriptions to raise money and that fund raisers were involved in seeking indulgences. But today, other countries are adapting the structured fund raising programs that have developed in the United States.

How did philanthropy become such an important part of American life? The history of America is, to an extraordinary degree, one of a giving, caring people.

It is one of strangers opening their hearts, homes, and pockets to aid those in need. We can learn a great deal about the philanthropic tradition by examining its roots. Beginning with our native culture, the concepts of stewardship and wise use of resources, community rather than private property, and intergenerational sharing and reciprocity inside the community have been important. The seventh-generation concept—that any action must be considered in terms of its consequences on the seventh generation into the future—is the root of modern environmental concerns ("Celebrating," 2002).

The colonists, with no formal government, engaged in voluntarism. The Jamestown Settlement and the Mayflower Compact represent early examples of voluntary association. Susan Ellis and Katherine Noyes (1990, p. 19) note: "Obviously, this system of government [in the American colonies] was dependent upon citizens willing to volunteer. All community members were welcome to discuss town problems and to propose solutions. Administrative officials were elected to supervise the implementation of plans decided upon by the town meeting. It is evident by a review of the titles and functions of such officials that most were unpaid and accepted the positions out of a sense of moral duty" to the community. Another key factor was the separation of church and state. Education, social services, and poor relief were functions of the church. When the church was separated from the public funding system, voluntarism and philanthropy became the primary source of support, leading to the development of new structures.

By the 1830s, Americans' generosity and their tendency to form associations were apparent in everyday life. They caught the attention of Alexis de Tocqueville. In *Democracy in America* ([1835] 1956, p. 198), he wrote:

> Americans of all ages, all conditions, and all dispositions constantly form associations. They have not only commercial and manufacturing companies, in which all take part, but associations of a thousand other kinds, religious, moral, serious, futile, general or restricted, enormous or diminutive. The Americans make associations to give entertainments, to found seminaries, to build inns, to construct churches, to diffuse books, to send missionaries to the antipodes; in this manner they found hospitals, prisons, and schools. If it is proposed to inculcate some truth or to foster some feeling by the encouragement of a great example, they form a society. Wherever at the head of some new undertaking you see the government in France, or a man of rank in England, in the United States you will be sure to find an association.

Robert Bremmer (1988) describes the development of philanthropy in the United States, beginning with the generosity the natives extended to Columbus. He also includes a list of important dates in U.S. philanthropy. Perhaps the earliest organized fund raising in the United States was the effort of a group of colonists to gather funds in England for the young Harvard College using a brochure titled "America's First Fruits" as their case for support. Bremmer notes the early efforts of Benjamin Franklin to institute secular charity. Franklin believed in direct solicitation, asking for a specified amount, asking for gifts based on the giver's means, asking for the largest gifts first, and inviting all potential donors to be part of a project.

Modern U.S. fund raising was influenced greatly by Charles Sumner Ward and Lyman Pierce, who organized a fund raising campaign for the YMCA of the United States in 1905 (Harrah-Conforth and Borsos, 1991). They influenced the structures that were used to raise funds and formed the first U.S. fund raising consulting firm. From these early initiatives came the fund raising consulting practice and the organized institutional fund raising efforts that are discussed in this book.

CHALLENGES FOR PHILANTHROPY IN THE TWENTY-FIRST CENTURY

Along with the challenges brought by rapid growth in organizations and philanthropic giving, a number of other matters affect the way fund raisers do their work.

Accountability

In 1993, William Aramony, then the president of the United Way of America, came under scrutiny for his lifestyle, such perquisites as flying the Concorde on trips to Europe, and potential personal gain. Aramony's activities ultimately led to his conviction for conspiracy and mail and tax fraud, for which he served a seven-year federal prison sentence (United Way of the Bay Area, 2001). It is difficult to say that Aramony's actions caused a greater call for accountability. These calls had begun prior to the 1990s. But the so-called Aramony scandal certainly galvanized the call.

In the mid-1990s, the calls for accountability became so loud that associations representing various voices in the nonprofit sector supported the development and passage of federal legislation to provide penalties for nonprofit executives and board members who are paid excessive salaries and who benefit personally from their relationship to nonprofit organizations. Known as "intermediate sanctions" because they impose fines as an intermediate step prior to the revocation of an organization's tax-exempt status by the Internal Revenue Service, the regulations provide a tool to help rebuild trust in nonprofit organizations.

Funders and donors have increased their gift restrictions and continued their call for accountability into the new century. Program evaluation, focus on results, and even impact studies to measure return on gifts have become more common. Fund raisers need to make certain that their organizations are prepared to respond. INDEPENDENT SECTOR (2000) has outlined a series of steps the philanthropic and nonprofit sector must take to ensure both narrow and broad accountability.

Narrow Accountability. According to INDEPENDENT SECTOR (2000, p. 7), "Narrow accountability refers to: (1) the formal responsibilities of individuals and organizations to report their actions to higher authorities (e.g. the Internal Revenue Service), (2) the specific reporting mechanisms they are instructed to use, and (3) the formal standards to which they are held." To ensure narrow accountability, nonprofit organizations must implement formal reporting structures to comply with applicable laws and regulations.

Broad Accountability. Broad accountability encompasses narrow accountability and builds on it by "expanding it in two important ways: (1) it broadens the set of higher authorities to whom individuals or organizations are potentially responsible, and (2) it broadens the criteria, expectations and standards to which these individuals and organizations may potentially be held" (INDEPENDENT SECTOR, 2000, p. 7). Otherwise considered to be "serving the public good" and "preserving the public trust," it can be expected that broad accountability is often "implicit and subjective." INDEPENDENT SECTOR suggests attaining broad accountability by "being able to account for the organization's implied promises to its constituents by pursuing its stated mission in good faith with defensible and transparent management and governance practices" (p. 8). In doing so, the organization is held accountable by the public's trust.

Blurring the Boundaries

In a fifteen-year period, nonprofit organizations increased both fee income and government funding at rates higher than philanthropy. So nonprofits have become more interdependent rather than more independent. At the same time, for-profit businesses have entered fields like health care, education, and social service that were once the sole province of the nonprofit sector. The Fidelity Charitable Gift Fund had become the second-largest recipient of philanthropic funds by the turn of the twenty-first century.

Many nonprofit organizations have adopted entrepreneurial models, sometimes forming for-profit subsidiaries to earn income that is used to support subsidized activities. Others earn marketing income through a variety of schemes, sometimes compensating staff on a commission basis for marketing and business income. Fund raisers are challenged by these arrangements because even though it might be ethical to be compensated on a percentage basis for market-based revenue, it is unethical to be compensated on a percentage or commission basis for philanthropic funds raised.

Changes in Tax Structures

For the remainder of this decade, fund raisers will debate the impact of the repeal of the estate tax on philanthropy. Major changes in the estate tax began in 2002 and will be fully implemented by 2009. Currently, the changes are set to expire the following year. Some research indicates that giving, especially planned giving, will be affected negatively; other studies show that the increased accumulation of wealth that will result will lead to increased philanthropy (Rooney and Tempel, 2001). A variety of other tax changes are pending. Lower tax rates might shift giving, as they did in 1986. Proposals to allow charitable gift deductions for nonitemizers over a certain amount will surely benefit philanthropy, as will proposals to allow individuals to roll over IRAs into charitable gifts and extend the deadline for claiming tax deductions for a calendar year to April 15 of the following year.

The Behavior of "New Donors"

There is much discussion about whether or not a "new donor" has emerged, and Chapter Seventeen is dedicated to this topic. One bit of wisdom is that the new donors are as different from each other as from the previous generation. Other observers have said that the new donors behave very much like the first generation of formal philanthropists, like Carnegie and Rockefeller. There are a few trends worth noting. Many donors today are interested in pursuing very distinctive projects. Many who accumulated wealth quickly in the 1990s are interested in pursuing philanthropy more quickly and at an earlier age. Venture capitalists who developed wealth through a distinct business approach have developed a "venture philanthropy" approach. The traditional model on which *Achieving Excellence* was built and on which most fund raising programs are operated is challenged by these new models. Sometimes the model of a sound organization with a good cause in search of donors is met head-on by a donor with a good project in search of a willing organization.

Engaging Constituents

The generation born between 1910 and 1930 has been called "the long civic generation" by Kristin Goss (1999) because they volunteered more (among other civic activities) than any generation before or since. Studies show that young people are coming back to volunteering, perhaps stimulated by new national service programs like AmeriCorps and Learn and Serve and through service learning and curricula like Learn to Give that teach about philanthropy in schools through youth organizations.

But young volunteers are challenging nonprofit organizations to do things differently. Studies show that they would rather volunteer on an ad hoc basis than make a long-term commitment. They prefer to provide direct service rather than become involved at the policy level. They want to volunteer with friends or coworkers and view volunteering as a social activity. Many nonprofit organizations lack the structures to engage volunteers on their terms, ultimately affecting fund raising. Fund raisers are challenged to develop new models and different methods to engage the next generation of volunteers.

Professionalization of the Sector

Management of nonprofit organizations has become more professional, and so has philanthropic fund raising. This trend is likely to continue. One study estimates that there are now more than 242 programs offering graduate and undergraduate degrees related to philanthropic studies and nonprofit management in colleges and universities and expects that number to increase to 400 by 2005 ("Building Bridges," 2001). Harland Bloland (2002), who has spent time analyzing fund raising as a profession, now concludes that fund raising has in fact become a profession.

This professionalization provides better use of resources, more strategic approaches, enhanced accountability, and more effective fund raising. Professionalization can help enhance and develop philanthropy. But professionalization also provides some challenges. It has the potential to diminish the volunteer experience and disengage volunteers if we do not see "managing" volunteers as a professional responsibility. Professionalization may cause fund raisers and others to focus more on their career development than on the needs of their organizations or donors. And it will surely continue to heighten the tensions surrounding compensation levels in the nonprofit sector.

OPPORTUNITIES FOR PHILANTHROPY IN THE TWENTY-FIRST CENTURY

The challenges just discussed, and others, will be more fully explored in the following chapters. And although nonprofits must rise to the fund raising challenges, they also have tremendous opportunities to expand philanthropy and to capitalize on the circumstances an expanded philanthropy will support.

The Wealth Transfer

As stock markets around the world climbed during the 1990s and the U.S. and global economies expanded, some analysts forecast a new "golden age of philanthropy" (Havens and Schervish, 1999). Havens and Schervish issued new figures on the transfer of wealth from one generation to another during a fifty-five-year period in the United States. They predicted not just an adjustment to the $10 trillion transfer we had all come to know but a minimum of $41 trillion based on 2 percent overall growth and $136 trillion based on 4 percent growth. They projected that even if philanthropy received only its current share of the transfer, an amount between $6 trillion and $25 trillion would make its way to nonprofit organizations and foundations. But Schervish (2000b) argues that to realize this "golden age of philanthropy," we must change the nature of much of organized fund raising. He challenges us to focus on the supply side of philanthropy, the donor, instead of the demand side, the needs of the organization.

The Supply-Side Model

The trend toward restricting smaller gifts that began in the 1980s has become a major factor in contemporary philanthropy. Schervish (2000b) argues that to maximize philanthropic support from individuals, we need to focus on the supply side of philanthropy. Major gift officers have long realized that the interests of the donor become more important as the size of the gift increases. Hank Rosso's philosophy of fund raising is based on the principle of understanding donor needs. The supply-side model focuses fund raising on the donor even more deliberately. Much of fund raising has been built on the demand side of philanthropy, looking at societal and organizational needs rather than donor needs. The demand-side approach, according to Schervish, has applied a "scolding model" to fund raising, essentially a sales approach, telling people about the needs of nonprofits and challenging them to give, to give unrestricted gifts, to give at certain times, and to give more and sometimes employing guilt, embarrassment, and coercion to stimulate a response.

Fund raising organized on the supply side must employ what Schervish (2000b) calls a "discernment model" that helps donors decide how to use wealth for philanthropy. Instead of telling donors how to give for what causes and in what ways, as the scolding approach implies, the discernment model focuses on listening. It asks donors questions about what their wealth means and how they might use it. It asks them to consider what they might do for the public good that will bring them happiness and satisfaction. The Rosso approach to major gift fund raising was to have the right volunteers ask the right prospect for the right amount of gift for the right cause at the right time. All these steps focused on the donor.

The supply-side focus helps us understand the direction in which philanthropy seems to be headed in the twenty-first century. If the model holds true for philanthropy, the next ten years are likely to bring two major tensions to the world of fund raising. One is the potential gap between organizational and societal needs and supply-side interests. Most organizations have already experienced a decline in unrestricted gifts and gifts for operating or infrastructure support. Emphasis on the supply side might make these gifts even scarcer. Fund raisers will be challenged to help organizations do better cost accounting to attribute operations and administrative costs to programs. And they will need to evaluate donors from a supply-side perspective about the other organizational needs, the demand side. Donors who are happy with their supply-side philanthropy must be drawn into deeper involvement with the organization, where they can learn more about organizational needs.

The other tension created by the supply-side model is the evaluation of the fund raising profession itself. A fund raiser employed by an organization who works on the supply side of philanthropy has the potential to expand philanthropy. In fact, Paul Pribbenow (2001) calls for a professional model where fund raisers assist donors in recognizing their values and aim to align both the donor's values and their giving. It is crucial, however, that those fund raisers who serve to link organizations and discerning donors be aware that all parties must be open, honest, and forthcoming with information to ensure a good match of values and objectives.

Fund raisers who become experts at using a discernment approach to help donors create philanthropy from their wealth in a meaningful way may create philanthropy for other organizations in addition to their own. Certain organizational employment arrangements for fund raisers are challenged by this model. How will organizations respond to fund raisers who generate philanthropy for others? Will organizations be able to adopt an attitude of abundance rather than scarcity?

The dynamics presented by the supply-side model and the discernment model challenge the way fund raisers are deployed. If we follow this new model to the extreme as presented in "Donor Interests: Time for New Approaches" (Tempel, 2001), it is possible that fund raisers should be employed by donors instead of nonprofit organizations.

Corporations and Foundations

As noted earlier, foundations have become a larger force in the total philanthropic picture. The growth of new foundations and of donor-advised and donor-designated funds in community foundations is one expression of the supply-side phenomenon. New assets in foundations, along with increases in foundation endowments through the performance of the equities market, have brought foundation grantmaking to $25.9 billion, or 12.2 percent of the total, in 2001, from $7.72 billion, or 7.3 percent of the total, in 1991. A recent report by the *Chronicle of Philanthropy* (Joslyn, 2001) indicated that the number of professional staff in foundations grew to 17,013 full-time and part-time staff members. Fund raisers are much more likely to be dealing with professional staff, full-time or part-time, when approaching a smaller foundation.

Corporate giving has diminished somewhat since 1991, when it was 5 percent of total philanthropic giving, to 4.3 percent in 2001 (AAFRC Trust for Philanthropy, 2002). If the economic slowdown continues through the first decade of the twenty-first century, it will no doubt continue to depress corporate giving levels. And fund raisers approaching corporations will need to know about the sophisticated ways in which corporations today support the nonprofit sector, a sophistication that will heighten if the economy remains sluggish.

Philanthropy Internationally

Philanthropy is present in all cultures, but in the United States, it is more formal, more highly structured, and a larger part of the economy than in any other culture. Increasingly, the Center on Philanthropy, its Fund Raising School, professional associations like the Association of Fundraising Professionals (AFP) and the Council for Advancement and Support of Education (CASE), and individual fund raisers are being called on to help build formal fund raising structures in other countries. Increasing wealth and a recognition of how philanthropy can play a role in building a more inclusive civil society are key motivators. There is much for the United States to learn from other countries. There are different and sometimes richer traditions. Often there are better uses of new techniques. And often there are lessons to be learned through foreign adaptation of U.S. models.

CONCLUSION

The first decade of the twenty-first century may be one of the most interesting periods of philanthropy in U.S. history. Even with a slower-growing economy and an unpredictable stock market, we may be on the verge of a golden age of philanthropy driven by wealth that has greatly increased since the first edition of this book was published. We may also have entered an age of new civic responsibility, of community, of caring for one another that seems to occur spontaneously following material crises (AAFRC Trust for Philanthropy, 2002).

But fund raisers will have to deal with a number of challenges to increase philanthropic response. Creative partnerships to deal with the blurring of boundaries between and among the sectors, balancing demand-side and supply-side tensions, engaging new types of volunteers, and perhaps even redefining their profession and the professional relationships established with organizations may be necessary if fund raisers are to play significant roles in a larger and more effective philanthropy in the United States and around the world.

CHAPTER TWO

A Philosophy of Fund Raising

Henry A. Rosso
Introduction by Eugene R. Tempel

I n this chapter, Henry A. (Hank) Rosso offers his philosophy of fund raising, a philosophy developed over a lifetime of work as a fund raiser, consultant, and teacher. The principles on which he founded The Fund Raising School in 1974 have stood the test of time and culture. So has his philosophy for fund raising. That is why his original chapter in *Achieving Excellence in Fund Raising* is included in this second edition unaltered and in its entirety.

A central theme in Hank's philosophy and in the way he approached his work was that "fund raising is the servant of philanthropy." He opened and closed the first chapter of his book with that theme. Fund raising is not an end in itself. When it becomes that, both the organization and philanthropy are diminished. Fund raising, in Hank's view, was only a means to an end that rested on organizational mission. The pillars that support Hank's central theme are as relevant today as they were in 1991.

The most significant of these pillars is the question "Why do you exist?" This question enables an organization to articulate its mission in terms of the societal values it is fulfilling. Mission is what gives us the privilege to ask for philanthropic support. Mission is particularly important in an era when nonprofit organizations are encouraged to develop new income sources, undertake market-based activities, form collaborations and partnerships, and approach venture philanthropists with confidence.

Hank's philosophy also rested on the role of the governing board. He saw governing boards as responsible not only for fund raising but also for stewardship of the organization's mission and resources. The governing board today must ensure the public trust of the organization if fund raising is to be successful. Heightened calls for accountability make the role of the governing board even more important today than it was in 1991.

Fund raising as the servant of philanthropy must be part of an organization's management system. This is a pillar of Hank's philosophy of fund raising that is also critical today. Fund raising cannot be a separate, isolated activity. Ensuring trust means conducting fund raising that is based on mission by staff and volunteers who are committed to the organization, who represent the organization with integrity.

Hank believed that philanthropy must be voluntary. Today this pillar of Hank's philosophy is more important than it was in 1991. The interest in self-expression through philanthropy calls for a more open approach by organizations. Pluralism becomes an important tenet. Another of Hank's beliefs is applicable here, that "fund raising is the gentle art of teaching people the joy of giving." Fund raisers must remember that giving is voluntary to ensure the long- term donor engagement and donor satisfaction that lead to increased philanthropy.

Perhaps the greatest contribution Hank made was to teach the substitution of pride for apology in fund raising. As the number of people engaged in fund raising has grown and fund raisers have sought a more professional approach, recognizing that fund raising is a noble activity based on organizational mission has been central to professional development. Another of Hank's statements about soliciting a gift is applicable here: "Set yourself aside and let the case walk in."

Hank's chapter is framed by the concept of fund raising as a servant to philanthropy. He explained the role of fund raising in terms that foreshadow the models currently needed to assist wealth holders in determining their philanthropy. He wrote that fund raising "is justified when it is used as a responsible invitation guiding contributors to make the kind of gift that will meet their own special needs and add greater meaning to their lives."

Today more than ever, fund raisers need a philosophy of fund raising. The call for accountability, the need to inspire trust, the leadership of volunteers, the involvement of donors in their philanthropy, and the new approaches to philanthropy discussed in the following chapters all call for fund raisers to be reflective practitioners who can center themselves with a philosophy of fund raising. Hank's philosophy provides an excellent beginning for us to develop our own philosophy.

A PHILOSOPHY OF FUND RAISING

Fund raising is the servant of philanthropy and has been so since the seventeenth century, when Puritans brought the concept to the new continent. The early experience of fund raising was simple in form, obviously devoid of the multifaceted practices that characterize its nature in the contemporary United States. These practices now make fund raising more diversified and more complex than ever before.

The American spirit of giving is known and respected in other nations. American fund raising methods are equally known and admired abroad, as foreign citizens who have attended classes taught by The Fund Raising School will attest. Ironically, the practice of resource development that is so much a part of the culture, necessity, and tradition of nonprofit organizations in the United States is not sufficiently understood, often misrepresented, and too often viewed with suspicion and apprehension by a broad section of our own population, particularly by regulatory bodies. Few still argue with the observation that fund raising has never been considered the most popular practice in this country.

Dean Schooler of Boulder, Colorado, a scholar and student of fund raising, takes the teleological view of a vitalist philosophy that phenomena not only are guided by mechanical forces but also move toward certain goals of self-realization. Indeed, fund raising is never an end in itself; it is purposive. It draws both its meaning and essence from the ends that are served: caring, helping, healing, nurturing, guiding, uplifting, teaching, creating, preventing, advancing a cause, preserving values, and so forth. Fund raising is values-based; values must guide the process. Fund raising should never be undertaken simply to raise funds; it must serve the large cause.

Organizations and Their Reasons for Existing

Organizations of the independent sector come into existence for the purpose of responding to some facet of human or societal needs. The need or opportunity for service provides the organization with a reason for being, as well as a right to design and execute programs or strategies that respond to the need. This becomes the cause that is central to the concern of the organization. The cause provides justification for more intervention, and this provides justification for fund raising.

The organization may *claim* a right to raise money by asking for the tax-deductible gift. It must *earn* the privilege to ask for gift support by its management's responsiveness to needs, by the worthiness of its programs, and by the stewardship of its governing board. An organization may assume the right to ask. The prospective donor is under no obligation to give. The prospect reserves the right to a "yes" or a "no" response to any request. Either response is valid and must be respected.

Each organization that uses the privilege of soliciting for gifts should be prepared to respond to many questions, perhaps unasked and yet implicit in the prospect's mind. These may be characterized as such: "Why do you exist?" "What is distinctive about you?" "Why do you feel that you merit this support?" "What is it that you want to accomplish and how do you intend to go about doing it?" and "How will you hold yourself accountable?"

The response to "Who are you and why do you exist?" is couched in the words of the organization's mission statement. This statement expresses more than justification for existence and more than just a definition of goals and objectives. It defines the value system that will guide program strategies. The mission is the magnet that will attract and hold the interests of trustees, volunteers, staff, and contributors.

The answer to "What is distinctive about us?" is apparent in the array of goals, objectives, and programs that have been devised to address the needs of the value system as well as serve as symbols of fidelity to it.

"How do we hold ourselves accountable?" is the primary question. It is a continuing call for allegiance to the mission. It acknowledges the sacredness of the trust that is inherent in the relationship with both the constituency and the larger community. The organization is the steward of the resources entrusted to its care.

It is axiomatic that change is a constant. Shifting forces within the environment quicken the pace of change, thus posing a new constant. Nonprofit organizations must always be prepared to function in the center of whirling pressure.

Organizations cannot afford to be oblivious to the environment that surrounds, and indeed engulfs, them. Forces within the environment such as demographics, technology, economics, political and cultural values, and changing social patterns affect daily business performance, whether this performance pertains to governance, program administration, fiscal responsibility, or fund raising.

To Govern or Not to Govern

Governance is an exercise in authority and control. Trustees, directors, or regents—the interchangeable nomenclature that identifies the actors in governance—are the primary stewards of the spirit of philanthropy. As stewards, they are the legendary "keepers of the hall." They hold the nonprofit organization in trust to ensure that it will continue to function according to the dictates of its mission.

The trustees must bear the responsibility to define and interpret the mission and ensure that the organization will remain faithful to its mission. Board members should accept the charge that trusteeship concerns itself with the proper deployment of resources and with the accompanying action, the securing of resources. Deploying resources is difficult if the required resources are not secured through effective fund raising practices. It stands to reason that trustees as advocates of and stewards to the mission must attend to the task of pressing the resources development program on to success.

Institutionalizing Fund Raising

Fund raising projects the values of the total organization into the community whenever it seeks gift support. All aspects of governance—administration, program, and resources development—are part of the whole. As such, these elements must be part of the representation when gifts are sought. Fund raising cannot function apart from the organization; apart from its mission, goals, objective, and programs; apart from a willingness to be held accountable for all of its actions.

Fund raising is and must always be the lengthened shadow of the nonprofit entity, reflecting the organization's dignity, its pride of accomplishment, and its commitment to service. Fund raising by itself and apart from the institution has no substance in the eyes and heart of the potential contributor.

Gift Making as Voluntary Exchange

Gift making is based on a voluntary exchange. Gifts secured through coercion, through any means other than persuasion, are not gifts freely given. They do not have the meaning of philanthropy. Rarely will gifts obtained under pressure or through any form of intimidation be repeated. These gifts lose their meaning.

In the process of giving, the contributor offers a value to the nonprofit organization. This gift is made without any expectation of a material return, apart from the tax deductibility authorized by government. The reasons for making a gift are manifold.

In accepting the gift, it is incumbent upon the organization to return a value to the donor in a form other than material value. Such a value may be social recognition, the satisfaction of supporting a worthy cause, a feeling of importance, a feeling of making a difference in resolving a problem, a sense of belonging, or a sense of "ownership" in a program dedicated to serving the public good.

Trustees, administrators, or fund raising practitioners so often misconstrue the true meaning of this exchange relationship, and they violate the acknowledgment process by offering a return of substantive value. This alters the exchange, reduces the meaning of philanthropy, and diminishes the gift in its commitment to the mission. The transaction is one of a material exchange, a self-centered quid pro quo with none of the spirit of philanthropy in the exchange.

Substituting Pride for Apology

Giving is a privilege, not a nuisance or a burden. Stewardship nourishes the belief that people draw a creative energy, a sense of self-worth, a capacity to function productively from sources beyond themselves. This is a deep personal belief or a religious conviction. Thoughtful philanthropists see themselves as responsible stewards of life's gifts to them. What they have they hold in trust, in their belief, and they accept the responsibility to share their treasures effectively through their philanthropy. Giving is an expression of thankfulness for the blessings that they have received during their lifetime.

The person seeking the gift should never demean the asking by clothing it in apology. Solicitation gives the prospect the opportunity to respond with a "yes" or a "no." The solicitation should be so executed as to demonstrate to the prospective contributor that there can be a joy to giving, whether the gift measures up to the amount or not. Fund raising professionals must teach this joy by asking properly and in a manner that puts the potential contributor at ease.

The first task of the solicitor is to help the potential contributor understand the organization's case, especially its statement of mission. When a person commits to contribute to a cause and does so because of an acceptance of and a belief in the mission, then that person becomes a "stakeholder" in the organization and that for which it stands. This emphasizes that philanthropy is moral action, and the contributor is an integral part of that action.

Fund Raising as a Servant to Philanthropy

Philanthropy is voluntary action for the public good through voluntary action, voluntary association, and voluntary giving (Payton, 1988). Fund raising has been servant to philanthropy across the millennia. Through the procession of the centuries, the thesis has been established that people want and have a need to give. People want to give to causes that serve the entire gamut of human and societal needs. They will give when they can be assured that these causes can demonstrate their worthiness and accountability in using the gift funds that they receive.

Ethical fund raising is the prod, the enabler, the activator to gift making. It must also be the conscience to the process. Fund raising is at its best when it strives to match the needs of the not-for-profit organization with the contributor's need and desire to give. The practice of gift seeking is justified when it exalts the contributor, not the gift seeker. It is justified when it is used as a responsible invitation, guiding contributors to make the kind of gift that will meet their own special needs and add greater meaning to their lives.

PART TWO

FUNDAMENTALS OF SUCCESSFUL FUND RAISING

The chapters in this part deal with institutional readiness for fund raising. According to the Rosso philosophy, an organization earns the privilege to ask for funds by making the case for support. This part begins with planning for fund raising and ends with a discussion of the total development plan, all built around the case for support. Fund raising is an ongoing process of interaction between the nonprofit organization and its publics. Chapter Three's focus on the fund raising cycle prepares the reader mentally for the other chapters in the section and also for the entire fund raising process.

Planning begins with a careful analysis of organizational strengths and weaknesses that affect fund raising. It also considers the threats and opportunities in the external environment. How well an organization delivers its services and modifies its programs in response to changes in the environment has an impact on its fund raising success.

Separate chapters focus on identifying constituents for fund raising and making the case for support. Constituency identification is based on the question "Who cares about us?" Case development begins with the question "Why do we exist?" The answers to these two questions are essential to planning for fund raising. Organizations cannot move forward in fund raising without understanding their constituents and a strong mission statement supported by program globalization.

The part ends with a discussion of the total development plan. The total development plan is a set of fund raising programs or activities to meet a variety of organization and donor needs through lifetime donor development. Not every organization can implement all aspects of a total development plan. But every organization can implement a plan that incorporates the concept of lifetime donor development. The total development plan reminds us of the ongoing nature of fund raising work.

Achieving excellence in fund raising depends on institutional readiness. Fund raising success is based on preparation of a fund raising plan built on the institution's case for support, its relationship with its constituents, and its interaction with its external environment. These elements lead the institution to its fund raising plan. Unless the institution has prepared itself well in these preliminary, but essential areas, fund raising cannot succeed.

CHAPTER THREE

Plan to Succeed

Timothy L. Seiler

In the first edition of *Achieving Excellence in Fund Raising,* Hank Rosso wrote the chapter titled "Understanding the Fund Raising Cycle." This revised and retitled chapter retains the concepts and principles of the planning model known as the fund raising cycle. The chapter emphasizes different points than Hank emphasized, but it retains the fundamental belief that the cycle is an effective planning tool to help fund raisers, both paid and volunteer, understand the manageable process that fund raising is. Each step of the process is explained in detail in the various chapters that follow.

Effective fund raising depends on effective planning and rigorous execution—actually, more planning than execution. The better the planning, the better the fund raising results. The fund raising cycle illustrates the principle that it is possible to ask someone for a charitable gift too soon. A premature gift solicitation usually leads to one of two outcomes: the donor refuses to make a gift, or the donor gives a token gift that is neither appropriate for his or her capacity to give nor adequate for the nonprofit's need. Neither outcome is what a fund raiser seeks or wants. Using the fund raising cycle avoids these outcomes and paves the way to the preferred response to a gift solicitation: "Yes, I'll make the gift you ask for." To paraphrase a winemaker's advertising slogan of several years ago, "We will solicit no gift before its time."

The first thing to note about the fund raising cycle is its name: the fund raising *cycle.* The fund raising process is continuous (see Figure 3.1). The ongoing nature is illustrated by the continuing arrows inside the steps of the model.

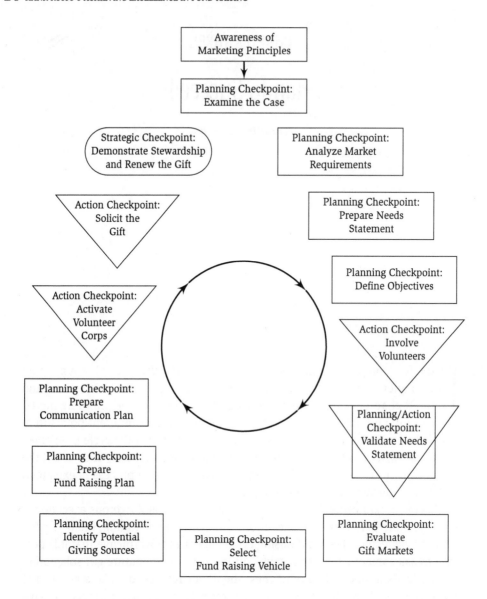

Figure 3.1. The Fund Raising Cycle.

Source: The Fund Raising School, 2002, p. 1-65.

These arrows represent the loop formed by the interrelated steps of the fund raising process. The complexity of the fund raising process lies in part in the reality that various constituencies from whom gifts are sought will be at different stages in the process. The fund raising manager must coordinate the various activities necessary for moving the constituencies through the phases in the cycle.

The second thing to note about the fund raising cycle is the number of discrete steps constituting the whole. Starting with the step labeled "Planning Checkpoint: Examine the Case" and proceeding clockwise around the cycle, there are fourteen steps. Soliciting a gift comes at step thirteen. Planning to solicit a gift therefore involves twelve steps. Skipping or shortchanging any of the steps leading to the solicitation will end in less than desirable results. Soliciting the gift (step thirteen) does not stop the process; it begins it anew. Thus the fund raising cycle is a continuous process of planning for and asking for charitable gifts.

Prior to taking the first step in the fund raising cycle is the nonprofit's need to understand marketing principles and how they apply to the fund raising process. Such awareness requires the nonprofit to develop feedback systems to measure and monitor the needs, perceptions, wants, and values of prospective donors. What do prospective donors seek for their own lives that they can find through involvement with the nonprofit? The better the nonprofit understands that exchange, the better it will manage its fund raising cycle.

The first step in the fund raising cycle, a planning checkpoint, is the examination of the nonprofit's case for support. The case is the sum of all the reasons why anyone should give charitable gifts to the organization. Each nonprofit must develop its own compelling case based on how it meets clearly defined and understood community needs. The case illustrates how the nonprofit serves the community, providing benefits and adding value.

The case must provide persuasive responses to these questions:

1. Why does the organization exist? The answer lies in the human or social problem or need addressed by the nonprofit. This is the organization's mission, its raison d'être.

2. What services or programs does the nonprofit provide to meet the need or solve the problem?

3. Why should prospective donors (individuals, corporations, foundations) provide gifts, and what benefits accrue to donors who make gifts?

The answers form the basis of the organization's mission. (Case and mission are covered more fully in Chapter Six.)

The next step is to analyze market requirements. The nonprofit must test its mission as articulated through its case against the wants and needs of the market or gift sources from which it seeks charitable gifts. Only the marketplace is a true test of the validity of the nonprofit's proposed solution to the human or social problems it addresses. Such market validation is crucial to successful fund raising.

If the markets do not understand or accept the importance of the needs being addressed by the nonprofit, fund raising faces a serious obstacle. Worse, if the markets do not even know of the nonprofit or the needs it addresses, fund raising is not possible. Donors will give to organizations they care about that address needs they care about.

In meeting clearly identified community needs understood to be of value to the potential donors, the nonprofit can formulate compelling arguments for why its work merits philanthropic gifts.

Next comes the preparation of a needs statement. This is the organization's plan for carrying out its work toward mission fulfillment. Program plans are projected for annual needs and for longer-term needs. Financial planning follows program planning and defines the resources required for carrying out programs and delivering services. This includes descriptions of sources of revenue needed to support the program plan. This is the justification for fund raising.

The preparation of the needs statement involves the volunteer leadership of the nonprofit, especially board members, selected major donors, and other volunteers who can affect the organization and its fund raising. The needs statement shapes future fund raising goals and objectives and must include not only annual operating needs but also longer-term fund raising plans for capital and endowment needs.

The next planning checkpoint is the definition of objectives. The programs for fulfilling the mission must be translated into specific, measurable action plans for providing solutions to problems the organization addresses. If the mission statement explains *why,* goal statements tell *what* and objectives state *how.* To be credible to the market sources, objectives must be realistic and achievable within the resources available to the organization. The acronym SMART helps clarify what objectives are:

Specific

Measurable

Achievable

Results-oriented

Time-determined

Specific illustrations of how the organization intends to do its work provide a visible link to program budgeting and to a rationale for fund raising.

Next comes the first action step in the fund raising cycle: involvement of volunteers. While earlier steps involved board members and selected other volunteers in planning, this step calls for action in developing and carrying out effective fund raising strategies. Because an effective gift solicitor is one who believes in and is committed to the cause, the earlier involvement steps prepare the volunteers to be effective solicitors of their peers. Historically, and still today, the most effective gift solicitation is that of a peer volunteer asking for gifts in a face-to-face solicitation.

One of the most effective ways to involve volunteers is in the validation of the organization's needs statement. Philanthropic support requires constant validation by the board and other volunteers. For volunteers to give and get philanthropic gifts, they must reaffirm the needs statement through continued involvement in analyzing the nonprofit's plans. Such involvement is critical before launching the fund raising program or campaign.

The next step in the cycle is an evaluation of gift markets to determine their ability and perceived willingness to fund the nonprofit's programs through charitable gifts. This step includes making informed judgments about which markets to approach and the gift amounts to be sought.

The most likely sources of gifts are individuals, corporations, foundations, associations, and government agencies. As explained in Chapter One, the most generous source has been individuals, providing approximately 83 percent of total philanthropy in recent years. Much individual wealth has gone into family foundations and community foundations in recent years, and thus foundations have been the fastest-growing source of gift funds.

Many nonprofits will not experience such a high percentage of gift support from individuals or even from individuals combined with foundations. The focus of market evaluation should be on building and sustaining as diverse a funding base as possible. The more diverse the funding base, the more likely the nonprofit can sustain itself in a volatile fund raising environment and can be more responsive to the needs of its market constituencies.

Planning continues with careful selection of fund raising vehicles (strategies). With the gift market evaluation completed, the fund raising staff and volunteers must now determine which fund raising techniques will be most effective in each market. Fund raising strategies or methods include direct mail, phonathons, special events or benefits (often called fund raisers), grant seeking, personal solicitations, recognition groups, and e-mail and Internet sites. Just as market evaluation calls for diversity of funding, so selection of fund raising methods should explore every opportunity for raising gift funds to carry out the organization's mission.

Fund raising programs include the annual fund, special or major gifts, capital campaigns, and endowment programs. The latter two often rely heavily on planned giving as a way for donors to make larger gifts than they typically make through annual funds or special gifts programs.

The successful fund raising program will analyze all the methods, test various ones, and evaluate their effectiveness through cost-benefit ratios and other measures of success. Long-term sustained fund raising effectiveness will match the various methods to the different gift sources to identify what works best in which markets.

Identifying potential gift sources is the next planning step in the cycle. This step distills and refines the gift market evaluation into lists of specific prospective donors. The prospective donors will be present in each market: individuals, corporations, and foundations. Each prospective donor is identified and qualified by three criteria: *linkage* to the organization, *ability* to give gifts at the level being sought, and *interest* in the organization's work.

Although many exercises in finding prospective donors begin with identifying individuals (and corporations and foundations) with the most money (ability), such exercises are futile. A funder who lacks interest in the work or a linkage to the nonprofit (such as a committed, involved volunteer) will not give just because of ability.

Volunteer involvement through a prospective donor development committee builds a priority list of specific giving sources. Furthermore, this type of volunteer involvement builds ownership of the fund raising plan and process among the volunteers.

The tenth step in the cycle is the preparation of the fund raising plan. The previous nine steps focused on analysis, or fact gathering, and planning. Preparation of the fund raising plan is a call to action. Fund raising staff draft the plan and involves volunteer leaders in refining and validating the plan. The plan should account for proper execution by allocating the resources necessary for implementing the plan. The plan should also include the management steps of monitoring and evaluating to provide for modification if needed.

The fund raising plan needs to spell out how much money will be raised for what programs in what time frame using which methods. The plan should include roles for volunteers and staff.

Understanding the organization's mission and its fund raising plan by those prospective donors who will be asked to make gifts is essential to successful fund raising. People give money to causes they know about and care about. Thus the next planning step is the preparation of a communication plan. For effective fund raising, communication must go beyond the dissemination of information. Communication must stir the emotions and the intellects of those from whom gifts are sought. Effective fund raising communication touches the heart and the head.

The goal of fund raising communication is to lead prospective donors to an understanding and acceptance of the nonprofit and its purposes and create a desire to share in seeing that the mission is fulfilled. Effective fund raising communication is a two-way interaction providing a means for donors to express concerns. Effective communication creates an opportunity for the exchange of values, which is fundamental for successful fund raising.

Fund raising is about relationships built on mutual interests and concerns. One of the saws of fund raising is that people give to people with causes. The next action step in the cycle is to activate a volunteer corps of solicitors.

Fund raising in the United States has been largely a volunteer activity, action taken by people so committed to a cause that they make their own gifts and then eagerly invite others to join the cause. No solicitation is more compelling, even today, than one done by a volunteer advocate who personally solicits gifts to support a nonprofit to which he or she is passionately devoted.

Though volunteerism in fund raising remains strong today, the trend, especially among large organizations, is to rely more and more on highly trained fund raising staff to solicit gifts, especially major gifts. Among universities and colleges, and to some degree among hospitals and medical centers, major gift fund raising is becoming more the purview of paid staff than of volunteers.

The effective nonprofit must renew and expand its volunteer corps of fund raisers to expand the base of donors. It is a generally accepted norm that one volunteer is needed for every five personal solicitations.

With twelve steps now completed, it is time to solicit the gift. Some gifts, from the board, the staff, and certain volunteers, will probably already have been part of earlier stages in the process. This step represents the carrying out of the fund raising plan into the broader constituency and is the culmination of all that has been done so far.

The solicitation step calls for already committed donors to visit personally those from whom gifts will be sought. The current donor makes the case for the organization, explains his or her own level of commitment, and invites the prospective donor to join in the fulfillment of the mission by making a charitable gift. The solicitation step is a dignified process of asking with pride for a philanthropic gift to help carry out the important work of the nonprofit.

Soliciting and receiving the gift is not the end of the process. In fact, it is only the beginning of a deepening relationship between the donor and the nonprofit. Proper gratitude for and acknowledgment of the gift must be expressed by the nonprofit. The nonprofit must also disclose how the gift will be used and demonstrate the highest level of accountability and stewardship in the appropriate, wise use of the gift.

Properly thanking donors, reporting the use of gifts, and demonstrating wise stewardship of contributed funds makes renewal of the gift possible. The renewal process, step fourteen, restarts the cycle. The case must be renewed by testing it again among the constituency. Renewal requires ongoing analysis of how effectively the nonprofit meets the requirements and fulfills the needs of its gift markets. The needs statement must be checked and rechecked to demonstrate the continuing effectiveness and worthiness of the nonprofit.

Fund raising is a multidisciplined process requiring extensive involvement of staff and volunteers in a series of interrelated steps described in the fund raising cycle. The main responsibility of the professional fund raising executive is to manage the process, serving as catalyst and coach for all involved in fund raising.

CHAPTER FOUR

Organizational Strengths and Vulnerabilities

Eugene R. Tempel

This chapter is based on Chapter Three in *Achieving Excellence in Fund Raising* (Rosso and Associates, 1991) and Chapter Seven in *Principles and Techniques of Fund Raising* (The Fund Raising School, 2002b). It is focused on the aspects and orientations necessary for an organization to be successful in fund raising. Hank Rosso said, "You can raise a lot more money through organized fund raising than you can through disorganized fund raising." Public perceptions about whether an institution is well organized have a great deal to do with fund raising success.

Fund raising is an active management process that is built on organizational strengths. And fund raising fails because of organizational vulnerabilities. This chapter examines the various organizational factors that enable fund raising to succeed as well as sometimes cause it to fail.

STRENGTHS AND VULNERABILITIES

Often an effort to provide for the public good begins with a single individual acting independently. Others might be drawn in to help support the effort with time or talent or money. Success might lead to organized voluntary association or ultimately to the formation of a nonprofit organization, qualified to receive philanthropic contributions eligible for the Internal Revenue Service's charitable gift deduction. It is through these formal organizations, meeting the requirements of section 501(c)(3) of the Internal Revenue Code or being organized as a church, that most philanthropic gifts are made. A nonprofit organization is able to engage volunteers and raise philanthropic dollars based on organizational strengths that reflect its understanding of the external environment. An inability to engage volunteers and raise funds is often a reflection of organizational isolation and weaknesses that leave the organization vulnerable to decline.

For an organization to be successful in fund raising, it must be connected to its external environment. It must understand the changing needs of that environment and its ability to respond to the organization's need for human and financial resources to remain functional. The organization must have management structures in place that interpret its mission in relation to changing external needs. An organizational tendency toward an open system or a closed system relative to the external environment has an impact on fund raising ability.

For nonprofit organizations to be successful in the twenty-first century, they must operate as open systems (Katz and Kahn, 1978), understanding that they are interdependent with their external environment, even if they are highly institutionalized with values that appeal to a narrow base of supporters. Research indicates that philanthropic giving is closely related to growth of the economy (AAFRC Trust for Philanthropy, 2002). Changing needs in society call for adaptations by nonprofit organizations. So do changing donor preferences.

Nonprofit organizations have a natural tendency to become closed systems. The attempt to build endowment reflects that tendency. A fully endowed nonprofit organization can become a closed system irrelevant to the common good and vulnerable to decline.

In the dozen years since the first edition of *Achieving Excellence in Fund Raising,* nonprofit organizations have begun functioning more as open systems. Professional management, competition, calls for transparency and accountability, changing donor behavior, and scholarship on best practices have all been responsible. Traditionally, higher education institutions functioned as though they could shape and control their outside environments. The intense marketing programs that colleges and universities have in place today indicate that they have come down from the ivory tower and gotten back in touch with the real world. Many higher education institutions have developed elaborate feedback systems to determine student preferences and have developed new services and arrangements to respond and sophisticated advertising and communications and incentive programs to recruit students they want.

When organizations desire or require a broad base of support or seek wider influence, they must be managed as open systems. Open system theory assumes that organizations are not independent of their external environments and that they have impact on and are affected by their environments. According to open system theory, organizations depend on a hospitable and supportive environment for supplies of human, financial, and material resources, as well as for consumption of goods and services.

To function successfully as open systems, organizations must continually monitor the environment and either adapt to changes or attempt to change inhospitable elements in the environment. Organizations that fail to adapt or fail to influence the environment eventually produce unwanted goods or unneeded services and lose their ability to attract vital resources.

Fund raising success depends on an organization's ability to adapt to surrounding conditions. A nonprofit organization exists to provide services for which there is a public or societal need, often on a small or local level. If that need is otherwise met, the organization's rationale for existence disappears. If it continues to provide staff and programs to fill the outdated need, it will be viewed as wasteful, inefficient, and unresponsive. Its sources of support will diminish, and it will be forced to shut down. For example, the Young Men's Christian Association (YMCA) was established in the nineteenth century in response to the need for a healthful Christian environment for young men who moved from rural areas to the cities for jobs. Had the YMCA not adapted to a new environment by abandoning its hotel business when that migration ended and shifted to filling other needs in the urban environment, it might not exist today. Similarly, the March of Dimes was founded in 1938 as the National Foundation for Infantile Paralysis, largely through the efforts of President Franklin D. Roosevelt. When a vaccine for polio was developed and the disease was eventually eliminated, the organization lost its rationale for existence. In this case, the organization found another health problem, children's birth defects, that required a solution and allowed the organization to adapt to other social needs.

Responding to changes in the environment is not as simple as meeting current needs. Organizations that respond to changing needs by making dramatic alterations to their own institutional value systems also risk their future. If traditional contributors fail to support an old institution in its newest efforts, those donors' contributions may be lost before a new support base is established. For example, consider a small Roman Catholic liberal arts college built on the tradition of providing a well-rounded education based on Catholic values in a highly personal environment. The college might respond to declining enrollments by orienting itself toward meeting needs for continuing education in local workplaces. The college risks losing its traditional student base entirely, however, and with it existing alumni support. The college may gain an expanded new student body and obtain private dollars from the community, but it will be a different institution with different potentials for fund raising.

Philip Kotler has made significant contributions by adapting marketing principles from business to nonprofit organizations (Kotler and Andreasen, 1987). He devised a scale that described an organization's orientation in one of three ways: unresponsive, casually responsive, or fully responsive. Unresponsive organizations function as closed systems, as bureaucracies. They do not encourage customers to submit inquiries, complaints, or suggestions; they do not determine customer satisfaction or needs or train staff to be customer-oriented. The casually responsive organization begins to look externally in its planning. It encourages its constituents to provide feedback and periodically measures constituent satisfaction. The fully responsive organization shares the characteristics of the casually responsive organization but also tries to improve its services based on new needs and preferences and prepares its staff to be customer-oriented.

Many nonprofit organizations cannot and should not become fully responsive to the market in order to enhance their fund raising. They must remain in harmony with the values and mission for which they were founded. Organizations with strong internal value systems that give rise to their missions should become highly responsive by actively involving their clients and potential contributors in the organization's affairs. Fund raising success depends on the sensitive inclusion of potential supporters in the life and spirit of the organization.

Kotler and Andreasen (1987) come to the same conclusion: "If a manager wishes the organization to be wholly customer-driven, he or she must directly confront the often unspoken fear that this type of marketing orientation will ultimately cause artists, surgeons, librarians, museum directors, and other nonprofit professionals to bend their professional standards and integrity to 'please the masses'" (p. 61).

Nonprofit organizations today are vulnerable to concepts of social entrepreneurship and market orientation. Donors often push nonprofits toward operating more market-based services, using a business model, with a focus on the bottom line. Some nonprofit organizations have had to deal with external pressures to balance bottom-line interests of donors and board members with topline, mission orientation.

Although nonprofit organizations do not exist to generate profits, their long-term survival depends to some extent on good business practices. Nonprofits that develop surplus income protect themselves from fluctuations in client fees and fund raising levels. The existence of surplus revenue also assures contributors that the organization has a future. Organizations that strive to provide the most effective services with the fewest resources are the most likely to generate surpluses. Organizations that are viewed as effective and efficient also have the best opportunity to attract philanthropic dollars. How well a nonprofit organization is managed also has an impact on its ability to raise money.

Accountability is a major force in nonprofit organizations today. Accountability encompasses not only how well a nonprofit is managed but also how well a nonprofit communicates its management and outcomes to its constituents. It is an organizational strength for a nonprofit organization to hold itself accountable to demonstrate good stewardship to its constituents.

Business techniques might be useful in managing nonprofit fund raising. However, the values and beliefs that give rise to these organizations often lead them necessarily to defy good business marketing practices. New service initiatives that abandon mission to enhance revenue production can harm philanthropic efforts. And when unpopular causes must be pursued, if the organization is to remain faithful to the requirements of its mission, it must defy marketing information in favor of its mission.

Sometimes fidelity to mission leads to conflict with sources of support. A conservative funding source might hesitate to support an organization that is serving a controversial cause because its employees, customers, or stockholders might object. A for-profit industry that manufactures a product to reduce tooth decay might be eliminated by the successful efforts of a nonprofit organization that seeks to eradicate tooth decay. Organizations that understand and manage this complexity put themselves in a position of strength when raising funds.

Fund raising is an effective test of organizational viability. As such, fund raising can become the catalyst for organization renewal and commitment. To be successful in fund raising, the organization must be viewed by potential supporters as responsive in its delivery of quality services. These services must be provided to constituents in an effective and efficient manner. Potential supporters must understand and accept the value systems that affect these services. An organization that lacks internal meaning has no basis for stimulating philanthropy.

By managing tensions between responsiveness to changing environmental factors and its mission, an organization can enhance its strengths and minimize its vulnerabilities. A simple SWOT analysis will enable an organization to conduct and succeed in its fund raising (Kearns, 1996). SWOT analysis can help an organization build on its *strengths,* minimize its *weaknesses,* and deal with *opportunities* and *threats* in its external environment. Such an analysis can help an organization focus on its strengths and reduce its vulnerabilities in institutional readiness, human resources, markets, vehicles, and management, the factors that are essential to successful fund raising.

Institutional Readiness

The premise of this chapter is that effective fund raising is built on organizational strengths and that organizational weaknesses and vulnerabilities can undermine fund raising efforts. With this in mind, an organization preparing itself for fund raising must analyze its strengths and weaknesses and inventory the resources that are essential for successful fund raising.

Fund raising based on the strengths of the organization assumes a dignity that flows from those strengths, obviating any need on the part of staff or volunteers to apologize for the solicitation process. Fund raising based on values and mission is a meaningful part of philanthropy. To take its case for philanthropic support to the public, the organization must have prepared itself internally to focus on its strengths.

An essential readiness element is the institutional plan. The plan attests to the stability and to the futurity of the organization based, as it should be, on an assessment of current and future social and human needs within the scope of the organization's mission. One of the greatest strengths that the plan can bring to the fund raising process is the affirmation that the organization is confident of its future and empowered by its vision of the future and a better society.

An effective plan must go beyond a description of programs. Programs must be drafted in economic terms if they are to provide a suitable foundation for fund raising. The plan must project annual income and expense requirements for each program, current and future. The plan should also identify special-purpose, capital, and endowment needs that are anticipated during the designated period. The organization is strongest when the prospective donor can accept the validity of the income and expense projections relative to past accomplishments and future program delivery. If financial accountability through the planning process can demonstrate efficient use of resources for effective programs, good stewardship has begun.

The financial plan should go beyond ordinary income and expense projections. It should state the amounts that must be raised for current program support through the annual fund; the amounts required for special projects, some immediate and urgent, others deferrable; the amounts required for capital projects; and the organization's endowment and cash reserve requirements. This comprehensive financial analysis, with its realistic assessment of anticipated revenue and gift production, forces careful evaluation of program proposals and responsible decisions when priorities are set.

Before the planning process can be initiated, the process itself should undergo scrutiny from the professional staff and volunteers of the organization to determine the extent to which it has involved the organization's primary constituency. A sensitive and responsive plan involves the professional staff and volunteers from the governing board as the plan's architects. Both groups must commit themselves to implement the plan and to evaluate it on a continuing basis, or the organization will be vulnerable during the fund raising process. The organization can benefit by generating a sense of ownership of the plan among the constituents. This can be done by inviting leaders within the constituency to participate in the planning activity. The more affirmation there is of the organization's mission through planning, the better the chances of winning the constituency's endorsement when the plan is finished. The plan will give substance to the various programs that have been devised to respond to the designated human and societal needs. From these program descriptions can be drawn the most salient and exciting expressions that can be used to promote and animate the case.

Human Resources

The first human resource strength in institutional readiness is the governing board. A thoughtfully structured, involved, and dedicated board of trustees is a symbol of responsible governance and an asset to the fund raising process. Conversely, a passive, uninvolved, and uninterested board is a problem.

It is essential that board members be actively involved in planning from the beginning delineation of the planning format through the periodic review and as part of the final acceptance of the plan with its definitions of program and financial priorities. By accepting the plan, board members accept the responsibility to give and to ask others to give in proper measure against the financial needs. This is trusteeship at its best. Finally, the board members must have integrity and credibility with the community, serving as the organization's first point of accountability to the public and as stewards of the public trust.

The board has a direct responsibility to press for the success of the organization's fund raising programs. To accomplish this, the board should have a fund raising or development committee on its roster of standing committees. Members of this committee should include the board members who have the strongest interest in the organization's mission and whose links with the community help initiate fund raising. This committee should meet regularly and actively develop, implement, and evaluate fund raising plans. Committee membership can be extended to non–board members who would be willing to give, ask, and work as advocates of the organization.

The second point of strength is the professional staff: the chief executive officer (CEO), individuals responsible for managing programs and finances, and the fund raising staff. The nonprofit entity's viability depends on long-term delivery of quality services that the public perceives as needed. This focuses attention on the CEO and the program staff. Filled with capable people, these positions provide organizational strength. The CEO is key in the fund raising process as a link to the board and to represent the organization in engaging donors and prospects. The CEO also sets the stage for organizational support of fund raising. Lack of CEO understanding, involvement and support is debilitating.

For fund raising to be effective over the long term, it requires the attention of someone who is competent to plan, organize, and manage the fund raising process. Fund raising management positions vary by organization as to the amount of time and the level of professionalism allotted to the task and range from volunteer to minimal part-time to full-time with a multiple-member professional staff, often a reflection of organizational age and size. The fund raising position of an organization is enhanced if it has full-time professional staff members at the helm who are dedicated to involving board members, other volunteers, and administrative, program, and support staffs so that they assist in the fund raising process.

The governing board and CEO must be prepared to become involved in fund raising. Board members must accept the organization as their own and support it financially as an indispensable first step in establishing institutional readiness. The final assessment of readiness is to determine the ability of board members, fund raising professionals, the CEO, and key staff members to come together as a development team. All must understand and accept that successful fund raising depends on the active participation of everyone on the team, both in the development and organization of fund raising programs and in asking for gifts.

That all team members embrace this concept is essential to the fund raising process. Under the definition of this process, the fund raising staff will provide the management services for the fund raising program. The volunteers will provide the links and leverage to the gift-making potential of the community. A properly developed governing board and volunteer and professional staff members are an essential asset when undertaking fund raising.

Sources of Support

Philanthropic funds originate in general areas of the economy referred to as "gift sources" or "markets." The five gift sources for fund raising activities are individuals, corporations, foundations, associations, and government. To some extent, every nonprofit organization has potential supporters among these markets. Opportunities for fund raising come from recognizing the potential for support among specific sectors of each market. Proper prospect development practices will make it possible to identify, cultivate, and solicit prospective donors within each sector.

Government funds are *not* philanthropic funds, but it is important to recognize that government funding has become a larger rather than a smaller source of revenue for nonprofit organizations. We are likely to see this trend continue, particularly for small neighborhood organizations and church and parachurch activities that provide neighborhood services.

Gift markets in the 2000s are significantly different from the gift markets from which organizations sought funds at the start of the 1990s, as noted in Chapter One. Foundations have become a more important source of funds, corporations take a more strategic approach, and individuals are more likely to be interested in program-related projects that allow them to express their own values and interests, many with private foundations to make their giving more formal. Understanding the values, interests, and needs of donors has always been important to fund raising but is even more important to success today.

Organizations today must have sufficient information about each prospect's interests, ability, and willingness to give. By accepting this basic principle of fund raising, the practitioner can understand that the organization will approach fund raising markets from its strongest position when it involves its board members, nonboard volunteers, and staff members in identifying, understanding, engaging, and soliciting potential contributors from any of the gift sources.

Fund Raising Vehicles

A nonprofit organization maximizes its potential for philanthropic support if it uses the full array of fund raising vehicles or approaches available to it. These include annual giving, special gifts, major gifts, the capital campaign, and planned giving. The organization's fund raising plan must take into account the human and financial resources it can commit to different fund raising activities. Today that includes use of a Web site for soliciting and accepting gifts and taking advantage of the various "e-philanthropy" opportunities available.

Organizations that depend too heavily on the annual fund through direct mail, telephone, and special events fund raising may incur high fund raising costs. Organizations that are dependent on one or two large individual, corporate, or foundation sources are vulnerable to the changing interests and funding capacities of these sources. The more comprehensive the fund raising plan is in making use of all the fund raising vehicles available to approach the full scope of funding sources, the stronger it will be.

For small nonprofit organizations, this can be a challenge, especially with major and planned gifts. But every organization can encourage bequests or giving through wills and use volunteer or pro bono consultants or a local community foundation to help with special opportunities for other types of planned gifts.

Management

Most experts agree that nonprofit organizations are more professionally managed today than they were a decade ago. But a Kellogg Foundation initiative for the first decade of the twenty-first century, called Knowledge Management in Nonprofit Management Education, is based on the evidence that professional talent is not uniformly distributed throughout the nonprofit sector. There is, however, some acceptance of the notion that even unsophisticated nonprofits are fairly efficient in the use of funds and effective in providing good services (Drucker, 1990).

Poor management or perceived poor management is a deficiency that leaves a nonprofit organization vulnerable to failure in fund raising. Sound management staff and processes are organizational strengths on which successful fund raising can be built.

The most successful organizations will have a management team of administrators, program managers, and fund raising managers who operate the organizations to some extent as an open system. This management team will involve its various constituents—clients, donors, trustees, volunteers, vendors, the community, and its own staff—in continued analysis and planning before executing programs and exercising management control over its programs. The successful organization will involve the same constituents in evaluating its programs as the management process of analysis, planning, execution, control, and evaluation (see Chapter Twenty-Three) begins another cycle.

Fund raising is a management process. It is based on the strength of an organization's programs to fulfill the organization's mission. Therefore, the organization must be well managed. Increasingly, managers of these entities are being called to account for themselves, illustrating to the public that they are good stewards of contributed funds and that the organization's programs are making a difference. In the strongest organizations, the fund raising manager has been successful in persuading the board of trustees and the CEO to dedicate significant portions of their time and energies to the organization's fund raising efforts.

Fund raising involves engaging constituents with the organization and helping them identify with organizational values and missions. It requires a comprehensive view of client constituencies, volunteers, advocates, and prospective contributors. Fund raising demands the mastery of professional technical skills and the ethical values that foster and protect philanthropy. It includes the management of planning and other efforts that precede many of society's voluntary actions for the public good.

Accountability

It is appropriate to end with a word on accountability. The organization that makes itself as transparent as possible, holds itself accountable to its constituents, and demonstrates good stewardship of its mission and its human and physical resources (see Chapter Thirty-One on stewardship) can engage in fund raising from a position of strength. The fund raising climate of the twenty-first century leaves organizations vulnerable to fund raising failure if they do not communicate with their key constituents; if they fail to invite key constituents inside their planning, management, financial, and evaluation processes; and if they do not report accurately on expenditure of funds. Accountability is not just a buzzword of the late twentieth century. Accountability has become an essential concept for nonprofit organization viability and success in the twenty-first century.

CONCLUSION

Fund raising success or failure is often related to organizational dynamics rather than fund raising strategies. Successful fund raising is built on strengths. Fund raising often fails because of organizational weaknesses or vulnerabilities.

First, to be successful in fund raising, organizations must operate as "open systems" while being true to their mission. Understanding the dynamics of the external environment whose gift support is sought is a key organizational strength. A sound plan for the future, developed with the involvement of key constituents, is an organizational strength in fund raising. It is also essential to have the CEO and the board involved in the process. Finally, the organization must have a communication plan through which it holds itself accountable to the public.

If organizations operate as "closed systems," focused internally with no plan for the future based on external needs, they are vulnerable to decline and failure in fund raising. Simply doing good work is no longer sufficient to ensure long-term success. More sophisticated donors and funders today are holding organizations to higher standards of accountability. Doing so demands professional management approaches that lead to institutional readiness for fund raising.

CHAPTER FIVE

Developing a Constituency
for Fund Raising

Timothy L. Seiler

E ffective fund raising requires intimate knowledge of the nonprofit's constituency, a distinct group of people with actual or potential interest in the organization. Some organizations have "natural" constituencies that are readily identifiable and generally accessible. Schools, colleges, and universities, for example, have students and alumni. Many educational institutions expand their constituencies to include parents and grandparents of current students. Hospitals have patients, often referred to in fund raising circles as "grateful patients." Arts organizations have patrons, members, and audiences. For Hank Rosso, constituency identification and development were at the heart of fund raising.

IDENTIFYING THE CONSTITUENCY

Organizations without a natural constituency still have constituencies. An organization may need to work hard to identify and build its constituency, but every nonprofit organization has its own constituency. At the very least, the constituency consists of people who need the nonprofit's services, who provide the services and direct the programs, who govern the organization, and who support the cause. In developing its constituency, an organization should expend the resources necessary to identify, inform, involve, and bond the constituency to the organization. The energy, time, and money invested in constituency development will be returned in multiples by serving the nonprofit through volunteers, donors, and advocates. The bond for this philanthropic activity is the nonprofit's mission.

The constituency is a set of interested persons serving the cause with passion. A synonym for *constituency* is *interested parties*. Interested parties include persons currently involved with the organization, those who have been previously involved, and those with the potential for future involvement. All constituencies also have active and inactive groups, interested and uninterested, close and distant. For fund raising purposes, it is essential to know the interests, needs, and wants of the people in the constituency because their level of involvement helps or hinders the nonprofit as it seeks to accomplish its goals. The constituency is made up of stakeholders interested in the health of the nonprofit.

A CONSTITUENCY MODEL

A helpful way to think about an organization's constituency is to visualize a set of concentric circles (see Figure 5.1). These widening circles represent the energy of an organization, which dissipates as we move outward from the center, much like the effect of a rock thrown into a pond. Where the rock enters the water,

Figure 5.1. The Constituency Model.

Source: The Fund Raising School, 2002, p. 2-17.

the action (energy) is highest. As the waves radiate outward from the point of entry, they become wider but weaker. That is how the constituency of a non-profit interacts with the organization. The closer to the center of the action, the greater the energy and the stronger the bond. The core constituency, then, is at the center of the concentric circles. Members of the constituency who are in the second, third, and fourth circles moving away from the center have a weaker bond with the organization. The farther away from the core the constituency segment lies, the lower the energy and the weaker the bond to the organization.

For the constituency model to affect fund raising positively, certain constituent groups should populate the inner circle, the core. The board of trustees, the senior management team, and major donors will ideally form the core of the organization. The trustees hold the organization in public trust and are respon-sible for the mission, vision, and policies of the organization. The senior man-agement team carries out the organization's programs to meet the community needs articulated in the mission. Major donors not only demonstrate their com-mitment to the cause through their gifts of substance but also serve as advocates for the cause. All three core components of the inner circle provide the energy for the organization and influence the direction of the organization.

Although these three groups are the critical ones to be in the central circle, large organizations might include additional groups: alumni boards, visiting committees, foundation boards, advisory committees, and friends groups, for example, might be part of the core constituency for complex organizations.

In the second circle are volunteers for program delivery and for fund raising; clients receiving the organization's services; employees who are not part of senior management; general donors who make gifts more modest than those made by major donors; members, if the organization is a membership organi-zation; and others involved with the organization, such as vendors, who have a stake in the organization but are not in the central circle.

All the components in the second circle are important because they provide a broad base of support and a potential for greater future involvement, includ-ing more strategic volunteer activity and major gift development.

The third circle, consisting of former participants, former board members, and former donors, represents a drop in energy as these groups are farther from the core of the organization. Although *former* refers to a state of what once was and might be taken as a negative, this circle holds the potential for reactivation and reinvolvement. Imaginative, open communication efforts might reveal that these groups would like to be invited back to participate more fully. If they once were participants, board members, or donors, they surely shared the values of the organization. Exploring how to win back their affections and their loyalty might move them back into the second circle and perhaps into the core circle. (Chapters Nineteen and Twenty-One provide suggestions for developing a com-munication process to invite people into the organization.)

The fourth circle, consisting of people with similar interests, is an ill-defined constituency segment. Constituents here are distant from the energy center. They typically know little of the organization, and the organization rarely knows much about them. This is the segment usually approached through direct mail in an attempt by the organization to acquire new donors. It is worth probing this segment, although the organization needs to recognize that returns from this segment are likely to be low for the time and energy expended.

The very last circle is the organization's universe. Every organization has such a constituency segment and often knows little about its giving potential. Involvement will be minimal, and whatever gifts come from this circle will probably be modest in size. But the gifts might be regular and long-lasting. The donors in this segment might give year after year, and the cumulative giving becomes substantive over time. This circle, too, is worth attention and energy.

Based on the Rosso model of fund raising, several principles of the circles model presented here are important. First, because energy is at the center and flows outward, the bond is strongest at the center. Fund raising, then, begins at the center of the constituency circles and is taken to the outer circles by the people in the inner circle—the board, management staff, and major donors. The constant challenge for the development program is to align the central players in the core circle. A dysfunctional fund raising program is one that finds the board or the management staff on the outer circles.

A second principle is fluidity in the circles. A major donor this year will be a general donor next year. Board members' terms expire, and they become former board members. Other changes occur in the constituency for many reasons: people change residences or occupations; donors' interests change; donors' financial capacity changes. Patterns in constituency development show that a 20 to 25 percent change annually is to be expected. Effective constituency development requires consistent involvement with all the circles in the model.

IDENTIFYING AND ATTRACTING LIKELY DONORS

One of the truisms of fund raising is that the best prospective donor is a current donor. Someone who has made a gift has demonstrated interest in and involvement with the organization. That donor is likely to consider another gift. Experienced fund raisers testify that every donor at one level is a prospective donor for a gift at a higher level. Working conscientiously with the constituency model will reveal the most likely candidates for renewed gifts and for increased gifts.

As stated in Chapter Three, the most likely donors are identified by three characteristics: linkage, ability, and interest. Linkage is contact. Often such contact is person to person, with peers of current donors. The personal contact, the linkage, makes possible a personal visit to the potential donor for the organization to make its case for a gift. Linkage can also be geographical, emotional, or professional. Think of it as networking. Linkage is determining who knows whom and who can arrange and carry out the visits necessary for successful gift solicitations.

Ability is a gauge of the gift source's financial capacity to give a gift at the level the nonprofit deems appropriate. Research by the nonprofit helps determine this capacity. Peer evaluations (linkage) of gift capacity are also effective in determining the ability factor.

Interest in the nonprofit and its work is essential. Even the most financially able gift sources will not make gifts to an organization in which they have no interest. Interest follows information and precedes involvement.

All three characteristics—linkage, ability, and interest—are imperative for identifying the most qualified and most likely prospective donors. It is most probable that these characteristics will be in greater evidence in the inner circles of the constituency model. Certainly it is important to test the principles across all the circles, but the most productive prospective donors will be found in the first two or three circles.

Some aspects of the constituency arise automatically. For instance, the client base becomes an immediate adjunct of the constituency because it acts in response to services offered. Trustees, management staff, and beginning program staff become an early part of an organization because they must make available the services that are needed by their clients. Contributors, volunteers, and advocates take longer to develop. They must be sought out and invited to become the philanthropic base that will augment and celebrate the organization's work.

The fund raising manager must be sensitive to the fact that there is constant interaction within and between the constituency circles and among the elements that make up each circle. Individuals gravitate toward the core circle as their interest is touched and then deepened; they drift away if their interest slackens, if they are ignored, or if their interests change or are neglected. A studied program of constituency involvement and thoughtful cultivation is necessary to maintain the vitality of the constituency base.

A responsible fund raising staff should assert itself continuously to develop an *awareness* within the constituency of the organization's mission, goals, and objectives; to foster an *understanding* of the service to that mission; and to invite constituency *commitment* to the organization through the process of making a gift. This gift-making process forges a strong bond of the constituency to the nonprofit organization and its mission.

An effective, externally oriented communication program is the first necessity. In developing any human relationship, it is necessary to get the attention of the subject, the person whom the organization wants to involve. The person must be made aware that the organization exists and that it exists for a purpose that may hold an interest for him or her. Awareness must be converted into understanding—first, of the guiding mission that delineates the human or societal needs that must be addressed, and second, of the programs that will respond to these needs. From awareness to understanding to acceptance is the direct path to involvement and the process that is so necessary for constituency development.

People will identify with an organization if they understand and can accept its reason for being, if they accept that the programs are valid and responsive, and if they strongly believe that the people associated with the organization are competent and trustworthy in their service to the mission.

Various techniques are applicable to this process of identifying and involving a constituency, particularly that segment who are likely to contribute funds and to volunteer time. One of the first and most effective instruments for constituency development is fund raising. The fund raising process is based on intelligent, purposeful communication with the amorphous and unidentified market, including prospective donors and current donors. A sensitively managed communication program will invite interest in the organization, its mission, its goals, and its programs. The outreach or public relations effort should include periodic newsletters that contain information of interest to the recipients. Too often these publications are self-serving instruments that extol the accomplishments of staff members while neglecting the concerns, questions, and curiosity of the constituency. Periodic surveys of readers' interests and reactions to the value of the newsletter might well evoke the kind of response that will correct the myopia of excessive self-interest.

Special events offer an opportunity to attract the attention of potential constituents. A special event can be any activity that is designed to accomplish a variety of objectives, one of which is to invite possible constituents to participate in the event and to learn more about the organization. Open houses, tours, runs and races, dinners, fashion shows, discussions, seminars, workshops, annual meetings, and book sales all qualify as special events. Properly staged events can serve purposes other than just raising money. They can encourage people to become part of the organization's expanding constituency base.

It is important to know and understand the concept of constituency circles, but this understanding must be translated into an understanding of the individual constituent in order to create and maintain the exchange relationship underlying effective fund raising and giving.

ROLES AND RESPONSIBILITIES THAT INFLUENCE GIVING

In identifying candidates for major gifts or for volunteer leadership positions, fund raisers are well served by a model known as the wheel of roles and responsibilities assumed by individuals (see Figure 5.2). These roles and responsibili-

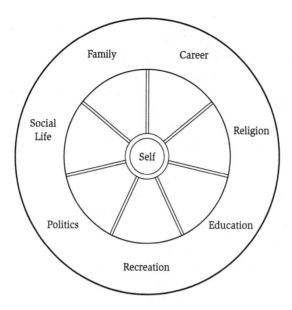

Figure 5.2. The Wheel of Roles and Responsibilities.

Source: The Fund Raising School, 2002, p. 2-19.

ties can help determine the behavior of constituents in relating to the nonprofit organization.

The individual who is a prospective major gift donor or leadership candidate is in the center of the wheel. Each spoke leads to a role or responsibility demanding a portion of the individual's time, energy, ability, and inclination to be involved with a fund raising program. The roles and responsibilities include family, career, religion, education, recreation, politics, and social life.

Family is of central concern to most individuals. The family will often have a positive influence on the gift-giving decision. But family interests can also hinder the major gift process. The fund raising executive needs to determine how the family role may affect the gift decision.

A career or profession will often influence a constituent's ability or inclination to help a nonprofit organization. Members of certain professions are conventionally viewed as likely to be major givers: attorneys, doctors, investment managers, and technology investors and entrepreneurs. Members of other professions—educators, nurses, social workers—are generally viewed as having little capacity to give. Effective constituency development goes beyond conventional attitudes and explores each individual for capacity and inclination, ignoring convention as the sole determinant.

Religion has been and continues to be a bedrock of philanthropy. Historically, giving patterns reveal that religion influences generosity to secular causes. It is true, however, that commitments to a house of worship can also reduce the financial capacity to give to other causes.

The role that education plays in an individual's life can be an important factor in major gift capacity. If a prospective major gift donor is paying tuition for family enrolled at private universities, his or her capacity to give to a nonprofit is likely limited for the duration of the educational process. If, however, the person places a high value on education because of the stature it confers, that can be a very important factor in determining interest in philanthropy in higher education.

Recreational interests can play an important role in the prospective donor's life. Some interests might be so costly as to reduce the potential for gift-giving. On the plus side, recreational interests provide a forum for involvement and interaction. The astute fund raising executive will determine how the nonprofit can meet the donor's interests through recreation.

Politics, or civic engagement, plays a role in most people's lives to the degree that it influences how people interact. Those constituents most actively engaged in communities of interest and shared values have wide-ranging connections, thereby expanding constituency circles.

Social roles are important to fund raising for how they build networks and make connections. A socially active, energetic constituency will extend itself widely, creating many opportunities for delivering the nonprofit's message. Broadening social contacts will assist in establishing helpful linkages.

These roles change many times during one's life. The fund raiser must recognize that on one hand, some of these roles might be in conflict with the organization's fund raising needs and will therefore militate against the making of a major gift. On the other hand, the roles might be compatible with the organization's needs and will form a basis of linkage to the organization, thus facilitating a major gift. The role of the fund raising executive, along with volunteers, is to identify the elements that provide a basis for the exchange relationship, focusing on the compatibility of shared values.

CONCLUSION

Constituency development is crucial for long-term, sustainable fund raising success. Most organizations have a larger constituency than they can interact with effectively. Organizations should spend the most time and energy identifying their constituencies and cultivating meaningful relationships with them, moving the constituents closer and closer to the center and bonding them to the core of the organization. Sensitive attention to the needs and values of the constituents will draw them more intimately into the mission of the organization.

CHAPTER SIX

Developing and Articulating
a Case for Support

Timothy L. Seiler

N onprofit organizations know intuitively that their work merits philanthropic gift support. If they assume that their gift sources share this intuitive knowledge, they are mistaken. A case for support is a *sine qua non*
for nonprofits. A case for support is the rationale underlying fund raising. For
Hank Rosso, it was the reason nonprofit organizations deserved philanthropic
support. Without a case for support, a nonprofit does not have a right to seek
support.

The case is the general argument for why a nonprofit deserves gift support.
The case is bigger than the organization and relates to a cause being served. The
case for support is an encyclopedic accumulation of information, parts of which
are used to argue that the organization deserves gift support for doing its work.

A case statement is a particular expression of the case. A case statement is
not as big as the case. That is, a case statement is a specific illustration of some
of the elements making up the case. Although the case is made up of numerous reasons why the organization deserves gift support, not every reason is
included in the case statement. A case statement focuses on or highlights critical factors important in arguing for gift support. A case statement selects and
articulates specific points from the overall case (Seiler, 2001; The Fund Raising
School, 2002b).

This chapter moves from the development of the case to the expression
of the case, distinguishing between the internal case and the external case.

49

The role of staff and volunteers in doing the work of case preparation is also described.

The preparation of the case begins with an understanding that nonprofit organizations raise money to meet larger community needs. Unmet social needs lead to the creation of nonprofit organizations, and the case for support is built on how well the organization meets those needs. The effectiveness of the case depends on how well the cause is served.

The case is the bedrock on which philanthropic fundraising is built. It is the urgent call for a solution to a problem, the meeting of a need. The persuasiveness of the case relates directly to the nonprofit's ability to solve problems and to adjust to meet changing market or societal needs. The case for support is the expression of the cause, addressing why anyone should contribute to the advancement of the cause. The case is larger than the organization's financial needs; it is larger than the organization.

Preparation, development, and validation of the case begin with staff. If the organization has on staff a development director, he or she should be the catalyst in the preparation and development of the case. The development professional typically serves as an interpreter of the concerns, interests, and needs of the external constituencies while also articulating the needs statement of the organization. The development staff not only know the organization internally but also interact regularly with external constituencies. The staff must be able and willing to bring back inside the organization what the perceptions of the organization are among the constituencies where gift support will be sought.

It is not uncommon for development staff to discover that not everything is perfect among the constituencies. Occasionally, constituents are misinformed or uninformed. Sometimes there are perceptions that the organization is not effective. Perhaps constituents lack confidence that gifts are needed or that they really make a difference. Finding out how to address these concerns will strengthen the case for support.

Development staff must know the organization from the inside out and must represent the constituency from the outside in. As Figure 6.1 shows, development of the case begins with the fund raising manager but includes the organization's key constituents, notably the CEO and members of the board. Getting others involved in the development of the case is important too. Seeking the ideas of key constituents—board members, volunteers, donors, and potential donors—is particularly effective in enlisting volunteer leadership for articulation of the case in fund raising. Having a role in developing and validating the case increases the enthusiasm of those who will articulate this case in their own words. They will question what puzzles them or challenge what disturbs them. If they are representative of others from whom gifts will be sought, their questions and challenges will strengthen the case for support.

Figure 6.1. Staff Constituency Participation in Case Development.
Source: The Fund Raising School, 2002.

WHERE TO START? WITH CASE RESOURCES

The development of the case begins with compiling information that provides the background for everything a potential donor might want to know about the organization. These *case resources* serve as a database or information bank, the platform on which the case statement is built. In fact, they are sometimes referred to as the internal case statement.

Case resources document the following aspects of the organization:

Mission statement

Goals

Objectives

Programs and services

Finances

Governance

Staffing

Facilities and service delivery

Planning and evaluation

History

A CLOSER LOOK AT EACH CASE RESOURCE

Information about all these aspects must be on hand in the organization's office and must be available, accessible, and retrievable when needed in connection with fund raising. Let's take a closer look at each of the case resources, which are summarized in Exhibit 6.1.

Mission Statement

A mission statement is a philosophical statement of the human and societal needs being met by the nonprofit organization; it explains why the nonprofit exists. A mission statement is an expression of the values in which the organization believes and around which it does its work.

Exhibit 6.1. Articulating a Case to Attract Donors.

Case Component	What It Must Articulate
Mission statement	An awareness of the cause; insight into the problem addressed by the nonprofit
Goals	The desired achievement that is expected to solve the problem
Objectives	What will be accomplished by reaching the goals
Programs and services	The nonprofit's service to people (including stories of how people benefit)
Finances	The expenses of providing programs and services, as a validation of the need for philanthropy
Governance	The character and quality of the organization as shown in its staff and volunteer leadership and governance structure
Staffing	The qualifications and strengths of staff
Facilities and service delivery	The available facilities; the advantages, strengths, and effectiveness of the mechanics of program and service delivery
Planning and evaluation	Program and fund raising plans and evaluation processes that demonstrate service commitments, strengths, and impact
History	The heroic saga of founders, staff, and others; the credibility implied by success over time

Source: The Fund Raising School, 2002.

A common misconception is that mission statements express what an organization *does,* as exemplified by statements such as "It is the mission of the agency to provide after-school care." This is a goal statement, not a mission statement. Any statement containing an infinitive phrase—*to deliver, to serve, to provide*—is a goal or purpose statement, telling what the organization does. A mission statement, by contrast, explains *why* the organization does what it does. An effective mission statement provides a base for identifying beliefs and values. A good mission statement often begins with the words "We believe" or "We value." For example, a shelter for animals might use the following mission statement: "Concern for Animals believes that all animals deserve humane treatment. Because we care about all animals, Concern for Animals provides shelter and food for abandoned and unwanted animals."

The following steps are suggestions for how to develop and write an effective mission statement:

1. Assert the dominant value the organization believes in.
2. Describe briefly the conditions preventing fulfillment of that value.
3. State briefly what needs to be done to alleviate the conditions in step 2.
4. Affirm that your organization challenges the conditions described in step 2 and carry out what is outlined in step 3.

The mission statement gives donors and potential donors an opportunity to identify the values they hold that are shared by the nonprofit organization.

Goals

Goals answer the question "What does the organization aim to do?" Goal statements are general expressions explaining what the organization wants to accomplish as it seeks to meet the needs or resolve the problems described in the mission statement. Goals are usually stated in ambitious terms not easily measured. Goal statements guide the organization toward fulfilling the beliefs expressed in the mission statement. Because organizations typically have multiple programs, goals will also be multiple. That is, the organization will have several program-related goals, including fund raising goals.

Objectives

Objectives differ from goals in degree of specificity. Objectives are more precise than goals and explain how the organization expects to reach its goals. The acronym SMART, introduced in Chapter Three, can help in crafting the statement of an objective, which should be *specific, measurable, achievable, results-oriented,* and *time-determined.*

Take the goal statement "To increase annual fund income." Objectives illustrating how to reach that goal might be "We will increase annual giving from individuals by 5 percent in the next fiscal year" and "We will increase corporate giving and corporate sponsorship by 15 percent in the next fiscal year."

Programs and Services

The programs and services component of the file should include descriptions of how the organization provides service to its clients. Stories of how recipients of services have benefited are an effective means for showing who benefits from the programs and services provided by the organization. Potential funders are more likely to be responsive to fund raising appeals when they recognize that real people are benefiting from the nonprofit's work.

One of the best ways to build this part of the file is to collect testimonials from clients and beneficiaries talking or writing about the organization's programs and services.

Finances

Financial information about the organization links budgeting with objectives and program descriptions. Information about finances gives a clear picture of how the organization acquires and spends its financial resources. This financial overview establishes and validates the need for philanthropic gift support and justifies fund raising. The financial overview also offers the opportunity to demonstrate fiduciary responsibility and prudent use of funds.

Governance

The issue of governance of nonprofits is critical in attracting charitable gifts. The governance structure of nonprofits indicates the character and quality of the institution. This part of the case resources file should contain relevant information about who sits on the board and how it functions. Complete dossiers on each board member and organizational material such as by-laws and conflict-of-interest statements should also be maintained.

This element of the case file should not be taken lightly. Governance often serves as a litmus test for potential contributors. The quality and integrity of the governing body reflect the strength of the nonprofit. Potential contributors have more confidence in nonprofits with boards who are serious about their commitment to governance and who hold the organization accountable to the public.

Staffing

Staffing reflects an organization's competence and professionalism. This part of the file should illustrate the credentials and qualifications of staff, both paid and volunteer. Staffing patterns reveal how the organization delivers programs and services effectively. This part of the file should contain résumés of all staff members.

Competent, skilled staff members, together with dedicated, energetic board members, offer a persuasive case for potential contributors to make charitable gifts. It is essential to keep this element of the file current. Staff should review their résumés at least annually, updating continuing education and professional development they participate in to improve their professional competence.

Facilities and Service Delivery

The description of facilities and service delivery should explain how people access programs and services. Facilities can be distinguishing factors; visibility, accessibility, and convenience are advantages for program and services delivery.

This file might also include plans for renovation, expansion, or new construction, which will help make the case for capital fund raising.

Planning and Evaluation

Information about planning and evaluation should describe the process used for planning and the measures taken for evaluation. Program plans precede fund raising plans; program plans validate the need for service, and fund raising plans demonstrate the need for philanthropic support.

Evaluation provides a means for demonstrating effectiveness and efficiency in programs and accountability and stewardship of philanthropic resources.

Planning and evaluation documents show that the organization takes its work seriously and holds itself accountable. This inspires confidence in donors and potential donors.

History

History is the heroic saga of the organization. In the record of its history, a nonprofit should focus on the organization's heroes and its accomplishments in terms of service to its constituencies. The history should capture the spirit of the people, both service providers and beneficiaries.

INTERNAL CASE AND EXTERNAL CASE AND THE DIFFERENCE BETWEEN THEM

With all the case resource elements in place, the case resources file, or *internal case*, is ready. An up-to-date and accessible case resources file (internal case) prepares the organization to develop expressions known as *external case statements* for fund raising. The external case statement tells the story to the constituencies.

Whereas the internal case is a database of information and knowledge, the external case statement orders and presents the information for communication, public relations, and fund raising. External case statements take the form of brochures, foundation (and corporation) proposals, direct mail letters, Web site development, campaign prospectuses, news releases, newsletters, speeches, and face-to-face solicitations. Hank Rosso defined the external case as "the case at work."

In making the transition from building the internal case to developing external case statements, the focus is on answering the following questions:

1. What is the problem or social need that is central to our concern?
2. What special services or programs do we offer to respond to this need?
3. Why are the problems and services important?
4. What constitutes the market for our services?
5. Are others doing what we are doing to serve our market—and perhaps doing it better?
6. Do we have a written plan with a statement of philosophy, objectives, and a program?
7. What are the specific financial needs against which private gift support will be sought?
8. Is the organization competent to carry out the defined program?
9. Who are the people associated with the organization: staff, key volunteers, trustees, directors?
10. Who should support the organization?

In writing case statements, it is helpful to remember that the purpose is to stimulate a potential donor to take a series of steps, ultimately ending in the decision to make a gift. The qualities that must exist in the writing and be present in the case statements to stimulate this sequence of reactions on the part of potential donors are excitement, proximity, immediacy, a sense of the future, meaning, and relevance.

Case statements need to excite the reader (or listener). Much of philanthropy begins with an emotional response to the external need as defined in the case for support. Proximity to the problem creates a sense of emotional awareness as does a geographical proximity. How real is the problem in the potential donor's life? How important, even urgent, is it that the potential donor take action to help solve the problem? This is a sense of immediacy. What happens if the donor delays in responding to this need? In addition to immediacy, the need to act now, there should also be a sense of the future. This is not a one-time action but an ongoing process. It is unlikely that all problems can be solved now, so what does the future hold as a promise to address the ongoing problems? What is the meaning to the donor? Case statements should communicate to the donor the values and benefits of participating that are of importance to that particular donor. The mission expressed in the case should connect to the donor's values.

Qualities such as these in the expression of the case achieve the desired sequence of responses by the donor (see Exhibit 6.2). Relevance grabs the attention of the donor and focuses on the importance of the problem or need the nonprofit addresses. A sense of nearness will interest the donor, building a sense of concern on the donor's part. The immediacy of the problem and the sense of the future instill in the donor the confidence that the nonprofit has defined the problem accurately and offers a compelling solution. This trust leads to a conviction on the part of the donor that the nonprofit will produce the desired results in addressing the problem. Excitement about what can be done will lead to the donor's desire to be part of the program because it will bring satisfaction and enjoyment. Finally, the importance of this project or program will move the donor to take action, to become a participant by making a gift to the nonprofit.

CONCLUSION

The essence of fund raising success is a fully developed case for support that articulates clearly and boldly the reasons the organization deserves philanthropic gifts. Those who solicit gifts for the organization should be familiar with the case, but they should not try to memorize case statements. Their effectiveness in soliciting comes from their immersion in the cause, their passion for supporting it, and their enthusiasm for inviting others to participate. The best solicitors are those who tell the story in their own words, with the integrity of their dedication to the cause.

Exhibit 6.2. Qualities and Responses.

Case Expression Qualities	Sequence of Response
Relevance	Attention
Proximity	Interest
Sense of the future	Confidence
Immediacy	Conviction
Excitement	Desire
Importance	Action

Source: The Fund Raising School, 2002.

Written case statements are effective stage scenery, and well-produced case statements play an important role in furthering the conversation between solicitor and donor. Donors, however, ultimately make the gift commitment to the credible solicitor whose testimony to the value of the cause persuades the donor to join.

Developing and articulating the case for support is the first step in planning for fund raising. Reviewing and testing the case at least once a year will validate that the nonprofit's mission is still compelling and its constituencies are well served.

CHAPTER SEVEN

The Total Development Plan

Timothy L. Seiler

As development and fund raising have become more formalized and professionalized, practitioners and volunteers alike have become more cognizant of the disciplined, systematic process that effective fund raising follows. Donors, too, have become more aware of the heightened level of conscious activity on the part of nonprofits to engage donors and prospective donors more fully and more intimately in the activities of the nonprofit.

The growing seriousness with which nonprofits and fund raising staff and volunteers take fund raising is seen clearly in two areas: the increase in the amount of continuing education and professional development and the increase in academic programs in nonprofit management and development in colleges and universities. For example, when The Fund Raising School moved from California to Indiana in 1987 to become part of Indiana University, there were approximately six hundred participants a year attending about a dozen courses offered in cities around the United States. At the end of fiscal year 2000–2001, more than six thousand participants attended regular and contract courses in twelve cities in the United States and in four foreign countries. In that same time frame, the number of nonprofit academic programs in colleges and universities increased from about a dozen to 242 undergraduate and graduate programs at 220 institutions.

This growth reflects the maturity of nonprofits and their growing understanding of the complexity of building and sustaining a disciplined fund raising program. More than ever before, nonprofit boards and staff realize that relying on fund raising special events and direct mail will leave them short of the funds required to sustain their programs and force them to operate at a level below their potential. Organizations are discovering that fund raising success year after year calls for a fully integrated plan that develops and nurtures a diversified funding base.

This chapter reflects on the components of the integrated development plan or the total development plan and suggests a model for building and sustaining effective fund raising and achieving excellence in fund raising.

PLANNING, COMMUNICATION, AND FUND RAISING

Development as an organizational process involves fund raising but goes well beyond it. Development involves growth of mission and hence includes planning, communication, and fund raising.

Planning calls for vision and leadership. It means setting direction for the future by answering the following questions:

Who are we?

What distinguishes us from our competition?

What do we want to accomplish?

How will we reach our goals?

How do we hold ourselves accountable?

These questions complement the organizational assessment discussed in Chapter Four. The answers to the questions address mission, goals, objectives, programs, evaluation, and stewardship (all addressed in other chapters, including Chapters Six and Thirty-One). Answering the questions provides a core script for communication. Effective communication programs include not only dissemination of information but also a means for interaction with constituencies. Good communication programs seek to engage constituencies in substantive exchange of ideas, allowing a forum for constituencies to articulate their interests and desires to the nonprofit. The best communication programs in the most effective development plans seek to nurture in-depth relationships with constituencies. They provide opportunities for constituencies to understand the organization's case for support, to endorse the case, and to become involved in the active articulation of the case.

Effective communication plans invite constituencies to join in sharing their own dreams and vision for contributing to fulfillment of the nonprofit's mission. Communication plans help cultivate relationships between prospective donors and the organization. They provide a means for involvement in the life of the organization.

Fund raising is an essential component of a development plan, and it is often the ultimate goal of the overall plan. Fund raising, however, is more than just asking for money. Effective fund raising includes identifying the most qualified prospective donors by focusing on their linkage to the organization and their interest in its work as well as their ability to make gifts. Fund raising involves the development of a relationship between prospective donors and the organization, a relationship fostered by mutual values and shared interests. As the organization makes its case and as prospective donors realize how their own interests are met by the work of the organization, fund raising becomes a process of the mutual fulfillment of the donors' and the organization's needs.

TYPES OF GIFTS

Historically, organizational financial needs have been classified into specific categories: ongoing program support, special-purpose needs, capital needs, and endowment needs. The fund raising programs for finding the needed funds have been the annual fund, special gifts, capital campaign, and planned giving (all explained more fully in Part Three). This model is still relevant today, although the special gift program is now often referred to as the major gift program. This is especially true in large fund raising operations most often found in colleges and universities, hospitals and medical centers, and large mainstream arts organizations such as metropolitan operas and symphonies, art museums, and urban theater groups. Major gift programs are often the natural outgrowth of successful capital campaigns and are a means of continuing the higher level of giving established during the capital campaign. A total fund raising program might be illustrated with a diagram resembling a four-legged stool (see Figure 7.1).

The annual fund is still the foundation of all successful fund raising. Donors contribute to the annual fund to support current, ongoing programs to fulfill the organization's mission. The ongoing programs are the organization's way of addressing the larger needs of the community. The programs provide solutions to the problems the donor and the organization agree need to be addressed.

The annual fund also serves to bond a large number of donors to the organization through recurring gifts. As donors develop a history of giving, they grow more interested in and involved with the success of the organization. This base of regular givers becomes the most likely core group of donors for other fund raising programs such as major gifts, capital gifts, and planned gifts.

Although special gifts in response to a special need or opportunity are still part of a total development program, they are now more often characterized as

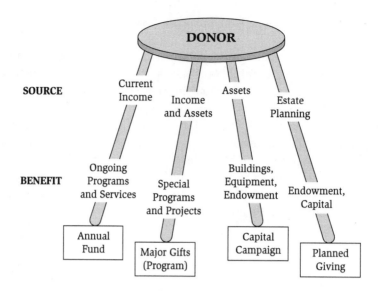

Figure 7.1. Four-Legged Stool of Fund Raising.
Source: The Fund Raising School, 2002.

major gifts. Major gifts are part of all campaigns, annual, capital, and endowment, and they also constitute a separate program that organizations maintain alongside the annual fund. A major gift is larger than the typical gift to the annual fund, raising the sights of the donor and bonding the donor even more closely to the organization.

Capital campaigns meet the organization's needs for increasing its own assets, renovating facilities, building new facilities, or acquiring land for expansion. Capital campaigns also support program development and expansion, and increasingly, they support endowment. The comprehensive capital campaigns today have included all components of the integrated fund raising plan: an increase in the annual fund, capital needs (including buildings and programs), and endowment.

Because capital campaigns seek very large gifts, donors typically make their gifts from their own asset base. Their gifts will generally be pledged over a period of years, typically the number of years of the campaign itself.

In the megacampaigns of today, capital campaigns can last five to seven years; some may actually last as long as ten years, although some definitions limit capital campaigns to seven years. In these larger campaigns, it is not unusual for donors to make multiple gifts or to extend their pledges.

Planned giving has been one of the most exciting growth areas in fund raising in recent years. Planned gifts, by definition, are gifts that are made in the present but whose value to the organization is usually realized at a later time, generally at the death of the donor or a surviving beneficiary. The most common forms for planned gifts are wills and bequests, charitable gift annuities, charitable trusts, and pooled income funds. Other types of planned gifts are life estates, insurance, and bargain sales. In the latter part of the 1990s, as employee pension plans accelerated in value, qualified pension plans became an exciting planned gift option for many donors.

While some planned gift instruments are highly sophisticated and technical and may be beyond the capacity of smaller nonprofits to manage, wills and bequests are the simplest form of planned gifts. Every nonprofit seeking to build a totally integrated development plan should be involved in planned giving at least through wills and bequests.

One of the conventional models of fund raising is the donor pyramid, demonstrating the typical process of donor involvement from annual gift to special or major gift to capital gift and ultimately to planned gift (see Figure 7.2). Although

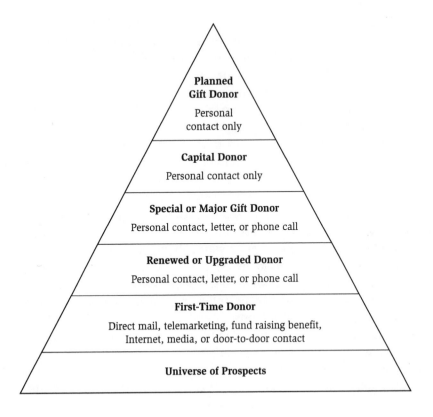

Figure 7.2. Donor Pyramid of Fund Raising Strategies.

Source: The Fund Raising School, 2002.

there may be an occasional exception—a donor's first gift as a capital gift, for example—this model is still valid today. Its primary value is in demonstrating the interrelatedness of all the components of the integrated development plan. Effective fund raising recognizes that the components are interdependent and manages the process of developing the components as mutually reinforcing.

PREREQUISITES FOR IMPLEMENTING THE INTEGRATED DEVELOPMENT PLAN

When Hank Rosso originally wrote this chapter, he outlined the prerequisites, the supporting elements, for successful implementation of the integrated development plan. Those elements still pertain today and are reprinted here. Certain requisites will command the attention of the governing board and the senior management team before this broader program of fund raising can be implemented.

• *Governance.* The statement of the overall needs, internal and external, and the plan to raise the funds that will address the internal needs must be reviewed, accepted, and approved by the governing board. It is essential that board members place their full support behind the plan by contributing to the best of their ability and by urging others to do so.

• *Management.* The chief executive must serve as the principal advocate for the continuing advancement of the organization into the future. The senior management group, with the full participation of board members, must articulate the values for the organization and participate in communicating these values to the constituency. The chief executive, as the primary link to the governing board and through the board to the larger constituency, must constantly champion the development program and the goals that it seeks to serve.

• *Programs and Services Staff.* Program accomplishments, not budget requirements, will attract generous gift support to the organization. The competence and the commitment of the program staff will provide the motivation for people to give and for individuals to involve themselves as volunteers. Program specialists make excellent "expert witnesses." As members of a soliciting team, they can effectively articulate the scope and worth of the programs. Key program staff members should team with board members and other volunteers to explain the organization's accomplishments to potential contributors.

• *Fund Raising Staff.* The ability of this staff to plan, organize, and administer programs will determine the outcome of the fund raising effort. However, administration is not the single factor that is most conducive to effective production. Other compelling factors are adequate budget, proper office space, competent support staff, and sincere acknowledgment by program and management staff that fund raising is an integral part of the total organization.

All four of the factors that contribute to the success of a total development program are interrelated and must not remain in bureaucratic isolation. None should be seen as weaker than or subservient to any of the others. All four are integral parts of the organization's structure and therefore interdependent.

ESSENTIAL SUPPORT

A number of elements must support the organization and its mission:

- Responsible board membership, competent management, quality services, concern for the individual, valid needs, and stewardship through open accountability will justify the case for philanthropic generosity.
- The statement of mission, the very foundation of the organization's case position, must be a statement of shared values or a philosophical expression of the human or societal needs that the organization is endeavoring to serve. The mission is a statement of the organization's reason for being.
- Proper communication methods require an acknowledgment of the constituents' needs and wants, an awareness of their perceptions and their requirements, and a readiness to design a public relations plan that will respond to these needs.
- Acceptance of fund raising as a management function and as a management process requires the acceptance of the chief fund raising officer as an important member of the senior management team.
- The involvement of board members, administrators, and program staff members with the development function is essential to ensure that key people become fully conversant with and supportive of the development objectives, policies, strategies, plans, and programs.
- The need to institutionalize the development function by weaving it into the fabric and endowing it with the power and the dignity of the organization is a fact of reality in a complex, somewhat turbulent, and always challenging environment. Fund raising must bear the mantle of the institutional mission as its symbol of honor.

To make the total development plan effective, the following components need to be addressed:

I. The Institutional Plan
   A. The plan must reach three to five years into the future as a design for the organization's strategy for addressing its mission, goals, and objectives.

B. The plan should set forth details of program support, special-purpose, and capital and endowment needs for the period of the plan. The dollar requirements can serve as a guide to fund raising programs for each year of the plan, as well as for the total period.

II. Full Board Involvement

A. A sense of personal "ownership" is an important motivating force to inspire board members, volunteers, and staff members to give and to work for the success of the program. Ownership can be generated by encouraging people to assist in determining needs, identifying prospects, and helping with solicitation.

B. The board is the constituency's energy center. It can mirror the constituency's interest. It should serve as a sounding board to receive and to reflect the constituency's feelings about the program and about the organization's readiness for major fund raising. It can and should present and represent the organization to its constituency.

III. Case and Cases: The Primary Document

A. Each request for gifts must have a case of its own drawn from the organization's larger case.

B. Each case must be exciting, compelling, and responsive to the prospective donor's interests and requirements for information.

C. The case must describe valid needs, and it must offer various gift options that will be suitable to the contributor's situation to facilitate the donor's gift-making capabilities.

D. The case must be renewed regularly if it is to have merit and if it is to have pertinence for prospective contributors.

IV. Volunteers for Fund Raising

A. Volunteers will play many roles willingly in the fund raising program once their commitment to the organization has been confirmed.

B. To encourage this commitment, volunteers must be meaningfully involved, properly recognized, and given a sense of importance. They must be made to feel that they are an important part of a worthwhile team serving a worthwhile program. Their involvement is making a difference.

C. Training for volunteers must have a major place in this transaction.

V. Planning

A. The total development program is a full-circle approach to the organization. It examines every aspect of an organization's being. The plan's final draft must be converted into a living document with meaning for each board member, each member of any advisory body, and each staff member, as well as for strategically important leaders in the organization's service area.

B. To be effective, the plan for total development should be prepared, evaluated, refined, and accepted by the people who possess the power to put it into action.

A fully integrated total development plan will be a necessity for sustainable fund raising success as the twenty-first century unfolds. Organizations that limit themselves to the lower-end activities of special events and direct mail deprive themselves of the opportunity to obtain high-impact major gifts or institution-changing capital or planned gifts. Fund raising that proceeds with pride in mission, boldly inviting large gifts from committed donors, will raise considerably more money through a total development plan than through hit-and-miss appeals designed only to keep the doors open.

Piecemeal fund raising activities and programs that do not integrate all four components of a fund raising program—annual fund, major gifts, capital campaign, and planned giving—limit their own opportunities for long-term fund raising success.

Organizations running only an annual fund will find themselves always stressed to keep the doors open by raising only what they need year after year. This strategy overlooks opportunities for major gifts for special programs or projects as well as opportunities to expand the organization's capital (assets) or to build long-term sustainability through an endowment. At the other extreme, organizations that concentrate only on endowment fund raising miss the opportunity to build enduring relationships and to expand their constituencies, hallmarks of an annual fund.

CONCLUSION

The totally integrated development plan recognizes the giving patterns of the majority of donors. The annual fund builds a large base of loyal donors who give repeatedly over many years. Their deepening commitment to the organization makes them likely donors for special gifts in addition to their annual gifts. The total development program recognizes that the annual fund and special or major gift programs form the solid base for the occasional capital campaign, which expands the asset base of the organization. A carefully coordinated orchestration of all the components of the integrated program acknowledges that the ultimate gifts made through planned giving will typically be the result of donors who have participated in the earlier stages of the total development program. This wisdom about fund raising has been substantiated by Schervish (1997), who found that major donors had developed a philanthropic identification with the organization through what he called "communities of participation." These are the very structures that the total development program promotes.

The chapters in Part Three on the annual fund, major gifts, capital campaigns, and planned giving address the strengths of each discrete fund raising program. Each leg of the fund raising stool plays a strategic role in the life of the organization's fund raising. The overall fund raising program (the four-legged stool), when it is fully integrated and carefully managed, positions the organization to conduct and manage fund raising at the most effective level.

The power and the efficacy of the total development plan are in bringing to bear the essential elements for long-term fund raising success. These include market-oriented programs and services; well-informed constituencies capable of and willing to serve the mission; a well-defined workable plan that can be monitored, evaluated, and adapted; dedicated leadership, staff, board, and other volunteers willing to work, to give, and to ask others to give; and a high level of professional accountability and prudent stewardship.

These elements, properly managed, with disciplined attention to the demands of organized fund raising, will carry organizations to higher and higher levels of effectiveness. The total development plan will raise the funds necessary for program support, special needs, capital needs, and long-term endowment needs. The total development plan demands commitment to hard work. It requires the investment of time, energy, and financial resources. Its returns are high.

BUILDING BLOCKS FOR SUCCESSFUL FUND RAISING

P art Three outlines the programs of a total development program introduced at the end of Part Two. Henry Rosso called these programs "vehicles" for fund raising, the term still used to describe them in The Fund Raising School.

The annual fund, the topic of Chapter Eight, is the base of a successful fund raising program. Not only does it provide support for the annual operating budget, but it also uses special strategies to recruit new donors, solicit repeat or renewed gifts from earlier donors, and upgrade or increase gifts from year to year. In most cases, larger gifts solicited through the programs outlined in the other chapters in Part Three are received from donors to the annual fund.

Many organizations now operate ongoing major gift programs as described in Chapter Nine, "Gifts of Significance." These might be special onetime gifts, large annual gifts, or gifts made in a capital or endowment campaign. Chapter Ten is devoted to endowment building. Endowment building is related to major gifts, capital campaigns, and planned giving, but it has become more common to have special initiatives dedicated solely to endowment.

Chapters Eleven and Twelve, on the capital campaign and planned giving, respectively, provide the structures and technical infrastructures needed to organize these two effective programs that help meet long-term major capital and endowment needs.

The total development program is based on the premise that a donor at one level is a prospect for a gift at a higher level. The fund raising vehicles outlined in Part Three must be integrated to make it possible for the organization to embrace the concept of lifetime donor development from the first annual gift to a planned gift.

Not every organization will be able to implement all levels of each program discussed here. But every organization should organize an annual fund that fits its size and scope. Other fund raising programs can be added over time as the donors to the annual fund increase and continue their gifts. Every organization can develop a program to inform donors about making bequests. It should be the goal of every organization to develop gifts of significance and planned gifts. They not only increase total gifts and contribute to capital and endowment needs but also help reduce fund raising costs or increase returns on fund raising investment.

CHAPTER EIGHT

The Annual Fund

Henry A. Rosso
Introduction by Robert Schwartzberg

In revising this chapter, which Hank Rosso wrote more than a decade ago, the first thought that came to mind was the old favorite, tried and true "If it ain't broke, don't fix it!" After numerous readings of the chapter and considerable thought, I realized that it ain't broke and I'm not going to fix it. Sure, I've made a few changes—a word or two here, a phrase or update there. But overall, this chapter is still Hank's, and it is as current, vital, and valid today as it was when he wrote it.

As a development officer and a fund raising practitioner for nearly a quarter of a century, I have continuously applied the lessons in this chapter, with great success. From planning to implementation, the lessons that Hank teaches are the steps to achieving the successful annual campaign that each organization requires as the foundation of its fund development efforts.

Over the years, it has become apparent that there is a greater need than ever for nonprofit organizations to have a strong and carefully thought-out annual campaign. Pay careful attention to this chapter, and compare your own annual fund raising campaign plans to it. If you have a plan for an annual fund raising campaign and apply the lessons in this chapter to it, your campaign will be much stronger. Conversely, if, like too many nonprofit organizations, you do not yet have a carefully thought-out, defined, and written annual campaign plan, this is an excellent opportunity to create a plan and a campaign in a manner that has proved to be successful over and over again.

THE ANNUAL FUND:
A BUILDING BLOCK FOR FUND RAISING

The annual fund is the building block for all fund raising. It serves to establish a base of donors that can serve as an effective device to involve, inform, and bond a constituency to the organization. It can further serve as an instrument that compels accountability to the cause the organization is serving.

With a successful annual campaign, the organization can go on to bigger and better things in addition to providing a steady flow of income for the programs, services, and activities it provides for the community.

Without an annual campaign, an organization often finds itself involved in crisis fund raising, which is also known as "give us money or we will have to drop the program, go out of business, fail to provide for people who need us—and it's going to be your fault!" With a successful fund raising program that is built around an annual campaign, this will not be the case. Instead there will be a carefully thought out, planned, and implemented approach to raising necessary money in an orderly and timely manner.

In formulating and executing programs in service to their missions, nonprofit organizations incur a variety of financial needs. Fund raising has the functional responsibility to secure money, gifts-in-kind, or noncash gifts, volunteer services, and a range of additional services from the community.

The annual fund is the cornerstone and the key to success for all aspects of the fund raising program. The objectives of this chapter are to identify the principles and techniques that pertain to the annual fund, to explain the "arithmetic of fund raising" that can facilitate the preparation of a plan, to describe a planning tool called the Ladder of Effectiveness, and to offer methods to apply these principles and techniques.

The focus of the discussion will be on individuals as primary contributors to the annual fund rather than corporations, foundations, associations, or government. The bulk of the money that is given away annually in the United States, historically around 75 percent (AAFRC Trust for Philanthropy, 2002), comes from individuals. It stands to reason, then, that they represent the most reliable source of givers to the annual fund. (Of course, corporations and foundations do give to the annual fund; their giving patterns are discussed in Chapters Fourteen and Fifteen.)

Reasons for Giving

People make philanthropic gifts for many different reasons. They are moved to give by the urgency of the community's needs. In addition, they will give because they respect the organization's commitment to carry out programs that are responsive to the needs that are central to its concern. However, an important axiom in fund raising says, "People will not give simply because the organization needs money." Contributors will not give just to help an entity balance its operating budget. Veteran fund raising professionals often use another axiom to emphasize one of the "carved in stone" principles of fund raising: "People do not give to people. They give to people with causes." To this piece of wisdom can be added another: "They give to people who *ask* on behalf of causes."

Individuals tend to give from three sources: discretionary or disposable income, their assets, and estates. The annual fund generally seeks funding from individuals' discretionary income. This statement does not seek to belittle the practice of sacrificial giving. People with strong religious belief or those who share a tradition of philanthropy, will tend to give sacrificially. For the most part, however, the bulk of contributors will not make any gift that will compel them to give up something important in their lives or cause them to change their standard of living. Nevertheless, they continue to give generously to causes.

Contributors will give for current program support, to meet a special need, for capital purposes, or to help build the organization's endowment holdings. This sympathetic broad-based giving pattern is not haphazard. The interests of the contributor must be nurtured. Involvement is invited through the annual solicitation of gifts to the annual fund. The very process of solicitation can encourage the contributor to become more knowledgeable about the organization, more understanding, and therefore more supportive.

For this important reason, the annual fund is much more than an unrelated series of special events, direct mail, phonathons, e-mails, on-line giving, broadcast faxes, and other activities. It is a thoughtfully devised and executed plan that creates a strong force of advocates who will dedicate themselves to the organization's advancement through their philanthropy and volunteer services.

The primary objectives of an annual fund should be the following:

- To solicit and secure a new gift, repeat the gift, and upgrade the gift
- To build and develop a base of donors
- To establish habits and patterns of giving by regular solicitation
- To seek to expand the donor base by soliciting gifts from new prospects
- To raise annual unrestricted and restricted money
- To inform, involve, and bond the constituency to the organization
- To use the donor base as a vital source of information to identify potential large donors
- To promote giving habits that encourage the contributor to make capital and planned gifts
- To remain fully accountable to the constituency through annual reports

Table 8.1 summarizes these points. The development process embodies the total development program outlined in Chapter Seven. The annual fund serves as the basis for the process and involves gifts through the major gift level.

The Arithmetic of Fund Raising

The annual fund can be enhanced by following time-tested working principles. Perhaps the most important principle of all is the one that pertains to the "arithmetic of fund raising." In planning for an annual fund, the arithmetic of fund raising concept directs the fund raising practitioner to determine the quality and number of gifts that are required to achieve the organization's goal. Decisions about the plan's strategies should be delayed until the following determinations have been made:

- What quality of gifts is required, and how many are needed in each category?
- What should be the ratio of prospects to donors?
- Does the donor base have the number of prospects to support the ratio?
- Is it realistic to expect that these prospects can be identified?
- If these questions cannot be answered clearly and factually, then is the goal for the annual fund realistic?

The use of such arithmetic to determine the number of quality gifts that are required to ensure the achievement of a fund raising goal had its genesis in the planning for capital campaigns. This planning device has been employed equally successfully as a method to determine the course of an annual fund. Such aids as *gift range charts* or *standard-of-gifts charts* are common in the capital campaign; they also have their application to the annual fund.

The Fund Raising School promotes the use of gift range charts in planning for both capital and annual fund raising campaigns. The chances for success will be made stronger if a determination can be made about the numbers and quality of gifts that must be produced to ensure that a goal is reached.

The arithmetic concept as it pertains to the annual fund means that a large amount of the money to be raised will come from a small number of contributors who are encouraged to provide what will necessarily be larger gifts. The formula is as follows:

The top 10 percent of the gifts received during the annual fund have the potential to produce 60 percent of the money required to meet the goal.

The next 20 percent of gifts will account for 15 to 25 percent of the money required.

The remaining 70 percent of gifts will cover the remaining 15 to 25 percent of funds required.

Table 8.1. The Development Process.

The Objective	The Process	What Is Required
Identify potential prospects	List development	Build lists of, identify, and research constituents
Convert potential prospects into qualified prospects	Test list effectiveness identifying linkages	Refine prospect development
Convert qualified prospects into initial donors	Build on linkages, test interest, ask, acknowledge	Solicit by personal contact via telephone, direct mail, and special events
Convert initial giver into donor of record	Build on interests and linkages, ask, acknowledge	Report use of gift, invite to renew
Increase the gift	Research, build on linkages, interests, inform, ask, acknowledge	Report, involve, invite to renew and increase gift, use gift club concept
Secure special gift ($1,000+)	Continue research through linkages, involve, build on interests, ask, acknowledge	Describe special needs and how money is used, solicit personally, invite to gift club membership
Secure major gift ($10,000+)	Use all linkages to validate as major prospect, ask, acknowledge, reward	Involve in institution: planning, case evaluation, needs determination, cultivation events, personal letters
Secure big gift	Continue involvement through linkages, add to interests, foster desire to give, ask, acknowledge, reward	Report, involve constituent as important advocate, involve through cultivation events, personal reports, personal contacts
Secure planned gift	Continue involvement, create feelings of belonging to and identifying with institution, foster mutuality of interests	Strengthen linkage, strengthen involvement

Source: The Fund Raising School, 2002.

It is generally accepted among professional fund raisers that 3 to 5 percent of contributors enrolled in an organization's donor base have the ability to make major gifts. When this supposition is applied to the gifts that are needed to properly achieve a goal, it follows that 10 percent of the gifts generated for an annual fund indeed have the potential to produce 60 percent of the funds received through gifts.

To make this principle work, the top two gifts that should be sought in the annual fund must each equal 5 percent of the goal. For example, if the goal is $500,000, then each of the top two gifts should be $25,000, for a cumulative value of $50,000. All other gifts in the arithmetic computations should scale down from the $25,000 level. The gift distribution can be evaluated by using the previously mentioned gift range *chart*. This planning tool aids the fund raiser in determining the optimal gift distribution. Tables 8.2 and 8.3 illustrate how the computations can be made.

In Table 8.3, the goal of $60,000 is more typical of the amount of money that would be sought by a smaller organization with limited current program support requirements. The purpose of the chart's goals of different sizes is to avoid the necessity of asking for smaller gifts, which are costly to raise. Such gifts should be acknowledged properly when received, but they should be less actively solicited than the larger gifts listed in the table.

Certain principles become apparent quite readily. The gift range chart gives form to the planning. The initial planning focus is not on a range of activity but on the more practical aspects of fund raising, the acquisition of large gifts that will make the critical difference in achieving the goal. From the two gift range charts, several concerns can be addressed. First, how many gifts and at what amount must the fund raising team produce to make the goal? Are the prospects available? If not, what can be done about it?

The chart is a flexible instrument. The ratio of prospects from the top of the chart to the bottom of the chart may be changed to coincide with the reality of the donor base and the availability of prospects. Flexibility pertains also to the numbers of donors and prospects that are required at each gift level. In some situations, it may be possible to secure more than the required two gifts at the top of each chart. Do not deny the reality of the figures, but be assertive when identifying prospects. Only through continual research will prospects be found.

It is easy to submit to the rationale that many small gifts will be easier to secure than the two largest gifts. But this will require that five hundred $100 gifts substitute for two $25,000 gifts in Table 8.2; this means that four hundred prospects must be solicited to secure the substituted one hundred gifts.

In Table 8.2, it is truly possible to secure 484 gifts from 960 prospects to reach the 60 percent mark, particularly if these prospects are part of the donor base that has a history of giving to the organization. Included in the prospect listing

Table 8.2. Annual Fund Gift Range Chart: $500,000 Goal.

Gift Range ($)	Number of Gifts	Cumulative Number of Gifts	Number of Prospects	Cumulative Number of Prospects	Total per Range($)	Cumulative Total ($)
25,000 +	2	2	10 (5:1)	10	50,000	50,000
10,000	4	6	20 (5:1)	30	40,000	90,000
2,500	18	24	72 (4:1)	102	45,000	135,000
1,000	30	54	120 (4:1)	222	30,000	165,000
500	110	164	330 (3:1)	552	55,000	220,000
250	320	484	960 (3:1)	1,512	80,000	300,000
	10% of gifts				60% of goal	
100	1,000	1,484	3,000 (3:1)	4,512	100,000	400,000
	20% of gifts				20% of goal	
Under 100	3,334	4,818	6,668 (2:1)	11,180	100,020	500,020
	70% of gifts				20% of goal	

Source: The Fund Raising School, 2002.

Table 8.3. Annual Fund Gift Range Chart: $60,000 Goal.

Gift Range ($)	Number of Gifts	Cumulative Number of Gifts	Number of Prospects	Cumulative Number of Prospects	Total per Range($)	Cumulative Total ($)
3,000	2	2	10 (5:1)	10	6,000	6,000
1,500	4	6	20 (5:1)	30	6,000	12,000
750	12	18	48 (4:1)	78	9,000	21,000
500	18	36	72 (4:1)	150	9,000	30,000
250	24	60	72 (3:1)	222	6,000	36,000
		10% of gifts				*60% of goal*
100	120	180	360 (3:1)	582	12,000	48,000
		20% of gifts				*20% of goal*
Less than 100[a]	400	580	800 (2:1)	1,382	12,000	60,000
		70% of gifts				*20% of goal*

[a]Average gift: $30.

Source: The Fund Raising School, 2002.

are individuals, associations, foundations, corporations, small businesses, and others who give to annual funds. The only relevant criterion here is, do they give to current program support?

In Table 8.3, sixty gifts are required from 222 prospects to achieve 60 percent of the goal. This can be easier than scheduling a host of special events or filing a host of grant applications with foundations and corporations. This is especially important to understand since most corporations and foundations prefer not to give for annual support purposes but rather for specific programs or projects.

The range of gifts dictated by the gift range charts gives eloquent testimony to the role of the annual fund in developing an involved and informed donor base. Within that base are individuals with the capability of making an extraordinary gift to the organization. Yet in many cases, the gift will not be made simply because the organization has not asked for it. It is axiomatic that the contributor will give only at the level of his or her perception of what the organization requires. If the gift is not actively sought, the larger gift in most cases will not be made. Rightly or wrongly, the potential contributor will assume that the larger gift is not needed or that the organization is unable to handle large gifts. This is especially true when gifts of appreciated stocks are involved, as is often the case with large gifts.

One of the many realizations that surface through the gift-scaling technique imposed by the gift range chart is that the potential for the large gift lies within the base.

The Principles Behind Effective Fund Raising

Fund raising is relatively straightforward as a concept, but it is a demanding taskmaster. Attention must be given to the simple management rules that can make a difference. One of the simplest of these rules is to scrutinize and analyze the gift potential in the donor base before making any effort to put the fund raising plan on paper. Ask and seek answers to the hard question: "Are there sufficient prospects within the base that have the capability to give at the level that is required?"

Profiling the base annually or semiannually provides the organization with a wealth of information about the potential giving patterns of its constituency. An understanding of this pattern can be a major benefit to the fund raising program. The following questions should be asked about the donor base:

- How many donors give annually?
- What is the frequency of the gift? Once a year, twice a year, or more often? How many donors give on a monthly basis? What is the date of the most recent gift?

- What is the level of giving? How many give $1,000 or more a year? $500 to $1,000? $250 to $500? $50 to $100? Less than $50?

- Is there a pattern of the gift being repeated but not upgraded over the years?

- Is a regular request made that the gift be upgraded?

- Do the records indicate the names of donors who give consistently to the annual fund as well as make special-purpose, capital, or endowment gifts during the course of the year?

- Is there a specific person identified as the solicitor of the gift?

- What is the pattern of giving by staff members, trustees, and members of advisory councils or non-board-related support committees?

This is prospecting, the eternal search for vital information that is so important to fund raising. It is an essential part of the fund raising office's knowledge. This information will enable the person planning the fund raising program to identify the potential gifts required by the gift range chart.

As the form in Table 8.4 shows, the data retrieved from the donor base as a result of this search can be organized easily to analyze the base's potential. These data should reflect the number and dominance of gift ranges over the past four years.

By replacing numbers of gifts with names of prospects, these data can be converted to a workable form. In Chapter Nineteen, Mal Warwick refers to the strategic qualification of donors and the acquisition of donor information. This measurement could be applied to all gifts of $100 or more. Gifts at this level show a greater tendency to repeat and to be upgraded, thus creating the opportunity for the solicitation of a special gift, major gift, or planned gift.

In fund raising parlance, *longevity* refers to the number of years that a person has been giving, *frequency* to the number of gifts made during the year,

Table 8.4. Form for Organizing Donor Data.

Gift Ranges ($)	Number of Gifts and Total Contributions ($)			
	Current Year	*Last Year*	*Two Years Ago*	*Three Years Ago*
1,000–5,000				
500–999				
250–499				
100–249				
50–99				

recency to the date of the most recent gift, and *amount,* of course, to the dollar value of the annual gift or the cumulative value of multiple gifts made that year. These bits of information become the determining factors in evaluating whether a donor of record might respond positively to a request for one of the larger gifts designated on the gift range chart.

Reckless guessing has no place in fund raising planning. Hard questions require hard responses. If a goal is to be justified, the justification must come in the form of hard information that the numbers of prospects required are indeed available and that the prospects do have the ability to give at the level indicated by the gift range chart.

In Table 8.3, for example, 222 prospects are potentially required to produce 60 gifts. Are the prospects available? If the response is yes, the plan should be activated to solicit each prospect with the hope that the designated gifts can be secured. If the precise number of prospects at the top level ($1,500 to $3,000) cannot be identified, the fund raising planners must make some serious decisions. Is the $60,000 goal feasible? The answer may well be yes if the prospects listed against the numbers required at the top of the chart are quality prospects. There is a better-than-average chance that they will make the gift if properly approached by the right soliciting team.

The prospect-to-donor relationship depicted on the gift range charts in Tables 8.2 and 8.3 may seem imposing and perhaps somewhat disconcerting to both the fund raising professional and the fund raising volunteer with little experience. The question asked may reflect such despair: "How is it possible to solicit so many prospects effectively? That will require an army of trained volunteers. How can they possibly be recruited to the task?" This is a reasonable reaction. The questions are logical and appropriate. If money is to be raised, prospects must be solicited. But first, the soliciting volunteers have to be recruited. This can be achieved with the understanding, in the planning stages, that this recruitment is not only indispensable but also a first priority. Recruitment, followed by proper training, will permit the assembly of a motivated cadre of volunteers who can and will be able to solicit the necessary gifts.

The Ladder of Effectiveness

The Ladder of Effectiveness (see Figure 8.1) may serve to allay some of the fears that naturally surface when the reality of solicitation must be confronted. By understanding how the different ways to solicit a gift will affect the results of the solicitation, volunteers can reduce their fear of rejection and develop realistic expectations of their choice of solicitation. In descending order, the ladder portrays the relative effectiveness of the various methods used to solicit gifts. Each step down the ladder indicates diminishing effectiveness in the soliciting procedure. Face-to-face solicitation by a peer of the prospect is far and away the most effective method; solicitation through the media or by direct mail is the least effective.

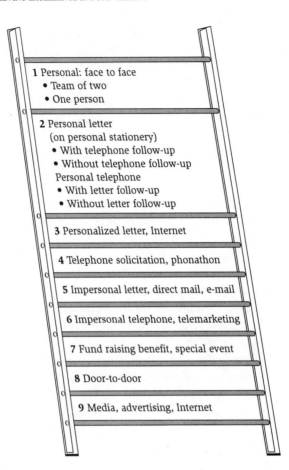

Figure 8.1. The Ladder of Effectiveness.

Source: The Fund Raising School, 2002.

Personal Face-to-Face Visit. A personal face-to-face visit by a team is far and away the most effective method. Two people make up the team: a peer of the prospect accompanied by the organization's chief executive, the fund raising officer, a program person, or another volunteer. The peer is a volunteer, the best link to the prospect, and an advocate for the organization; the staff person is the expert witness, there to answer any questions and to make sure that the volunteer makes the ask.

A face-to-face visit by one person can be an effective approach if the person is knowledgeable about and committed to the organization's mission and feels comfortable about soliciting. If the person is uncomfortable or reluctant to solicit, do not risk an ineffective solicitation, which can be awkward for both the solicitor and the prospect.

Solicitation by Letter. A peer writes to friends, colleagues, and family members on personal stationary, ideally with a preaddressed reply envelope enclosed, to encourage and facilitate a response to the solicitation. Follow-up strategies include a phone call to the prospect a day or two after the letter has been received. Another option would be to wait seven to ten days. If there is no response by then, the solicitor phones the prospect to follow up on the solicitation.

If the prospect fails to respond to the letter appeal and the solicitor declines or fails to place a follow-up call to request the gift, then usually a gift will not be made.

Solicitation by Phone. A personal telephone call placed by a peer, with or without a follow-up letter, will have a similar result as the solicitation by personal letter. The chance of eliciting a gift is far greater with a follow-up letter or even a reminder e-mail than without such follow-up. In fact, it is often the follow-up that motivates the prospect to make the gift. A response mechanism included in the follow-up letter or e-mail will make it easier for the prospect to make a gift.

Each of the procedures discussed so far requires some form of personal contact and often follow-up with each potential donor. In Table 8.2, each of the 222 prospects listed against the $1,000+ gift level represents a major opportunity to secure a gift. Each prospect must be approached on a personal basis by no less than personal visit or a personal telephone call.

If at all possible, the personal approach should even be extended to the prospects in the $250 to $999 categories. These prospects are too valuable to the program to be relegated to the impersonal approaches. An impersonal approach to the potentially major contributor is a grievous error of strategy.

The descent down the ladder continues, with the understanding that the remaining steps are far less effective in obtaining substantial gifts.

Personalized Letters and E-Mail. Once you have identified all of the prospects who will be contacted personally by visits, telephone calls, or personal letters, the organization now turns to its "house list" of other known prospects: donors, lapsed donors, clients, staff members, individuals who receive newsletters, and any other constituent with an active tie to the organization. The personalized letter should include the prospect's name and address in the letter; both letter and e-mail should use the name in the salutation. Upgrading and renewal mailings are sent to appropriate segments of these lists. Many organizations are successfully adapting the personalized letter to a personalized e-mail. Whenever possible, identify people who prefer being contacted by e-mail; build a separate list of these people, and tailor solicitations to these e-mail prospects.

Impersonal Letters and E-Mail. Impersonal letters and e-mailings are also known as direct mail and have a unique place in the annual campaign. It is not an efficient tool in raising funds for the organization, but it is a useful way to acquire new donors. An organization must continuously seek new donors to replace those lost through attrition. The least expensive way with the largest reach is through direct mail or the Internet. Mail and e-mail lists can be purchased, rented, borrowed from other organizations, or obtained from current board members and friends of the organization, government lists, and other sources. Since these lists are made up of *potential* prospects, not prospects, the response will not be nearly as successful in raising funds as the personalized letter. It is a fact, however, that a donor acquisition mailing can cost more than it brings in and yet still be considered successful if it enables the organization to obtain new donors.

Impersonal Telephone Calls. Impersonal telephone calls, often made as part of a phonathon, though successful for some organizations, are not an effective fund raising tool. Whether they are conducted by volunteers, the organization's staff, or paid telemarketers, they can be counterproductive and annoying to the recipient. In addition, though "cold calling" may obtain pledges, the amount collected can often be far less than the amount pledged. Add to this the increasing use of voice mail, answering machines, and caller ID, and the organization will find it necessary to make numerous calls just to get to speak to a person and not a machine.

Fund Raising Benefits and Special Events. These are activities that are staged for a variety of reasons, one of which is to raise money for current programs and operating support. Typical special events will produce 50 percent net revenues for the organization. Other valid reasons and benefits include opportunities to educate the community about the organization's work; to recognize and honor volunteers, donors, and other supporters; to improve the organization's image in the community; and to recruit and involve volunteers.

Door-to-Door Soliciting. Very few organizations use this arduous method of fund raising, and even then, not with a great deal of success. Local schools, especially the students from sports teams and bands knocking on doors in the neighborhood, often have good success, especially after announcing their intentions in local newspapers and on posters in the community.

Communicating Through the Media. Advertising space in newspapers and airtime on radio and TV are costly and require a strong emotional appeal or a natural disaster of major proportions, such as a hurricane or earthquake or the tragic terrorist attacks of September 11, 2001, to elicit what are essentially impulse givers to respond. Newspaper articles and feature stories are good for publicity but rarely generate much in the way of contributions.

Part Five provides details on special strategies that can be used in the annual fund, including direct mail, the Internet, and special events.

The Annual Fund Calendar

When should an organization raise money? Whenever it needs money to carry out its programs and to deliver its services. When is the money most urgently needed? Every day of the year. So when should the organization raise money? Every day of the year.

This ancient wisdom applies today as much as in decades past. But variations in interpretation may be necessary. Fund raising every day of the year would be difficult and somewhat tiring. Taking advantage of the entire year, all twelve months, is a wise use of time. This permits sufficient time for the planning, research, volunteer recruitment, cultivation, and solicitation of the critically important major donors.

July and August are heavy vacation months in the United States, so fund raising is sometimes less successful. However these months can offer manifold opportunities for cultivation visits of prospects and donors. The pace of fund raising drops off, time becomes available to review what has been accomplished, and the opportunity to adjust and fine-tune the fund raising activity is at hand. A planning draft can be prepared for revision, updating, and expansion during the final months of the year.

Planning includes analysis—that is, a prodding curiosity about the diversity of financial needs that will affect fund raising plans in the fiscal year ahead. In addition to current program support, will there be a need to raise special-purpose, capital, and endowment money? How will this affect the annual fund plans?

The solicitation of gifts in person, by mail, by phone, through special events, and through grant applications is a year-round activity. A wisely developed plan will provide for multiple mail solicitations at carefully selected times during the course of the entire year. Some of these will be donor acquisition mailings. Others will involve upgrading mailings and appeals for special-purpose gifts.

The year's fund raising calendar will include scheduled dates for special events, some designed to raise operating funds, others planned for the purpose of attracting attention to the organization or contributing to the luster of its image, and still others as fun-filled activities to recruit, involve, or recognize volunteers.

Perhaps one of the greatest results that can accrue through the use of a year-long annual fund calendar is flexibility. This enables work to be done with annual major gift prospects in accordance with their requirements and without the artificial constraints of an unrealistic timeline imposed by the organization. Volunteers' time must be put to judicious use throughout all of this, something that a flexible timetable would also permit. Sensitivity to the importance of building and maintaining relationships with major contributors demands it.

Building the Annual Fund Team

Team building is important in the annual fund raising process. The volunteer as a member of the team becomes a strategic force: an advocate, a peer, a link to the larger community, and an asker without a vested interest. It is essential to involve key volunteer leaders, beginning with the governing board, in the membership of an annual fund committee, either as a stand-alone committee or as a subcommittee of the board development committee.

The fund raising officer, either a development officer or an annual fund director, serves in a staff support relationship to the annual fund committee. The staff professional in this support position assumes responsibility for preparing the annual fund plan in draft form for review, study, modification, and acceptance or rejection by the annual fund committee. To enhance the workability of this plan, early in the planning stage, the fund raising person must involve the chair and other strategic members of the committee. This takes delicate handling. At no time should the fund raising professional lose control of the preparation process. Ownership of an idea can be negotiated. The wisdom and involvement of the committee should be included from the beginning. Certainly its wisdom and involvement are needed during the implementation period.

After accepting the annual plan, the primary function of this committee is to execute it. In accepting the plan, the committee as a whole attests to the validity of the financial needs that justify the goal. It acknowledges that the goal is reasonable and achievable. It gives evidence of the committee members' willingness to make their own gifts at the level of their capabilities at the beginning of the program, as well as to join in the soliciting process by asking other prospects to do the same.

As stewards of the organization, committee members can perform yeoman service to the cause by assisting staff members in identifying potential contributors within the constituency. Prospect research is a staff responsibility. This research can be expanded and enriched significantly through a working partnership of staff and informed volunteers who have knowledge of the financial structure of the community in which the fund raising is to be accomplished.

The annual fund should be the province of a subcommittee of the development committee. As a management force for the annual fund, this subcommittee should invite to its membership those individuals within the community who are willing to contribute the time, energy, and talent needed to ensure a successful, productive undertaking.

CONCLUSION

To sum up, the annual fund is all of the following things:

- The annual definition and validation of program and special needs
- The securing of funds for the year's operating needs

- A sensitive outreach effort to identify existing and potential constituents and to invite their continuing involvement with the organization
- Inquisitive and continual prospect research that identifies every potential gift source
- The enrollment of capable volunteers who will provide leadership and will give and urge others to give
- The building of links between the volunteer leadership and potential large-gift donors
- A process that seeks to build a strong donor base by soliciting and securing a gift, repeating the gift, and upgrading the gift
- The productive solicitation of that critical 10 percent of donors who have the capacity to give 60 percent of the annual contributions
- The efficient compilation of records that constitute the information bank used in planning all fund raising programs
- The acceptance of the principle that people tend not to give to people but to people who ask on behalf of a cause
- The acceptance of the principle that the right time to ask for the gift is when the organization needs the money for worthy programs and services
- The making of annual gifts, special gifts, big gifts, and planned gifts as a statement of conviction and commitment to the cause that the organization serves
- The strategic procedure of asking the right person to solicit the right prospect for the right amount of money for the right reason in the right way at the right time
- A coordinated plan of fund raising that uses each fund raising vehicle in a disciplined, interrelated fashion to ensure maximum income to meet the nonprofit organization's annual program and special needs
- The ongoing process of seeking and receiving supportive testimony to the fact that the organization is responding to human and social needs through valid programs that merit community support

The annual fund is all of this and more. It is the fund raising event; the donor acquisition, renewal, and upgrading letter; the special gift letter; and the personal letter soliciting a major gift. It is also the phone calls, the door-to-door asking, collection boxes on store counters, car washes, bake sales, e-mails, and Web sites. These are the impersonal, mechanical ways to ask for money used by persons who are uncomfortable with or inexperienced in the face-to-face, personal solicitation that represents the more dynamic, more effective form of fund raising.

Hank Rosso's definition of fund raising is constantly applied to the annual fund: "Fund raising" he said, "is the gentle art of teaching people the joy of giving." And by people, Hank meant individuals. Not corporations, not foundations, but people—members of the community, the organization's constituency, its board and clients. Fund raisers must focus on the fact that the greatest single source of charitable contributions, year in and year out—as noted earlier, historically, about 75 percent—is individual gifts, and when bequests are included, the figure surpasses 80 percent. It is the job of the development officer to enable people to experience the joy of giving their gifts as much as their gifts benefit the organization.

An annual fund raising campaign requires a carefully thought out plan and timetable, people with the right abilities in the right roles, and most of all, the willingness and ability to ask for gifts. "Secure the gift, renew the gift, upgrade the gift" is the watchword of the annual fund. It is the most effective strategy to invite, involve, and bond the constituency to the organization, making it the organization's primary strength. This strength will enhance the organization's ability to raise funds for current program support, for special purposes, and for capital and endowment development because the organization will be asking a constituency that has been properly informed and conditioned by an effective annual fund to provide that support.

CHAPTER NINE

Gifts of Significance

James M. Hodge

Nonprofit organizations large and small rely heavily on major gifts to reach annual fund objectives as well as to ensure the success of capital campaigns. The Rosso model of a total development program depends on personal solicitation of major gifts to complete the donor pyramid. The definitions of a major gift vary as greatly as the institutions themselves. One thing is certain: major gifts are inspired that have a significant impact on the development program and the institution. Such gifts make it possible to launch new program initiatives, transform the physical plant, and endow vital components of nonprofit organizations. Defining major gifts by their size alone is insufficient to characterize the role they play in an organization's vitality. One group's definition may be $1,000 while another's may be $1 million. Frequently, major gifts are defined as gifts that constitute 1 to 5 percent (or more) of the gifts to an annual fund drive goal or ½ to 1 percent of the gifts to a capital campaign objective.

Gifts of significance come in many forms. They may be substantial cash contributions, gifts of appreciated securities, or in-kind gifts such as contributions of valuable art or tangible personal property. Often major gifts are in the form of multiyear pledges given outright or through planned giving vehicles such as bequests, charitable trusts, or gift annuities. Regardless of the form they take, gifts of significance usually come from donors who have contributed several smaller "gifts" over a period of time.

Hank Rosso's philosophy was that every donor at one level was a prospective donor for a gift at a higher level. Leaders in the field of development have posited models of gifting leading to the major or ultimate gift. Perhaps one of the best examples is that espoused by David Dunlop (2000). Dunlop classifies gifts as "annual," "special/capital," and "ultimate." His work details the size, frequency, types, and characteristics of gifts on a continuum. In this model, major gifts are ten to twenty-five times larger than the annual gift; they are infrequently requested and require considerable thought on the part of the benefactor prior to confirming a commitment. These and other similar models of major gifts presented by Dunlop give form and context to the work of major gift officers.

Although most models focus on the size, type, and purpose of major gifts, a new or perhaps renewed paradigm of major gifts is emerging in the philanthropic literature as well as in the practice of development. These are models of ever-deepening relationships between the development officer and the nonprofit and benefactor's values and the institution's mission. Such models consider how the value systems of donors overlap with the core values and mission of the organization.

These are the models of transforming philanthropy (see Exhibit 9.1). The theory behind such models is based on the "why of giving" far more than the "how of giving." Gifts of significance are given to organizations that earn the trust and confidence of benefactors. Big ideas compel those philanthropically minded individuals to invest in, partner with, and commit to meaningful contributions to worthy organizations.

Relationship-based models of philanthropy require the development officer to be an "agent of change" as articulated by Sheldon Garber in a thoughtful essay (1993). As an agent of change, the development officer is charged with participating in the articulation of the institutional mission, probing the core values of prospective major benefactors through values-based inquiry, and developing a deeper sense of the role and meaning of philanthropy in one's life.

Linkage, ability, and interest apply in major gift fund raising. Regardless of the model of philanthropy, there are two essential aspects to the work of major

Exhibit 9.1. Stages of Transforming Philanthropy.

Transational Stage: Giving	Transitional Stage: Naming	Transformational Stage: Changing
Ask and give	Give and name	Partner and change
Smaller gifts	Major gifts	Gifts of significance
More frequent	Less frequent	Rare
Acquaintances	Friends	Soul mates

gift fund raisers. Development officers must work with volunteers to determine both the *financial capacity* of prospective benefactors and the *inclination* those benefactors may have to make a gift to a specific organization. Determining donor capacity requires the development officer to explore indices of wealth from public records, garner information from volunteers who know the prospective benefactor, and draw conclusions based on interactions with the benefactors themselves. Some development offices have full-time staff whose job it is to search databases and sources of wealth to determine the financial capacity of prospective benefactors. (Using information in the fund raising process is explored more fully in Chapter Twenty-Six.) With or without such research staff, it is imperative that the development officer have all possible knowledge about prospective benefactors before formulating a request. Arthur Frantzreb (1991), in describing benefactor research, states the need to know the "interests, concerns, hobbies and eccentricities; education; family history, spouses and children; experience in the nonprofit world; residences; civic, social and fraternal positions; and religion" of potential major benefactors (p. 120). This information serves as a basis for evaluating donor capacity and inclination to make a major gift. Paul Schervish, in his studies of the wealthy, has postulated that the truly wealthy have the advantage of satisfying all their comfort needs in life and that such individuals no longer have to expend energies on accumulating wealth. Rather than focusing on asset accumulation needs, the truly wealthy can explore ways their resources can have a meaningful impact on the world (Schervish and O'Herlihy, 2001, pp. 3–4). These individuals have the capacity to make a difference in the world and truly leave a legacy of caring through philanthropic gifts. In order to secure gifts of significance, one must cultivate relations with those of significant resources. But mere indices of wealth capacity alone do not suffice to inspire major gifts. Both an inclination to do good in the world and a specific interest in the organization are required for the realization of a major gift. Instead of merely chasing money, the development officer and volunteers must be cognizant of signs of wealth but must place more emphasis on individuals with a charitable nature.

Seeking natural partners is the prime responsibility of the major gift officer. Who are "natural partners" for one's organization? First and foremost are present donors to the nonprofit. Major gifts generally come from donors who already believe the institution's mission and case for support. Other potential major donors are volunteers who are governing board or committee members; the nonprofit's constituencies (alumni, former campers, members, and so on), and philanthropically minded individuals in the community. More and more studies are finding that individuals who are deeply religious and spiritual are more likely to use philanthropy to vote their values and to find meaning in their lives (INDEPENDENT SECTOR, 2002). Indeed, more than half of all individual gifts to nonprofit organizations have historically been directed to religious institutions.

Searching for wealthy individuals who are spiritual and committed to making the world a better place is an important activity for major gift officers. Major gift programs must focus more time and attention on donors who believe in the organization and wish to propel it to new levels of service, efficiency, or effectiveness.

Using benefactor wealth research and referrals from board members, volunteers, and major donors, the development officer creates a list of individuals with the capacity to make a difference in the organization. It is then the officer's responsibility to develop a plan to involve those donors in the life of the organization. For it is through involvement that philanthropic gifts of significance arise.

Numerous models describing stages in the solicitation of major gifts have been postulated over the years. The Fund Raising School (2002) uses an eight-step model (see Exhibit 9.2). As donors are further involved in the life of the nonprofit organization, they develop an "ownership position" in the good that is done through the organization. As donors increase their "equity share" in the institution and see their personal values overlap with the institution's mission, more and more significant gifts are made to further the cause.

How does the development officer engage potential benefactors in the mission of the organization? Once natural partners are discovered, it is through genuine relationship building that the development officers promote major investments. Asking donors to volunteer on important committees, raise funds, share their expertise, and serve on the governing board are some of the most common ways of building ownership. The key is not so much a technique but rather the spirit behind the technique that is important. Potential major benefactors are in constant demand and volunteer burnout is rampant, but a surefire

Exhibit 9.2. Major Gifts: The Eight-Step Solicitation Process.

1. Identification

2. Qualification

3. Development of Strategy

4. Cultivation

5. Solicitation and Negotiation

6. Acknowledgment

7. Stewardship

8. Renewal

Source: The Fund Raising School, 2002.

way to propel an organization into the arena of major gifts is to authentically involve donors in the mission of the nonprofit. Perhaps the highest form of reverence we can demonstrate to donors is to genuinely ask their opinions. Institutions need to involve donors and volunteers in important projects where their input is valued and their advice is sought. It is not through disingenuousness that major gifts arise. The wealthy, like all of us, are tired of being manipulated politically for votes, economically to purchase products, and philanthropically to make gifts. The proper stance to take in relationship-based philanthropy is not to manipulate but rather to inspire, not to push someone to make a "transaction-based" gift but rather to make the mission and its work so real and important as to compel or "pull" a donor to make a gift. As Tom Morris said in his book *If Aristotle Ran General Motors* (1997), pull is the "lure of an attractive goal or a strongly desired good, recognized by Plato and Aristotle as well as by many other great thinkers of the past . . . embodying a valued ideal. It attracts us and calls us to put forward our greatest efforts. The greater the ideal, the greater the power it can have in our lives" (p. 63).

WHAT WORKS IN MAJOR GIFT FUND RAISING

Fortunately, in the past several years, practitioners in the field of philanthropy and professors in our nation's universities have begun to explore more deeply why benefactors make major gifts and why donors say they do not make gifts. This donor-centered research is both refreshing and instructive. *The Seven Faces of Philanthropy* (Prince and File, 1994) categorizes wealthy donors into seven motivational types. This important work looks at understanding the interests, concerns, needs, and motivations of wealthy individuals toward the role of philanthropy in their lives. By developing an understanding of such motivations, the development professional can better plan how to authentically involve a particular prospective benefactor in the work of the nonprofit. Cluster analysis by Prince and File revealed four important donor segments: "affiliators," who look for social and business linkages through nonprofit activities; "pragmatists," who see personal financial advantages through support of nonprofits; "dynasts," who are heirs to family affluence and to the tradition of philanthropy; and "repayers," who want to reciprocate benefits they or someone close to them received from a nonprofit.

Simply put, donors make major gifts because of a sense of obligation to the nonprofit, the greater community, or the world. Gifts of significance arise out of the true interests, values, and passions of the prospective benefactor. Regardless of the particular motivation for giving, the role of the major gift officer is to engage the donor in the important work of the nonprofit and deepen the benefactor's involvement in the organization's mission and value systems.

It is also instructive to note why fund raisers fail or why donors refuse to make major gifts to nonprofits. Sturtevant (1997) identifies four of the most common reasons that major gifts fail to materialize: institutional leaders and development officers neglect to establish basic trust between the organization and the prospective benefactor; fund raisers fail to show the inherent value of the nonprofit's mission, vision, and services; nonprofit leaders don't help donors to connect with the institution and serve the benefactor's interests and needs; and fund raisers fail to instill a sense of urgency for the request. Donors do not make major gifts because of a mismatch of interests between donor and institution; a premature request before the donor was ready to give; a failure to ask for a specific amount; being asked too many times by the organization or by competing nonprofits; and a lack of connection between the solicitor of the gift and the donor.

INQUIRING AND INSPIRING

Given the anecdotal findings of professionals in the development field and the recent research of social scientists, we are better prepared to understand the motivation of major donors. The next question confronting nonprofits is how we best position our institutions and our prospective benefactors for success in the area of major gifts. Hank put it best when he said, "Fund raising is the gentle art of teaching people the joy of giving." He long understood and practiced the idea of "transforming philanthropy." He knew that major gift work was the result of relationship building. And like Sheldon Garber, he understood the need for development officers to be agents of change in the lives of their organizations and benefactors. What skills, then, do development professionals working in the area of major gifts need to succeed? Simply put, they require inquiry skills that will help them understand the values and motivations of potential major benefactors and train and manage volunteers, the ability to articulate the institution's mission, and the creativity and passion to inspire the benefactor to action. Being a successful major gift officer and volunteer fund raiser does not require having all the answers about the prospective benefactor, but it does require that development professionals and volunteers know all the right questions to ask of both the institution and the donor. As agents of change, development professionals and volunteers must be involved at the highest levels of decision making in the nonprofit. They must not only be skilled at articulating the mission but also be involved in creating the mission and moving the organization to greater levels of efficiency and effectiveness.

The following are some key questions the major gift officer must ask of the institution:

- Is our mission relevant, important, and easily articulated?
- Can we use outcome measures to determine if we are advancing the mission?
- How can we better involve volunteers and donors in the good that is done through our organization?
- Who best articulates our mission and vision for the future?
- Who would be a natural partner with a particular benefactor?
- Who is responsible for developing the relationship with a specific benefactor?

Every nonprofit must identify the "vision master," a leader who brings the mission to life for benefactors. Just as important, each institution must identify the staff members with the skills to transform vision to action, to make things happen so as to advance the mission through definable steps and acts. Finally, the major gift officer must be a primary person to advance the relationship between the prospective donor and the institution. This is where donor and institutional values overlap and the "dance of philanthropy" is performed (see Figure 9.1). Some institutions discover that the vision master and best relationship developer may be the organization's president or chair of the board of directors. For other nonprofits, there will be many hands in the work of eliciting major gifts. It is wise to have multiple links between the nonprofit and the benefactor. This prevents reliance on few people to raise major gifts that can be devastating when and if the major players leave the nonprofit.

There are questions major gift officers must ask themselves as well. To paraphrase Payton (1988, p. 74), who posed the most piercing question of all: Do we as professionals work *for* philanthropy or *off of* philanthropy? Why are we doing this important work? For major gift work is less of a job than it is a calling. Development professionals are not selling products; they are rather promoting visions

Figure 9.1. Values Overlap.

and possibilities for the betterment of humankind. This is serious work taken seriously by the professionals engaged in it. O'Neill (1993) saw development professionals as moral trainers. Major gift officers are moral trainers whose work is about ethical inspiration (Rosso's "teaching the joy of giving"). Hence one must ask, are we serving as role models for philanthropy? Are we making important philanthropic gifts ourselves? Do we serve as "soul models" of well-examined lives? And perhaps most important of all, are we devoted to helping donors find meaning in their lives through acts of philanthropy? Many prospective major benefactors know how to accumulate "means" but not "meaning" in their lives. One way of looking at major gift work is that development officers, volunteers, and donors are on a long walk together to find meaning in life. Meaning can be found through philanthropy.

As important as it is to be an agent of change through professional introspection and probing the mission and values of the institution, the great work of development is done through exploring a benefactor's values in an atmosphere of trust. Using a process Dunlop (2000) refers to as "nurturing inquiry," major gift officers ask defining value questions of donors. The classic work by Kübler-Ross (1969) on death and dying teaches that on their deathbeds, individuals do not measure the value of their lives by their net worth or accumulations; rather they measure their life's meaning based on whether or not they made a difference in the world and whether they're leaving a lasting legacy. It seems apparent that through philanthropy, development officers and volunteers can help donors provide meaningful answers to those deathbed questions. For this is the essential partnership in philanthropy: our institution's mission and the donor's value system equals more than either can accomplish separately. This makes the essence of major gift work "helping people arrive before they depart!" This requires changing major gift work from role models in business to soul models in philanthropy. How are these transformations accomplished? By inquiring about the donor's core values and passions through values-based questions. By asking important questions, we help donors transform from motivations that are intrinsic to extrinsic, from self-centered to other-centered, and from independent to interdependent. Transforming major gift work is about changing "me-centeredness" to "we-centeredness."

QUESTIONS OF VALUES

Before elucidating some of the key values questions, it is important to set the rules of values-based inquiry. Before one asks important questions regarding values, it is necessary to establish an atmosphere of trust. Two essential components for an atmosphere of trust are permissions and protections. These are assurances to the donor that before we probe core values, we will seek their permission to enter a deeper relationship. Beyel (1997, p. 52) calls it "philanthropic informed consent." This is a discovery process whereby the development officer and the donor engage in a moral and ethical dialogue. This may be as simple as asking permission to inquire about closely held values, but more often it is an intuitive process, much like knowing when it is safe to ask an acquaintance a question we would normally ask a close friend. The second important way of establishing trust is to ensure that any information divulged will remain private and confidential. This means that the development officer must guard all insights gained and not mention them to the donor's family, friends, or colleagues or in visit reports. Some key donor questions include these: What values do you hold most dear? Who has inspired you in your life and your work? How does one make a difference in the world? What is your legacy in the world today or in the world of tomorrow? Can you finish your legacy alone? How much is enough money to leave to heirs? Is there ever too much money to leave to heirs? What is the most satisfying philanthropic gift you have made and why? Which one of the nonprofits you support does the best job of keeping you involved in its mission? What kinds of reports do you want and expect as stewardship for your major gift? How do you prefer to be invited to make a charitable gift? These are only a few samples of key questions the major gift officer must ask while developing a relationship with each benefactor. The questions are asked at appropriate stages in the relationship. They are meant to be stretching questions but can seem impertinent if they come too early in a relationship.

In addition to the individual contacts between officer and donor, strategic questions may be considered when the donor interacts with other members of the nonprofit board or staff. One highly successful way to ask many of these questions is through a donor profile interview. In this setting, a donor is asked to participate in a profile of his or her life and philanthropy. These questions help turn dreamers into dream makers for your institution. For it is a truism that once they have fulfilled their own personal goals and dreams, highly successful individuals will often transform into major benefactors who will fulfill the dreams of others through the nonprofit.

BUILDING AN OWNERSHIP POSITION

The most important role for the major gift officer is to forge a close relationship between a donor and the nonprofit, including its volunteers. In the life and mission of the organization, one important device in this relationship building is philanthropic storytelling to elucidate to the benefactor great things that others have done to advance the organization's mission through philanthropy. Storytelling allows the development officer to comfortably make maps for donors to follow with their own personal gifts. A part of the cultivation and relationship-building process may be to ask the donor to make investment or "step" gifts to the organization. Charitable step gifts are smaller gifts given to the nonprofit that allow the organization to demonstrate how it uses contributions and how it reports on the impact of such gifts. It is important to ask for these smaller gifts, as they allow the donor to open a window into the nonprofit and provide the nonprofit with the opportunity to further involve the donor through meaningful stewardship and appropriate recognition. Solicitations of step gifts allow the development officer to determine if the proposal harmonizes with the donor's core values. But rather than asking merely for any "starting gift," it is paramount to consider what sort of gift will further involve the donor in the nonprofit and might naturally lead to additional gifts. The major gift officer should ask, "Does this proposal have the potential to grow into more substantial gifts by the donor?" A step gift request for a partial academic scholarship can lead to further requests to endow that scholarship and at some time in the future perhaps name the academic unit wherein the scholarship lies. Although step gifts are common ways to encourage major gifts, it is not unheard of for a first gift to a nonprofit to be a major gift. Development officers and volunteers must be alert to those unique individuals who can quickly catch a vision and make major initial gifts to the nonprofit.

Another way to involve donors in step gifts is to "borrow their collections." Often potential major benefactors have accumulations that can be appropriately used by the nonprofit. These may range from art collections to private planes. By borrowing these accumulations, the nonprofit recognizes their value and demonstrates to the donor that their collections, as well as their donations, will be respected and used wisely.

THE REQUEST OR INVITATION

Most of the work of a proposal is done prior to writing the request and making the appointment with a benefactor. Donor values have been explored, an appropriate gift amount has been considered, and the proposal team has been carefully selected and has rehearsed the solicitation in detail. The major gift officer must ask several questions: Have we come to know this donor sufficiently? Has this donor been involved meaningfully in the work of our organization? Is this an appropriate time for this request? Have we got the amount and the purpose right?

In setting up the specific meeting to discuss a proposal, it is important that the potential benefactor know that the purpose of the visit is to be asked for financial support for an important project. This avoids fund raising by stealth or surprise and is the respectful thing to do. Where will the major gift proposal be made? The site should be chosen with the donor's needs and comfort in mind. Usually it is at the donor's home or place of business. Sometimes it takes place at the nonprofit, particularly if the request requires a tour or on-site demonstration of how the donor's gift will be employed by the nonprofit. Public settings such as restaurants for major gift solicitations can be disastrous. A waiter may interrupt or stumble just as the proposal reaches its apex, spoiling both mood and decorum. Regardless of the setting, the major gift officer must be sure to ask, "Are all the decision makers at the table?" This means that appropriate leaders of the organization, the donor and spouse and family, and legal and financial advisers, as appropriate, must all be on board. The proposal itself must be clear and include the gift amount, project goals and means of measurement, recognition options for the gift, and a plan for reporting or stewardship after the gift is made. A preproposal rehearsal will make certain that at the right time, the right person makes the specific request: "We are requesting your consideration of a leadership gift of (*specific amount*), which will be the catalyst for making this project a reality."

STEWARDSHIP AND RECOGNITION OF MAJOR GIFTS

Once a gift commitment is entered into, the process of stewardship begins (more on this topic is explained in Chapter Thirty-One). To ensure that there is no "donor regret," to steal a term from the for-profit world, the organization must provide stewardship of the gift and send regular and meaningful reports. Reports on construction progress, thank-you letters from scholarship recipients, financial reports, lab tours, photos, and personal visits with progress reports are simply the best way to strengthen donor ties to the nonprofit. Stewardship is both ethical and essential following receipt of major gifts, and it is the smart thing to do to encourage future gifts from the benefactor.

Donor recognition is another way to involve benefactors in the nonprofit. "How would you and your family like us to acknowledge your generous gift?" is an appropriate inquiry. Recognition should be as personal as possible, reflective of the uniqueness of the nonprofit and the gift and appropriate to the size and importance of the contribution. Other major donors in waiting will examine how your institution respectfully recognizes and exhibits stewardship for gifts of significance.

MANAGING THE MAJOR GIFT PROCESS

Whether a major gift officer heads a one-person shop or is a part of a large and complex major gift team, the key to major gift success is an organized system for the identification, involvement, and solicitation of potential major benefactors. The literature is rife with examples of how to manage the major gift process. Successful programs can be managed using simple index cards or sophisticated software programs. (Exhibit 9.3 provides a guide for managing the major gift process.) Regardless of the format, every institution must identify the

Exhibit 9.3. Developing a Strategy for the Major Gift Process.

Benefactor Biographic Information

- Name, address, phone numbers
- Family information, marital status, children
- Degrees, interests and hobbies
- Governing board and committee memberships
- Interest areas for potential major gifts
- Other pertinent publicly known information

Financial Information

What is known about the prospective benefactor's financial information and ability to make a major gift?

- Public information on stock and real estate ownership
- Previous gifts to the organization and other charities
- Other pertinent public financial information

Linkages

- Who are the individuals, staff, and volunteers closest to the prospective benefactor?
- Who are the donor's natural partners?

Strategy

- Who should be involved in the relationship building, proposal development, and the request?
- For what specific purpose is the gift being sought?
- What is the proposed gift amount?
- Who will present the proposal?
- When will it be presented?
- What specific steps or next actions must be accomplished before a proposal can be made? By whom? By when?
- Are there any roadblocks to this proposal, and if so, who can remove them?
- What coaching, rehearsals, or strategy planning sessions will be necessary?

Specific Next Steps

- Set up a reminder system, manual or computerized, to monitor next steps and for revision of strategies as appropriate.
- Determine what actions should be taken, by whom, and by when.

top twenty-five to one hundred potential major donors whose philanthropy can have a significant impact on the organization.

Once identified, each donor should be assigned an individual file. Files should be developed with respect for the donor and include only information that is pertinent to the potential major gift. This information will be useful in determining what types of nonprofit projects will resonate with the donor's value systems. Private and potentially embarrassing information about donors has no place in these files. A good guide is only to place information, notes, or comments on donor contacts that could be read by the donor without embarrassment. Files should include the names of natural partners who are centers of influence in the donor's lives. Vital is information about regular meetings with institutional leaders to discuss the donor, his or her deepening involvement in the nonprofit, a realistic potential gift amount, and details of any projects of great potential interest.

Specific ways to further the donor's involvement and interests can then be documented. Essential to this management process is the appointment of the relationship manager, the person responsible for advancing the relationship using volunteers and other aides as appropriate. Many management plans suggest that a specific number of personal visits and other donor contacts are required between the major gift officer and the potential major benefactor during a given period of time. I believe, however, that it is not the frequency of the encounters that is important but rather how deep an impact the development officer or other institution leaders and volunteers have on a donor's sense of belonging to the nonprofit. Visit numbers are less important than meaningful encounters with predetermined objectives that increase donors' "equity share" in the nonprofit.

CONCLUSION

Some specific techniques of major gift work have been explored in this chapter, along with ways to approach and manage the major gift process, but when all is said and done, it is still the spirit behind the major gift process that determines its success. If, as major gift officers, we operate on the "push "or "scolding" model of development (Schervish, 2000b, pp. 2–3), we will have neither long-term success in the field nor satisfaction in our work (see Exhibit 9.4). It is through Schervish's "discernment model" that we respect donor wishes in the fund raising process. If we compete with other nonprofits for perceived limited charitable dollars, we will look like avaricious children squabbling over a parent's estate. In major gift fund raising we must stay focused on long-term possibilities. We cannot be distracted by immediate needs. Success in major gift fund raising comes from a vision for what the organization can become and what

Exhibit 9.4. The Scolding and Discernment Models.

Scolding Model	*Discernment Model*
You must give . . .	• Is there something you want to do?
• The right amount	• Is there something you want to do for others?
• At the right time	• Is there something that would offer you deeper identity and satisfaction?
• To the right causes	
• In the right ways	

Source: Paul G. Schervish, The Spiritual Horizons of Philanthropy," in E. R. Tempel and D. F. Burlingame (eds.), *Understanding the Needs of Donors,* New Directions for Philanthropic Fundraising, no. 29. Copyright © 2000 John Wiley & Sons, Inc. This material is used by permission of John Wiley & Sons, Inc.

services it can provide in the long term with those major resources. We owe it to ourselves, our profession, and the dignity of donors to approach our work with the enthusiasm and respect it deserves. Schervish (2000b) helps us do just that with his idea of "supply-side philanthropy." This elegant theory postulates that it is not through competition for an illusionary and limited "pie of philanthropy" but rather through inspiring individuals toward gifts of significance that the true growth of philanthropy will occur. This theory implies that the only limits to philanthropy are those that we impose on ourselves and our institutions through misinformed notions of this important work and the transforming effect philanthropy can have on the lives of our benefactors. If we follow Schervish's advice and focus on improving the "quality of giving" over the "quantity of giving," we will achieve both greater respect for the work of development and great philanthropic success in the process.

CHAPTER TEN

Building Endowment

Edward C. Schumacher

T hink of endowment as putting money away "for a rainy day"—only these pennies last not just through one wet season but through many. Or picture an endlessly blooming rosebush that keeps producing beautiful flowers as long as it is tended carefully and pruned judiciously. That's endowment—gifts given to provide an income for all time.

WHY BUILD ENDOWMENT?

An endowed fund acts as a self-sustaining funding stream, one that may prove crucial to the financial stability of a nonprofit organization both in the present and into the future. Such a fund offers protection from the uncertainties of the economy and the instability of many other forms of funding. As outlined in Chapter Seven, endowment building is an important part of the total development program espoused by the Rosso model and one of the four major fund raising results. Both capital campaigns and major gift programs outlined here in Part Three can produce endowment gifts. However, this chapter deals specifically with types of endowment and special endowment initiatives that can be developed in mature fund raising programs.

Providing a stable income source is not the only enticement of endowment. By creating an endowment fund, an organization showcases its long-term mission and vision, renews its commitment to donors and clients, and even begins to portray itself as a vehicle of fund investment and enhancement. Endowment funds often attract large current and deferred gifts; donors can feel committed to the present mission and also buy a bit of immortality with a contribution that lasts long beyond their lifetime.

Endowment Today

Although endowment funds have been part of the overall fund raising programs of major institutions for some time, most nonprofits have not created and could not create endowments. Today things have changed; many more nonprofits have begun to use endowments to stabilize their finances and ensure their future. This chapter defines and describes endowment, provides tools for assessing readiness for endowment building, and offers ideas for beginning the process of endowment fund raising.

Endowment Defined

Endowment is a fund of money to be held in perpetuity as directed by the donor. The money in this fund is invested in stocks, bonds, and other vehicles, and an annual income is derived from this investment; the principal remains intact. The return from the investment of this money may be used for the purposes of the nonprofit or as the donor directs.

Most endowments are permanent endowments; the principal cannot be touched and is invested in perpetuity to provide an enduring source of funding for an organization. This funding may be for specific projects or programs, or it may go into the general operating fund. Gifts to endowments can be made from many sources, including cash, property, or securities, and may be received as a lump sum or, in the case of deferred or planned giving, over time. Even monies earned from special events can be designated for endowment simply by placing them in a general or special endowment fund.

There are three generally recognized types of endowment funds: true endowment, term endowment, and quasi-endowment. We have already described a true endowment: the principal cannot be touched; only the earnings are spent. These earnings include interest and dividend income and in some cases portfolio appreciation as well. Most of these "true" funds are established by a donor, through a gift or bequest, with provisions that direct the earnings to a specific project or program. These funds are often named, and the original donor may add to the principal over time.

A term endowment functions as a true endowment until a specified event occurs, a specific period of time elapses, or a predetermined date is reached, at which time the principal may be spent. The income from term endowment may be either restricted, usually by donor instructions, or unrestricted, that is, not specified by donor instruction but designated for a specific use by the organization.

An organization may establish a quasi-endowment. This fund may be treated as an endowment but is not truly subject to the rules of true or term endowment; rather, it functions more like a reserve account. Investment earnings are spent for programs and projects, while the principal is protected; however, earnings can be used for various purposes, and the main fund may be utilized. This fund may be established with gifts or current operating funds and is generally used at the discretion of the board of directors.

Endowments may be held and managed by the organization receiving the funds, but they are often held and managed by an outside organization, usually a community foundation, a private foundation, or a private financial institution.

History and Growth

Endowment is not a new concept; many private universities were founded with large endowments, and some long-established nonprofit groups boast very old endowment funds. Two late-twentieth-century trends, however, boosted both the need for endowments and their chances of success.

Beginning in the 1980s, nonprofits saw their government and private corporate funding drop dramatically; organizations were forced to become more creative and sophisticated in their search for dollars. In the 1990s, the stock market exploded, and investment profits rose radically. In numbers tracked by INDEPENDENT SECTOR (2001b), the total dollar value of receipts from endowment and investment income increased from $5.1 billion to $31.5 billion between 1977 and 1996.

More recently, the growth of community foundations as agents for nonprofit endowments has spurred the creation of endowment funds among even the smallest of organizations.

The current world of endowment funds and fund raising is an unbalanced one. A study conducted in 2000 by the Spectrem Group found that groups in the United States held nearly $600 billion in endowments (Billitteri, 2000). According to the 2000 National Association of College and University Business Officers (NACUBO) Endowment Study (Klinger, 2001), colleges and universities hold the lion's share of these funds, with more than $239 billion in endowment assets, and yet, says NACUBO, only a limited number of nonprofit higher education institutes in the United States have endowments. The same study shows that forty-one universities and colleges held endowments worth $1 billion or more, with Harvard holding the largest single endowment in the nation, valued at nearly $19 billion (Manetta, 2001).

INDEPENDENT SECTOR (2001b) has compiled statistics that show that education and scientific research receive more income from endowment and investment than any other part of the nonprofit sector, but slowly other sectors are creating and benefiting from endowment funds. In the two decades from 1977 to 1996, arts and culture organizations saw their receipts from endowment and investment rise tenfold, from $100,000 million to $1 billion. In the same period, social and legal services increased their receipts from endowment and investment, with income rising from $200,000 million to $1.8 billion.

Despite this growth, endowment funds remain misunderstood and underutilized. At the same time, continuing struggles for funding and an uncertain economic future make endowment ever more desirable and necessary.

ENDOWMENT FUND RAISING

There are many ways to include an endowment fund in your general fund raising program. Endowment can be integrated into your planned giving program (see Chapter Twelve) by establishing an endowment fund and soliciting planned gifts specifically for this fund or by promoting the establishment of named endowment funds as part of the planned giving process. You may choose to solicit endowment gifts as you would annual gifts (see Chapter Eight)—asking on an ongoing basis for current cash or equivalent gifts for the fund through face-to-face meetings or special mailings.

It has become quite common to include an endowment fund raising element within a capital campaign (see Chapter Eleven); this is an obvious combination as you raise money to build a facility and solicit the funds to ensure its long-term use and maintenance at the same time. You may wish to conduct a strict endowment campaign, which follows the general rules and structure of a capital campaign but focuses solely on building the endowment fund.

Strategies

Successful endowment fund raising combines the best techniques used for annual giving with the special strategies employed in capital campaigns. For endowment fund raising efforts to succeed, there must be an ongoing year-round process of cultivation, solicitation, and recognition; it can never be set aside or considered finished. Endowment campaigns may be used to kick off the start of a fund, but the fund needs to always be part of the organization's overall fund raising plan. A permanent staff member should be assigned to run the endowment program year-round, to make it a priority for the organization, and to promote it to the whole community.

The strategies used to cultivate and solicit endowment gifts mirror those used for major gifts and capital gifts. Endowment fund raising is generally focused on a small group of donors and aims to generate large gifts over a period of time; therefore, the pace of this fund raising is often slow. Large amounts of time are spent on cultivation, proposals are specially tailored for each prospect, and numerous one-on-one meetings must take place.

Planned Giving

Endowments are often confused with planned giving or estate gifts. Although many endowment gifts come in the form of planned gifts, it is important for both the organization and its donors to distinguish between the two. As discussed in Chapter Eleven, planned giving refers to giving vehicles, such as charitable remainder trusts, life insurance, donor-advised funds, or wills, which direct donations to a nonprofit organization during the life of the donor or upon the donor's death. An endowment is the actual fund of monies that have been given to the organization, with the direction that only the income from its investment be spent. An endowment may be funded in part by a planned gift, and many planned gifts are designated as endowment gifts, but they are not to be confused.

GETTING READY FOR ENDOWMENT FUND RAISING

Most nonprofits can have an endowment. Endowment fund raising can be as simple as a wills-and-bequests program or as complicated as a full-blown planned giving program. In either case, there are some factors that must be in place before you start. There should be a clearly defined fund raising staff position, that of development officer or other similar job title. In addition, there should be an annual fund or other ongoing giving program, volunteers, and a donor base. Access to a community foundation or the other legal and financial organizations needed to run an endowment are also necessary. Although a planned giving program is not a prerequisite for beginning an endowment fund, as mentioned before, one ought to be in place to ensure the success of the fund.

Since so many nonprofits are now doing endowment fund raising, there is no need to start from scratch. Create a study group, which includes the development director, the board finance chair, the board fund raising chair, and other interested parties, to embark on a research project. Research the endowment funds of other similar organizations, interview someone in your community who has helped start an endowment fund, and interview someone from the local community foundation; even if you don't use the services of the foundation for your endowment, it will have plenty of knowledge about such funds. All the information the study group gathers will be valuable later when the process of education begins.

This study group will also want to conduct a brief internal feasibility study to see if the organization is ready to start an endowment fund raising program. This feasibility study is really a set of answers to a long list of questions designed to help you assess your chances for success.

Assess Your Donor Base

Begin the study by analyzing your donor base to ensure that you have endowment donor potential. Compile information on the number of active donors you have and the number of donors at each giving level. You need not only look at the highest giving levels; even donors who have consistently given $500 a year to your organization for two or three years may be potential endowment donors.

Prospect research, both informal and formal, is an important component of good endowment fund raising. It is essential that the capacity of prospects be assessed and that time is spent seeking information that points to leadership gift prospects.

Look especially at your top donors. What is their cumulative giving over the past five years? Have they given planned or major gifts? Review your planned giving program. How many donors do you have, and what types of gifts have they given?

What is the age range of the donor list? What is the age range of your top ten donors? Are they good candidates for planned gifts, and are they in a phase of life when they are looking at wills and making plans for their estates?

How many of your current board members are among the top ten donors? Board members are often good first endowment donors, just as they are good first capital and major gift donors.

Assess Your Fund Raising Program

This is perhaps the most important part of the study. Do you have the donor base to make the investment in endowment fund raising worthwhile? Look closely at your annual giving program: How old is it? How much income does it generate each year? What size gifts do you receive? Are donors segmented by gift size and approached differently based on gift size? Do you have major donors, corporate and foundation donors? The answers to all these questions will help you determine how big to make the endowment program and how fast to get it going.

Assess Your Organization

How old is your organization? Institutional age generally denotes stability, and endowment donors want to give to stable organizations. Does the community know who you are, what you do, and how you do it? Is your mission accepted by the community as an important one? Are the organization's values clearly stated and demonstrated in public documents and public acts? Do you have a long-range plan in place that shows you know where you are going in the future?

Does the organization maintain a comprehensive list of names and addresses of members and constituents, business prospects, clients served, and other interested parties? Is there a program or system for keeping past board members involved with the organization? Are there publications and other vehicles for promoting endowment giving?

Is the organization financially sound, that is, can it meet its current operating needs and cover any deficits through annual and other giving?

Assess Your Leadership

You will need the right people in the right places in order to pursue endowment fund raising. Think about the members of your board: Are they the movers and shakers of the community? Are they committed to the organization? Are they committed to building an endowment? Are there leaders among the group who are able and willing to lead fund raising efforts?

Does the board participate in other fund raising endeavors, as both fund raisers and donors? What percentage of the board gives to the annual fund or gave to your most recent capital drive? How many board members have named the organization in their will or given another type of planned gift? As with all fund raising, an active board whose members are willing to give and ask others to give is essential. Endowment fund raising will require intense board education: members cannot simply support the idea of an endowment program; they must understand how endowment works.

An endowment program is a time-consuming endeavor. Both the CEO and the development director must be committed to making it a success. You will need to determine who will oversee the endowment fund raising effort, how much time that staff member will devote to endowment, and how those efforts will balance with the person's other responsibilities. Details such as who will provide administrative support or research support for the program need to be determined before the program is launched.

It is important to make a commitment with funds as well as ideas. Obviously, you will need to fund a position or part of a position to run the program, but you will also need a budget for training the staff, for cultivating donors, and for paying legal and financial fees associated with the program and all the printing, mailing, and other costs associated with fund raising.

Assess Your Systems and Records

If you do not possess a fully computerized, accurate, and up-to-date donor database, you are probably not ready to begin an endowment program. If you do have a database, consider whether it allows for timely and appropriate gift processing and whether it has the capacity to handle the detailed research and cultivation information necessary for endowment fund raising. Are funds available to purchase a new system, if one is necessary, or to enhance the current system? How will the records of endowment giving be incorporated into those of annual giving and capital giving? Endowment dictates that detailed, complex records can be kept over time; you will want to track endowment income and outcomes, perhaps even as they relate to individual donors.

The legal and financial aspects of endowment require that an organization have established and written gift policies and procedures. Take a careful look at these policies. Do they outline how to accept securities, real estate, bequests, or tangible personal property? Do the policies address investment practices, fund management, board oversight, and stewardship? Donors will want answers to all these questions.

THE PLANNING PROCESS

The planning process for developing an endowment initiative should involve key constituents and result in organizational policies related to endowments. Following are some of the aspects organizations should consider.

The Committee

The board should create an endowment advisory committee (EAC), and a staff member should be assigned to this committee. The EAC will draft strategy, goals, and directions related to endowment creation and fund raising. The board then reviews the plans and sends them to the finance and development committees for approval. The staff develop a basic endowment fund raising plan and plan an endowment retreat.

The Endowment Retreat

There will be many questions to be answered at the endowment retreat: Which type of endowment will you have? Who will manage the endowment? How will the CEO, board members, and others be involved in the endowment program? Who will train them? How will the endowment program be integrated with the organization's current fund raising programs? What cultivation activities will be introduced? Who will solicit prospective endowment gift donors? Who will develop written materials for endowment? What programs or projects will you choose to endow?

The endowment retreat is the beginning of a long process of education. Many board members, even those with sophisticated legal and financial background, do not truly understand endowments. As mentioned before, they may have endowment funds confused with planned giving or other giving vehicles or view them as something too complex and overwhelming for nonprofits to undertake. The education process begins with the board and will continue with staff and donors as the endowment moves forward.

Legal and Professional Counsel

The creation and management of an endowment fund requires expertise in several legal and financial matters. Whom do you need to bring in to do this work? Are there people already in your organization who can take on this work, or do you need to hire outside agents? Do you already have relationships with organizations that can advise you in these matters? Be cautious. Just because a board member is a lawyer does not mean that he or she is qualified to run an endowment fund. That said, some organizations do rely on board, staff, and volunteers to create, invest, and manage their endowment funds. Others choose to hire trust companies or financial advisers to do the managing.

Institutionally Related Foundations

It is possible and often preferable to establish a separate and independent (501)(c)(3) organization, sometimes called a "foundation," to raise and manage an endowment. Tied to the organization through bylaws, articles of incorporation, and linked boards, an institutionally related foundation can bring added staff and resources to endowment fund raising efforts.

The Community Foundation

Another option open to nonprofits is the use of a community foundation. These grantmaking organizations are in the business of investing funds and supporting nonprofits. They can help you establish your fund and administer it for very reasonable rates. They may also offer better fund growth, as your fund is often pooled with those of others; investment expertise; and greater visibility for the fund through their networks and publications.

Donor-Advised Funds

Donor-advised funds have grown in popularity and assets over the past few years (Billitteri, 2001). Commercial brokerages, community foundations, federations, and even some charities have set up donor-advised funds, in which donors may give cash or other assets, claim a charitable deduction, have the funds invested, and help direct the resulting monies to charities. Charities that choose to oversee such funds for donors usually require that the donors give them some portion of the funds in the account each year. Considered a planned giving vehicle, donor-advised funds could be used to augment the organization's own endowment fund. If you wish to offer donor-advised funds, be aware that they are complicated and may be perceived as competing with local community foundations.

The Case for Endowment

As with other types of fund raising, the success or failure of endowment fund raising can depend on the case presented to prospective donors. The development of a case should be comprehensive and cover all the components of the organization's success. Specifically, the organization needs to address both the nature of endowment funds and the reasons for giving to endowment. The case documentation (see Chapter Six) will serve as your main educational document to help donors understand the benefits of endowment giving.

Endowment is attractive and important to donors for a number of very different reasons. Those reasons need to be customized to meet the needs of each specific donor. Here are some to consider: Endowment giving can translate into a little immortality, as the gift lasts long beyond the giver's lifetime. The gift can be made now, but in the case of many giving vehicles, the donor retains use or benefits from the funds until death. There can be many tax savings, including capital gains and estate tax relief. All these need to be highlighted in the case statement.

Documentation

To build an effective endowment fund raising program, the following documents should be in place in the nonprofit organization: (1) a statement of board responsibilities related to endowment; (2) a statement of rules for fund raising and the creation of new endowments and rules for making additions to existing endowments; (3) a statement that includes gift transfer rules, rules for the receipt of gifts, accounting policies, and procedures for endowment; (4) written investment policies, goals, and procedures; and (5) templates for distribution and endowment reports.

LAUNCHING THE FUND

As discussed in Chapter Three, the concept of the fund raising cycle is at the heart of Hank Rosso's fund raising philosophy. The fourteen steps of the cycle, when put into place, can be used to prepare for and carry out many types of fund raising, including endowment fund raising (see Figure 3.1 in Chapter Three).

Endowment fund raising is simply good fund raising. It can be done in a campaign format like a capital drive or in a lower-key, continuous mode like an annual fund. In either case, some of the basic premises remain the same. The first gifts to the fund should be leadership gifts, which set high giving expectations and encourage other donations. Endowment fund raising highlights multiyear pledges and multiyear vehicles and both current and deferred gifts. It is a very intense type of fund raising, with emphasis on nurturing close relationships and spending one-on-one time with prospects.

Much like planned giving, endowment fund raising has to work hard to prove itself successful. Endowment fund raising is generally not quick. It takes time to develop relationships and to discuss the importance of an endowment gift. Often the commitment to endowment is made today with a gift to come later. The numbers don't always look so good when they do not coincide with money in the bank. Staying the course is essential to get the outcomes you want. Be clear about your goals and the reality of endowment giving so that the board and others can understand what a successful endowment fund looks like.

Prospect Identification

Every organization can find endowment prospects. The information on individuals in Chapter Thirteen is helpful here. However, some organizations have the advantage of having a constituency more suited to endowment giving. Generally, endowment donors are fifty years old or older, are past donors to the organization, and have a long history of giving. They may also have made an endowment gift to another institution. Prospect research, both formal and informal, can provide insights into your donor base (see Chapters Thirteen and Twenty-Five). This ongoing process may look at a wider range of donors than you suspect. You want to look not only at individuals with high incomes but at those with large asset bases as well. Look closely at real estate holdings, art collections and collectibles, and other tangible property.

The most likely prospect is already a donor to your organization and is someone who would like to see your organization continue to prosper beyond his or her life. Devoted donors such as these make great prospects for endowment giving.

Marketing Your Endowment

Whether you are conducting a campaign devoted solely to endowment or with endowment as one element or are simply beginning your endowment program, you will want a prestigious event to kick off the fund raising. A well-done event can mobilize the volunteer leadership, provide an opportunity for prospect cultivation, and deliver your case in a wonderfully exciting setting. It is a great way to kick off a general marketing program as well.

You can use all the same vehicles to promote endowment that you use for planned giving—brochures, newsletters, special events. Once donors fully understand endowment, they are generally eager to participate. Package the endowment carefully, stressing the permanence of the funds, being specific about how they will be used, and focusing on naming opportunities. Gift agreements can often be used as part of the marketing program. Each gift agreement, like each giving proposal in a capital campaign, can give very specific information about the donor's gift and its uses. Designate and promote special types of gift giving for endowment; perhaps place all anniversary, birthday, and memorial gifts in the endowment fund.

Be creative when generating naming opportunities. We all know about naming buildings or naming endowed chairs in a university department, but you can name many things within your organization. Name a program or project, name a staff position, name a classroom; name anything that is relevant to your group. It may seem odd at first, but it can be very attractive to a donor to know that her gift, say, to a food bank, creates the "Mary White Endowed Food Distribution Fund," thus ensuring that the food bank always has the funds to hire a well-qualified person for this important staff position.

The Endowment Discussion

It is in the discussion of endowment with prospective donors that we get to make our case. One of the truly different components of endowment fund raising is the nature of the conversation held with prospective donors. It is only in endowment that we can use words like *legacy, perpetuity,* and *heritage.* Here we have powerful language that gets people's attention and helps them see beyond their own lives. This is truly doing good forever. Good endowment fund raising recognizes and uses the power of these concepts to involve donors in comfortable discussions about the vision and mission of the organization beyond their lives.

Endowment also offers the opportunity to memorialize the donor, the members of the donor's family, or close friends or to honor someone important to the donor. Once again, this recognition carries with it a "forever" connotation.

Solicitation

People give to endowment for many of the same reasons they give to other funds:

- They believe in the cause and were asked to give to it.
- They believe in the cause and have a linkage to it.
- They believe in the asker.
- They are dedicated to the specific project or program within the organization that the endowment will fund.
- Their business or industry will gain from the gift.
- They would rather give to your organization than to the government—they want the tax advantage.

But endowment giving has its own special enticements: donors like the idea of perpetuity—giving beyond their own lifetime; they are pleased to know that their gift will grow with sound investment and spending practices; and they may be impressed with the investment advice and proposed management of the endowment.

Within your endowment campaign, create a structured individual solicitation drive. A four- to eight-week drive provides a set amount of time for those involved in solicitation to make their calls and requests. Certain times of the year are considered best for asking for bequests for endowment: late spring, when people reexamine their wills or draw up new ones in preparation for long summer trips; winter, when people plan winter vacations and year-end tax moves; between Thanksgiving and Christmas, when people are in a charitable mood; whenever tax laws change; and around special anniversaries in your organization's or donors' lives.

One of the best methods for cultivating, soliciting, and ultimately recognizing endowment donors is to create a special "endowment club." Club membership is attractive to many donors; if they know their friends are going to the club meeting, they want to go as well. The club is also an easy and effective way to involve board members in endowment giving and fund raising. Even the naming of the endowment club can be part of the process of board involvement.

The club gives the organization a chance to know the donors better, special opportunities to thank the donors, and a vehicle to stimulate and maintain interest in endowment giving. It is difficult to know the exact amount you will raise from bequests, trusts, and cash gifts, but statistics seem to show that for every fifty members in the club, you will realize $1 million. About 5 percent of the club members will eventually give 95 percent of your endowment gifts (Public Management Institute, 1980, p. 44).

There are several ways to solicit potential members for this type of club. The president, board chair, endowment committee chair, or executive director of your organization may sign a letter announcing the formation of the "Heritage Club" and asking for help in locating donors who may qualify for membership in it. The letter should be mailed to board members, staff members, major donors, and long-term friends.

Donor Recognition and Stewardship

Endowment giving needs to receive special recognition. Donors have placed great trust in the organization and have assumed long-term financial accountability. Make sure they know how the funds are doing, how important the ability to rely on the endowment as an income source is to the organization, and ways in which the organization is acting as a responsible steward of the fund. Remain responsive, no matter how long ago the gift was made. You have stressed its perpetuity; you must make the relationship between organization and donor a permanent one as well. Regular written reports on the progress of the endowment, on how the funds are currently affecting the life of the organization, and who the donors are is an essential component of both recognition and stewardship.

Find unique ways to honor the donor. Hold an annual anniversary party to showcase endowment results; this not only gives recognition but also provides an opportunity for further giving to the fund. Use your club as a way to recognize donors. Hold special club meetings, bring financial advisers in to speak with club members, and recognize the club in all general organization publications.

Recognize that endowment fund raising is not a onetime effort. It is labor-intensive. By its nature, it is an ongoing process of cultivating and soliciting gifts, investing and receiving income from these gifts, and recognizing the givers and the overall results of the gift. Plan to stay dedicated to your endowment fund raising program. Constant stewardship of past donors and of current prospects is essential. Both staff and volunteers must stay tuned in to the needs of the donors. Make sure stewardship and donor recognition are in your long-range plan and your long-range staffing plan.

CONCLUSION

Nonprofit institutions have evolved into crucial and essential partners in our communities, acting as a "safety net" and emerging as both a civilizing and a stabilizing influence in society. Despite their crucial role, nonprofits have been consistently underfunded and are often forced to rely on inconsistent and unpredictable funding sources. Endowment building may be one solution for nonprofits as they struggle to meet the ever-growing needs of our society. And as the idea of endowment building becomes more popular with donors and the practice more common with nonprofit organizations, fund raisers will need to grow more sophisticated in their development and management of endowments.

CHAPTER ELEVEN

Capital Campaigns

Robert Pierpont

A capital campaign is an intensive fund raising effort designed to raise a specified sum of money within a defined time period to meet the varied asset-building needs of an organization. These needs can include the construction of new buildings, renovation or enlargement of existing buildings, purchase or improvement of land, acquisition of furnishings or equipment, and additions to endowment. All of these are asset-building objectives. All can have a place in developing a goal for capital fund raising.

This chapter draws heavily on Hank Rosso's original chapter "Asset Building Through Capital Fund Raising" in the first edition. The revisions reflect contemporary practice—especially the much larger goals prevalent today, the longer length of campaigns, and the declining use of on-site residential management—as organizational staffs have grown in experience and sophistication. Some of the best thoughts are based on Andrea Kihlstedt's work writing The Fund Raising School's capital campaign course.

CAMPAIGN TYPES

The best-known form of capital fund raising is the traditional, or classical, intensive campaign that has a specific goal related to building construction, renovation, or expansion. This is generally referred to as "bricks and mortar" fund raising. In its early years, it also earned the interesting sobriquet of the "once in a lifetime" campaign because of the size of the goals and the size of the gifts that had to be solicited to meet those goals. That reference faded quickly. It is not unusual for organizations to schedule capital campaigns every five to ten years, one after another.

The comprehensive, integrated, or total development program, discussed in Chapter Seven, is based on long-term comprehensive analysis of the organization's diverse needs: current program support, special purposes, capital, and endowment. Once identified, all of the needs are incorporated into a single goal and addressed through a fund raising program spread over as many as ten years. The integrated development program includes annual fund and other fund raising programs that are slower-paced and lack the intensity of the traditional capital campaign. These fund raising programs are discussed in the other chapters in Part Three.

CAMPAIGN CHARACTERISTICS

This chapter's primary focus will be on the principles applicable to all forms of capital campaigns. Two main characteristics set them apart from other fund raising activities: (1) the gifts solicited are much larger than those generally sought during an annual fund, and (2) pledges are emphasized as commitments payable over a number of years convenient to the donor or through the transfer of appreciated real or personal property. The campaign may be for bricks and mortar alone or combined with endowment. Some institutions also add the annual support anticipated over the duration of the campaign solicitation period. The megagoals announced by large institutions often are the result of "counting everything" during a five- to seven-year campaign period.

Another characteristic is the involvement of strategically important volunteers who are able and willing to commit their gifts and also provide access to or solicit from other potential donors. This "human capital" in the form of dedicated volunteers is a precious resource. Its availability—or lack thereof—can affect the outcome of the effort.

Discipline is the nature of intensive campaigns. They require unremitting attention to details, from responsible preplanning analysis through goal setting and leadership enlistment to program execution and conclusion.

PRECAMPAIGN PLANNING

The analysis process starts with the determination of the various asset-building needs that will make up the goal. Too often in too many nonprofit organizations, too little attention is given to this most important aspect of campaign preparation. The project cost statement is incomplete, carelessly contrived, or unrealistic in identifying and estimating the costs of these needs. Lack of realism and objectivity at this stage will cause serious problems later when potential donors will test their intent to give against their acceptance of the validity of the needs statement.

Volunteer Involvement

The planning stage is the time to begin to involve volunteers—key governing board members and others whose capacity to give or get top-level gifts or pledges is great. As they work with staff to develop the campaign goal, they will become intimately familiar with the various projects, the collective cost of which will lead to a preliminary goal. This involvement also begins to familiarize them with the organization's vision and mission.

During the precampaign period, when the size of the campaign goal is being considered, the management team and board members of the organization must examine the eligibility of each capital need suggested for inclusion in the goal: Which needs should be included? Are they all valid? Are they all urgent? Are they all of equally high priority? Involving key governing board members and other volunteers at the goal-setting stage can help introduce objectivity and discipline to the process. Remember: involvement leads to investment!

Preliminary Goals and Project Costs

Costs relating to construction, such as architecture, engineering, land acquisition, site preparation, furnishings, equipment, start-up, and endowment, are essential parts of a comprehensive needs analysis. Other costs also should be included as part of the total project. These are the hidden costs that, if forgotten, will complicate the financing process during or after the construction period. These include the following:

- *Fund raising costs.* All expenses that will be incurred in conducting the capital campaign are a logical part of project costs.

- *Attrition costs.* Capital campaigns should attract pledges to be paid over some number of years—usually three to five. Some of the value of these pledges will be lost through nonpayment. In a properly conducted campaign, however, this nonpayment should not exceed 5 to 10 percent of the goal. These losses should be anticipated and incorporated into the project's cost projections.

- *Inflation and cost overruns.* What impact will inflation have on project costs? What will actual costs be when the building is finished and ready for occupancy and use? It is difficult to estimate what the actual costs will be when the project has been completed, but during planning, a contingency factor for inflation and cost overruns should be included in the computations of cost.

Other financing may be a critical element in setting the campaign goal. In many cases, sources other than philanthropy are available to help cover the costs of new construction and substantial renovations. Colleges and universities can borrow from state agencies under the provisions of the federal Higher Education Facilities Act. Dormitories and student union buildings produce revenue from operations, some of which can be applied to amortizing this debt. Similarly, hospitals have the capacity to borrow through bonds and repay them from increased charges covered directly by patients or from third-party reimbursements—private and government medical insurance.

THE FEASIBILITY OR PRECAMPAIGN PLANNING STUDY

What happens before capital fund raising starts is the most important part of the work. Questioning, measuring, qualifying, verifying, listening to hard answers to hard questions, and weighing judgments expressed by potential key volunteer leaders and potential key contributors are all parts of strategic market testing. This process is called the feasibility study or the precampaign planning study. In straightforward terms, it is a thorough examination of the institution's readiness to ask and the constituent's preparedness and willingness to give—and if appropriate, to serve as a volunteer committee leader or member.

Staff Versus Counsel

The questions most often asked are these: Can the organization conduct its own feasibility study? Should the staff fund raising person undertake the task of interviewing key constituents? Is it necessary to retain professional counsel to conduct a study?

It is quite difficult for an inexperienced fund raising staff member or the executive staff member without experience in fund raising to undertake this sensitive assignment. A staff person often does not know what questions to ask, how to evaluate the answers, or how to judge the campaign's feasibility. Objectivity is important to the process, and the staff and prospect may both find it difficult to be objective.

In exceptional circumstances, when staff members have developed long, cordial, and confidential relationships with key leaders and donors, they may be able to "test" feasibility through conversations with donors known to be ready to consider the top-level gifts needed for success. Some institutions with very sophisticated and experienced chief development officers have been through several campaigns in recent years. They frequently skip the formal study process because they and their board members have the confidence that the gifts needed are in sight—especially the very large ones needed for success. Some governing boards resist conducting a study simply because they are convinced that the new campaign goal can be met this time, just as it was the last time and perhaps several times before. Nevertheless, if there is any uncertainty about the goal to be tested, retaining experienced fund raising counsel is a wise investment.

Study Interviews

How are the names of intended interview respondents selected? To gain the insights required to determine the campaign's feasibility, a list of key interview candidates is drawn up. This list can range from as few as thirty names to as many as one hundred or more. It may include senior managers, program staff members, governing board members, current major gift donors, potential big gift donors, and campaign leadership candidates. It certainly should include the prospective donors who can give or influence the top ten to twenty gifts needed.

Most interviews are in-depth, lasting about an hour. All information gathered during the interview is held in confidence; if it is divulged, it is with the promise that its source will not be attributed. Only in this manner can sensitive information crucial to the progress of the campaign be elicited from interview respondents.

Study Questions

Straightforward answers are required to the hard questions that will make a difference in the course the campaign will take. The following questions are indicative of the type usually asked during the feasibility study. They seek information about the nine most important components of the capital campaign.

The Appeal (Case). Is the case or argument for a capital campaign well defined? Does it reflect the institution's mission, goals, and objectives? Does it have strong appeal? Will the organization's constituencies understand it? Will it motivate potential donors to be unusually generous? Are the needs valid? Do they reflect a sense of urgency? Are they understood and accepted as valid by the constituency that will be asked to give?

The Goal. Is the proposed goal realistic for the constituency? If not realistic, why not? What are the problems?

The Prospects. How many gifts will be required, and at what level? Do potential sources for these gifts exist? Are the gifts expected to come from individuals, corporations, foundations, or associations? How many from each category, and in what range? Is it possible to secure one gift worth 10 percent or more of the goal? Two gifts each worth 5 percent or more of the goal? What solicitation strategies will be required to meet the goal?

The Leadership Potential. If the campaign is to succeed, leaders must be able to give and help solicit upper-level gifts, especially at the start. Can this quality leadership be enlisted, first, from the membership of the governing board and, second, from the larger constituency? Who is the best possible candidate to be the general chairperson for the campaign? What is the proper strategy to enlist this person?

The Timing. Is this the proper time for a campaign? Are conflicting campaigns in progress or contemplated in the near future? What impact will they have? What amount of time is required to ensure the success of this campaign: a year, two, three, more? (Current practice is three to five years and not more than seven. Fund raising programs of longer duration usually cannot sustain the intensity.)

The Public Relations Requirements. Are there public relations problems that will have to be resolved before any campaign can start? What public relations or promotional activity may be needed to motivate the community to support this program?

Staffing. What staffing will be required? Should an outside professional firm provide it? Should people be added to the existing staff? What are the short-term and long-term benefits of these options?

The Budget. What budget will be required to finance the campaign? How much will it cost to raise the goal? Is that cost reasonable? Will management and the governing board make these funds available? What budget control and reporting methods will be required for proper accountability?

PLANNING AND PREPARING FOR THE CAPITAL CAMPAIGN

Validating the needs that justify the capital fund raising and placing them in a priority order is a logical first step. Testing the validity of the needs and the reality of a goal is a reasonable second step. Building the plan around leadership enlistment, identification of top-level gift prospects, the development of time-lines and designs for essential activities, and the solicitation strategies that will flow from all of this must follow. This section will address the essentials of planning and preparing for capital fund raising, drawing on the findings, conclusions, and recommendations determined in the feasibility study.

Articulation of the case for a capital campaign merits priority consideration at the beginning of the planning and preparing period. Staff members, trustees, and volunteers who are not experienced in this specialized form of fund raising will tend to express the case for the campaign in simple terms: "We need a new building. We're trying to raise one million dollars to build the building. We're asking you to give so that we can start construction." This is not a convincing case expression. As the saying goes, "People don't buy Buicks because General Motors needs the money."

People give because they believe in the organization. They can identify with its mission and goals. They know the people who are part of the organization, and they hold the same values. People will not give because the organization feels that it should have a new building. The case must be stronger, more compelling, more exciting, and more inviting to persuade prospects to give at the level required by capital fund raising.

The definition of the overall case for the organization (see Chapter Six), with its statement of mission and goals, precedes the preparation of a case for the capital campaign. The rationale for this level of fund raising must come from the mission statement. It is the mission that identifies the human or societal needs that are at the center of the organization's concern. The programs or strategies that serve the mission, goals, and objectives give evidence to the needs that will justify the capital fund raising goals. Simply put, new building construction, purchase of land, acquisition of technical equipment, additions to endowment holdings—all capital needs—must contribute directly to program advancement, program improvement, or enhancement of services. "This will help us teach better." "This will help us serve more people." "This will help us satisfy your health care needs more efficiently and more effectively."

One of the oldest maxims of fund raising is that "people don't give to causes; they give to people with causes." Indeed they do. In contemporary fund raising, this maxim might be modified a bit. People give to people with causes, but they give to causes that they know, understand, and believe in strongly.

GIFT RANGE CHARTS

As noted previously, the capital campaign is a demanding taskmaster. The most demanding of its disciplines is the unremitting focus on large gifts and the requirement that enough of these gifts must be secured at the very beginning of the campaign to establish a pattern for others who follow.

What is meant by "large gifts"? Capital campaigns seek to secure 90 percent or more of the required funds from 10 percent or fewer of the contributions that are received. To ensure this quality production, at least one gift at 10 percent or more and two gifts each worth 5 percent or more of the goal are sought at the beginning of the campaign.

This standard of giving can be set out in a gift range chart or standard-of-gifts chart (see Tables 11.1 and 11.2). This instrument provides a method to

Table 11.1. Sample Gift Range Chart: $10 Million Goal—Three- to Five-Year Pledges.

Type of Gift	Number of Pledges	Number of Prospects	Pledge Size	Total for Size	Cumulative Total	Percentage of Goal
Lead Gifts	1	3–5	$1,000,000	$1,000,000	$1,000,000	
	2	6–10	500,000	1,000,000	2,000,000	42.0%
	4	12–20	250,000	1,000,000	3,000,000	
	8	24–40	150,000	1,200,000	4,200,000	
Major Gifts	12	36–60	75,000	900,000	5,100,000	
	20	60–100	50,000	1,000,000	6,100,000	35.5%
	30	90–150	30,000	900,000	7,000,000	
	50	150–250	15,000	750,000	7,750,000	
Special Gifts	80	240–400	9,000	720,000	8,470,000	
	120	350–600	6,000	720,000	9,190,000	21.6%
	240	720–1,200	3,000	720,000	9,910,000	
General Gifts	All others	Many	Under 3,000	90,000	10,000,000	

Table 11.2. Sample Gift Range Chart: $10 Million Goal—Five-Year Pledges.

Type of Gift	Number of Pledges	Number of Prospects	Pledge Size	Total for Size	Cumulative Total	Percentage of Goal
Lead Gift	1	5	$1,000,000 +	$1,000,000	$1,000,000	
	1	5	750,000–999,999	750,000	1,750,000	47.5%
	3	15	500,000–749,999	1,500,000	3,250,000	
	6	30	250,000–499,999	1,500,000	4,750,000	
Major Gifts	12	48	100,000–249,999	1,400,000	6,150,000	
	24	96	50,000–99,999	1,300,000	7,450,000	39.5%
	50	100	25,000–49,999	1,250,000	8,700,000	
Special Gifts	70	210	10,000–24,999	700,000	9,400,000	
	100	300	5,000–9,999	500,000	9,900,000	12%
General Gifts	All others	Many	Under 5,000	100,000	10,000,000	

determine the quality of gifts, the quantity of gifts, and the number of prospects that will be required to ensure achievement of the goal.

The gift range chart has its origins in the real-world observations of the Italian economist Vilfredo Pareto of a century ago, who noted that 20 percent of the effort yields 80 percent of the results. In the 1950s, Si Seymour, a prolific writer and fund raising consultant, developed the "rule of thirds" for capital campaigns, in which he observed that the top ten gifts should amount to one-third of the goal, the next hundred gifts another third, and all the others the final third.

Experience has shown that 5 to 10 percent of the donors are providing 85 to 95 percent of the goal. A similar pattern holds true in the world of for-profit sales, where sales managers note that 20 percent of their sales staff sell 80 percent of the products and that 20 percent of their customers buy 80 percent of their product.

The gift range chart applies these rules to capital campaigns and illustrates how many gifts of what size a campaign probably needs to reach its goal.

Several rules should guide the formulation of a gift range chart:

- Above all, the lead gift should constitute 10 percent or more of the goal,
- About 40 to 60 percent of the goal should come from the ten to fifteen largest gifts.
- About 33 to 50 percent should come from the next 100 to 150 gifts.
- About 10 to 20 percent of the goal should come from all other gifts.

Different gift range charts may be developed for various uses. The first use of the gift range chart is usually during the precampaign study when the higher prospect ratio at the top is preferable because it focuses on the need for large lead gifts. Because the precampaign study often uncovers genuine prospects for the top gifts, the ratio of prospects to gifts can be reduced during this stage. In fact, many campaign veterans have seen the top gift virtually assured by one prospect during the study process.

Once the precampaign study has been completed, the revised gift range chart serves to guide the donor recognition program in which the levels of recognition must be in keeping with the gifts needed. For example, if four gifts of $250,000 each are needed, the donor recognition program should provide six to eight naming or recognition opportunities at that level. In this way, donors may be presented options to name spaces or, if appropriate, endowments. At the lower levels, donors are often listed in categories grouping them by amounts and naming the categories—"benefactor," "patron," and so on. Plaques listing such groups are then used to acknowledge these donors. Many organizations have developed very imaginative ways to display names of donors. Examples used by others should be investigated to stimulate creativity in this area. Donors will appreciate the extra effort.

The gift range chart provides a good guide for evaluating the number of prospects needed for a specific campaign goal. The traditional ratio of prospects to gifts needed in a pro forma gift range table is 5:1 for the top third gift levels, 4:1 for the middle, and 3:1 for the bottom. This ratio is based in part on the reality that some donors will give at lower levels than expected. Their gifts will be credited to lower levels, thereby reducing the need for prospects in those levels.

Some practitioners believe that more accurate ratios are the reverse: 3:1 at the top, 4:1 in the middle, and 5:1 or more at the bottom. Those who use this approach are convinced that better prospect research improves the probability of strong results at the top while the limited volunteer effort at the bottom requires a higher ratio because the large pool of low-rated prospects will be solicited by phone or mail.

Table 11.1 is a sample gift range chart for a $10 million goal payable in three- to five-year pledges. At the top levels, the projected pledge amounts are divisible by five. Lower levels are divisible by three. The difference is designed to acknowledge that pledges made in the lead gifts and start of the major gifts phases (the quiet phase) can be paid over a longer period of time, allowing donors to stretch their commitment over five years, which should encourage larger commitments. And because they are to be secured at the start or early part of the campaign, waiting five years for full payment fits with the organization's financial plans. Pledges at the lower levels, with three-year payments, will have been paid in full at about the same time or even earlier. This sample chart depicts an organization with a reasonably broad base of prospective donors—some 1,700 to 2,800 of them. The range of three to five prospects at each level acknowledges a degree of uncertainty because the organization has not conducted a capital campaign recently and intends to use this sample chart initially to test potential in a campaign planning study.

Table 11.2 depicts a sample gift range chart for a $10 million goal payable in five-year pledges. It portrays the potential for an organization with a well-developed but narrow or limited donor base. The number of prospective donors thought to be available for most of the gifts needed are fewer than one thousand. The ratio of prospects at the top is 5:1, in the mid-range 4:1, and at the lowest level 3:1 because the planners are being cautious in their projections for the top gifts but confident of the potential at the lower levels. Further, the organization's donor recognition program includes multiple opportunities for pledges at the top and middle ranges. For example, the projected $1.4 million from twelve major gifts assumes eight pledges of $100,000 and four of $150,000. Recognition is available at both these levels and will be used to set donors' sights on pledging these amounts.

Note another difference in the charts. While both depict a range of gifts from the largest to the smallest, only Table 11.2 portrays a range under the heading "Pledge Size"; Table 11.1 has only a single amount. Either approach is acceptable. The purpose of these charts has not so much to do with the labels or even the arithmetic as it does with their uses: first, to be tested in a planning study; second, to set donors' sights on what gifts are needed to succeed; and third, to help keep score and highlight shortfalls. It is not uncommon to adjust the table during the campaign—not frequently, but to reflect actual results versus plan. When tempted to adjust or modify the table, be mindful of the need to reflect the number of prospects needed. If all prospects have been exhausted at a level that still has not reached its total for size, either new prospects must be identified or an adjustment for making up the shortfall in that level must be made. Keeping track of progress by the number of gifts actually committed at each level may reveal more than projected at the upper levels (much to be preferred) or shortfalls leading to the need to find more gifts at lower levels. This may be a sign of trouble and should be carefully evaluated. As noted earlier, making up for failures at the top is difficult.

SEQUENTIAL FUND RAISING

The gift range chart and the listing of prospects by giving potential provides a guide for sequential fund raising. This is the technique of classifying prospects according to their assessed giving potential and then approaching top prospects first in sequence, assiduously avoiding any solicitations at lower levels until the solicitations at the top have been successful.

Sequential fund raising is based on four axioms of campaign fund raising:

- The ten largest gifts set the standard for the entire campaign.
- A failure to adhere to the top-down pattern lowers giving sights across the board.
- Extended solicitation and participation at lower levels will not offset major gaps in the upper ranges.
- Once the big-gift-first sequence has been seriously violated, the entire program is in jeopardy.

LEADERSHIP AND CAMPAIGN MANAGEMENT

Capital campaigns are more reliant on volunteer leadership than any other form of fund raising. The four components of the leadership team are the governing board, board or nonboard campaign chairpersons and committee members, executive and key program staff members, and fund raising staff members. Each serves in a different functional relationship to the campaign.

The Governing Board

The governing board must be the activating force for any capital campaign. As the primary stewards of the nonprofit organization, board members hold the power to approve or disapprove capital projects and the fund raising activity that will support them. It stands to reason that if the board members exercise their authority as stewards to approve the expenditure of funds for capital development, they must accept the parallel responsibility of helping to raise the funds by giving generously—in proportion to their ability—and participating in the solicitation of others. If they are unwilling to invest in the organization, how can they expect others to invest?

Nonboard Volunteers

Ideally, the general chairperson of the campaign should come from the governing board. But under certain circumstances, this may not be possible, practical, or wise. Board membership may be geographically dispersed, coalitional, lacking in leadership capabilities, or constituted of program experts who lack the socioeconomic clout that is so precious to fund raising. This is not a rare condition today, nor will it be in the future. In these situations, campaign planners must be prepared to look elsewhere for capable people who can provide the spark of energy that makes a campaign succeed. A properly developed constituency holds unexpected potential. Campaigns are times when this potential must be tested and invited into the leadership ranks.

Executive and Program Staff

The chief executive officer (CEO) and key program staff members can exert considerable influence to help manage the campaign to success. The CEO as the visionary and program staff members as expert witnesses are able to speak eloquently about the mission and program strategies. They can serve as information resources and assist in the cultivation and solicitation of gifts. In most cases, the chief executive officer is the best-informed person and must therefore be the spokesperson for the campaign. He or she also must be a motivator who can help generate enthusiasm for and confidence in the cause.

Fund Raising Staff

At times, in-house fund raising staff members can function as managers of the campaign, provided that they have the experience and can afford to meet the time demands of the campaign. Experienced staff members with larger organizations can handle the assignment; overburdened staff members with a smaller organization will find it difficult, if not impossible, to cope. Historically, more experienced outside professional counsel was retained to direct the campaign on a full-time resident management basis. Today, with the increasing sophistication of fund raising staffs, the decision is not so obvious. Some organizations use the occasion of a campaign to build their staffs, hiring people who have been successful campaign directors elsewhere. Many that do so anticipate having larger staffs after the campaign because they expect to need them for the next campaign or for the increase in ongoing fund raising that often follows a successful campaign. Further, thanks to the high demand for good fund raising personnel, there are opportunities for staff members to find career advancement in other organizations.

If internal fund raising staff members decide to assume full responsibility for directing the campaign, the objective counsel of an outside consultant will be helpful. In either case, internal or external professional staff members must assume full responsibility for planning, organizing, and managing the campaign.

Fund raising staff members who have experienced campaigns make certain that key leaders are involved in the more important campaign decision-making process: they help make the vital decisions that will affect the course of the program. Staff members make sure that the top leadership is provided with the information and guidance required for wise decision making.

Certain components should be noted on an organizational chart that depicts the campaign's working elements (see Figure 11.1 for an example). The primary element on the chart is the "campaign cabinet," "steering committee," or whatever the management committee calls itself. This cabinet or committee comprises the most capable campaign leaders who can be enlisted. It is headed by a general chairperson and staffed by the campaign director.

This managing group is made up of eight to ten thoughtfully selected individuals who possess the willingness, creative energy, and socioeconomic clout to stir the constituency to action, to enlist other leaders of equal caliber, and to solicit the quality gifts that will make a difference in achieving the organiza-

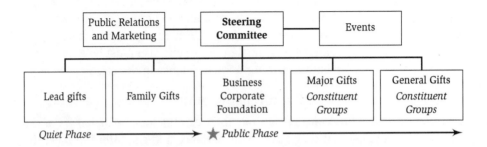

Figure 11.1. Campaign Structure.

Source: The Fund Raising School, 2002.

tion's goal. This steering committee's responsibility will be to approve and to execute the plan, to identify strategic prospects with the ability to make lead gifts, and to accept the charge to help solicit these prospects.

Any final delineation of the organizational chart will depend on the requirements of the campaign plan and whether it is complex in structure or neat, clean, and tight enough to discharge the task in the most efficient and effective manner possible. The caliber of the leadership; the availability and natural clusters of qualified prospects; the willingness of the trustees to give, to ask, and to work; and the organization's fund raising experience will determine the hierarchy of the chart and the campaign's timetable. The committees should be recruited in sequence, as they are needed, but well in advance in order to get on the calendars of the busy people most likely to do the best job. In some campaigns, this may be months in advance. In the major gift phase of the campaign, it may be advisable to organize by constituent groups—classmates, neighbors, professions, grateful patients of a particular department, or other clusters with common characteristics.

Establishing Goals

Generally, the senior management team consults with appropriate program staff members to make certain judgments about a possible campaign goal. These judgments are reviewed with the appropriate board committee and then with the entire board. A tentative goal will emerge from these discussions and is the one to be tested during the feasibility study. The study's findings, particularly those pertaining to the goal, are discussed by the fund raising staff, the trustees, and other influential volunteers who may be involved. Acceptance of the main and subsidiary goals should not be considered final until they have been cleared and accepted by the campaign steering committee. This is common sense. Those who have to assume responsibility for raising the money should be given the opportunity to accept the goal or to suggest any modifications they feel are necessary. Emotional and intellectual acceptance by the people who are key to the completion of the program is essential at this point.

The overall goal is the primary goal. Subsidiary goals reflect the obligation of various campaign divisions—personal gifts, staff and trustees, employees, corporations, foundations, associations, and others. In addition, there are divisions necessitated by the soliciting strategies, such as strategic or "pacesetter" gifts, major gifts, and general gifts. All are subgoals. All must be properly managed.

Assignments of goals to subordinate units must be based on realistic expectations of what these divisions are capable of producing. Are valid prospects available to each unit? Have these prospects been properly evaluated with suggested giving amounts appended? Are judgments about giving potential based on accurate information secured from reliable sources? Has the proper person been identified to solicit the right prospect for the right gift at each level?

Support Services

Support services can make a difference in a capital campaign. Sufficient to the purpose, they will help to advance the program. If they are inadequate, they will inhibit its progress. Before any serious activity can be set in motion, arrangements must be made to provide a competent staff, adequate campaign office space, and clerical staff trained in data management, the proper use of telephones, faxes, and e-mail, and working with volunteers.

The office staff will have as its daily concern such routine but sensitive details as records and research, prospect tracking, proposal preparation, volunteer assignments, gift recording and acknowledgment procedures, and campaign promotional materials.

The Budget

The budget is the description of the program in dollar terms. It should provide for sufficient funds to meet the expenditure requirements of an active, forward-moving campaign. Too tight a budget can be inhibiting; too generous a budget can invite questions and criticism from the campaign steering committee and possibly from prospective donors.

Campaign costs vary significantly. Small campaigns, for a few million dollars, will cost more proportionately than large campaigns for hundreds of millions. Local community campaigns should be less expensive than national campaigns with heavy travel costs or regional campaign offices. (See Chapter Twenty-Eight for more on costs.)

As a percentage of the campaign goal, costs as low as 5 percent and as high as 15 percent may be expected—such levels are acceptable. Emphasis on costs can be counterproductive. The better measurement is return on investment (ROI). Campaign costs of 12.5 percent, for example, should be shown to be as an ROI of 8:1. In other words, every $1 invested in the campaign budget will produce $8 of gross income, or a net of $7.

A good approach to determining an overall budget is to survey colleagues and comparable organizations to learn from their experience. This approach will often help the parties asked to approve budgets by demonstrating that other organizations with which they may be familiar—and may even admire for their success—have successfully campaigned at a comparable level of cost.

Campaign budgeting must also consider whether the costs are over and above ongoing fund raising operations or if part of the costs will be covered by assigning present staff to campaign responsibilities. The most obvious case is when the chief development officer decides to direct the campaign by hiring a "number two" to take on the annual fund and other ongoing fund raising efforts. How that change is reflected in the budget will affect the calculation of costs. Another issue is whether in a large organization, for example, major gift officers will reorient their efforts toward capital pledges during a campaign and then return to the ongoing major and planned gift programs after the campaign. If so, are their salaries and expenses to be calculated as campaign costs?

Of course, if this is the second or third campaign conducted over the past fifteen to twenty years, history will be an excellent guide for budgeting.

Basic budget elements and their percentage of the overall budget are typically as follows:

Personnel	50 to 60 percent
Materials and events	20 to 30 percent
Overhead	10 to 20 percent
Contingency	5 percent

These ranges are only ballpark figures. The multiple variables and experience in similar situations all must be weighed in developing the campaign budget.

SEQUENTIAL SOLICITATION

Out of the accumulated wisdom of legions of capital campaigns emerges an imperative: to be effective, fund raising must be "top down and inside out." The "top down" part of the equation pertains to a strategy known as sequential solicitation. As noted earlier, if the top gift is at the level required by the gift range, all other gifts should relate to it. The top gift will set the standard for all of the remaining gifts. If it is too low, other gifts will drop accordingly, and the outcome of the campaign will be in doubt. Sequential solicitation is a necessity for goal attainment in capital campaigns. It forces a focus on the larger gifts and discourages a preoccupation with the smaller gifts at the bottom of the gift range chart.

"Inside out" means that all fund raising should start with the "family" inside the organization—the governing board, senior management, program staff, and employees. This is a critical part of the quiet phase of the campaign. With the completion of this phase, the program reaches out to the external constituency, reports what the board and the family have been able to accomplish, and invites others to join in support.

If a governing board approves a program that will involve significant capital expenditures and the money to cover these expenditures will have to be raised through a capital campaign, board members must commit themselves to contribute generously. Others will be less inclined to support a campaign that appears to lack generous support from those who hold it in trust. It is ideal when the largest gift comes from inside.

CAMPAIGN PHASES

As should be clear, campaigns proceed in phases from preplanning to an end—preferably with commitments totaling the announced goal or more. A simple illustration of the phases is shown in Figure 11.2. Note the "kickoff." Prior to going public, the goal may be adjusted to reflect results in the earlier phases—sometimes called the quiet or silent phase. Once that phase has succeeded in raising an impressive aggregate total of insider commitments and most, if not all, of the top-level, pacesetting lead gifts, it is time to announce or kick off the campaign. An event is often organized to recognize the donors to date and to stimulate enthusiasm among those remaining to be solicited—and confidence in the ultimate success throughout the organization. Kickoff events may take a great many forms. They are most effective when they are fun events that convey the message of success to date in a spirit or mode reflecting the organization's unique personality and mission. Campaigns should be announced to the broad constituency only once the leadership is confident that the goal is in sight.

There are a number of questions to ask at this point:

Are there enough prospective sources in sight to fill the pool of prospects as depicted in the gift range chart?

Are the right people ready to serve as the volunteers needed to solicit at least the next level of gifts, often labeled major gifts?

Is there a valid plan for soliciting the large number of smaller special and general gifts needed to wrap up the campaign in a timely manner?

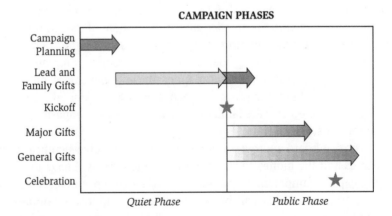

Figure 11.2. Campaign Phases.

Source: The Fund Raising School, 2002.

If the answer to any of these is no, more planning and preparation will be needed before kicking off. Many organizations that ignore this advice have found their campaigns floundering, often leading to disappointing results.

TESTING READINESS FOR A CAPITAL CAMPAIGN

Crucial to the success of any capital fund raising program is the readiness of the institution to take on this complex, intensive, energy-demanding exercise. It is demanding because it focuses on attention to details, requires control, and insists on quality of leadership throughout. The "Test for Readiness for a Capital Campaign" in Exhibit 11.1 offers fund raising practitioners, managers, and trustees of nonprofit organizations an opportunity to assess their preparedness for a capital campaign.

As in all instruments of this type, the test score is not the final word in measuring readiness, but it is valuable in alerting staff members and trustees to any weaknesses that may hinder capital fund raising. Scores reflect perceptions, with a higher score reflecting greater readiness than a lower score.

CONCLUSION

A successful campaign depends on the strengths of the organization. The following are fifteen essential elements that should be in place or in sight to give everyone involved the confidence to proceed with any capital campaign, regardless of goal size.

1. A case rooted in well-developed advance organizational planning with a sound defensible business plan for the application of the funds needed to meet the goal

2. An involved and committed governing board

3. An informed constituency with a history of support and the apparent potential to provide the funds needed to meet the goal

4. A chief executive officer prepared to support the campaign intellectually and emotionally and to recognize that campaigning is not time for business as usual

5. Adequate budget for the incremental costs of campaigning in hand or within reach

6. Qualified staff with the requisite campaign experience or openness to retaining outside expertise, as needed

7. Recognition of the absolute importance of soliciting in sequence, from the top down, and establishing an early pattern of pacesetting and exemplary gifts to motivate others

8. Prospect research and rating programs to identify and evaluate the potential sources of support in sufficient numbers to yield three to five prospects for each gift needed at various levels

9. Involved board and possibly other volunteers willing to serve first on a campaign planning committee and subsequently on other committees, as needed

10. A procedure for testing the campaign plan in advance through a planning or feasibility study involving volunteers and staff

11. Other volunteers to work with staff to organize committees, develop solicitation strategies, and make presentations to prospects.

12. Adherence to a schedule with deadlines for action and accountability

13. Publicity and printed materials prepared in phases and released or produced as needed

14. Events to announce the campaign, report progress, publicize significant gifts, and recognize donors and volunteers

15. Contagious enthusiasm about the campaign's goals and objectives throughout the organization

Exhibit 11.1. Test for Readiness for a Capital Campaign.

Institutional Plans. Has a three- to five-year plan been prepared by senior staff members and approved by the board? Does the plan identify capital as well as current support needs for the planning period? Have staff and board members committed themselves to meet these financial needs through fund raising? *Score:* 0 to 5

Case. Does a written statement of the case exist? Does it identify the mission as an expression of the organization's values? Can a strong case be made for capital fund raising? *Score:* 0 to 5

Constituency. Has the organization identified its constituency beyond those who are closely involved with its programs? Has it analyzed the constituency for fund raising purposes by asking who the potential contributors might be? Has a constituency cultivation program been devised to involve the constituency? *Score:* 0 to 5

Market Involvement. Do staff-members and trustees know the makeup of the market? Are they knowledgeable about market needs, interests, and inclinations? Does the organization have a history of interacting with its markets and their various segments? Is fund raising structured so that it appeals to the specific interests and requirements of different market segments? *Score:* 0 to 5

Gift Support History. Has the fund raising program historically sought gifts for current program support, special gifts, capital, and endowment? Has this gift experience been catalogued in a way that enables staff members to analyze the potential for a capital campaign? Has the fund raising program been active in its approach to larger donors: individuals, corporations, foundations, and others? Does the fund raising staff spend time periodically evaluating the potential of its donor base? *Score:* 0 to 5

Prospect Development Plan. Is an active prospect development plan in place? Does this plan include the presence of a prospect development committee? Do staff members and volunteers devote time periodically to discuss large gift prospects? Has this prospect research information been recorded in a manner that will make it available to staff members and volunteers for use in their fund raising assignments? *Score:* 0 to 5

Record Keeping. Is a proper record-keeping system in place? Does it provide for responsible storage and retrieval of confidential information? Are gift-receiving, gift-recording, and gift-reporting procedures in place? Will these procedures permit the appropriate acknowledgment of gifts in a timely manner? *Score:* 0 to 5

Communication Program. Is the communication program a two-way system of informing and receiving feedback from the constituency? Is the feedback heeded when a new

Exhibit 11.1. Test for Readiness for a Capital Campaign, Cont'd.

communication program is designed and the materials are prepared? Does communication go beyond simple data dissemination—printed words on paper—to encompass a more sensitive program that seeks to inform and involve people? *Score:* 0 to 5

Fund Raising Staff. Is a competent, qualified staff available to plan and direct the capital campaign and to provide the level of support that volunteer leadership will require? Is this staff able and in a position to devote its full energy and time to this fund raising assignment? Will the rest of the staff, management, and program and support staff give their full support to the fund raising team during the period of the campaign? *Score:* 0 to 10

Involved Governing Board. Have the members of the governing board asserted themselves as primary stewards of the organization? Have they been active in planning, approving, and clarifying policy; supervising management of resources; and generating resources through fund raising? Has the board been responsibly involved in the planning process for the capital program? Are members willing to give according to their abilities and to ask others? *Score:* 0 to 15

Potential Large Gifts. Large gifts are the top ten or twenty gifts that are required to produce 40 to 60 percent of the campaign goal. The top gift ideally should be a minimum of 10 percent of the goal, and the next two gifts each should equal 5 percent of that goal. Have valid prospects for these gifts been identified? *Score:* 0 to 15

Fund Raising Leadership. Does the organization have as part of its actively involved constituency a quality of volunteer leadership that will give the energy, enthusiasm, and drive that is necessary to press the campaign on to success? Will this leadership be willing to give and ask at the level required, and will it commit itself to do so? *Score:* 0 to 20

Scoring the Test

The maximum score is 100. Very few organizations can score this high. A score of 75 to 100 indicates a reasonable chance for success. A score of 50 to 75 means there are problems that may have to be addressed before any decision can be made to move forward with a campaign. A score below 50 serves as a warning that the organization is not ready and that there may be problems that will have to be addressed before any efforts can be made to start a campaign.

Note that the score for the last four items—fund raising staff, involved board of trustees, potential large gifts, and fund raising leadership—totals *60 points.* If there is a serious readiness weakness in this area, plans for a campaign should be put on hold until these weaknesses can be corrected or eliminated.

Source: The Fund Raising School, 2002.

CHAPTER TWELVE

Establishing a
Planned Giving Program

Dean Regenovich

Since the early 1900s, individuals have relied on specific charitable instruments—bequests, charitable gift annuities, and various charitable trusts—to fulfill their philanthropic desires. However, it wasn't until the mid-1970s that nonprofits experienced a significant surge in planned giving activities. Most of this activity was centered on the establishment and marketing of charitable bequest programs, which continues to be the cornerstone of most successful planned giving programs. *Giving USA* (AAFRC Trust for Philanthropy, 2002) reports that of the $212 billion contributed in 2001, bequests accounted for $16.33 billion, representing 7.7 percent of all contributions made in 2001.

Beginning with the tax legislation enacted in 1986—which dramatically increased capital gains taxes—professional financial advisers and donors turned to other charitable planning instruments such as the charitable remainder trust to fulfill a philanthropic desire and simultaneously avoid, minimize, or delay the capital gains taxes. An aging donor population and an unprecedented growth in asset value further strengthened the attractiveness of other planned giving instruments such as the charitable remainder trust and the charitable gift annuity. A survey conducted by the National Committee on Planned Giving (2001) reports that life income vehicles—charitable remainder trusts and charitable gift annuities—have increased in popularity, with 2 percent of Americans indicating that they have created one or the other (or both) of these types of instruments in 2000. This is more than triple the 0.6 percent of respondents in 1992 who reported making a life income planned gift.

Some nonprofits responded to this "new" giving opportunity by hiring individuals to master the technical aspects of planned giving. Other nonprofits, primarily because of budgetary constraints, have instead found creative ways to "market" the basic planned giving opportunities, such as bequests, to their constituencies.

The important point to recognize is that planned giving should become part of your development efforts, regardless of your organization's size, mission, age, budget, in-house expertise, or prior giving history. Hank Rosso challenged all nonprofit organizations to work toward a total development program that included planned giving (see Chapter Seven). The material contained in this chapter is designed to assist you in determining the level of planned giving activity appropriate for *your* organization. Your organization's planned giving program may end up looking remarkably different from the planned giving program at the nonprofit across the street. That is OK, for planned giving programs can be built over time, with additional layers added to the program once a particular level has been achieved. This chapter also contains a brief overview of the "core" planned giving instruments as well as a discussion regarding the marketing of planned gifts and how to identify viable planned giving prospects.

INSTITUTIONAL READINESS

Institutional readiness depends on giving consideration to the organization and its staff, its board, its planned giving professional, and its policies and guidelines.

The Organization and Staff

Not all nonprofit organizations are prepared to implement a comprehensive planned giving program. In fact, most small to midsize organizations, particularly those in existence for a short period of time, do not have the financial resources and personnel to allow for an all-inclusive planned giving program. But it is important to recognize that no matter how old the organization is or how limited the resources are, there are ways to begin a planned giving program that can be enhanced over time.

First, make sure organizational plans exist before developing a planned giving plan. Does the organization have a strategic plan that outlines goals and objectives for the next three to ten years? Is the mission statement clear, and does it accurately depict the organization as it exists today? Is there a case statement that clearly and concisely describes what the organization does, why the organization must do it, and how it proposes to do it? If the organization's mission and case statements are unclear, the planned giving program will most likely experience only limited success.

Since some planned gifts benefit the nonprofit organization at some future date, donors must be comfortable with the stability and permanence of the organization. How long has the organization existed? Will the organization be in existence thirty years from now to receive the planned gift? Is the organization growing or shrinking? These are some of the questions donors will ask before contemplating a planned gift for the benefit of an organization.

Potential planned gift donors may also be interested in the financial stability of the organization. Does the organization have the capacity to satisfy current operating expenses? Does the organization have a history of balancing its budget? Will the organization be a responsible steward of the gift? Does the organization have the financial staff to account for and invest the gift properly? Will the organization ultimately use the gift in accordance with the donor's wishes? Donors are expecting greater accountability from organizations today; organizations must consequently be prepared to provide financial reports and information concerning overall financial performance and in some cases the performance of specific funds established by the donor.

People give to people with causes. Planned giving fund raising involves developing close personal relationships with individuals. To be successful in planned giving, organizations must have knowledgeable development staff who are capable of clearly articulating the organization's mission and programs, as well as a point person who has the ability to explain the various planned giving options to donors and their financial advisers in an understandable manner.

The Board

The planned giving program must have full support from all members of the board. They must understand the role planned giving plays in ensuring the growth and long-term stability of the organization. In addition, they must be willing to assist the development department with the planned giving program and play an active role in it.

Before introducing a proposed planned giving program to the board, first educate the board as to what planned giving is all about. Show them not only how planned giving benefits the organization but also how it can provide significant benefits to donors. Consider conducting a brief seminar for the board to address the various planned giving options and help them understand how planned giving would be used to complement the organization's existing development efforts. Don't hesitate to bring in an outside consultant or a third party who can articulate the merits of planned giving clearly and concisely.

There is no better way to begin a planned giving program than by securing planned gift commitments from individual board members. Do this by meeting with each board member individually, rather than making a broad appeal to the entire board. By participating in the planned giving program through their own personal commitments, the board members will send a strong message to the organization's constituency that these types of gifts are important and should be made in addition to participating in the annual fund.

The board must be willing to provide the financial resources necessary to begin implementing a planned giving program. An effective program will be built around the development of long-term personal relationships with donors. This is a labor-intensive process that may require adding a new development professional to the staff whose primary responsibility is to spend time outside of the office developing the personal relationships. Financial resources may also be needed to market the planned giving program. It is not imperative that the organization develop new print materials to promote the various planned giving opportunities. At the outset, it may be sufficient to incorporate planned giving messages into existing publications.

Because planned giving is a process dependent on relationship building, the board must recognize that the organization may not experience immediate results in the form of completed planned gift arrangements. Some planned gifts may occur within a six-month period; others may take years to complete. Each donor will ultimately decide when he or she is ready to make the gift. For that reason, the progress of a planned giving program should be based more on the contacts made and relationships built than completed arrangements or dollars in hand.

The board can provide leadership to the planned giving program by publicly endorsing it, identifying prospective donors, introducing development staff to prospective donors, and assisting in the solicitation of planned gift prospects.

By properly educating the board members at the outset and using their time judiciously throughout the process, you will find that most will vigorously endorse and support the planned giving program. Along the way, be sure to keep them informed and share with them your progress and success stories in the planned giving area.

The Planned Giving Professional

Due to budget constraints and limited manpower, many nonprofit organizations are not able to hire a full-time development professional whose sole responsibility is planned giving. Therefore, it is common for many organizations to ease their way into planned giving by marketing a selected number of planned giving opportunities, rather than the full menu of available arrangements.

Organizational responses to planned giving inquiries from individuals can be handled in a number of ways. The organization can assign that responsibility to a development officer whose sole responsibility is to raise money—preferably a major gifts officer—who is interested in adding planned giving to his or her list of responsibilities. This approach will cut down on that person's ability to travel and develop relationships with donors, for it will require devoting a certain amount of time to technical training, developing planned giving policies and procedures, identifying planned giving prospects, and marketing the planned giving program.

A second option is to rely on friends of the organization who have experience working in charitable estate planning and related areas. These friends could come from a variety of professions, including attorneys, certified public accountants, certified financial planners, bank trust officers, certified life underwriters, and stockbrokers. Although these individuals may be able to provide the organization with the technical support necessary to respond to planned giving inquiries from interested donors, it is probably not advisable to rely on these professionals to develop the personal relationships with donors that are so crucial to the success of a planned giving program. The professional advisers are best suited to handle functions such as drafting planned giving instruments, accompanying the development professional on a personal visit when the donor has decided to make a gift and is now contemplating how the gift should be structured, and assisting in developing planned giving policies and procedures.

A third option is to hire a development professional whose primary responsibility is planned giving. This person may or may not have previous development experience as a major gift or annual fund development officer. A growing number of planned giving officers are coming from the for-profit world. These individuals may have previously practiced law, served as a bank trust officer, or held a position in the financial services industry and are seeking a career change or have an interest in serving an organization whose mission they are passionate about.

It is not imperative that the planned giving officer be an attorney, although it is advantageous if that individual has some familiarity with the technical issues involved in planned giving. Some of the best planned giving professionals have come from nontechnical backgrounds and learned the technical aspects of planned giving through independent study, attending seminars, and hands-on training.

What attributes should a nonprofit organization look for when hiring a planned giving officer? The following characteristics merit attention:

- *Good interpersonal skills.* The ideal planned giving officer has the ability to develop meaningful personal relationships with donors.

- *A proactive mind-set.* An effective planned giving officer must spend significant time outside the office developing personal relationships with donors, rather than being consumed with in-office administrative details. Approximately 30 to 60 percent of a planned giving officer's time should be spent visiting donors and their professional financial advisers.

- *Simplicity and understanding.* Individuals skilled in explaining the technical aspects of planned giving with simplicity and understanding will experience a high degree of success in planned giving. This same skill is also important when training other development staff, the board, and volunteers.

- *A thirst for knowledge.* The tax laws surrounding planned giving are constantly changing, so an effective planned giving officer must be willing to stay abreast of tax law changes and case law developments that affect charitable gift planning.

- *Articulateness and perceptiveness.* Not only is the planned giving officer responsible for explaining the technical aspects of planned giving and identifying the donor's financial objectives, but that individual must also be able to clearly articulate the organization's mission and programs and identify the donors' philanthropic objectives.

Planned Giving Policies and Guidelines

Before embarking on a planned giving program, written policies and guidelines governing the program should be developed. It is highly recommended that board approval be a prerequisite to the implementation of such policies and guidelines. Once the board has approved, development personnel, volunteers, and donors must adhere to the parameters contained in the document, thereby positioning the planned giving program to move forward with unity and clarity.

The following is a list of issues a nonprofit organization should consider addressing in its policies and guidelines document:

1. Will the organization offer charitable gift annuities to its donors?

2. Will the organization serve as trustee of charitable remainder trusts and charitable lead trusts? If not, is it the donor's responsibility to secure a trustee?

3. Will the organization administer charitable trusts or charitable gift annuities? If not, who will serve as the third-party administrator?

4. What minimum amounts and other limitations should be established for each of the planned giving instruments? What is the minimum gift amount the organization is willing to accept for a charitable gift annuity? What is the minimum gift amount the organization is willing to accept for it to serve as the trustee of a charitable remainder trust? Are there minimum age requirements the donor must meet before the organization will enter into a charitable gift annuity contract? Are there maximum payout percentages the organization is willing to offer for charitable gift annuities and charitable remainder trusts?

5. Who in the organization has the authority to accept gifts of appreciated property, particularly real estate and closely held stock? Is board approval required before such assets may be accepted?

6. Who in the organization is authorized to negotiate the terms of a planned giving instrument, such as a charitable gift annuity or charitable remainder trust, with a donor? Is board approval required before the document may be executed?

7. Who in the organization has the authority to sign the planned giving document on behalf of the organization?

Here are some specific guidelines to consider incorporating into a policies and guidelines document:

1. *Percent payout rate on charitable remainder trusts.* The payout rate on charitable remainder trusts must be at least 5 percent but should generally not exceed 10 percent.

2. *Minimum age requirements and funding levels for charitable remainder trusts.* If the organization is willing to serve as trustee, the minimum age of an income beneficiary should be fifty-five. The minimum funding level should be $50,000.

3. *Percent payout on charitable gift annuities.* It should be the organization's general practice to use the gift annuity rates established by the American Council on Gift Annuities.

4. *Minimum age requirements and funding levels for charitable gift annuities.* The organization should not offer charitable gift annuity contracts to donors under age fifty-five. The minimum funding level should be $10,000.

5. *Trustee.* Most organizations should not serve as trustee of charitable remainder trusts and charitable gift annuities. In such instances, the donor is responsible for selecting a trustee.

6. *Real estate.* All proposed gifts of real estate must receive board approval before accepted.

7. *Donor-centered philanthropy.* All arrangements entered into with donors should always have the donor's best interests in mind, provided that the terms of the arrangement do not violate the organization's policies and guidelines.

8. *Legal counsel.* Donors should be advised to consult with their legal counsel before entering into any legal arrangements with the organization.

9. *Confidentiality.* All information about a donor or named income beneficiaries, including names, ages, gift amounts, and net worth, should be kept strictly confidential by the organization unless permission is obtained from the donor to release such information.

PLANNED GIFT OPTIONS

Planned giving generally involves one of three gifting methods—current outright gifts, expectancies, and deferred gifts. A common misconception in the planned giving industry is that all planned gifts are "deferred gifts." Some planned gifts are structured to provide immediate benefits to the nonprofit organization, others provide deferred benefits to the organization, and still others may involve a combination of methods, whereby a current outright gift is combined with a deferred gift or an expectancy to achieve the donor's philanthropic and financial objectives.

Current Outright Gifts

Gifts of assets such as stock, real estate, and tangible personal property, although given for the current use and enjoyment of a nonprofit organization, qualify as planned gifts by virtue of their dollar value and the fact that they are combined with other assets. These gifts are generally made jointly by spouses and require significant contemplation and planning, unlike annual fund gifts, which are often made spontaneously in response to a mail appeal and satisfied by writing a check from income.

Stock

Appreciated stock—publicly traded or closely held—is the most common type of noncash gift. Nonprofit organizations prefer gifts of publicly traded stock because it is highly liquid—it can be sold instantaneously by a phone call from the owner to the broker—and it has a readily ascertainable fair market value, published daily in newspapers like the *Wall Street Journal.* Closely held stock, by contrast, may be difficult to value and requires the services of a qualified independent appraiser, which could take several weeks to complete. Such stock may also prove to be illiquid in that it may be subject to restrictions prohibiting it from being gifted to a nonprofit organization, or it may be unsalable if a ready, willing, and able buyer cannot be found. Individuals who started their own companies may have a significant percentage of their wealth in closely held stock.

Real Estate

Real estate is the second most common type of noncash gift. There are a number of issues a nonprofit organization should address before accepting a gift of real estate. Is the estate subject to a debt? Are there liens or encumbrances on the real estate? Is the donor the sole owner, or is the property jointly owned with others? Once accepted, will the organization be able to sell the property within a reasonable period of time, and if not, does the organization have funds available to pay for insurance, taxes, and maintenance? Will the organization retain the property and use it for its exempt purpose? Have environmental tests been conducted on the property to ensure that it is not contaminated?

Many organizations require board approval before accepting gifts of real estate. Some even create a real estate checklist that must be satisfied before the proposed gift is presented to the board. Since most organizations are not interested in entering into the real estate management business, acceptance of a gift of real estate may be predicated on the ability to sell the property within a short period of time.

When deciding on which assets to give currently to an organization, donors often choose to give the most highly appreciated assets, thereby entitling the donor to a charitable income tax deduction equal to the current fair market value of the property. This is a more attractive option for the donor than to sell the property and become liable for capital gains taxes on it. Furthermore, if the donor gives appreciated assets to the organization and the organization sells those assets, all capital gains tax is avoided thanks to the organization's tax-exempt status. So this arrangement is advantageous from both the donor's and the nonprofit's point of view.

Charitable Lead Trust

A charitable lead trust is a trust arrangement that pays current annual income to the nonprofit organization for a specified period of years, with the trust principal reverting to the donor or the donor's family when the trust ends. The annual income payment by the trust is similar to an outright gift of cash, for the charity is free to use the cash as soon as it is received, subject, of course, to any restrictions placed on the gift by the donor. The charitable lead trust is probably the most sophisticated of all the planned giving instruments, so it is advisable to seek the assistance of an experienced charitable estate planner before entering into this type of arrangement.

Expectancies

Expectancies involve a promise by a donor to make a gift to the nonprofit organization at some future date; however, that promise may be revoked at any time prior to the donor's death. Since the gift is not a completed gift during the donor's lifetime, the donor does not enjoy the benefit of a charitable income tax deduction when the expectancy provision is created. The most common types of expectancies are bequests, retirement plan and IRA designations, and life insurance designations.

Bequests. Bequests are the backbone of all planned giving programs and historically are the most popular planned giving method used by donors. Donors like bequests because they are easy to understand and do not require the donor to part with assets during life. This provides the donor peace of mind knowing that assets are available to satisfy unforeseen expenses such as medical or nursing home costs. Charities like bequests because they are easy to explain, require very little cost to promote, and once in place are rarely revoked.

A bequest is a written statement in a donor's will directing that specific assets, or a percentage of the estate, will be transferred to charity at the donor's death. Since most individuals should have a will and since bequests can be for any dollar amount, nonprofit organizations should consider marketing bequests to their entire constituency, regardless of age and net worth. If you do nothing else but regularly include sample will language in your organization's communication devices, you will have initiated a planned giving program that will pay dividends to your organization for years to come.

Retirement Plans and IRAs. A second type of expectancy gaining in popularity among donors involves naming an organization as the beneficiary of a retirement plan or IRA. For many individuals, retirement plan assets represent the single largest asset in their portfolios. Like the bequest, it is easy to understand and easy to implement. This gifting opportunity merely involves obtaining a beneficiary designation form from the retirement plan administrator and naming a charity as the entire, or partial, beneficiary of the retirement plan assets upon the owner's death. A donor may achieve significant income and estate tax savings by naming a charity as the beneficiary of the retirement plan assets rather than a noncharity—sometimes the tax savings is as much as 75 cents on the dollar.

Life Insurance. A third type of expectancy, life insurance, may be attractive to donors because it affords donors the opportunity to make a gift with a sizable face value for a minimal outlay of cash. Donors may give an existing policy, either fully or partially paid, or a new policy. Similar to a retirement plan designation, the proposed gift to charity is accomplished by naming the charity as a beneficiary of the policy on the beneficiary designation form. Upon the donor's death, the charity will receive all, or a portion of, the proceeds from the policy. The donor is entitled to a charitable income tax deduction equal to the cash surrender value of the property and any future premiums paid only if the charity is named as the owner and beneficiary of the policy.

Deferred Gifts

Deferred gifts involve irrevocable transfers of cash or property not available for the charity's use and enjoyment until some time in the future. Although the gift is complete, thereby entitling the donor to a current charitable income tax deduction, a future event such as the donor's death or the expiration of a specific term of year will cause the charity's interest to come to fruition. The most prevalent types of deferred gift arrangements are charitable gift annuities and charitable remainder trusts.

Charitable Gift Annuity. A charitable gift annuity is a simple contract between the donor and the charity whereby the donor makes an irrevocable transfer of cash or property to the charity. In return for the contributed property, the charity agrees to pay a fixed amount of money each year for the lifetime of one or two individuals. The payout rate offered by a charity will depend on the number of annuitants and their ages. The annuitants have the option to defer receiving their annuity payments until some future date, provided that this decision is made at the time the contract is entered into.

Many charities offer charitable gift annuities to their donors because they are easy to explain and require minimal administrative time and expense to implement. Charitable gift annuities are attractive to donors who are interested in making a gift to charity but are unable to make a current outright gift—they require an additional stream of income in return for their gift.

Most states regulate charitable gift annuities; a charity should therefore familiarize itself with state restrictions, regulations, and reporting requirements before initiating a charitable gift annuity program. The charity must be concerned with requirements not only in states where it has offices but also in states where the charitable gift annuity donors are domiciled.

Charitable Remainder Trust. A charitable remainder trust is an irrevocable trust in which the donor transfers cash or property to a trustee and in return the donor or other individuals named by the donor as income beneficiaries receive income from the trust for life or a specified term not to exceed twenty years. When the trust terminates, the corpus is distributed to the charities named as the charitable remainder beneficiaries.

There are two main types of charitable remainder trusts—the charitable remainder annuity trust and the charitable remainder unitrust. Although the two are similar in many ways, they do have a few differences, the most significant being the method by which the annual income paid by the trust to the income beneficiaries is calculated. Another major difference is that annuity trusts do not allow for additional contributions once funded, whereas unitrusts allow for additional contributions at any time.

A charitable remainder annuity trust pays a fixed dollar amount, annually, based on the initial fair market value of the property transferred to the trust. For example, if a donor transfers $100,000 to an annuity trust and selects a payout percentage of 5 percent, the named income beneficiaries will receive $5,000 per year until the trust terminates, regardless of whether the trust principal increases or decreases in value over time. Thus annuity trusts are generally favored by donors who are more interested in receiving a fixed income than they are in chancing market volatility.

A charitable remainder unitrust, by contrast, provides fluctuating income payments to the income beneficiaries, based on a fixed percentage of the annually revalued trust corpus. For example, if a donor transfers $100,000 to a unitrust and selects a payout percentage of 5 percent, the named income beneficiaries will receive $5,000 in the first year. But if in the second year the trust grows in value to $110,000, the income beneficiaries will receive $5,500, thereby enjoying the benefit from the appreciation experienced by the trust. Alternatively, if in the second year the trust drops in value to $90,000, the income beneficiaries will receive only $4,500 in the second year. Market volatility will thus have a direct impact on the income payments received each year by the income beneficiaries.

The payout percentage provided for in the trust document must be at least 5 percent. Most charitable remainder trusts have payout percentages of 5 percent to 10 percent, depending on the number of income beneficiaries and their ages. Charities that serve as trustees can determine the payout percentage offered for each particular trust, but charities that do not serve as trustees are not in a position to dictate the trust's payout percentage. Many charities choose not to serve as trustees because of the legal fiduciary responsibility one assumes as trustee.

MARKETING PLANNED GIFTS

Developing a planned giving program internally within a nonprofit organization is not enough. Thought must be given to how the organization will market the fact that it is in the planned giving business, to whom it should direct its appeals, and which planned opportunities to promote.

For organizations just getting started in planned giving, it is unrealistic to expect that a comprehensive program offering every available planned giving opportunity must be introduced. Many organizations develop planned giving programs on a piecemeal basis, first introducing revocable arrangements such as bequests, retirement plan designations, and life insurance designations and later introducing irrevocable arrangements such as charitable gift annuities and charitable remainder trusts. If an organization is not in a position to respond to inquiries concerning the more technical instruments such as charitable remainder trusts, it is probably a good idea not to market that particular giving option. Donors must be left with the impression that the organization is capable of answering questions accurately and fully explaining the benefits of a particular opportunity to both the donor and the organization.

Not every available planned giving opportunity will be marketed to an organization's entire constituency. In some instances, it may be prudent to market a particular giving method to the entire constituency but other giving methods to a narrow segment of the constituency. Age, family situation (living spouse, children, grandchildren, and so on), prior giving history, level of affluence, and involvement with the organization are some of the factors to consider when determining which gift opportunities will marketed to a particular donor.

The essence of a successful planned giving marketing program is to educate and inform the organization's constituency about the various gifting opportunities available to help individual constituents accomplish their philanthropic and financial objectives. Communications regarding the organization's planned giving business should send the message that it is looking to the future to address long-term goals and objectives. Consequently, many donors may choose to direct their planned gifts for endowment purposes rather than to support current operating expenses. Be prepared to share with your donors the various endowment opportunities that the organization has available.

Print Materials

The development of print materials may be the first step in disseminating planned giving messages to the organization's constituency. Print materials may include brochures, newsletters, inserts, ads, stand-alone mailings made up of a cover letter and accompanying illustration, and the integration of planned giving messages throughout all facets of the organization's communication pieces.

Brochures and newsletters are commonly used by organizations to market planned giving opportunities. There are two basic approaches to consider with brochures. The first is the creation of a comprehensive brochure containing a brief explanation of each available planned giving opportunity. Such brochures tend to be widely distributed because they cover all available planned giving opportunities, from the most basic, bequests, to the most sophisticated, charitable lead trusts. An all-inclusive brochure may be particularly attractive to organizations with a limited budget since design and printing expenses will be kept to a minimum.

The second approach is the creation of a series of planned giving brochures, each describing in detail a particular planned giving method. For example, individual brochures may be created for bequests, charitable gift annuities, retirement plan and IRA designations, charitable remainder trusts, and so on. These brochures are typically not intended for widespread distribution but rather are available to share with donors expressing an interest in supporting the organization who require additional information about a particular giving method.

Regardless of which approach is taken, there are a number of companies who offer generic brochures that can be purchased and imprinted with the organization's name and logo. Many of these companies also offer nonprofit organizations the option of custom-tailoring the generic brochure so that it includes photos and mission-related information and stories about the organization and its donors. By weaving the organizational information into the generic text, an organization is able to produce a brochure with a look and message consistent with its other development and communication pieces.

Some organizations assume the task of preparing the entire planned brochure in-house. Although there is merit to this approach in that it is completely written and produced by individuals who work for the organization and therefore know its mission well, before embarking on a project of this magnitude, an organization should ask itself, "Do we have the manpower and technical expertise in-house to produce an effective brochure that is technically sound, conveys a clear and understandable message to our constituency, and can be produced in a timely fashion?" An organization may conclude that the planned giving officer's time is better spent out of the office developing relationships with key donors, rather than behind a desk preparing brochures.

Each brochure should contain a reply device giving donors the opportunity to request additional information, indicate that they have already included the organization in their will or estate plan, request an illustration, or request a personal visit from the planned giving officer. Donors who take the time to respond to mailings are prime planned gift prospects and should be contacted immediately through a personal phone call to gather additional information and schedule a personal visit.

The mailing of a planned giving newsletter on a regular basis (quarterly, semiannually, annually) is another way to market planned giving opportunities to the organization's constituency. Each newsletter may focus on a specific planned gift opportunity and contain a story about a donor who has used that particular method in the past to benefit the organization. Some nonprofit organizations have been successful in securing newsletter sponsors, such as law firms or banks, who are willing to underwrite the cost of producing the newsletter in exchange for placing the firm's name on the newsletter. Newsletters typically lend themselves to widespread distribution—donors of record, volunteers, professional financial advisers, and so on—for the cost-per-newsletter drops significantly once a certain production volume has been attained.

One-page planned giving inserts or ads in existing organizational publications may be a cost-effective way to communicate with a broad base of the organization's constituency. For instance, if a hospital or university regularly sends a health-related or alumni magazine to its constituency, an insert or ad inside the magazine highlighting the opportunity to support the organization through a bequest or charitable gift annuity may generate interest and cause new planned giving prospects to surface.

Integration with Annual Appeals

Nonprofit organizations interested in marketing planned giving opportunities to their constituency should consider reviewing existing communication devices to find ways to incorporate planned giving messages. Something as basic as including a line on the annual appeal card giving donors the opportunity to tell you they have included the organization in their will or estate plan or they would like additional information about a particular planned giving method is a cost-effective way to identify planned gift prospects. It is also a way for organizations with a limited marketing budget, who do not possess the financial resources to produce brochures or newsletters, to begin placing planned giving messages in front of their constituency.

Stand-Alone Mailings

Virtually for the cost of postage alone (currently just a nickel per letter at the nonprofit rate), stand-alone mailings, highlighting a particular planned giving method, consisting of a cover letter and accompanying illustration, can be a cost-effective marketing strategy. For example, mailing sample bequest language with a cover letter signed by a key board member, volunteer, or leader within the organization, extolling the benefits of a particular planned giving method to the donor and the organization, can be conducted with minimal time and expense.

Revocable planned giving methods, such as bequests, retirement plan designations, and life insurance designations, are typically marketed to a broader base of donors than irrevocable planned giving arrangements, such as charitable gift annuities and charitable remainder trusts. This is due to the fact that revocable arrangements are easy to understand, can be implemented with minimal effort, and can be designated for any dollar amount, large or small. Since irrevocable arrangements appeal to a narrower segment of an organization's constituency, consider segmenting marketing messages based on age, level of affluence, prior giving history, involvement with the organization, or some combination of these factors.

Seminars

Planned giving seminars are an excellent way for an organization to educate its constituency about the various planned giving opportunities and create an awareness that the organization is prepared to discuss such plans with donors and assist them in facilitating such gifts. Seminars can be designed for a variety of audiences, including donors, volunteers, board members, faculty, and professional financial advisers.

The audience will dictate the level of technical content presented at the seminar. It is important to keep donor and volunteer seminars concise and understandable. This may by the first opportunity the donor or volunteer has had to learn about the various giving methods, so you want to be sure they leave the seminar with a clear understanding of what was discussed, rather than feeling confused or overwhelmed. Donor and volunteer seminars should avoid presentations involving deep technical discussions about specific planned giving methods. Discussions about bequests, retirement plan and life insurance designations, charitable gift annuities, and in some cases charitable remainder trusts are best suited for these types of seminars. Securing a well-respected professional financial adviser from the community to participate as a presenter will lend credibility to the program, but make sure this individual is capable of presenting the material in an understandable fashion for nonprofessionals.

Seminars for professional financial advisers should be more technically oriented than donor and volunteer seminars. Many, but not all, financial advisers understand the basics of planned giving, so these presentations should provide a more thorough analysis of the specific instruments and address the income, capital gains, and estate and gift tax benefits available through each instrument. Offering continuing education credit may make the seminar particularly attractive to the financial adviser.

Personal Visits

The most important aspect of marketing is ensuring that once an individual responds to a mailing, a personal call is made immediately by the planned giving officer to answer questions, provide additional information, and schedule a personal visit. Many planned gifts are completed as a result of the organization's ability to build a personal relationship with the donor and identify ways to involve the donor with the organization. Letters, e-mails, and telephone calls are not substitutes for personal visits but should be used in addition to the visits. Depending on one's job responsibilities beyond fund raising, all development officers should attempt to make a certain number of personal donor visits per month. In the early stages of a planned giving program, it is sometimes more prudent to gauge the planned giving officer's progress on the number of personal visits made rather than the number of planned gift arrangements closed or dollars raised.

Planned Giving Recognition Society

The impetus for creating a planned giving recognition society is to identify individuals who have included the organization in their will or estate plan. Donors may neglect to notify the charitable organization that it has been included as a beneficiary in the estate plan. Such omissions are sometimes intentional, but usually the donor simply fails to think about notifying the organization. Creating a planned giving recognition society and marketing it to the organization's constituency creates a heightened awareness among individuals that the organization is interested in learning about their future plans to benefit the organization. It also provides an opportunity to begin building relationships with those donors and identify ways to involve them in the organization's activities.

The charitable organization is free to choose which planned gift arrangements qualify one for membership in the society. Many organizations make membership all-inclusive in that any one of the various planned giving methods qualify one for membership, regardless of dollar amount and regardless of whether the commitment is revocable or irrevocable. Some organizations require the donor to provide a copy of the legal document that references the donor's gift, while others are comfortable taking donors at their word and merely require a written statement from the donor summarizing the gift arrangement.

Planned giving recognition society brochures explaining the impetus for starting the society, the organization's mission, a brief description of the planned gift methods that qualify one for membership, a roster of current planned gift donors, and an explanation of what action must be taken to become a member are sometimes created to help market the society. These brochures are typically sent to planned gift donors of record, board members and volunteers, annual giving donors beginning with those individuals at the highest annual giving levels, and professional financial advisers.

An annual event exclusively for society members, such as a luncheon or dinner, is used by some organizations as a way to thank members for their participation. Most planned gift donors do not expect organizations to give them tangible objects such as plaques or paperweights. In fact, some donors are adamant that the organization refrain from using gift dollars for anything other than activities and programs directly supporting the mission of the organization.

PROSPECT IDENTIFICATION

Planned giving prospects come in all ages, levels of affluence, family situations, philanthropic objectives, and financial objectives. It is a mistake to pigeonhole planned giving prospects into a narrowly defined set of characteristics. Sometimes planned gifts are made by donors you least expect, so it is important not to overlook a prospect or segment of your prospect population because of particular characteristics. With that said, where do you begin? Some organizations begin the prospect identification process by analyzing individuals who are currently on the radar screen, namely, those individuals who have previously made planned gift commitments to the organization or are supporting the organization on a regular basis through annual fund commitments. Don't feel as though the process of identifying planned gift prospects must begin by identifying "new" prospects with no previous gift history. It is more likely than not that those individuals who become planned gift donors have a history of previous giving or involvement with the organization.

Current Planned Gift Donors

First, identify individuals who have current planned gift commitments in place. Perhaps they have named the organization as a beneficiary in a will, retirement plan, or life insurance policy. As discussed previously, a donor has no obligation to notify an organization that it has been included as a beneficiary. For that reason, some organizations create planned giving recognition societies in addition to including one-line responses on annual appeals that provide an opportunity for the donor to notify the organization that a planned gift commitment is already in place. Once current planned gift donors are identified, it is the planned giving officer's responsibility to contact those donors, thank them for their commitments, and attempt to begin building personal relationships with those donors. Not only will this provide an opportunity to obtain details about their planned gift commitments, but it will also create an opportunity to convert revocable arrangements, like bequests, into irrevocable commitments.

Annual Fund Donors

Second, analyze donors who have participated in the organization's annual fund. In particular, look at the number of years they have participated. Individuals who have made annual fund gifts for each of the last ten years or eight of the last ten years are sending a message that they are interested in the organization and are willing to support the organization on a consistent basis. These same people may be interested in learning how they can support the organization in a more significant way, either during their lifetime or at death. Because some planned gift arrangements offer income to the donor in return for their gift and provide various tax benefits to the donor, some donors may conclude that they are capable of making a gift they did not think was otherwise possible or are capable of making a gift at a level that is much higher than they ever expected.

Board, Volunteers, and Staff

Next, look at individuals who have a history of direct involvement with the organization. These individuals may be former or current board members or trustees, volunteers, administrative and professional staff, former donors, and community leaders. The linkage to the organization exists or did exist at one time—it is the planned giving officer's responsibility to determine if ability and interest are still present. Keep in mind that most individuals have a variety of charitable interests, so even if interest in the organization is not at the highest possible level, an individual may still be interested in supporting the organization, particularly through an estate plan arrangement that does not require a current outlay of cash or assets. Not all planned giving prospects have a high net worth. There may be many individuals of moderate wealth who would be willing to entertain the idea of making a current transfer to an organization in return for a stream of income or willing to include an organization as a partial beneficiary in a will, retirement plan, or life insurance policy. In addition, don't overlook donors who fall below certain annual giving levels, such as $500. Some individuals, even though interested in a particular organization, will never make a significant commitment to that organization during their lifetime because they are conservative or need the peace of mind that they will have sufficient assets available for unforeseen emergencies such as major medical expenses. However, these same individuals may be willing to make a significant gift to the organization at death through one of the various planned giving methods.

Professional Financial Advisers

Networking with professional financial advisers, particularly those practicing in the local community, can sometimes lead an organization to new prospects. Clients sometimes look to their professional advisers, such as attorneys, accountants, financial planners, and trust officers, for advice in satisfying philanthropic objectives. Many financial advisers actively promote various planned giving instruments to their clients, recognizing that some clients will lose control over a certain percentage of assets at death due to estate taxes. With proper lifetime planning, some planned giving instruments can allow individuals to redirect dollars that would have otherwise been lost to the government in the form of taxes to their favorite charities, thereby allowing the individuals themselves, rather than the government, to determine how their hard-earned dollars are spent.

Some organizations formalize their network of financial advisers by creating a planned giving committee that meets periodically to create gift acceptance policies, review prospect lists, prepare articles for planned giving newsletters, and learn more about the organization's mission. Many professional advisers welcome the opportunity to learn more about an organization's mission, the programs it offers, and the people it serves. Creating opportunities for advisers to come to an organization's site and observe firsthand the organization and its people as they carry out that mission may leave an indelible mark that may cause advisers to think of the organization when discussing philanthropic alternatives with their clients.

CONCLUSION

To be successful, planned giving programs must be carefully planned and designed to meet the needs of each particular organization. Commitment from institutional leaders is critical. As gift planners, we must address each donor's philanthropic and financial objectives. Never lose sight of the significance of your organization's mission to the donor. Planned gifts are rarely strictly for tax considerations. A belief in the organization's mission is generally the driving force behind most planned gifts. Once a donor has decided that your organization merits support, helping the donor understand the various giving opportunities and how to make the gift in the most advantageous manner becomes the responsibility of the charitable gift planner.

Like other areas of development, success in planned giving requires the ability to develop meaningful relationships with your constituency. People give to people with causes. Understanding your donor's motivations and objectives—which is accomplished primarily through personal contacts and relationship building—is far more important than understanding the technical nuances of planned giving. Begin to develop relationships with your top prospects, learn the gift planning process, and recognize that most planned gifts require the efforts of a team of individuals who understand their roles and those of the other parties involved. Success will follow.

PART FOUR

SOURCES OF FUND RAISING

The chapters in Part Four provide insights into the various sources of philanthropic support available to nonprofit organizations. In addition to the aspects covered in the first edition of *Achieving Excellence,* this edition includes new chapters on women as donors, new approaches to philanthropy in the twenty-first century, and cultural diversity in philanthropic giving.

Every organization should set as its goal to create a base of philanthropic funds that includes diverse sources of support. The more funding sources in the organization's donor base, the less likely the organization is to be affected by events that might have an impact on any one of those sources, such as a corporate merger or a change in fortune of an individual major donor.

The largest percentage of philanthropic support continues to come from individuals during their lifetimes. When bequest income is included, individuals account for about 83.5 percent of total giving each year (AAFRC Trust for Philanthropy, 2002). Chapter Thirteen, on individuals, provides insights for identifying potential donors, engaging them with the organization, and sustaining them as donors over time.

Corporate giving in the twenty-first century is very different from its twentieth-century counterpart. New models for corporate giving, corporate sponsorship, and community engagement are aspects of corporate social responsibility. Chapter Fourteen provides guidance on approaching corporations.

Chapter Fifteen focuses on foundations, which have become the second-largest source of philanthropic support. With more than fifty-five thousand private and community foundations in existence today, every organization should develop expertise for approaching foundations. Many new private foundations are small and run by family members, but they often support local organizations and may be an extension of individual philanthropy. Local community foundations have increased in number, have grown dramatically in size, and provide additional opportunities for local support.

The last three chapters in Part Four provide special insights for fund raisers. Women have become a more significant force in philanthropy. Chapter Sixteen helps us understand how women as donors differ from men and how organizations can engage them. Chapter Seventeen reminds us that many new donors today are as different from each other as from the previous generation of donors. That may always have been true, but the twenty-first century has brought with it several new and innovative approaches being used by younger donors. Finally, the demographics of the United States are changing. Chapter Eighteen discusses different cultural approaches to philanthropy. Organizations must be aware of the cultural aspects of philanthropy if they hope to achieve a donor base that reflects the diversity in their communities.

CHAPTER THIRTEEN

Individuals as Donors

Margaret M. Maxwell

At its heart, fund raising is really about people: Nonprofit organizations exist to make a positive impact on the lives of all types of people, and it is people who make decisions about which causes they will support, even if the funds they give away are not their own, as in the case of corporate or foundation donations. And because fund raising is about people, the truism that "people give to people with causes" is most evident with individual gift fund raising—and therefore most intimidating to many organizations because of the extremely personal nature of conversations about money. Nevertheless, individuals represent the largest donor market segment, significantly surpassing the funds given by corporations or foundations.

Hank Rosso described several fund raising concepts that particularly apply to developing relationships with individuals that result in philanthropic gifts: the LAI (linkage, ability, interest) principle, the constituency model, the Ladder of Effectiveness, and the use of prospect research in developing an effective fund raising plan. These concepts are described in detail in other chapters but are discussed here along with some demographic and giving trends to show how nonprofit organizations develop relationships with and solicit gifts from individual donors. This chapter explores how Rosso's concepts of fund raising can be applied in the constantly changing environment of individual philanthropy.

BACKGROUND

Individual giving has always been the major facet of American philanthropy. The nation's founders' deliberate disassociation of church and state gave early citizens the opportunity to invent new models of relationships between individuals and their communities. The result was a system where individual effort could—and did—help create common good and where volunteerism by individuals was seen as an essential part of making democracy work. Alexis de Tocqueville observed some 170 years ago that Americans seemed to have moved beyond the "alms to the poor" type of giving into a more philanthropic mode that emphasized improving society as a whole. As he noted in *Democracy in America* ([1835] 1956), Americans seemed to have an inclination to give and serve, banding together in voluntary associations to achieve common goals.

Early traditions of American individual giving have evolved into a financial powerhouse, accounting for approximately 83 percent of all funds donated. Although the actual percentages of individual, corporate, and foundation giving have changed slightly over time, the overwhelming dominance of individual giving in the American philanthropic landscape has remained constant since *Giving USA* began tracking annual philanthropy in 1960.

Giving by individuals shows no signs of abating in the future, especially given the much talked about transfer of generational wealth. Individuals from several demographic segments—the Depression-era and World War II generations through the baby boomers—have amassed great wealth over half a century of thriving economic conditions. As individuals in these age groups die and pass on their estates, nonprofit organizations are poised to be significant beneficiaries. Estimates of the size of this wealth transfer have been revised upward to more than $25 trillion in new donations to nonprofits over the next fifty-five years (Havens and Schervish, 1999).

Whatever the eventual size of the wealth transfer, the message to fund raisers remains the same: Making connections with individuals provides the greatest opportunity for nonprofits to acquire the financial resources to fulfill their mission. To be effective with this type of fund raising, however, nonprofits must understand the basic principles behind successfully engaging individuals with the causes they are passionate about.

ELEMENTS OF INDIVIDUAL GIVING

Hank Rosso described five important concepts that fund raisers must understand in order to be effective at raising funds from individuals. These concepts are outlined here and discussed further in the following sections of the chapter:

- Organizations must be able to identify their *constituent groups* (as discussed in Chapter Five).

- Analyzing an individual constituent's *linkage, ability, and interest* will determine whether the person should truly be considered a prospective donor to the organization (as discussed in Chapters Three and Five).

- The process of discovering the connections between a donor or a prospective donor and a nonprofit organization is called *prospect research* (discussed in Chapter Ten).

- The most effective fund raising results from having a donor plan that focuses on the *six right considerations* in making connections between organizations and individual donors (discussed in this chapter).

- Ultimately, the first four concepts are applied most effectively if people are willing to ask other people to join them in supporting organizations that address societal needs. The Ladder of Effectiveness (discussed in Chapter Eight) describes a hierarchy of asking strategies that can be used to involve individuals most effectively with organizations.

Constituency

As noted in Chapter Five, an organization's constituency is identified through the following question: Who should care about what a particular organization does? This question, if contemplated by an organization's board and staff, should generate a significant list of responses. Ideally, the individuals who are most vested in the mission and the work of the organization should include all board members and the leadership of the staff as well as major gift donors. Beyond these three constituent groups, the organization should be able to develop a long list of other groups of individuals with varying degrees of connection to the organization, for example:

The individuals served by the organization (clients)

Other current donors

Volunteers who help carry out the organization's work

Other employees

Former participants in all of these groups

People who are interested in the general type of cause the organization represents

Fund raisers refer to this list of potential individual donors as "constituent groups." Not all members of a constituent group are likely to become donors to an organization, however.

People can be simultaneous members of many constituent groups that connect them with numerous nonprofit organizations. Imagine an individual who graduated from college, is a regular churchgoer, and who feels grateful to the local hospital for taking good care of her father when he had a heart attack. She also volunteers time in her child's school and works in a social service agency. This person has multiple connections to worthy organizations that have touched her life significantly. Which ones will she give to? A review of the LAI principle here is useful.

Linkage, Ability, and Interest

The LAI principle helps an organization determine who among a group of constituents should be considered as a prospective donor. *Linkage* refers to the human connection between the organization and the individual. A board member, a staff member, a volunteer—anyone connected directly to the organization—can help provide the link that connects the organization with the prospective individual donor.

Ability is the qualifier that organizations most often consider as the primary determinant of giving: Is the prospect financially capable of making a gift? This qualifier, however, is the least reliable indicator. Countless studies have affirmed that individuals who financially might be considered least able to give are in fact the persons who give the greatest percentage of their income to charitable causes. Nevertheless, ability to give must be considered as a factor when determining who should be asked to participate in the cause.

The final indicator, *interest,* refers to a prospective donor's personal preferences for becoming involved in an organization. Does the individual have a personal interest in the problem that the organization is addressing? Or does the person's interests really lie with other causes?

Ideally, a nonprofit organization will develop a prospect list of individuals who evidence all three qualifiers—a direct link to a person who is involved in the organization, a personal interest in the cause represented by the organization, and an ability to make a financial contribution, if motivated. The process of discovering the connections between an organization and its constituents is known as prospect research.

Prospect Research

Using information in fund raising is discussed more thoroughly in Chapters Ten and Twenty-Six. It is included here to illustrate how donor market development is achieved. The purpose of conducting prospect research is to uncover the connections between an organization's mission and a potential donor's personal philanthropic goals or personal values in order for the organization to issue the right kind of invitation to participate. There are two basic types of sources that nonprofits look to in seeking information about prospective donors: people and reference materials.

People research is gathered during one-on-one interviews with individuals who know the prospective donor or in prospect rating meetings that are held with a small committee established by the organization just for this purpose. (Although these third-party sources can provide valuable information about prospective donors, they do not substitute for the best source of people information, the prospective donors themselves.)

Reference material research uses resources from libraries and a vast array of other sources. Since the late 1990s, access to the Internet has made gathering this reference information quicker and much less expensive for most organizations. Researchers who used to spend days traveling between public libraries and records offices gathering information about individuals now have these same resources available at their fingertips. In addition, electronic screening services have increasingly enabled organizations to match their lists of prospective donors against a variety of lists, include some of those identified in Exhibit 13.1, to determine which individuals warrant additional background research.

It is important to emphasize that prospect research about individuals is not "gathering gossip." Rather, it is the systematic acquisition and documentation of relevant information to enable the organization to connect appropriately with current and potential donors. Because of the personal nature of this research, adherence to the strictest ethical standards is vitally important (see Exhibit 13.2).

Having quicker access to more sources of information is undoubtedly a benefit to fund raisers; knowing how to use the information appropriately to acquire new or upgraded donors is the real challenge most organizations face and the one that is addressed through planning.

The Six Rights

The data-gathering process involves identifying prospective donors who are interested and able to make a gift and who have a link to the organization. Creating knowledge out of these data comes through Rosso's "six right considerations in the gift solicitation" planning process. The hypothesis behind this planning is that fund raising success is maximized when the *right* person asks the *right* prospect for the *right* amount of money for the *right* cause at the *right* time and in the *right* way. Done properly, research can identify who or where the strongest link is between the organization and a prospective donor and what the prospect's potential giving capacity is. The process of donor cultivation— inviting prospective donors in to see the organization and to get to know the people who carry out its work—helps the organization gather additional information from the prospective donors themselves. Ultimately, the combination of the research and cultivation processes enables the organization to develop a unique "six rights" plan for each individual donor.

Exhibit 13.1. Sources of Prospect Research Data on Individuals.

- Telephone directories (including yellow pages for professional listings)

- ZIP code directories

- *Who's Who in America*

- Other *Who's Who* volumes (thirty-four additional special areas or subjects are covered)

- The Marquis *Who's Who* books: *Who's Who in the West, Who's Who in Law, Who's Who in Finance and Industry,* and so on

- Social registers

- The *New York Times* Index of Names

- Index to the *National Cyclopedia of American Biography*

- *Standard & Poor's Register of Directors and Executives*

- *Dun & Bradstreet's Million Dollar Directory*

- *Dun & Bradstreet's Reference Book of Corporate Managements*

- *Dun & Bradstreet's Middle Market Directory*

- *Walker's Manual of Western Corporations*

- Prospectuses of public corporations

- Official summary of security transactions and withholdings

- The Quantas *Compendium of Directors,* published by PC Research Services (includes salaries, stock holdings, and directorships of major corporate individuals)

- Proxy statements: Send a postcard request to a publicly held corporation for its most recent proxy statement and annual report. Proxy statements contain biographical information on a company's executives and directors, their salaries, shares of stock owned, and bonuses.

- Taft publications: *People in Philanthropy: A Guide to Philanthropic Leaders, Major Donors, and Funding Connections; The Taft Trustees of Wealth: A Biographical Directory to Private Foundation and Corporate Foundation Officers; America's Wealthiest People: Their Philanthropic and Non-Profit Affiliations;* and *Guide to Private Fortunes*

- City or county clerk's office or county courthouse: Probate and will information is arranged chronologically by date of death and then alphabetized.

- Tax assessment office for real and personal property values

- Local newspapers (especially the business, social, and obituary sections)

- Bulletins, newsletters, and magazines of organizations similar to yours or covering your constituency

Exhibit 13.1. Sources of Prospect Research Data on Individuals, Cont'd.

- Directories and membership lists of local clubs and organizations (social, civic, political, recreational, professional, business, and so on)

- Newspaper morgues (libraries)

- Influential contacts

Sources: Adapted from Exhibit 17.1 in the first edition of *Achieving Excellence* and from Allen, 1991, p. 219.

Exhibit 13.2. Prospect Research Statement of Ethics.

Prospect researchers must balance the needs of their institutions to collect, analyze, record, maintain, use and disseminate information with an individual's right to privacy. This balance is not always easy to maintain. The following ethical principles apply, and practice is built on these fundamental principles:

A. Confidentiality

Confidential information about constituents (donors and non-donors), as well as confidential information of the institutions in oral form or on electronic, magnetic, or print media, is protected so that the relationship of trust between the constituent and the institution is upheld.

B. Accuracy

Prospect researchers shall record all data accurately. Such information shall include attribution. Analysis and products of data analysis should be without personal prejudices or biases.

C. Relevance

Prospect researchers shall seek and record only information that is relevant and appropriate to the fund raising effort of the institutions that employ them.

D. Accountability

Prospect researchers shall accept responsibility for their actions and shall be accountable to the profession of development, to their respective institutions and to the constituents who place their trust in prospect researchers and their institutions.

E. Honesty

Prospect researchers shall be truthful with regard to their identity and purpose and the identity of their institution during the course of their work.

Suggested Practice

A. Collection

1. The collection of information shall be done lawfully, respecting applicable laws and institutional policies.

2. Information sought and recorded includes all data that can be verified and attributed, as well as constituent information that is self-reported (via correspondence, surveys, questionnaires, etc.).

Exhibit 13.2. Prospect Research Statement of Ethics, Cont'd.

3. When requesting information in person or by telephone, it is recommended in most cases that neither individual nor institutional identity shall be concealed. Written requests for public information shall be made on institutional stationery clearly identifying the inquirer.

4. Whenever possible, payments for public records shall be made through the institution.

5. Prospect researchers shall apply the same standards for electronic information that they currently use in evaluating and verifying print media. The researcher shall ascertain whether or not the information comes from a reliable source and that the information collected meets the standards set forth in the APRA Statement of Ethics.

B. Recording and Maintenance

1. Researchers shall state information in an objective and factual manner, note attribution and date of collection, and clearly identify analysis.

2. Constituent information on paper, electronic, magnetic or other media shall be stored securely to prevent access by unauthorized persons.

3. Special protection shall be afforded all giving records pertaining to anonymous donors.

4. Electronic or paper documents pertaining to constituents shall be irreversibly disposed of when no longer needed (by following institutional standards for document disposal.)

C. Use and Distribution

1. Researchers shall adhere to all applicable laws, as well as to institutional policies, regarding the use and distribution of confidential constituent information.

2. Constituent information is the property of the institution for which it was collected and shall not be given to persons other than those who are involved with the cultivation or solicitation effort or those who need that information in the performance of their duties for that institution.

3. Constituent information for one institution shall not be taken to another institution.

4. Research documents containing constituent information that is to be used outside research offices shall be clearly marked "confidential."

5. Vendors, consultants and other external entities shall understand and agree to comply with the institution's confidentiality policies before gaining access to institutional data.

6. Only publicly available information shall be shared with colleagues at other institutions as a professional courtesy.

Source: Excerpted from Association of Professional Researchers for Advancement (APRA), *APRA Statement of Ethics*, Sept. 30, 1998. Used with permission.

It is important to note that neither research nor cultivation is completed overnight and to emphasize that ideally, a unique plan is created for each prospective donor. Finding the interest of a particular individual and the personal connection that links this person to the organization can take months or even years, depending on the size of the gift being sought. Obviously, no organization can afford to conduct this type of planning with every individual on its constituency list. It is therefore vitally important that an organization desiring to raise major gifts from individuals engage in appropriate prospect screening and research in order to organize its work with prospective donors most effectively.

Embedded in the "six rights" planning process is the important assumption that the most effective way to raise funds from individuals is by involving volunteers who ask their peers—people they already know—to help join them in solving a problem they both care about; the solution to the problem, of course, can only be realized by making a gift to the organization.

The Ladder of Effectiveness

Rosso's Ladder of Effectiveness describes a hierarchy of strategies used in soliciting gifts from individuals and is taught as an essential part of The Fund Raising School. The Ladder of Effectiveness is covered in detail in Chapter Eight (see Figure 8.1) but abbreviated here for the sake of individual giving. The most effective method—peer-to-peer solicitation conducted in person—is also the strategy that holds some organizations back from engaging in an individual gift program. Because talking about money is a cultural taboo that causes many people a great deal of discomfort, encouraging a volunteer to ask a peer for a financial contribution is often seen as putting both individuals in an uncomfortable situation. But money will have to be discussed. What if the prospective donor says no? And is it appropriate to put people in a situation that we know is "socially improper"?

To answer these questions, it is useful to look at the real dynamics of the solicitation process. Volunteers who care about an organization's mission are inviting others—who research suggests might also have an interest in the cause—to become part of something that they both care about. Ultimately, a gift will be made if the prospective donor comes to understand and believe in the mission of the organization as strongly as the volunteer does. Thus the asking process is not really about money; instead, it is about developing a shared relationship between an organization and the people who care about the cause being addressed.

Face-to-face solicitation with a peer is the most effective individual gift strategy—especially when an organization is raising major gifts (as in a capital or endowment campaign) or seeking upgraded gifts in an annual fund drive. When seeking first-time gifts from individuals, organizations generally rely on strategies that are farther down on the Ladder of Effectiveness—direct mail, telephone, and e-mail—as the means of asking for the gift. Although these less personal strategies may take away some of the perceived discomfort of asking for a gift, they are generally not as successful as face-to-face solicitation. These strategies are more successful, however, when the communication is sent by a peer—someone actually known to the recipient of the letter, phone call, or e-mail.

THE CHANGING DYNAMICS OF INDIVIDUAL GIVING

The basic concepts of individual gift fund raising described in this chapter have been part of fund raising for decades and fund raising training for nearly thirty years since Hank Rosso established The Fund Raising School. And their basic truths—constituents, LAI, prospect research, "six rights" planning, and the Ladder of Effectiveness—have remained essentially unchanged during that period of time. The environment in which individual gift fund raising is being conducted in the early twenty-first century, however, is significantly different than in the last century. New generations of donors are "coming of age" philanthropically; a broader group of people with a more diverse cultural background has access to greater financial resources; new motivations for giving seem to be emerging even from among the "traditional" giving demographic; and new vehicles for giving are available for channeling individual philanthropy.

Generational Differences in Giving

Each generation of people alive today has been shaped by the times in which it lived. Adults who grew up during the Great Depression or World War II, times when everyone was expected (or forced) to make personal sacrifices and when economic prosperity was unknown among the broad population, have very different attitudes toward money than adults of the baby boom generation. The baby boomers have now reached middle age after a lifetime of unprecedented economic growth. Wealthier and more numerous than any preceding generation in American history, the sheer size of this group would make anyone assume that its philanthropic interests could have a major impact on individual gift fund raising. And they do. Partly due to the size of this group and because its members are now in their prime earning years, the nation has seen an explosion in the number of nonprofit organizations created and funded since the early 1980s.

However, there are other trends that are having equally dramatic impacts on philanthropy in the twenty-first century. The group of adults born between 1965 and 1980—the "baby busters" or "Generation X"—are generally regarded as less politically and civically engaged than their parents or grandparents, although evidence also indicates that they volunteer more actively than their predecessors for causes that they are passionate about. "Echo boomers," the children of the baby boom generation, were born between 1980 and 1995 and grew up at a time when computers were as much a part of their households or classrooms as telephones were in previous generations. Thus their comfort with and use of technology is greater than any previous age cohort's.

Although there is no monolithic descriptor that encompasses every member of any of these generation groups, it is important for fund raisers to understand that generational differences do have an impact on how nonprofit organizations appropriately connect with individuals, effectively communicate with them, and successfully invite them to become involved as philanthropists. It also affects the size of gift that these individuals might consider making to a nonprofit organization and the type of information they seek (or require) from an organization before determining whether they should support it.

Unsurprisingly, perhaps, individuals who have grown up in relative affluence believe they are capable of giving larger gifts (particularly to annual funds) than individuals who grew up in relative poverty. Although there are expectations on both sides, Nichols (1990) has noted that post–World War II generations tend to make larger first-time annual gifts than donors in the pre–World War II groups. However, particularly if they are part of Generation X, these donors likely will expect much more specific information about how their funds will be used before agreeing to make a gift. This generation's members' expectations about information sharing are not limited to nonprofits; they also set the same requirements for other institutions, such as corporations or political parties, before they choose to purchase a product, accept a job, or vote for a particular candidate. Also unsurprisingly, generations that have grown up with greater ease of access to information thanks to technology expect information to be delivered more quickly than those who are not familiar with the Internet, faxes, or e-mail communication.

Nonprofit organizations must understand that these generational differences exist and explore the makeup of both their current constituent groups and the quality of the linkages they have with prospective donors in order to undertake or expand an individual gift fund raising program. "One size fits all" fund raising will not ensure future success for any organization, particularly one that is trying to diversify its donor base beyond the current group of donors and attract benefactors from new generational groups. It is especially important to understand this point in light of another important trend: the changing demographics of the population.

Demographic Changes

People are living longer, so the population is aging. More women than ever are employed full time in the workforce. People are delaying marriage and having children—including second families—at a much broader range of ages than ever before. Thanks to changes in technology, medicine, immigration policy, and social attitudes, these significant demographic changes in the American population are strikingly evident in the first decade of the twenty-first century. The implications of these changes on individual giving have challenged nonprofit organizations to rethink their assumptions about who prospective donors are and what types of gifts they are capable of and interested in making at the various stages of their lives.

The old rules about individual giving looked at demographics as the primary indicator of when an individual was an appropriate prospect for a particular type of gift. Adults in the household formation stage of life—twenty- to forty-year-olds who were marrying, building careers, and raising children—were generally thought of as being financially capable of making gifts primarily to annual fund drives. The best prospects for significant-size gifts to capital campaigns were thought to be the forty- to sixty-year-olds, who still were earning significant salaries but whose primary expenses—their children's education and their mortgages—were behind them. And planned giving prospects were defined as individuals over age sixty who were preparing for their retirement at age sixty-five. (Because the average life expectancy was only sixty-eight to seventy years in the mid-twentieth century, however, planning for retirement at age sixty-five really was the same thing as estate planning.) In most cases, the old rules also assumed that the male of the household was the primary wage earner and ultimately the primary decision maker about where charitable gifts were made.

The old rules no longer apply. Although most individuals still begin careers in their early to mid twenties, the age at which marriage, children, and household formation occurs has been significantly pushed back. As a result, it is not unusual for adults in their early fifties to be sending their first child off to college and finally beginning to save for retirement. And as the average life span for both men and women in the United States has risen over the past century to more than seventy-five years, retirement planning is no longer for a brief period of time. The growth of women as vocal, independent decision makers about all types of financial matters, including philanthropy, has also changed assumptions about how to approach individuals (or couples) effectively in asking for a gift. The implications of these and other demographic changes are that nonprofits have been forced to rethink campaign strategies, communication messages, and cultivation and solicitation approaches in their work with individual donors. One rule has not changed, however: researching prospects to find their linkage, ability, and interest is more important than ever.

Cultural Groups and Giving

Chapters Sixteen, Seventeen, and Eighteen discuss important contemporary aspects of individual donors. Each provides additional information to the summaries presented here.

Until the mid-1980s, most research about individual gift fund raising looked only at the white middle-class population and, more specifically, the white middle-class *male* population. As women became more numerous in the workplace, however, research about women as philanthropists also became more prevalent. Now, especially as some regions of the United States are seeing that the white "majority" population has in fact become a minority group, there is growing interest in understanding the nuances about the giving interests and habits of the new majority populations—primarily Hispanics, African Americans, and Asian Americans.

Generally speaking, members of these minority groups have also been generous in sharing their financial resources with needy causes. However, the types of causes they support and the asking methods they respond to are very different from those revealed in the research on white males. More than the larger population, members of these subgroups need to find personal connections to the causes that they support or have a personal relationship with the individual doing the asking. Often the "cause" is really a relative or a friend who needs assistance rather than an organization serving a broader societal need; thus the giving done by individuals in these cultural groups is generally more informal and personal than "institutional." Family, the church, and education are the connections and interests that have the broadest appeal, according to the W. K. Kellogg Foundation (Dennis, 1999).

Because of the size of these population groups and their overall buying power, nonprofit organizations cannot afford to ignore them just because they don't respond in the "traditional" way to requests for support. Successful nonprofits spend the time to find personal connections between themselves and these growing communities in order to issue appropriate invitations for involvement—generally using face-to-face and peer-to-peer methods rather than direct mail or telephone. The results are worth the effort.

In 1985, for example, the United Way of Central Indiana began an effort to involve more African Americans as both volunteers and donors in supporting the work of its member agencies. By bringing together some key African American community members to assess, plan, and help implement a strategy to accomplish this goal, the United Way was successful in raising a significant number of new leadership-level ($1,000 to $2,500) annual gifts. In its first year, this new strategy yielded only six new donors; by 2001, the annual giving effort had grown to involve more than 250 African American leadership-level gifts.

New Donors

In the late 1990s, as entrepreneurial activity, particularly in the information technology sector of the economy, reached new heights, a new type of philanthropic giving emerged. Participants call this new method "venture philanthropy" or "high-engagement philanthropy" and describe it as a way of looking at donations as an investment rather than as just a gift. Venture philanthropists see themselves as long-term strategic partners in building community well-being or creating social change by linking long-term grantmaking with noncash assistance. But like venture capitalists in the for-profit sector, they have performance expectations of the nonprofits that they choose to partner with. In *Venture Philanthropy, 2001: The Changing Landscape,* Mario Morino (2001) of the nonprofit Morino Institute describes venture philanthropists as helping to strengthen the nonprofit organizations in which they invest by

- Addressing organizational issues
- Helping attract and retain key management and board members
- Assisting in the development of product and distribution channels
- Helping leverage partnerships through their strategic relationships with other organizations and with other organizations in which they have invested
- Creating and executing development and expansion strategies
- Developing financial plans, improving fund development, helping establish new revenue sources, and creating syndicated funding by bringing together other venture philanthropy investors and foundations
- Helping management leverage strategic benefits, ranging from management development to technology applications, to strengthen the organization and magnify its effectiveness
- Providing access to industry and subject matter experts and knowledgeable advisers

Venture philanthropy funds numbered about fifty in 2002, investing in eighteen states as well as nations in Europe, Asia, and South America, according to the Morino Institute. In addition, many other individuals have chosen to become involved in high-engagement philanthropy outside of the structure of a venture fund. Whether part of an established fund or operating as an independent investor, venture philanthropists face a similar challenge: how to measure the success of their investments. Unfortunately, there is little agreement about how to evaluate success. Instead, most funds or investors work with their nonprofit partners to establish individualized metrics—and often make future funding of the organization contingent on its ability to meet those standards.

Even though this form of giving by individuals is relatively new, it follows the same principles of individual giving explored in this chapter. Linkage, ability, and especially interest are the key indicators of prospective matches between an organization and a venture philanthropy donor. If anything, the nature of the ongoing relationship between the two is stronger than most organizations usually seek to forge with constituents.

New Vehicles for Giving

Finally, individuals are using a variety of new methods for practicing philanthropy other than making gifts directly to organizations. These range from establishing new foundations to employing donor-designated or donor-advised funds to carry out philanthropy.

Community foundations and Jewish federations have historically offered a variety of vehicles for individual philanthropy, including donor-advised funds. As community foundation assets grew during the 1990s, the number of new donors establishing these types of funds also grew.

In 1992, Fidelity Investments established a donor-advised fund to help individuals tie their philanthropic activities in to their financial planning. Fidelity offered current and new customers the opportunity to create a personal giving fund with a minimum gift of $10,000. Fidelity also helped educate its customers by offering information about how to determine which causes they cared about in order to develop a personal giving strategy and how to research potential grantees organizations that address these causes. Other investment firms and banks and nonprofit organizations have created donor adviser funds and charitable gift foundations as well.

Bypassing these types of funds, whether offered by community foundations or financial services companies, has also become popular as thousands of wealthy individuals and families have chosen to create their own private foundations instead. The Foundation Center (2001) estimates that the number of grantmaking foundations stands at fifty-six thousand at the turn of the twenty-first century. Most of these new foundations were created by individuals or families to channel their personal philanthropy to the nonprofit causes they care about. With this growth, there has also been an explosion in the number of advisers who help these wealthy individuals think through their personal interests and then establish guidelines and procedures to help potential grant recipients apply for funds. Thus finding connections not only to potential donors but also to their advisers is increasingly important for nonprofit organizations.

CONCLUSION

Individuals will remain the greatest source of funds to nonprofit organizations as long as organizations remember that fund raising is really about making personal connections with people. Generational attitudes, demographic changes, and the emergence of new giving vehicles such as venture philanthropy or charitable gifts funds offered by financial services companies may challenge nonprofits to ensure that they are continuing to connect effectively to new groups of individual donors who have diverse interests. However, the basic principles of individual gift fund raising have not changed. Identifying all of the organization's potential constituent groups—including demographic groups who may not have been traditionally included in the organization's thinking and planning—and then researching their linkages to the organization, their ability to give, and their interest in the organization's work remain the keystones of inviting individual philanthropy. In addition, the emerging trends validate the strengths of peer-to-peer, face-to-face solicitation as the most effective means of asking for individual philanthropic gifts. As nonprofits seek to expand their donor bases, they must continually study the external environment in order to understand how these principles can be applied most effectively given changing conditions in the philanthropic landscape.

CHAPTER FOURTEEN

Corporate Giving and Fund Raising

Dwight F. Burlingame

Business support of private action for the public good has been for a long time an integral part of the philosophical reason for why corporations have supported nonprofit organizations as a way to increase the quality of the environment for business. The rationale of "the healthier the community, the more business one will be able to conduct" is often cited as a reason for corporate giving. In addition, in America, the ability to establish a company or corporation is given by the state; therefore, the company has an ultimate responsibility to provide for the social well-being of citizens as it goes about conducting its business.

In the twenty-first century, companies and nonprofits will be concerned with several major issues as they seek to articulate their relationships. Among them will be a concentrated focus on ways of interaction that benefit both the company and the nonprofit. Gifts to nonprofits from corporations will need to prove their value to the company. Will the current United States philanthropic model be replicated in other parts of the world? How will international giving be most effective? These two questions will be high on the list of issues for U.S.-based companies as well as non-U.S. companies operating globally. Small companies will continue to prove to be a challenge for nonprofits to articulate benefits to local owners. Whether large or small nonprofit, whether large or small company, asking how the relationship benefits each party will continue to dominate the corporate-nonprofit relationship. Within this environment, the imperative echoed by Hank Rosso years ago is especially cogent to the corporate-nonprofit gift relationship. "In accepting the gift, it is incumbent upon the organization to return a value to the donor in a form other than material" (1991a, p. 6).

HISTORY

In practice, corporate support of charitable nonprofits is a twentieth-century invention. Most historians point to the support of the YMCA by the railroads in the late nineteenth and early twentieth centuries as a way to provide "safe" housing for workers as the beginning of corporate philanthropy. Of course, an enlightened self-interest was clearly at work in the beginning as it is in most of today's corporate giving. In fact, many of the ways that corporations provide for support of nonprofits today can be more clearly characterized as self-interest rather than interest for others or for the public good. This realization is an important one for anyone doing fund raising work for nonprofits, for it sets the context for the corporate development program to be successful in seeking gifts and other support from the business sector.

The development of regular giving programs by companies to charitable organizations began in the United States in 1936. Hayden Smith (1997) refers to this as the modern period and chose this date because it is the first time that we had recorded figures of corporate giving on federal corporate income tax forms. Corporate giving was recorded at about $30 million in 1936 and had increased to nearly $10 billion at the beginning of the twenty-first century. According to *Giving USA* (AAFRC Trust for Philanthropy, 2002), most of the growth in corporate giving is the result of increases that took place in the last quarter of the twentieth century. Much of the increase in corporate giving can be attributed to the increase in the number of businesses in the country as well as the elimination of some legal impediments. Most important was the 1953 case of *A. P. Smith Mfg. Co.* v. *Barlow,* in which the New Jersey Supreme Court refused to overturn a decision by management of the Smith Company to make a gift to a charity. For an informative history of corporate involvement with nonprofits, see Muirhead (1999).

CORPORATE SUPPORT FOR NONPROFITS

Corporate support of nonprofits in 2001 accounted for just over $9 billion, which represented about 4.3 percent of all charitable gifts (AAFRC Trust for Philanthropy, 2002). This represented about 1.3 percent of corporate pretax income, down from 2.3 percent in 1986. Many factors have contributed to this decline, including a changing philosophy of the role of corporate giving, the executive officer's role, increased global competitiveness, and the definition of corporate giving. However, depending on the purpose of the nonprofit, the percentage of income received from corporate giving varies from nothing to close to 100 percent. Among subsectors, for example, giving from corporations varies widely. In education, 14.7 percent of gifts came from corporations, while almost nothing was given to religious organizations. Consulting the most recent issue of *Giving USA* is the best source for the most recent breakdown of corporate giving to subsectors.

Meaningful expectations of what corporate gifts might provide to the overall revenue of a nonprofit will depend mostly on the congruence of the corporate and nonprofit missions. Examples of gifts to "controversial" causes having affected particular market segments of a company have been widely disseminated. Consequently, many companies work to support causes that directly affect their client markets and are viewed to be "safe" gifts. Further, there is a somewhat tenuous relationship between the for-profit and the nonprofit because of the fundamental differences in function—private gain versus public purpose. In addition, the differences in their respective environments, one based on a social caring network and the other on business management practices, serve to add to somewhat less than complete trustfulness between the two groups.

MODELS OF CORPORATE GIVING

Understanding the company perspective on why giving is of value to it is a helpful perspective to bring to bear to the fund raising process and for soliciting companies for support. Burlingame and Young (1996) articulated four major models of why corporations give to nonprofits:

- Corporate productivity or neoclassical model
- Ethical or altruistic model
- Political (external and internal) model
- Stakeholder model

Corporate Productivity Model

This model comes out of the notion that the only way to justify shareholder profits' being spent on giving to nonprofits is that it will in some way benefit the bottom line of the company and thus increase its ability to make more money. This may be done directly by giving cash or company product or indirectly by improving company morale or worker productivity. Enlightened self-interest is the mantra of this model as long as the long-term goal is to increase profitability. The challenge for the fund raiser is to identify aspects of his or her organization that will facilitate the public image of the company, to identify projects that will increase employee morale and will help market corporate products (often through sponsorships or cause-related marketing techniques), and to research efforts that might lead to lower corporate costs for such activity.

Ethical or Altruistic Model

The classical idea of corporate philanthropy is represented by the ethical model. It is based on the idea that corporations and their executives have a social responsibility to society, and through their discretionary resources, they will partner with nonprofits in seeking solutions and meeting needs of citizens. Fund raisers will need to make the case for how their organizations meet the needs of the community and how their projects involve employees in community efforts to solve local problems, and they will need to be aware of the preferences of the leadership of the company.

Political Model

External and internal variations of the political model exist in most corporations. The external paradigm is built on the premise that corporations use giving as a means to influence and build relationships that will help limit governmental influence over them. The corporate giving program serves as an important liaison with community power centers. To be successful in operating under this model, fund raisers will want to emphasize aspects of their programs that build closer relationships between the nonprofit and the company, efforts that serve as an alternative for government provision of service, programs that minimize the need for government intervention, and programs that serve to enhance the public image of the company.

The internal paradigm is predicated on the idea that the corporate giving officer is a player in a larger corporate game in which his or her worth to the company is based on what power and benefit giving can provide to the respective company unit. Corporate giving officers must demonstrate how their work helps the personnel, marketing and sales, research, and public relations departments. Giving that is consistent with this model includes employee volunteer plans because they improve employee moral, research grants to nonprofits that facilitate short- and long-term products and goals, and corporate sponsorship and cause-related types of activities. The fund raiser will want to consider various departments of the company as potential sources for support—be it gift or other income arrangements. Being able to provide evidence of how the nonprofit can facilitate the multiple goals of the corporation will be imperative.

Stakeholder Model

Stakeholder theory is based on the premise that the modern company must respond to multiple groups that have an interest in what the company does— and not just focus on the shareholders as the primary stakeholders. Employees, customers, suppliers, community groups, and governmental regulators compete for the attention of the management of the company. Consequently, to have an effective corporate giving program, the corporation must respond to the various stakeholders. Fund raisers will want to identify aspects of their programs that can meet the need for volunteer projects, employee benefits that nonprofits can provide, and other activities that benefit consumers of company products.

In many ways, the stakeholder model emphasizes the idea that all the models may be in operation at a company in any particular time. In the current global context, the political environment is more complex, and stakeholder groups are more diverse. In part because of these changes, there is even greater pressure to show a better bottom line. Fund raisers for nonprofits need to give due consideration to these models as they interact with companies to provide support for their organizations.

APPROACHING THE CORPORATION FOR SUPPORT

The four models provide a context for nonprofit managers and fund raisers to understand why a company gives. Whether it is for marketing purposes, supporting community infrastructure so that business can succeed (commonly referred to as enlightened self-interest), influencing government and public policy leaders, social investment, or simply "doing good while doing well," it is also important to remember that there are arguments against corporate giving to charitable causes. A philosophical perspective that argues that the business of business is business and not giving shareholder profits away is often heard. Many businesses are unfamiliar with industry giving practices and the time required to make effective grants. Such observations suggest that nonprofits and their fund raisers must continue to educate business leaders about the advantages of corporate giving, whether it is in the form of donations of time, cash, other assets, in-kind support, or more direct relationships such as sponsorships and cause-related activities. Curt Weeden (1998) provides an effective and comprehensive argument for why and how corporations do social investing.

HOW CORPORATIONS GIVE

The most commonly sought gift from a corporation or its foundation is cash for special and new projects and for capital campaigns. Corporations are less likely to give to operating support, but there are notable exceptions. Still prevalent are requests for cash to support a special event, such as a table at a recognition event or sponsorship of a race.

Matching gifts for employee contributions are also common.

In-kind contributions may be the largest form of support by companies for nonprofits. The most common form of in-kind contributions are company products and employee time. In many communities, executive loan programs are available.

Sponsorships and cause-related marketing income for nonprofits have increased rapidly, primarily because they provide a vehicle for the company to expand its marketing efforts through mutually beneficial agreements with nonprofits.

Reasearch and development support from companies provide income for a few nonprofits, especially those in education and health. Care needs to be taken in order to ensure that contractual understandings are made clear to both parties.

RESEARCHING POTENTIAL BUSINESS SUPPORT

Linkage, ability, and interest are important in any fund raising effort, as Hank Rosso and The Fund Raising School have so aptly taught. In corporate gifts, linkage is paramount. The importance of operating in the same territory as the company is especially important. Companies work under the premise that they need to help the social infrastructure of the communities in which they operate in order to have a stable environment for good business.

There are many research sources to use in identifying potential contributors. The Foundation Center and the Taft Company publish the most frequently used directories of potential companies from which to seek gifts. In addition, regional and local information can be found at public and research libraries as well as local donor forums. Valuable information for your listings can also be obtained from business journals and newspapers, shareholder reports, professional publications, public recognition reports, personal communications, Chamber of Commerce directories and service clubs, and Internet database sources.

The best way to obtain support from the business community is to have built good relations with your neighbors. Maintaining a simple file of potential supporters with notes about the companies, who the leaders and middle managers are, along with their contact information, annual reports or social responsibility reports, press clippings, and other relevant facts will go a long way toward building a potential corporation donor file that can serve the nonprofit. Corporate giving guidelines are also an important part of this file. Ongoing updates reflecting new businesses that have moved into the area, which corporations have expanded or downsized in the last year, and which corporations are making grants in the same area in which your organization works are important components to be included.

Reviewing your organizational demographics is also an important part of doing corporate research. Knowing which of your donors represent or work at corporations is a must. Periodically review all of your corporate and corporate foundation donations, not only for stewardship purposes, but also with an eye toward who should be on your donor list that isn't. Knowing the form that the company's donations were in is also important. Understanding your organization's mission and how it might be congruent with a potential company donor is an important result of the research effort.

CULTIVATION

Fostering corporate relations is an ongoing process. With a focus on mission and a strategic plan to guide the cultivation, a successful and ongoing relationship can be built between the nonprofit and the company. This relationship is often built on various levels, from initial introductions, committee and board service, and volunteer participation in delivering service to clients to financial commitments. Involvement in special events and site visits and reading about the organization in annual reports and newsletters all are part of making the company representatives an integral part of what your organization does.

Solicitation is the actual process of asking for support for various programs and projects. Cultivation should always precede solicitation. The ideal form of solicitation for most corporate involvement is a person-to-person request. Often the proposal will not be acted on at the time of the request, since many corporations make awards at committee or board meetings. The request will be most successful if there has been personal contact prior to discussing the project for support. Involvement of volunteers will increase the potential for success. Effective volunteer participation presupposes that the volunteer will have been briefed on the specific proposal and is therefore able to articulate the needs of the nonprofit. Volunteers can provide assistance in opening doors, endorsing proposals, making corporate or personal gifts, signing thank-you letters, and participating in other recognition activities.

After a meeting or verbal contact, completing a contact report is crucial. This document should indicate the essence of the contact and serve as a record of the information shared and commitments made for future action. Include only essential information, in such a way that you would not be embarrassed if the potential donor were to read the contact report.

Follow-up phone calls, personal visits, and correspondence all contribute to a successful solicitation. Once an organization secures funding for a project, continued contact is important in maintaining a relationship that will extend to the longer term. The old rule of saying thank you at least seven times is as true with corporate givers as it is with individual donors. In addition to the thank-you letter for support, thanks can be expressed by forwarding press clippings of the announcement of the gift, by recognition at committee or board meetings, by a telephone call, by personal visits, by announcements in newsletters, by acknowledgment in donor clubs or other recognition activities, and by reports on progress and activity made possible by the company gift. And of course thanks can be given as a preface for the next request for continued support.

DEALING WITH REJECTION

Rejection of a proposal should never be taken as the final word in your efforts to build a relationship with a company. Many fund raisers would argue that it is only a matter of time until your organization and the potential donor company find an opportunity for funding. Rejection of a particular proposal should always be followed up with a cultivation note of thanks for considering the proposal. Call to arrange for a follow-up meeting with a company representative to determine what caused the proposal to fail, how it might be improved, what kind of proposal the company might consider, and what the nonprofit should do to increase its chances for success. Also, after an initial rejection, the company may be able to suggest other potential partners who might welcome the proposal.

If the company is not in a position to make a cash gift at a particular time, opportunities for sharing of volunteer support, in-kind products, or other non-cash support should be explored, with the goal of keeping corporate representatives up-to-date on the mission of the nonprofit and its progress in meeting stated goals. In essence, rejection can be taken as an opportunity to review your overall corporate giving program. How many company gifts did you receive in the past year, and from whom? What levels of support do you have? Do you have opportunities for further logo or name recognition? What industry groups are missing on your organization's donor lists? These and other questions will suggest ways that you might also use certain gifts for leveraging other giving. Bringing other partners into your family of donors is not only a benefit for diversifying your funding base and thus increasing the chances of program success; it is also a perceived good to corporate supporters to have multiple investors to share risk and to demonstrate the potential for success.

SPONSORSHIP, BRANDING, AND CAUSE MARKETING

Toward the end of the twentieth century, significant increases of funds to non-profits from corporations came in the form of sponsorships and cause-related marketing projects. As noted by Burlingame (2001), cause-related marketing is defined as a company's providing dollars to a nonprofit in direct proportion to the quantity of a product or service purchased by consumers during a particular period of time. Continuing the period of time from a short-term to a longer-term relationship between the company and the nonprofit is generally referred to as "cause branding."

Sponsorship, by contrast, is not directly tied to consumers' purchasing behavior. However, it does represent company investments, of cash or in kind, in return for access to a particular activity, event, or cause represented by a nonprofit. Such activity is not gift giving in the true sense but rather an investment by a company in a nonprofit with an expected return.

Cause-related marketing grew from about $450 million in 1984 to close to $10 billion in 2000 (Cone/Roper, 1999). Cone, Inc., in Boston is one of the best sources for information on the size and scope of cause-related marketing and branding. It is important for the professional fund raiser to be aware of this activity and to be involved with decisions about nonprofit and corporate ventures. Both parties need to be beneficiaries, and therefore clear understandings need to be worked out between them.

Opportunities

Companies engage in sponsorship and branding relationships with nonprofits for a variety of reasons:

- To create greater public trust in the company
- To enhance the company's image or reputation
- To build "brand awareness"
- To create goodwill now and for the future
- To increase profits for the company
- To attract investors
- To increase employee morale and attract and retain employees
- To provide a competitive advantage

Nonprofits, for their part, engage in such partnerships for different reasons:

- To gain more revenue
- To obtain in-kind services or resources
- To diversify income streams
- To facilitate greater capacity to provide a service
- To enhance the organization's reputation
- To increase public recognition and build greater community awareness of the cause
- To attract more volunteers and donors

Research has shown that companies that engage in sponsorship, cause-related marketing, and branding do increase sales and improve employee morale while enhancing the image of the company (Cone/Roper, 1999). Thus it is important for fund raisers to be aware of these findings as they negotiate programs with companies.

Challenges

Most of the disadvantages associated with cause-related marketing, sponsorships, and branding rest with the nonprofit and the negative reactions such activities may cause in some donors because of their view of the company. In addition, the commercial nature of the activity may decrease trust in the nonprofit among the public. Further, donors or potential donors to the nonprofit may think they have already contributed their fair share by participating in the cause-related marketing activity and thereby cause a decrease in gift income. The potential for gifts from other companies in the same industry group may also decrease if those companies feel that they have been "co-opted" by the corporate partner.

Companies may find such arrangements problematic because achieving the financial expectations from the effort can prove difficult. The effort may require more time, more accounting procedures, and more patience than the partners anticipated. Cultural clashes may develop, only to increase with company turnover, mergers, and other changes in the business environment. These issues argue for a considered arrangement, approved by the nonprofit board, that is reevaluated regularly with an eye toward continuous improvement and with a clearly understood exit strategy.

CONCLUSION

Corporate giving has gone full circle; once part of direct business activity, it turned more toward public good purposes before returning to being mainly business-driven. Craig Smith (1994), in his seminal article in the *Harvard Business Review,* noted that the practice today is for companies to invest in partnerships with nonprofits that will advance their business interest at the same time that it positively effects social change.

The issues for the twenty-first century in corporate giving and fund raising will be focused in three areas:

- How corporate support assists in legitimizing other fund raising efforts of the nonprofit.

- Industry development as the dominant model of corporate giving. This will be particularly true for global companies as they seek way to use their giving to continue to be successful in foreign environments.

- How corporate giving can assist other units of the company in meeting their goals as the company seeks to be a good corporate citizen.

An exciting opportunity for fund raisers exists as they go about articulating their organizational mission to potential corporate funders and partners. Making the right match will continue to be the challenge for both the company and the nonprofit. Moving companies into the inner core of the nonprofit constituency circle will continue to be important for nonprofit organizations.

CHAPTER FIFTEEN

FOUNDATION FUND RAISING

Gwendolyn Perry

A s reported in Chapter Two, Hank Rosso's philosophy on fund raising states the process is at its best when it strives to match the needs of the nonprofit organization with a contributor's need and desire to give. This match applies especially to foundations as a source of philanthropy.

Foundations as a source of funds require particular study and approach. They operate as structures that provide opportunities for a donor to give and for nonprofit organizations to receive. They are usually governed by strict guidelines regarding the scope and deductibility of contributions they receive and the distribution of their funds to nonprofit organizations.

The case for support is particularly important in approaching foundations for contributions. Hank's philosophy of fund raising focuses us on the relationship between a foundation and a nonprofit, built on a mutual desire or interest in improving a civic or public good. Nonprofit organizations are the mechanisms through which most foundations carry out their public responsibilities.

DEFINING THE FOUNDATION

A *foundation,* as defined in the *NSFRE Fund-Raising Dictionary* (Levy, 1996), is an organization created with designated funds from which the income is distributed as grants to not-for-profit organizations or, in some cases, to people.

During the past decade, foundation assets (commonly referred to as endowments) and distributions from those assets have made significant headlines, with several foundations passing the $10 billion level in endowments and some providing single distributions in excess of $100 million, according to annual reports compiled by the Foundation Center (2001). Simultaneously, the number of foundations has grown exponentially, to more than fifty-six thousand by 2002 (AAFRC Trust for Philanthropy, 2002). Foundations provide a significant amount of support for the nonprofit sector, second only to individual support, and exceeding 12 percent of the actual dollars of charitable giving (AAFRC Trust for Philanthropy, 2002).

Foundations are often attractive to nonprofit organizations as a funding source because they have clear, printed guidelines for the disbursement of funds and have the potential to provide significant monetary support for a program or operations. To gain the most benefit from requests to foundations, it is important to understand the different types of foundations and the distinct characteristics of each type.

Keep in mind, too, that proposal writing and grant seeking are enterprises with dissimilar results. A program of solitary proposal writing will not necessarily provide funding support for an organization. Developing a culture that encourages appropriate relationships with foundation staff and investments in a foundation relations program will help establish systematic and measurable goals for foundation support in a fully developed fund raising program.

This chapter will serve as a guide to developing a foundation relationship program, including a review of current foundation trends and basic foundation fund raising strategies.

TYPES OF FOUNDATIONS

There are four basic types of foundations: independent, corporate, community, and operating.

Independent Foundations

As defined by the Internal Revenue Service (IRS), independent foundations are private foundations established to provide support or distributions to tax-exempt organizations through grants. Assets of independent foundations are usually established through gifts from individuals or families and often carry the names of the original funders.

During the years of wealth creation in the late 1990s, the expression "family foundation" has become common to describe an independent foundation with noteworthy involvement and decision making by living family members, both immediate and extended. The size and administration of independent foundations vary widely.

Large, well-established independent foundations generally have a full-time staff, often in proportion to the size of assets. Smaller foundations may have only one full-time person dedicated to daily operations; family foundations may include family members as needed. Independent foundations often define specific areas of interest for funding or limit grants to a specific geographical area. Examples of large independent foundations include the Ford Foundation, the W. K. Kellogg Foundation, and the Lilly Endowment.

Corporate Foundations

Another type of private foundation, the corporate foundation generally receives its assets from an associated for-profit company or business and often serves as a grantmaking vehicle for the company. Its mission and funding interests will often mirror the business interests of the company. A corporate foundation may work in concert with any other corporate giving program and often has a separate board of directors, usually composed of employees and individuals related to the company. More detailed information about approaching corporations is included in Chapter Fourteen.

As a funding source, giving by corporate foundations has changed substantially in the past decade. Most corporate foundation giving reflects the company's products and consumers' interests, both current and potential, and decisions from corporate foundations are directly influenced by employee involvement and interest in the nonprofit organizations seeking support. The management of corporate foundations differs from one to the next. Many corporate foundations have an individual dedicated to receiving, processing, and administering proposals and grants. Others may combine foundation responsibilities with employee duties. The ExxonMobil Foundation and the SBC Communications Foundation are examples of corporate foundations.

Community Foundations

Community foundations continue to grow rapidly as a segment of the foundation world, with assets growing at twice the rate of independent or corporate foundations. Unlike other foundation structures, community foundations generally both receive gifts and make grants through special IRS provisions. As public charities, they must receive assets from a large pool of donors and consequently fund a wide range of community needs. By definition, most community foundations limit their interests and grants to a particular geographical area.

The rapid increase of community foundation assets is attributed to several factors, including the rise in asset values for individual donors and the seeding and incubation of small donor-advised funds. The sharing of costs, reduction in administrative duties, enhanced return on well-managed investments, and ability to remain involved with grants attract donors to advised funds at community foundations.

Community foundations generally have unrestricted funds, donor-advised funds, and donor-designated funds. With a donor-advised fund, a donor retains the right to make suggestions to the community foundation as to which qualified 501(c)(3) organizations or causes should receive grant money from this fund. A donor-designated fund allows the donor to select the specific nonprofit organizations or causes that will receive grants based on the fund's income. Both funds are established with a permanent gift to the community foundation and allow the donor an immediate tax deduction under IRS rules. The community foundation usually specifies that the gift be combined and managed with other foundation investments.

Many community foundations consider a primary mission to support communitywide initiatives and develop unrestricted funds for this purpose. Some community foundations are experimenting with a staff system that reduces general unrestricted grants and works specifically with donor advisers and endowed funds to create a communitywide funding system.

Operating Foundations

Operating foundations seldom make grants to other nonprofit organizations. Because they are dedicated to conducting research and promoting programs to support the work of the original charter or governing body, the IRS mandates that they spend at least 85 percent of their income in support of their own programs. Although operating foundations are not usually a source of cash grants, they are often a source of useful publications and information for nonprofits engaged in complementary research, work, and programs. In addition, operating foundations often serve as conveners in a particular body of knowledge and may provide nonprofits with opportunities for engagement with other practitioners and experts.

TYPES OF SUPPORT

Foundations commonly provide five types of support: operational or unrestricted, program, capital, pilot, and challenge or matching. Operational or unrestricted grants are made to support the ongoing operations of a nonprofit with no conditions for their use. Program grants support a specific set of activities and plans. Capital grants generally provide support for building construction funds, large equipment purchases, and endowment growth. Pilot grants award start-up funding for new programs at a nonprofit organization for a limited period of time. Challenge or matching grants support an effort to encourage philanthropic giving in a constituent segment.

As a potential funding source, foundations have several unique features, including a requirement for independent foundations to distribute a minimum percentage of their endowment through grants to qualified 501(c)(3) organizations. There are a number of excellent resources on the current scope and size of the foundation sector. The Foundation Center, publisher of the *Foundation Directory,* and its Web site (www.foundationcenter.org) provide reports and ongoing research. The Council on Foundations a membership organization for foundations, and its Web site (www.cof.org), provide resources and publications on a range of topics from starting a foundation to measuring and evaluating programs supported by foundation grants.

GROWTH OF FOUNDATIONS IN THE UNITED STATES

In addition to the numbers of foundations and their grants, other statistics on the foundation field are impressive. In particular, the growth of independent and community foundation assets between 1995 and 1999 eclipsed any previous period of growth. Many factors are believed to support the increase: impressive gains in the U.S. stock markets, increased gifts to all foundation types, and the rise of megafoundations in the western portion of the United States. Traditionally, large foundations have been located in the East and Midwest, largely a result of the individual fortunes that established them during the Industrial Age. The gains in information technology, based largely in the West, helped fuel this geographical shift.

Since 1990, nationwide, more than 33 percent of all large foundations have been established, tripling the rate of growth in the 1950s, when foundations experienced an 11 percent increase in number, according to the Foundation Center (2001). The average age of donors also decreased during the same period as many younger foundation donors sought to take advantage of tax incentives and establish a history of giving for their young families.

Growth in giving was more modest in corporate foundation grants. The slower growth of corporate foundations was influenced in part by modest transfers of cash and assets to foundation programs.

TRENDS IN FOUNDATION SUPPORT

Foundations are defining more clearly their interests and expectations of grantee organizations. They are also requiring more extensive evaluation of funded programs and organizations. Foundations continue to learn from past grants and use this information to make better and more effective grants for the future. Collaboration among foundations is on the rise, as is the trend of supporting organizations that communicate and work together. Foundations are also emphasizing effective governance and management of organizations in making grant decisions of any type.

In conjunction with the growth of foundation assets, professional staffing has increased. Joslyn (2001) indicates that full- and part-time staff had grown to more than seventeen thousand by the turn of the twenty-first century. Several trends have emerged as new directions for foundation support. We shall examine six of these.

Evaluation

Emphasis on evaluation of grantees and foundation activities is increasingly visible. The literature on nonprofits indicates that early attempts at evaluation by foundations served two purposes: checking for accountability to grant financial policies and expediting grantee renewal decisions. Foundations continue to evaluate grants using these criteria, but the scope of evaluation has changed and grown to help foundations gauge the success of a programmatic field of interest and to help shape future grants. In many foundations, these learning opportunities affect future grant recipients by focusing on particular segments of a program and providing helpful advice about past success and disappointments.

Foundations are also encouraging grantees to implement an evaluation plan during the preparation and planning of a foundation request. For foundation grant recipients, more extensive postgrant evaluation, often by external evaluators, may be required at the conclusion of a program. An objective review of the progress of a particular grant and program is intended to help organizations focus on program results and impacts.

Collaboration

Collaboration is a mutually beneficial and well-defined relationship entered into by two or more organizations to achieve common goals. This relationship includes a commitment to a definition of mutual relationships authority; accountability for success; and a sharing of resources and rewards. In an attempt to avoid replication of services and funding of programs, foundations and their grantees are participating in more collaborative efforts than ever before. Foundations are also interested in seeing stronger and more inclusive programs based on the expertise and client bases of cooperative organizations. For the grantee organizations, the potential for more substantial financial support and the power of a larger group working on an identified need can have a substantial impact on a community problem.

Professionalization of Grant Application and Distribution Processes

More foundations are carefully defining their policies and procedures about distribution of funds. In an effort to fund appropriate projects and reduce the time nonprofits spend preparing proposals outside foundations' interests, many foundations now clearly explain their areas of interest, application procedures, distribution plans, and timelines. In addition, foundations now seek evidence that a nonprofit operates with effective board governance and competent staff management, a long-term fiscal and program plan, and a mission related to social needs about which the foundation is concerned.

Charitable Gift Funds at Financial Service Firms

During the late 1990s, charitable gift funds at for-profit financial services firms experienced an incremental rise in managed assets. The *Chronicle of Philanthropy* reported that by 2000, the assets of the top three funds had surpassed the assets of the top eleven public charities (Larose, 2002, p. 11). The premise of these gift funds, such as the Fidelity Gift Fund and the Vanguard Charitable Endowment Program, is to allow donors to make irrevocable gifts to the fund and recommendations on the future distribution of those funds. For the donor, the advantages are an immediate tax reduction, the opportunity for the corpus of the fund to increase in value with the help of professional money managers, and the ability to remain anonymous with potential grantees. In the nonprofit community, concern is expressed over the fee structure of the funds and the control given to financial services professionals rather than community and nonprofit experts. Nevertheless, according to the *Chronicle of Philanthropy*, at the end of 2000, for example, the assets of the Fidelity Gift Fund exceeded $2 billion (Larose, 2002, p. 11). It will be important to watch the continued growth in these funds and the future impact of their funding decisions on the nonprofit community and whether these foundations offer new opportunities and challenges.

Emphasis on Diversity in Board Governance

According to the U.S. Census Bureau, only half of the nation's population is expected to be non-Hispanic white by the year 2025. Increasingly, foundations expect this diversity to be mirrored in the leadership of nonprofit institutions in the United States.

Increasingly, foundations are requesting that nonprofit boards of directors reflect the diversity of the communities and populations they serve. Some foundations require that nonprofits actively recruit in a way that encourages diversity, and some ask for evidence of board diversity composition. Simultaneously, the boards of community and private foundations are maturing and changing with the population shift.

Capacity Building

Campobasso and Davis, in *Reflections on Capacity-Building* (2001), define capacity building as the development of an organization's core skills and capabilities, such as leadership, management, finance and fund raising, programs, and evaluation, in order to build the organization's effectiveness and sustainability. It is the process of assisting a group to identify and address issues and gain the insights, knowledge, and experience needed to solve problems and implement change. Capacity building is facilitated through the provision of technical support activities, including coaching, training, operational assistance, and resource networking. As with any idea in its organizational infancy, capacity building is still broadly defined and working through several shifts in approach and application. Many foundation programs have begun to develop a focus on building internal and external resources to support nonprofit programs. Programs like the Organizational Impact Program at the David and Lucile Packard Foundation have devoted important resources to define and develop capacity building as an interest area.

BEFORE APPROACHING A FOUNDATION

Foundations are interested in funding nonprofits with diverse financial sources. It is important to consider a foundation grant one part of a fully diversified development plan. Support from clients, friends, and community members is an important tool in demonstrating a clear mission, broad community support, and a solution-focused organization.

Preparation is key in submitting foundation requests, and the first step is researching the foundation to determine any linkages and interest. The specific strategies described here are general rules. Adaptations may be necessary, depending on the culture of the organization and foundation.

Careful attention to the following advice will not always result in a foundation grant. Foundations are approachable because of their clear guidelines and structured timelines, but foundation fund raising is similar to all fund raising in that the most successful partnerships are built on trusted relationships established over time.

A nonprofit with clearly established priorities from its governing board and executive staff will have fewer difficulties in determining appropriate foundations to contact than organizations without clear operational mandates and strategic plans in place.

MAKING A REQUEST

As with all fund raising, the written request or proposal is the final result of intensive and thorough preparation. In foundation fund raising, it includes a review of the requesting organization's mission, identified needs, and the foundation's preferred interests. The Fund Raising School (2002) suggests using Hank's LAI (linkage, ability, interest) principle in qualifying your foundation prospects. Using this principle, ask three sets of questions about each prospect:

1. Does the foundation have any previous relationship with my organization? Does my organization have any friends, staff, or constituents with connections or influence at the foundation? Determine any linkages that exist or should exist before approaching the foundation.

2. Does the foundation have the assets and make grants of the size necessary for my program? Review current and past grant information to determine typical gift size.

3. Does the foundation have any interest in funding the type of program my organization is proposing? Has the foundation funded in this grant area previously? Review guidelines and funding interests.

Several tools exist to help nonprofit organizations find information on foundations. Many nonprofit and for-profit companies produce annual compilations of foundation information for a fee, but some of the best resources cost little or no money. Because the IRS governs foundations, each year they must make a Form 990-PF (commonly referred to as a 990 or Form 990) available to the public.

Although this form has always been available to the public, in 1998 the IRS made obtaining the form easier and less time-consuming. Many foundations now produce the Form 990 on their Web sites for immediate viewing as an Acrobat Reader file (*.pdf file). The Form 990 provides basic information, including board of directors, total grant amount distributed, grant recipients, and awards. Many independent, corporate, and community foundations publish an annual report, listing much of the same information and providing more detailed descriptions of their support.

Foundation guidelines are an important piece of information to determine the suitability between a foundation and a potential program. Guidelines establish the current interests of the foundation, usually by program type or geographical area; give specific procedures for preparing a grant proposal; provide typical funding parameters; and define deadlines for submitting a grant request. After reviewing the selected foundation information, carefully check the application for submission instructions and formatting.

Only after completing the preliminary research is the nonprofit ready to begin an initial conversation with a foundation. The next step is, preferably, an initial phone call to the prospective foundation to discuss the proposed program or project and the likelihood of funding in the current operational year. Nonprofits may also discover more specific information about a particular foundation's operations and interests. This initial conversation with a foundation representative does not ensure that a proposal will be funded, but it provides more information for the nonprofit organization in preparing a request.

Some foundations do not accept unsolicited phone calls. In these instances, it is useful for the nonprofit to prepare a brief letter of inquiry to the foundation, indicating the parameters of the program and how the program will benefit the larger community. Unless specifically requested, do not include any budget numbers in the initial inquiry and focus instead on the proposed project.

THE PROPOSAL

If an initial inquiry letter or phone call has been positively received and the
tinuation of the funding discussion,
package. The details of the package
ished guidelines of the foundation.
ain the following items:

:ontact information

al should articulate the identified need
se to solve the problem.
ge, provide a copy for your organiza-
fore submission to the foundation. The
he cover sheet mentioned earlier) to
al.

JNDATION

proposal will likely follow an internal
process is often published in the foun-
posal is received and recorded in a cen-
tral processing area. It is then reviewed to ensure that all necessary materials
are included and that it generally fits within the foundation's guidelines. In
small foundations, a single person often completes both tasks. Large foundations may have these steps completed separately.

A program staff person will review your proposal to determine its applicability to foundation priorities. If this review is successful, you may be contacted for further information or to arrange a site visit. Remember that the grant officer with whom you interacted now becomes your advocate. A site visit, or program visit, is an opportunity for foundation staff to get a better grasp of your project and its proposed outcomes. It is also an opportunity for the nonprofit to articulate ideas, connections, and impacts that could not be included in the original proposal. While it is important to prepare for the site visit, the nonprofit should not attempt to orchestrate or manipulate staff, participants, or outcomes.

THE GRANT DECISION

If the organization has successfully received a grant from a foundation, the opportunity for an extended foundation relationship begins. Provide immediate and appropriate thanks and recognition to the foundation. Depending on the length of a program, the nonprofit may be required to submit intermediate reports, or the foundation may contact the nonprofit several times for updates on progress. Continue to remain in contact with the foundation. The program's success is important to the foundation, and its staff will provide support and guidance throughout the program's duration.

At a minimum, a nonprofit will be required to provide a postgrant evaluation at the conclusion of the program period. The level of evaluation proposed at the outset of the project will also determine the level of contact and reporting to the foundation. In addition, the relationship developed may provide future funding opportunities for new programs at the organization.

A proposal denial does not preclude a relationship with the foundation. A number of factors, including timing, the current foundation portfolio, and future commitments, may influence a decision. Thank the foundation for considering your request, and accept your current denial letter. At the conclusion of the grant process, some foundations will discuss the reasons for denials and may offer advice for resubmitting a proposal.

Nonprofits should keep in mind that the number of foundation proposals submitted is not an accurate measure of foundation fund raising performance. Strong relationships and focused proposals are keys to a strong track record with foundations.

CONCLUSION

Working with foundations can be an exciting and successful process for many nonprofit organizations. Clearly defined programs and strategies of research and relationship building can lead to organized and appropriate grant propos-

als that may result in foundation support for an organization's ongoing operations and special programs. If an organization is successful in receiving foundation support, the impact of a single grant can provide greatly needed funding
to implement an important program or provide vital support for an organization. Successful foundation fund raising results from clear, specific research, a
focus on similar interests, and a dedication by both the foundation and the
nonprofit to support organization of the missions of the communities and
causes they serve.

CHAPTER SIXTEEN

Women as Donors

Andrea R. Kaminski

The Rosso model emphasizes valuing philanthropy from the donor's perspective. A successful fund raising program recognizes that the values of the donor must connect to the values of the organization. Women as philanthropists are different from men as philanthropists. This chapter is designed to assist professionals and volunteers in engaging women to become donors.

In 1992, fifty women leaders in philanthropy gathered at the Wingspread Conference Center in Racine, Wisconsin, to explore ways to inspire and empower more women as philanthropists. Sponsored by the University of Wisconsin-Madison's Center for Women and Philanthropy and the Johnson Foundation, the conference brought together women with different perspectives; the convening included development professionals, foundation trustees and staff, scholars, and philanthropists themselves. The conference produced a national agenda for advancing women's philanthropy (Thompson and Kaminski, 1993).

Most notable among the achievements has been a general recognition of the potential of women's philanthropy, in terms of dollars and impact, as well as a recognition that women have unique motivations, giving patterns, and expectations for their philanthropy. Research in the past decade indicates that women prefer to give to organizations with which they feel personally connected. Development professionals can help women fulfill their potential as philanthropists by strengthening that sense of connection through donor education and relationship building.

Women have a long tradition of voluntary giving to improve the communities in which we live. Centuries ago, religious women in Europe were creating orphanages, hospitals, and homes for the destitute. More than a century ago in the United States, Emma Willard and Mary Lyon applied their fortunes and talents to pioneer education for girls and women equal to that offered by the best schools for boys and men. Jane Addams created Hull House to meet the needs of the poor and of new immigrants in Chicago. Madam C. J. Walker, the daughter of emancipated slaves who became an influential entrepreneur and philanthropist, uplifted her gender and her race through her gifts to such organizations as the National Association for the Advancement of Colored People (NAACP), the YMCA, and the YWCA (Bundles, 2001).

Committed women who could not give large amounts of money to support education were adept at raising funds from others. For example, Spelman College was founded by Sophia B. Packard and Harriet Giles, two friends who were commissioned in 1879 by the Women's American Baptist Home Mission Society of New England to study the living conditions "among the freedmen of the South." They raised several thousand dollars from the black community, as well as from major philanthropists on the East Coast.

WHY FOCUS ON WOMEN AS PHILANTHROPISTS?

It is clear that women have long been givers. What has changed is that today, more women have more control over much more money than ever before, and more women view philanthropy as an opportunity to help shape the future of society.

Consider the facts:

- There were almost 1.6 million female top wealth holders in 1995, with a combined net worth of over $2.2 trillion. The average net worth for the group was $1.38 million, slightly higher than for male wealth holders, and the females carried less debt (Internal Revenue Service, 1999).

- In 1999, there were 9.1 million women-owned firms, employing almost 28 million people and generating over $3.6 trillion in sales (National Foundation for Women Business Owners, 1999).

- There are more than seventy women's funds across the United States, up from the "original eight" created in the 1970s (Women's Funding Network, 2001).

- A study of giving in Indiana found that men and women give equally, on average, when controlled for income and educational level (Center on Philanthropy at Indiana University, 2001).

- An estimated $41 trillion to $136 trillion will be passing from one generation to the next by 2044 (Havens and Schervish, 1999). Women tend to marry older men, and women live on average seven years longer than men. Consequently, women will be deciding what becomes of much of this wealth before it is passed down to the next generation.

WHAT DO WE KNOW ABOUT WOMEN AS PHILANTHROPISTS?

We know that women have money and that they give. But what do we know about *how* women give? What are women's motivations, fears, expectations, and giving patterns? A number of qualitative studies have examined women's giving patterns through focus groups and personal interviews with hundreds of women nationally (UCLA Foundation, 1992; Shaw and Taylor, 1995; Taylor, 1995; National Foundation for Women Business Owners, 1999). The Women's Philanthropy Institute continues to conduct focus groups with women philanthropists, including several groups in 2001 for Rutgers University and Oregon State University (Women's Philanthropy Institute, 2001a).

Other studies have produced a more quantitative measure of women's giving, as well as comparing women's giving patterns with those of men (Peter D. Hart Research Associates, 1999; National Foundation for Women Business Owners, 2000; Sterling, 2000; National Committee on Planned Giving, 2001; Marx, 2000).

These studies indicate that women have the same core motivations for giving as men do—altruism, gratitude, the desire to make a better world. However, women approach giving differently from men. This is consistent with studies that have found that there are gender differences in communication styles (Gilligan, 1993), as well as in the way men and women approach management in the workplace (National Foundation for Women Business Owners, 1994, 2001). This is a result of women's socialization in a society that has long had a double standard in its economic, social, and power structures.

THE SIX C'S OF WOMEN'S GIVING

The culture of women's giving is described by Shaw and Taylor (1995). These authors detected certain recurring themes in their discussions with women philanthropists. These philanthropic motivations are not necessarily unique to women, but they are clearly of particular importance to women. Further, the women philanthropists interviewed, personally and in focus groups, by Shaw and Taylor and the Women's Philanthropy Institute have indicated repeatedly that these issues are often overlooked in fund raising programs, which, the women say, have been developed to appeal to male donors. Shaw-Hardy (2000) summarized these recurring themes in six words beginning with the letter *C—create, change, connect, collaborate, commit,* and *celebrate*—and together they define the culture of women's philanthropy.

Create

Women often give to create a new institution, as Jane Addams, Sophia Smith, and Mary Lyon did. In other cases, women create new programs in existing institutions, like Lorene Burkhart, who endowed the Center for Families at Purdue University, which focuses research and education on the well-being of families.

Change

Women give to bring about social change. Mary Elizabeth Garrett did this in 1881 when she gave $350,000 to Johns Hopkins University to establish a medical school on the condition that the medical school open its doors to women (Fisher, 1993). In the focus groups, women often say that rather than provide general support to maintain an organization, they prefer to target their gifts to particular programs that promise to bring about change. For this reason, we recommend against trying to appeal to women donors by offering them an opportunity to "help keep the institution great."

Connect

Women often seek a sense of personal connection with the program or project they fund. Fund raisers can often fulfill this desire for a sense of connection by providing continuing information after the gift has been made. Women donors want to know how their money will be used, how the project is progressing, and how it is helping people.

This is consistent with the findings of a study by Deloitte and Touche (1998), which found that women seek to build a close working relationship with their financial advisers. The women in this study expressed a desire for ongoing guidance and information from their financial advisers, and women seek the same type of partnership with people connected with the projects they fund.

Collaborate

Women like to work together as a group—this accounts at least in part for the fact that they often don't respond to competitive fund raising appeals. The women's funds, women's giving circles, and women's philanthropy councils in higher education are examples of collaborative philanthropy. These programs usually engage in donor education and involvement, which build a sense of connection.

The high value women place on collaboration and connection is consistent with what we have learned about women's management styles in business settings (National Foundation for Women Business Owners, 1994). Women managers in general foster cooperation, consensus, and networking. That's how women do business.

Commit

Women are committed to the causes they support—they want to give not only their money but also their time. According to INDEPENDENT SECTOR (IS), volunteering is still more significant among women than men. In its 2001 national study of giving and volunteering, IS found that 46 percent of women and 42 percent of men reported that they had volunteered in the past year. And people who volunteer give more financially. IS found that giving households that volunteer gave an average of $2,295, compared to $1,009 from households that do not include a volunteer (INDEPENDENT SECTOR, 2001a). Over the six biennial national surveys INDEPENDENT SECTOR has conducted on giving and volunteering, contributing households with a volunteer gave more than twice the percentage of household income than contributing households in which the respondent did not volunteer. Even in periods of uncertain economic conditions, as in 1991 and 1993, this relationship held.

Women's commitment to volunteerism goes back to the days when all that most women had to give was their time, and so they raised money with events. Now more women are capable of making major gifts and can have more impact on the organizations they support by doing so. It is up to the development profession to help them understand and realize that potential. At the same time, it is crucial to affirm women's contributions of unpaid service and make them aware of opportunities for meaningful volunteer involvement.

Celebrate

Finally, women like to celebrate their accomplishments and have fun with philanthropy. This is also grounded in women's tradition of raising money through events. Events are still an important way to recognize the contributions of major donors and volunteers and also to have fun.

GENERATIONAL DIFFERENCES

Of course, every donor is an individual who has been shaped by unique socioeconomic and family influences. In addition to gender, there are differences based on generation, region, religion, ethnicity, and race. Individuals with inherited wealth are likely to view giving differently from those who have earned it in their adult lives. Understanding these differences can be helpful when working with donors.

It is also important to understand that these differences can be additive. For example, the issue of gender may compound generational difference. While both men and women who came of age during the Great Depression are likely to want to hold on to their savings for a rainy day, for women this fear is heightened by the fact that they may never have brought home a paycheck.

Pacesetting research by Cindy Sterling (2000), director of gift planning at Vassar College, indicates that in planned giving, women are more likely to give through bequests, while men are more likely to make life income gifts. This was backed up by a recent survey by the National Committee on Planned Giving, which found that more than half of charitable bequest donors are female (53 percent, compared to 47 percent men). Conversely, 56 percent of charitable remainder trust donors are men, compared to 44 percent women (National Committee on Planned Giving, 2001). Sterling speculates that a bequest may feel "safer" to women, who may fear outliving their resources, than an irrevocable, income-producing gift.

Women of this generation may feel that "my husband earned that money." As widows, they may believe their responsibility is to safeguard the family money, spend as little of it as possible, and then pass it on to their children. Or they may believe the money should be given, out of a sense of loyalty, to the causes and institutions that the husband supported. Mature women often defer to male financial advisers or family members in their financial and philanthropic decisions.

Women in this generation have often devoted a life of unpaid service to family and community, and they rightfully may not believe that society values these contributions. They may be suspicious of administrative costs, and they may restrict their gifts to programs or scholarships, rather than supporting operating funds.

Women born between 1931 and 1945 represent a "sandwich generation." They share many of the characteristics of the mature generation but may have been influenced by the feminist writings of Betty Friedan (1984) and others. Many women in this cohort entered college and the workforce before the days of affirmative action or at midlife. Either way, they were pioneers.

Women in this generation tend to be wary of issues related to money and power, and they prefer to give to programs that serve the traditional interests of women—child welfare, education, and health care (Shaw and Taylor, 1995).

Baby boomer women, born between 1946 and 1964, are more likely to earn their own money and make their own money decisions. Although boomers have tended to be spenders rather than savers, men and women in this generation have begun to take more interest in planning for retirement.

Of course, it is critical to begin planning now for how to reach the next generation, often called the baby busters, especially in light of the great wealth that has been generated by the high-tech industry. Like the mature generation, the busters have been shaped by economic uncertainty in their childhood. They were born into a period of economic recession, corporate downsizing, and high divorce rates. Women in this generation know that they cannot count on anyone—husband or employer—to support them.

If there is anything uniform about the buster generation, it is a resistance to being typecast as uniform in any way. The Women's Philanthropy Institute has found that women in this generation resist a separate focus on women. At one seminar, a young woman said that women and men are now equal in the workforce and in society, and therefore separate programs will only "ghettoize" women. Unfortunately, salary studies do not support her claim (National Endowment for Financial Education, 2000).

OVERCOMING THE BARRIERS TO WOMEN'S PHILANTHROPY

Although socialization has resulted in unique giving patterns for women, it has also led to unique reasons why women hold back in their giving. Some of these barriers are internal fears that the women themselves have to overcome. Donor education will help. However, the most pernicious barrier, one that came up again and again in the focus groups, is that women don't believe they are being asked to give at the same level as men. This was even found in a 1999 study of high-achieving businesswomen conducted by the National Foundation for Women Business Owners. More than half the women in the study donate $25,000 or more annually, yet one out of four said they do not think they are taken seriously by the fund raising community.

MOTIVATING WOMEN AS PHILANTHROPISTS

In focus groups and interviews, women philanthropists have illuminated ways that development officers and nonprofits can partner with them to shape a better world for future generations. They have described what motivates them as philanthropists, as well as what turns them off. Following are suggestions for transforming a nonprofit's everyday development procedures to help reach, involve, and motivate more women as major donors and volunteer leaders:

1. Concentrate fund raising efforts on relationship building. Potential women donors may first identify themselves through volunteer work.

2. Examine what women see when they look at your organization. Review your boards, committees, administration, and publications. Are women represented? In leading roles or supporting roles? Women want to see that your nonprofit affirms and values their expertise and talent.

3. Review your standard development procedures. Are the six C's represented in your work? Do women know about opportunities to be involved in *creating* new programs? Do they know how the programs will bring about *change*? Are there opportunities for meaningful volunteer involvement? Do you provide ongoing information so they feel *connected*?

4. Analyze current giving statistics, broken down by gender. Choose a time period—say, the past three years—and answer the following questions:

What percentage of donors were women?

What percentage of total gift dollars came from women?

What percentage of members of major gift clubs or higher giving categories were women?

What percentage of your planned gifts and of the total dollars given in planned gifts came from women?

What percentage of those on prospect tracking are women? (How many women are you actively talking to about major gifts?)

Note that the results of this inquiry will depend in part on how your nonprofit credits contributions, in particular those from married couples. When looking at the raw data, it may be impossible to know which spouse had more influence on the philanthropic decision. Start by examining how your nonprofit credits joint gifts; you may want to recommend a change in policy for the future. A recent study of women's philanthropy programming at research universities found that all of the development offices surveyed used systems, including BSR Advance, Ascend, or Millennium, that are capable of crediting spouses separately when a gift is received from a married couple (Marcello, Van Dien, and Vehrs, 2000).

5. If you do nothing else, direct at least 50 percent of your fund raising calls toward women. The fact that women have been giving in greater proportion than they are being asked can mean one of two things: that asking is detrimental (and we should all lose our jobs) or that the potential for women's giving is enormous. I believe it is the latter because the women in the focus groups have said they do not believe they are being asked at the same level as their male peers. Imagine the good work our nonprofits could accomplish if we helped women realize their philanthropic potential!

6. Partner with both partners. If your development office is working with a committed couple, learn about both spouses or partners, and try to include both in solicitation calls and recognition. Often older women hold back in their giving because they are afraid their adult children will not approve. They may feel they need permission to give. And nearly as often, the adult children, when they hear about their mother's intention, are supportive and proud. Building a relationship with the family builds trust, and the relationship may continue even after the woman donor passes away.

7. Pay attention to stewardship. How you accept the gift, acknowledge the donor, and maintain the relationship is crucial. In the research, women have expressed an overwhelming preference for personal, as opposed to public, recognition. Men might say the same in a similar situation—this suggests another area for further investigation. As more new groups—women, young entrepreneurs, and minorities—enter major gift philanthropy, the best approach is to talk with your donors about recognition and listen to their preferences.

MODEL WOMEN'S PHILANTHROPY INITIATIVES

Over the past decade, an increasing number of nonprofits have identified the need for special programming to reach and involve more women as donors. Women's initiatives are important vehicles for institutional change at the leadership and governance levels. Outstanding women donors and volunteers are often identified and cultivated through these programs. These women are then invited to serve on institutional boards and committees, increasing the talent pool for the institution and empowering the women.

Institutions of higher education were the first nonprofits to create women's philanthropy initiatives, but the trend has spread in the past few years to other nonprofits. The Women's Philanthropy Institute (2001b) maintains a resource list on the top programs. There is no single best program for all nonprofits or all communities. The program model that is best is one that takes into consideration such factors as the demographics of the women and the culture of the organization.

Women's Major Gift Club

Members of a women's major gift club give in their own names to support the nonprofit overall or the programs of their choice. The Women's Philanthropy Council of the University of Wisconsin Foundation, founded in 1988, has ongoing educational programming in geographical areas, with a forum held at the university every other year. Model women's giving councils also exist at Purdue University, the University of Tennessee, and Oklahoma State University. At the University of California, Los Angeles, UCLA Women and Philanthropy has a $25,000 minimum gift or pledge required for "Circle Membership." However, annual membership in the council at large is possible with a $1,500 gift.

The United Way of Greater Greensboro (North Carolina) increased its giving by at least 10 percent in 1998–1999, in part because of an effort led by philanthropist Bonnie McElveen-Hunter to motivate women to make donations of $10,000 or more (Marchetti, 2000). Under McElveen-Hunter's direction, the United Way approached businesswomen, women who were active community leaders or volunteers, and housewives with financially successful husbands. In some cases, the women's husbands were asked to make gifts in honor of their wives. McElveen-Hunter began by making her own gift in honor of her mother. She made forty-three personal visits and obtained forty new donations from or in honor of women. Then she persuaded Merrill Lynch to place a $50,000 full-page ad in the *Wall Street Journal* featuring a photograph of the women. Her own publishing company designed the piece.

Women's Leadership Council

Some nonprofits have created a council that advocates for women in the organization and provides mentoring and other opportunities for leadership. For example, the President's Council of Cornell Women advises the university president on issues important to university women and helps attract and retain outstanding women on campus. Philanthropy is just one part of the mission of these councils, and the members often do fund raising for specific projects or programs. An example is the National Council of Ohio State Women, which raises money for Critical Difference for Women, a campus program providing scholarships and research and professional development grants.

Focus on Connection

Some nonprofits prefer not to create a membership council, opting instead for a less structured initiative that provides programming of interest to women with the goal of connecting more women to the cause. The finest example of programming for women without a membership council is the Annual Colloquium for Women of Indiana University (IU), a program inviting high-achieving alumnae to hear faculty or famous women. Invitees are women who are major donors or prospects and present or potential volunteer leaders for the university. Interestingly, the women who regularly attend the colloquium have expressed a desire for more active involvement. As a result, the IU Foundation is exploring the possibility of creating a women's fund to be named after Sarah Parke Morrison, the first female graduate of IU. The foundation is also considering the possibility of creating a membership organization for women donors, similar to that at UCLA. The colloquium and women's fund would be part of the overall initiative.

The World Wildlife Fund (WWF) established the Women and Conservation Initiative to recognize and expand the critical roles women play in using and managing natural resources. The initiative offers recognition awards, as well as gender sensitivity training, technical assistance, and tools to assist WWF field staff in increasing women's participation in conservation activities.

A Women's Campaign

In 1998, Rita Hauser led a group of four women to create the Women's Challenge Fund at Harvard University. The four women pledged up to $15 million in matching gifts for donations from women ranging from $25,000 to $250,000.

The challenge resulted in $15 million raised in seventy-seven business days and another $4 million raised in an additional thirty-three business days. Approximately 44 percent of the donors made their first-ever or first large gift to Harvard, and more than 38 percent increased the gift they were already intending to make in order to participate in the challenge (Castle, 1999).

Another leading example of women's philanthropy took place in Columbus, Ohio. The YWCA is housed in the Griswold Building, the only downtown Columbus edifice built, owned, and operated by a group of women (Schwarzwalder, 1998). In 1990, the YWCA board of directors convened a committee to weigh the relative advantages of renovating the dilapidated structure or moving to another site.

To affirm women's skills and abilities, the board selected only women for this committee, which included architects, bankers, real estate professionals, and lawyers. They eventually chose to renovate for two reasons: to preserve the historical significance of the graceful Griswold Building and, because the city of Columbus promised substantial funding, to maintain the YWCA as a downtown residence for low-income women.

In all, city, county, and state agencies yielded nearly $8 million in grants and loans. It was up to the board to raise the remaining $7 million in private funds, the largest such goal in the history of Columbus.

In 1994, the board appointed a fifty-member, all-female campaign cabinet. Abigail Wexner, wife of Leslie H. Wexner, chairman of The Limited, was general chair for the campaign. After viewing the dilapidated building, she called in a pledge of $1 million toward the campaign in the annual phonathon and committed to raising the remaining $6 million. Consistent with the YWCA's tradition of community involvement, funds were raised from small businesses, religious congregations, civic organizations, union and trade associations, YWCA members and friends, and the general public.

Karen Schwarzwalder, CEO of the YWCA, wrote: "From its inception, this project demonstrated the abilities of the contemporary woman, and many donors made contributions simply because they wanted to be in support of a women's project" (1998, p. 111).

Women's Giving Circle

The giving circle is a most exciting model for women's collective philanthropy. In a women's giving circle, members contribute equal shares to a pooled fund and decide democratically on the distribution of the funds (Shaw-Hardy, 2000). Some women's giving circles are the creation of a group of individual women acting on their own desire to invest in the future health of their community. Other circles are organized under the sponsorship, and in support of, a particular nonprofit. For example, the Seven Generations Circle of Women, in Columbus, Ohio, was founded in 1997 to celebrate the twenty-fifth anniversary of

Action for Children, a local child care resource center. The Women's Philanthropic Healthcare Fund in Boise, Idaho, supports programs of interest to the members at the Saint Alphonsus (Hospital) Foundation. There are also women's giving circles benefiting Oklahoma State University, California State University at Long Beach, the University of Wisconsin-Eau Claire, and other institutions of higher education.

Women's giving circles bring new individuals into major gift philanthropy and provide an opportunity for many of the members to be involved in directing a larger gift than they could currently make themselves. This experience can also inspire and embolden donors who are capable of giving larger amounts but have been holding back. A women's giving circle, like any collaborative program, provides an enjoyable opportunity for women to learn more about money and philanthropy.

Sondra Shaw-Hardy (2000) encourages giving circles to make the contribution from members at least $1,000 annually for two to five years. This amount is significant for most donors, and the pooled fund will be capable of making a genuine impact in the community. This amount may be a stretch for many women, but it helps women of modest means think of themselves as philanthropists.

In New York, members of the WellMet Group contribute $5,000 each annually for three years to a donor-advised fund in the New York Community Trust. In Traverse City, Michigan, the Three Generations Circle of Women is sponsored by the Women's Resource Center. Half of each member's $1,000 annual contribution stays with the center. The other half goes into the pooled fund, which may be invested in other projects in the community.

Perhaps the most exciting—and educational—aspect of a giving circle is that the members are actively involved in grantmaking. There is usually a grants committee that researches and recommends specific projects to the membership, which makes the final decision by vote. Shaw-Hardy advises giving circle organizers to recommend that each member serve on the grants committee with some frequency. She points out that the experience helps donors learn how to plan their own philanthropy, as well as experience the joy of directing larger gifts. In its first year of grants, the WellMet Group will give out grants of up to $20,000 for two purposes: to help emerging or grassroots groups and to help organizations that encourage people to become self-sufficient. The circle's sixteen members have formed two groups of eight to research and identify organizations that are doing such work.

Giving circles generally provide education for women in financial issues and philanthropic leadership. The Seven Generations Circle sponsors the three-part Leadership Institute, bringing in nationally renowned experts on women's philanthropy. Giving circles are most educational for women who are discovering their philanthropic potential. However, many experienced philanthropists enjoy the collegiality of the group, as well as the meaningful opportunities to mentor younger—or newer—women donors.

Women's giving circles are donor-focused. Almost as much attention is paid to providing education and support for the members as to the grantmaking, according to Shaw-Hardy (2000). Yet, she points out, there is usually little in the way of individual donor recognition.

A SUCCESSFUL WOMEN'S PHILANTHROPY INITIATIVE

A successful women's program depends on a number of elements.

Committed Staff

A women's philanthropy program is major gift work, and it takes cultivation. Women donors want to work with a staff member who is as dedicated to the effort as they are—one who is committed to staying with the nonprofit and the program for three to seven years.

An Active Volunteer Committee

To heighten a sense of connection and ownership, it is crucial to involve a core group of women volunteers in developing the mission, purpose, goals, and tone of the program. At the same time, it is important not to try to include a large number in the initial planning. The core volunteer committee should be made up of women who are established financial donors to the organization and respected leaders in their community. This core group should develop a mission statement and work with the staff representative to decide on the overall format of the program.

Donor Research

Listen, listen, listen to your women donors. Find out what they like about your organization, as well as what they want to change. You may want to run focus groups or conduct a series of personal interviews with women donors. While generating valuable information about their views of your organization and your fund raising efforts, this research will also help bond the donors to the institution. After you have finished the focus groups or interviews, share the findings at a recognition event for the women who participated in the study.

Organizational Commitment

It is equally important to communicate to the women that the program is not an auxiliary. Enlist the support of your CEO, the board chair, or a well-respected donor to communicate that the program is an opportunity to become involved in advancing the organization's central mission.

It is critical to include all development staff as you plan and initiate your women's program. By keeping people aware that the program is designed to increase women's giving to the entire organization, you will help avert "turf wars" between development staff. It is equally important to communicate the important role of male development officers in advancing philanthropy by women. Women donors will support the programs they care about, regardless of the gender of the fund raiser. What is important is for the asker to understand women's motivations, fears, and expectations with respect to philanthropy and to support them in their philanthropic endeavors.

Full Philanthropy Education

It would be a mistake to make fund raising the sole focus of your women's initiative, because women are also seeking a sense of connection, a chance to learn and talk with others, leadership opportunities, and an opportunity to celebrate and have fun. However, it is also a mistake to neglect to mention up-front that philanthropy is a critical part of the program. The women may feel manipulated if you try to introduce fund raising at a later date. It is best to introduce the subject of philanthropy from the outset, along with a program of philanthropy education that celebrates and enhances their giving to your organization and other nonprofits.

Donor education seminars and publications enlighten women donors while solidifying their connection with your organization. The discussions should begin with the concept that philanthropy involves gifts of time, talent, and treasure and that nonprofits need all three to function at full capacity. The Women's Philanthropy Institute has developed an innovative donor curriculum that takes women through progressive stages of development as philanthropists: motivation (why be a philanthropist?), knowledge (how to maximize my impact as a philanthropist), and leadership (motivating others to become philanthropists).

The United Way of America (2001) has suggested the following additional "best practices and key components" to ensure the success of a women's initiative:

- An inaugural kickoff and annual event with strong keynote speakers
- Underwriting for events
- A stated mission
- Goals for members and dollars raised
- Specific strategies to attract targeted groups of women, such as women volunteer leaders, business leaders, homemakers, lawyers, and doctors
- Opportunities for women to gather for substantive issue-focused meetings
- Opportunities for women to direct their money to specific areas of concern

- Strategies to recognize and involve women who are currently giving
- Social opportunities for spouses and partners
- A personal solicitation
- Challenge grants
- Ongoing evaluation

CONCLUSION

Women have emerged as leaders in business, government, and the professions who bring a new approach. Now they are poised to make a major impact with their philanthropy. They are passionate in their commitment to making a better world. They are seeking connections and guidance to help them make active choices about what becomes of their wealth—how much they spend, how they invest, how much goes back to society in the form of taxes, and what they accomplish through strategic philanthropic giving.

Though much has been accomplished, there is still much we can do to promote philanthropy by women. Professionals and volunteers working in the nonprofit sector can continue to inspire and empower women in their emerging role as philanthropists. We do this by recognizing their potential as major donors and learning about their motivations, preferences, expectations, and fears with regard to giving. We do it by asking women to give and demonstrating stewardship of their gifts to maintain their sense of connection. We encourage women's philanthropy by providing guidance through donor education and development programs, as well as in every contact we have with women donors and their families. By partnering with women philanthropists, nonprofit fund raisers can help them discover the joy of philanthropy.

CHAPTER SEVENTEEN

Trends in Major Donor Behavior and Innovative Approaches to Philanthropy

Lilya Wagner

Hank Rosso taught us to focus on the unique characteristics, interests, and values of each individual donor or funder. So the fund raising structures in this book are adaptable to the "new donor." Even when "new donors" challenge the models, there are ways for traditional models to accommodate nontraditional donors.

In mainstream philanthropy, the donor-donee relationship is often a "compliance relationship," in which nonprofits feel they have to jump through hoops to meet certain requirements and qualify for certain funds. This relationship, however, has taken on new dimensions, as exemplified by observable trends in major donor behavior. A philosophy of "I will help you succeed" is more prevalent than ever before, and there is increasing commitment to strategic partnership. In recent years, philanthropists have contributed not only their money and expertise but also their networks. They plan for maximized growth or impact. They believe in quantitative performance assessment. In short, the trends that philanthropists are exhibiting can be characterized as follows:

- Investment in organizations, not projects
- Proclivity toward social investment
- Commitment to significant long-term capitalization (as opposed to short-term or start-up funding)

- Hands-on management participation (direct participation in operating decisions and probably a seat on the nonprofit's board)
- A drive to get things done

Researchers and writers whose works have addressed the twenty-first-century donor point out the trends and practices and how these differ from yet build on traditional philanthropy and fund raising. This chapter defines the terminology that has entered the fund raising lexicon, defines the variety of major donors that have emerged in this decade and their emerging roles and practices, and discusses how the new donor fits into a comprehensive fund raising program. Equally important is consideration of how new approaches to giving compare with traditional philanthropy, what future projections can be suggested, and caveats regarding the maintenance of a balance between what is tried and true and what is a trend. As Reis and Clohesy (2001) note, it seems reasonable to "value the new models as enhancers of current organized philanthropy, adding more design options of philanthropic approaches to the spectrum of societal challenges and opportunities" (p. 3).

EMERGING MAJOR DONOR TRENDS

An entrepreneurial spirit evident in the early years of the twenty-first century has increased propensity to give. What motivates major donors to be generous is their own financial ability, a cause consistent with personal values, the organization's reputation, and the organization's performance. The philanthropists capable of giving large sums of money are concerned with the organizational vision and mission. They believe in helping the needy, giving back to the community, organizational accountability, and the chance to make a difference. They focus grants in a specific field, and some seek out "sector investments," in such areas as health care or the environment. As donors, their ability to leverage resources or make things happen is the characteristic that most distinguishes them. They are interested in direct service.

Reis and Clohesy state, "The extraordinary mass of financial capital produced by the economy in the late twentieth century, along with the creative force of a new generation of innovators, has formed a wellspring of new ideas for philanthropy" (2001, p. 2). An entrepreneurial focus; greater emphasis on partnerships among business, government, and nonprofit sectors; and new wealth as well as new social innovation are dramatically affecting the philanthropic scene—and therefore nonprofit organizations and fund raising.

As an example of a significant trend affecting major donor behavior, venture philanthropy has perhaps received the most attention due to comparisons with venture capitalism; indeed, both functions share characteristics and behaviors, and venture philanthropy is often the preferred practice of the newly wealthy. In the closing months of the last century, the expression "venture philanthropy" entered the sector's vocabulary. Letts, Ryan, and Grossman (1997) published an article in the *Harvard Business Review* that is widely regarded as the venture philanthropy manifesto. They criticized traditional foundations for investing in program innovation rather than nonprofit infrastructure and capacity building. Nonprofits often couldn't carry out the program activities that the donor was funding due to inadequate institutional support. Letts, Ryan, and Grossman defined the problem but left it up to the practitioners to implement solutions. As it turned out, many "new" donors took the initiative and provided funding on their own, not always at the behest of the nonprofit.

Experts in the field and the media declared that a new type of generosity was exerting its influence. The coverage they provided, as well as the experience of nonprofit organizations and fund raisers, raised awareness of venture philanthropy and created excitement about its potential.

However, venture philanthropists are not the only ones who have been identified as exhibiting unique characteristics of donor behavior. In fact, the term is less relevant than the philanthropic traits and behaviors exhibited by the new type of donor, and these traits are shared by donors described by other designations, included the high-tech donor, the social entrepreneur, the engaged grantmaker, and the investor. These donors challenge the donor development process (discussed in Chapter Seven) and the Ladder of Effectiveness (discussed in Chapters Eight and Thirteen), since many make major gifts as their first gifts to organizations. Clearly, at the heart of defining the new major gift donor is entrepreneurship. Jed Emerson (2001) defines entrepreneurs as individuals who have the ability to identify unusual or one-of-a-kind opportunities, pursue those opportunities in innovative ways, find or leverage new resources, make decisions on the direction of their enterprise, and assume risk as they do so. Yet one might ask how different these behaviors are from those described in the Rosso model discussed in Chapter Seven and throughout much of this book. Generally speaking, major donors have for many decades desired to see effective results from their donations, have had at least some involvement in the activities of an organization, have been influential in attracting new resources, and have assumed risk when giving to nonprofit organizations. That is what the Rosso model teaches.

What is a new trend, however, is the tendency of philanthropists to borrow principles from the practice of venture capitalists in the business world. They believe in the idea that the best investments require more than money to achieve success. It also takes talent, expertise, and strategic thinking. Results and accountability are expected from the organizations they support.

Another example of a new type of major gift donor is the "social entrepreneur." This donor is focused on social issues and opportunities to create and sustain social values. Innovation plays a major role here as well, and a high demand for accountability to constituents is integral for the social entrepreneur. As Reis and Clohesy state, "Social entrepreneurs are changing civic and human services, leadership and institutions to encompass market-based approaches for appropriate scale, impact, and sustainability" (2001, p. 6). They are driven by sustainability and entrepreneurial or enterprise-based solutions as they create social value through innovation and leveraging of financial resources.

Perhaps in the near future, designations for major donors may derive from their source of wealth, such as the use of the designations "high-tech philanthropist," or "Internet-based philanthropy," frequently used terminology in the early twenty-first century. Terms that often enter the language of researchers, writers, and practitioners when discussing the new donor are *business and social responsibility, philanthropy as social venture capital, venture partnerships, corporate citizenship, nonprofit enterprise,* and *social capital.* These terms may well describe traditional and accepted ideas, but for many people, they indicate a revolution of ideas and practices in philanthropy.

IDENTIFIABLE CHANGING MAJOR DONOR BEHAVIORS

Although differences in language and terminology describing trends in major donor behavior exist, the characteristics of the new donor are similar, with few differences among designations indicating preferences in the practice of philanthropy.

High-engagement philanthropists are no longer content to write a check and let the money be invested and distributed by others. Rather, they want to be involved in the decision making, and they seek charitable organizations that satisfy their needs. They are hands-on, do much research, and demand accountability and results. In short, today's wealthy are seeking out causes for which their dollars can make a discernible difference. They are the movers behind the biggest shift in philanthropy since the days of the Rockefellers and the Carnegies and in many ways represent a return to those days. Many new donors are under forty and are not waiting to distribute their wealth. However, unlike traditional philanthropic practices, they don't give to any idea that comes along or respond to an unresearched plea. They make sure (as much as possible) that their money tackles a problem that can be solved. Consequently, they may devote only 10 percent of their efforts to making the grant and the rest of the time to the recipient.

These major donors are transforming philanthropy even as they transform businesses. As summarized in *Time* magazine, "Many of today's tech millionaires and billionaires are applying to philanthropy the lessons they have learned as entrepreneurs. They want to make sure their charitable investments benefit their ultimate 'customers'—those in need—and don't get lost in red tape and bureaucracy. This has caused some tension with the nonprofit organizations that have traditionally been the recipients of such largesse" (Greenfeld, 2000, p. 50).

Sometimes nonprofits may not be ready to deal with the increasing and changing demands of philanthropy. They may have been functioning on a smaller scale and may not have the resources, including people, to do the additional work. A solution offered by the new donor may be to offer technological expertise and experience at running lean, efficient organizations. They scrutinize each charitable cause like a potential business investment and want maximum return in terms of social impact.

Peter Hero (2001a), writing about the emerging patterns of what he defines as a new philanthropy, summarized the characteristics of major donors. They select a small number or perhaps even one charitable venture; they focus on prevention and not just symptoms; they donate not just money but also time, involvement, connections, and other resources; they stay involved over time; they build organizational capacity; they provide sustainability in funding; they expect agreed-on performance measures; and they plan an exit strategy at a point when they feel they can withdraw. Betsy Streisand (2001) added, "Strange to say, many young millionaires move full time into charity because while they no longer need money, they do need something to do. They often end up with both (p. 42)."

According to Emerson (2001, p. 21):

> Much of classical philanthropy is focused upon what may be called "transactive philanthropy," an approach to charitable giving that emphasizes the awarding of grants. Within transactive philanthropy, the value of the grant-maker is based upon the size, number and perceived "innovation" of grants awarded. While one may periodically fund an evaluation of a program, the primary definition of success is placed more on the act of giving than upon long-term impact. It is important to recognize that transactive philanthropy is a positive part of the nonprofit capital market. Some organizations with proven track records of success simply deserve additional financial support without the requirements of massive amounts of evaluation. Other causes should be supported simply because it is the right thing to do—this is charity in its purest sense and should not be underrated."

Having explained the classical model, Emerson goes on to explain "investment philanthropy": "Within an investment approach to philanthropy, the purpose of grant-making is not simply to make grants, but rather to invest in the enhanced capacity of organizations to execute their strategies with the greatest degree of effectiveness possible" (2001, p. 21).

One of the critical differences between transactive philanthropy and investment philanthropy is accountability. Although donors have always desired accountability, it is now of primary importance. Also important are greater organizational capacity and maximization of social return on investment. Major donors are not content just to be philanthropic and support charitable causes. They want to ensure effective organizations and skilled management. They contend that behind every effective program is good management.

This new breed of philanthropist scrutinizes each charitable cause like a potential business investment, seeking results in terms of social impact. This leads to the erroneous impression that new philanthropists seek results but traditional philanthropists do not. However, for the new philanthropist, focusing on outcomes is paramount. The top irritant for a venture philanthropist is a perceived lack of credibility and reliability. This kind of donor doesn't find the "write a check and walk away" charity appealing. He or she is interested in the potential for great changes. "Where and how can I make a difference?" is a universal motivation for any donor, but the new donor puts a greater emphasis on this than donors of previous generations.

The major donor of today also may not like the word *philanthropy*. The current trendy terminology includes "investment," "social investment," "venture philanthropy," and "giving back to the community."

Nontraditional forms of giving are spreading among the wealthy. They increasingly demand that nonprofits prove outcomes in ways that are familiar to them in their own environment—the business world. They are eager to have a more direct role. They want to address the other side of extraordinary wealth—provide direct service in addressing the problems of poverty, hunger, lack of access to health care and housing, and education. They tend to shy away from and are skeptical of established organizations. They want fresh initiatives. Many favor giving through their own foundations, trusts, or gift funds. Major donors often realize that what they are doing is becoming more connected, more engaged, to the work of the nonprofit sector. Basically, this means greater involvement than before.

Whether all this will change the nature of philanthropy itself, as some observers predict, remains to be seen. But what is sure is that there has been a burst of philanthropic activity by the newly wealthy, and major donors are changing their views on how philanthropy should be practiced and what it should accomplish. Instead of desiring to leave a legacy, many donors work toward discernible and measurable change. Indeed, some young philanthropists describe their activities as a second career. Their attitude is, "There are no tax advantages to giving after you're dead, so why not do it now?"

The aim of proponents of the emerging trend in major gift activity is to catalyze a new generation of donors and encourage them to build the capabilities of nonprofit organizations. They propose to do this through strategic management assistance that is provided to leverage and augment financial investments. In addition to gifts that are their investment, the givers also share technological expertise, leverage their network of contacts, and help organizations empower themselves to achieve their missions instead of trying to redefine them.

INTEGRATING TRENDS IN MAJOR
DONOR BEHAVIOR INTO EXISTING MODELS

The new major donor, especially the entrepreneur, is an increasingly important type of donor for charities to cultivate but also presents some fund raising obstacles. Many fund raisers are unsure how to even find them. They aren't easy to locate in public records that, for example, list stocks in publicly traded companies and commercial real estate. Giving by entrepreneurs is on their time, not the charity's. They are unlikely to respond to appeals to give by a deadline imposed by the charity. Fund raisers may even have to make "elevator pitches," or become accustomed to asking and giving on the run. Often there is just one chance to ask, and only one. And entrepreneurs want fund raisers to be direct, which implies a great demand for readiness in stating the organization's case and making the appeal. This sometimes produces tension between the demand side and the supply side of philanthropy, causing astute fund raising professionals to adapt to the changing face of philanthropy and be flexible among evolving environments and trends. Rosso's principles on making a case are timeless, and learning how to adapt these principles when addressing the new donor of any era is essential for success.

New donors may not respond to invitations to serve on charity boards or participate in other activities that involve a time commitment, yet building relationships is as important as ever because otherwise an organization and its mission may not become apparent to the donor seeking a cause in which to invest and be involved.

Because new donors are success-oriented and achievement-focused, organizations may need to tout that they are on the cutting edge and the best in the market. Appropriate publicity about what makes a particular organization unique, credible, exciting, and extraordinary is vital to becoming noticed by the new donor.

Philanthropists exhibiting these changing characteristics often enjoy breaking with tradition. They like new ideas and will invest in such much more readily than in maintenance of existing programs. In addition, they are enticed by immediate gratification and appreciation. However, there is the tendency not to have the kinds of social connections that traditional donors have, and they may therefore not be likely fund raising volunteers.

The new major donor may have come by wealth quickly and may not be comfortable with it. The individual may be young and have limited experience in philanthropy, and may need or seek out advice on how to become philanthropic.

As already noted, new donors have a hands-on style and a tendency to direct or restrict their gifts. They will probably adopt an investment model for philanthropy, and because they may be suspicious of the philanthropic establishment and large institutions, questions of accountability and credibility are paramount, and organizations soliciting new donors must shape their appeals accordingly.

The Rosso model, while essentially remaining valid, has to be modified when considering the new philanthropists. These modifications are appropriate to accommodate current trends. The traditional donor development process may not work for them as well as it has in the past—they may take their time in becoming known, but when interested, may go directly to the top of the giving pyramid. The new donors may enter at the major gift level and remain there through long-term engagement with the institution. Of course, big donors have always demanded big outcomes. But now philanthropists have a universal tendency to apply to philanthropy lessons learned in their business ventures— strategic thinking, respect for innovation, a belief in the values of measurement, accountability, and return on investment. They are not likely to throw money at piecemeal plans, stopgap measures, or isolated initiatives aimed at current problems. They are also interested in the intellectual process of arriving at comprehensive, long-range solutions. Good ideas are even more important than money. Fund raisers must show respect for their intellectual ability and can-do attitude. "Although they understand the importance of money to charities, they believe that ultimately ideas, not money, will make the difference in improving society" ("Fundraising and the New Wealth," 2001, p. 22).

The donor's advisory team takes on new importance as well. Money managers, investment house strategists, financial advisers, lawyers, consultants, and private bankers may all become involved as new donors require and request help in deciding how and where to give and how to manage their assets, maximize their returns, and minimize their tax burdens, all at the same time. "The new philanthropists have changed the course of business history, often reinventing themselves along the way, and they hope to do the same through philanthropy" ("Fundraising and the New Wealth," 2001, p. 23).

Table 17.1 provides a summary look at major donors' behaviors and practices compared with emerging trends and activities of the new donors.

CONCLUSION: LESSONS LEARNED AND FUTURE PROJECTIONS

It is too early to judge whether or not changing philanthropic trends and behaviors will achieve the results promised by today's benefactors. Often they ask, "Will it be possible to add significant value to the nonprofit organization beyond the capital investments by more direct intervention and involvement?" Nonprofits have been conditioned, by human and financial constraints, that incremental growth is to be expected and accepted, and they have some difficulty accepting the expectations of cyberspeed change, intensive involvement, and

Table 17.1. Traditional Philanthropists and New Donors Compared.

Behavior, Attitude, or Practice	Traditional Philanthropist	Today's Major Donor
Terminology	Major donor, philanthropist	Venture philanthropist, social entrepreneur, social investor, Internet-based philanthropist, high-tech donor
Approach to philanthropy	An organization in search of donors who have an interest in the cause.	A donor with an idea, project, program, or interest in search of an organization.
Function of philanthropy	Citizens hold taxable resources in the private domain but give for the public good.	Similar to traditional philanthropy, but more focused on market-based philanthropy, an expansion of the boundaries of philanthropy.
Purpose of philanthropy	Philanthropy is a means to help others.	Equity and "ownership" are emphasized, along with measurable results and financial sustainability.
Motivation for philanthropy	Philanthropy occurs according to donor's perception of need and possibility.	Donor seeks cause that holds high personal interest.
Philanthropic process	Philanthropy is providing resources to organizations that ask and make a case for worthwhile projects.	Focus is on a limited number of organizations, maybe only one, and contact is often donor-initiated.
Range of desired effectiveness	Philanthropy ranges from simple charity to strategic change investment.	Focus is on organizational effectiveness and capacity building.
Interaction of sectors	Clear definition of sectoral boundaries	Blurring of sectoral boundaries

Table 17.1. Traditional Philanthropists and New Donors Compared, Cont'd.

Behavior, Attitude, or Practice	Traditional Philanthropist	Today's Major Donor
Philanthropic commitment	Commitment to public responsibility	Commitment to public responsibility plus market models
Pace of wealth development and types of wealth creation	Wealth creation takes place over a lifetime.	Rapid new wealth is being created, especially due to technological advances.
Types of projects and funding	Projects with time limits, based on models, partial funding for project, short-term (seldom for more than one year), project or program funding, some demand for account-ability; organizational endowments	Long-term engagement and funding, emphasis on capacity building, demand for performance measures, small number of projects or just one, significant contribution to budget as well as in-kind gifts and services; private foundations
Interaction with donee	Some collaboration	High level of involvement
Risk taking	Little risk for funder	High level of sharing the risk

changes to the "business as usual" way of operating. Experts and researchers sometimes wonder whether a return-on-investment mentality can always be translated to social good, improved lives, increased volunteerism, and the advancement of civil society. There is also concern that trends in philanthropy fail to make significant headway in addressing fundamental questions of social and economic justice; the models that have emerged so far do not match attitude with substance.

Mark Kramer (1999), writing in the *Chronicle of Philanthropy,* notes that there are limitations on transplanting successful for-profit models into the very different culture and goals of the nonprofit world. The tools of the venture capitalist will not work in philanthropy. He points out that there are key differences between the for-profit and nonprofit worlds. First is the failure rate. One out of ten investments will be a home run, two to three will break even or make a modest profit, and more than half will fail outright. Can those odds work in philanthropy, and will the public tolerate philanthropy's failure rates? There is no simple way to measure social benefits like monetary returns. We can't waste dollars on nine programs that accomplish nothing in the hopes that one will succeed. Then there's the matter of control. Venture capitalists control their portfolio companies. No such control is possible over nonprofits.

Other issues arise from how nonprofits function. Nonprofits can't change their goals or missions as easily as may be necessary to meet the expectations of venture philanthropists. Growth rate is another issue. Social change doesn't happen fast—at least not as fast as a venture capitalist may expect. Finally, there is the question of expertise. The majority of nonprofit organizations are inexperienced in and unprepared for absorbing the kinds of strategic management support that many philanthropists are tying to their financial investments. Nonprofits sometimes underestimate what is expected of them, and there is considerable strain in carrying out their end of the partnership. Therefore, a dissonance exists between expectations and reality, sometimes disappointing both the funder and the organization. In addition, philanthropists may not have training in the field they support and therefore may not be able to give wise advice. Kramer concludes, "Doing philanthropy well is a difficult and unique endeavor. Its lessons should be learned from those who best understand and practice it, not by borrowing metaphors imported from some other field" (1999, p. 72).

The implications for the future are mixed. A valid question to ask is, will a modified Rosso model, based on higher expectations, more specific performance measures, and stringent evaluation be more effective than the traditional model that tends to be based on trust that the receiving organization will "do good"? Perhaps not. However, some change being driven by the new philanthropists is good: measurable results, better performance, higher expectations. These will continue to shape the profession of fund raising and the act of giving.

The belief that wealth creation for the purpose of addressing social change will influence philanthropists is both exciting and challenging. As Reis and Clohesy observe, "The practices of these new philanthropists are challenging more experienced leaders in philanthropy to think about changing roles and relationships with grantee partners, using new tools and approaches that stretch philanthropy beyond traditional grantmaking and into more opportunistic and market-based models" (2001, p. 11).

In philanthropy, as in most societal changes and developments, the new and the established must work together constructively and respectfully. Trends in major donor behavior may change, but what remains constant is the dedication of people committed to nonprofit organizations who help provide solutions to societal problems. Nothing in life is static; change occurs on all fronts. The new donor is responding, and will continue to respond, to changes in the U.S. economy, culture, and society. The fund raising professional will in turn respect, acknowledge, and work with these changes while making it possible for major donors to use their resources for the benefit of nonprofit organizations and their communities.

CHAPTER EIGHTEEN

Embracing Diversity in Fund Raising

Lilya Wagner

H ank Rosso was personally committed to extending the work of The Fund Raising School to diverse populations. The Rosso emphasis on understanding the interests and needs of the donor fits well with the engagement of diverse populations. Successful ventures between The Fund Raising School and Native Americans in Philanthropy, the Hispanic Stewardship Partnership, and the Thurgood Marshall and United Negro College Funds illustrate this adaptability.

Today nonprofit organizations are increasingly embracing diversity as a mission and organizational value. They are seeking to do the right thing as well as access the economic growth and power of Hispanics, African Americans, Asian Americans, and other diverse population groups. It's not just the right thing to do; it's a useful perspective in building and managing credible, comprehensive fund raising programs.

At the same time, diversity presents a challenge to fund raisers. No longer can they function under the assumption of "one size fits all," something the Rosso model taught us to avoid. Diverse groups have identifiable, valuable, and significant philanthropic characteristics and traits. Therefore, fund raisers find that in order to be successful, they must tailor their fund raising appeals to the prospective donors' customs and sensibilities.

Not to acknowledge and work with diversity in U.S. populations is to ignore much potential income for nonprofit organizations. Reis and Clohesy (2001) note, "As these populations grow in numbers they will continue to grow in influence and resources. The philanthropy of women, communities of color, and youth are likely to have a substantial influence on traditional philanthropic institutions. Already these populations have created new philanthropic institutions and networks that more closely resemble their social and ethnic cultures and attempt to solve issues they consider to be of most importance" (p. 124). Some diverse or minority populations haven't attained the income levels of the majority population. But there are signs of emerging wealth and purchasing power. Entrepreneurial activity is rising, education levels are increasing, and individuals are flourishing in the professions, especially in the legal and medical realms.

According to Michael Anft (2002), "Besides rising wealth, minority donors also offer great potential for generosity. Federal income-tax data suggest, for example, that black and Hispanic homeowners tend to give a higher proportion of their incomes to charity than do white homeowners" (p. 4).

In this chapter, we will consider use of terminology, challenges presented by understanding philanthropic practices of diverse population groups, the giving habits and preferences of four major ethnic population groups, cautious generalizations that can serve as a foundation for further understanding, and guidelines for developing comprehensive fund raising programs and understanding diversity among donor groups.

DEFINING DIVERSITY

The use of language in defining diversity presents many challenges. Even the commonly used phrase "fund raising in diverse communities," often encountered in the titles of books and articles, can be disputed. Perhaps it would be more correct to say "fund raising across, within, among, for, or with diverse communities," because any discussion of fund raising among population groups other than the majority in the United States may well imply cross-cultural fund raising for the mutual benefit of various population groups.

Primary to any discussion of diverse populations, a consideration of what culture means is valuable for providing a foundation or framework. According to Wilson, Hoppe, and Sayles (1996), "Culture strongly influences how one behaves and how one understands the behavior of others, and cultures vary in the behaviors they find proper and acceptable." (p. 1). There is the external culture, which is exhibited in outward behaviors and traditions that are readily discernible, such as a performance of a mariachi band, and internal culture, which is less evident, such as the way people think about situations and conceptualize information. Culture can be most easily explained as a people's way of life. The authors of *Philanthropy in Communities of Color* explain culture in this way: "All cultures construct reality differently; within each unique cultural community, beliefs and behavior have meanings that are often not shared or understood by the outside world. Some cultural meanings are manifest and easily recognized; others are latent and subtle, requiring systematic observation in order to produce accurate analysis" (Smith, Shue, Vest, and Villarreal, 1999, p. 3).

For the fund raising professional, therefore, consideration of cultural elements is vital prior to any fund raising activity. Unfortunately, many fund raisers approach a relationship and solicitation from their own perspective, leaving themselves unprepared for cultural differences that can easily be misinterpreted and misconstrued. Smith and colleagues point out that ". . . the cultural dimensions of gift-giving, financial assistance, sharing, and the distribution of income and wealth all have a variety of meanings from culture to culture. . . . The uses of wealth, prestige, and power are also important to the cross-cultural analysis of charitable behavior" (1999, p. 3).

In addition to the difficulties presented by perceptions of other cultures, terminology also offers challenges in any discussion of diverse populations and philanthropy. Should the correct designation for diverse populations be "people of color," "minorities," or "ethnic groups"? And is the correct terminology "African American" or "black"? "Hispanic" or "Latino"? "Asian American" or "Pacific Islander"? Labels may get in the way more than they help when identifying and qualifying donors.

Naturally, people of diverse populations would prefer to be identified by their actual country of origin or their source of national orientation. Mexicans or Mexican Americans, for example, would rather be distinctive than lumped into an overall designation such as "Hispanic." Chinese may have few similarities with Pacific Islanders, yet they usually come under the same appellation. For the purposes of this chapter, the following guidelines will be used.

To identify population groups that are often referred to as "minorities" or similar terms, we will use "people of diverse populations." Although preferences differ vastly among people of diverse populations as to specific nomenclature, for purposes of clarity and ease, the following will be used, sometimes interchangeably (based on terminology found in current literature):

African American or black

Hispanic or Latino

Asian American or Asian/Pacific Islander

Native American

PROBLEMS AND CHALLENGES OF DIVERSE POPULATIONS AND FUND RAISING

Jill Moss Greenberg (2002) identified six forms of bias that can serve as barriers to understanding populations outside our own source of identity and inhibit good working relationships. These readily apply to philanthropy and fund raising.

1. *Exclusion and invisibility.* This is the most fundamental form of bias and the most difficult to detect. It can range from unintentional to determined exclusion. It means excluding both people and information about people, such as their contributions to history. Exclusion and invisibility diminish the value given to some groups. If diverse population groups' philanthropy is ignored or they are considered to be poor givers or even incapable of giving, we are expressing a distinct form of bias as fund raising professionals.

2. *Stereotyping.* Stereotyping portrays members of specific groups as having characteristics in common, negative and positive. It is harmful because it implies that a certain population group is homogeneous rather than having a range of individual roles, beliefs, preferences, and behaviors. Stereotyping is, however, different from intelligent generalization, which provides a foundation for further individual understanding of cultural and ethnic characteristics leading to philanthropic behavior.

3. *Imbalance and selectivity.* Presenting only one interpretation of an issue, situation, or group results in a one-sided, skewed, or simplistic view of complex issues, situations, or people. For this reason, the astute and sensitive fund raiser must move beyond generalizations and understand each donor or donor group as completely as possible; in other words, the same thorough prospect research principles must be applied to all potential donors.

4. *Unreality.* This is the tendency to exclude underlying facts or issues that clarify. Substantive or controversial topics may be glossed over, restricting information that helps understanding. Again, the implication for fund raisers is that stereotypes and sheer lack of knowledge inhibit an understanding of and respect for populations that are "new" and different from our usual donor groups.

5. *Fragmentation and isolation.* Isolating or separating the experiences of minority groups from those of the majority population implies that these experiences are unrelated to those of the majority population. Differentiating in this way leads to exclusion or invisibility.

6. *Linguistic bias.* Language frames perceptions, perspectives, and attitudes. Slurs can categorize people. Therefore, great care must be taken to use nomenclature that is comfortable for diverse populations. This is not an easy task, as we have already discussed, but a necessary one.

Reluctantly, we must restrict our discussion to four major ethnic groups and do so without sufficient consideration for subcategories. We do, however, acknowledge that African Americans, Asian Americans, Hispanics, and Native Americans have been isolated from much of the broader mainstream philanthropic discussions and therefore have created their own philanthropic structures and practices. The structures and practices differ somewhat from each other as much as they differ from the white majority in the United States, but there are also some similarities across the various groups.

In general, fund raising professionals don't approach diverse donors responsibly. Unwarranted assumptions about each population's philanthropy color our viewpoints. Finding ways to appeal to ethnic generosity is a daunting challenge. There is no one model for fund raising among minority groups; there are many different models (Anft, 2002). Compounding the challenges is the fact that ethnic groups have been stereotyped as receivers, not givers, of charity.

The following discussion of diverse population groups' philanthropy will prove that many commonly made assumptions are incorrect and even harmful.

DIVERSE GROUPS AND PHILANTHROPY

The amount of giving by diverse population groups is estimated to be consistent with that of other populations in the United States, but the ways in which they give and to whom they give vary (Smith et al., 1999). Differences also show up among ethnic groups. Asian Americans tend to give to family- and health-centered charities, while Hispanic donors, accustomed to government and church help on social issues, give more often to religious institutions and mutual assistance groups that provide aid to impoverished community members (Anft, 2001).

Data about the U.S. population, based on the 2000 census, are presented in Table 18.1.

Hispanics or Latinos

Hispanics or Latinos come from more than twenty countries. They vary greatly in levels of affluence and education. According to the Hispanic Market Web site (http://www.hispanic-market.com):

Table 18.1. Breakdown of the U.S. Population by Race, Income, and Poverty Status, 2000.

	Non-Hispanic Whites	Hispanics	African Americans	Asian Americans	Native Americans
Racial identification[a]	69.1%	12.5%	12.1%	3.6%	0.7%
Average annual household income	$44,366	$30,735	$27,910	$51,205	$30,784
Percentage living in poverty	7.7%	22.8%	23.6%	10.7%	25.9%

[a]1.9 percent of respondents indicated "other" or "multiracial."

Source: U.S. Bureau of the Census.

- 89 percent list Spanish as their first language.
- 70 percent speak Spanish at home.
- 70 percent watch Spanish-language television.
- Some people with Hispanic names do not speak Spanish.

The Hispanic Federation's 1999 Latinos and Giving survey found that two-thirds of Hispanics contribute to a charitable cause, 48 percent give to churches, and 36 percent give to nonprofits.

According to Michael Cortes (2001), the nation's nonprofit sector has been slow to integrate Latinos into its mainstream institutions and strategies. Organized philanthropy seems slow to respond to Latino community needs and aspirations. Mainstream nonprofit institutions neglect Latinos, and Latinos in return are less likely to view the formal nonprofit sector as a vehicle for addressing their problems, aspirations, and values. Therefore, more Latino nonprofits are being formed.

Generalizing about Latino philanthropy is difficult because there are variations, while there are also distinctive philanthropic traditions that all populations have in common. They give relatively little time and money to mainstream charities except churches. They send money to family, kin, and communities outside the United States. They provide caretaking services to the young and the old. They help newcomers to the United States. Hispanic philanthropy tends to be personal, intimate, one-to-one relationships (Cortes, 2001).

Philanthropy in the general U.S. tradition is not well understood by Hispanics. For them, philanthropy is a "social thing" or good for business. Giving, therefore, is mostly one-to-one donations to relatives or gifts to church. In other words, although Hispanics give generously in informal ways and through non-institutional means, the idea of organized philanthropy is relatively new to them.

Fund raisers, however, have shaped the current state of Hispanic philanthropy. On the average, Hispanics receive only fifteen to twenty solicitations per year. Nevertheless, in spite of generally being ignored by nonprofits, gifts from Hispanics tend to be consistent, even if small.

Hispanic culture values one-on-one contact. It requires a very personalized approach when donating to a cause. Hispanic people come from a "high-context" culture, and they see things in terms of relationships. For this reason, Hispanics have an initial reluctance to go outside of their arena. They will work inside their communities and then go out to support larger Hispanic projects.

Whites are more fact-, statistic-, and task-oriented, while Hispanics are more cause-, relationship-, and motivation-oriented. Whites articulate their tradition of giving by keeping statistics and records. Hispanics are now in the learning stages of articulating their traditions and keeping accurate records.

Hispanics tend to give to causes that have an impact on their values, beliefs, and culture. As many Hispanics in the United States have made gains in economic status, their values and giving patterns have come to reflect those values. For instance, it is not uncommon to have wealthy conservative Hispanics give to traditionally conservative causes. Generally speaking, because Hispanics are still in middle- or lower-income classes, the appealing causes for Hispanics are often assistance to family members in need of financial or other emergency need; activities that promote their heritage and culture; education, especially in terms of scholarships for Hispanics; social justice issues; community development; and disaster relief for communities or countries in which they have a heritage.

Philanthropy in the Hispanic community is often based on people's understanding of giving. Because Christianity is widely practiced throughout Latin America and among U.S. Hispanics, and the act of giving is taught as a Christian principle, giving is often seen in terms of time, talent, and treasure. Therefore, giving of time through hands-on involvement such as volunteering is given the same value as a cash gift. Also, a cause that is church-based is more likely to receive approval than one that is not.

History and politics also have an impact on giving. For instance, for recent Latino immigrants, having lived under governments that are not accountable to their citizens may have engendered a sense of distrust. In the United States, local governments are often guilty of the same lack of responsiveness and accountability to Hispanic communities. Moreover, Hispanics have not always been treated with the same respect accorded other immigrant communities by U.S. society.

As a result, trust becomes a major issue. The person asking is very important; so are how the request is formulated and the asker's accountability.

A survey of Hispanic professionals who were asked for advice on fund raising among Hispanics yielded these recommendations (Wagner, 1999, pp. 102–103):

> Be sincere in your approach to the community, do not assume anything, and take the time to build the trust needed in order to be accepted by the Hispanic community in which you may find yourself working.

> "Know the community, know the issues, know the language, be in a teacher mode, and don't take anything for granted."

> "Consideration and patience have to be exhibited as a result of the historical neglect by dominant institutions of the Hispanic community. A sudden rediscovery of Hispanics cannot easily undo years of neglect. Be prepared to answer questions like, 'Why are we now prospects when we weren't before?'"

> "Hispanics are always willing to help. You have to be sincere with them. You have to earn their trust because too many people have tried to use them."

> "Listen to the reasons behind established practices before proposing new ones."

African Americans

Records on African American giving in the United States reveal more than 250 years of "philanthropy among friends." Data also show, as time goes on, increasingly higher rates of giving as well as the use of philanthropic activity to bring about social change.

Based on the research of Emmett Carson (1993) and other scholars, there are eight distinctive characteristics of African American philanthropy:

- The "axiom of kinship," meaning shared values and identification with other African Americans
- The power of "collective giving," in which each member contributes to a common pool
- The desire to leave something as a legacy to other generations
- Thanksgiving and joy in giving
- The importance of seeing the "face" of the need
- Equal value placed on gifts of time and talent
- Making giving affordable
- Ownership of the gift

African Americans often don't view what they do to help others as philanthropy. In a general sense, they tend to help more informally and within families and neighborhoods, and helping other African Americans usually comes first. Philanthropy is perceived as a strategic activity of larger institutions. The church continues to be the primary institution through which African Americans become engaged in helping others. Giving tends to be validated when the appeal comes from a respected, charismatic leader such as the senior pastor. To this end, a culture of trust is established. Conversely, African Americans will tend to maintain a sense of doubt and suspicion should the appeal lack leadership credibility or integrity.

Moreover, African Americans tend to be reluctant to make donations to general funds and charities, preferring to focus on specific causes and individuals. African Americans consider donations of knowledge, skill, and time to be of considerably greater value than money.

African Americans most frequently support the following causes:

- Assistance to family and friends
- Religion
- Education and scholarships
- Civil rights
- Youth programs, especially for at-risk youth
- Human services

- Health care and research

- Community and economic development

African Americans make gifts through many vehicles, including churches; mutual aid societies; fraternities, sororities, and other social groups; historically black colleges; community service groups; and black federated campaigns. Making gifts on a personal or situation basis is more common than on an organization level (Hall-Russell and Kasberg, 1997).

Advice for those who might work with African American causes and donors includes the following:

African Americans value personal contact over mass-produced solicitations; direct mail is likely to be unsuccessful.

African Americans are less likely to have wills; only 28 percent of African Americans have wills, compared to 51 percent of whites.

African Americans see giving motivations as "obligations."

"Uplifting the race" is a significant motivation.

Asian Americans and Pacific Islanders

There are nearly 10 million Asian Americans and Pacific Islanders in the United States, and they represent more than forty distinct ethnic groups. Their most significant traditions are helping each other through mutual aid societies and family, neighborhoods, and self-help groups, although Asian American philanthropy is becoming more formalized among latter generations.

Practices and traditions vary according to how long the donor has been in the United States; there is significant variation because immigration to America spanned from the early 1700s to the present. According to Janice Gow Pettey (2001, p. 108), Asian Americans tend to support programs that strengthen the family; promote education, health care for all, and long-term health care for the elderly; and facilitate employer-employee efforts for the poor. They consider philanthropy as a repayment for community debts.

Gow Pettey warns that no single form of Asian American philanthropy exists. Practices are as diverse as populations themselves. The following generalizations, made cautiously, may be presented. Extended family and ethnic members of their community are more important than organized charity. Sending money to needy relatives and friends in the home country is essential. There is often a reluctance to raise money for charitable causes because of a need to "save face" and be successful. Gifts are made to reciprocate instances when they feel indebted; they want to "repay" a perceived debt as soon as possible. Asian Americans tend to give to their own community groups, thereby helping maintain ethnic identity. Planned gifts are not commonly made, and Asian Americans often make gifts to mark ceremonial events, such as births and funerals.

There is a tradition of stressing group needs and values over those of the individual. They would be willing to give to mainstream groups if their family association has endorsed the idea. Giving among Asian Americans differs greatly from one generation to the next. Younger generations may abandon the idea of sending money to their parents' homelands. In general, however, most Asian Americans who still have ties to their home countries send gifts of money and material goods back to relatives and friends. Among Asian Americans, giving is often thought of as sharing, not charity.

Asian Americans use five main vehicles for charitable giving:

- Family (in America and in country of birth), extended family, and friends
- Family associations, by ethnicity
- Church or temple
- Ethnic nursing homes, community centers, cultural institutions, civic associations, and sports programs
- Mainstream organizations that have strong history of serving Asian community

When approaching Asian American population groups, the following guidelines may help the fund raiser in tailoring the funding request:

Approach them with quiet dignity. Cheerleading is not part of the culture.

Serve before you ask. If Asian Americans are underrepresented as service recipients, they will likely continue to be underrepresented as donors.

Personalize. Relationships form the cornerstone of philanthropy, and for the Asian community, this tendency is even more pronounced.

Language is an issue. Information translated into native languages will have greater impact.

Members of the Asian community feel strong ties to organizations with which they have a history or a connection.

Memorial gifts are a popular form of donation.

Remember that family and community are paramount to early generations of Asian Americans.

Different generations of Asian Americans react differently—those who have been in the United States a long time (several generations) act more like traditional donors.

Don't insult any ethnic group. Understand holidays, ways of giving gifts, and the significance of certain colors.

Be sensitive to labels. Explore what is accepted terminology among the population segments you serve and will ask.

Donors continue to feel a sense of loyalty to programming that is relevant to them.

Preferred methods of solicitation are the following, in order of preference:

- Mail correspondence from a familiar organization
- Personal solicitation from someone known
- Giving at work
- Mail correspondence from someone known
- Phone call from someone known

Native Americans

Not unlike other major population groups discussed in this chapter, Native Americans are also made up of diverse subgroups. What they have in common is a strong tradition of giving and caring for each other as well as others outside of their immediate communities. Native Americans traditionally redistribute what they have and are very generous. The distinction between sharing and charity is also important. Sherry Black (2001) writes:

> Native communities are comprised of a network of individuals, families and kinship relationships that is also interconnected with nature and the environment. This connection is made through spiritual values, leadership and cultural roots. Western culture, on the other hand, tends to fit life into compartments— family, volunteerism, spirituality and community are often separate, for example. Individualism tends to take priority over community. Because of the differences in culture, a wide gulf exists between methods of Native giving and that of Western philanthropy. Goodwill efforts in the Native tradition are holistic in nature, encompassing all parts of the interconnection, whereas Western philanthropy tends to divide giving into categories. Sharing and reciprocity, rather than charity, are a hallmark of Native philanthropy [p. 41].

According to Gow Pettey (2001, pp. 124–125), the most common forms of giving among Native Americans are as follows:

- Informal personal giving
- Public charities
- Tribal giving programs
- Workplace giving programs
- Private foundations

The most common interests for donors are

- Education
- Cultural preservation
- Economic development
- Youth
- Elderly services
- Arts
- Health care
- Rehabilitation services such as drug and alcohol addiction counseling
- Environmental or natural resources
- Emergencies and disasters

Native Americans prefer to make anonymous and need-based gifts. They respond to personal appeals rather than mail appeals and prefer to give to people they know well. The disparaging concept of the "Indian giver" is erroneous; in Native American tradition, both the giver and the recipient are equally honored, and gifts are passed on. Native Americans also prefer to give directly to the recipients, which are carefully selected.

The foregoing summary of philanthropy among diverse populations presents only highlights. Deeper study is required when considering the philanthropic habits and preferences of diverse populations and tailoring fund raising programs accordingly. Amassing background information will help reduce fear of the unknown, will avoid mistakes in planning approaches to groups or individuals, and will remind us that despite the generalizations, the individuals with whom we speak are distinct individuals and different from each other.

Arab Americans and Other Groups

Other populations besides those related to the four major ethnic populations should also be considered. For example, attention has begun to be focused on nonprofit institutions that celebrate Arab Americans, a diverse group of people, including Muslims and Christians, who have emigrated from areas of the Middle East and North Africa. Only recently, according to Debra Blum (2002), have organizations started to systematically cultivate and solicit individual donors.

As with the other diverse populations, complications are caused by some Arab traditions. Charity is ordinarily approached informally. Giving is often based on emotion and not on tax or estate planning, and gifts go first to one's family members or directly to someone in need. Arab Americans tend to donate to their religious institutions and to send money to family members or charities in their homeland before contributing to a U.S. organization.

Arab Americans who have been in the United States for many years may give generously to nonprofit organizations but at the same time may not contribute to or even know about Arab American groups (Blum, 2002).

Other diversity issues are evident. These include gender, age, and ethnic groups who often do not feel comfortable being included in the sorts of broad categories that are usually used when discussing diverse population groups. For example, many persons from ethnic groups who immigrated several generations ago to the United States may still cling to cherished traditions and characteristics that set them apart, and these will clearly define their philanthropic tendencies and preferences. Some ethnic groups, such as refugees from the Balkan states, may not find it comfortable to be lumped with white Americans. Also, recent arrivals from Africa may not be compatible with African Americans when it comes to customs and traditions.

It is not within the scope of this chapter to fully explore philanthropy among diverse populations. The purpose has been to study characteristics that provide a starting point—a framework or foundation—for consideration of donor information and to urge the fund raising professional not to ignore differences in philanthropic attitudes and practices.

CAUTIOUS GENERALIZATIONS REGARDING DIVERSE POPULATION GROUPS AND PHILANTHROPY

Generalizations about groups can be dangerous, even if one's intentions are good. This is especially true when expressing generalizations about those with whom we lack experience or knowledge. Even if the generalizations are not offensive (unlike many that have been perpetuated over time), they may be unrealistic, unfair, and stereotypical. All diverse communities contain individuals who do not closely identify with a specific group and resent being categorized according to racial and ethnic generalizations.

However, generalizations can provide us with some basic information from which we can develop further knowledge that is more specific, accurate, and individualized.

Philanthropy in diverse populations often begins with the nuclear family. Although this is usually not considered philanthropy, it does present a groundwork for developing philanthropic habits and practices. Also, in many cultures, family reaches beyond the immediate members to include more distant relatives and even people regarded as relatives even though not blood kin. Smith and colleagues (1999, p. 147) refer to such family members as "fictive kin."

Religion often plays a significant role. Special occasions, such as birthdays and confirmations, are a platform for giving and volunteering. The religious traditions of Protestants, Catholics, and most other religions all promote and teach philanthropic values, although with differing emphases.

Mainstream philanthropic organizations are often shunned. The concept of not giving to strangers is prevalent in most cases. An exception is the wealthy, who may ignore their own ethnic causes and join the ranks of other major donors giving to large organizations and well-known causes.

Other similarities in giving can be seen across cultures. People of color are generous philanthropists, but in ways not recognized by the nonprofit world and the IRS, primarily because most ethnic philanthropy is informal and not recorded in tax returns and Gallup polls. The following are some identifiable similarities of giving among diverse populations:

- The convergence of wealth accumulation, education, career growth, and increased earning capacity allows many to become philanthropists in their own right.

- For many cultures, philanthropy is seen in the broadest sense—gifts of time, talent, and treasure—and revolve around family, church, and education.

- Direct and informal support is provided to children, the elderly, and community members.

- The level of immediate need is important.

- Planned giving is seldom a priority.

- There is some distrust of traditional nonprofits.

- Most groups are highly influenced by leaders—religious, community, professional, social, and family.

- Diverse populations often give for reasons unrelated to tax and economic issues.

- Much philanthropy is focused outside of the United States without regard for tax benefits.

- Reciprocity is an accepted concept. Helping people in ways they themselves were helped often motivates giving in diverse populations.

- Caretaking activities provided by government and nonprofit groups are usually taken for granted among populations. This is usually not the case among other ethnic groups, who see caretaking responsibilities as their own.

RESPONSIVENESS TO DIVERSITY AND DIFFERENCES: STEPS TO TAKE IN SHAPING A FUND RAISING PROGRAM

Commenting on the new rules for engaging donors of color, Emmett Carson (2000) says, "To engage donors of color, nonprofit organizations must understand the importance and interconnectedness of morality, market, and mission" (p. 74).

Diana Newman (2002) points out that the traditional donor pyramid works well for organizations that raise most of their charitable gifts from white donors but is not applicable for many cultures because of its hierarchical nature and the element of time involved in the donor development process. She presents a continuum of philanthropy that begins with families concerned with survival and basic needs, moving to those who help others who have less, and concluding with people who will invest in their communities and institutions to accomplish common and visionary goals. The continuum, therefore, as it moves from left to right, involves activities she labels "survive," "help," and "invest."

In terms of fund raising practice and changes that may be necessary to consider when fund raising among diverse population groups, Newman (2002) devotes several chapters to advice on how fund raising programs should be enhanced or even restructured. No doubt how-to books and articles will quickly follow on the heels of the volumes on diversity in fund raising that appeared in the late 1990s and early 2000s.

CONCLUSION

A review of the literature in fund raising among diverse populations indicates that traditional fund raising principles have to be adapted to changing donor populations. The fund raising professional needs to consider variations on donor approaches, including one-on-one solicitation, direct mail, use of the Internet, and telephone solicitation. Prospect research strategies must be redefined to capture information that is relevant and suitable to diverse donor identification and cultivation. Volunteers representing various ethnic groups will need to be recruited and trained.

Before modifying or enhancing fund raising strategies and practices, however, organizations must commit to diversity, both internally and among constituents and donors, to modifying the organizational mission so that it reflects this commitment, and to providing any necessary training or programs that enhance awareness of diversity issues. To accomplish this, an organization must have top-level leadership support as well as diversity in its ranks. A needs statement should be crafted that identifies the organization's status regarding diversity, its willingness to embrace diversity, and how diversity issues fit into the organization framework. Focus groups can provide excellent feedback and advice. Best practices can be developed through study and research, and a transformational program can be established.

Given the diverse populations of the United States and the fact that what we now call minorities will make up nearly half of the population by 2050, nonprofit organizations have a stellar opportunity to increase giving from diverse groups in the coming years. This fact provides our organizations with numerous opportunities to understand and interact with individuals offering diverse differences in languages, values, and cultural practices. It is a movement away from homogenizing everyone toward accepting and embracing cultural richness in our lives.

PART FIVE

SUCCESSFUL FUND RAISING METHODS

The chapters in Part Five provide information on special fund raising strategies and approaches. Two of the chapters are new to this edition of *Achieving Excellence*, one on using the Internet and one on special events. The special methods for fund raising presented in these chapters will aid organizations in their annual fund work and in determining the appropriate application of these new strategies to the total development program. (Additional information on specific approaches to individuals, corporations, and foundations can be found in Parts Three and Four.)

Direct mail, the topic of Chapter Nineteen, is a way of contacting large numbers of potential donors, lapsed donors, and current donors of small gifts. Less expensive than more personalized mail and telephone approaches, direct mail is generally the most effective and efficient way to build a donor base or get fund raising started.

The Internet has become an important tool for communicating with donors, accepting contributions from donors, recruiting new donors, renewing donors, acknowledging gifts, and providing information on planned giving. Chapter Twenty outlines how the Internet can be used at different levels of the total development program.

Special events are important to all organizations. For some they are a way of recruiting new donors; for some they are a way to thank donors; for others they are a way to engage their constituents. For all they are a public relations opportunity. Chapter Twenty-One provides guidance for developing successful special events.

Grassroots organizations can often be successful by using special approaches that are different from the generally accepted principles outlined in this book. Chapter Twenty-Two provides guidance for grassroots organizations in adapting the material in this book to their special situation.

CHAPTER NINETEEN

Direct Mail

Mal Warwick

To Hank Rosso, fund raising was "the gentle art of teaching people the joy of giving." Most fund raisers view direct mail as anything but gentle—a mechanistic, marketing-driven process that seems to bear little relation to the major gift fund raising, planned giving, and capital campaigns that comprise the backbone of traditional fund raising. But in this chapter, you'll read about a strategic, donor-centric approach to direct mail fund raising, one harmonious with Hank's philosophy, one that puts to work the methods and mechanisms of direct marketing in the service of fund raising. By providing superlative donor care to individuals recruited through the mail and carefully tracking and respecting their behavior and their preferences, many nonprofit organizations have learned that direct mail can become the engine of a dynamic and lucrative fund raising program, yielding hundreds or thousands of high-potential major and planned giving prospects.

In the years following the Second World War, when postage was cheap and the mail was first widely put to work to raise money for the fast-growing nonprofit sector, direct mail was viewed as a tool to generate gifts from people who wouldn't otherwise be reached by charity fund raising drives. For two decades thereafter, direct mail continued to be seen by most fund raisers as a cost-effective way to secure small donations—mostly first-time gifts—from the public at large. Its function was therefore to recruit (or, in the inelegant language of the field today, to "acquire") new donors.

In that unsophisticated environment, many charities persisted for years without even taking the trouble to solicit repeat gifts by mail: it was cheaper for a nonprofit organization to mail to the general public—possibly including previous donors as well as new prospects—in much the same way as it had in previous years.

Direct mail fund raising has come a long, long way since those not-so-good-old days. Nowadays, fund raisers can use direct mail to support their work with donors at every stage of their life cycle:

- *New donors.* Surveys repeatedly show that "I got a letter" is the reason most often cited by donors for giving a first-time gift to charity. For most nonprofits, direct mail is far and away the most cost-effective means to make the case for giving to a broad list of prospective donors. Even those large national charities that are able to use television to prospect for new donors often find that direct mail is more cost-effective (or helps them reach markets they wouldn't otherwise reach).
- *Active donors.* Experienced fund raisers know that a single gift does not a donor make. Only once a first-time donor has given a second gift is it prudent to call this an active donor. Typically, only about one-half of first-time donors ever give again to the same charity. By contrast, it's common for two-thirds of two-time donors to give a third gift. Direct mail is widely and successfully used to "convert" first-time donors into active donors.
- *Committed donors.* Donors who give an average of two or three small gifts every couple of years are the bread and butter of most direct mail fund raising programs. But to generate a level of revenue that will truly help sustain a nonprofit organization requires either much more frequent or much larger gifts. Donors who are unable to give large gifts can express their commitment with *monthly* gifts that, over time, will mount into the hundreds or thousands of dollars. Direct mail is an effective tool to recruit and retain monthly (or committed) donors.
- *High-dollar donors.* Most direct mail fund raising programs solicit—and receive—gifts of less than $100 each. Until the 1980s, larger gifts were unusual, and direct mail was only rarely used to ask for them; those that came in almost always represented the spontaneous generosity of the giver, not the fund raiser's intention. Increasingly since the closing years of the twentieth century, direct mail has been used effectively to solicit gifts of $500, $1,000, and occasionally much more. In appearance, in production quality, and in their message, these solicitations are typically very different from the direct mail packages used to solicit small gifts, but the principles underlying the process are the same.
- *Major donors.* One charity's "major donor" can be another's small fry. Many broadly based nonprofits classify anyone whose annual giving reaches

the $1,000 level as a major donor. Other organizations may draw the line at $25,000—or even $1 million. But wherever the line falls, direct mail is coming into wider use all the time to communicate with and sometimes solicit major donors. However, no one would confuse the sort of highly personalized packages mailed to major donors with "junk mail."

• *Legacy donors.* With a charitable bequest through a will or a trust, almost any donor can become a major donor. Bequests—typically amounting to tens of thousands of dollars—come from donors whose lifetime giving may have been modest (typically, a series of gifts of $100 or less over a number of years); in fact, many such legacy donors have *never* previously contributed to the organizations named in their wills. Donors in higher tax brackets or with more complex financial needs might choose instead to leave a legacy through some form of "planned giving" involving a charitable gift annuity, a pooled income fund, or a charitable trust. Direct mail is playing an increasingly prominent role in cultivating legacy prospects and marketing these and other legacy giving options.

From the fund raiser's perspective, then, direct mail can be an almost endlessly flexible tool. But direct mail isn't limited to the tactical applications to which it can be put in the fund raising process itself. Direct mail can play a strategic role in the life of a nonprofit organization.

DIRECT MAIL AND THE FIVE
FUNDAMENTAL FUND RAISING STRATEGIES

All fund raising strategies fall into one of five distinct categories, each one of which serves a unique strategic function—not just to raise funds but also to support a nonprofit organization in the pursuit of its mission. Taken together, the five strategies (*growth, involvement, visibility, efficiency,* and *stability*) encompass the full range of strategic directions that a nonprofit is likely to pursue at any given time in its organizational development (Warwick, 2000). Direct mail can be used effectively in specialized ways in the service of every one of these five strategies:

• *Growth.* If growth in its donor base is an organization's top priority, direct mail can be uniquely useful almost all the time. Donor recruitment is the classical first use of direct mail. It's the strategy of choice for most nonprofits seeking to reach out widely to attract new members.

• *Involvement.* If a nonprofit places a premium on involving its donors—to participate in grassroots lobbying, for example, or to volunteer or to patronize its productions—direct mail can be used not just to advertise these opportunities but sometimes to play a direct role in the involvement process as well. For instance, a nonprofit group involved in lobbying might include a petition or a postcard to an elected official in a fund appeal. Similarly, a museum might mail free tickets to an upcoming exhibition or discount coupons for use in its retail shop.

• *Visibility.* The work of many nonprofits is hampered by a low public profile and low name identification. Direct mail can often help address this problem— all the while recruiting new donors and generating revenue for the organization. The mail itself—which is a form of advertising, after all—can breed familiarity with the organization's name, logo, and mission. Devices included in the mail, such as decals, name labels, or bumper stickers, can multiply the mail's impact by reinforcing the organization's visibility.

• *Efficiency.* If an organization seeks to lower its cost of fund raising, increasing its use of direct mail to recruit new donors is probably not a good idea. Direct mail donor acquisition can be cost-effective, but it's rarely a revenue generator. However, direct mail can help build a monthly giving program, which can be extremely efficient. The mail can also be used to recruit, cultivate, and upgrade high-dollar donors with gifts of $1,000 or more.

• *Stability.* An organization that is overly dependent on one or a very few sources of revenue is likely, sooner or later, to give some thought to diversifying its fund raising program. If stabilization becomes the top priority, direct mail can be highly useful in a variety of ways: launching a new, low-donor recruitment program; upgrading responsive low-level donors to monthly giving; upgrading responsive mid-level donors with high-dollar solicitations; or promoting bequests and other forms of legacy gifts.

By now you might be wondering how this ultraflexible tool could possibly work in all these circumstances. A full answer to that question would require a lot bigger book than this, much less a single overview chapter. But it does seem appropriate to examine some of the basic elements of direct mail fund raising, so we'll put down our field glasses now and take up a microscope in the hope of gaining insight into how direct mail works.

HOW DIRECT MAIL WORKS

Donor recruitment and donor development are the yin and yang of direct mail fund raising. Without a steady stream of new recruits, a donor development program will shrivel, since donor attrition—due to death, changed economic circumstances, attraction to new causes, or other reasons—will shrink any donor file all too quickly. Conversely, donor recruitment is rarely profitable enough to be worth the trouble in the absence of an intensive program of donor development that will help a nonprofit develop larger contributions from its new donors. In fact, today donor recruitment is usually evaluated in terms of the investment required, or "acquisition cost," the average net cost of recruiting a new donor (the difference between a mailing's total cost and its total revenue, divided by the number of donors recruited).

Broadly speaking, donor recruitment makes use of large mailings involving tens or hundreds of thousands, even millions, of letters. The purpose of these "prospecting" or "acquisition" mailings is to bring in the largest possible number of new donors at an affordable acquisition cost. By contrast, donor development mailings—sent to those who have previously contributed—are designed to maximize the value of existing donors; donor development mailings are intended not just to generate high net revenue but also to educate and cultivate donors, increasing their loyalty and responsiveness. The most effective donor development mailings are designed on the basis of the individual behavior that donors have demonstrated in their relationships with the organization. For most nonprofits, donor development mailings are comparatively small, involving only a fraction as many letters as donor recruitment mailings (although in very large, mature programs, the relative sizes may be reversed).

Recruiting new donors from lists of people who are perceived to be good prospects typically yields a very modest response. Depending on the circumstances, that response might range from a fraction of 1 percent of the number of letters mailed to as much as 7 or 8 percent. Typically, these days, acquisition response falls between 0.5 and 2.5 percent (and for most nonprofits, toward the low end of this scale). Response to donor development solicitations is ordinarily much higher, ranging from 2 or 3 percent to as high as 50 percent. The difference in response is largely due to the difference in the lists used: cold prospects in the one case, hot ones in the other. Similarly, the average gift in a donor recruitment mailing is typically lower than that in a donor development mailing for the same organization (because first-time donors who contribute small amounts are typically not included in resolicitation mailings and because some donors increase or "upgrade" their gifts when resolicited).

Choosing Acquisition Lists

The art of donor recruitment requires great skill in the selection of lists. Most lists of prospective donors are, by definition, an unknown quantity. Since they have never before responded to an invitation to contribute to your organization, you can only use educated guesswork about the likelihood that they will respond to your mailing. However, there are several characteristics that predispose prospective donors to welcome your invitation. In approximate declining order of predictive value, those characteristics are as follows:

- They have written your organization expressing interest in contributing.
- They have phoned or e-mailed your organization asking for information.
- They have previously given tax-deductible gifts to similar causes or institutions.

- They have previously given tax-deductible gifts to causes or institutions whose donors are demographically similar to yours.

- They subscribe to periodicals that focus on the issues your organization addresses.

- They have previously given tax-deductible gifts to other causes or institutions.

- They subscribe to periodicals whose readers are demographically similar to your donors.

- They have demonstrated their responsiveness to direct mail by purchasing goods—and they share key demographic characteristics with your donors.

- They live in neighborhoods with demographic characteristics similar to those of your existing donors.

- They appear on lists that are "compiled" by list brokers from a variety of sources and are claimed to have affinity for your mission or to have contributed to similar organizations.

Note that two characteristics stand out above all others in this list: demonstrated donor behavior and proven responsiveness to direct mail. Many seemingly high-potential lists frequently prove to be hugely disappointing because they lack these characteristics. Among the best examples are lists of physicians who fail to contribute in significant numbers to health-related causes (unless they're already donors and direct mail responders) and lists of people who have attended a charity's fund raising event.

Choosing lists is an art. And that's true in donor development mailings as well as in donor recruitment.

Segmenting Your Donor File

Successful donor development rests on the principle that some donors will be able to contribute more than other donors. There are four properties of a donor that help determine potential in the cold arithmetic of direct mail fund raising:

- *Recency.* How recently a donor's last gift was received is an excellent indicator of the likelihood that he or she will give again in response to another appeal. Forget the "logic" that people who have recently given will choose to wait awhile before giving again. There is a very high correlation between recency and responsiveness in subsequent direct mail fund raising.

- *Frequency.* The greater the number of times a donor has given to your organization, the higher the likelihood that he or she will give again when you ask. Frequency is usually measured in terms of the number of gifts received during a recent period, typically twelve, twenty-four, or thirty-six months. A group of donors who have given twice during that time will probably give more than twice as much as an equal number of one-time donors, and those who have given three times will almost certainly give far more than three times as much as single-gift donors.

• *Giving level.* Donors who typically give gifts of $10, $15, or $20 can be a reliable and even lucrative source of funds for a nonprofit organization—so long as they give frequently. However, equally frequent donors at higher levels—$50, $100, or more—are worth disproportionately more. Those whose gifts are more generous are, presumably, either more affluent (or at least freer with their money) or more committed to the cause, or both.

• *Source or channel of first gift.* It's a truism that people who respond to direct mail are people who have acquired the habit of responding to direct mail. The corollary of this proposition is that people who are accustomed to responding to telephone appeals or attending special events *will not typically* respond to direct mail. When selecting donors to include in a direct mail appeal, it's not always wise to include those who have previously contributed only by other means.

The process of selecting donors to include in an appeal mailing (called *segmentation*) requires taking all four of these donor properties into account. By doing so, a fund raiser may fine-tune a mailing so that it is as cost-effective as possible.

Naturally, a smaller mailing, limited to those donors who have given most generously, most recently, and most frequently, and who are proven direct mail responders, is likely to yield the greatest revenue at the lowest possible cost. Such small, selective mailings also allow the organization to concentrate its attention on those donors who have demonstrated the greatest interest in its work, a high priority in donor development. A larger, more inclusive mailing may have other objectives: maximizing the number of current donors, for example, or giving everyone an opportunity to contribute at year's end (when donors are most likely to be responsive).

However, important as it is, list selection—whether in donor recruitment or in donor development—is far from the only factor that determines the success or failure of a mailing.

FACTORS THAT MAKE THE
MOST DIFFERENCE IN A DIRECT MAIL CAMPAIGN

You are the most important ingredient in any direct mail fund raising program you might undertake. Half the response to direct mail is determined by your organization's track record and the power of your message, the quality and visibility of your organization's leadership, the ties of your work to issues of broad public concern, and the amount of publicity you get. The other half of the response is affected by factors under the fund raiser's control. That 50 percent breaks down this way:

- *List selection.* This is by far the most important ingredient you can control. Call it 25 percent of the recipe, or about as much as all the other controllable elements combined. The most brilliant appeal for the most dynamic organization in the world won't work if it's mailed to the wrong lists.
- *The "offer."* Next is how you structure the request for funds: what you ask for and what you tell donors they'll receive in exchange (even if that's strictly intangible). Call it 10 percent of the total picture. Every mailing must be built around a "marketing concept"—a simple, straightforward connection between the offer and the market or intended audience.
- *Copywriting.* The actual wording of your appeal may account for 5 percent of the total picture. Most direct mail experts consider the letter itself to be the single most important element in a direct mail package, and experience shows that a conversational and personal style is most effective (Warwick, 2001). But it will work far better if the outer envelope, response device, and all other package elements reinforce the marketing concept of your appeal.
- *Format.* The size, shape, and color of the envelope, the character of the inserts, and the extent of personalization may all have significant bearing on the results. The right format choices can be as important as the copy—about 5 percent of the total. However, more often than not, the "right format" in donor recruitment mailings is a standard, white, business-size outer envelope mailed via nonprofit bulk rate and containing an 8½-by-11-inch two-page or four-page letter, response device, and reply envelope. In any case, everything in a direct mail package must fit together to form an effective whole.
- *Design.* Once the format is set, the designer's skill with type, color, and placement can have an equal (5 percent) influence on the outcome.

There is a sixth factor in the equation, virtually impossible to assign a fixed value. It's *timing.* Timing comes into play in one of two ways: either through the phenomenon of seasonality (because donors tend to be more responsive at the end of the year and at the beginning of the year and less so in midsummer, for example) or because natural or historic disasters preoccupy the public. Timing matters—sometimes a lot. There's just no way to know in advance when its true power will be felt.

Now let's take a brief look at direct mail "packages."

THE ELEMENTS OF A DIRECT MAIL PACKAGE

These days, in direct mail fund raising in the United States, at least four components come into play: the letter itself, the outer envelope (or "carrier"), a reply envelope, and a response device (sometimes called a "coupon").

Many direct mail fund raising packages include other elements as well. Brochures are commonly used. Experience has shown that general brochures distract the reader from the action elements of the package, namely, the letter and response device. However, when a brochure is specially developed for a particular mailing, it has the potential to improve the results. Other inserts are also popular:

- "Lift letters" (or "lift notes") that highlight an important endorsement or a new argument that supports the case for giving
- "Buckslips" that characteristically illustrate a premium or special benefit available to those who respond by sending gifts
- Other items such as copies of press clippings, memoranda from field staff, photographs, or membership cards
- "Front-end premiums," which is a fancy way of describing the freebies often included in direct mail packages to entice the reader to open the envelope (and induce guilt)—such items as address labels, bookmarks, decals, or calendars

Direct mail fund raising packages come in a myriad of sizes, shapes, colors, and formats. In the United States, standard, business-size letter packages are the least expensive and the most common, using 8½-by-11-inch letterhead paper and #10 carrier envelopes with windows. In the simplest package, the addressee's name and address appear only once, usually on the response device, and are positioned to show through the window on the outer envelope. Larger-quantity mailings may involve unconventional shapes and sizes and include a half-dozen or more instances of "personalization," in which the addressee's name appears in many different places. (In small quantities, multiple, personalized, "in-line" packages such as these are often prohibitively costly.)

Just as it's sometimes wise to employ a more costly format to achieve higher impact, additional elements such as lift notes and front-end premiums can be effective in boosting response and, despite their cost, increasing the cost-effectiveness of a direct mail appeal. Just as often, however, a simple letter package will do as well as anything else.

Currently, direct mail package costs (including postage, printing, and the cost of "lettershopping," or addressing and assembling the contents into packages, affixing postage, and mailing) vary from a low in the range of 25 to 30 cents to a high of $5 or more per package. Ordinarily, less expensive packages are used most widely in donor recruitment efforts, and the most expensive (and most personalized) ones are used almost exclusively in donor development. Thus a typical donor recruitment mailing of 100,000 letters might cost a total of, say, $30,000 to $50,000, while a donor development letter (such as a special appeal for funds) mailed to 10,000 donors might run $8,000 to $20,000 or more.

Now that we've touched on the cost of direct mail, it seems appropriate to take a look at the revenue we might reasonably expect to generate.

BENCHMARKS FOR EVALUATION IN DIRECT MAIL FUND RAISING

There are three levels of assessment in a direct mail fund raising program: individual mailings, the direct mail program, and the development program as a whole. To gain a full appreciation of the value of direct mail, it's necessary to view the realities at each of these levels.

• *Individual mailings.* In all mailings, we look at the rate of response expressed as a percentage and the average gift, and we compare cost with revenue. However, these three measures only scratch the surface. The true success of a donor recruitment mailing is usually calculated in terms of the acquisition cost—the net cost to enlist a new donor. A select few nonprofits are fortunate enough to recruit donors at a profit; many others typically pay an average of between $2 and $25 per donor; some are willing to invest $100 or even more, because their donors are worth so much more to them. In the case of donor development mailings, the key to assessing the results is to compare the cost of the mailing with the amount of revenue it generates. Some mailers measure the "fund raising ratio or cost," or the number of cents it costs to raise a dollar. Others calculate the ratio of revenue to cost, or return on investment, while still others look at net revenue per donor mailed. They all amount to much the same thing, however: typically, a donor development mailing will generate between two and ten times its cost (depending on a host of factors far too numerous to discuss here).

• *The direct mail program.* Viewing the direct mail program as a whole requires us to take into account not just the net revenue that results from donor development mailings but also the net *investment* typically entailed by donor recruitment mailings. A large program focused on efficiency might limit the investment in prospecting to a level sufficient to replace donors lost to attrition; such a program could easily generate between four and eight times its costs in revenue (translating into a fund raising cost of 12 to 25 cents per dollar raised). A smaller program, or one geared to a growth strategy that thus requires heavy emphasis on donor recruitment, might yield only two or three times its costs (creating a fund raising ratio of 33 to 50 cents per dollar raised).

• *The development program.* From a larger perspective, the principal reason to sustain a direct mail fund raising program might have little to do with the net revenue it generates—an amount that in many cases is decidedly modest when viewed against the organization's budget as a whole. For many fund raisers, the principal functions of direct mail recruitment and donor development are to identify and cultivate prospective major donors and prospective planned giving donors. Thus viewed, the principal benchmarks to evaluate might be (1) the number of direct mail donors who reach a predetermined threshold (say, $1,000), at which point they become candidates for cultivation as possible major donors, and (2) the number of direct mail donors who express interest in charitable gift annuities, bequests, or other forms of planned giving.

In other words, establishing benchmarks to evaluate the success of a direct mail fund raising program requires a clear understanding at the outset of what the program is intended to accomplish. There are few absolutes in direct mail fund raising.

There are, however, basic principles involved in direct mail fund raising. They are the ten most important things about direct mail fund raising.

1. *Direct mail fund raising is a process, not an event.* Direct mail is a way to communicate with lots of people and to build rewarding relationships with them. Skillfully used (in combination with other direct response techniques), direct mail can lead donors through all the stages of the fund raising cycle. Individual mailings are mere building blocks in the relationship-building process; the only way to promote genuine donor development is through a continuing, year-round sequence of communication that includes many mailings in the course of a year.

2. *The true rewards from direct mail come only over the long haul.* The principal virtue of direct mail is that it can generate steady, predictable, undesignated income. Still, the richest rewards from a direct mail fund raising program may come in the form of bequests or other forms of planned gifts—and such a gift may not come until fifteen or twenty years after a donor is recruited by mail. The success of a direct mail fund raising program is often evaluated by comparing the acquisition cost for new donors with the demonstrable long-term value they bring to the organization—benchmarks that cannot be reliably calculated in fewer than five years' time.

3. *Cost is less important than cost-effectiveness.* It costs money to raise money. Sometimes net revenue rises when an investment in a mailing is enlarged. In any case, the sheer cost of a mailing is less important than its outcome. It usually pays to invest more in top donors and less in the least responsive and least generous donors. Cheaper is not always better.

4. *The list is paramount.* It's worth emphasizing over and over again: the list is by far the most important factor in a mailing. The difference between mailing to alumni or nonalumni, to more accomplished alums or more recent alums, to donors or nondonors, to direct mail responders or nonresponders, or simply to one list that has proved to be responsive instead of another that hasn't, can make or break a mailing.

5. *Next comes the offer.* The offer you make to the recipients of your mailing is next in importance only to the list. If you're mailing to solicit an annual gift or membership renewal, it's important that the offer appear front and center in the package. In fund raising, the offer revolves around the fundamental reason you're mailing—for example, whether to recruit new donors, renew existing donors' annual support, enlist them in a monthly giving club, secure special gifts, or persuade them to remember your organization in their wills. Each of these "marketing concepts" requires a very distinctive letter.

6. *Segmentation is the key to cost-effectiveness.* Whom you include in a mailing list and whom you exclude determines the outcome of a mailing. It rarely makes sense to mail an appeal to everyone in your donor file. Almost always, such an effort will be far more cost-effective if you exclude those who haven't contributed during the last two or three years or who haven't contributed more than token gifts. Equally important, by "segmenting" your list, you can reserve special treatment for your top donors (first-class postage, personalization, higher production values). Special treatment like this frequently pays off in bigger returns in the short run—and more numerous legacies over the long haul.

7. *Annual giving provides the structure for direct mail fund raising.* One of the most basic assumptions in direct mail fund raising is that donors must be encouraged to give at least one gift per year; less frequent giving is unlikely to produce enough net revenue to justify the effort. In many organizations, an "annual campaign" or "annual fund" serves as the vehicle to inculcate this idea in donors' minds. Other organizations adopt a "membership" structure and often employ a "renewal series" to urge donors to meet their implied obligation to contribute at least once annually. The renewal series, based on the model of magazine subscription renewal notices, entails sending members a series of notices—usually between three and ten—until they respond with gifts. This approach is usually very cost-effective and promotes donor loyalty as well. Even nonprofits that maintain neither an annual fund nor a membership campaign are likely to mail a year-end holiday appeal to their donors every year.

8. *Testing leads to incremental improvements over time.* The distinguishing characteristic of direct response—which includes direct mail, telemarketing, direct response television, and e-mail marketing—is that its results are precisely measurable. If you want to know which of two offers will produce the better results, you can (normally) construct a test, simultaneously mailing letters containing one offer to group A and letters containing the other offer to group B, with the two groups chosen at random from the same list so that they are statistically identical. Testing allows direct mail fund raisers to boost results over time by identifying (and then putting to work) the most successful lists, offers, and messages.

9. *Repetition is essential.* Success in direct mail fund raising, as in any area of marketing or advertising, requires that materials have a consistent "look and feel" over time. This normally means using the same logo, theme, slogan, or "tag line" long after the organization's board members and executives have concluded

that they're boring. Repetition reinforces donors' views of an organization. In modern parlance, it helps a nonprofit establish and sustain its "brand identity."

10. *Without timely and accurate record keeping, direct mail is impossible.* The donor database is the sine qua non of direct mail fund raising. Without an up-to-date database, fund raisers can't measure results, segment, test, or assess the success of their development program. And building relationships with donors requires detailed record keeping, too: otherwise, how could we know which donors are strong performers and which are weak?

I've called these the ten most important things about direct mail fund raising, but in reality they all apply to direct response in general. Ten or twenty years ago, that might have been of little interest to most fund raisers who used direct mail. Nowadays, though, direct mail fund raisers cannot ignore the roles of telemarketing, on-line communications (see Chapter Twenty-One), and video (including television) in the fund raising process. The very context in which we practice has changed.

In recent years, the context has changed in one other, very important respect: the advent of government regulation of the fund raising process. Legislation in more than forty states now requires many direct mail and telephone fund raisers to register, pay annual fees, and submit frequent financial reports to charity regulation offices. In fact, the process has become so complex and onerous that a cottage industry of specialized attorneys and accountants has come into being to help bear this load.

THE CHANGING CONTEXT: DIRECT RESPONSE

Today, direct mail rarely stands alone. To maximize returns and to enhance the long-term value of direct mail donors, more and more direct mail specialists are incorporating other communications media into their donor recruitment and donor development programs. For example, telemarketing is often effectively used to boost renewal rates, to recruit monthly donors, to upgrade donors to high-dollar annual giving clubs, or for other important tasks. E-mail and Web sites are used to supplement donor or member services—with free electronic newsletters, for example—as well as to attract and cultivate prospective donors or members. For some nonprofits, direct response television is a cost-effective way to recruit new donors—but their donor development efforts are built on direct mail communications.

In this new context, direct mail fund raisers are learning how to integrate mail with communications using other direct response media. Integration complicates the fund raiser's life with potential schedule conflicts and with more intricate list segmentation. Should you send the same message to donors recruited through a television infomercial featuring a high-profile celebrity as you send to those who enrolled through a direct mail package in which the letter was signed by a staff member? No! Yet integration offers the promise of synergy—and with it, increased net revenue.

Fund raisers are also coming to understand that direct mail must be seen as an essential ingredient in an organization's development program as a whole. This requires integrating direct mail efforts (and the resulting donor or member base) with activities to secure major gifts and planned gifts. This kind of integration is easier to describe than to accomplish, but the added revenue potential it brings is too substantial to ignore.

Integration—both with other forms of direct response and with other fund raising activities—is the new reality direct mail fund raisers must learn to live with.

IS DIRECT MAIL DOOMED TO DIE?

In the mid-1990s, following the advent of the World Wide Web, it became fashionable for fund raisers to speculate that sooner or later (and many thought much sooner), direct mail would die because donors would quickly gravitate to e-mail and the Internet to express their philanthropic preferences. There are those who assert that in five or ten years, on-line giving will dwarf all other giving channels, reducing or even eliminating direct mail fund raising.

I consider myself an optimist about on-line giving and an enthusiastic advocate for its use, but I also believe that direct mail will continue to play a significant role. I believe it's a safe bet that in 2010, billions of letters will still be delivered by hand, and millions of donors will still insist on using the mail to send contributions. And those generous individuals will still prefer to receive information from the causes and institutions they support. A thorough understanding of direct mail will enable fund raisers to meet the expectations of those donors, promoting philanthropy by serving them in the manner they prefer, just as others might prefer the Internet.

CONCLUSION

Direct mail came into its own during the twentieth century. It continues to play a major role in the twenty-first. However, all too many fund raisers continue to think of direct mail in the last century's terms—recruiting and renewing donors in a stand-alone program with no meaningful connection to the broader development picture. By approaching direct mail as the flexible tool that it is and viewing it in terms of its potential to recruit new donors and also serve major gift, planned giving, and capital campaign fund raising, today's fund raisers can gain an enormous advantage for the organizations they serve.

CHAPTER TWENTY

The Internet as a Fund Raising Vehicle

Theodore R. Hart

Although many aspects of fund raising have grown and changed since the first edition of *Achieving Excellence in Fund Raising* was published, no change has demanded or received more attention than the arrival of *e-philanthropy,* or the use of the Internet for philanthropic purposes. In the first edition, Hank Rosso eloquently stated that "fund raising cannot be a separate, isolated activity." So it is with the Internet. To succeed using the Internet as a fund raising vehicle requires integration of on-line techniques with the organization's off-line activities as well as other on-line efforts in support of its mission and programs.

Professional fund raisers are typically expected to be familiar with a wide range of fund raising techniques or strategies, and some have developed specialized skills. The growth of e-philanthropy has required even the most seasoned professionals to learn new skills and to reevaluate how they approach nearly every aspect of fund raising. This is not to suggest that e-philanthropy has taken the place of any traditional fund raising methods; actually the opposite. E-philanthropy tools add a new dimension of efficiency and require high levels of integration with every off-line approach to attracting philanthropic support. Although some organizations may be tempted to treat e-philanthropy as a specialty area to be administered separately from other fund raising methods, much in the way some might have a prospect research specialist on staff, doing so would diminish the overall effectiveness of these tools and deny the opportunity to fully benefit from them. This chapter will provide an overview of e-philanthropy techniques nonprofits can use as part of the total development program to cultivate and maintain steward relationships, communicate and invite advocacy for their cause, and solicit contributions on-line.

DEFINING E-PHILANTHROPY

E-philanthropy is a set of efficiency-building Internet-based techniques that can be employed to build and enhance relationships with stakeholders interested in the success of a nonprofit organization.

E-philanthropy is the building and enhancing of relationships with volunteers and supporters of nonprofit organizations using the Internet. It includes the contribution of cash or real property or the purchase of products and services to benefit a nonprofit organization and the storage of and usage of electronic data and services to support relationship building and fund raising activities

SEPTEMBER 11, 2001

There is no date we can refer to that marked the beginning of direct mail or planned giving. But after more than two years of strong growth in both its effectiveness and its infrastructure, e-philanthropy came of age on September 11, 2001.

In the days and weeks following the terrorist attacks on the United States, the world turned to the Internet as a vehicle for its charitable response to the tragic events. The level of on-line philanthropic activity in the weeks following these events was so extensive that the experience has become a defining moment in U.S. philanthropy.

Contributors were aided by several for-profit Web sites that quickly linked their on-line credit card processing systems to create an opportunity for millions of their visitors to make a contribution to relief-related organizations and funds. The American Red Cross reported that for the first time in its history on-line, donations outnumbered those given via their toll-free number, by a three-to-one margin. A Red Cross spokesperson said, "Clearly, the power of the Internet is huge" (Christensen, 2001).

In November 2001, the America Online Time Warner Foundation and America Online, Inc.; the Cisco Foundation and Cisco Systems, Inc.; and Yahoo!, in partnership with more than twenty nonprofit foundations and associations, launched a robust, multifaceted charity portal aimed at allowing all nonprofits and donors to make use of the Internet to benefit charitable causes. Network for Good (http://networkforgood.com) incorporated the assets of AOL Time

Warner's Helping.org in hopes of making donating, volunteering, and other tools available at no cost to all charities, big and small, whether they have a Web site or not.

ENGAGING THE DONOR

The true strength of e-philanthropy-based methods lies in their ability to do more than simply function as a novel way in which to raise money. The Internet is an ideal platform from which to reach, inform, and engage potential donors, many of whom may be beyond the reach of normal fund raising channels. Communication and relationship building are key components to the Rosso approach to fund raising and remain so in the successful use of these techniques.

Charities seeking success on-line should approach the Internet as a communication and stewardship tool first and a fund raising tool second. Any seasoned fund raiser will tell you that when you can build and enhance a relationship with a prospective donor, you have a much higher chance of successfully soliciting a gift.

Whether the solicitation for support comes via news broadcasts reporting on a tragic event or in the form of an e-mail message from a charity, donors must still be asked for support if organizations expect to receive it. Although there are many more on-line donors now than there were prior to September 11, 2001, these contributors are not surfing the Web looking for a cause to support. These experienced e-philanthropists are much more likely to be inspired to contribute based on the mission, the stated need, and the opportunity to give presented by a charity they have likely already supported off-line. But to obtain their support, *they must be asked!*

Local and national charities that do not offer their supporters the opportunity to communicate and contribute on-line are not reaching their full potential and are not preparing for the future. Every nonprofit has the opportunity to reach out to more donors and prospects than they could ever afford to contact using traditional methods of direct mail, telephone, or personal visits, but they must cultivate an on-line relationship before asking for support. This cultivation and solicitation must be part of an integrated fund raising program that includes both on-line and off-line fund raising techniques.

BACK TO THE FUTURE

The arrival of e-philanthropy is not the first time that nonprofit organizations and fund raisers have adapted to new technologies. Radio, television, newspapers, telephones, fax machines, computers, electronic databases, and direct mail have all affected the way we raise money. Some of the new methods that have evolved are more successful than others, and not all of them have been used with equal success by all nonprofits.

Each new advance in technology has created a particular set of challenges for nonprofits and their donors; each has triggered a corresponding set of fund raising norms. For nonprofit organizations, the Internet provides an unprecedented and cost-effective opportunity to build and enhance relationships with supporters, volunteers, clients, and the communities they serve. Connecting with supporters on-line provides a new means for converting interest in a mission to direct involvement and support.

"Make no mistake," one scholar wrote, "the e-philanthropy revolution is here to stay, and it will transform charitable giving in as profound a way as technology is changing the commercial world. Charities that have dismissed e-philanthropy as a fad, or run from it in confusion, will sooner or later need to become reconciled to it. If they don't, they risk losing touch with donors and imperiling the vitality of their work" (Austin, 2001).

To harness the power of e-philanthropy, nonprofit organizations must remember two things:

1. E-philanthropy should be seen as a set of relationship-building tools first and fund raising tools second.

2. Nonprofit Web sites and the use of e-mail for promotional purposes will succeed when integrated into every other form of communication used by the nonprofit (direct mail, brochures, planned giving, newsletters, telephone, radio, print media, and so on).

Michael Johnston (2002, p. 47) points out, "Lawmakers are only now coming to grips with the legal ramifications of Internet tools such as e-mail and the Web. It's inevitable that they'll pay increasingly close attention to these ramifications, since there are genuine issues of privacy and security for regulators to consider."

The Internet challenges existing charitable regulation. As a set of tools, e-philanthropy crosses the boundaries of traditional jurisdictions by giving even the smallest organizations the ability to communicate and solicit support on a global scale. But in the absence of specific regulation related to the Internet, many regulators are attempting to apply current laws to on-line activities. Scores of states and local municipalities are attempting to require registration of every charity whose on-line donation opportunities are accessible via the Web to citizens of those jurisdictions.

If all charities were required to register in all states, provinces, counties, and municipalities, the cost in both money and time to maintain such registration would extinguish the use of the Internet for philanthropic purposes. The National Association of State Charity Officers (http://www.NASCOnet.org) has issued a document known as the *Charleston Principles,* which call for a fair and equitable approach to on-line charity registration. Though not law, the document is a set of guidelines that all states are urged to consider enacting. In addition to this important effort, the ePhilanthropy Code of Ethics was established by ePhilanthropyFoundation.Org. Nonprofits that follow these principles can be confident that their on-line efforts are consistent with sound ethical practices—and more important, they will send a signal to donors that the nonprofit is knowledgeable about and committed to the ethical use of the Internet in its cultivation and solicitation of support.

NEW OPPORTUNITIES

The Internet provides donors with an easy way to contribute, using the Web to fulfill their charitable intentions. As e-philanthropy has emerged, organizations have discovered that consistent and deliberate e-mail communication driving traffic to the organization's well-organized and informative Web site has become the key to success.

Years of experience in the off-line world have taught fund raisers that attention to detail, privacy, security of information, and honesty in reporting while building a case for support are key components to any successful solicitation of support, whether that support comes in the form of volunteerism, advocacy, or contributions. Through the appropriate use of permission-based e-mail, a nonprofit can provide its donors with increased access to information and more timely details regarding the stewardship and solicitation of their charitable support. This increased access and detailed information help strengthen the relationship and trust between the nonprofit and supporters. To earn this trust, nonprofit organizations must become accustomed to increased levels of scrutiny and demands for evidence that the charity is well managed and provides service consistent with its mission.

Building a Web site is not enough. Success on the Internet requires an integrated strategy that embraces standards for protecting and preserving donor relationships. For-profit vendors have developed a wide array of services to help "power" nonprofits' Web sites.

As charities look at various services, they should start by understanding the strategic objectives for their Web site. It is not necessary to have all the "bells and whistles" before engaging prospects and donors on-line. It is advisable to start small and build slowly. Begin with collecting e-mail addresses, communicating via e-mail, and offering the opportunity to give on-line via an encrypted Web page.

Taking the time to plan ahead can often mean the difference between mere use of the Internet and the development of a successful e-philanthropy strategy.

The exact mix of strategies and techniques are as varied as the number and types of nonprofits that deploy them.

E-philanthropy techniques fall into six categories:

1. Communication, education, and stewardship
2. On-line donations and membership
3. Event registration and management
4. Prospect research
5. Volunteer recruitment and management
6. Relationship building and advocacy

The particular mix of tools and services for each organization will vary widely; organizations should always evaluate options and test assumptions. Incremental improvements and additions of services will help supporters and staff become accustomed to using the new technology and communicating via the Internet. Only by testing can the organization learn which techniques perform the best.

Communication, Education, and Stewardship

The first step toward building on-line donations, a volunteer base, and a clearer communication of the organization's mission with a larger audience using the power of the Internet is to identify whom you want to reach, what you want them to do, and what will inspire them to accept the organization's invitation to take action, volunteer, or give.

Use of the Internet as a stand-alone solution is not effective. Although some observers have predicted that e-philanthropy will eventually replace many traditional approaches to soliciting support, that will not be the case. Just as television failed to kill radio yet changed it significantly, the Internet will change traditional forms of fund raising, not by eliminating them but by altering their utility and increasing their effectiveness.

Just as there are no shortcuts to long-term success off-line, there are similarly no short cuts on-line. E-philanthropy methods permit an organization to communicate and engage supporters not only through a Web site but also directly via e-mail, which can direct attention back to the organization. But it takes time to build effective communication tools.

As part of an integrated communication and fund raising strategy, e-philanthropy offers effective and efficient opportunities for nonprofits to communicate with a much wider audience than they might otherwise have the resources to do. Direct mail, telephone, radio, television, personal visits, and other traditional means of communication with supporters all have significant personnel, printing, postage, or other costs associated with them.

The organization's Web site should reflect the mission of the organization; outdated content on a Web site indicates that there is nothing new to share. The Web site must be a true resource for up-to-date information related to the charity's mission and provide ample opportunities to support and communicate with the charity.

Supporters who begin or maintain an on-line relationship with an organization have expectations of communication different from those of their off-line counterparts. In most cases, people who communicate via the Internet will expect to receive an automatic electronic response.

Integration. By promoting on-line resources and services through integration with traditional marketing and communication channels, organizations significantly increase the effectiveness of overall operations while providing additional options to supporters.

- *Direct mail and telemarketing.* Every direct mail and telephone appeal should provide the opportunity for supporters to give by mailing in the response form or by making a gift or pledge on-line. In the case of telemarketing, those who might be at their computer when the call is placed could be directed to an on-line audio or video message that can enhance the telemarketer's message and could then be prompted to give on-line.
- *Print material and literature.* Every publication and printed item should include the organization's Web address. Wherever the address or phone number for the nonprofit is printed, the Web address should also appear. Large and expensive-to-produce publications like an annual report can be posted on a Web site in portable document format (pdf). Directing donors and supporters to download and print the file not only saves money but also expands the number of people who can access the report and become comfortable with on-line interaction within the organization.
- *Brand building and promotional opportunities.* Public service announcements (PSAs) and paid advertising and marketing efforts on television and radio and in print are often means organizations use to get their message to a wider audience. By directing those hearing or viewing these messages to a Web site, the nonprofit is able to make a more comprehensive appeal for support of its mission and provide additional information.
- *Press.* Press conferences, television and radio appearances, and public speaking engagements are prime opportunities to promote on-line resources. Nonprofits should establish an on-line press room, providing in a downloadable format background information, press releases, photos, and other material of interest to the media. This will give the press an opportunity to learn about the organization at any time, day or night.

Getting the Word Out. The on-line environment offers several opportunities to communicate with potential supporters. There are four essential aspects to getting the word out on-line:

- *E-mail.* This is the most powerful and most cost-effective on-line communication tool available to nonprofit organizations. In accordance with the ePhilanthropy Code of Ethics, it is important that supporters "opt in" to nonprofit e-mail lists. This means that they give permission to receive e-mail from the nonprofit; permission should never be assumed. Even after permission is granted, the supporter must also be given the option to have his or her name removed from the e-mail list at any time. This is known as "opt out."

Several vendors have developed services that make it easy for organizations to use e-mail and the Internet for soliciting donations, outreach, education, and advocacy strategies. The integration of the organization's Web site (content and encrypted on-line donor forms) and e-mail (pushing the message to supporters), along with direct mail, telephone, and other campaigns, not only provides additional options for donors but also gives them the opportunity to become more informed and engaged donors.

- *Search engines.* Search engines provide ways of searching the Internet—instantly. Each has its own criteria for cataloguing the resources of the Internet. Yet no single search engine searches more than 16 percent of the Internet. Therefore, it is important to register the organization's Web site with several of the leading search engines.

- *"Pass-along" marketing.* Although it is highly unlikely that anyone receiving a direct mail appeal from a charity will make several copies, address envelopes to their friends and family, and mail copies of the letter urging that they also support the organization, it is highly likely that the recipient of an electronic communication will send copies to others. Through "virtual marketing," we ask the recipient of an e-mail to send the message along to other people who might be interested. Within seconds, the message can be sent to scores of people on the recipient's personal e-mail list. Very important to the success of this method is the fact that the message is now being sent by a friend or family member, thereby increasing the chances of its being read, following a proven fund raising method.

- *Send to a friend.* Visitors to a nonprofit organization's Web site are often looking for expert information related to the mission of that organization. By offering the option to send an article or link to a Web page on the site to a friend, the utility of the Web site's content is further enhanced. Once again, the power of this feature is that the recommendation is coming from a trusted friend or family member.

On-Line Donations and Membership

Most visitors to a Web site go there because they know or care something about the organization or its mission, and they are seeking information. Effective sites offer multiple opportunities for visitors to support the organization through advocacy, volunteerism, or donations, often on each page of the Web site.

The Internet's impact in an organization is measurable. Response rates are more quickly and accurately measured than in other media. This combination of price and response measurement makes e-mail, particularly e-mail newsletters, very attractive to nonprofits.

On-Line Donations. The technical details of establishing and owning a secure e-commerce server can be overwhelming; however, with the variety of vendors and several free services available for processing on-line gifts in accordance with ethical and security standards, most nonprofits have the opportunity for professional assistance to undertake the creation of a "home-grown" on-line donation solution. According to the ePhilanthropyFoundation.Org's *Tips for Online Giving,* charities should offer Web sites that use encryption technology to ensure appropriate security for on-line donations and data transmission. Before entering any information, donors should be able to verify that the page requesting their credit card information is secure (encrypted). The letters https://—rather than http://—should precede the page's URL, or there should be an unbroken key or padlock symbol located in the corner of the Web browser.

Planned Giving On-Line. Planned giving can often seem complicated to both donors and nonprofits. For donors, education is an important component for learning how they can match their charitable intentions with their estate plans. Nonprofit organizations face the challenge of identifying individuals who may support their missions with planned gifts—and then providing them with the details they need to choose the right planned giving vehicle. For both large and small nonprofits, and for donors and prospects, the Internet is increasingly becoming both a strong marketing tool for planned giving and a great resource for information. The Internet can be an effective vehicle to promote and enhance planned giving efforts, allowing nonprofits to provide detailed information regarding tax-wise giving to more of their donors and prospects and allowing prospects to model different planned giving approaches.

Information. It is relatively easy for most nonprofits to put planned giving information on their Web sites; keeping the site updated and legally accurate is more difficult. Several services provide Internet-ready tools that are regularly updated and kept compliant with changing tax laws. These tools are a cost-effective way to provide compelling and effective planned giving content.

Many donors are turning to the Internet to investigate for themselves how a planned gift would work, instead of calling an adviser or asking a charity for a planned giving illustration.

To meet the needs of these donors, charities can include on-line tools and gift planning calculators on their Web sites. This information makes available to donors information and resources that had once been the exclusive purview of accountants, lawyers, and planned giving professionals. Providing these tools gives another reason for donors to visit the Web site.

Marketing. Once planned giving information is available on the charity's Web site, it is time to invite donors and prospects to visit. Most board members and staff members hesitate to discuss planned giving with donors and prospects for fear they'll be asked questions they can't answer. The Web site provides a valuable tool in reaching out to these donors by providing self-explanatory planned giving pages. Local attorneys, financial planners, and other advisers should be contacted and made aware of the content and services available. These advisers are often asked by their clients if they know of reputable organizations they might support via the will or planned giving vehicle. Advisers not wanting to appear to have a conflict of interest will often offer several options. They are much more likely to advise in favor of organizations they feel are prepared and understand the concepts and topics on which they are asked for advice. Sometimes it takes traditional communication vehicles like brochures and letters to get prospects and advisers to the Web site.

Event Registration and Management

As discussed in Chapter Twenty-One, e-philanthropy special event management makes event registration easier for nonprofits and event attendees. On-line services are available to send event invitations, organize volunteer activities, maintain income and expense records, and provide high-quality registration and attendee services. Golf tournaments, walks, and silent and live auctions each have specialized registration and item organization needs. Several on-line services have been developed to address one or more of these specific requirements.

Surveying the participants from the prior year's event can enhance special event planning. An on-line survey form can be e-mailed to participants to obtain their feedback. There are several free and fee-based on-line survey tools available.

Prospect Research

Although an incredible amount of information about fund raising prospects is available on-line, it's important to pay close attention to the management and use of information gathered. Whether you subscribe to the Association of Professional Researchers for Advancement (APRA) (http://www.aprahome.org) code of ethics or develop your own privacy policy, it is important to protect sensitive and confidential information. (Prospect research and individuals as donors are discussed more fully in Chapters Ten and Thirteen, respectively.)

Manual Prospect Research. It is estimated that the Internet now contains more than half a trillion Web pages and is growing daily. The challenge is to determine which structures are most likely to support fund raising. Indexed Web sites offer an easier approach to finding helpful databases. These sites have been developed to aid access to information databases and Web sites.

Internet Prospector (http://www.internet-prospector.org) is the very best customized nonprofit site for doing manual prospect research over the Net. The site is set up as a road map to resources that have direct bearing on gathering information on prospects. Staffed by a national network of volunteers, this nonprofit site provides a unique service that "mines" the Internet to report on resources of use to prospect researchers.

Several university development programs have developed Web sites cataloguing useful Web sites and resources for use by their own fund raising staffs, and many of these sites are open to the Internet public.

Electronic Screening. The Internet makes it possible for charities of all sizes to obtain helpful information regarding the capacity of their key prospects to make a major gift. There are several free and paid access databases available to nonprofits seeking to identify prospects with wealth. Several companies have developed services that make it possible to match a charity's prospect database to specific information about persons with private wealth, philanthropists, inside stock traders, private company owners, high-net-worth professionals, and corporate and foundation executives and trustees. Remember that wealth is only one of the three factors—linkage, ability (wealth), and interest—required for defining a prospect.

Volunteer Recruitment and Management

The Rosso approach to fund raising depends on volunteers. The Internet provides tools that can enhance relationships and improve communication. Recruiting volunteers on-line is an excellent way to reach nontraditional volunteers, including populations that might be underrepresented in an organization's volunteer ranks (seniors, ethnic minorities, people with disabilities, and so on).

There are several on-line resources available that can help with technical assistance, resource sharing, training, and consultation. Organizations interested in posting volunteer opportunities on-line have several options to obtain help in locating volunteers, tracking them, and managing their activities.

Virtual Volunteer Management. The Internet can be used to increase communication, coordination, education, and collaboration with and among volunteers. The Internet can help volunteers, particularly those who work away from direct supervision, feel more connected to the work and mission of the organization. Here are some examples:

- E-mail is an easy and free way to communicate with volunteers quickly and give them opportunities to communicate easily with nonprofit staff.
- An on-line "ask a peer" discussion group for volunteers is an ideal tool to help them collaborate, share what they have learned, and increase teamwork.
- Regular e-mail updates on important organizational news and volunteer activities can help in volunteer retention.
- Volunteer manuals, guidelines, statistics, and other information that volunteers may find helpful to their service can all be posted on-line, making them available at any time.
- On-line calendars can help volunteers remember important assignments and deadlines.

According to the Virtual Volunteering Project (http://www.serviceleader. org/vv), "virtual volunteering" refers to volunteer tasks conducted in whole or in part via the Internet. Virtual volunteering combines technology with off-line volunteer recruitment and management efforts. Organizations can expand their reach by attracting volunteers from new areas and increasing their level of participation.

Privacy Concerns. When an organization asks donors or members for demographic and personal contact information, it is implicitly asking them to trust that it will not misuse the information they provide. Organizations must address privacy concerns. Information will not be given and donations will not be made on-line if members and donors don't trust that their information will be used responsibly.

To increase the likelihood that the trust supporters have for the charity will be transferred to the on-line environment, nonprofits should do all of the following things:

- Publish their privacy policy on the Web site and at other places where such information is requested or required
- Review and strengthen internal security and use of confidential information
- Ensure that supporters can control the information collected about them, including removing their name from lists for future on-line communication or solicitation

- Respond promptly to complaints and all forms of electronic communication
- Consider seeking certification from one of the well-known privacy trusts such as TRUSTe or BBB*OnLine.*

Shopping and Bidding. Shopping sites, auction sites, and others can give supporters an opportunity to show their support by encouraging them to shop or bid to benefit the charity of their choice. To date, few of these options have raised significant revenue for charities. Allocations of staff time should focus on improving the Web site, developing an effective e-mail communication program, and integrating these efforts into traditional forms of fund raising. Even though additional services have failed to generate quick and easy money for nonprofits, it may be appropriate to use these services as options on a charity's Web site, provided that the items being sold or the auction event is in some way tied to the mission of the organization.

Learn and Share On-Line. The Internet provides many opportunities to reach out to colleagues and professionals who share an interest in most topics of e-philanthropy. There are several services that allow others to learn from colleagues and share experiences.

PRSPCT-L features discussion of prospect research issues, developments, sources, and techniques. To subscribe, send an e-mail to listserv@bucknell.edu. In the message, type "subscribe prspct-l < your real name > ." To post a message, send it to prspct-l@bucknell.edu.

Charity Channel (http://www.charitychannel.com) hosts more than fifty discussion groups on a wide range of topics including annual giving, planned giving, and e-philanthropy.

Relationship Building and Advocacy

For some organizations, the promotion of their mission by e-mailing an elected official, signing an electronic petition, receiving electronic "action alerts," or forwarding e-mail messages to friends, coworkers, and family serves an important role in building and enhancing on-line relationships.

An on-line advocacy campaign can serve as a successful way to rally support and an excellent way to build an e-mail database. Making effective use of the organization's Web site and e-mail database requires careful planning. The messages in the action alerts should reflect and reinforce those of print media and the Web site. It is important to identify specific goals for on-line advocacy.

Follow-up to these prospects or donors through traditional direct mail or other methods should refer to the initial e-mail contact; for example: "Last month on-line you joined with 75,000 other dedicated Americans who are joining the fight for tougher drunk driving laws. Today, we are writing to ask for your help."

To support the details of this effort, several on-line services have been developed.

Since the initial contact with potential supporters was on the occasion of an advocacy campaign, it is important to provide appropriate follow-up. Charities might consider proposing additional advocacy activities, an invitation to volunteer, or a suggestion to make a charitable gift to support ongoing efforts related to the initial advocacy request. The purpose is to turn potential donors acquired during an on-line activism campaign into donors.

CONCLUSION

E-philanthropy techniques have brought to the nonprofit world an unprecedented opportunity to leverage technology for the benefit of the charity and convenience of the donor. Even small nonprofits today can get to the Internet through low-cost and free services available over the Internet and through local providers. In every organization, time and resources are spent on recruiting and retaining charitable support. This support is based on relationships built and missions fulfilled. Hundreds of options exist to develop solutions for each of the six categories of e-philanthropy outlined in this chapter. Use of the Internet enhances these efforts by providing efficient and effective communication tools tied to robust, secure on-line services. These services empower donors to use information and support charitable causes anytime and anywhere.

CHAPTER TWENTY-ONE

Special Events for
the Twenty-First Century

Alan L. Wendroff

To paraphrase the twentieth-century century philosopher Martin Buber, who wrote, "All real living is meeting" (1958, p. 11), *all real fund raising is meeting!* As discussed in Chapters Nine and Twelve, successful fund raising, especially major and planned gifts, has always been conducted in a one-on-one, face-to-face manner. How do special events relate to this type of fund raising? A special event is the program in the annual development plan that can link the nonprofit agency, the donor, and the community. Special events are the catalyst that can illuminate the nonprofit's mission statement by demonstrating visually and graphically the reason for the agency's existence. Special events introduce the nonprofit board members and staff to current and potential donors and future lay leadership.

This chapter will lead you through the steps needed to produce a successful special event. Throughout the process, we will use actual examples to illustrate points that will assist in your ultimate decision making about producing a special event.

As discussed throughout this book, Hank Rosso's philosophy taught us that nonprofit fund raising involves identifying common values among a donor, a nonprofit agency, and the community. The process of identifying and exchanging these values involves achieving doable goals by a partnership between the donor and the nonprofit agency. Each goal represents a component of the special event. The whole produces a successful event. The following seven goals serve as the basis for excellence in special event fund raising:

1. To update the nonprofit's mission statement to educate the community as to why the nonprofit exists
2. To motivate and educate lay leaders, volunteers, and professional staff
3. To recruit volunteers (and future board members and supporters)
4. To expand the nonprofit's network in the community
5. To market the nonprofit for the benefit of the community
6. To obtain endorsements for the nonprofit from community leaders
7. To receive financial support by achieving the first six goals

A nonprofit can go one step further with the seven goals by stating its current situation, what it requires now from a successful event, and its future needs (see Table 21.1).

Table 21.1. Determining Special Event Goals for the Nonprofit Organization.

Special Event Goals	Current Situation	Required Now	Required in Two Years
Money	Fund raising = $80,000	$105,000 to meet budget	$150,000
Motivation	10 of 25 board members active	20 out of 25 active	25 active board members
Volunteer recruitment	35 active volunteers	60 active volunteers	100 active volunteers
Network expansion	1,500 names on donor and prospect list	2,500 names	3,500 to 5,000 names
Current donors	750 active donors	1,250 active donors	2,000 active donors
Marketing	Local name recognition	Countywide name recognition	Regional name recognition
Mission statement and marketing	Limited program, one location	Multiple-county programs and locations	Regional program sites
Endorsements solicited	Very few	Local government and corporate recognition	State and regional recognition

Source: Alan L. Wendroff, *Special Events: Proven Strategies for Nonprofit Fundraising.* Copyright © 1999 John Wiley & Sons, Inc. This material is used by permission of John Wiley & Sons, Inc.

SPECIAL EVENT MODELS AND ELEMENTS

The special event and the seven goals form the core of a strategic and tactical fund raising plan. There are five basic models of special events that can be used to produce a variety of particular events:

1. Communitywide events: races, marathons, and 5-, 10-, or 20-kilometer runs with costumes (such as the Far Side run, in which runners dress up like characters from Gary Larson's cartoons); galas put on by large arts organizations like the symphony, opera, ballet, and museums; raffles, cook-offs, fashion shows, unique home and mansion tours

2. Testimonial events: tribute and award dinners, luncheons, breakfasts, and receptions of all types; recognition events where someone is honored

3. Sporting events: golf, tennis, bowling, and softball tournaments

4. Theater and art gallery openings: previews of exhibits, new movies, and stage plays; open artists' studios, galleries, and showplaces for the exclusive use of the nonprofits' guests, with a percentage of each sale to the agency

5. Auctions: live and silent auctions held as stand-alone events or in combination with testimonial and sporting events, such as honoree dinners and golf tournaments

Events to benefit your nonprofit can take virtually any form. A low-cost example is that old favorite, the round-robin dinner. Guests purchase tickets from the nonprofit. They go from one volunteer's home to another for each course of the dinner and sample the cooking of the best amateur chefs and bakers. Guests enjoy going to one volunteer's home for salad and another for soup. It is very cost-effective for the nonprofit agency, since almost all of the food and drink is donated.

The following elements are key to producing a successful event in conjunction with the seven goals. These are the steps in the planning process you need to complete before the event actually raises money:

1. Setting the seven goals

2. Strategy: planning the event

3. Organization: partnering with volunteers, developing the tactical plan

4. Administration: logistics, leadership, motivation to tie the process together

MISSION, VISION, AND GOALS

ɔ preached the importance of mission statements throughout his pro-
career. All fund raising programs that make up the nonprofit's annual
ment plan rely on a cogent mission statement that answers the question
do we as a nonprofit exist?" Donors will not support an organization
ɔse it has administrative needs. Donors make gifts to nonprofits with whom
they share values as reflected in what the nonprofit does to benefit the community, region, state, and country.

The vision statement explains the organization's plans for the future. In reality, it is the mission statement with a timeline wrapped around it. It informs
donors that their investment beyond the current year's gift will reflect their values with the organization on a continuing basis. Based on the mission statement, goals can be implemented that will allow the nonprofit to achieve its
mission and vision.

The special event is an excellent way to display mission and vision statement
values to guests who have purchased tickets to the event. At the event reception, the creative development officer can set up small TV viewing stations
around the periphery of the room or, if the event is out-of-doors, exhibit programmatic displays in covered booths. Some programs lend themselves to visual
graphic displays in booths staffed by a professional and a volunteer. All guests
should receive the agency's brochure when they register at the event.

Possibilities are limited only by the imagination of the planners. Special
events can either be dull as a rubber chicken entrée or as exciting as a rock concert. Most of the special events that a nonprofit will choose to produce fit into
the five basic models outlined earlier in the chapter. These models can stimulate the event producers to think of other variants where they can use their talents to plan and build events that their constituency will enjoy and support.

SOME ACTUAL EVENTS

In the following examples, the first, a two-part event, was designed for an organization with a limited natural constituency, people with similar but very specific interests; the other featured event was crafted to attract donors from the
entire community.

A health organization, drawing members from a specific medical discipline,
wanted to honor one of its founders by producing an event that not only would
attract colleagues to pay homage to the founder but also would establish a

unique annual program. The committee decided to hold an all-day professional conference, attended by specialists in their medical discipline from around the world who would receive continuing education unit credits for attending. A dinner at which the founder of the organization would receive recognition from his peers rounded out the program. This model attracted fellow professionals, as well as a secondary audience of people who were helped by the founder over the years, and of course the founder's close friends and family.

Many of the conference attendees also attended the dinner; tickets were priced attractively to encourage attendance at both events.

In contrast, the Institute on Aging, a San Francisco agency providing services to senior citizens, the fastest-growing group of people in the country, designed an event to reach out to the entire community. The majority of people in the United States provide some kind of support to their mothers and fathers, aunts and uncles, and will participate in and support legitimate agencies that help this group of people live out their lives in dignity and comfort. Because people in San Francisco eat out at a higher rate than in most other U.S. cities, a food-related event was a natural choice.

The planners dubbed their event "Dinner à la Heart" and scheduled it for the Tuesday before Valentine's Day. (Tuesday is traditionally a slow day for restaurants.) The institute asked restaurants to participate either by donating a certain number of dinners (say, six to twelve) or by donating a free dinner for every dinner that is paid for at a discounted price. It then grouped the restaurants into several price categories and organized the marketing of the event much like a testimonial dinner.

The restaurants were interested in working with a well-known, respected nonprofit that would draw future patrons to their restaurants, and the nonprofit, by selling the dinners at retail prices, was able to raise funds for its programs. A total of one thousand donor-diners participated that first year in what has become an annual event.

Events can also borrow from the five basic models—for example, by having a silent auction or a program journal complete with paid tribute pages from the friends of the honoree or nonprofit agency.

RECRUITING VOLUNTEERS

Recruiting leadership for the event begins with recommendations from the nonprofit's board of directors, advisory committee, and special event executive leadership. The agency's board is responsible for appointing the development committee members, who in turn decide who will be the most effective overall event chair. The event chair can come either from the leadership of the agency or from the group of supporters who are volunteering their time because your agency is honoring a prominent head of a local corporation or founder of a respected institution.

There are two specific committees that are vital for a successful event, serving as the structure and fund raising arms of the event. The *executive committee* is composed of the event chairperson and various cochairs, and the communitywide *event committee* is recruited from the nonprofit's natural constituency and the colleagues and friends of the executive committee members. The executive committee can meet as often as once a week, depending on the size of the event; however, the normal frequency is once or twice a month until two weeks before the event. The event committee usually meets only once, eight or ten weeks prior to the event.

To ensure success, the event chair must actively share his or her resources with the event committee. These resources are the lists of potential event supporters from the private records of the event chair and the cochairs and introductions these leaders can make for the agency from the political and professional worlds.

The strategy that nonprofit leaders and professional staff should use in making the event happen is called *reverse networking*. Before signing up the first available chair or cochair, make a list of people you would like to work with as your ideal leadership. Then, with the assistance of your board of directors and other agency leaders, arrange introductions and meetings with those people. To recruit people for executive volunteer positions, you must be prepared. Attend these meetings with documents that make up a case statement for your event. The following items should be included in the case statement portfolio you bring to these meetings:

- An up-to-date mission and vision statement
- A comparison chart, based on the seven goals, outlining the agency's current situation and what is required in the coming programmatic year plus future needs
- An event organization chart
- A "master event timetable"
- A draft budget of revenue and expenses
- An agenda for the executive committee and community committee meetings

After the initial face-to-face meeting, attendance at the executive committee can fall off dramatically. And ordinarily, only 60 to 70 percent of the members who have signed up will attend the one-and-only meeting of the community-based event committee. As you will see in the next section, using the Internet can significantly increase attendance at meetings by increasing volunteer motivation.

VOLUNTEER MOTIVATION AND INVOLVEMENT

Motivating volunteers is one of the most important tasks in achieving a successful fund raising program and especially a special event. When the nonprofit agency's professional staff treats volunteers in a respectful manner and makes good use of their skills, it will motivate the volunteers. Too many nonprofits ask their volunteers to do only menial work—stuffing envelopes, licking stamps, and brewing coffee. These tasks should be performed by mailing houses and the person who pours the last cup from the coffeepot.

Nonprofits that are producing their first special event tend to overlook budget expense items and feel that only volunteer labor will rectify the problem. This compounds one problem with another. If you must ask your volunteers to perform basic tasks, balance the situation by also scheduling them for the fun and high-profile positions: greeting guests at the event, assisting VIPs who are scheduled to attend the event, and performing the many other people-oriented tasks that make up a special event.

Write a volunteer job description outlining what volunteer jobs are available, what they require, and how they will be organized (for a model, see Figure 21.1). Interview your potential volunteers, and talk about their background, interests, and reasons for volunteering for the agency. Treat your volunteers with respect, and they will exceed your expectations. They will ask to work at your other functions (fund raising and programmatic), and they will tell their friends what an enjoyable time they have when they volunteer at your agency. Frequently, volunteers become your future lay leaders—board members and monetary supporters.

Most nonprofits are computer-literate: they work extensively with word processing, spreadsheet, and database programs. If you already have an installed database program from a provider, a module probably exists that can take care of your requirements. The software application you are working with usually has a database program that you can use to keep track of the event reservations, payments, who needs to be invoiced, contact e-mail and telephone numbers, and special requirements such as vegetarian meals or at whose table people want to sit.

Special event committee meetings have been the Achilles' heel of event organization. Putting special event committees together using the face-to-face physical meeting is the preferred method because of the instantaneous networking

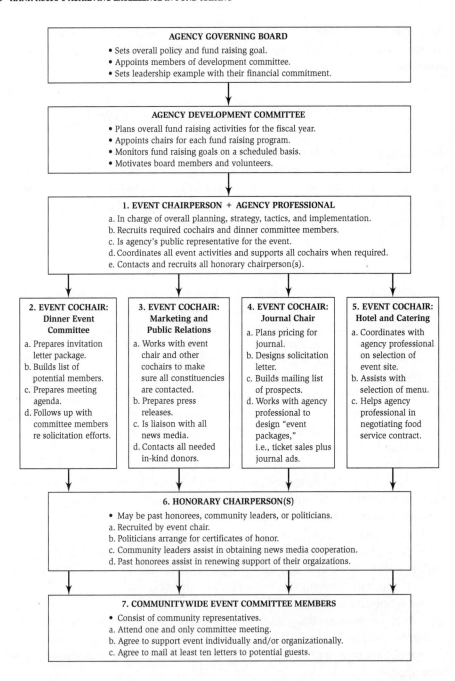

AGENCY GOVERNING BOARD
- Sets overall policy and fund raising goal.
- Appoints members of development committee.
- Sets leadership example with their financial commitment.

AGENCY DEVELOPMENT COMMITTEE
- Plans overall fund raising activities for the fiscal year.
- Appoints chairs for each fund raising program.
- Monitors fund raising goals on a scheduled basis.
- Motivates board members and volunteers.

1. EVENT CHAIRPERSON + AGENCY PROFESSIONAL
a. In charge of overall planning, strategy, tactics, and implementation.
b. Recruits required cochairs and dinner committee members.
c. Is agency's public representative for the event.
d. Coordinates all event activities and supports all cochairs when required.
e. Contacts and recruits all honorary chairperson(s).

2. EVENT COCHAIR: Dinner Event Committee
a. Prepares invitation letter package.
b. Builds list of potential members.
c. Prepares meeting agenda.
d. Follows up with committee members re solicitation efforts.

3. EVENT COCHAIR: Marketing and Public Relations
a. Works with event chair and other cochairs to make sure all constituencies are contacted.
b. Prepares press releases.
c. Is liaison with all news media.
d. Contacts all needed in-kind donors.

4. EVENT COCHAIR: Journal Chair
a. Plans pricing for journal.
b. Designs solicitation letter.
c. Builds mailing list of prospects.
d. Works with agency professional to design "event packages," i.e., ticket sales plus journal ads.

5. EVENT COCHAIR: Hotel and Catering
a. Coordinates with agency professional on selection of event site.
b. Assists with selection of menu.
c. Helps agency professional in negotiating food service contract.

6. HONORARY CHAIRPERSON(S)
- May be past honorees, community leaders, or politicians.
a. Recruited by event chair.
b. Politicians arrange for certificates of honor.
c. Community leaders assist in obtaining news media cooperation.
d. Past honorees assist in renewing support of their orgaizations.

7. COMMUNITYWIDE EVENT COMMITTEE MEMBERS
- Consist of community representatives.
a. Attend one and only committee meeting.
b. Agree to support event individually and/or organizationally.
c. Agree to mail at least ten letters to potential guests.

Figure 21.1. Event Organization Chart for a Special Event: Duties and Responsibilities.

Source: Alan L. Wendroff, Special Events: Proven Strategies for Nonprofit Fundraising. Copyright © 1999 John Wiley & Sons, Inc. This material is used by permission of John Wiley & Sons, Inc.

that occurs when committee members socialize at the one-and-only event committee meeting. The Internet, used in conjunction with an actual meeting, is a very effective way to make sure people who cannot attend the meeting obtain up-to-date information at a time that is convenient for them. It also allows committee members who attended the meeting to double-check the information they received at the meeting. For all committee members, the Internet Web site can provide daily or weekly updates of reservations and other revenue, press releases, and marketing information.

Internet Web site programs, known as Application Service Provider (ASP) sites, can supplement physical meetings and telephone calls. Such Internet sites as www.kintera.com, www.blackbaud.com, and www.etapestry.com provide a variety of services for nonprofits, including database programs and tools that allow nonprofits to put on special events and to organize and conduct the committee meetings for a successful event.

At the event committee meeting, which is where community volunteers learn how to make the event a success, the members are asked to make their own commitment to the event and to contact at least ten potential guests by letter, by telephone, or in person. This information is posted on the Internet site, complete with sample letters that can be written in the sender's style. The letters can be sent via e-mail directly from the site. A hyperlink embedded in the letter connects to a secure site where guests can make their reservations and other financial transactions.

A committee member who cannot make the scheduled meeting or a live presentation on the Web site can access the information on this site at his or her leisure. This technology changes and improves almost daily, so it will become easier to communicate live on the Internet and plan an event from beginning to completion, with all documentation and guest information recorded on your database.

MARKETING AND PUBLIC RELATIONS

Marketing (public relations and advertising) is the process of getting your agency's name, mission, and programs as well as your special event's name, date, and location to the nonprofit's natural constituency and the community at large.

Writing a Marketing Plan

A marketing plan should contain at least the following information essential to the success of the event:

- Identification of potential attendees
- Organizational values to be promoted
- Programs to be supported through the event
- Communication vehicles
- Training of key staff and volunteers
- Public relations to promote the event
- Implementation of the marketing plan

For each item on this list, it might be helpful to construct a grid using "Strategy," "Person Responsible," and "Outcome" as column headings.

Special events can use the seven goals outlined earlier in this chapter as a basis for writing a marketing plan. Phillip Kotler is quoted as noting that "marketing is a way to harmonize the needs and wants of the outside world with the purposes and the resources and the objectives of the institution" (Drucker, 1990, p. 84). A special event is an excellent marketing and fund raising program that can bring the prospective community supporters into a forum where they can learn about the work of your agency. Remember, a special event is the only fund raising program where donors pay to come to your house.

Special Event Marketing Examples

Your marketing plan will identify the constituency you are aiming at for potential attendees and communicate your programs and the values they provide to your community. The plan will be a guideline for training your volunteers and will describe the public relations techniques you use and how to implement them.

Implementation of the marketing plan means that every piece of paper—stationery, announcements of any kind, business cards (on the reverse side), and media public service announcements should mention the special event: day, date, time, and location.

Internet Web sites provide another way to market the event. First, if the nonprofit has its own Web site, the home page should present all of the pertinent information about the event. Second, if the agency has a Webmaster, it should design a page for the special event, if at all possible. (Sometimes this can be done by a volunteer.) This page should have basic information about the event and on how to become involved with the event and the nonprofit. This section can also present logos from corporate and other sponsors. The site can include a hyperlink to a page where supporters can reserve seats and tables, take out ad pages, and make donations for support of the event and the nonprofit. These same sponsors of the event, or any organization connected with the event that supports the nonprofit, can put a banner on their own Web pages giving the basic information about the event.

These marketing strategies, combined with the work of the members of the event committees, will produce a positive reaction toward the fund raising program and the work of the nonprofit.

THE SPECIAL EVENT BUDGET: AN EXAMPLE

The budget in Exhibit 21.1 is based on the special event that is put on most often, a meal (breakfast, lunch, or dinner) at which the agency honors someone or celebrates an anniversary. You can also combine an event of this sort with an auction, a dinner dance, or a celebrity performance. Theatrical performances, gallery openings, and sports events like golf tournaments can use the basic model as a template to design their unique events, which may include a meal.

The most important section of the special event budget is the potential revenue sources. Revenue comes from event seat sales; ad journal advertising; in-kind donations of wine, printing, and advertising; and underwriting or sponsorship of many of the items that constitute the expense items incurred when producing a special event.

Expenses are always with us, and when planning a special event, you cannot realistically estimate the expenses until you calculate the potential number of event participants. And before you calculate the potential number of guests, you have to know how many people you can accommodate at the venues available in your community. If you are putting on the event in a metropolitan community, you will probably have a variety of sites to choose from with capacities of one hundred to one or two thousand guests. A rule of thumb that you can use for this calculation is the square footage that a table of ten guests requires. Most sites have round tables 60 or 72 inches in diameter. Sixty-inch round tables require approximately 110 square feet, and 72-inch round tables need 132 square feet. If the site available for the event has 5,000 square feet available for a seated dinner, then you can realistically serve forty-five tables of ten, or 450 guests using 60-inch rounds, and thirty-eight tables of ten, or 380 guests using 72-inch rounds. After figuring the parameters of the optimum attendance at your event, you can calculate a realistic number of potential attendees.

The number of guests invited to an event will set the potential expenses for postage, number of meals, printing, and so on. There is no hard and fast ratio between the number of invitations mailed and the positive responses you will receive. Factors like the prominence of your honoree and the event chairperson, the uniqueness of the event, the newsworthiness of the event, and the agency's reputation in the community all go into the calculations for an attendance

Exhibit 21.1. Revenue and Expense Budget Items.

Revenue Source	Number	Cost per Unit	Total Cost	Percentage of Total Revenue
Individual reservations	400	$100.00	$40,000.00	71.51%
Event sponsor	3	$1,200.00	$3,600.00	6.44%
Event cosponsor	3	$800.00	$2,400.00	4.29%
Donations (3% of total revenue)			$1,678.05	3.00%
Ad journal: (10% of total revenue)			$5,593.51	10.00%
Sum of cash items			$53,271.57	95.24%
In-kind donations (5% of total revenue)			$2,663.58	4.76%
Total revenue:			$55,935.15	100.00%

Expenses	Number	Cost per Unit	Total Cost	Percentage of Expense Divided by Total Revenue
Food	400	$26.00	$10,400.00	18.59%
Beverage	80	$14.00	$1,120.00	2.00%
Corkage (only if wine is donated)				
Postage (formal invitations + return cards)	4,000	$0.37	$1,480.00	3%
Printing (invitations, forms, stationery)			$2,000.00	3.58%
Ad journal (print 80% of estimated total attendance)			$2,000.00	3.58%
Awards			$250.00	0.45%
Decorations			$500.00	0.89%
Miscellaneous			$400.00	0.72%
Subtotal			$18,150.00	31.95%
In-kind offset			$2,664.00	
Total expenses			$20,814.00	36.71%
Net revenue			$35,121.15	62.79%

equation. At a minimum, plan to use a 5:1 ratio between invitations mailed and potential guests attending the event. Therefore, if you mail two thousand invitations, the *potential* attendance might be four hundred. Obviously, the more invitations you mail, the more opportunities you have to attract guests. To ensure a healthy attendance, the wise nonprofit professional will make sure that the event has recruited a large community-based event committee. These people agree to assist you in marketing the event and are expected to attend. If you budget the event for four hundred attendees and recruit seventy-five community committee members, you can count on a minimum of between 75 and 120 attendees (or the equivalent in dollars if the member cannot attend but gives you an equal donation). Looking at the attendance with a conservative eye, you can calculate approximately 20 percent paid attendance from the committee, before the invitations are mailed. Once estimated attendance has been calculated, you can fill in the expense figures.

The sample budget in Exhibit 21.1 shows the usual revenue and expense lines an agency will use when planning an event. Dollar amounts are included because they illustrate the percentages you can aim for when planning your event. Obviously, you cannot construct a budget that reflects accurate prices for every community. The sample budget shows expenses as about 37 percent of total revenue. This percentage varies, due to the same factors that were cited for potential guidance. More established events with higher sponsorships will have a lower expense percentage. By using your committee chairs and members, it is possible to lower the cost by having beverages, printing, and many other items donated to the agency for the event. The closer you can bring the expenses to no more than 30 percent of total revenue, the more motivated your lay leadership will be to get involved with your future events and the greater the net profit you will make for the agency.

EVALUATING THE EVENT

Evaluation of your event is based on comparing the stated goals (both quantitatively and qualitatively) with what actually happened. The quantity aspect of the event is easy to evaluate: count the money, attendees, and participation of the volunteers and lay leadership. Measuring the qualitative impact of the event takes a higher degree of sophistication and should be done by the senior professionals and executive board members of the agency. Questions like the following should be asked and answered:

What impact did the event have on introducing the agency's programs to the community?

Should you produce this event again next year?

Is the event a part of the agency's long-term planning?

Were the lay leaders of the agency involved with the planning of the event, and did it motivate them?

What did unaffiliated community leaders talk about after the event?

THE MASTER EVENT TIMETABLE

The master event timetable (MET) is a special document that summarizes the entire event (see Exhibit 21.2); planners will refer to it every day. The MET is designed for a six-month lead prior to the day of the event. This is the minimum time that you need to produce a successful major special event; nine to twelve months is a more usual time frame for event planning. The MET can be expanded to meet a longer time requirement. For example, the week 1 tasks can be accomplished over the course of two weeks if the MET is expanded to twelve months. Smaller organizations with small-scale special events may work with shorter time frames.

The last task noted for week 1 is "Set date and choose site for your event." This is a crucial task. For testimonial meal events, you must establish a date that accommodates the honoree and not a date that is convenient for the agency. Too many nonprofits set the date and are very arbitrary about changing it.

There are various key weeks in the MET. Week 5 sets the date for the communitywide event committee meeting in week 14. Week 19 is the time when personal letters from the committee members are mailed to their lists of prospects. Weeks 20 through 26 witness the final push for reservations. Week 27, the week after the event, is acknowledgment and evaluation week. If you want supporters and volunteers to return to next year's event, you must thank them promptly. Evaluate the event while it is fresh in your mind.

CONCLUSION

Special events fill key needs for nonprofit organizations. They make the organization known to the public, involve volunteers, reward donors, and raise money for the annual fund. Special events are public events. Careful planning is required to ensure that they meet the goals and purpose set for them and succeed in the eyes of key constituents and the public. Special events can play key roles at all levels of the total development program and should be considered a useful strategy by major and planned gift officers as well as the annual fund manager.

Exhibit 21.2. Master Event Timetable:
A Weekly Schedule of Tasks to Accomplish to Produce a Successful Event.

Week	To Do This Week	Person Responsible	Date Done
1	• Have governing board set up special event committee		
	• Select type of special event for your agency		
	• Recruit event chairperson		
	• Complete revenue and expense budget		
	• Recruit one or more honorees or special guests		
	• Prepare event timetable		
	• Update agency's mission statement (if needed)		
	• *Set date and choose site for your event*		
2	• Chairperson recruits cochairs		
	• Prepare preliminary list of prospect names for event committee and invitation list		
	• Set up computer program		
3	• Recruit honorary cochairs		
	• Complete cochair recruitment		
	• Set date for event chair and cochair meeting		
	• Obtain additional names from chair and cochairs		
4	• Establish marketing and public relations guidelines		
	• Prepare press releases		
	• Prepare "save the date" notices		
	• Prepare draft of event invitation package		
5	• Set agenda for event chair and cochair meeting		
	• Secure additional names for event committee from chair and cochair		
	• Set date for the "one and only" event committee meeting		
	• Discuss other sources of revenue with event chair and cochairs		
6	• Start negotiations with site and catering managers		
	• Continue recruiting committee members		
	• Obtain insurance and governmental permits		
	• Mail "save the date" notice to all prospect names on invitation list		

Exhibit 21.2. Master Event Timetable:
A Weekly Schedule of Tasks to Accomplish to Produce a Successful Event, Cont'd.

Week	To Do This Week	Person Responsible	Date Done
7	• Select printer and mailing house		
	• Determine size and layout of invitation package		
	• Determine volunteer requirements and outline volunteer duties		
	• Continue recruiting committee members through week 9		
	• Work with ad journal cochair and set up solicitation campaign		
8	• Prepare event committee information kits		
9	• Mail event committee invitation letters		
10	• Continue to add names to event invitation list through week 16		
12–13	• Hold event committee meeting		
14–15	• Secure final mailing lists from committee members		
16	• Design site layout, sound system, and decorating scheme		
17	• Complete in-kind solicitations		
18	• Mail event invitations		
	• Follow up with event committee members and other prospects		
19	• Have event committee members mail personal letters to prospects		
20	• Prepare checklist for items and people needed at the event		
21	• Secure first deadline for ad journal copy; e-mail or telephone all advertisers who have not submitted a camera-ready ad		
22	• Start the *final push*: e-mail or telephone committee members for reservations and event journal ads		
23	• Secure final ad journal copy and camera-ready material; send to printer		
24	• Reconfirm all speaker and special guests arrangements		
25	• Pull everything together—you are almost there!		
26	• *EVENT DAY*		
27	• Send out acknowledgments—thank everyone involved		
	• Evaluate the event		

Source: Alan L. Wendroff, *Special Events: Proven Strategies for Nonprofit Fundraising.* Copyright © 1999 John Wiley & Sons, Inc. This material is used by permission of John Wiley & Sons, Inc.

CHAPTER TWENTY-TWO

Fund Raising at the Grassroots Level

Kim Klein

My first experience with Hank Rosso was grassroots fund raising exemplified. In 1977, five women who were part of a feminist collective called the Coalition for the Medical Rights of Women called Hank to ask him about The Fund Raising School. They wanted to go but did not have the money and were nervous that there would be no other grassroots organizations in the training. Hank replied that he would be happy to meet with them at his house and help them create a fund raising plan. They brought a tape recorder and sat in his living room, plied with cookies and coffee by his wife and assistant, Dottie. He spent three hours with them. He helped them write a job description for a fund raising coordinator, and shortly after their meeting, I was hired for that job. It was my first full-time development director job. These women were my coworkers and board in one, as I was the only staff. They gave me the tape, and I listened to it more than a dozen times. Years later, when Hank and I taught together, he always asked about the group and each of the women he had met. He always remembered their names, even though, to my knowledge, he never saw them again.

This story illustrates what has come to be known as the Hank Rosso philosophy. Hank believed in being of service and saw fund raising as a service profession. He believed, and exemplified his belief, that fund raising was about relationships—about remembering people's names and respecting their work. He believed that anyone could do fund raising and any group could raise more money than it was raising by applying the principles he had identified as central

289

to successful fund raising. He was thorough and methodical as a practitioner and as a teacher.

Although he did not come out of a grassroots fund raising background, he had great appeal for those of us who have made our home in grassroots fund raising because of his down-to-earth, step-by-step approach and his undisguised respect for the grassroots activists who came him for training. He demonstrated that fund raising strategies could be adapted to any kind of situation, and he constantly sought new ways to promote that philosophy.

GRASSROOTS FUND RAISING: WHAT IT IS AND WHAT IT IS NOT

The *Doubleday Dictionary for Home or Office* defines *grassroots* as referring to "ordinary people, especially those apart from the centers of political power or influence" or to "the primary source or foundation."

This definition provides an excellent starting place for understanding grassroots fund raising, which is a subset of all fund raising. Grassroots fund raising can be planned and implemented by "ordinary people" rather than professionals and does not require being close to sources of money or power. A grassroots organization starts like this: Some people have an idea. Perhaps they see a pressing social need and want to respond. Or they have an artistic vision and wish to create a cultural vehicle to express it. They believe that a change is needed in law or public policy, or they want to protest a structural injustice. They get together in a living room or a school cafeteria and plan how to create the change they wish to see. Their plan must include raising money, and before long, they have created an organization. They start their fund raising with a garage sale or a bake sale; they canvass their neighborhood; they seek donations from local merchants, religious congregations, friends, and colleagues. They send a few appeal letters, and they even identify some of their acquaintances whom they can ask for $250 or $500. This is grassroots fund raising—it does not require much research or technical knowledge; it allows people to use the skills they have—friendliness, sincerity, and a genuine desire to see something get done—to raise money. Grassroots fund raising does not require much front money and does not take a lot of time to see results. Many grassroots organizations don't even have staff.

Later, a grassroots organization may decide to grow to do more work or to work more effectively. It may seek and receive foundation funding in order to expand its response to a proven need. It may eventually have a lot of foundation or even government funding and may even develop an endowment, but if it is a smart institution, it will still use some grassroots techniques. Most institutions in the United States started off as grassroots efforts, and many still use grassroots fund raising techniques as part of their overall fund raising plan.

Generally speaking, a grassroots organization has a budget of less than $500,000 (in fact, many have budgets of under $25,000, which means they do not have to file a Form 990 with the Internal Revenue Service every year). It is run by a team of board members or volunteers and may have part-time or one or two paid staff and generally works in a specific and limited geographical area. The work of grassroots groups spans the gamut of political and social issues, and often grassroots organizations are part of larger grassroots movements.

To understand the vast range of groups that fit the grassroots definition, it is helpful to note that grassroots organizations make up the majority of nonprofits in the United States. They account for more than half of the organizations incorporated as 501(c)(3) nonprofits and the majority of the more than eight million groups that operate in the United States without any tax designation. Grassroots groups often face one another in legal and legislative battles over environmental issues, gun control, abortion, housing, water rights, rent control, the death penalty, and other contentious matters, but many grassroots groups can also be found providing essential human services such as day care, food banks, and homeless shelters and running community centers, historic preservation projects, and arts councils. Neighborhood block associations, soccer clubs, beautification projects, and the like usually use only grassroots fund raising techniques and operate mostly on volunteer time. Grassroots coalitions made up of large and small groups often come together to get out the vote before an election or to speak for or against very local concerns such as a big chain store moving in and putting local merchants out of business or national concerns such as nominees to the U.S. Supreme Court. Grassroots organizations form choirs, theaters, and small orchestras; they publish poetry, newspapers, and novels. Sometimes they work locally to help people far away, as in spontaneous relief efforts for victims of hurricanes or earthquakes.

Grassroots fund raising includes almost all strategies that involve raising money from individuals and does not include raising money from government, foundations, or corporations. In the past ten years, the massively increased number of foundations has meant that many grassroots organizations have applied for and received small foundation grants. As many people have left working for grassroots organizations to work in corporations, and as many technology corporations are started and run by classmates of staff and volunteers of grassroots groups, we have also seen more corporate donations to small organizations. Again, the corporate and foundation strategies are dependent on personal connections, as is all fund raising, grassroots or otherwise.

THE HISTORICAL RECORD

To understand the importance of grassroots organizations, it is useful to look at a few historical examples of what ordinary people, working on shoestring budgets, have been able to accomplish.

From the beginning of the colonial settlement of what would become the United States, there have been grassroots groups. The very first charity organized by women was begun in Philadelphia in 1778 by freed slaves. Known as the Free Africa Society, it provided an early version of insurance. For 25 cents per week, members were assured of money to tide them through emergencies.

Another of the first charities organized by women was the Society for the Relief of Poor Widows and Children, formed in New York City in 1797. During the first winter of the society's existence, it helped 98 widows and 200 small children by enrolling the children in schools and teaching the women sewing as a source of income. The society raised money by charging its women-only members $3 per year and taking contributions from men.

Building churches and schools and carrying out the work of these self-help societies characterized the majority of grassroots efforts through the 1700s. Starting in 1830, however, people added to these activities by organizing around the issue of the abolition of slavery. Freed and escaped slaves formed underground networks, and white people worked in hundreds of abolition societies, which grew to more than a thousand by 1837. The campaign to abolish slavery was always a grassroots movement rooted in churches and funded through the small contributions of thousands of members.

Another set of successful grassroots organizations was born of the temperance movement of the late 1800s. The most famous of these organizations was the Women's Christian Temperance Union (WCTU), created in 1874. The WCTU itself survived primarily by using the fund raising strategy of "parlor meetings" (today's house parties). WCTU donors were almost entirely women of moderate means, and yet in 1889, the money raised in just the Chicago chapter allowed the WCTU to run two day nurseries, two Sunday schools, an industrial school, a shelter for four thousand homeless or destitute women, a free medical dispensary that treated more than sixteen hundred patients, a lodging house that provided temporary housing for fifty thousand men, and a low-cost restaurant.

Between the end of the Civil War in 1865 and the passage of the Nineteenth Amendment in 1920, the most important grassroots movement was the drive to obtain women's suffrage. Two groups are of interest here: the all-women National Women's Suffrage Association and the American Women's Suffrage Association, which admitted men. Formed in the late 1860s, these two organizations coexisted for more than two decades before merging to become the National American Women's Suffrage Association, now the League of Women Voters.

The money needed for this movement (which took more than fifty-two years, forty-seven campaigns and state constitutional conventions, and nineteen successive Congresses to succeed) was supplied by hundreds of thousands of women and men through small and large gifts, special events, membership fees, and bequests.

The suffrage movement also provides a good example of how grassroots fund raising often leads an organization to much more sophisticated fund raising. By the late 1800s and early 1900s, Susan B. Anthony, Alice Paul, Lucy Stone, and other leaders had attracted many very wealthy women to their cause. Elizabeth Eddy left $50,000 to Anthony. Mrs. Frank Leslie left a $2 million bequest.

The civil rights movement provides yet another excellent example of numbers of grassroots organizations using grassroots fund raising in strategies to bring about phenomenal social change. One of the most famous examples was the Montgomery bus boycott of December 1955. For 381 days, not a single African American rode the public buses in Montgomery, Alabama. The campaign cost $3,000 a week, and all of the money was raised in African American churches. Every night, participants at church rallies would contribute dollars, quarters, and even pennies.

More recently, the large and diffuse environmental movement has been funded primarily through grassroots fund raising. One dramatic example comes from Washington State. In 1999, the Northwest Ecosystem Alliance, an environmental advocacy group with a budget of $650,000 and a membership of three thousand, was able to raise $13.1 million to save a 25,000-acre wilderness area called the Loomis Forest from being logged, in a period of only nine months. The grassroots fund raising component was assigned to raise $650,000 in gifts of under $10,000, looking at hundreds of gifts in the $50 to $500 range. Ultimately, that component raised $1.5 million through a combination of house parties, personal visits, and direct mail and phone solicitation.

GRASSROOTS FUND RAISING STRATEGIES

In the wide world of fund raising strategies, there are some that are fairly easily adapted to the grassroots environment and others that will not work at all. The most easily adapted are special events, mail appeals, public speaking, and personal face-to-face solicitation. Let's look at each of these and see how a grassroots group could put them to work raising money.

Special Events

Everyone is familiar with the very large golf tournaments, award luncheons, and black tie dinner dances that raise $100,000 or even $1 million. They cost thousands of dollars to put on and take paid staff and dozens of volunteers working for months. In small towns and rural communities, special events of small nonprofits form the basis of the social life of the town. (The mechanics of developing special events is described in Chapter Twenty-One.)

A grassroots organization can raise $5,000 or $10,000 with three or four months' lead time and a handful of volunteers. Take, for example, a dinner dance. Rather than in a hotel ballroom, the dance can be held in the community center or the school gymnasium, free of charge. Teenagers in the group can be put in charge of decorations. Lots of paper streamers and balloons make it festive. Food can be provided by members or, to make it more fun, can be the focus of a competition. People might pay a small fee to enter the food competition in different categories, such as main course, salad, or dessert. They must bring enough food to feed fifteen people. People attending the event get a small sample of each entry and get to vote on which is the best. They then pay a small fee for a larger portion of the courses that they liked. In reality, most will be full after the sampling, so the group will not run out of food. A cash bar can provide extra income. (Be sure to check local regulations about serving alcohol.) Later, dancing can be provided by a local band that is trying to become better known and is willing to perform for a low fee or free. Alternatively, music for dancing can be provided by a DJ who is a friend of one of the members. Marketing and advertising the event is done largely by word of mouth and on posters hung in the neighborhood where the event is being held. Public interest radio and television often have community calendars, so it is not hard to get your event publicized. Each board member sells ten tickets at $10 or $15 each. This is generally not too hard either. With 150 people attending, at $10 per person, plus each person paying on average $10 more for extra food or drink, plus the entry fee of the food competitors who each pay $15, an organization can easily gross $5,000. Expenses will include buying drinks to sell, printing up tickets and attractive certificates for the winners of the food contests, and possibly mailing thank-you notes to volunteers after the event is over. Expenses could be as high as $1,000, giving the group a net of $4,000 and a core of involved constituents. As the years pass, more and more people want to enter the food contest, and more people want to come.

A chocolate lovers' festival, put on by a group with a total budget of $75,000, was organized along the lines just indicated and by the fifth year was netting $40,000! It attracted top chefs from every restaurant in town, in addition to laypeople entering their favorite brownies or best hot chocolate.

The dinner dance is just one example of how adaptable events are. Each aspect of the event should be conceived as a separate component, and components can be added or deleted according to the number of volunteers and amount of time available. A silent auction can be added to the dinner dance, or a live auction could replace the dance or be added to it. An afternoon barbecue at the beach could replace the dinner, and games could replace the dance. That kind of event would focus much more on families with young children. Tea and dessert followed by a lecture would appeal to a more academic or older crowd.

The secret is to do as much as possible at very low or zero cost and to charge for as many things as you can without having people feel that they are being "nickel-and-dimed" to death. Advertising must be effective so that the maximum number of the right people are attracted to the event at minimum cost. Grassroots groups know how to take advantage of free services, such as public service announcements, community bulletin boards, or e-mail listservs. Word of mouth is the cheapest and most effective advertising and marketing vehicle.

Raising Money by Mail

Chapter Nineteen provides in-depth information on direct mail. Mail provides another avenue for grassroots groups. Of course, the kind of sophisticated testing of packages and premiums that requires five thousand or ten thousand names just for the test is not available, but very focused list acquisition can bring in impressive returns. For example, a large organization tests a mailing to two thousand people and gets a 1 percent response (considered good in direct mail terms). It attracts twenty new donors, who give an average of $40 each, for a gross of $800. The organization will probably spend 50 cents each on the mailing, which means it will spend $1,000 to raise $800, or $10 to acquire one donor. They will make this money back over the next couple of years, as these donors renew and give extra gifts. Direct mail experts would say that is very respectable.

A grassroots group doesn't have the option of tying up money like that. So participants get their board members to each bring in ten to fifteen names and send out two hundred letters first class, with personal notes from the board members on each letter. They spend more on postage but nothing on list acquisition. They may even use a rubber stamp for the return address on the return envelope, and they hand-address the carrier envelope. So they also spend 50 cents each on these letters, for a total expense of $100. This highly personalized approach brings a 10 percent response, or twenty new donors, who each give $40, for a gross of $800. The difference between this group and the larger group is that our grassroots group walks away with a $700 income from the first mailing. The other difference is that ten board members each spent an hour or two getting the mailing out. The secret here is to find a source of names of prospects. Board members' friends are good, but the scope is finite. People who use the service the group provides or come to its events may constitute dozens or even hundreds of potential prospects. As with big direct mail appeals, not every appeal will be successful.

Also, the long-term success of a mail program is in the quality and consistency of renewals and extra appeals. Because grassroots groups rely a great deal on volunteers and overworked staff (if they are lucky enough to have staff), it is critical that every step in any fund raising strategy be written down so that a neophyte can easily figure out what to do. Everything should be as systematized as possible. The newsletter committee plans exactly what is going in the newsletter, when copy is due, who is doing the design and layout, how it will be proofed, who is taking it to the printer, and who is picking it up. It is important that production stay on deadline; otherwise, the membership committee's spring appeal may arrive on the same day as the newsletter—not an example of good timing.

For a mail appeal program to be effective, the organization must invest in a good database and keep it up-to-date. There are many free or inexpensive databases available to grassroots groups that are easy to use. Organizations should be cautious never to promise something they cannot deliver. For example, an organization shouldn't tell people they will get a newsletter three times a year unless the organization is reasonably certain it can produce and distribute one three times a year.

Finally, as with all fund raising, "acknowledging the first gift is the key to getting the second," as Hank Rosso said at least five thousand times.

Public Speaking

Public speaking is a wonderful way for grassroots groups to get their message out. There are hundreds of local organizations that need speakers on a monthly or quarterly basis, and if an organization develops a reputation for having good speakers, it will have more invitations than it can accept. Each speech will end with a low-key pitch for money, unless the speaker has permission to do a more assertive one. Speakers always close with something like this: "Thank you all for coming. If you want to help, there are three things you can do. You can do one of them, two of them, or all three of them. One, you can write a letter to your congressional representative expressing your views on this issue. Two, you can come down to our office and volunteer—all skills are useful and no skills are required. Three, you can support our work financially. All the information you need for these options is in the brochure I am handing out now."

A brochure is handed out with a return envelope attached. Some organizations will allow speakers to pass a basket at the end of the talk. Also, some organizations actually pay an honorarium, meaning that the speaker is actually paid to describe the important work his or her group is doing.

Often public speaking becomes the vehicle for collecting names for mail appeals. If that is the plan, the speaker will say, "If you would like more information about our group and how you can help, please sign up at the door." Then have a sign-up sheet available. It is critical that a mail appeal be sent promptly after gathering names.

Groups that use public speaking as a serious income stream as well as a way to get their message out need to develop a "speaker's bureau." People who are familiar with the issues the organizations addresses and who are comfortable in front of a crowd form the core group of this bureau. They create written materials for speakers to use, such as answers to difficult questions, narrative descriptions of programs and budgets, quotes from famous people in support of their work, and tips on how to handle disruptive audience members or how to structure a speech for a particular audience. Copies of notes and speeches are kept for each member of the speaker's bureau to use, and when possible, speeches are tape-recorded so that the speakers can review their presentations and everyone can learn and improve.

A shelter for battered women that had a speaker's bureau generated $10,000 a year from honoraria and thousands more from donations. Ultimately, the speaker's bureau led to the creation of a full-time training program when the shelter received a contract from a statewide law enforcement agency to train police officers in how to respond to domestic violence calls.

Personal Solicitation

Personal face-to-face solicitation is a grassroots strategy. Generally, a grassroots group doesn't have a long track record or any other trappings of success, such as a fancy office or well-known board members. The volunteers trade a lot on their reputation for integrity and thoughtfulness to raise money. People give $500 or $1,000 not because they have heard of the group and not because they are going to get a lot of recognition but because their friend Terry says that the group does good work and they trust Terry.

Personal solicitation is both the easiest and the hardest strategy for almost anyone. It is the easiest because volunteers just have to talk to their friends, who are, presumably, easy to find and comfortable to talk with. There is no real cost involved, except for the time of the volunteer and perhaps the cost of taking a friend out for coffee or lunch, and the meeting can be set at the convenience of the volunteer and his or her friend. It is the hardest because it requires asking for money and running the risk of rejection or of offending the friend. Hank was very clear that asking for money in person was the cornerstone strategy and that there were two things to keep in mind when asking: we have the right to ask, and the prospect has the right to say no. He further emphasized that many people will say no, and there is no disgrace in having your request declined. Many people will also say yes and be grateful that they were asked. Hank always noted that a request for money is an invitation and an opportunity being given to the prospect. For various reasons, the prospect may turn down the invitation, but there is no begging or apology required in asking.

Grassroots organizations often find that their personal solicitation program is their most lucrative and that the relationships they build with donors lead those donors to introduce the organization to other donors, to invite the organization to speaking engagements, and so on, as illustrated earlier in the history of grass-roots organizations.

THE COST OF FUND RAISING

The most formidable issue for any organization is the cost of fund raising, and for grassroots groups, finding even front money that can be repaid from the proceeds of the strategy is very difficult. Without front money, grassroots organizations settle for cramped offices, no clerical help, underpowered computers, old photocopy machines, and other less than ideal conditions. They spend a lot of time trying to get things donated and doing things as cheaply as possible. For example, if a large institution needs a new computer, it buys it. A grassroots group will spend hours trying to get someone to donate it, often winding up with a computer that can't run the newest versions of software on its archaic operating system. Group members can't use the computer but feel bad telling the donor that, so they keep it in the office and put a plant on it. Meanwhile, they send out a special appeal to their membership or hold a garage sale to raise the money to buy a decent computer. This whole process puts them six months behind the larger institution, which was able to fill its computer needs immediately.

In spite of, or more likely because of, the problems they have with money, grassroots groups often operate at a high level of efficiency. Fired by enthusiasm for their work and belief in their cause, a few people will do a huge amount of work and do it well, accomplishing a lot each day. The director of a grassroots group may not only write the direct mail appeal but, along with her volunteers, be the one that folds the letters, puts the labels on the envelopes, and sorts the bulk mailing while answering the phone (there is no secretary), sweating through a hot summer day (there is no air conditioning), and coordinating the efforts of the volunteers who are there to help. Often the director is paid one-third to one-half as much as her counterpart at a larger institution. Ironically, she may have more skills than her peers at bigger organizations because she has had to develop a wide range of skills to run the grassroots organization—bookkeeping, budgeting, administration, public relations, program development and evaluation—that other agencies are able to divide among more specialized personnel.

Grassroots organizations must learn a fundamental premise of business: one has to spend money to make money. Furthermore, some problems can be solved only with money. High-quality equipment will usually have to be purchased. Staff need to be paid living wages and need some benefits, particularly health care, if they are to really focus on their work. Dreary, poorly lit, badly insulated offices will save money in rent, which will then be spent in increased numbers of sick days, lack of productivity, and high staff turnover. One reason Hank encouraged grassroots organizations to attend The Fund Raising School along with members of a wide variety of other types of organizations was so they could experience what larger nonprofits took for granted. Grassroots activists often left The Fund Raising School courses and made major changes in their working conditions, which enabled them to raise much more money.

GRASSROOTS FUND RAISING: PEOPLE POWER IN ACTION

Grassroots fund raising can galvanize people to act, and this is its most valuable element. If an organization is working to change a law or to save wilderness or to end discrimination, it will need thousands of people to agree with its position. Facing the choice of one person giving $100,000 or one thousand people giving $100 each, the organization is far better off choosing the latter, because now it has a thousand little ambassadors discussing their issue with their friends and colleagues, which leads to more money and may eventually lead to a gift of $100,000 as well. Getting a large number of donations from a lot of people is also key to helping a group become more visible. By definition, grassroots groups are too new, too controversial, or too small to have been publicly accepted or become widely known. Many lack the skills to attract media attention or to be taken seriously. As a result, they have little name recognition. This means that much of their fund raising involves explaining their case to people, which makes their fund raising efforts much more time-consuming for the amount of money raised.

When all is said and done, though, the essence of grassroots fund raising is the essence of all fund raising: building relationships. "People give to people with causes," and these groups are full of people with causes. Successful fund raising of any kind requires ingenuity, commitment to the cause, love of people, common sense, a willingness to ask for money, and an understanding and deep appreciation of human nature. Many grassroots groups raise money with only these in place. They lack technical skills and are often weak in areas like keeping records on donors, understanding prospect research, knowing how to write foundation or corporate proposals, getting money from the government, or setting up planned giving programs.

CONCLUSION

Ultimately, any successful fund raising program will probably have a grassroots component. The test that the public (or some segment of the public) wants a charity to exist and to be able to avail itself of the many financial advantages of being a nonprofit can best be met through grassroots fund raising techniques. Does the organization have a group of volunteers who are willing to devote a large number of hours, without any reward besides a free pizza at their meetings and possibly a round of applause at their annual convention, to get a much larger number of ordinary people to give small and large donations? These donors themselves will receive little material reward for their gift beyond a heartfelt thank-you note and a newsletter. The work of the group is the reward, for the donor, for the volunteer, for the staff, and for the greater good. At its heart and at its best, this is how all fund raising works.

PART SIX

MANAGING SUCCESSFUL FUND RAISING

Hank Rosso used to say, "You can raise a lot more money with organized fund raising than you can with disorganized fund raising." Part Six covers the various aspects of managing the fund raising program. Fund raising is a management function that should be integrated with other management functions of the organization. This part of the book provides insights into management and leadership that will help fund raising executives manage the total development program.

The Rosso philosophy of fund raising is built around volunteer involvement in the fund raising process. In addition to other functions of management and leadership, the first two chapters, Twenty-Three and Twenty-Four, cover the "management" of volunteers and the development of volunteer leadership. We return to these topics again in Chapter Twenty-Five in the discussion of the trustee's role in fund raising.

Chapters Twenty-Six and Twenty-Seven discuss the range of information that must be managed for successful fund raising and how technology can be used in managing information and the various processes that support fund raising activity.

It costs money to raise money. The successful fund raising program has a budget to support the necessary activities. The successful fund raising manager understands the benefits and costs of various fund raising activities and can assess the risks and potential returns of new fund raising initiatives. Chapter

Twenty-Eight provides guidance in developing fund raising budgets and analyzing fund raising costs. Investment in fund raising and concepts of return on fund raising investment are explored.

Consultants play valuable roles in managing the fund raising process, from evaluating the fund raising program to conducting feasibility studies to providing advice and assistance during capital campaigns. Consultant involvement must be skillfully managed for maximum results. Chapter Twenty-Nine provides information on using consultants.

CHAPTER TWENTY-THREE

Managing the Fund Raising Program

Elizabeth A. Elkas

This chapter deals primarily with management of the fund raising process. It is a complement to the discussion of leadership in the following chapter. It is based partially on the original chapter (Grace, 1991) in the first edition of *Achieving Excellence* and the work of The Fund Raising School (2002b).

CHALLENGES IN NONPROFIT MANAGEMENT

Regardless of the size of an organization, fund raising managers face issues every day that are challenging and costly in time, resources, and emotional energy. Generally, the larger and more complex the organization, the more intense and varied the subjects. Large or small, though, all nonprofit leaders need to have the necessary management skills, organizational procedures, staff members, and systems in place if they are to navigate through demanding issues. Hank Rosso described managing the fund raising program as the "gentle exercise in helping people work together productively" (Rosso, 1991b, p. 131). Compare this image to that of a private sector business leader directing a company. You may initially conjure up radically different thoughts about the two leaders' styles, yet ultimately, the successful fund raising manager stands shoulder to shoulder with the business manager in producing measurable and progressive results.

Effective fund raising managers have learned to draw from each side of The Fund Raising School's "cube"—institutional readiness, human resources, management, markets, vehicles, and dynamic functions—to successfully fuse people, ideas, and programs for the good of the organization. Though all-inclusive, the management process is not static. Wouldn't it be wonderful for an organization to be able to unfold a mature management plan from day one or for a new manager to be in full swing on the first day on the job! In reality, we all know that management is a process developed over time to suit the specific needs of the nonprofit and its people. Care must be taken to nurture and continuously evolve the management process to allow it to grow with the organization.

Today a number of critical issues confront fund raising managers and their organizations, including these:

- Experiencing rapid change in the environment
- Answering the demand for more services from limited resources
- Addressing the call for greater accountability from board members and donors
- Finding a balance between the urgent needs of today and goals of the future
- Defining leadership roles of the board, staff, and volunteers
- Keeping pace with the latest changes in technology for efficiency and up-to-date information
- Energizing and unleashing the inner motivations of staff and volunteers, even when resources are limited

The series of high hurdles that nonprofit managers must jump over to accomplish their missions can be daunting. There is, however, a universal element in every successful organization: its *people*—the leadership, board members, staff, volunteers, and donors who inspire and are inspired by the organization's potential. In the words of Hank Rosso, skilled fund raising managers are in the "delicate position to assert quiet leadership, of having to accomplish much through persuasion" (1991b, p. 131) as they inspire people to focus their efforts for the benefit of the organization. It's certainly not a task for the faint of heart or the devoid of determination, but much can be done to accentuate an individual's managerial abilities.

FUND RAISING MANAGERS AND THEIR RESPONSIBILITIES

"Nothing great was ever achieved without enthusiasm," wrote Ralph Waldo Emerson in 1841. While Emerson's observation remains applicable to leaders in many professions, it is especially true in the world of fund raising management. The enthusiastic fund raising leader is regarded as the keystone by many individuals in the organization—the CEO, professional staff, support staff, board members, volunteers, and donors. To complement their positive outlook, such leaders must develop systems for communication to flourish, productivity to increase, and institutional goals to be realized. Several tenets hold true for all good fund raising leaders—perhaps none as essential as an earnest belief in the mission of the organization and loyalty to serve. Here's what the enthusiastic leader will look like:

- A person who ensures accessible, open communication at all levels of the organization
- A confident and caring leader who is articulate and influential by helping people work together
- An individual who is trustworthy and fair
- A considerate, good listener
- A person who has respect for staff and volunteers as well as donors and board members
- A clear goal setter who inspires staff to stretch for an attainable mark
- A person who will acknowledge a job well done as well as provide constructive feedback
- A leader who inspires others to be creative and optimistic
- A professional who is proud to be known as a fund raiser
- A person who exemplifies a code of ethics through speech and actions
- An individual who recognizes the importance of the philanthropic process to the sector

The very best fund raising managers are both problem solvers and solution enablers in that they encourage the people around them, including the board, to think and act creatively for the good of the organization. Successful fund raising management is the convergence of good people relationships and good business practices. The key word is *relationships*. Relationships are built around people. It is people who dream and need and plan and carry out the business of fund raising. Without effective relationship building, the best of business practices will suffer or, at best, recycle the same air. Similarly, without implementation of a good business plan, the most dynamic of people encompassed by a nonprofit will be neither completely fulfilled nor utilized to the utmost of their ability. A tight weave of mastered technical skills and pervasive ethical values creates trust, shared goals, excitement, and a path to effective results.

What is a "successful" development program? What do we truly want to accomplish? What am I doing to get us there? How do I measure our results? What can we do to reach our goals—and reach them faster? Will we be able to grow the program to the next level? How can we keep our volunteers satisfied? Can we raise more money given the resources on hand? Is the staff able to carry out our goals? These are all good questions asked by those who want to see their nonprofits serve the public interest. Each of these questions calls upon a similar issue—effective fund raising management. Whether with a part-time or full-time staff person, effective fund raising management happens when people and programs come together by responding to needs and obtaining gifts.

MEETING THE CHALLENGE THROUGH BASIC MANAGEMENT FUNCTIONS

The management process used by The Fund Raising School includes six separate functions involving planning, implementation, and assessment. They are analysis, planning, execution, control, evaluation, and professional ethics.

Analysis

Management begins with analysis. Ultimately, the process of planning is borne out of the analysis of many aspects of the organization, including the mission and case, human resources, the environment, internal and external communication, and finances. Goals and objectives should be outlined in the fund raising plan, along with specific action plans that you intend to implement. It is also important to include the people within the institution who are essential to realizing success and prioritizing goals. Ultimately, analysis answers the question "Where are we today?"

Planning

As important as the resulting plan itself is the process of planning. (Much more about this important topic can be found in Chapter Three.) "Are we headed in the right direction?" and "What are we doing to get us where we need to go?" are logical questions to pose. Regard the plan and the planning process as avenues for continually assessing the goals of the organization—looking down the road instead of at your feet. No one intentionally goes through planning to get stuck in a rut, but it can happen. Too little planning or no planning at all results in unclear or, worse yet, unrealistic expectations and directions for the development function on the part of the CEO, board, staff, and volunteers. The cause of no planning and its end result are usually the same—fear, mistrust, inertia, and apathy. Conversely, too much planning prevents people from moving forward. A manager shouldn't yoke self and staff to the finite specifics of the plan without acknowledging the importance of flexibility to respond to new opportunities and unforeseen challenges. Change will and should happen along the way. The plan will serve as something of a global positioning satellite the majority of the time, but on occasion you may have to build a new road to get where you need to go.

How often should the planning process be conducted? It is recommended that plans be developed and refined annually. This is known as *strategic planning* (covering the next six to twelve months). A *long-range plan* (generally one to five years or more) may also be reviewed and updated annually, thereby ensuring its relevance to the present as well as future growth and direction. Individuals in important decision-making roles should be called on to actively participate in the planning process, and their input should be integrated into the plan, not tacked on as an addendum to the final product. These individuals include the CEO, board, staff members, major donors, constituents, and volunteers. According to Joseph Mixer, "Those parties most affected by the plan will give it greater support if they are consulted and involved during its creation" (1993, pp. 96–97). Encouraging prudent risk taking and innovative thinking has its rewards as people work through the process individually and collectively. Among the areas assessed should be the program, the organization (board and staff), and the development function (fund raising, marketing, and public relations). Done correctly, the planning process is an energizing experience, empowering each participant as a stakeholder in its realization. A spillover benefit is that of building trust, confidence, understanding, and collegiality within the team.

Execution

Once the development plan evolves into a finalized document, the fund raising manager must implement the plan and assign responsibilities. If never executed, the plan is nothing more than a work of fiction sitting on a shelf. This is not a onetime deal! You wouldn't think of exercising once a year and then saying, "I'm glad that's over for another twelve months!" Just as a regular physical workout may energize, build muscle, and get the blood flowing, you need to keep up the implementation process, or else you will slide back to your former condition. It is the role of the chief development officer to lead the organizational charge with energy, optimism, and a commitment to investing time in the process. The leader needs to take seriously all the duties that only he or she can assume. Keep in mind that staff who helped devise the plan are filled with expectations and excitement and have an earnest desire to see that the plan is implemented. Secrecy has no place here. Copies of the plan should be distributed to all to make everyone aware of it and comfortable with it. Delegating responsibilities within the plan and in implementing the plan will help build stronger and more capable staff eager to promote cooperation instead of competition. Along the way, it's wise to check that people know why you are asking them to take on various tasks, thereby confirming their understanding and sense of ownership. Without such affirmation, communication can become splintered and the plan a burdensome workload. Time management is especially important for staging the desired outcomes of the plan. Setting schedules in advance and meeting regularly infuse enthusiasm and confidence in all.

Control

Control is the process of building procedures, policies, and reporting mechanisms into your system. It is designed specifically to manage people *and* paper! It's the resulting endpoint of all of the hard work, creativity, and hours that went into planning and execution. For example, if the nonprofit sought a solution to its problem with sending acknowledgment letters within twenty-four to forty-eight hours of receiving the gift, the control is the system by which this was addressed, remedied, and maintained. Measures—through staff and resources—are put into place to accomplish the desired outcome. Control is the effective implementation of systems and guidelines to establish standards within the organization. Effective nonprofit organizations are well stocked with controls for mandating procedures and expectations within reasonable time frames and continue to invest time to study and update such issues.

Evaluation

Management includes assessment. Managers need to regularly ask two blunt questions of themselves and of their staffs. "Are we accomplishing what we set out to do?" and "How well is it working?" The candor with which they answer these questions is usually telling of the success they will realize. Evaluation is the process of holding the mirror to oneself to assess programs and people. Is what we're doing getting us what we want? What do we need to change? How effective is this year's annual fund? How about the corporate giving program and the training sessions for new board members? Wise is the manager who sees a problem in the organization and addresses it with tact, concern, and dignity. If the organization continues to lose money on its direct mail appeal, the problem needs to be studied and addressed in a timely manner. Such problem solving leads to growth of the organization and maturation of the manager as a competent and efficient leader who engenders the respect of the staff. It's the gentle nudge in action.

Evaluation needs to be conducted through two scopes—one for programs and the second for individuals. Both are revealing. Programs should be assessed for impact, dollars realized, and overall success. For example, results of the special event should be monitored carefully and, when possible, compared to past events. Was the special event successful in attracting the desired audience? Did the volunteer structure work well? Was communication about the event effective? Was the service good? Is a follow-up survey called for? How much money was raised? How could the event be improved next year? Evaluation leads naturally to analysis, making management an ongoing cyclical process.

Professional Ethics

Management must be done in a professional and ethical way. It's the charge of the fund raising leader to initiate such a stance and to demonstrate it to all, including the CEO, board, staff, donors, volunteers, constituency, and community. Fund raisers must act ethically, using judgment that reflects not only the highest standards of the organization and the profession but also the self-worth of the individual. (More about ethics can be found in Chapter Thirty.) At times, development officers face conflicting issues when soliciting gifts from donors who request special favors that benefit them unfairly. For example, a fund raiser would be compromised ethically if she were to solicit and accept a leadership gift for the school she represents knowing that in return for the gift, the donor expected that his child, with insufficient grades, will be admitted to the school. It is the duty of the fund raiser to act with strength and courage to decline such a gift and explain why it is not permissible. She must be able to ask for a gift with a positive attitude and confidence knowing that she is the embodiment of the organization. In turn, she must feel that she has the full backing of her supervisor and the organization to use her ethical judgment in asking for and receiving a gift. With heightened competition for donor dollars, especially those coveted extraordinary gifts needed to reach annual and capital campaign goals, ultimately, the fund raising manager must champion what is right and acceptable in the realm of gift receiving among staff and volunteers and not exert undue pressure on reaching dollar goals at the expense of ethics. Likewise, it is incumbent on the fund raising leader to set the pace with self and staff on making an energized presentation to be a part of the future and to be cognizant of that role. "The practice of gift seeking is justified when it exalts the contributor, not the gift seeker," explained Hank (Rosso, 1991a, p. 7). The fund raising leader knows to recognize the balance of meritorious staff recognition and adulation.

Successful fund raisers are able to look confidently into the eyes of a donor and ask for a gift. They understand that they are giving the donor an opportunity to be involved with something bigger than the donor himself or herself. Organizations such as The Fund Raising School, the Council for the Advancement and Support of Education (CASE), the Association of Fund Raising Professionals (AFP), and the Association of Healthcare Philanthropy (AHP) have done an exceptional job in responding to the need for professionalism by developing certificate programs.

THE MANAGEMENT MATRIX

The six components just described—analysis, planning, execution, control, evaluation, and professional ethics—are the elements of a *management matrix*. The management matrix (see Table 23.1) forms a superstructure or grid for integrating

Table 23.1. The Management Matrix.

What Must Be Managed	Analysis	Planning	Execution	Control	Evaluation	Professional Ethics
1. Human Resources						
2. Information Resources						
• Internal						
• External						
3. Financial Resources						
• Gifts						
• Investments						
• Expense budgets						
4. Physical Resources						
5. Relationships						

Source: The Fund Raising School, 2002.

the elements into a cohesive and comprehensive development *management process.* Fund raising managers can use the matrix as a tool as they address each area of the grid to assess the effectiveness of their development operation, knowing that a strength or weakness in one area will certainly have a spillover effect for other components. The process of working through the matrix and periodically updating it is highly valuable in measuring the progress of the ever-evolving development operation.

DEVELOPMENT OFFICE ORGANIZATION

Whether in a sixty-year-old nationwide nonprofit or one that is newly incorporated and serving a small community, hiring staff is a big investment. The investment is in the future life of the organization and the careers of individuals in the nonprofit sector. As with any job, new and longtime staff members function best when they know exactly what their fund raising managers expect of them and how they can be most effective. A comprehensive job description is essential. Not only should the description be a part of office records, but it should also be freely shared with staff members during the interview process. Job descriptions give staff members a sense of the magnitude and responsibility of their positions and serve as a guidepost for future performance reviews and professional growth.

Professional Staff Responsibilities

Not surprisingly, fund raisers are hired to raise money! Yet at times, the purpose of their job is reshaped by forces in the environment or by organizational necessity. It's helpful for the fund raising manager to have clearly spelled out expectations. Many organizations have developed fund raising target goals for the number of donor contacts per month or year as well as the goals for dollars to be raised. These methodical systems facilitate tracking of activities leading to donor commitments. The number of contacts and specific dollar goals need to be developed with the input of the development officer to reflect the organization's maturity, donor base, and staff size. A large and established nonprofit may expect major gift officers to carry prospect portfolios numbering 100 to 150 individuals with a gift potential of $100,000 or more. The number of meaningful donor contacts anticipated per month could be in the upper ranges of 30 to 40. Conversely, a small new organization may look for its lone development officer to raise the $35,000 annual fund goal on a part-time basis. It is extremely helpful, yet too often neglected in small shops, to determine goals with regard to the number of contacts and gift ranges for prospects. Accordingly, it is most reasonable for the prospect base to be asked for lower-level gift amounts to reflect that figure.

What is more difficult to measure on paper, yet equally as important, is the *quality* of a contact with a prospective donor. After a visit with the fund raiser at the animal shelter, is the donor feeling more involved and gratified about her relationship with the shelter's people and programs (in addition to her love for the animals)? Progressively and carefully building relationships with people in a position to respond financially is an essential ability for the development officer. Reflective fund raisers and their managers are well aware of this dynamic and track such relationships accordingly.

If the staff member is to have supervisory responsibilities, these should be clearly enumerated in the job description, including the person's role in evaluating support staff. If the development officer is to have duties such as implementing computer programs or attending regular meetings and events, those should also be outlined in the description. Imagine the dismay of a young woman who with much anticipation accepted a position with an organization in New Jersey assuming it was a Monday-through-Friday, 8-to-5 workday. Once on board, she learned that her manager expected her and other professional staff members to clock sixty or more hours per week, including evenings and weekends! She hung on for six months before quitting. In the end, both she and the nonprofit lost valuable time and resources. Professional staff should also be encouraged to establish short- and long-term goals, create job descriptions for new staff, serve as liaisons to board members and volunteers, and be accountable for human and monetary resources utilized. In shops of more than one person, staff should meet weekly or biweekly to discuss current activity and progress.

Staff Retention

One of the most turbulent issues for fund raising managers today is staff retention. Fund raising professionals leaving one job for another have become an all-too-frequent occurrence and can pose serious problems for nonprofits. The financial and emotional costs of recruiting and training new staff members are high (from hundreds to many thousands of dollars). Damaging is the loss of unrealized gift income during the time a position is open. And when a new professional does come on board, it frequently takes six to twelve months before she is prepared to actively solicit and receive substantial new donor dollars. When an employee, especially one who is more senior, chooses to leave for another job, out walks every relationship he has worked hard to nurture between the donor and the organization. Connectivity to the donor is hampered or may even be lost altogether; if the relationship does continue, it may never regain the same depth.

What is causing fund raisers to gaze at greener pastures? Salary has much to do with it as the field expands. Competition for professional staff has skyrocketed, along with the growth of U.S. charities (Schwinn and Sommerfield, 2002). Many nonprofits are offering very attractive recruitment packages to lure talent, especially senior professionals, to their camps; perquisites may include club memberships, automotive privileges, educational opportunities, housing, and other enhanced benefits. Ultimately, this causes something of a chain reaction in the marketplace, with many search firms now aggressively involved in helping nonprofits fill positions. Other factors include the perceived or actual realization by fund raisers that they may not be fully valued or appreciated by their boards or bosses. Criticisms include feeling underutilized by the board, having limited authority and influence in the organization, experiencing burnout, working absurdly long hours, and being handed unrealistic expectations, including a constant pressure that they, as fund raising experts, can and will fix all money woes . . . or else!

Although it is good that fund raisers are able to move on to better-paying and more challenging positions, ultimately, it is better for the organization to retain the staff it has invested in. But can't the same thing happen to a fund raiser all over again at a new job? Of course! And if a productive individual accepts a job elsewhere, how much will it really cost the organization to fill his position, including lost gift income in the intervening time while hiring a replacement? The price may be steep. What other elements lead to discontent? One study (Duronio and Tempel, 1997) revealed that fund raisers aged sixty and above reported working sixty hours per week, while the average for everyone else in the survey was forty-eight hours. Considerable hours away from family and home can take their toll on the dedication of an employee and lead to burnout.

How can you prevent staff exodus? Positive solutions to deal with these pressures include instituting flexible work hours and building a higher level of staff recognition. Make your environment one filled with caring, fun, and esprit de corps. Also, regularly ask people what they like and dislike. As simplistic as it sounds, the results are usually eye-opening, for everyone appreciates having a voice in the office. Fund raisers, just like anyone else, seek genuine understanding and appreciation for a job well done. Other factors that can make a discernible difference to staff are to provide room for professional and personal growth and a clear opportunity for promotion within the organization. Consider implementing or adjusting goals to be realistic and attainable—development people thrive on gentle pressure, yet they may choke on an impossible quest! As fund raising manager, it's your job to listen to the staff (hear the current desires) and look ahead (anticipate the future needs). The payoff will be a happy and productive team of fund raisers who want to invest their future with the organization because they can see a meaningful place for themselves.

Support Staff Responsibilities

Often the "first face" encountered by an organization's external constituency, a welcoming support staff member with a pleasant, helpful attitude makes a positive difference in setting the tone for clients, members, donors, and board members calling in or stopping by. A support assistant at an Indiana health care nonprofit was assigned to call donors who made gifts of $100 or less. She telephoned a woman to thank her for her recent $100 gift—the first personal call the donor ever received from the organization. When the donor realized that the caller simply wanted to express thanks and *not* ask for another gift, the donor was taken aback. As the support staff member concluded the call by saying, "You have a nice day," the donor interrupted and said she had never before received such a call asking "for nothing." The donor requested further information from the organization—over time resulting in a $1.5 million bequest, credited to the initial good work, gentle manner, and quick thinking of a support staff member. The lesson here is that each contact we have with donors and our constituency is a seed planting for the future—and everyone in the organization serves as a "fund raising seed planter," whether or not it is written in the person's job description.

Clearly, support staff members are an integral part of the development team and should be regarded as such by the fund raising manager. As with professional positions, their numerous duties need to be captured in written job descriptions that are communicated to all. These duties may include clerical and administrative responsibilities required for effective support of one or many staff members. Specific job requirements may include general correspondence and writing of letters, scheduling and handling the details for meetings, and taking minutes of board and staff meetings. It is also important for support staff to accurately process gifts and record information in the database, conduct research when needed, and organize time effectively to stay on top of the workload. Wise is the fund raising manager who realizes that effective support staff and volunteers are the backbone of a growing shop. As such, these valuable employees should be encouraged to continue their education and, if possible, receive financial help with attending courses and seminars for professional growth. It's an appreciated vote of confidence and a morale booster.

Staff Evaluations

Staff members, both professional and support, need be regularly evaluated one-on-one with a fund raising manager to provide feedback on performance. This may take place on a periodic basis and should certainly be conducted no less than once a year. In advance of the meeting, it's helpful to encourage staff to assess their *own* performance and how to improve it. The meeting itself is an ideal time to earnestly praise staff performance and initiative, to point out difficulties they may be having, to constructively reprimand when needed, to solve problems, to seek their ideas, and to set future goals. It's also helpful for managers to ask how they may help staff members do their job more effectively. People want to feel valued by the organization and their colleagues. A kind word or deserved praise goes far in sending a message of value. Given the fact that few nonprofits are in a position to compensate at a high dollar level to show appreciation, recognition of deserving staff is especially important. Likewise, if criticism is called for to change a person's behavior, it should be done in the most constructive way possible. The evaluation, if done with honesty and care, is a lift to the individual as a contributor to the success of the mission and also serves to enhance his or her feeling of self-worth.

Volunteers

Volunteers are the emotional heart and soul of many nonprofits. Often they serve as a consistent and much needed workforce that makes the organization function. "Managing" this wellspring of expertise, energy, and enthusiasm is an important component of any successful operation—in fact, recognizing the importance of the volunteer base, some larger organizations hire staff just to coordinate the volunteer function. Without clear direction, volunteers can become bored, feel underappreciated, and, over time, lose interest. To add luster to a strong volunteer base, it is essential for volunteers first of all to understand what is expected of them. For example, how will a community library use a team of volunteers to help with the annual fund? How will the volunteers be recruited? What are the various jobs they may take on? Will they be asking for gifts? Is there a need for volunteers to write thank-you letters? Who provides training, and how often is it given? Answering these questions in advance of recruiting and accepting volunteers will help ensure smooth involvement and help avoid misunderstandings in volunteer job performance. Just as with paid staff, it helps immensely to have written job descriptions for volunteers, including expectations regarding hours, reporting structure, specific duties, event involvement, and interaction with donors, if appropriate. Similarly, as we review and assess the performance of paid staff, some organizations annually review the year with volunteer staff. Such a review also provides a good opportunity to set goals for the coming year and to ask volunteers if they would like to take on new responsibilities. If, as occasionally happens, a volunteer's actions or words are not in keeping with the organization's standards, the fund raising manager must take appropriate action to change the behavior or to remove the individual from that position. By far the vast majority of volunteers are a wonderful enhancement to the operation as well as an economic windfall. Keep in mind, too, that some of our best donors may emerge from our volunteer ranks.

Sharing information with our volunteers gives them a sense of importance and makes them feel like insiders who know about the internal workings and goals of the organization. It also deepens their appreciation and understanding of the nonprofit's mission. Depending on the organization, it may be appropriate to have the volunteer annually sign a letter of commitment stipulating what he will take on, thereby reaffirming his involvement and recognizing the generosity and importance of his time commitment to the organization. It is essential that the fund raising manager carve out time and resources to appropriately recognize and reward volunteers. Such recognition doesn't need to be costly, but it should be meaningful for the individual. Too often, organizations with long-time volunteers tend to assume that life goes on as usual without pausing to give sincere thanks. Likewise, when asking a volunteer for her impressions on volunteer recognition, she may respond that she gets her satisfaction from doing her part to help out. True, but it is important for the organization to find an appropriate way to express thanks—primarily for the volunteer but also to communicate to others involved with the organization that volunteers and the act of volunteering are valued and appreciated.

POLICIES AND PROCEDURES

Management of the fund raising process requires written policies and procedures related to a number of aspects of the program to provide guidance to staff and volunteers.

Gift Processing and Acknowledgment

Having a set of systems and guidelines in place is an especially valuable tool for saving time, money, and staff power, as well as to achieve more accurate and comprehensive communication. Such procedures are indispensable in the area of gift processing and gift acknowledgment. The standard for gift acknowledgment is high yet appropriate: within twenty-four to forty-eight hours of receiving the gift, the nonprofit should contact the donor to extend an expression of gratitude. There is no better way to demonstrate to the donor the value your organization places on the gift, as well as to exhibit accountability for receiving the gift. Such a response may be handled a variety of ways, including a personal visit, letter, phone call, or e-mail. All gifts should be acknowledged, and written documentation, including a mention of the gift amount, is generally required for tax purposes.

Prospect Research

Each nonprofit needs to determine what is a reasonable and ethical amount of information to collect with regard to a donor or prospective donor. (See Chapters Thirteen and Twenty-Six for more information on this topic.) Where will the information be filed, will volunteers have access to it, and what types of information will and will not be gathered and stored? Will information be purchased? Simply because financial and other revealing information is available in the public domain, does that mean it is to be collected? What are the ethical principles driving the organization, and does the policy fit? Much discussion has taken place with regard to this subject. Several organizations, including The Fund Raising School, the Association of Professional Researchers for Advancement

(APRA), and the AFP, have written codes on the subject that would be helpful to all nonprofits in developing their standards of ethical operations.

Internal Gift Reports and Communication

Do you know where your fund raising dollars stand as of today? What gifts and pledges are expected in the coming months? By the end of the fiscal year? This is valuable information to the fund raising manager as he plans ahead and looks toward successfully helping the organization reach its funding goal. Still, it is surprising that not all fund raising managers have ready access to such crucial information, instead being dependent on the financial manager or another individual for such data. It is very important to share this information with fund raising staff and the board so that they can respond accordingly in their cultivations and solicitations. The figures on gifts and pledges received should not be a mystery until the end of the fiscal year, when there is no longer time to respond. If possible, such vital data need to be shared with appropriate staff on a monthly basis.

Effective fund raising directors appreciate the value of sharing information internally and consequently seek to empower the support and professional staff. One idea is to circulate a single file that contains the copies of letters to donors and prospects that were mailed out and received during the previous week. Some organizations refer to this as the "rainbow file" because it covers the spectrum of current donor activity. The rainbow file also contains copies of gift cards, gift reports, proposals, and other written correspondence, including relevant newspaper articles and e-mails. (Personal correspondence and sensitive materials are excluded from the rainbow file.) The file, with a checklist of staff names on the cover, is circulated among all appropriate individuals in the fund raising office. This provides an ideal way for professional and support staff to share information and be in the know. Whether through nature or through practice, many people have a tendency to collect an overabundance of paper. The rainbow file is a good way to cut down on that habit, and it's surprisingly helpful in exchanging vital information. Once the contents of the file have been circulated to all in the office, the papers are then added to the donor files under the names of the individuals, corporations, and foundations.

Regardless of the size of the office, all development staff should be encouraged to use one central filing system for donor records—including donor research and donor gift information (the exception again would be highly sensitive donor information). The benefit of this policy is that it cuts down on information being "siloed" in the desk drawer of a staff member, rarely if ever to be seen again, especially if the person leaves the organization and mistakenly takes the documents along. Moreover, central filing of donor records guarantees that when donor information is needed, it is readily available and not inaccessibly locked away. An added benefit is that all donor records are stored in one place, thereby reducing the need for filing cabinets in individual offices. Interestingly, circulating the rainbow file and then using a central filing system works especially well in larger offices where there could be timely changes in the records of particular individuals. Sharing these data improves internal communication among staff members involved in the progress of donor relationships and also indicates to staff that they are a vital element in responsibly handling confidential internal information.

Record System and Maintenance

Although each organization has its own format for recording key data electronically (manual forms are acceptable if no computer is available), specific basic components must be included, such as donor name, address, phone number, e-mail address, date of gift, gift amount, pledge amount, payment schedule, and purpose of gift. It is also important to record if gifts or services were received in exchange for the gift, if the donor wishes the gift to be anonymous, if the gift is a memorial and, if so, who should be notified, and whether the gift is eligible for a corporate match.

The office staff structure needs to clearly define who has access to computerized donor records and who has authorization to make changes and updates to the system. If free reign in changing data is given to too many people, the integrity of the information will be compromised by becoming duplicative, inaccurate, or overlooked. If possible, it's best for those who make record changes in the system to add their initials after entering the new information—thereby keeping a record of who made the change and when. Typically, the fewer people entering information, the more accurate it will be. Essential to the entry process is verification to ensure the accuracy of the data. This responsibility should be carried out by a staff member different from the person who entered the information. When the time comes for the purchase or upgrade of hardware and software, it is desirable to involve several people in the decision-making process, including those who enter and access information and the development leader and other fund raisers. Although price may be a factor in your purchase, make sure the new system can accommodate your current and future needs. Sometimes the best "bargain" at first blush may end up costing more in the long run.

Resource Materials

In building a comprehensive development office, there should be a resource area that serves as a small library or reference area. The fund raising director should take the lead in purchasing fund raising books and ordering periodicals to be made available to staff and volunteers. It's also an ideal spot to gather fund raising materials such as annual reports, direct mail samples, and brochures from other organizations to contrast styles and stimulate new ideas. All in-house materials pertaining to case development, mission statements, and printed materials should also be available at this central location for all staff to access.

Office and Other Physical Requirements

The quarters housing the development office say much to people who visit them. Whether large or small, finely appointed or modest in appearance, the important question remains, "How is a visitor made to feel?" Is the space emotionally austere, or does the office reflect the spirit of the organization and its people? Is the office adequately marked and well lighted? Is someone stationed at the entrance to warmly greet and direct guests, or must a visitor embark on a lonely hunt? Are shelves orderly and clean, or are files and old magazines scattered about? Is the first impression that of a professional organization? Would it be apparent to a visiting donor that this organization understands its purpose and donors are cherished and welcomed?

Resources must be spent on furnishing the development office to reflect its importance to the organization. At the very least, staff members need usable work spaces, a storage area, and an appropriate room to accommodate visitors, including a conference room for private meetings with donors, staff, volunteers, and vendors. Ideally, the development office should be located in close proximity to the director or president of the organization, both reflecting the importance of the development operation and enhancing accessibility to the organization's leadership. Over time, the fund raising leader's planning should include the purchase of additional office furniture and equipment needed to communicate effectively. This includes a good telephone and conferencing system, a computer, a copy machine, a fax machine, and other professional tools.

MANAGING THE STEWARDSHIP PROGRAM

Developing a comprehensive stewardship program is one of the wisest investments a nonprofit can make toward a healthy future. (Chapter Thirty-One is dedicated to this important topic.) Stewardship is about your donors and how you carefully involve them with your organization. Stewardship is a belief, a communication tool, a mind-set, and yes, even a philosophy for how the organization interacts with its donors during the time between receipt of a donor's current gift and a possible next gift. Effective stewardship helps the organization breathe deeply and sustain our ties to donors. Think of stewardship as a point along a perfect circle. As we plot the fund raising cycle (see Figure 3.1 in Chapter Three), at the top of the circle (12 o'clock), the developmental process in initiated by examining the case. It is only when we have come nearly full circle (10 o'clock) that the solicitation is made and the gift realized. Good stewardship leads to a repeat gift from the donor, starting the circle over again. Not surprisingly, the best future donor is one who already gives to the organization. "To yield effective results year in and year out, however, relationships with donors must be managed scientifically, which requires hard work," succinctly notes Kathleen Kelly (1998, p. 387).

Successful organizations draw on that ability to enhance their stewardship programs, for it results in a more informed, involved, and engaged donor population. We need to exhibit that we are responsible users of their gifts. An annual report detailing the organization's year, as well as a personalized statement on the usage of *their* specific gift, reflects time and money well spent.

Recognizing the power of stewardship, many nonprofits are investing in staff and resources to expand their stewardship programs. Customized donor plans that address specific interests are clearly part of good planning, research, event, communication, and major gift elements. Nurturing relationships with these donors expresses our appreciation for their financial commitment and something more—their participation and ultimate care for our mission. While the investment may be attractive to building long-term investors, some board members and others in leadership positions fail to see the merit of committing dollars today with no immediate payback in sight—at least for the next budget year. A fund raising leader will look to exert positive influence to grow this aspect of the development program over time. Although the cost for added staff time, events, and publications is very real, the investment ultimately leads to greater donor connectivity, understanding, and gift dollars.

CONCLUSION

In an environment of perpetual change and demand on nonprofits' human and financial resources, the role of the fund raising manager and leader is pivotal to the organization. Managing the fund raising program is an extremely important function that will lay the groundwork for future internal and external relationships. As Hank Rosso said, the fund raising leader employs a "gentle exercise" in drawing out and accentuating the strengths and diverse talents of professional staff, support staff, board, volunteers, and donors. Although a development office is a multidimensional structure, when all the elements of The Fund Raising School cube are successfully addressed, the people and programs of the organization are exhilarated and able to work collaboratively to achieve maximum potential. *Good plans come from good planning!* The planning process coalesces all aspects of effective fund raising management—people, policy, and procedures—to create and affirm opportunities and expectations. With a genuine focus on individuals and a commitment to mission, the fund raising leader is a builder—a builder of relationships, a builder of communication bridges, a builder of plans and futures, and a builder of an organizational framework around which these elements will flourish. The result of this labor is rewarding. It yields enhanced communication, a system of ambitious yet achievable goal setting, and an organized and functional office structure. Best of all, though, is the burgeoning growth and empowerment of staff and volunteers who will achieve heightened fund raising successes.

CHAPTER TWENTY-FOUR

Leadership
and Team Building

Kay Sprinkel Grace

Hank Rosso taught us that successful fund raising was having the right person ask the right prospective donor for the right amount of gift for the right cause at the right time. Much of this book is dedicated to the process for getting everything right. Often the right person is a board member, volunteer, or key staff person who must exercise leadership in making the proposal and soliciting the gift.

The Rosso model of lifetime donor development requires the exercise of leadership in all aspects of operating a nonprofit organization. As donors continue their involvement over time and as the organization engages donors more meaningfully in its mission and its vision for the future, leadership becomes ever more critical. Leadership among staff and board is needed to define and articulate a mission and vision for the organization that will attract major donors. Without organizational leadership in which donors have confidence, fund raising cannot be successful. But fund raising itself requires leadership. Board members, volunteers, and staff must be willing to serve as advocates for the organization, make the case for support, and ask for gifts if the fund raising program is to reach its full potential.

Chapter Twenty-Three dealt with management in fund raising. This chapter is dedicated to leadership in fund raising. Not all managers are leaders, but all leaders need to be capable managers. The public is attracted to—and philanthropists invest in—nonprofit organizations with strong board and staff leadership. Fund raising itself is a leadership task. It takes leadership to create a vision for the future, to present a stimulating case for support, and to convince the public that change is needed.

There are as many definitions of leadership as there are writers about leadership. The descriptions applied to leaders are familiar to everyone: "is a visionary," "gets things done through others," "is inspiring," "creates teams," and on and on. Asked to generate a list of attributes of leaders, few people have a problem. So why does strong leadership seem to elude us? Why do boards have such difficulty attracting and developing leaders? Why do executive directors burn out, and why do so many choose to do this job only once? Clearly, leadership, as it influences public confidence, donor investment and satisfaction, and perception of overall performance, is a continuing quest among aspiring organizations and the prevailing practice of organizations that are viewed as successful. In our sector, we look to effective board and staff leaders to do all of the following:

- Have and share a vision that will attract and retain both thoughtful donor-investors and strong volunteer leaders

- Give form and direction to the donor and fund raising process—from identification of potential donors through renewal of current donors— that supports successful donor involvement and the fund raising process

- Evidence an unwavering commitment to transparency in accounting for and reporting the impact of donor investment

- Be effective managers of people, ideas, and tasks involved in the fund raising process

There is no way to separate the requirements of institutional leadership from those of successful fund raising. Long-term donor and fund development depends on solid leadership by staff and volunteers. Strong leadership on an ongoing basis is needed to attract other strong board members and volunteers, to recruit the best administrative, program, and development managers, and to create increasingly loyal networks of community supporters, donors, and volunteers that sustain nonprofits. When we speak of leadership in donor development and fund raising, we are talking about the board, volunteers, and staff leadership in our organizations. The leadership of the board, volunteers, and staff to engage donors in the plans and programs of the organization is critical to securing significant investments of money and time.

This chapter will explore new ideas and challenges in leadership and new roles for leaders, as well as review the principles of leadership that remain the same. It will examine the challenges the sector faces in attracting and developing leaders and provide examples and ideas for recognizing, encouraging, and nurturing leadership in your organization. It will also look at leadership as it applies to fund raising and the major gift process, an aspect of leadership that The Fund Raising School has developed and evolved for more than a decade.

PERFORMANCE DEMANDS ON LEADERSHIP

In recent years, nonprofit organizations have undergone intense scrutiny. The flourishing of philanthropy at the close of the twentieth century gave donors and funders new access and insights into our sector. In our communities, the need for human, social, and educational services has called nonprofits into new roles, and shifts in funding for the arts, culture, and the environment have also led to new demands for nonprofit partnerships. Sustaining nonprofit services to our communities has never been more important. A distracted world runs the danger of neglecting its deepest community needs, and so the need for strong leaders in our sector is growing. In this environment, nonprofit leadership is essential both to operate in a manner to sustain confidence and to help raise the funds essential to support needed programs.

Communities look for nonprofit leaders with wisdom, vision, skill, and integrity in whom they can trust to serve and solve the problems we face in our communities. The lessons we learn and apply in times of great challenge can become the platform for improved performance and service in what we hope will be better times ahead. Across the sector, we want to hire managers and enlist volunteers who have these powerful and essential leadership attributes. We also hope that they will be able to manage, inspire, evaluate, communicate, anticipate, listen, articulate the mission, and engage others—particularly donors—in the purpose and plans of the organization. A tall order? Perhaps. But these leaders do exist, and to attract them, organizations must be aware of the internal and external forces at play in our sector and its donor and fund development challenges.

Increasing demands on philanthropic organizations to meet stringent requirements for transparency, accountability, and measurable action intensify the leadership challenges presented by our already chaotic, Internet-speed, time-driven, and pressure-ridden external environment. These new expectations place incredible challenges on leaders in a variety of areas.

Mission and Values

Increasingly, people give to solve problems. Potential donors search for organizations that are addressing concerns they deem important (for example, mental health, public or private education, or domestic violence). They evaluate these organizations, choose the ones they want to support, and make "philanthropic investments" because they believe the organizations serve or even help resolve these issues. For these donors, the core consideration is *values*. If donors are concerned about the issue of aging, for example, the values they look for may range from quality of life to dignity to independence to protection and safety. Donors expect that these values, as expressed in the mission, will be acted on by the organization and that programs and outcomes will validate those values. Leaders must affirm those values in their actions and communications and must continually inform and engage donors in ways that assure them that what they invested in is indeed coming to pass. Challenging as it is to quantify the mission impact, doing so is essential. People evaluate leadership on the basis of the impact the organization is having on an issue about which they care and whether the problem is being served or solved well by the organization.

Partnership

It is important that we advance a new perception of the sector, emphasizing that we are not "charities" that need a handout but rather nonprofit organizations that are full partners with the community and donors in addressing community issues. Although our sector will always be viewed as the "charitable sector" and will serve to invite and satisfy the "charitable" instincts of our most thoughtful citizens, leaders today must be able to present the sector in a new way. Among those who have undertaken a campaign to shift our thinking are Peter Hero, president of the Community Foundation Silicon Valley in San Jose, California, and Peter Drucker, a proponent of new ways to relate to donors. As long ago as 1991, Drucker was telling readers that people no longer give to charity; rather, they buy into results. Hero (2001b) believes that our sector needs to be known not as the charitable sector or even the nonprofit sector but as the *public benefit sector*. He challenges the idea of referring to our sector as "nonprofit," reminding us that we are the only sector that defines itself by *what it is not*. Leaders today need to articulate the notion of our sector as full partners in a united effort by communities (defining the needs), nonprofit organizations (meeting the needs), and donors (funding programs that meet the needs) to continually strengthen our communities and their organizations. This is the model that ensures high-impact philanthropy (Grace and Wendroff, 2000). Leaders today must be willing to challenge their organizations to achieve this level of performance.

Results

The paradigm shift from a focus on the needs of the organization to communicating the results or impact of its work has been dramatic (see Schervish, 2000a, among others). As articulated throughout this book, people give because organizations *meet* needs, not because they *have* needs (Grace, 1997). Successfully led organizations are those that have mastered Drucker's admonition that people buy into results. When that article appeared, many nonprofits were still conducting tin cup fund raising, and their leaders were still promoting the needs the organization had, not the needs the organization met. The transition to the new way of positioning organizations for investment has not been complete—many social and human service organizations still present an image of being needy rather than meeting needs—but it has been significant. A big job of leaders is to ensure that this transition has been made in their organizations.

Evaluation of the Venture Philanthropy Movement

The "venture philanthropists" have been greeted by nonprofit organizations with responses that range from enthusiasm to caution to fear. (See Chapter Seventeen for a more complete discussion.) These are donors who may be new to philanthropy but are eager to see changes in social, educational, environmental, cultural, or other services in their communities. They often offer multiyear funding, but frequently their demands for programming, accountability, and involvement exceed those of other donors and the tolerance of the organization. Organizations whose ability to quantify results, engage venture philanthropists in the mission, and stand firm about what they can and cannot achieve have welcomed this new kind of investment. Leadership from board members, CEOs, and fund raisers is essential for an organization's success in this environment. Those who have felt uncertain about their ability to deliver on expectations yet are reluctant to raise concerns have been cautious to the point of refusing such support. Many organizations have resisted this kind of funding because they feared that venture philanthropists would change the culture and the practices of their organizations. This is a failure in leadership that can have a negative impact on fund raising. Much has been written about social entrepreneurship (see Dees, Emerson, and Economy, 2001, 2002), and controversy has raged over whether the investments of venture philanthropists are appropriate. The decision is clearly left to the leadership of the organization and to the particular aspects of the offered gift. If, however, the concerns are related to outcomes, accountability, and transparency, organizations that do not raise their own standards will find themselves losing not just venture philanthropy but other kinds of investments as well. From a leadership standpoint, the positioning of an organization to attract and utilize multiyear venture capital should be a major goal—along with the honing of internal systems (accounting, reporting, and stewardship) that will convey standards and capacity that a venture philanthropist will respect and honor. Fund raisers who are unable to move their organizations toward these goals will achieve less not only with these donors but with other donors as well.

Donor Expectations

It is not just the venture philanthropists who have increased expectations about our sector. Other dissatisfied donors cite a number of reasons for discontinuing or reducing their support, including chronic neglect of stewardship of the donor, carelessness with stewardship of the gift, inaccurate (or no) reporting of ways in which a gift was used, resistance to demands for transparency (even when privacy is not threatened), failure to communicate impact on the issue that secured the gift, and resistance to donor involvement in the work of the organization. To neglect any of these leadership practices is foolish fund raising practice, and to resist appropriate involvement of major donors is a breach of leadership responsibility and opportunity. Increasingly, donors want to be involved in some way with the organizations they fund. They want to join the organizations' leadership as advocates and often as askers. Whereas involvement in the work of a nonprofit used to be more characteristic of women's philanthropy, we now see that men and women both want some kind of involvement. Leaders on both staff and board who understand this need and are willing to accommodate it in appropriate ways are on the leading edge for successful twenty-first-century philanthropy.

The proliferation of articles about philanthropy in the popular press in recent years has highlighted this new phenomenon. It is one to which the sector must adapt as it accommodates donor interest and involvement in organizational boards and committees and the programs that deal with the issues that the organization is addressing.

THE WINDOWS AND MIRRORS OF LEADERSHIP: LOOKING OUT, LOOKING IN

The staff, board, or fund raising leader must realize that it is only by looking through the windows of our organizations into our communities that they can gain the information and perspective they need to provide appropriate leadership. Leaders must focus externally. Our vision must extend beyond our organization's capacity to effectively act on its mission to encompass a vision of the way our community (geographical, social, cultural) could be if our dreams and programs were realized. Organizations that persist in looking only in mirrors will eventually find themselves so out of touch with the external environment that their programs, practices, and fund raising activities are no longer relevant. One organization, a venerable statewide cultural organization in a large state, spent several years doing a "self-study," handsomely funded by a national foundation, that ultimately found that another organization had so invaded the nonprofit's territory and membership that the next decade promised only decline and near-death. Not until a courageous executive director came in and made some bold decisions about location and programming did this organization begin its renaissance. Thanks to its strong leadership, that organization is alive and well today, in a new era of operations focused on the needs of the community. The mirrors have been minimized, and the windows increased in number and size. One of the great challenges of fund raising leadership is to keep up with the trends in the community. Keep looking through the windows by tapping into United Way or community foundation demographic databases, attending conferences with similar organizations, engaging new and different constituencies on boards and committees, and engaging the public or information sources that will keep programming relevant and current to community needs and the case for support that is consistent with ongoing donor and organizational aspirations. Keep the windows clean by ensuring board composition that is broadly representative of the community and includes fund raising leaders. You should also make sure that board meetings always include a "mission message" from a person in the community who benefits from or contributes to the success of your programs. This helps energize the fund raising leadership of the board. Conducting a market-focused zero-based planning process every three years or so is also a vital responsibility of leadership; asking the question "Are the programs we offer meeting the needs of this community, or are there other things we should or could be doing?" is a healthy exercise. Answering that question requires leadership from the board and staff. Fund raisers will find the answers useful in attracting and satisfying funders and donors.

In addition to understanding the external environment, leaders have to know the organization, its people, its culture, and its vulnerabilities. Organizations with healthy programs and leadership demonstrate a spirit of internal teamwork, openness, transparency, respect for differing styles and opinions, and accessible communication avenues that are used by board, staff, and donors. These factors contribute to fund raising success. Twenty-first-century philanthropists are demanding more performance from our organizations. There is growing evidence that due to increased knowledge of and involvement in philanthropy, coupled with a temporary or long-term reduction in available funding, the number of organizations people are willing to support that are working to serve the same mission will shrink. Donors are looking for collaborations that increase impact and reduce administrative cost. Redundancy is not tolerated in tight times or when people gain knowledge of the ways in which organizations could reduce overhead by working together. To survive this scrutiny and the potential narrowing of the provider field, an organization must find the right balance between internal stability and external awareness. Sadly, resistance to collaboration still flourishes in our sector, with people protecting donor and prospect lists and staff jobs when they should be looking for the best way to accomplish the mission—even if it means joining forces with other organizations. It takes leadership to work with other organizations, and it takes leadership to work with donors on the importance of organizational infrastructure.

NEW TEAMS AND CHANGES IN LEADERSHIP STRUCTURE

Great energy currently surrounds the evaluation of traditional board structures and models. BoardSource (formerly the National Center for Nonprofit Boards) has framed the issues and invited stellar thinkers like Richard Chaitt (1996) to analyze existing models and propose new ones. It is evident that sometime during this decade or the next, the natural evolution of boards may be accelerated by a new model that addresses some of the predominant issues in nonprofit board leadership. Most of these issues directly affect the operation of the administrative, program, and board teams that contribute to the success of fund raising, especially the major gift programs. In The Fund Raising School's advanced course in major gifts, we focus not only on the major trends affecting board leadership but also on the internal passages an organization makes as it progresses through its life cycle. We examine the ways in which the various stations on an organization's life cycle affect the nature and performance of leaders, and we match that with the phases of fund raising (vendor, facilitator, strategist) developed by Hank Rosso (The Fund Raising School, 2002). Using the organizational life cycle developed by Ichak Adizes (1979), students are challenged to look at their own board structure and practices and ask themselves if they are matching their board leadership growth cycle to their organizational growth cycle. They are asked to look at whether they are stimulating the kind of involvement that leads board members to be enthusiastic facilitators and strategists in raising money, rather than just vendors selling raffle tickets and tables at events and putting notes on direct mail solicitations. Most confess they are not. Board leadership in annual fund activity is very useful. But without board leadership, the major gift program cannot succeed.

Board practices that encourage the spirit of leadership, team building, and the willingness to become major gift advocate-askers include the following:

- Make sure that meetings engage members in the mission and plans of the organization. Avoid agendas that are predictable (or nonexistent), and do not allow dialogue to be dominated by only a few speakers or to go on too long.

- Permit everyone to participate, not just a few; do not cause anyone present to feel excluded.

- Make decisions in a manner that is inclusive, rather than having most decisions made at an executive committee level. Boards want to be hands-on participants, not rubber stamps.

- Keep the focus on the mission at board meetings, and demonstrate mission fulfillment through discussions about program and client success.

- Include everyone in the organization's vision for the future.

Board members engaged in this way are able to recruit other volunteers to the fund raising program and take on the leadership responsibilities required to raise funds, especially major gifts, for the organization. To build leadership, ensure leadership succession, and create teams that work effectively not only within the organization but also with others in similar organizations to advance a larger shared mission, changes often need to be made in leadership structure. The strengthening of leadership in a nonprofit begins with the way board members, volunteers, and staff are recruited; it is reinforced by the extent and quality of the orientation they receive, is increased by the importance of volunteer and board service that is conveyed in the recruitment and orientation process, and is stabilized by the degree to which people are involved around the tasks and with the kind of interaction that is motivating to them. All of these leaders have an impact on the fund raising process, but in the leadership course at The Fund Raising School, we look to the motivation of board members to be leaders and advocate-askers. We rule out "letterhead" board members and those who are recruited in haste to meet a deadline. Volunteer and board leaders must be recruited from a position of strength that reflects their values in relationship to the organization. This enhances not only their overall leadership involvement but also the role they are willing to play in fund raising and donor development. There is a further aspect to encouraging volunteer leadership: board members and others are most effective and most engaged in fund raising when they are treated like major donors (which they are, even if they do not make a major gift, because of the time, linkages, and expertise they offer). Stewardship of volunteers, beginning with the board, is as important as stewardship of the donors and their gifts. Leadership flourishes where there are positive feedback and encouragement.

What are the implications of these observations about leadership motivation for fund raising? How can organizations better organize their boards, committees, and board-staff interactions to stimulate the greatest possible leadership for fund raising? Let us look at some changes that are occurring in leadership practices in organizations.

Boards

In addition to implementing the kinds of practices cited in this chapter and keeping meetings stimulating and focused on the mission, there are other leadership development practices emerging in pacesetting organizations:

- *A recruitment process that is systematic,* based on a matrix keyed to the institution's strategic vision and goals and guided by procedures and policies that are followed by everyone. Strategic recruitment can be balanced from time to time for particular donors and prospects with the "opportunistic" enlistment of someone who brings very special skills for special organizational tasks or linkages for particular prospects and donors. But most organizations find that their leadership grows more effectively when the recruitment is well structured to reflect leadership needs. Job descriptions for board members and volunteers and some form of contract, agreement, or statement about mutual expectations will enhance recruitment and lead to stronger leadership, especially in fund raising.

- *Orientation* that is inspiring, uncovers motivation through interaction, and is highly informative not only about the organization but also about the responsibilities and expectations of board members and volunteers, especially expectations for activities related to giving and getting involved in fund raising.
- *Opportunities for leadership development and succession* that are clearly communicated and encouraged. Bright people who see no room for advancement on a board or in volunteer structures will find other organizations to serve.
- *Thorough mission orientation for everyone,* including individuals recruited to boards for their special expertise (finance, legal). A major problem with the leadership fabric of some boards is the "two camp" issue: some members are on the board because of the passion they feel for the mission, and others are there in a legal, financial, or liaison capacity. This divides and dilutes the leadership roles of those who must serve as advocate-askers in the fund raising process. All board members, regardless of where they fit on your matrix, should be recruited because they have an interest or passion in the organization.
- *Application of the rule of thirds* as it applies to board composition. One-third of your board should have your organization as its top philanthropic priority, one-third should have your organization among its top three priorities, and one-third should bring expertise, connections, or visibility—as well as the potential to move into the other thirds in time. Sometimes you can get the first and last characteristics in one person. But if your board is tipped heavily to the last third, you are probably having problems with leadership development and succession as well as fund raising. If your board is already entirely in the top two-thirds, you will probably have greater success recruiting additional volunteers and involving the board in fund raising.
- *Annual board and volunteer self-evaluation and leadership assessment* to embed the importance of board and volunteer service and provide a confidential opportunity to assess issues that might otherwise stand in the way of effective leadership. The BoardSource (http://www.boardsource.org) self-assessment is quite comprehensive. The Fund Raising School (2002, 101-Sec. V-42) has additional instruments. Self-assessment provides an excellent platform for the annual renewal of the strategic plan, revealing areas of satisfaction, strength, and opportunity in the overall management of the role of the board and of other volunteers in advancing the mission and goals of the organization, including its fund raising program.
- *Opportunities for involvement as volunteers* before people come on the board and after they have left the board, to provide growth and continuity in leadership. One very successful social service organization *requires* people to serve on a volunteer committee before they can be considered for the board. Other organizations effectively assign community leaders to fund raising committees or special task forces not with the idea of bringing them on the board

but with the purpose of tapping into their skills or network for a specific purpose. Still others engage former board members (a neglected and wasted resource in most organizations) in ad hoc or standing committees or task forces, capitalizing on the years of experience and advocacy these individuals have accumulated, to help raise funds or otherwise advance the organization.

LEADERSHIP AND TEAM BUILDING FOR FUND RAISING

Throughout this chapter, the focus has been on board members, volunteers, and staff who serve as members of the fund raising team. The board chair and the CEO are the most influential team the organization can assemble for key donor prospects.

The lines between board and staff responsibilities has grown increasingly blurred, and the relationships between volunteers and staff have become more complex. The sense of partnership—of pairing leaders in ways that make the best use of the skills and practices of each—is growing. This development of partnerships leads naturally to board and volunteer engagement in fund raising.

Policy Development

Volunteers who are involved in policy development are more likely to accept the commitment necessary to provide leadership for fund raising. Today, most policies are developed by staff, with board and other volunteer input, and are then taken to the board for their approval. Then they are implemented by the staff.

Marketing and Other Staff-Relieving Functions

Involvement of talented board members and other volunteers in membership and institutional marketing and other budgeting and staff-relieving tasks has increased dramatically. This practice also supports board and volunteer involvement in fund raising. Involving volunteers is an excellent way to supplement diminished resources while increasing volunteer motivation and developing volunteer leadership. Furthermore, because board members and volunteers represent the world beyond the organization, those who have marketing expertise frequently also know the marketplace better. Getting board members and volunteers involved in marketing or other tasks can be the best way to encourage leadership and expand organizational capacity—but the rules and expectations have to be made clear at the outset. Staff members should work with volunteers to define the job and the partnership and agree on expectations before the work begins.

Fund Raising, Especially for Major Gifts

Fund raising provides one of the best leadership involvement opportunities for board members, volunteers, and staff in our sector. At many universities, large independent schools, and large cultural organizations, solicitation is an increasingly staff-dominated process. One reason that staff members resist volunteer involvement is that they are evaluated not by the number of board members or other volunteers with whom they build strong relationships but by how much money they raise. They feel that raising funds is their exclusive responsibility. The Fund Raising School stresses the importance of the partnership in major gift fund raising—a porous partnership in which staff and board work collaboratively to identify, qualify, develop strategy for, cultivate, solicit, and steward donors. The leadership benefits of engaging board members and other volunteers in the major gift process are numerous, not the least of which are joy, participation, satisfaction, accomplishment, ownership of results, and a heightened sense of engagement. We see repeatedly that when people articulate the mission and vision, they become even greater believers in it; when they volunteer their time to call on other members of the community, it has a positive impact on those they are approaching for money. Finally, when a successful meeting is completed, they have seen the donor's joy of giving and have experienced the rewards of asking. They have become brokers between the institution's vision and the donor-investor's dreams and leaders in the larger process of stabilizing their organization in the service of its mission. Developing fund raising leadership among board members and volunteers is key to fund raising success. A review of fund raising and major gift advertisements in the *Chronicle of Higher Education* and the *Chronicle of Philanthropy* indicates that most institutions are committed to volunteer involvement in the fund raising process.

To provide the leadership necessary for fund raising teams to succeed, the expectations and contributions of individual members and volunteers must be made clear. Board members and volunteers typically expect staff members to prompt them in carrying out their leadership tasks; to prepare material, including case expressions and background material on prospects; and to carry out follow-up work. Staff members typically expect board members and volunteers to embrace and model the values of the organization, to become advocates based on the case for support, to open doors and ask the right prospects for gifts, to make the calls and appointments they promise, and to be donors themselves. Both volunteer and staff roles require leadership. In a team solicitation, typically the board member or volunteer exercises leadership by identifying with the organization, revealing support levels, and asking for the gift. The staff member of the team exercises leadership by articulating a vision for the future, focusing on external needs being met by the organization, and discussing the boundaries of the organization related to donor impact. Fund raising teams function best when they work together over time and take time to practice and rehearse the complementary leadership roles.

CONCLUSION

Robert Waterman, in *The Renewal Factor* (1985), challenges us to build on our successes; to move on, using the best of work; and to leave behind what has become outdated or what doesn't work if we are to renew and revitalize our organizations.

Fresh organizations are in the best position to engage board members and volunteers and are more likely to be successful in fund raising. John W. Gardner (1990) identified nine tasks of leaders that are as relevant in this century as they were in the last. They include envisioning goals, affirming values, managing, and serving as a symbol. All of these apply to fund raising.

Fund raising begins with the leadership of the board. Decades of work with hundreds of boards and thousands of board members have yielded the following observations regarding effective nonprofit leaders:

- They have an inspiring community-focused vision and enroll donors, community members, and others in that vision.

- They keep donors and volunteer leaders engaged through thoughtful stewardship of their gifts, time, interests, ideas, and needs.

- They remember that leadership in donor and fund development depends on a commitment to relationships and the knowledge that ultimate resource development is not just about money but also about building, nourishing, and maintaining those relationships.

- They live their organization's values, which are evident in the organization's marketing, programs, decisions, people, and results.

- They avoid mission drift by focusing on the mission as a bigger issue than the organizational entity, and they encourage collaborations with other organizations that are pursuing similar values and missions.

- They engage in continuous institutional renewal through regular strategic planning and systematic board recruitment, enlistment, orientation, and involvement.

- They communicate with transparency about financial performance, values, and mission-related results and their impact in the community.

By exercising leadership in these areas, board members help position the organization for successful fund raising.

We have a rare opportunity to provide leadership in a world that is weary from corporate excesses and governmental inability to act decisively to solve chronic social problems and stimulate needed cultural enhancements. To confront the challenges of the new century—which have made themselves apparent already—these principles can become the platform for leadership in your organization. They are the principles that will develop leadership and ensure the best possible leadership succession, and they are the principles that will provide the context for implementing the critical management and fund development practices that nonprofits need to master.

Among these principles, enrolling others in the vision is the most durable and most crucial. After establishing and enunciating the vision, effective leaders must *keep* it, *share* it, *grow* it, and *use* it.

Without strong vision, organizations founder. Vision is the platform for planning. It is the inspiration for action and the motivation for hard work and the energy for fund raising. It is what inspires transformational gifts by donors and community leaders. Leaders have to build other leaders. Vision is the lure for new leaders, and its advancement is the reward that keeps current leaders involved. It is also the way donors stay inspired. It is what causes them to renew and increase their gifts.

CHAPTER TWENTY-FIVE

The Trustee's
Role in Fund Raising

Skip Henderson

Imagine yourself in a new job, attending your first board meeting. You are being introduced by the head of the search committee that has just selected you as the organization's fund raiser. The speaker is describing the personal pleasure received through leading the board to its recognition of the need for a professional fund raiser and then proceeding with the hiring process. Finishing with pride in the organization's progress and enthusiasm for the future, the speaker sighs with relief that fund raising responsibilities are now in the hands of a skilled professional; other matters can now go forward—fund raising can be taken off the board agenda.

Excited and hopeful, you are initially enthused by the new career opportunity. You are pleased to have been hired by a board that is eager to seek philanthropic funds and support. You listen while the head of the search committee finishes your introduction and welcomes you to the organization. You notice the sigh of relief as the search committee chair sits back, stating, "Let's welcome our fund raiser and then get on to our other responsibilities. . . . The board has done its part. We can now look forward to reports of fund raising success."

Your hope and enthusiasm are dimmed as you politely acknowledge the board's warm welcome.

This scene reflects the dilemma faced by many organizations and fund raising practitioners: on one hand, you have boards, consisting of thoughtful, responsible people, committed to the pursuit of an important mission, yet on the other hand, the same boards operating with a misconception about the nature and process of fund raising. "Fund raising" is interpreted in its most limited meaning, collecting money, with the implication that the process begins and ends with asking friends and strangers for money.

This misconception is fed by the term *fund raising* itself. Use of the term implies, as one could expect, that fund raising is primarily the collection of monies when in fact the activity encompasses a myriad of ways in which an organization is sustained, developed, and advanced. Although collecting money is a significant element of the fund raising process, successful fund raising demands that the process be more—that it build institutional strength and spirit and ensure that an organization improves its capacity to support and sustain its means of addressing mission objectives, all board responsibilities.

Fund raising is a complex process with a potential for multiple results. Fund raising accumulates essential resources and builds the institution's capacity to expand mission activities and secure the institution's future. While accumulating resources and assets, good fund raising enlists a strong and growing constituent base led by an involved board of directors that recognizes, enjoys, and commits itself to sustain the institution's direct and indirect benefits.

These are the boards that recognize that *fund raising* means "institutional advancement" or "development." These are the boards that have approached prospective supporters not with *"Please give us . . .,"* reflecting a temporary or momentary relationship, but rather with the offer of an embracing, long-term partnership, *"Please join with us."* Fund raising for these organizations and their boards becomes an ongoing community development process rather than a one-dimensional fund-collecting procedure.

Returning your thoughts to the meeting in progress, you consider strategies for reaching the board and shifting its perception of fund raising. You're determined to initiate efforts for building the board, its individual members, the staff, and the organization's constituencies into a development team, advancing and sustaining mission activities.

Although dollar goals have been set for you, you consider board education and engagement as your first priority; in fact, you know it's the means for meeting your funding objectives.

Your observations and consideration prompt a recall of Hank Rosso's teachings on the role of board members as stewards holding institutional values and assets in trust for the community and for the future. Hank stated in the first-edition version of this chapter that board members must be willing to espouse the cause of an organization through fund raising and that the hallmark of successful programs was board involvement in fund raising.

THE BOARD AS TRUSTEE AND STEWARD: A MORAL RESPONSIBILITY FOR FUND RAISING

This chapter draws on Hank Rosso's original chapter as he addressed board member fund raising roles and responsibilities. The chapter's objective is to provide guidance for fund raisers and volunteer leaders working with boards made up of decent, caring people, serious in their desire to be good stewards, yet unaware of or unable to recognize the need and full importance of their direct participation in fund raising. As Hank stated in the original edition of his book, "Much is lost, in fact, if the effort is not made to involve even the most reluctant trustee in fund raising" (Rosso, 1991b, p. 135).

This chapter considers both the collective governing board and the individual board member's role as trustee or steward. Varied aspects of a board's responsibility are related to fund raising functions. The chapter explores the roles associated with meeting board fund raising responsibilities and provides ways in which fund raising practitioners can engage and motivate board members in those roles.

Whether a person is a member of the governing board of a major nationally renowned institution or a community based local service, the legal charge is the same—be responsible for protecting and nurturing organizational values and assets. This responsibility follows the trust placed in the hands of the board and its members by the community. The trust establishes that governing boards and their members serve as trustees or stewards protecting, preserving, and nurturing an institution's values, ideals, mission, capital assets, monies, and reputation. On top of the board's legal responsibility for stewardship as it governs activities and protects assets, it has an added moral responsibility for stewardship of organizational values and ideals. Irrespective of legal or moral considerations, the import of the community's trust extends from the tangible to the intangible. Responsibility involves all organizational components, including governance, management, program operations, community relations, and the fund raising or development efforts essential to sustaining each element.

In addition to moral and legal responsibilities imposed by the community's trust and the responsibilities reflecting allegiance to constituent interests, board actions themselves impose and accelerate fund raising responsibilities. As new programs are established and expanded budgets are approved by a board, an obligation for board member support follows. It would be irresponsible for board budgeting procedures to set program and operating objectives unrelated to known income sources and then designate the deficit as a unilateral charge to the development office.

The Fund Raising Board: Acting Collectively

An outmoded and admittedly jaded picture of a fund raising board is that of an elite assemblage of well-connected, affluent members merging social and charitable interests. On this type of fund raising board, attention is focused on the collection of money from wealthy peers, business associates, and exclusive club contacts. This view also suggests a board, though genuinely concerned about the cause, that is bound more by an institution's current cachet than by the task of meeting mission objectives, institutionalizing values and ideals, and ensuring service for the future.

A more contemporary and more accurate image of a fund raising board is a group of individuals who seek to build an institution, establishing and sustaining a record of mission accomplishments. This eager board recognizes and seizes development opportunities and new sources of support. Such a board is willing to invest, ready to act, and determined to engage, cultivate, invite support, and celebrate its fund raising success. Though constantly thinking of fund raising opportunities, such a board is not mercenary—it is missionary—and it reflects the larger constituency of the organization.

Certain characteristics define a fund raising board. Effective fund raising boards may have some or many of these characteristics. Development practitioners can protect and nurture the ones already attained and encourage the acquisition of the readily attainable. An assessment of a board's status might include the following criteria:

- The board maintains organizational worthiness, measuring all organizational elements against best practices, cost-benefit analysis, and ethical standards.

- The board collectively and its members individually participate in all fund raising activities and events, seeking 100 percent board member participation at a significant level within the means of each member.

- The board understands the concept of investing in fund raising. It budgets adequate funds, sustains proven methods, and creatively explores new approaches. The board hires competent staff, provides administrative support, and pays competitive salaries. The board looks to fund raising expenditures as an important investment with a calculated return.

- The board spends the fund raising budget prudently, engaging in continuous strategic and rational planning.

- The board brings unanimity—a single strong voice—to case arguments articulating community needs and benefits achieved through the use of funds contributed. It seeks a well-grounded case for each fund raising initiative.

- The board expands the organization's volunteer fund raising leadership cadre through the attraction and involvement of nonboard community leaders. It creates a special bond among allies capable of providing leadership to the cause, and it makes the interpersonal bonding process inclusive, not exclusive.

- The board actively networks with appropriate and potentially supportive constituencies. Its members carry the organization's message wherever it will be heeded.

- The board understands fund raising's need for policies that guide and preserve efficient, effective, and ethical practices. The board establishes protocols and policies for gift acceptance, recognition, and fund management. It subscribes to standards established by national philanthropic authorities.

- The board maintains oversight through reports and evaluations that consider fund raising progress in terms of net income, expenditures, and donors acquired, retained, and upgraded. It seeks reports that monitor the participation of key constituent segments and the success of fund raising activities within that segment.

- In the same light, the board considers its own performance indicators and timely attainment of action benchmarks.

- The board honors donor rights and the obligation to expend gifts explicitly for purposes detailed in the gift solicitation.

- The board recognizes and celebrates contributors, ensuring that they receive fulfillment and meaning through their gifts and their association with the organization.

- The board brings joy to the process of giving.

The Governing Board Member: Individually Responsible

Organizational theorists differ in the primacy assigned to a board member's individual responsibility. Hank Rosso was clear on fund raising as a prime board responsibility, stating, "In this role of primary steward, a trustee must be more than an overseer, a custodian, a casual adviser, a 'sometime' participant, an absentee member, a misguided volunteer apt to confuse administration with governance, or a vociferous adversary maintaining steadfastly that gift making and gift seeking are *definitely not* the responsibilities of a board member" (1991b, p. 134). A board's charge, according to Hank, includes the responsibility "to acquire, to conserve, and to manage the corporation's resources in a responsible manner." Trustees, Hank maintained, are "the visionaries, the advocates for the organization and its fund raising plans, spokespersons for the urgency of the needs and the validity of the programs. As volunteers without a vested interest, they can give powerful testimony to the worth of the services and thus justify the gift" (1991b, p. 136). Indeed, as noted earlier, much is lost if board members are not involved in fund raising.

John Carver (1990) portrays the fund raising responsibilities of a trustee as adjunct to three prime board functions: (1) providing linkage to stakeholders and constituencies; (2) setting explicit policies that govern, establish, and maintain the institution's work; and (3) ensuring that the executive is performing on behalf of the other two responsibilities. Carver allows that the function of fund raising, though not monitoring the results, can be delegated to staff, retaining the stewardship responsibility—and its fund raising imperative—in the board room. For Carver, the board's most important fund raising responsibility is to ensure that the organization is worthy of funding and that these three prime responsibilities are the means by which a board establishes institutional worthiness.

Kathleen Kelly (1998) considers that board participation in fund raising is not a matter of choice. For Kelly, board fund raising is not voluntary; it is accepted as a tacit condition of joining a board. She suggests that the responsibility be addressed through three trustee fund raising roles: "to lead by example, to endorse objectives, and to provide a network for reaching prospective donors" (pp. 446–447).

Deriving from Kelly's argument that participation in fund raising is promised in the acceptance of the board assignment is the argument that board fund raising responsibilities flow from the trustee's particular and unique position in an organization. Lilya Wagner (1994) argues that a board member's position provides power, potential, and uniqueness, and by virtue of holding the position, board members have an obligation to raise funds. Wagner's point is that board members are in a position to succeed in fund raising and therefore demands are justified for them to exercise what can be called—though she does not use the term—the "bully pulpit" of their office. The demand, however, is not sufficient unto itself. Wagner insists that fund raising practitioners must persuade board members that they do, in fact, hold positions of power and uniqueness—that board presence gives authority to the fund raising process.

Additional board fund raising responsibilities flow from characteristics unique to board members. If a member is a specifically delegated or implied representative of a particular constituency, locale, culture, or demographic, then responsibility accrues for that board member to use that link to identify, attract, and solicit contributed income from the represented group.

Varied Roles, Multiple Responsibilities

Whereas expectations are universal, capabilities are not. Organizational and fund raising literature anticipates that the trustees will be well connected in the community, well versed in and committed to organizational values, and capable of giving or accessing gifts at a major level.

There are indeed boards composed of the movers, shakers, and social elite. They are, however, the exception, though they may often be the most visible to the general public. One marvels at successful annual campaigns going over a campaign's dollar goal or achieving its mark ahead of schedule—or is astonished by the capital campaigns for major institutions like museums, universities, and hospitals that achieve campaign goals with 80, 90, even 95 percent of gifts coming directly from board members or through their personal activities. Most often, such board members are practiced in social and philanthropic skills. They were "to the manor born," obligated by affluence and its resultant prestige to participate in civil society as generous citizens.

The majority of boards reflect other types of citizens. Novelist P. D. James's "miscellany of people" is an apt description of many of our nonprofit governing boards. They are not well-orchestrated collectives of movers and shakers, and seldom are they groups of persons of influence, high stature, and power. Neither are they, as might be desirable, representative of key stakeholders and constituencies or experts on professional and management matters related to an organization's area of interest.

Especially in community organizations, governing boards are most often made up of our neighbors, friends, and acquaintances. They are colleagues, business associates, or fellow club members—people who agree that the effort is worthwhile and are willing to serve at our side. They may be unknown to us and unfamiliar with the organization, as when board fairs attract strangers to our cause. Board membership is urged on any or all contacts who have displayed a modicum of civic interest or availability. Sometimes an organization's recruitments are conducted according to a rational strategic board development plan; more often they are instigated by a need to fill a board roster, accommodate annual turnover, or maintain meeting quorums.

The miracle—or at least a marvel—is that our organizations end up with memberships of decent, sacrificing, thoughtful people, more often than not serving and meeting responsibilities with care and distinction.

Though not usually captains of industry, citizens of the year, heirs to wealth and philanthropic traditions, or public luminaries, the people our nonprofits gather are good, willing people—your kin and neighbors, distinguished by a generosity of spirit and a willingness to serve. They need explicit direction in performing essential fund raising roles. (A discussion of board composition and development can be found in Chapter Twenty-Four.)

As Steward. The responsibility for stewardship is paramount. The roles flowing from this key responsibility are numerous and complex. For the individual board member, the key element is recognizing fund raising as essential to the care and nurturing that stewardship implies. Proper stewardship unabashedly keeps fund raising continuously on the agenda, recognizing that it is essential to mission accomplishment and to the building process that will advance the institution toward its goals. (A more complete discussion of stewardship can be found in Chapter Thirty-One.)

The stewardship role or attitude is never abandoned. It requires that questions be posed and progressive approaches considered for all the elements involved in preserving organizational values, assets, relationships, and mission accomplishments. Areas requiring fund raising stewardship attention include planning and goal setting, mission relevancy, prospecting, case development, leadership or volunteer utilization and development, solicitation processes, recognitions, accountability for donor intent, contributed fund management and investment, and budgeting for an adequate and capable support system.

As Donor. Trustees can meet their fund raising responsibilities by undertaking a variety of tasks and roles. Fundamental demands are made of all board members; accepting the role of donor is one that is critical. Service as a trustee, no matter how active and committed the individual, cannot substitute for a financial contribution, nor will a token contribution suffice.

Why doesn't a contribution of time and effort suffice? One reason, suggests Kim Klein, a noted fund raising consultant and publisher of the *Grassroots Fundraising Journal,* is that in our society, money has symbolic value. Whether we agree with the premise or not, the manner in which we use money expresses something about who we are and what we value, about how our own personal philanthropy—the dollar amount we contribute to the institution whose care has been entrusted to us—reflects our valuation of the institution. Consider a trustee involved in a solicitation being asked, "How much have you given?" and responding, "Well, I give of my time and advice." The response that one is not giving to an organization whose case one is espousing undercuts any appeal for a donor prospect to join in support of the cause.

Collectively, in terms of the board itself, the same considerations hold. Significant gifts are hard to draw to a campaign lacking full board support expressed through a high percentage of individual board contributions at the level deemed significant.

While people are generous, the competition for their philanthropic interest is so intense that appeals not fully backed by all organizational trustees and management leaders will be less than compelling. This point is exemplified by the number of grantmakers, foundations, and corporations whose application procedures preclude receiving proposals from agencies lacking 100 percent board member participation as financial contributors.

A variety of approaches have been developed to establish guidelines for board giving. Some suggest that giving be at a level equal to a trustee's highest gift to any other nonprofit. A gift of $250 to an organization where you are responsible as a trustee and a gift of $500 to another organization for which you bear no formal responsibility suggests a peculiar and less than enthusiastic response to the cause entrusted to the board member's care. Exceptions to this rule might be made for gifts to a faith group or alma mater, traditional recipients of a donor's larger gifts.

Some boards encourage "stretch gifts." These are gifts beyond one's normal giving limits. Equity among board members with unequal means or giving capabilities is achieved when each stretches beyond his or her normal giving pattern. One person's gift of $50 may represent a stretch equal to another person's gift of $500.

Many boards establish a minimum expected gift level; each trustee is expected to contribute at the given amount or more. Such a policy ensures full participation and provides for equal gift amounts from board members, though the equity established does not extend to the proportionate ease or burden the gift may represent in each board member's financial situation.

Two additional problems arise with the establishment of minimum board giving levels: those able to give more may not consider a higher level of gift; and those unable to meet the established level are excluded from board membership.

As Solicitor. When trustees exclaim, "I'll do anything but raise funds!" they are actually referring to a small, albeit significant, part of the fund raising process. "People give when they are asked to give," reads one of Hank's maxims. The "request" requires an "asker," a person willing to consummate the relationship between donor and organization by explicitly requesting a gift. It is this solicitation itself that draws the most resistance from board members. Some trustees will never be able to undertake the task. The so-called taboo of money may be so ingrained in the social mores of some trustees that they will never be able to ask directly for a contribution in spite of their commitment to a powerful cause. Although soliciting is an important role for board members to undertake, there are other important trustee fund raising roles, short of direct personal solicitation, where trustees can be helpful. These include writing letters of thanks, signing appeal letters, and opening doors for others. Often these activities serve as training for personal solicitation.

As Prospector. A board member can reveal potential donors by engaging in an identification, prospecting, and evaluation process. The role calls for a constant search, seeking persons or populations with interest in the cause and the capability of providing support and then assessing each prospect's link to the organization and how that link can strategically lead to gift giving.

As Advocate. Advocacy means associating oneself with the cause and willingness to be public, even vocal, about that association. "Did I mention that I'm on the board of this great organization?" you might say. "Let me tell you about its important cause." This is not a prelude to a request for money, though it may lead eventually to additional support; this is a genuine expression of a board member's engagement. It is a means by which a leader can build awareness of and interest in the cause and draw people they know to consider joining in a cause that may be mutually shared.

As Visible Attendee. Attending events hosted by the organization is essential for all board members. If specific events are important to the organization's mission, board members need to be in full visible support. And even if mission objectives are not involved, board members should consider the value or rationale for the event in determining whether to risk not attending.

Being visible is an extension of being an advocate. It means being seen on the donor rolls, at events, as a personal representation of civic engagement on behalf of the cause; it is "wearing the association on your sleeve," modeling your personal allegiance and commitment in a public manner.

As Team Builder. This role ensures that the board backs up policies and provides budgetary support for enhancing communication between professionals and volunteers and between internal and external constituencies. It involves the infiltration of fund raising considerations throughout the organization, its personnel, and constituent groups.

MOTIVATING BOARD MEMBER FUND RAISING SERVICE

The *exchange principle* states that a person acts or contributes in direct proportion to the value received from the action or gift. Accordingly, we surmise that the exchange principle underlies and determines the extent of a board member's fund raising effort and involvement. A board member's motivation to participate in fund raising will reflect how meaningful gathering support for the organization is to the member.

An action plan or agenda can be developed for introducing motivational practices. But prior to considering helpful practices, it is wise to examine responsibility and role expectations established as board members are recruited and enlisted in board service.

Effective fund raising organizations have a board that is not only fully engaged in varied fund raising roles but is also cautious and selective in recruiting and enlisting new members. Effective fund raising organizations employ a strategic board recruitment procedure that gives significant weight to a potential candidate's fund raising attributes. The recruitment plan considers desirable board changes, creates or identifies appropriate candidate feeder systems, and develops adjunct committee responsibilities or assignments that locate and track potential candidates, thus permitting their movement onto the board at the appropriate time.

The enlistment process for building a competent board is no different from that undertaken in a successful individual donor program. If an organization is having difficulties recruiting board members, it is probably true that it also has no substantial individual donor base and no effective identification, cultivation, and solicitation process. To compound matters, in situations where the need for board members is critical and the organization lacks a fund raising culture, recruiters may well be shying away from discussing the board's fund raising responsibilities and expectations.

Fund raising is often considered an onerous task that abuses relationships by intruding in areas of personal finances and values. Such portrayals must be countered through training, experience, and collegial encouragement for board members to see the importance and fulfillment possible through fund raising for a cause. Fund raising must rest on the case for support, not on personal relationships. Performance recognition and rewards, though intangible, must be readily discernible by board members and particularly by individuals considering board membership or new to board service.

Board members are ordinary people asked to take on extraordinary responsibilities. Engaging them in fund raising requires inculcating a level of sophistication about civic affairs, personal confidence, and a comfortable perception of their own self-image as an advocate for the cause. Board members need a sense of their stature as appropriately reflecting the responsibility they hold. Boards need to be introduced to the pivotal role they play as leaders of an institution seeking a symbiosis of forces among donor, institution, client, mission, needs, ideals, and the demands of the cause.

Board recruitment procedures need to emphasize the personal pride that follows entrustment as well as the responsibilities and roles that entrustment entails. There is pride in meeting public responsibilities and being placed in a position of trust. There is pride upon being selected, chosen, and acknowledged as having the capacity to care, value ideals, and be responsible. Yet the power of that pride is too often diffuse as organizations fail to highlight the presence and value of their board and its members. Board stature and prestige must be celebrated.

Oliver Twist laments the desire to "be a hero in one's own life story." Bolman and Deal (1995) speak of the need for meaning and fulfillment and the opportunity trusteeship offers for finding that meaning: "The gift of significance lets people find meaning in work, faith in themselves, confidence in the value of their lives, and hope for the future" (p.113). Board membership and its outreach responsibilities need to be presented in a fashion that engenders recognition of the personal rewards entailed. Prospective board members need to be made aware that promoting ideals and a cause and attracting others to the cause and to support of the cause lead to respect, meaning, and fulfillment. It provides for recognition among one's peers and one's betters—be that in a social, civic, or professional context. Fund raising offers rewards of association, stature, and pride in accomplishment for the benefit of the public.

IMPLICATIONS FOR THE DEVELOPMENT PROFESSIONAL

The exchange principle underlies and determines volunteer involvement and motivates gift giving. By extolling a board member's importance and the fulfillment possible through active involvement in the fund raising process, board fund raising will be significantly enhanced. Prospects should be made to realize that board membership involves not only roles and responsibilities but also rewards.

It is the fund raising professional's responsibility to develop a board engagement plan for promoting, engaging, and maintaining involvement on the part of the board and each board member.

For each board member, the practitioner needs to do all of the following:

• *Understand the values held dear by each board member.* How does the exchange principle apply to each member? What motivates this person's other service? How can these motivational forces be applied? How can the personal benefits received from fund raising efforts be promoted?

• *Assess each member's competencies, special talents, or attributes.* How can each board member be put to best use? Is a member with strong social skills encouraged to participate in cultivation and solicitation activities? Are there other appropriate and meaningful activities for volunteers with skills in other areas? Is there an identifiable role for each board member? Is there a conscious plan to encourage members to serve in their appropriate roles? Is there hidden talent to be encouraged and drawn on?

• *Increase each member's knowledge about the organization, its mission, its accomplishments, and who benefits and how.* It is difficult to get people to talk to others about money and especially to ask for a gift. It is even more difficult for people to feel competent in their asking approach. There is a fear of not knowing and appearing uninformed. Build comfort levels by helping board members articulate the values and ideals underlying the organization's work. Start with the ideals and values that connect to their emotional and passionate content. From why things are done, move on to what is done and how it is done. Encourage board members to be knowledgeable, but assure them that they need not know all details and can respond to a request for details by referring the question to staff.

• *Introduce reluctant members to fund raising through "low-impact" fund raising activities* that build confidence and understanding of the fund raising process. Can people unfamiliar with fund raising be assigned as part of a team hosting a grantmaker site visit or meeting to provide information to a significant prospect? Provide less demanding experiences not requiring a direct face-to-face solicitation. Encourage volunteers to be enthusiastic with friends about the organization they are serving. Focus on enlisting interest rather than asking for funds. Let seeking contributions emerge in its own time and manner.

• *Draw attention to the specific achievements of each member's participation.* Submit internal written and verbal board reports that can highlight achievements and tell the story of members active in the fund raising process. How can the mundane activities be recognized to encourage further efforts? Can the people involved in the accomplishment of particular objectives be rewarded without being patronized?

• *Encourage board members to value, accept, and use the "bully pulpit" and status aspects of their board membership.* Provide opportunities for board members to take pride in their office and their association with the organization's achievements. When networking or attending a service club lunch or an associated nonprofit's reception, invite a board member to join you. Have the person represent the cause and help draw others to the organization.

• *Emphasize the board's trustee and stewardship responsibilities.* Draw attention to and develop assignments around board governance responsibilities. Keep board considerations and activities related to larger governance issues. While encouraging board outreach, cultivation, and solicitation responsibilities, discourage involvement in operations and the day-to-day management processes. Board members are responsible for moving the organization toward a successful and sustainable future. They should focus on that future, using professional staff to manage the present.

• *Set collective board goals.* Consider the impact of establishing fixed board member contribution levels or solicitation goals. Will these deter desirable board prospects from membership? Will these serve to embarrass or stratify the board as stature is accorded to those achieving higher levels? Can the board set participation and board gift campaign goals with success or failure accruing to the entire board and not specific members?

• *Emphasize mission over money.* Talk about the fund raising process as advancement, development, community enrichment—not the accumulation of funds. Incorporate mission achievement stories in reports. Translate numbers into needs being met. Describe those needs with stories of people and the community. Let fund raising rest on the case for support.

• *Teach philanthropy.* Showcase ways in which people in your community contribute, not just within your organization's constituency. Present national per capita giving statistics. Promote fund raising activities as critical but not unique to your organization. Community needs are met and enrichments provided through the philanthropic fund raising process.

- *Be expansive.* If your organization is worthy, there is no need to restrain its outreach for support. Help board members recognize that people give, that people like to give, that people gain meaning from giving, and that solicitors are agents for personal meaning and fulfillment and engagement of others in building a better community and a better world.
- *Remind board members that they serve as ambassadors of the cause,* not fund raising goals, and of the mission's imperative that it overcome antiquated cultural notions of fund raising as begging or violating friendship protocols.
- *Remind board members when they approach a prospective donor with fear and anxiety to consider Hank Rosso's instructive dictum:* "Step aside and let the cause walk in."

CONCLUSION

There are boards and board members whose fund raising involvement measures up to the responsibility they accepted with board membership. It's an involvement that leads naturally—even comfortably—to advocate for the mission, proudly present organizational accomplishments, attract donors, and build an institution carrying cherished values and ideals into the future.

There are board members, described as ordinary people, who have been asked to take extraordinary responsibility. In the process, they have become extraordinary people. Board members engaged in fund raising elevate their own stature by becoming a voice for high and worthy communal values and ideals. They can, in modest manner or grand ways, be heroic. Meeting board responsibilities through facilitating and actively participating in fund raising processes offers the opportunity to enrich their lives with meaning and fulfillment as they enrich the community.

Board members need to remember Hank's dictum, quoted several times in this book, that "fund raising is the gentle art of teaching the joy of giving." As they consider their fund raising roles and responsibilities, they also need to remember and heed Hank's corollary—that there is equal joy in getting.

CHAPTER TWENTY-SIX

Thinking Strategically About Information

Sheree Parris Nudd

ank Rosso's definition of a prospective donor as one who has linkage, ability, and interest leads us to information. But information about prospects today can be overwhelming. Development professionals would do well to take seriously Thoreau's dictum to "simplify, simplify, simplify." Thanks to modern technology, we can now store more information in less time and in less space than ever before. But here, too, Murphy's Law is fully operative: first, the more information you have stored, the more difficult it is to focus; second, the nonprofit across the street is just as likely to collect the same amounts of data as you; and third, donors today are bombarded by sophisticated (and not so sophisticated) fund raising appeals.

It is ironic that out of today's computerized efficiencies, volumes, and so-called personalization, the old-fashioned handwritten letter or note has emerged as today's ultimate status symbol because it is ultimately personal. How well nonprofits make productive use of information almost certainly determines their success or failure in the pursuit of philanthropy.

EVALUATING INFORMATION

One of the hardest myths to conquer is that "bigger" and "more" equate with success. Nothing could be further from the truth; in reality, both can be counterproductive. The beginner tends to equate size with progress; the seasoned veteran knows that success is continual prioritizing and then acting on those priorities. Although insightful information can make all the difference in the world for an organization, information gathering must not become an end in itself. It is essential to find a happy medium. We must think strategically about how much information and what types of information will be useful in donor development.

Development professionals and volunteers must avoid getting bogged down thinking they have to fill in every detail in a donor record and find every little piece of information before they *do* anything. One must not be like the salesperson who has the best prospect list in the company—detailed, alphabetized, and immediately accessible—but who ends up spending time improving the prospect list instead of making sales calls!

ELEMENTS OF SUCCESSFUL FUND RAISING

There is a fascination to pages of computerized data that is difficult to resist. Surely, you think, all those names, addresses, and other bits of data will automatically translate into a higher and higher level of success. But that's not necessarily so: one must keep in mind that *information gathering for its own sake costs money but does not raise any.*

Whether it is called development, advancement, attracting philanthropic resources, cultivating voluntary support, or "friend raising," the key to fund raising success is *relationship building.* The process of building relationships is supported by and works in tandem with information gathering (see Figure 26.1).

The challenges of the future will require identifying, building, and maintaining relationships with an organization's most important prospects and contributors—and doing so better than ever before. Continued success (and in some cases continued existence) will depend on the ability to develop and maintain a close relationship with the few individuals who have the ability and the willingness to make a difference for the organization.

How few? For many charitable organizations, 80 percent of their dollars have traditionally come from 20 percent of their donors. For many charitable institutions, 90 percent of their dollars come from 10 percent of their donors. (Both figures are reflected in the donor pyramid discussed in Chapter Seven.) One would think that with this reality, professionals working in philanthropy would be in the throes of profound information-gathering shock as everyone restructured development procedures and priorities. Instead, for most it remains "business as usual." Yet for nonprofits to live up to their potential, a sense of priority must be explored.

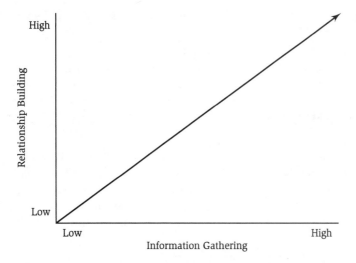

Figure 26.1. Information and Relationships: One Depends on the Other.

This model shows that a decision to increase the investment in information gathering must correlate with the organization's ability to achieve the same growth in the relationship with the donor or prospect. It would make no sense for the development office to collect extraordinary amounts of information on the richest family in the country if the organization had no connection to it through constituents or board members.

DETERMINING THE ESSENTIAL

Fund raising futurists see the next decade as one that mandates a new order based on the premise that effective philanthropic endeavors are dependent on the practitioner's ability to develop and coordinate highly meaningful relationships with those who can help the organization generate greater and greater levels of success.

What this all means is that a higher priority exists than being a great team player and competent office manager. It means that profuse green foliage does not count; only harvested fruit does. It means that development officers must allocate their time and energies such that the 10 percent to 20 percent of the donors or prospects who have the potential to deliver 80 percent to 90 percent of the needed funds are carefully and tenderly cultivated and that they are never far from mind.

It means that in spite of the daily blizzard of paper and electronic messages, these professionals must find a time and a place, away from the telephone, away from *everyone* and *everything*, where they can dream, plan, conceptualize, and prioritize. It means constantly breaking through the barrier of the *routine* to accomplish the *essential* so that voluntary financial support can become all that it can and should be.

And not a week should go by without significant attention being given to the care and cultivation of those at the top of the major donor list!

INFORMATION GATHERING: AN INVESTMENT

"Investment" implies that resources (adequate budget, time, staff, and staff effort) must be invested in the information-gathering process. As will be true of all major expense categories, the dollars spent to create, develop, use, analyze, and retain information about donors should be continually scrutinized. Just as it would not do at all to scrimp on the concrete in the foundation during the construction of a new home, it is equally inappropriate to provide inadequate funding for the information-gathering process.

In addition, an investment in information gathering means an investment of energy—maintaining a pervasive and constant awareness of information that surrounds the philanthropy professional. Whether it is scanning the business and social columns in the newspaper, reading trade magazines aimed at the industries from which funding is being sought, asking for information while networking with colleagues, or picking up on signals from donors, relationship building is a process that knows no time boundaries, keeps no office hours, and never stops.

A development officer was visiting with a foundation executive and his wife in their home. The foundation executive had responded to the development officer's request for an appointment to discuss a forthcoming proposal. While in their home, the development professional, an accomplished pianist and musician, spotted a beautiful piano in the living room. She remarked about it and her interest in music. A lively conversation ensued. The participants talked about their favorite types of music. The hostess, upon declaring her love for ragtime, pulled out a piece of sheet music and asked the development officer to take it home with her and return in the near future to play it.

When relating this story, the development officer admitted, "I confess that I could never do justice to ragtime. So during my next visit, I offered to play another piece, a specially arranged version of 'Amazing Grace.' They seemed so pleased. I had no idea that all those years of practicing the piano could add to my repertoire of fund raising skills!"

And the foundation executive and his wife? They raved about the fund raiser who played the piano for them. They were just as pleased about the $500,000 challenge grant they were able to give her institution.

Will music continue to be a topic in conversations? Does this experience and information contribute to relationship building? Without a doubt! On her travels, this same development officer has been known to pick up a souvenir or item with particular meaning for a volunteer or two (such as the chocolate tennis balls from Ghirardelli's for her tennis tournament chair) before she shops for her family! Strategic information is useful.

Not the Same for All

Basic information gathering is the same for everyone. Institutional development officers need to know correct addresses and how people prefer their names to be listed in recognition publications. Donor histories are a must for all. Each donor receives information about the organization in the form of letters, newsletters, publications, and annual reports. But that is where the sameness stops.

As noted, a disproportionate share of the needed funds is likely to come from 10 percent to 20 percent of the donors. This fact alone underscores the importance of the judgments made when it comes to investments in information gathering, cultivation, and nurturing of donors. Although it is important to attract gifts of all sizes (and new donors whatever the gift level), organizations cannot afford to develop additional information on everyone.

Of course, all donors receive appreciation. All donors deserve multiple thankyous for gifts, large and small. However, one of the development officer's most important jobs in making productive use of strategic information is knowing when to shift gears in nurturing groups of donors and individuals in a special way.

The development officer has a fiscal responsibility to allocate information-gathering dollars wisely, remembering always to direct such funds to channels where the ratio of return per dollar is at a maximum.

Where to Invest in Information Gathering

A decision to move a particular donor to a higher information-gathering status will depend on the type of gift that the donor is capable of making (see Figure 26.2) and the method of fund raising that will be used to solicit the gift.

Paul Wisdom (1989, pp. 148–149) developed this idea when he wrote: "Development is not only contact-intensive but also paper-intensive. Prospects must learn a good deal about the institution, its programs, and its people before they will support it. They need to know what it is, why it's important, its quality, what it will do for them and for others, and why the institution needs their support. Conversely, the fund raiser also needs to know a great deal about prospects in order to maximize chances of success."

You should target much of the consequent information gathering on discovering whether or not an individual qualifies as a major donor prospect (MDP), however your organization defines it; typically, this is someone having the capacity to make a onetime gift of $5,000 or more. Once a person is identified as an MDP, the research efforts and contacts are more strategic. Development officers need to find out certain information about each individual in order to

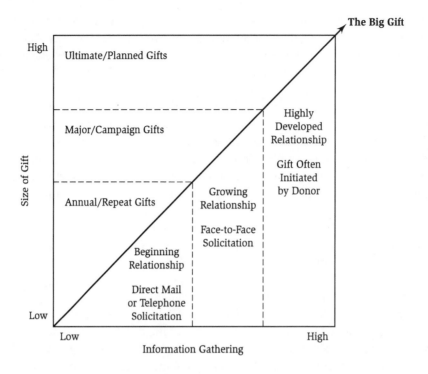

Figure 26.2. Giving Is Built on Relationships.

This model illustrates the dependence of big gift fund raising on information gathering and relationship building. The higher the gift (or the anticipated amount), the more one invests in the types of activities that build relationships, and the more essential it is to gather appropriate information.

devise and develop a successful cultivation strategy. Ultimately, each prospect will be asked for a major gift, ideally at the right time for the right purpose in the right amount at the right location and with the right person or persons asking. Strategic information helps make certain we get these aspects right.

A national survey of senior development professionals and consultants suggests that an average of nine separate cultivation activities should take place before a major solicitation (Fisher and Quehl, 1989). The cultivations can take place in a variety of ways and settings. They may include such things as a personal letter from a faculty member, an alumni volunteer, a dean, a development officer, a vice president, a department head, or the president; a phone call from any of these individuals; a personal visit at home or at the office; an invitation to lunch or dinner; attendance at an athletic event or play; a visit to an art exhibit; or even a suggestion for a golf match or a fishing trip. The event may not even be university- or college-related, as long as an institution-related person is involved. The nature and style of these events depends on the ongoing research that determines the interests of the prospect. All of the events are designed to develop a good person-to-person relationship that will ultimately bring success.

FACTS AND FIGURES: NOT MUCH BY THEMSELVES

For major donors and for those who are on the cultivation track for ultimate gifts, one must go beyond facts and figures to discover the essence of the donors' interests and participation. Why do they give? What dreams can they help turn into reality? What gifts will be inherently gratifying to the donor? How must organizations present additional opportunities for action? This information can be found in both likely and unlikely places. One of the most likely and most dependable places to learn about the prospect is directly from the prospect.

It is not difficult to obtain information about prospects from public sources or even from peers, friends, or associates. But what differentiates successful development programs from less successful ones? *Listening* to the donor and listening well makes all the difference in the world. By tuning in to individual prospects (like noticing the piano), professionals can tailor requests and proposals to specific values, likes, and interests and even discern the amount to ask for or whether to name a "hoped for" amount.

A corporate giving officer may talk about the sizes of gifts that his or her company typically gives. A foundation representative may expound on the board's philosophy and desire to make a national impact by awarding small grants over a wide geographical area. Still others may talk about focusing on a few projects and awarding large gifts to "really make a difference."

By listening intently to what the prospective donor is saying, the development professional can pick up on strategic information that will help in the cultivation and solicitation process.

Not all donors will be as direct as one foundation executive encountered by an inexperienced development director. Because two gifts had arrived in the office on the same day for the same piece of equipment, she asked for an appointment with one of the donors. She thanked him for the gift and asked whether the institution had permission to use the $3,000 grant for a different piece of equipment.

The donor graciously said that the gift could be used accordingly but continued by saying something the young woman will never forget.

"You know," he said thoughtfully, "I was disappointed that you didn't ask for more." She mentally picked herself up off the floor and stuttered an apology. "That may be because I'm new to this, and I certainly will try to do better in the future," she promised.

Rest assured that she saw to it that the foundation executive *never* had that problem again! The development director nurtured that relationship, asked thoughtful questions, and continued to tune in and listen to that executive. The foundation's support grew and eventually totaled several hundred thousand dollars, including a grant that is the largest gift ever given by that particular foundation, before or since!

Really listening also means using "intuitive listening." An example of this is told in the words of a chief development officer. During one casual conversation with a donor visiting the office, they talked about likes and dislikes, tastes and eccentricities. The donor mentioned that even though he can't really tell a "good" cup of coffee from a "bad" one, it drives him crazy to drink out of a foam cup. "I don't care what it tastes like, but I want to drink out of a real cup," he remarked with a chuckle.

A little thing? Insignificant? Maybe. Maybe not. But you can be sure that if any member of the staff offers refreshment to this particular donor, it will be served in a *real* cup!

NEGLECTING TO ASK:
CONDUCT UNBECOMING A DEVELOPMENT OFFICER

Development professionals should adopt the motto "When in doubt, take the direct route." For example, ask the donor about preferences when preparing a request letter for a foundation or a corporation, and then ask questions such as these:

"Would you prefer that I send you a formal or an informal request?"

"Would you prefer that we ask for funding for one piece of equipment, or should we include a choice of several items for your committee?"

"May we send you a proposal asking for consideration of a gift in the $50,000-to-$60,000 range for the XYZ project?"

If the gift range is unrealistic, the prospect approached in this way will often give an indication of whether the amount should be raised or lowered.

Notice that these questions are not vague, nor do they imply that one is on a "fishing trip." A question like "Could you give us your ideas of what our organization should ask you for?" will give the impression that the organization doesn't know its priorities or has yet to define its critical needs.

After a lengthy cultivation process and several modest gifts from one grant-making entity, a hospital development professional realized that the funding committee might consider a *much* more significant gift. A conversation with the foundation officer revealed a key piece of information that shaped the institution's approach to the grantmaker. The foundation executive asked, "What do you think of challenge grants?" The development professional answered with a smile, "We like them!" "Well, I think they're good, too," the foundation officer replied.

Of course, the proposal requested a challenge grant. By meeting the foundation's conditions of raising $500,000 in cash from other donors, that hospital qualified for a dollar-for-dollar matching grant.

As a result of development professionals' using listening skills and asking carefully phrased questions, corporate executives have been known to offer their help in critiquing proposals and actually helping rewrite portions of those proposals before they are forwarded from the local corporate branch to the national headquarters for funding.

INFORMATION GATHERING: EVERYONE'S JOB

Every staff member, and every volunteer for that matter, should play a role in gathering information. Bits and pieces of information, learned by various people in various ways, contribute to the overall picture *when the information is incorporated into the donor file.* If important pieces of information do not get into the donor file, they don't contribute to the groundwork of knowledge management; they do not become part of the basis for cultivating that donor.

When everyone on staff is an information gatherer, it is a natural step to involve everyone in prospect cultivation and donor acknowledgment, to make everyone a thank-you sayer—in short, to make everyone a fund raiser.

INFORMATION AS AN OBLIGATION

In the fund raising field, odds are that a development officer will not be in one institution or position for an entire professional career. Thus when a development officer moves on, the information that is left behind will be one of the key criteria by which career and character will be judged for years to come.

Simply raising a lot of money is not enough to brand a development professional a success. The information left at an institution—validating one's work, outlining donor relationships, detailing the next steps for future cultivation— will clearly demonstrate how those dollars were raised. Dollars raised without good record keeping and documentation and without top-notch donor files can lead organizational leaders to assume that it was a fluke or that most of that money would have come in anyway and can force organizations to start from scratch with potential major donors.

The highest praise that one development professional can give another is to say, after joining an organization, "The person I followed did a *fantastic* job. I could tell exactly what had been done with the major donors every step of the way. It was easy to continue those relationship-building steps because of the information I had at my fingertips." Smoothing the transition with donors, volunteers, and staff for the incoming development officer and leaving a legacy of information and record keeping is not an optional exercise. It is integral to the professional fund raiser's life and work.

A SPECIAL NOTE TO THE CEO

The organization's president or CEO is ultimately responsible for the information-gathering activities of the development staff. The staff cannot be expected to maximize fund raising without the necessary tools and access to information resources. The most sophisticated computers and software programs will be of no help if there are barriers to accessing data and information. In some organizations, the barriers exist simply because the development function is never a high enough priority to get attention and programming time from the information services department.

Making sure that the development officer is in the "inner circle" in receiving administrative and institutional information will not only enhance the organization's ability to attract gifts but will also save some embarrassing moments. For example, one development officer was about to send off a grant request for an existing program (the proposal had been approved by the administration a few weeks before) when the grapevine carried the news that the program had abruptly been eliminated!

Information can also help the CEO evaluate the productivity of the development program, but only if the right questions are asked. Consider the following:

Do you know how to tell if your development program is making progress, and do you play a key role in cultivating donors?

Have you requested information from your development officer lately on donor trends and renewal rates in addition to dollars raised?

Do you know how to judge if goals are "stretch" goals?

Is your involvement in and evaluation of the development process as thoughtful and as focused as a state inspection, a Joint Commission review, or a visit by the accrediting committee for your organization?

Have you gathered enough information and done enough intuitive listening to figure out what makes your development officer tick?

Do you share key information about prospects with your development officer?

If the CEO cannot answer these questions with a resounding "Yes!" mixed messages are being sent to volunteers, donors, and staffers.

MANAGING THE KNOWLEDGE

Just as nonprofit organizations have learned to manage information about best practices and organizational outcomes, they must learn to manage information about prospects and donors.

All the information in the world will not help raise money unless time is spent analyzing it and applying it to the cultivation process needed to secure repeat gifts, upgraded gifts, special gifts, major gifts, and ultimately planned gifts.

For nonprofit organizations, it is no longer a question of whether or not to use a computerized system for tracking donor records and managing fund raising. Rather, determining the features a system must have for the process of capturing and analyzing information is paramount. (Determining the type of system needed by one's particular organization is addressed in Chapter Twenty-Seven.)

TAKING THE DONOR'S VIEW

Ultimately, all information gathering should lead to one thing: *the process and practice of taking the donor's view in cultivating the philanthropic partnership with the organization.*

Reviewing major donor and major prospect files and information constantly, especially before making an appointment, visiting, or soliciting, gives continuity to the efforts of volunteers and staff. (Chapters Nine through Twelve cover various aspects of major gift fund raising.)

One development professional performs a "debriefing by dictation" after every visit with a major donor prospect. These resulting documents take the form of file notes or contact reports and include a summary of the visit, new items learned about the donor during conversation, and general and specific thoughts about the next steps to be taken in the cultivation process. (Interestingly, the word *document* is derived from the Latin *docere,* which means "to teach").

Some of these notes remind the professional about a person's pace or "style." For example, one grantmaker, after a quick and friendly greeting, likes to get right down to business; another likes to chat for a while about the community, family, or the organization, and it can sometimes take fifteen or twenty minutes to get to the meeting's appointed topic.

Reviewing the file documents before the appointment helps the development professional match the pace of the prospect or donor, anticipate conversations and questions, and consequently *make that time as full of relationship building as possible.*

TRACKING THE CULTIVATION OF MAJOR DONOR PROSPECTS

Besides the at-the-fingertips types of information available on the "giving history" reports of donor-tracking systems, the development staff will need to keep individual files for major donor prospects. The Milton Murray Method (M^3) for tracking cultivation for major donor prospects uses two file folders (yes, paper) for each prospect (Rosso, 1991b). One contains data and information: items that range from newspaper clippings to public tax records. The second file folder holds a correspondence file with the most recent information at the front, such as letters, contacts, phone or e-mail conversations, and visits.

A page inside the front cover of the correspondence file lists one-line entries (much like a table of contents) that summarize the documents contained in the file. This kind of file with this much detail is kept only for donors who have made or have the capability of making a major or "ultimate" gift to the organization and is in addition to the electronic files.

People intimately involved with the organization can define what qualifies as a major gift. Some organizations "start counting" gifts of $10,000 or more; for others, a gift of $1,000 is considered a leadership gift. Whether a gift is major is not determined solely by its amount. Rather, the *relevance* of the gift to the overall well-being of the institution and the capability of the giver are paramount. In this vein, there are no "big" or "small" campaigns. Instead, there are only "tough" and "tougher" campaigns. Thus strategic information becomes critical.

THE TWO-WAY FLOW OF INFORMATION

Approach information flow (or knowledge management) as a two-way transaction. Collecting information and gathering facts and figures about donors and prospects is an incoming process. Information flow also has an outgoing function that is concerned with the concept, frequency, and method of communication with donors and the centers of influence in the organization's service area. All of this activity is successful when it creates progressively nurturing relationships and leads toward giving transactions that become increasingly gratifying to the donors.

Besides using information as an institutional voice (see Exhibit 26.1), there are multitudes of ways to use donor information in a manner that augments and validates relationships. As the maxim says, "People rarely give to causes or institutions; people give to people with causes." Credibility must first be established

Exhibit 26.1. Information Treasure Chests: Eleven Essentials.

If you are new to your organization, you need to immediately assess what information is available to you. Quickly assemble some basic information to have at your fingertips. If you are not new to your organization, it's a good idea to use this section as a checklist and periodically run your information files through a "relevance review."

1. *Information on the Organization.* Such information would include the organization's history, who it serves today, and its philosophy (vision statement). You also should be able to access (within seconds) a copy of the organization's mission statement, articles of incorporation and bylaws, statistics on clients served, and plans for the future. A one-page fact sheet about the organization may be the item you use most.

2. *Information on Needs.* The "never-finished" case statement that is constantly revised and updated is a sign of a vibrant and dynamic organization. But if your agency has a "never-started" case statement instead, you have some work to do! Also, can you (or anyone on your staff in your absence) pull out a list of named gift opportunities upon request?

3. *Information on the Fund Development Effort.* Such information should include current and historical annual plans, evaluations and accomplishments based on the plan, project reports for special events, results from and examples of direct mail projects, development audits and studies done over the years, and charts and graphs showing the growth (or need for growth) of annual and capital funding efforts. Also add pie charts to show the sources of contributions in comparison with national trends.

4. *Information on Successes.* Gifts received, challenge grants met, people served, families helped, children educated, lives saved—all should be part of this file. Also include human interest stories that illustrate how your organization has made a difference in the community.

5. *Information on Donors.* Besides the information covered elsewhere in this chapter, consider collecting written comments on the reasons that donors have given to you. Were they or a family member dramatically affected in some way? The major donor with eye problems who designated gifts for the ophthalmology department, the community leader whose volunteer work started in speech and hearing because she had a deaf daughter, the businessman whose life was turned around when he was a young student by a caring teacher at his alma mater—all of these are examples of important pieces to be included in the information treasure chest.

6. *Information on Solicitors.* If you have enumerated solicitors' likes and dislikes, interests and hobbies, you will do a better job matching them with potential givers. You may also need to record who should *not* be assigned—such as the overenthusiastic volunteer whose brash manner turns your current donors into former donors!

Exhibit 26.1. Information Treasure Chests: Eleven Essentials, Cont'd.

7. *Information on Key Institutional Players.* Make sure you have copies of the CEO's résumé and information on other prominent players (physicians, professors, researchers, and scientists, for example) who are affiliated with your organization. Keep a current list of board members handy, along with business address, home address, phone and e-mail information, and spouse information.

8. *Information on Your Nonprofit Sector or Industry.* Establish a clip file on education, health care, the arts, social services, children's issues, or whatever it is that your organization is about. Then find ways to share pertinent thoughts and issues with your volunteers and donors.

9. *Information on Giving and Philanthropy.* Professional organizations serving non-profit and fund raising interests publish a plethora of information about giving and philanthropy. Stay current with the trends and find a way to share "big picture" information with your donors and volunteers. Don't scrimp on your resource library. When new books on fund raising hit the shelves (or the mail-order catalogue pages), buy them and *read* them.

10. *Freestyle Information.* You will also want to develop resources on topics that particularly appeal to you. I collect quotes on philanthropy and volunteering. Some of my colleagues collect cartoons about fund raising, giving, special events, and so on, and I contribute to their collections. I also find myself latching on to any article I can find about trusteeship and what makes a good volunteer—not for the sake of filling a file folder but with the thought of how the information might be shared with our volunteers and used to expand the strengths of our efforts.

11. *Personal Information.* Get into the habit of keeping information on your own personal and professional development and accomplishments in fund raising. Keep track of your contributions to professional organizations (service, writing, or chairing committees, for example). This information makes the process of applying for and maintaining your professional accreditation much simpler. It also lends itself to establishing a periodic "personal audit" of accomplishments, plans, sources of satisfaction, and the next goals to be set!

---

before any serious thoughts of giving manifest themselves. Information and astutely orchestrated dialogue (written and oral) will engage the donor and gradually build solid foundations for donor relationships.

In the early stages of a donor relationship, one can always acknowledge the anniversary of a gift. For example, "It was one year ago today that your gift helped culminate our capital campaign. We just wanted to tell you again how much that gift has meant in influencing others to give."

Acknowledgments of birthdays and anniversaries might be included as the relationship grows. Successful fund raisers know that prospects must also be involved in nonsoliciting experiences for future gift requests to be received positively.

Only when development professionals feel passionately that the relationship with the donor is more important than the gift requested can they be truly effective. Such sincerity shines with laserlike clarity and acts as a safety net to prevent carelessness or inadvertent manipulation and misuse of information in connection with giving.

Information must travel up and down in the organization, as well as back and forth between the institution and its donors. Development officers should make information accessible to those who need it, making sure that vital information is passed along to the right people above and below them. Donors will feel much more comfortable about investing in an organization whose leaders "have it together," who are communicating from the staff level all the way to top volunteers and administrators.

DONOR INFORMATION: HANDLE WITH CARE

Keeping information confidential does not necessarily mean keeping it secret. Rather, it refers to the sensitive gathering and perceptive, judicious, and ethical use of strategically important information about prospects. In the wrong hands, detailed information could possibly hurt either the prospective donor's reputation or the institution's. Consequently, it's essential to safeguard confidential files.

A case in point: researchers in a certain college development office routinely ordered business profiles from a commercial service to research alumni donors who owned businesses. But they failed to provide adequate safeguards to maintain confidentiality and restricted circulation. One day, instead of directing the corporate profile to the appropriate in-house researcher, a student worker inadvertently mailed the information to the donor himself. The alumnus called the college development office. "If you want to know something about my business, all you have to do is ask me," he announced and hung up the phone. Needless to say, a few seconds' carelessness rankled the donor and compromised the work of many years.

IDENTIFYING THE RIGHT SOLICITOR

Gathering information on committee members and volunteers, particularly those who will solicit gifts for the organization, is another important piece of the information pie.

Is the prospective solicitor pleasant? Persistent? Is the solicitor sensitive to the right time to ask? Confident enough to do the asking? Does the solicitor have good taste, a sense of appreciation for the donor, and the ability to cultivate and nurture the prospect? Will the solicitor express gratitude appropriately when the gift is made?

Good fund raisers have a highly developed sensitivity to nuances, those almost imperceptible gradations of expression that no true professional ever disregards. These individuals well realize how easy it is to undo years of toil. Those who do not possess this sensitivity should never be unleashed on a donor or prospect.

During a joint multimillion-dollar capital campaign being conducted by several hospitals in a metropolis in the Southwest, a small group gathered to evaluate the giving ability of potential donors.

When Mr. Prospect's name came up, one of the committee members expressed his doubts that Mr. Prospect would give to the campaign. "He's been in town for thirty years and has never done anything for the community."

A second committee member commented, "Well, I think he might give $2,500 if he were asked in the right way."

A third committee member spoke up: "I met Mr. Prospect as he got off the train when his company in New York sent him here. I know him fairly well. Although it is true he hasn't done much, I think that if he were asked in the right way, in due time he might be convinced to give $25,000." Of course, the third volunteer was asked to interact with Mr. Prospect!

At this juncture, a young development officer was assigned to the volunteer to help him educate, cultivate, and inform Mr. Prospect. The staff member went through his calendar and wrote down the name of the volunteer every four to six weeks. This reminded him to communicate periodically with Mr. Volunteer about Mr. Prospect. Whenever a campaign milestone was reached, the development officer made sure that Mr. Volunteer had the particulars about the news to share with the prospect.

Occasionally, Mr. Volunteer would take Mr. Prospect to a baseball game. A relationship of mutual respect developed. Over a period of time, this volunteer visited with Mr. Prospect, communicated with him, and even enlisted Mr. Prospect's daughter's support for the cause.

About a year and a half after those initial conversations, Mr. Prospect became Mr. Donor when he gave a gift of assets to the campaign. It was immediately converted into a cash total of $800,000!

That experience demonstrates the value of matching the right solicitor with the right prospect based on strategic information; it also shows how the development staffer sets into motion the succession of notes, calls, and visits that in combination solidify the relationship over time, resulting in a contribution.

CONCLUSION

Managing fund raising information to support relationship building is demanding yet exciting. This brief introduction can but scratch the surface of this rapidly changing field.

Fund raisers must continually ask themselves these questions: How much information should we gather? How much cultivation should we do? How long does it take to build a relationship for a lifetime gift?

At a gallery, an artist was asked, "How long did it take you to do that painting?"Without batting an eye, he replied, "Thirty-one years and three hours." The entire span of his artistic career was focused and condensed into each painting he created!

The same is true of nurturing donors: The process spans years. Each experience and exchange is woven like a different-colored thread into the relationship tapestry. A proverb says, "Kind words can be short and easy to speak, but their echoes are truly endless."

Thinking about information strategically means gathering information on prospects, donors, and volunteers that is useful in developing strategies for securing repeat and upgraded gifts in the total development program. Thinking strategically about information means keeping and managing information in such a way that you would not be embarrassed to share the donor's file with the donor. Managed well, strategic information gathering has far-reaching effects on the relationship building that ultimately leads nonprofit organizations toward fund raising success.

CHAPTER TWENTY-SEVEN

The Effective Use of
Technology in Nonprofits

Janice Kercheville
Jim Kercheville

Technology was drastically different and much more fundamental when Hank Rosso articulated his philosophy of fund raising in the original edition of *Achieving Excellence* than it is today, but its use by nonprofits remains consistent with his basic philosophy. In fact, Hank's references still deliver a valuable lesson for the leaders of nonprofit organizations: technology should be a servant to fund raising and other nonprofit functions.

The use of the Internet in fund raising is discussed in Chapter Twenty, and Chapter Twenty-Six describes the strategic use of information. This chapter focuses on the use of technology in nonprofits and how it supports the fund raising process.

Hank Rosso's central theme was that "fund raising is the servant of philanthropy," in other words, that fund raising was a means to an end. He noted that fund raising must be tied to an organization's mission and a part of its management system, not a separate, detached activity.

This is an important perception for nonprofit organizations and how they approach technology—and not just for fund raising but for every aspect of their operations. Technology is a means to an end. It must be aligned with mission. It must be fully integrated into an organization's management and day-to-day operations. It must support the long-term fund raising and donor development process.

Technology enhances the potential for success in fund raising in two ways. First, it enhances the efficiency of an organization by standardizing many of the approaches to communicate with and account to its constituents. Second, it has the potential to support the fund raising and donor development process directly and make it more sophisticated and efficient. Technology can enhance a great many routine processes, including handling incoming phone calls, distributing reports, managing budgets, and storing and evaluating information about organizational outcomes. The better the organization manages, the better access it provides to its constituents and clients, and the better it can report its successes to donors and other key constituents, the more likely it is to be successful with fund raising. But integrating the organization's information and database with the fund raising systems is essential. The fund raising process depends on computer systems to manage donor records, track gift expenditures, and generate gift acknowledgments and stewardship reports. It can include mailing and printing technology to solicit new gifts, and it might include telephone equipment to run a phonathon or cell phones and Palm Pilots for major officers. The long-term donor development process depends on computer technology to help manage prospect engagement, volunteer assignments, and solicitation teams.

At the dawn of the twenty-first century, many nonprofits had still not embraced this message. They had not demonstrated much awareness of the many ways modern technology can improve the efficiency of operations and support the fund raising process. Whether because of a lack of funds, a shortage of technology expertise on staff or among volunteers, disinterest, or fear of the unknown, nonprofits were behind the curve of technology growth in the booming 1990s. They now have a long way to go to close the digital divide, not only between the nonprofit and for-profit sectors but also between small and larger nonprofits. There are some encouraging signs of progress, though at a slower and more deliberate pace than one might want.

Adopting new technologies is always a challenge, but there are a few basic approaches that every organization should follow. First and foremost is *planning*. Nonprofits must approach technology as they would any other management function, defining its purpose, its intended outcomes, its link to mission, its various elements, and their applications. They must also communicate to the organization and its stakeholders how technology can best be used throughout the organization. Special attention should be paid to planning the technology needed to manage the fund raising process, which in too many cases is merely an afterthought.

Of course, planning can't be done in a vacuum. It requires a thorough understanding of what technology is available today, what may be on the horizon (or how an organization can keep its systems flexible enough to allow for future growth and enhancements), the pros and cons of alternative applications, and cost.

A TECHNOLOGY PRIMER

Starting a plan means understanding the elements that go into it and how they can best be used. With technology, the target is constantly moving.

"Technology" is a many-splintered thing, a vast area to which many fear to go. It can be as basic as a simple telephone system or as complex as a centralized, multilocation computer system providing a common database to staff and administrators.

Phone systems are probably the best understood and most widely used form of technology in organizations. But they can range from the basic PBX system to full-featured systems that offer conference calling, voice mail, direct in-dial, and a menu of options for callers. The phone system can be a bank of phones used for creating a hot line or soliciting gifts during a phonathon. Telephone-Internet hookups through various service providers facilitate conference or training sessions with audio and video capabilities. One trainer can easily train targeted staff or volunteers at a variety of locations.

Technology includes the copying machines and printers for letters and reports. It includes the LCD projectors and PowerPoint programs to make presentations to boards, committees, and volunteer fund raisers. For some, it includes teleconferencing and videoconferencing capabilities. More advanced technical support for an office operation can include a linked network of computers and peripheral devices (such as printers, modems, and CD-ROMs), connected through a local area network (LAN)—usually within a single building or campus. Smaller operations may use a personal computer (PC) as the office server, a shared computer on the LAN. As the size and needs of an office expand, so does its computing support—through a single, fast, and powerful PC or an integrated network of multiple servers, superservers, or mainframe. The more computing power, the more functions: control of voice mail, e-mail, and a variety of "back office" functions such as accounting, personnel data, and customer or donor records. For multiple-office operations, data communications support may be managed through a wide area network (WAN), which links, usually via telecommunications lines, more than one LAN.

Planned with foresight and organization objectives in mind, data communications and telecommunications systems are most efficient if they are integrated—each subsystem with the ability to communicate with others—and designed to allow future migration, or growth as the organization's programs and fund raising efforts, donor base, and fund raising volunteers and staff increase.

Such systems are rare in the nonprofit world, but an appreciation for how technology can make an organization more efficient, improve its communication with key stakeholders, and enhance the sophistication of its fund raising program is growing in the nonprofit community.

A report from Knowledge Works on e-Philanthropy (2001), underwritten by the W. K. Kellogg Foundation, notes that foundations and nonprofits alike are using the World Wide Web "to improve basic administrative and information services: grant applications, conference and membership registrations, technical assistance services, and knowledge diffusion. This last arena—knowledge management—looms large on the social impact horizon" (p. 15).

Such organizations represent technology leaders in the nonprofit sector; however, they are not the norm. They are models for success, even if in some cases their application of technology is in only parts of their organizations. Widespread and full-scale introduction in nonprofit operations is still on the road ahead.

The Knowledge Works study revealed a steady growth in nonprofits' adoption of new technologies, including a move toward greater use of the Internet. As nonprofit leaders learn more about the value and efficiency of such applications—along with demonstrated successes—a faster adoption curve should be evident. In varying degrees, ongoing studies by Knowledge Works and others indicate that nonprofits are embracing technology for the following purposes:

- To solicit and receive donations
- To recruit new volunteers or members
- To match volunteers with work assignments
- To link visitors to the organization's knowledge base (materials, information, resources, and so on)
- To provide Internet-based services for board and volunteer development and strategic planning assistance

REALIZING THE POTENTIAL

The various studies of technology show us that people in nonprofits see the potential benefits of technology but haven't quite gotten the hang of using it. Their toes are in the water, but they are reluctant to leap into the technology rapids. The use by the for-profit sector of e-mail, the Internet, and other computer-based services is second nature and fully integrated in the normal workday. But many nonprofit leaders admit that they check their e-mail only occasionally during the workweek or wait until the workday is over. The problem, clearly, is not simply a lack of access to technology but rather an attitude about using it.

No one can predict which factor—lack of access to technology or personal attitude toward it—will be more difficult to change. However, knowledge and experience will go a long way toward resolving both issues.

Nonprofit and fund raising leaders need to make sure they don't get lost in the technological jabberwocky of bits and bytes, hardware and software, RAM and modems, but instead recognize that the digital pieces, properly assembled, add up to a more efficient way to communicate with key constituencies in support of the organizational mission.

There are a lot of wrong ways to go about integrating technology into any operation. Knowing where the potholes are in the technology road—and outside expertise can help identify them—will provide reassurance that the organization will not only stay intact but grow with new technology. Many organizations make mistakes when facing the decision to embrace technology. Some of the most common mistakes are the following:

- A lack of planning for the immediate and distant future
- Taking too short-term a view or failing to lay a proper foundation for future technology development
- Failing to examine technical systems or hardware in light of the organization's mission and primary functions
- Investing in outdated or obsolescent technology
- Failing to plan or budget costs and time for the training necessary for staff to use the new technology efficiently (or to demand this of a vendor)
- Not integrating the organization's databases
- Not looking beyond the technical aspects of new systems and recognizing their communication value with staff, volunteers, board members, donors and prospects, and the community

TWO ESSENTIALS: PLANNING AND COMMUNICATION

The integrating threads for weaving a technology success story for the nonprofit organization are planning and communication. In essence, they are opposite sides of the same coin: the plan itself is an excellent communication tool.

A surprising number of organizations—nonprofit and otherwise—bring technology into their operations without thinking much beyond the immediate system or two they are putting in place. Planning for technology is a bit of a chess game in which thinking several steps ahead is imperative (and cost-efficient too).

The plan begins with the organization's mission, what it seeks accomplish, and what its priorities are. For example, is the goal to raise money for a particular cause, issue, or need? Is it to mobilize volunteers for some community good?

Is it to develop advocacy on a particular public issue? Is there a general need to improve communication—with current or potential donors, volunteers, or staff?

Theodore R. Hart, the president and CEO of ePhilanthropyFoundation.org, told us, "Start by looking at the end product of what you're trying to accomplish. If you have a lot of donors, a lot of volunteers, or a lot of data you need to manage, you need to look at what data enhancements you can make to accomplish those goals. In other words, if you need more volunteers, find the systems to build and enhance what you're doing in that area" (interview with authors, December 4, 2001).

A technology plan should integrate with the organization's business plan, if one exists, or vice versa. Each area of the operation should be examined for its potential use and benefit from technology. For many nonprofits, however, an initial list may be staggering, an overwhelming menu of needs. This is where developing a plan with both timetable and budget is essential and where the organization can set its priorities for technology integration. It is essential to maintain fund raising functions such as storing and retrieving gift histories and financial information, texts such as the case for support, donor trip reports, and volunteer management systems.

Integrating modern technology into the nonprofit organization doesn't have to break the budget. A growing number of services are available to nonprofits free or at minimal cost, and access to the Internet is particularly cost-efficient. Certain commercial enterprises offer nonprofits creative and low-cost ways to improve operational efficiency, raise money, and provide services.

There's at least one key point about introducing technology into an organization on which technology and nonprofit experts agree: don't try to do everything at once. Smaller steps in implementing technology, adding technical enhancements, will increase efficiency over time without putting a major strain on finances. Start somewhere, however, with an eye toward which aspect of the nonprofit's operation can most benefit from a technology jump start.

THE PLANNING PROCESS

A technology plan helps identify the starting point and the priority need for meeting the organization's mission. Howard Feingold, president and founder of Technology Plus, Inc., has been providing technical consulting to nonprofit and for-profit businesses for nearly two decades. His advice always begins with the plan, ideally written for nontechnical decision makers, not technical managers. Feingold recommends a three-step process:

1. *Definition of requirements and recommendations:* Defining short- and long-term requirements for technology performance that will support organization objectives.

2. *Developing options*: Outlining the range of options for each of the selected recommendations from phase 1, with a pro-and-con analysis of each option (cost, staffing needs, outsourced versus in-house technology, and so on)

3. *Implementation planning:* Completion of the plan, with a detailed implementation schedule, budget, migration strategies, and staffing and training requirements.

The plan can be developed in concert with outside resources, with nonprofit management, and with board and volunteer involvement. The process not only serves to integrate operational and technical priorities but also provides a communication foundation for the organization's key stakeholders—and perhaps an important reminder or even restatement of mission and goals.

A technology plan provides a sound, albeit evolving, plan for ongoing systems development. As such, it is a foundation that avoids implementing technology piecemeal and facilitates integration of all voice and data needs. The plan serves as a road map that keeps the organization from painting itself into an expensive, inefficient technical corner by identifying how the organization can migrate to new technology in the future. The organization must ask itself such questions as these: Should we buy or lease? Should we wait for the introduction of new software? What new technologies will we be able to move to in the future? How functional and flexible is the telephone system? Are gifts to the organization of older equipment useful, or do they raise additional maintenance and support issues?

If the organization is national or international, with far-flung affiliate offices, a wider perspective on planning is required. Centralized information technology support personnel may be appropriate, and a consistent design of systems across the nonprofit's network is critical. A basic element such as the same protocol for e-mail addresses in the various offices of an organization can facilitate faster, easier communication. The international Juvenile Diabetes Research Foundation, for example, has centralized information technology (IT) support stemming from its New York headquarters, which lessens the burden on smaller, local offices to develop and implement technology designs of their own.

In the fast-changing world of technology, planning must remain flexible. "All plans are dynamic," Feingold told us. "They offer a good overview of the future, but they need regular reassessment and tweaking as conditions change. We recommend annual reviews at minimum and more frequent reviews if possible to ensure that technical and operations objectives stay in sync" (interview with authors, December 15, 2001).

Feingold observed that many of the nonprofits he's worked with know they need more modern technology but typically are unwilling or unable to spend the necessary dollars. The result may be a piecemeal and overly cautious approach that results in hardware or programs that won't function smoothly on an integrated basis or present major hurdles to evolving technology systems. Nonprofits will frequently have to resort to donated equipment that may not be the best, so they are trapped into using outdated computers and programs, again making migration to future systems more difficult and more expensive.

He warned that nonprofits can fall into the trap of buying in to new systems without planning for the necessary staff training and orientation. "Teaching staff and others how to use the technology is critical," he noted. "An organization should leverage vendors in any way they can to get the training that goes with new technology, whether they purchase or lease, and that can include video and multimedia backup."

GETTING THE KNOWLEDGE

How, then, and where do nonprofits get the knowledge and experience, the tools and technology to become a full participant in this ever-expanding technology dance? Close to home, most nonprofit observers will agree.

Small and medium-sized nonprofits, and even some larger organizations, don't have the wherewithal to integrate an IT function into the organization. IT professionals are in high demand, and nonprofits find it tough to offer competitive salaries. *Volunteer* IT expertise is another matter. Nonprofits can add experts to their boards who bring with them in-depth knowledge and experience of technology to complement community and business leaders, a staple on nonprofit boards, offering financial, organizational, human resource, and other business acumen to the nonprofits' operations. Developing a trusted relationship with outside vendors is also a must.

According to Jay Love, CEO and one of the founders of eTapestry.com, very few nonprofits will be able to develop their technology internally. A few national nonprofits or university-based or major medical organizations have the resources to develop an internal staff, but the great majority in the nonprofit arena will need to find new trusted advisers.

"Historically," Love explained, "the older, more established business provided tools to allow the nonprofits to manage databases and direct mail data or do their lockbox processing. However, they haven't had more established players saying, 'We'll be your trusted partner for Web site development or on-line donations.' Those and other new tech-based services have had to come from fairly new businesses coming into this market" (interview with authors, December 3, 2001).

Love noted that two things can happen that will facilitate a nonprofit's adoption of new technologies: as newer tech-oriented companies become more stable and demonstrate success, they can become new trusted advisers; and older trusted suppliers need to adapt and bring out products and services that meet the needs for integrated electronic management of nonprofit operations, especially those that are useful to fund raising. That's already happened in the for-profit world, but movement in the nonprofit arena has been slower.

INTEGRATING THE DATABASE

For the digitally challenged—and for many who have gotten past the first steps of adapting technology—the array of computer hardware (computers and peripheral equipment that make up a data network) and software (the brains that drive the systems and provide myriad applications) can be a bit daunting. (A handy reference for the sophisticated as well as the wanna-be technophile is *Newton's Telecom Dictionary* [Newton, 2002]).

All roads of the digital world lead to, or begin with, the database. It's what nonprofits could benefit from most. As Hart pointed out, "An integrated database allows for the sharing of information organizationwide and not just a donor database. Any data that are in the institution should come from a common database. Everything stems from that, including internal accounting and budgeting data, human resource information, resource information for those dealing in community and media relations, and record keeping on donors and volunteers" (interview with authors, December 4, 2001).

Mary Duffy (2000) describes some of the most common, useful database applications for nonprofits. These include the following:

- *Information and referral (I&R) databases.* These are lists of organizations that offer a broad range of information and services. A client or member of the public may request a referral, and services or organizations matching their criteria can be retrieved from the I&R database. In order for this type of database to be useful and effective, the list of services and service providers must be kept current and complete.
- *Donation databases (donorbases).* These allow nonprofits that rely heavily on fund raising for income to track information about actual and potential donors and all donations. A donorbase at minimum should be able to generate donation reports, allow the organization to sort donors in a variety of ways, record multiple donation and donor details, create and sort lists of potential and current donors, and print letters, labels, and a variety of reports. A donation database should be connected to the accounting system and to other databases, such as membership or client databases, and should anticipate fund raising growth and programmatic changes in its design.
- *Client or contact management databases.* These can range from very simple to very complex. Beyond just basic contact information, organizations sometimes require additional information regarding people preferences and schedules

(such as when is the best time to call someone or what days a volunteer is available). Sorting options give such databases even greater functionality. The ability to provide information about referrals, client services, and program impacts is as crucial to the fund raising process as asking for the gift.

TAPPING IN TO THE INTERNET

Access to the World Wide Web and communication via the Internet offer nonprofits unparalleled efficiency and value. Whereas building and integrating a database can be costly, Internet access is relatively inexpensive, while its value is limited mostly by the imagination and energy of its users. Web access and e-mail—either for internal or external communication—allows easy, virtually instant interactive communication with a nonprofit organization's key stakeholders, including donors, volunteers, board members, event participants, the community, the media, and staff. Nonprofits have attained a high level of Internet access and e-mail capability by now, but they have not yet learned to use these for successful fund raising. This is unfortunate, since the speed, flexibility, and wide reach of the Internet offer the nonprofit organization a relatively easy way to build efficiency in the management of operations, improve communication, and conduct fund raising. Hart observed, "It's essential for an organization to understand that it can accomplish much more via the Internet, compared to the inefficiency of much of what they do now, day to day, with direct mail and other traditional forms of communication" (interview with authors, December 4, 2001).

How might nonprofits make the best potential use of the Internet? Important areas include the following:

• *Fund raising.* There is a vast array of innovative approaches to Internet fund raising: e-mail campaigns, donations via the charity's Web site or an advertising banner, event management, donor management, planned giving, and corporate internal campaigns, to name just a few. With the number of people accessing the Internet growing explosively and with the younger generation particularly sophisticated in its use, the potential of Internet fund raising can't be ignored. What nonprofit organizations must realize, however, is that on-line fund raising is not a stand-alone answer to giving. It is one more method that should be integrated into the organization's total funding efforts, developed in the context of its mission and long-range plans. (For a more complete discussion of Internet fund raising, see Chapter Twenty.)

• *Web site.* Increasing numbers of nonprofits have established a presence on the World Wide Web. The value of an organization's Web site is greatly diminished, however, if its information is allowed to grow stale. With regular attention, the site can be a lively, even interactive, source for donor, volunteer, board, and community information. News releases, volunteer opportunities, event publicity and registration, ongoing or special funding campaigns, and analyses of pressing community needs are just some of the facets of a well-designed, energetic, and informative Web site. All these activities can be developed to support the fund raising process.

• *Volunteer recruitment and matching.* This can be carried out through the organization's own Web site, in direct e-mail campaigns, and via several national Web sites that permit the posting of volunteer opportunities: engaging them with the institution, soliciting them as donors, and enlisting them as volunteer fund raisers.

• *E-mail.* Michael Stein and Marc Osten (2001) collected from colleagues a list of seventy-two reasons to support the pronouncement that e-mail is still the top Internet application—the "killer app," as Michael Gilbert (2001) labeled it. The list included the following attractive aspects of e-mail:

Improved operating efficiency (reduces phone tag; great way to coordinate appointments and meetings; can be accessed around the clock, seven days a week; saves money on long-distance fees)

Enhanced collaboration (quick way to send files to colleagues for feedback, great way to thank people, facilitates brainstorming)

Improved information and knowledge management (can help organize information and tasks, provides access to unique information and people)

Improved marketing (preferred way for most media people to receive news releases)

Deeper personal relationships with funders (broadens issue awareness, drives traffic to a Web site)

Stein and Osten also cited a variety of other benefits, not the least of which is that e-mails are fast, easy, and cheap. E-mail is also a great way to renew and upgrade smaller gifts and provide stewardship to current donors.

There is reason to expect growing participation in the digital world by nonprofit organizations. With technological price and expertise often a real or perceived barrier, the growing accessibility of application service providers (ASPs, such as eTapestry, NPower Convio, and 3rdSector.net) and nonprofit-focused consulting organizations (such as ePhilanthropyFoundation.org, The Alford Group, Coyote Communications, and Summit Consulting Collaborative), along with a wealth of *free* Web sites offering information specially tailored for nonprofits, the reasons for saying "we can't do this" are diminishing.

ASPs offer any organization the advantage of state-of-the-art technology without extensive investment in hardware or software. Through a remote data center accessed via the Internet or a private network, ASPs provide just what the name implies—applications, software-based services and solutions, plus all the information technology infrastructure and support services needed to deliver them. Basically, ASPs allow organizations to outsource some or nearly all of their information technology needs on a subscription basis.

ASPs come in a variety of sizes and shapes, tailored for large or small organizations, by location, by specific need (such as human resource services), or for specific industry or operation—including nonprofit or government organizations. Several provide integrating fund raising and donor development functions.

As Mark Dennis, president of The Alford Group, told us, "Technology has arrived in the nonprofit sector, but it's not yet well understood. That's because it's up against a major assumption in the field of philanthropy—that people give to people with good causes. Another way to say it is that people build on relationships, and philanthropy is all about relationship-building." But technology can be useful in building and "managing" those relationships.

Given this historical philosophy, Dennis said, the tone of philanthropy has been very relational. In this case, "the cause of the institution must have a voice and a face."

And technology, Dennis added, "has not been depicted as either the voice or the face. I think that is part of the challenge today. Technology is doable, everyone understands the ease of it, and it's becoming more accessible. At the same time, it may lack the relational connection with the actual person."

MAKING THE DECISION

We have outlined here but a few of the technology applications that organizations can take advantage of to improve operating efficiency.

Vendors promise solutions for all technology needs. Caution, homework, and asking the right questions are useful habits to employ in response.

The organization or outside technology experts will want to look at hardware and software needs for the next three to five years, starting with a review of internal capacities: current capabilities, needs not now being met, what technology can be retained, and what staffing levels are required to support new technology.

Bountiful information and advice are available on the Internet for the expert or novice, including nonprofit-focused Web sites, as noted earlier. Another is Access Innovations, Inc. (http://www.accessinn.com), which provides background and updates for clients or potential clients about development in the information industry. A checklist of questions from Access president Marjorie M. K. Hlava covers issues that prospective technology users should address throughout the process of selection and implementation, among them the following: How easy will it be for the end users to operate the system effectively? Do you want your system to be multifunctional? What is the growth potential? How secure is the system? Who is going to maintain the software and the hardware? Can you have a demonstration of the system? What training is required, and who will provide it?

When selecting a vendor, there is long list of issues to address, including how long the vendor has been in business; what type of technology or business partnerships it has; how many employees it has in product development, sales, services, and other relevant areas; and how long the product has been on the market and how many customers currently use it.

The process can be daunting and perhaps impossible without expert advice. The benefits of technology, however, are worth learning to navigate through the technical information and sales pitches. Technology and information needs change rapidly, and the guardians of the technology of any organization need to stay on top of the latest trends and developments. This can be difficult for smaller organizations, but volunteers and consultants with the necessary expertise can be particularly valuable. Although engaging independent technology consultants will initially add to the cost, the advantage of having an expert not connected with a specific vendor or product can provide economic and operating efficiencies in the long run.

If there is one theme that characterizes the technology reviewed in this chapter, it is *communication*. Communication as a path to information sharing, fund raising, and relationship building, integral to almost every nonprofit's activities, may be the most important benefit of organizational technology. Whether it is communication with current and prospective donors, volunteers, board, management, or staff, technology—computer and telephone system networks, Internet, e-mail, and all the rest—provides an extremely fast and efficient way to put forth an organizational message and to receive immediate responses to it. Something as simple as a cell phone is a relatively inexpensive and extremely effective way to maintain accessibility with staff members who are frequently out of the office on business. The wise use of technology will contribute both to the efficient operation of the organization and public perception that the organization is professionally managed. Both the reality and the perception are essential to fund raising success.

CONCLUSION

It may be ironic that something as cold as technology can become a strong link to building warm relationships, not only between nonprofits and their donors but also with other key stakeholders: volunteers, staff, and the community at large. Technology can be a powerful servant of philanthropy, not an end in itself but a more efficient way to achieve organization goals and communicate these achievements to key constituents. Using technology must begin with planning, must be fully integrated with all of an organization's activities and systems, and must link directly to the organization's mission. To build on Hank Rosso's thoughts once more, technology, like fund raising, draws both its meaning and its essence from the ends that are served: communication, efficiency, flexibility, speed, cost-effectiveness, and revenue generation and fund raising. The non-profit organizations that integrate technology into their day-to-day operations and support not only general operations but also the fund raising and donor development process will discover that they have acquired a valuable and hard-working servant.

CHAPTER TWENTY-EIGHT

Accountability and Budgeting

Assessing Costs, Results, and Outcomes

James M. Greenfield

D emand for accountability on nonprofit organizations' results is increasing among their publics. What outcomes have these public benefit programs produced for the funds expended? What difference have the arts and health-related programs made to the culture and wellness of people in the community? What public benefits from these charitable services can be seen in terms of quantifiable outcomes? While boards of governors and chief executive officers of nonprofit organizations are working to address these concerns, the absence of any national standards for performance measurement of nonprofit organizations continues to be a major handicap. "Many opinions and assertions are put forth about the effectiveness and desirability of nonprofits, but evidence is scarce. Especially limited is information about whether nonprofits are better or worse at achieving certain goals than for-profit firms or government enterprises would be" (Weisbrod, 1988, p. 2).

This chapter addresses several areas for performance measurement of a nonprofit organization. The areas are broad—institutional mission, governance, operations and financial management, strategic planning, budget allocation, and marketing and communication—and we also examine how fund raising is dependent on each for its success. Each area is appropriate for performance evaluation, but as Hank Rosso (1996, p. 9) pointed out, "organizational fund raising is a discipline that requires cooperation from each component of the organization that is endeavoring to support its programs through volunteer gift giving. It cannot be the total effort of one person. The task is too complex. The organization seeking the funds must put its support behind the person charged with the responsibility to prepare the plan and to administer the action required by the plan." Fund raising results are inextricably tied to each of these internal operating areas, along with local environmental factors that aid or thwart success, such as economic conditions, access to wealth, history of fund raising activity, image and reputation, and popularity and respect. Fund raising does not operate in a vacuum; it requires that the organization make careful plans and establish its priorities of need; it must also acknowledge that gifts and contributions are among a variety of revenue resources available to further an organization's mission, vision, and values. Moreover, organizations differ in how they perform fund raising, and fund raising performs differently in every organization. Fund raising works best when it operates in close synchronization with the organization's mission and its financial and strategic plans, is coordinated closely with its marketing and communication activity (all seek to reach the same audiences), conducts a variety of solicitation programs with an established corps of volunteer leaders and trained solicitors, receives reliable levels of annual support, offers a variety of avenues for public participation, and possesses an experienced, trained staff of fund raising professionals with adequate space, budget, and systems. Given such a favorable mix of positive ingredients, questions about accountability in fund raising performance should be able to be answered.

ON BEING ACCOUNTABLE

There are larger questions of accountability, much tougher to answer, that must also be addressed besides fund raising performance: How has the organization used gifts and contributions from a willing public to accomplish its goals and objectives? What measurable outcomes can it document? Can it quantify how its programs and services have been of direct benefit to the community it serves? Performance evaluation of all these areas is required, but this work is not easy. Further, when compared with for-profit companies and their use of "bottom line" measurement of profits only, there is no accepted set of uniform standards against which nonprofit organizations can be measured.

American nonprofit organizations are quite alike one another in several respects, and this is helpful in any assessment of their accountability. With formal Internal Revenue Service and state approvals, each is privileged to hold identical exemptions from federal and state income, sales, and property taxes and can verify to all donors that their charitable contributions are eligible for deduction from personal or corporate income tax. In exchange for these privileges, nonprofit organizations are obligated to report to their community on outcomes and benefits its citizens receive in exchange for their personal support as advocates, donors, and volunteers. They must be able to demonstrate an exacting accountability for delivery of quality programs and expanded services; for ethical conduct in all relationships, be they with clients or customers, board members or employees, donors or volunteers; and for stewardship of their assets, including all funds raised and received as well as how these funds were used, and for their employees, facilities, and equipment. Exhibit 28.1 offers one measurement tool the board of governors can use to evaluate fulfillment of the mission in its annual board assessment. There can be no substitute for the highest standards of conduct in every area of a nonprofit organization's daily activity because in the end, it is the public's confidence and trust in a good performance that enables the organization to operate successfully. Without such confidence, trust, and commitment by members of the public to give of their time, energy, talent, and personal funds, any organization cannot long survive.

Accountability is no longer optional; people want to know what the organization is doing with "their money." Results can be measured and monitored and the conclusions published. Organizations must also go beyond minimal report-

Exhibit 28.1. Assessment Criteria for the Mission.

	Score				
	Low				High
1. Fulfills a "charitable" purpose	1	2	3	4	5
2. Completes annual public reporting requirements	1	2	3	4	5
3. Provides high quality of service	1	2	3	4	5
4. Offers accessibility to service	1	2	3	4	5
5. Increases public awareness of the cause	1	2	3	4	5
6. Addresses five advocacy measurements	1	2	3	4	5
7. Adequately uses audits and auditors	1	2	3	4	5
8. Is financially accountable	1	2	3	4	5
9. Stimulates innovative ideas	1	2	3	4	5
10. Provides programs of value to the public	1	2	3	4	5
11. Develops new leadership	1	2	3	4	5
12. Is guided by written policies and procedures	1	2	3	4	5
Median Score					

Source: James M. Greenfield, ed. The Nonprofit Handbook: Fundraising, 3rd ed., 2001, p. 156. Copyright © 2001 John Wiley & Sons, Inc. This material is used by permission of John Wiley & Sons, Inc.

ing standards. They must be willing to share operating details as well as sensitive information including financial decisions in order to keep a sometimes skeptical and even cynical public willingly supporting their mission and vision. Exhibit 28.2 is a tool to evaluate routine operations and management areas on an annual basis. Where possible, the public wants to see results as quantifiable, measurable outcomes. Financial reports are one area of particular interest, as these are commonly used to evaluate for-profit companies. These must also be meticulously correct, clearly presented, easy to read, accurate, and fully accessible to the public. In summary, there can be nothing private about a public benefit corporation, including the conduct of its board, managers, donors, and employees engaged in support of its mission, vision, and values, which exist only to benefit others.

Exhibit 28.2. Environmental Audit for Operations.

	Score				
	Low				*High*
1. Aging of the population	1	2	3	4	5
2. Debt financing	1	2	3	4	5
3. Coalitions, mergers, and acquisitions	1	2	3	4	5
4. Costs of supplies and services	1	2	3	4	5
5. Disclosure	1	2	3	4	5
6. Ethics and professionalism	1	2	3	4	5
7. Financial conditions	1	2	3	4	5
8. Globalization	1	2	3	4	5
9. Government regulation	1	2	3	4	5
10. Leadership development	1	2	3	4	5
11. Management competency	1	2	3	4	5
12. Pressure for cash	1	2	3	4	5
13. Profitability	1	2	3	4	5
14. Public confidence	1	2	3	4	5
15. Technology	1	2	3	4	5
16. Wages and benefits	1	2	3	4	5

Median Score

Source: James M. Greenfield, ed. *The Nonprofit Handbook: Fundraising,* 3rd ed., 2001, p. 160. Copyright © 2001 John Wiley & Sons, Inc. This material is used by permission of John Wiley & Sons, Inc.

Herein lies the basic quandary: How do nonprofit organizations quantify and report the outcomes of their charitable programs and services? To begin, the organization must operate in full public view, with open and complete willingness to disclose all of its activities, including its financial affairs. It must be committed to excellence and dedicated to serve every purpose defined in its mission—its reason to exist. Its statements of vision and values help explain its credo of higher purposes as well as its future intentions. Further, it must do the work to monitor its own performance, evaluating the quality of its programs and services with regularity. And it must report fairly and frequently on its results. Routine financial reports, such as the annual audit statement and annual information return (IRS Form 990), are public documents; copies must be provided upon request. With such documentation and its disclosure, the public can review such indicators of success as financial performance, evaluate the benefits provided by the organization, and be informed about their free choice to continue to support its good works. In contrast, without open and full disclosure of these and other results, doubt, uncertainty, and suspicion are more likely to arise, and gifts will not be forthcoming.

How should a nonprofit organization demonstrate accountability for its fund raising activities? How effective are its fund raising programs in conducting public solicitations? How cost-efficient is it when using the organization's budget money to ask for contributions? Answers begin with budgeting for fund raising, a variety of gift reports, and multiple assessments of the results.

ASSESSING BUDGETS AND COSTS

To begin, three principles of budgeting are advocated. First, nonprofits must recognize that the fund raising program is a *profit* center, not just another cost center. Donors and volunteers make investment decisions with their support, whether as wealth or work, with the expectation of a healthy return to benefit both the organization and the community it serves. Second, budgeting for fund raising should be based on recognition that each solicitation program, method, and technique used is a separate financial enterprise. Each requires budget support for its preparation and planning, materials, gift processing, donor recognition, training, and evaluation with direct costs used in its execution. Thus each method experiences its own separate level of direct expense along with internal support in the form of indirect and overhead costs to be measured against its results. Third, budgeting is both a planning and management function. It is a financial plan to perform specific tasks linked to goals and objectives. And it is a management function for supervision and reporting on progress. Evaluation of both is required to demonstrate success.

Budget areas for a comprehensive fund raising program are similar to those for a small office operation. Salaries and benefits may represent half the budget and may include a variety of employment arrangements, as shown in Exhibit 28.3. Labor costs should be based on the same employment plan as all other organizational employees. Direct expenses are an array of traditional areas, as displayed in Exhibit 28.4, and may add personnel costs as consultant fees or in purchased services. Direct expense areas require careful preparation to determine how each cost element (e.g., office supplies, printing costs, postage and mailing) is allocated to each solicitation method in use along with necessary back-office support functions. The recommended method for budget preparation is first that each solicitation program should develop its own separate budget for personnel and direct expenses along with estimates of indirect and overhead costs, all to be consolidated into the overall fund raising budget plan. Each nonprofit organization will prepare separate budget request forms that will use different labels from other organizations for the same expense categories, in order to match up with how their expense accounting system is structured. Also, these same elements should try to mirror IRS Form 990 and its expense criteria (Part II, lines 22–44), also needed to comply with annual disclosure requirements.

Fund raising should be understood to be an investment of organizational budget with the expectation of positive returns, "profits" as net income to support operating expenses for current programs and services. A variety of fund raising methods and techniques are available to organizations to invite their public's interest and support, each with its own separate levels of performance effectiveness and efficiency. These methods also work in concert with one another. Finally, budgets for fund raising are management tools to monitor performance, measure results, and manage the process. Each solicitation method should be measured against the results achieved, preferably against prior years' performance using the same method. An evaluation of year-end "bottom line" results (total costs measured against total gift income) will be misleading with respect to actual solicitation activities and their separate performance characteristics. For example, in Exhibit 28.5, the current fiscal year result of $603,100 from a budget of $131,115 (a cost-benefit ratio of 22 cents to raise $1) suggests the likely outcome of a similar performance next year. However, behind the $603,100 were three bequests for $85,000 that cannot be repeated. Actual funds raised were $518,100 (a cost-benefit ratio of 25 cents to raise $1), a more accurate base for future budget and results planning. Finally, most fund raising methods require up to three years to demonstrate their individual levels of prospective effectiveness and efficiency. This multiyear performance analysis also permits reliability in forecasting future results the organization can count on to fulfill its own financial goals and objectives.

Exhibit 28.3. Departmental Budget Worksheet—Personnel and Benefits.

Category	Current Fiscal Year		Budget Year
	Budget Year to Date	Actual Year to Date	Estimate
Salaries and Benefits			
Director of Development			
Director of Individual Giving			
Director of Corporate Giving			
Director of Foundation Giving			
Director of Special Events			
Support Staff #1			
Support Staff #2			
Part-Time Staff #1			
Part-Time Staff #2			
Temporary Staff #1			
Temporary Staff #2			
Volunteer Staff In-Kind Service[a]			
Subtotal Salaries			
Fringe Benefits (_____%)			
Pay Increase (_____%)			
Subtotal Benefits			
Total Salaries and Benefits			

[a]Do not include in total.

Source: Connell, J. E., "Budgeting for Fund Raising." In James M. Greenfield, ed. *The Nonprofit Handbook: Fundraising,* 3rd ed., 2001, p. 82. Copyright © 2001 John Wiley & Sons, Inc. This material is used by permission of John Wiley & Sons, Inc.

Exhibit 28.4. Departmental Budget Worksheet—Direct Expenses.

	Current Fiscal Year		Budget Year
Category	Budget Year to Date	Actual Year to Date	Estimate
Office Operations[a]			
Books, Subscriptions			
Computer Equipment			
Conferences and Staff Education			
Consultant Fees			
Donor Recognition			
Dues and Memberships			
Entertainment			
Equipment Maintenance			
Insurance		.	
List Fees			
Office Supplies			
Office Rental			
Printing Costs			
Postage and Mailing			
Purchased Services			
Rental Equipment			
Telephone Equipment			
Telephone Charges			
Travel Nationwide			
Travel Local			
Total Office Expense			

[a]May include indirect and overhead costs, along with direct expense areas.

Source: Connell, J. E., "Budgeting for Fund Raising." In James M. Greenfield, ed. *The Nonprofit Handbook: Fundraising*, 3rd ed., 2001, p. 83. Copyright © 2001 John Wiley & Sons, Inc. This material is used by permission of John Wiley & Sons, Inc.

Exhibit 28.5. Summary Budget Request with Estimated Expenses and Revenue.

	Previous Year	Last Year	Current Fiscal Year	Coming Fiscal Year
Budget				
Labor costs	$66,009	$74,164	$79,800	$90,259
Nonlabor costs	43,594	50,026	51,315	50,000
Total budget	$109,603	$124,190	$131,115	$140,259
Gift Revenue				
Gross revenue	$342,738	$563,384	$603,100	$655,000
Minus expenses (budget)	109,603	124,190	131,115	140,259
Net revenue	$233,135	$439,194	$471,985	$514,741
Cost of fund raising	32%	22%	22%	21%
Return	213%	354%	360%	367%

Source: James M. Greenfield, ed. *Fund-Raising Cost Effectiveness: A Self-Assessment Workbook*, 1996, p. 24. Copyright © 1996 John Wiley & Sons, Inc. This material is used by permission of John Wiley & Sons, Inc.

The end results of proper budgeting are the realization of the anticipated revenue and the control of expenses. Budgeting is a major leadership task of fund raising professionals, an essential process that consumes the time and talents of staff and volunteers. Budgets are both evaluation and planning tools, designed to measure the [financial] performance of fund raising efforts. A budget may be an important part of other administrative tasks, such as the formulation of grant proposals, determining program support, and establishing new programs and campaign efforts. A budget may also serve as an occasional reference on program progress or as a step-by-step guide for financial development. Budgeting is used to both plan and control fund raising efforts. Budgeting forces the fund raising director to evaluate past program results and to make decisions on future activities. It is not an isolated function, and to be successful it must be based on realistic institutional planning. The budgeting activity must be a well-conceived process that forms a [financial] plan of action for future fund raising efforts [Connell, 2001, p. 53].

Finally, there are a variety of routine daily activities in an operating fund raising program that do not produce any revenue. These support functions include planning and preparation; performing data entry to record and deposit every gift; preparing gift reports; attending staff volunteer committee and board meetings; conducting staff training; preparing budgets; attending activities, benefits, and special events; and evaluating results. These areas constitute indirect costs and overhead expenses that must also be allocated back to each individual solicitation program in operation. Direct costs such as printing, postage, food, entertainment, equipment rentals, and telephone and Internet charges are finite budget expenses, but they are not easy to allocate to each of the solicitation activities they support. Other budget expenses such as staff time (salaries and benefits), heat, light, and rent are also not easy to allocate among the several programs in use. Further, to allocate salary and benefit expenses for employees against individual solicitation activities first requires a time analysis study. By tracking each employee and the hours each spends daily in these support functions as well as direct solicitation programs, realistic salary and budget figures can be assigned to each activity. Some fund raising managers resist such evaluation and staff time analysis studies ("they don't raise any money"), but the work is necessary for an accurate understanding of how staff and budget are aligned with results of each of their ongoing solicitation activities. The combined allocation of direct costs with complete indirect and overhead expenses to each solicitation method is the only means to arrive at an accurate cost-benefit assessment of fund raising performance.

REPORTS OF GIFTS AND CONTRIBUTIONS RECEIVED

The key to useful reports of fund raising results is good preparation. It begins with actual data entry at the time each gift is received, which should capture information about the method used to solicit each gift (and the solicitor, if involved), along with the name, amount, date, and purpose or use of the funds the donor has specified. Gift reports should be developed to not only display the results of each and every solicitation but also to illustrate how each method is performing this year as compared to past years, its status in completing its assigned goal, its use of budget resources, and its cost-benefit measurements.

Three primary reports are recommended to collect details necessary to display these results. Exhibit 28.6 tracks the *sources* of gifts, as important as counting the number of donors in each group who participate. Average gift size is a bonus, to understand how effective the solicitations for each audience were, along with a measurement of the donor's confidence and trust in the organization. Exhibit 28.7 reports the *purposes or uses* that donors specify for their gifts that must be matched to the goals set as support required for these priority programs and services. Average gift size illustrates the level of conviction, expressed as how much was given as well as the relationship to the gift use options offered in the solicitation message. It also signals potential future interest in these same areas, should the needs require. Exhibit 28.8 tracks each *solicitation method used*, again counting the number of gifts, gift income, and average gift size, by solicitation method, which serve as prime indicators of the effectiveness of each method to perform well and raise the funds needed.

Exhibit 28.6. Gift Report on Sources of Gifts Received.

Sources of Gifts	Number of Gifts	Gift Income	Average Gift Size
Trustees/directors	15	$25,500	$1,700
Professional staff	21	3,025	144
Employees	65	3,675	57
New donors (acquisition)	285	8,030	28
Prior donors (renewal)	282	18,010	64
Corporations	17	8,500	500
Foundations	12	38,800	3,233
Associations/societies	6	2,850	475
Bequests received	3	31,500	10,500
Unsolicited gifts	42	2,950	70
Other gifts received	12	21,500	1,792
Grand Total	760	$164,340	$216

Source: James M. Greenfield, ed. *Fund-Raising Cost Effectiveness: A Self-Assessment Workbook,* 1996, p. 15. Copyright © 1996 John Wiley & Sons, Inc. This material is used by permission of John Wiley & Sons, Inc.

Exhibit 28.7. Gift Report on Purposes or Uses of Gifts Received.

Purposes or Uses of Gifts Received	Number of Gifts	Gift Income	Average Gift Size
Unrestricted Funds	225	$34,519	$153
Temporarily Restricted Funds			
Capital/equipment purposes	295	$26,950	$91
Programs/services purposes	138	18,500	134
Education/training purposes	14	22,500	1,607
Research/study purposes	15	26,450	1,763
Staff/employee purposes	58	3,016	52
Other restricted purposes	12	905	75
Subtotal	757	$132,840	$175
Permanently Restricted Funds			
Unrestricted endowment	2	$6,500	$3,250
Restricted endowment	1	25,000	25,000
Subtotal	3	$31,500	$10,500
Grand Total	760	$164,340	$216

Source: James M. Greenfield, ed. *Fund-Raising Cost Effectiveness: A Self-Assessment Workbook,* 1996, p. 16. Copyright © 1996 John Wiley & Sons, Inc. This material is used by permission of John Wiley & Sons, Inc.

Exhibit 28.8. Gift Report of Solicitation Activities and Results (by Program).

Solicitation Activities	Number of Gifts	Gift Income	Average Gift Size
A. Annual Giving Programs			
Direct mail (acquisition)	285	$8,030	$28
Direct mail (renewal)	282	18,010	64
Membership dues	0	0	0
Donor clubs	0	0	0
Support groups	0	0	0
Telephone gifts	0	0	0
Benefit events	2	12,850	6,425
Volunteer-led solicitations	65	3,675	57
Unsolicited gifts	42	2,950	70
Other gifts received	16	21,500	1,344
Subtotal	692	$67,015	$97
B. Major Giving Programs			
Corporations	17	$8,500	$500
Foundations	12	28,800	2,400
Individuals	36	28,525	792
Special projects	0	0	0
Capital campaigns	0	0	0
Bequests received	3	31,500	10,500
Subtotal	68	$97,325	$1,431
Grand Total	760	$164,340	$216

Source: James M. Greenfield, ed. *Fund-Raising Cost Effectiveness: A Self-Assessment Workbook,* 1996, p. 17. Copyright © 1996 John Wiley & Sons, Inc. This material is used by permission of John Wiley & Sons, Inc.

With three solid reports in place, the addition of full budget details will complete the picture (see Exhibit 28.9). The original budget as approved and actual expenses incurred can now be compared to gift income received by each solicitation method, yielding *cost per dollar raised by solicitation method.* In this exhibit, overall "bottom line" results suggest that for the $603,100 in gifts received, actual expenses were $79,800 in direct costs (labor/payroll) plus $51,315 in indirect and overhead expenses (nonpayroll costs), a total of $131,115, yielding net income for the organization's use of $471,985. These figures suggest a cost-benefit ratio of 22 cents to raise $1 plus a return on investment of 360 percent in twelve

Exhibit 28.9. Year-End Gift Report.

	Gift Amount	Budget Approved	Budget Expended	Cost of Fund Raising (%)
A. Annual Giving Programs				
Direct mail (acquisition)	$35,500	$14,500	$14,798	42
Direct mail (renewal)	76,500	1,500	1,620	2
Membership dues	48,500	550	585	1
Benefit events (3)	59,600	20,000	21,747	36
Volunteer-led solicitations	82,000	1,200	1,250	2
Subtotal	$302,100	$37,750	$40,000	13
Direct Costs: Annual Giving				
Labor/payroll		$62,000	$63,050	
Nonpayroll costs		37,750	40,000	
Subtotal		$99,750	$103,050	34
B. Major Gifts Programs				
Corporations	$45,500	$3,500	$3,250	7
Foundations	65,000	3,500	2,015	3
Individuals	145,500	3,800	4,200	3
Bequests received	45,000	200	1,850	4
Subtotal	$301,000	$11,000	$11,315	4
Total	$603,100	$48,750	$51,315	9
Net Income	$471,985			
Direct costs: Major giving				
Labor/payroll		$18,000	$16,750	
Nonpayroll costs		11,000	11,315	
Subtotal		$29,000	$28,065	
C. Expense Summary (A + B)				
Direct costs		$80,000	$79,800	
Indirect costs/overhead		$48,750	$51,315	
Total		$128,750	$131,115	22
Return				360

Source: James M. Greenfield, ed. *Fund-Raising Cost Effectiveness: A Self-Assessment Workbook,* 1996, p. 249.

months, an impressive record. Presentation and explanation of this report can help boards, chief executive officers, donors, and volunteers understand the "profitability" of well-managed fund raising activities and provide insight into the performance characteristics of the separate solicitation methods in use. When it is time to prepare the next year's budget, to calculate anticipated income as well as required expenses, this summary report will be a most valuable tool.

ASSESSING RESULTS

To achieve an understanding of the accountability of fund raising performance, organizations need to review their results for at least a three-year period. This exercise will also be essential in forecasting future years' results with reliability and will aid the organization in setting standards of performance expected of all its fund raising activities. Nonprofit organizations are quite unalike, even within the same industry group. For example, the fund raising performance of a five-person office at a small liberal arts college of twelve hundred students located in central Connecticut cannot be compared fairly or equitably with a staff of eighty professionals at nearby Yale University. Reasonable guidelines on fund raising cost for each type of solicitation activity are available (see Exhibit 28.10). These performance rates are applicable after *three or more years* of continuous experience. Organizations can use them to monitor performance of each of their individual solicitation methods as one measuring stick for their solicitation activity.

A more in-depth analysis is to apply the Nine-Point Performance Index to each and every solicitation activity (see Exhibit 28.11). Use of this measurement tool adds a consistency of various performance indicators as applied to each fund raising method in use. For example, direct mail acquisition seeks first-time donors to the organization; critical indicators are how many donors replied with money (percent participation), followed by their average gift size. If the response rate is below 0.5 percent and average gifts are less than $25, this program is not working well and needs attention in order to be successful; the mailing lists selected may be faulty, the amounts requested may have been unclear, the organization may be unknown or unpopular, or the message about the purpose or use of the funds for community benefit may have been uninspiring. When renewing current donors, also by mail, critical indicators will again be percent participation (how many donors were retained) and average gift size, plus how many upgraded or increased their gifts. Here if the response rate is above 50 percent and average gifts increased because 10 percent of donors upgraded their prior gift levels, this program is performing well. Acquisition and renewal solicitations, both using direct mail, perform quite differently. As another example,

Exhibit 28.10. Reasonable Cost Guidelines for Solicitation Activities.

Solicitation Activity	Reasonable Cost Guidelines
Direct mail (acquisition)	$1.25 to $1.50 per $1.00 raised
Direct mail (renewal)	$0.20 to $0.25 per $1.00 raised
Membership associations	$0.20 to $0.30 per $1.00 raised
Activities, benefits, and special events	$0.50 per $1.00 raised (gross revenue and direct costs only)[a]
Donor clubs and support group organizations	$0.20 to $0.30 per $1.00 raised
Volunteer-led personal solicitation	$0.10 to $0.20 per $1.00 raised
Corporations	$0.20 per $1.00 raised
Foundations	$0.20 per $1.00 raised
Special projects	$0.10 to $0.20 per $1.00 raised
Capital campaigns	$0.10 to $0.20 per $1.00 raised
Planned giving	$0.20 to $0.30 per $1.00 raised

[a]To calculate bottom-line total costs and net proceeds from a benefit event, calculate and add the indirect and overhead support expenses to direct costs incurred and subtract from gross revenue.

Source: James M. Greenfield, ed. *Fund-Raising Cost Effectiveness: A Self-Assessment Workbook,* 1996, p. 281. Copyright © 1996 John Wiley & Sons, Inc. This material is used by permission of John Wiley & Sons, Inc.

take one of the ever-popular benefit events; the critical indicator will be whether the event can achieve a direct cost ratio of 50 cents per $1 raised in net proceeds to be deemed financially successful. If an event budget included all the indirect and overhead expenses (value of volunteer hours, staff salaries and benefits, cost of committee meetings, telephone calls, gift processing, guest seating, program planning, and so on), no benefit event is likely to produce any appreciable net income for the organization, considering all the work required for a successful event.

The final evaluation tool for fund raising performance is to measure growth in giving for the organization. Fund raising is supposed to be a growth program. With a solid organizational case statement, a budget and staff, volunteers, and a good effort by all, each program should be able to increase the number of donors, the average gift size, and net income each year. It also should be able to increase the percentage of those who respond to invitations to give and be able to reduce the average cost per gift while increasing the return on investment. Exhibit 28.12 illustrates cumulative growth over three years in both number of donors and percent participating at 31 percent, which is most impressive. So is the 30 percent growth in net income coupled with the 15 percent reduc-

Exhibit 28.11. Nine-Point Performance Index.

Basic Data

1. Participants	= Number of donors responding with gifts
2. Income	= Gross contributions
3. Expense	= Fund raising costs

Performance Measurements

4. Percent participation	= Divide participants by total solicitations made
5. Average gift size	= Divide income received by participants
6. Net income	= Subtract expenses from income received
7. Average cost per gift	= Divide expenses by participants
8. Cost of fund raising	= Divide expenses by income received; multiply by 100 for percentage
9. Return	= Divide net income by expenses; multiply by 100 for percentage

Source: James M. Greenfield, ed. *Fund-Raising Cost Effectiveness: A Self-Assessment Workbook,* 1996, p. 31. Copyright © 1996 John Wiley & Sons, Inc. This material is used by permission of John Wiley & Sons, Inc.

tion in average cost per gift and 11 percent cut in fund raising costs. These figures represent a comprehensive "bottom line" analysis of overall fund raising performance, including a return on investment for the organization's commitment of budget dollars at 333 percent in one year, impressive performance indeed. Where else in the organization is there such a positive ("profitable") financial result?

ASSESSING OUTCOMES AS COMMUNITY BENEFITS

For a nonprofit organization to demonstrate that it can deliver value to its community, it needs to evaluate itself beyond fund raising prowess using several criteria matched to an assessment of community needs. These criteria may include the following quantifiable areas:

- Improving the performance of its current programs and services with higher quality and for more participants
- Calculating and communicating its measurable outcomes to staff, volunteers, donors, the public, and others

**Exhibit 28.12. Report on the Overall Rate of
Growth in Giving Using the Nine-Point Performance Index.**

	Two Years Ago	Last Year	Annual Rate of Growth (%)	This Year	Annual Rate of Growth (%)	Cumulative Rate of Growth (%)
Participation	1,355	1,605	18	1,799	12	31
Income	$448,765	$507,855	13	$571,235	12	26
Expenses	$116,550	$123,540	6	$131,850	7	13
Percent participation	39%	44%	13	52%	18	31
Average gift size	$331	$316	−4	$318	0.4	−4
Net income	$332,215	$384,315	16	$439,385	14	30
Average cost per gift	$86.01	$76.97	−11	$73.29	−5	−15
Cost of fund raising	26%	24%	−6	23%	−5	−11
Return	285%	311%	9	333%	7	16

Source: James M. Greenfield, ed. *Fund-Raising Cost Effectiveness: A Self-Assessment Workbook,* 1996, p. 272. Copyright © 1996 John Wiley & Sons, Inc. This material is used by permission of John Wiley & Sons, Inc.

- Identifying where it can provide more effective programs and services with defined strategies that it can implement more broadly
- Developing new approaches that will respond to changing community issues
- Defining internal values as programs funded by the community that are delivered back to the community
- Recognizing progress as increased support of volunteers, numbers of donors, and amounts of public gift support

The effort to identify these elements or another series of criteria and to commit the organization to pursue them must be rigorous, must receive the commitment of the board and senior management, and must be assigned to a team of employees including public representatives. This team must also be empowered to examine the work performed by the organization and to initiate data collection methods required to capture essential information that will define measurable outcomes. It must be understood that this entire process is being performed in order to establish the organization's outcome measurement process. It is not intended or directed at any specific employees or current programs, nor will it be used in evaluating anyone's personal performance. It reflects a commitment to demonstrate fulfillment of the mission and delivery of quality programs and services that meet community needs.

An illustration of this sequence of activities in a nonprofit organization begins with community needs assessment, which must be measured against the organization's own mission statement. This exercise, seen as a "circle of accountability" (see Figure 28.1), begins with assessments of how the mission matches up with defined community needs. In response, strategic plans are prepared by the organization to define those programs and services plus the budget required to address these needs. Fund raising goals are prepared to invite the public to help meet these needs, and through active solicitations and other activities, community needs are communicated widely, inviting the public to help achieve the organization's goals. The precise nature of these communications, defined as quality programs and services provided by the organization, will also supply answers to the public's need to know how its funds will be used to make a difference. People also need to know, as precisely as possible, how the gift amounts requested fit with the expected value delivered back to the community. The organization conducts these priorities through rigorous application of staff and financial resources to defined programs and services during its annual

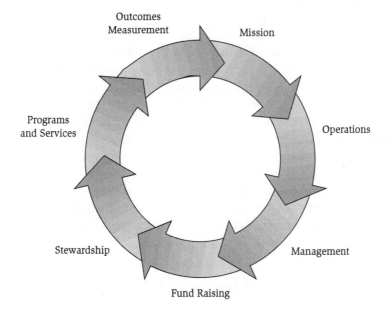

Figure 28.1. The Circle of Accountability.

Source: Greenfield, J. M., and Dreves, J. P., "Fund-Raising Assessment." In James M. Greenfield, ed. *The Nonprofit Handbook: Fundraising,* 3rd ed., 2001, p. 155. Copyright © 2001 John Wiley & Sons, Inc. This material is used by permission of John Wiley & Sons, Inc.

operating year. At year end, these operations result in outcomes that can be measured and reported as quantifiable benefits delivered back to the community, completing the circle of accountability. With such solid efforts, the organization is now prepared to answer the following questions, defined as community benefits delivered:

- Has the organization made a difference in the life of the community?
- Can the results be measured against the mission through its programs and services?
- Is the organization effecting change in the community and in its industry?
- Is the organization providing a direct benefit to community residents?
- Has the organization improved community residents' quality of life?
- Can the organization demonstrate both quality and quantity in terms of having made a positive difference?
- How well is the organization accomplishing these things in light of the funds it receives?

On the surface, these are challenging questions for any nonprofit organization. They are also achievable areas of performance measurement. United Way of America has initiated a national program committed to addressing community benefits, complete with an instruction manual and workbooks. It has also defined aspects of a measurement report to demonstrate community benefits: "Outcomes may relate to behavior, skills, knowledge, attitudes, values, condition, or other attributes. Examples of outcomes include greater knowledge of nutritional needs, improved reading skills, more effective response to conflict, getting a job, or having greater financial stability. Outcomes are benefits or changes for individuals or populations during or after participating in program activities. Outcomes are influenced by a program's outputs. They are what participants know, think, or can do; or how they behave; or what their condition is, that is different following the program" (United Way of America, 1996, pp. xv-2). These changes can be measured against the philanthropic support the organization reviews when budgets accurately record gifts and other income.

CONCLUSION

Every nonprofit organization has a wealth of examples of how it has helped people. What is needed is the homework to document more than numbers of people served. Report on how people's lives have been influenced. Link these activities with the community's assessment of its own needs to demonstrate where the effective partnership with nonprofit organizations bears fruit worthy of continued support. The remaining challenge is accurate public perception of honest accountability. The future will test even further the levels of accountability that nonprofit organizations must continue to address. The final arbiters will be volunteers and donors, the "best friends" every nonprofit organization has. Their motives are never to hesitate to point out all the warts and blemishes each organization still has while remaining steadfast in their support, because they are convinced that they are the means to help it perform even better.

CHAPTER TWENTY-NINE

Selecting and Working
with Fund Raising Consultants

Jim Reid

Hank Rosso's approach to fund raising included professional management of the process. For some organizations, that means looking beyond the expertise of the organization. Part of the human resource team for fund raising is often made up of people from outside the group of those who already have some defined role, such as staff, board, or volunteers. Consultants both in general services and with certain specialties can be a valuable resource to the nonprofit fund raising team on many occasions.

Most nonprofits arrive at a point when the assignments they face in fund raising exceed the talents or the time that their existing staff can give to the tasks at hand. Rather than make the investment or take the risk of adding staff in a potentially short-term need or when the opinions of experienced fund raisers who are in a position to be totally objective observers are needed or when the pressing needs of the organization do not leave time to build a staff for the task ahead, the hiring of a consultant makes strategic as well as pragmatic sense.

In any of these cases, the hiring of a fund raising consultant is a major decision that can have a significant impact on the organization and its programs. Consultants may also be used across the full range of fund raising functions, from analyzing initial strengths and organizational readiness through the design of each of the component parts of a comprehensive program to the intense efforts of a capital campaign or the creation of highly tailored planned giving programs. Also, since charitable organizations are often slower in the implementation of strategic and long-range planning efforts, consultants are frequently used to help facilitate that work as a part of the preparation to raise funds and to define the case for charitable support of the organization. Therefore, the selection of the right consultant to meet the particular needs of the organization at any given time is a crucial activity.

Each consulting area in the fund raising process has some unique features. It makes sense to examine those areas, with an eye toward the needs and the defining features of the services a consultant should be expected to provide in each.

INSTITUTIONAL READINESS

There are occasions in the life of a nonprofit organization when a "window of opportunity" presents itself. Frequently, a new fund raising initiative is necessary to realize the opportunity presented. On those occasions, consultants can provide the objective review and assessment of the organization's existing capacities and projections of success in either a special effort or campaign or the creation of a whole new permanent initiative in the fund raising area. These assessments of capacity usually result in not just a conclusion about what is possible but also a list of specific actions and steps that should be taken either to correct deficiencies in preparation or to begin the initiatives that will help the organization reach its potential.

ANNUAL CAMPAIGNS

Consultants working with organizations that are structuring (or restructuring) their annual giving efforts frequently bring a broader vision and a wealth of experience and examples from other clients that allow the current client organization to see opportunities for variety in its program. Consultants should also be expected to help plan the program against a set of expectations and costs for each solicitation technique in the annual fund arsenal of activities, assembling the new effort within the budget expectations and limitations of the client.

In the area of annual fund consulting, there are specialists who concentrate specifically on the techniques of direct mail and special events. Each of these specialties can be highly complex activities within the annual fund appeals. Consultants with these concentrations bring to the client organization some very realistic projections about what to expect as results from these techniques, based on the numbers involved in the planning and the costs of conducting the activities. Those projections are sometimes very sobering to client organizations who have heard about "miracles" that can be achieved.

CAPITAL CAMPAIGNS

The intense activity of capital campaigns provided the first arenas where turning to fund raising consultants for technique and operations became the norm. It was logical, convenient, and comfortable to hire a consultant to come in and "do all the dirty work" of the campaign and then leave so that the staff and the board of the client organization did not have to get enmeshed in the details. This mind-set was just as fallacious then as it is now, but it illustrates the value of the objectivity that an outside team can bring to the process of preparing and implementing an intense fund raising effort for a specific period of time. The conduct of capital campaigns requires a higher staff commitment from the organization than is normally present on an ongoing basis. A consultant, as an adjunct staff member, can provide the extra human resources as well as the expertise in the particular organizational strategies required in campaigns. In those cases, the consultant becomes the "manager of the campaign" and a valuable asset to its success.

In the instances just described, as in all consulting usages, the client should retain the primary working relationship with both volunteers and donors. Consultants should *not* become the organization's main avenue of communication with either volunteers or donors. That relationship is the custodial responsibility of the cause or the organization, not the consultant.

In other instances, the organization may be well staffed and not in need of extra personnel but in need of steady advice on the structure, timing, and logic of a capital campaign. In those cases, the consultant can provide objective advice on the best activities and planning techniques and be a mentor to the staff and volunteer leaders of the campaign.

PLANNED GIVING PROGRAMS

Planned giving is a highly specialized area of fund raising activity, and consultants with very specific experience in the negotiation of planned giving instruments as well as the structuring of the programs for planned gifts into the total development program that is already in place can be very useful to organizations that are embarking on a planned giving effort for the first time. Consultants should be expected to have very specific suggestions about which instruments are the most suited to the case for support of the organization, how those instruments should be promoted within the organization's development marketing effort, and which donors in the organization's database would be the best to approach first in the initiation of the program.

COMMUNICATION AND MARKETING

The arts of marketing, sales, and communication are closely allied with those of fund raising and were in fact the parents of the original fund raising profession, and those skills are still a major part of carrying the message of charitable organizations to their constituents. Consultants in the communication and marketing fields generally provide good counsel to charitable causes in the analysis or creation of communication programs. It is best if the consulting firm has experience with nonprofit organizations, since the basic motivations and philosophies of the nonprofit sector require an understanding that for-profit marketing specialists may not have.

PROSPECT IDENTIFICATION

Several other chapters, including Chapters Thirteen and Twenty-Six, discuss prospect research using electronics sources. The advent of widespread access to the Internet over the past decade has completely changed prospect research for fund raising. Thanks to the accessibility on the Internet of a wide variety of information regarding individuals, corporations, and foundations, a certain capacity to do prospect research at the organizational level with local staff has become a major element in the preparation for fund raising. The Internet prospect research sources themselves are very changeable, however, making regular visits to each site a necessity. Luckily, there are now specialist consultants who spend their time exploring the sources and locations that are available. These specialists can be hired on a project-by-project or source-by-source basis, and their fees are structured accordingly. An organization that needs specific references on a particular source or a broad analysis of a list of sources from its own records can turn to these prospect research consultants to provide that analysis.

Research specialists also counsel clients on the services and research capacities that can be built into the organization's own resources, and their assignment should include not only a list of the services to install and libraries to build and visit but also some initial training for the organization's staff on the use of these resources.

BOARD AND STAFF TRAINING

The most significant and most underutilized source of charitable support for nonprofit causes continues to be major gifts. The approach to individuals for their support, either personally or as decision makers for their corporations and foundations, requires not only an understanding of the philosophies of philanthropy but also an understanding of the dynamics of face-to-face negotiation of a gift. The preparation of a team of volunteers and staff to overcome the fear of asking is one area of training in nonprofit organizations where the assistance of consultants can be useful. Fund raising training specialists, including those at The Fund Raising School, can bring not only a curriculum of training to prepare good askers but also a philosophical attitude of success and pride in the process of asking that will empower the organization's team to be effective in this most productive arena in fund raising.

In addition, all of the specialty areas mentioned so far are places where staff and volunteer training are needed.

SPECIAL EVENT PLANNING

Though frequently regarded as the cornerstone of some organizations' fund raising programs, in reality most special events serve a broad range of positive purposes in a nonprofit enterprise. Consequently, a consultant or specialist in fund raising event design can be helpful in designing an event that maximizes all of the positive benefits of holding the event and makes the often extensive preparations worthwhile. Consultants in this area often bring significant human resources to the effort from their own staffs, making their presence very advantageous. Note that the fee for such consulting service should not be based on a percentage of ticket sales or participation income, as that is considered unethical in the profession. Staff must be clear about the distinction between marketing and advertising income, on the one hand, and philanthropic contributions, on the other.

STRATEGIC LONG-RANGE PLANNING

Successful fund raising for an organization depends on a well-developed strategic long-range plan that lays out a vision for the future of the organization and indicates why it is important to the community it serves and the constituency that it represents. Thoughtful donors are most often inspired by the dreams and plans of the organization (and dismayed when those are not present or articulated in the fund raising effort). It is this absence that often brings the need to improve or initiate fund raising in the organization in the first place. These two realities are often the reason why fund raising consultants for charitable organizations are called to assist in the process of planning, visioning, and strategic decision making. The process in the nonprofit world is procedurally similar to that in the commercial arena but differs in both the philosophy of application and the nature of the "product" being offered to the community. Seasoned fund raising consultants from most of the previously discussed specialties are usually excellent planning consultants and can be very helpful in the strategic planning process that validates the organization's needs for the funds being raised. They bring to their consulting assignments discipline, procedures, and objectivity, all of which makes them very useful to the strategic and long-range planning process.

EXECUTIVE SEARCH

There are consulting firms whose consulting service focuses on finding organizational executives for nonprofit and for-profit firms. They serve as virtual brokers for executives and organizations in search of each other, and they come with a wide variety of clients on both sides of the brokerage and a wide variety of operational techniques and fee structures. They are most often used when an organization already knows its most immediately accessible market for the position is insufficient and wants a broader search beyond its own contacts. National and international organizations, highly specialized institutions, and others with broadly defined constituencies and purposes are those most often using the services of executive search consultants. Such specialists should provide the organization with a fairly lengthy list of potential candidates for the position, based on selection criteria developed in advance with the assistance of the consultants. They will also suggest places for advertising the position and some of the ways to evaluate the *curricula vitae* that are submitted. These consultants usually charge a flat fee or a percentage of the first year's salary plus direct expenses.

ORGANIZATIONAL READINESS

Consultants can bring valuable services to organizations, but they should not be regarded as miracle workers or reservoirs of everything that an organization needs to succeed in a particular activity or program. There are some requisites that the organization needs to have in place before a consultant can be expected to render real service.

Although it is frequently true that the range and scope of a consultant's work is expanded after work has begun, that is usually true because the client organization has failed to realize the need for the broader consulting agenda before the contract was secured. It would be useful to review some of the items in the readiness agenda that the organization should have in place before it is prepared to make maximum effective use of the consultant's presence (and obtain the maximum value for the fee it will pay).

Desired Outcomes

An organization in search of a consultant should have, in advance, a list in broad terms of the deliverables or desired outcomes it wants from the consultant—the amount of a goal, the end products of a process, a time frame for productivity. These will be somewhat negotiable, depending on what the consultant brings to the table in the discussions prior to contract.

Organizational Commitment

Consultants should rarely be expected to come in and "do it all." The organization should be prepared to make a significant commitment of the human and financial resources necessary to work with the consultant on the tasks ahead. Usually a single individual in the organization should be designated to serve as the primary contact when the consultant finds it necessary to navigate organizational structures and protocols. Organizations are built by and with people, and people are political in almost every facet of their relationship to the organization. A consultant's work can be jeopardized in the early phase of the work if the consultant runs afoul of the internal politics of the organization. Most consultants are aware of this potential and sensitive to internal politics but can nevertheless be greatly aided by the presence of a designated primary contact.

In most cases, the work of the consultant also depends on spending a significant amount of time with the major decision makers in the organization in the areas of the consultant's work. A commitment from those people is part of being ready to use a consultant. Volunteer leadership time is an essential ingredient in that commitment as well.

Financial Resources

In addition to the consultant's contracted fee, there are always ancillary expenses such as travel, lodging, telecommunications, possible publications and printing, internal conferences or retreats, and a number of other miscellaneous expenses that are a part of the successful use of a consultant. Without the organization's commitment of these necessary financial resources, consultants and their clients are often frustrated in producing the results outlined at the start of the project.

The organization's commitment to these financial requirements, from the highest levels of its structure (governing board and executive management), should be in place before the consultant is signed to a contract.

Staff Expertise

The advice and recommendations of a consultant frequently require a certain level of both understanding and capacity to respond from the staff of the organization. Of course, the consultant may, in fact, be a training agent to accelerate the expertise of the staff, but an assessment of what is present before the arrival of the consultant is an important part of the process of preparation. As mentioned earlier, some organizations already have a large enough team in place to conduct a capital campaign, but the presence of the consultant will be to organize and monitor the team as it performs according to a design that the consultant prepares. Without a team in place, the organization should seek a different type and level of consulting services for its campaign.

Volunteers

The presence of volunteers drives the ultimate success of any fund raising program in the long term. Therefore, the volunteers' existing experience and availability to the consultant are parts of the preparation process before hiring a consultant. Consultants often stipulate that a committee of volunteers for the project be designated to work with the consultant during the contract period and to be the initial group to which the consultant will make his or her report.

BENEFITS OF WORKING WITH CONSULTANTS

Though much has already been mentioned about the value of working with consultants, several additional features deserve specific mention.

The objectivity and the technical expertise brought by consultants is part of the very definition of the consulting practice in almost every field of consultancy. These values are based on the experience the consultant has amassed while being involved often in the activities about which the consultant advises. It has been said that "a consultant in his own back yard is a prophet without an audience!"—testimony to the value of the objectivity that consultants bring to projects in which they have not previously been direct participants.

The arrival of a consultant is often a demarcation line, a boost to project momentum or the point at which it is regained. The investment and commitments needed to bring the consultant to the task become the energy behind that momentum.

The training and motivating of volunteers and staff, as well as the strategic planning elements of consultancy, have already been mentioned. Furthermore, consultants' objectivity, experience, and analysis of the constituency also make them excellent writers or editors of the textual materials produced in the fund raising effort. Their knowledge of the effectiveness of language used in similar circumstances or organizations is especially valuable when creating new documents.

UNREALISTIC EXPECTATIONS

Successful long-term fund raising in an organization depends on the relationships it builds with its major donors in all the different areas of giving. Those relationships are the most precious assets for the organization, and their management is the organization's responsibility. That responsibility is the job of the organization's staff to develop, maintain, and pass on to succeeding members of the staff. Consultants should not be hired with the expectation that they can bring new major donors to the organization as a result of the consultant's relationships with those donors on earlier projects. However, their *knowledge of major donor programs* may be of assistance in helping the new organization start building relationships with its own major donors.

Similarly, a consultant cannot guarantee the commitments from the volunteers that are necessary for success. Volunteers are motivated through relationships with nonprofit organizations, which must accept ultimate responsibility for volunteer programs.

Consultants make excellent trainers in the art of solicitation, as already discussed. So do special programs like The Fund Raising School. But they should not be the solicitors in an organization's fund raising appeals—again because the relationship should stay with the organization. Consultants might go along on solicitation calls and participate as witnesses to the organization's role in the community, but they should not be sent out on their own.

Since people will work hardest for the things that they help create, an organization should avoid expecting a consultant to create an entire program and then bring it to the organization for implementation. Staff and volunteer involvement in all the steps of the process ensures that it will continue to function when the consultant is no longer part of the process.

HIRING A CONSULTANT

Hiring a fund raising consultant is much like selecting any other professional service provider. The organization doing the selection wants evidence of previous work in the relevant field, success in that work, evidence of credentials that certify preparation and training, and comments from others who have had successful experiences with that professional.

A number of consulting firms belong to the American Association of Fund Raising Counsel (AAFRC). The AAFRC has a code of ethics for consultants and provides guidelines for selecting counsel. Smaller or single-person firms may be affiliated with the Alliance for Nonprofit Management. In any philanthropic market, there will be chapters of practicing professionals such as the Association of Fundraising Professionals (AFP), the Council for the Advancement and Support of Education (CASE), the Association for Healthcare Philanthropy (AHP), the Association of Professional Researchers for Advancement (APRA), the AAFRC, and the National Committee on Planned Giving (NCPG), whose members will be happy to provide a list of the active consultants in the organization's operating area. That listing should provide brief information about credentials and contact information.

Credentials

Within the fund raising profession, there are several organizations to which practitioners may belong, depending on their particular specialization, from general practice to planned giving and prospect development. All of the recognized organizations accept the certification first developed by the predecessor organization to the Association of Fundraising Professionals (AFP) and the Association for Healthcare Philanthropy (AHP), known as the CFRE (Certified Fundraising Executive). This credential recognizes both academic preparation in fund raising and performance on the job for a period of time. It is generally recognized as a standard of achievement and diligence on the part of individuals an organization might choose for general fund raising consulting. The AFP offers an advanced version known as the ACFRE, which is a more senior level of certification. The AHP offers an advanced certificate as well, the FAHP (fellow of the AHP).

Although there are fund raising consultants operating without any of these credentials, they are usually in such a specialized field that the lack of the credential does not necessarily compromise the quality of their experience in their specialty. In any case, an organization seeking consulting advice should always inquire about the consultant's certifications.

Experience

The evaluation of a consultant's experience depends to some extent on the organization's activities and expectations and its needs for service. However, there are several types of information that are important to know. The amount of time the consultant or consulting firm has spent on charitable fund raising or related activities is very important. So are the types of organizations and communities where the experience was obtained and the positions, staff or executive, in which it was obtained. The amount of money raised relative to the budgets of previous client organizations is the best indicator of fund raising success. It will give an indication of the importance of charitable income to the organizations served and also of the teamwork and organizational attention required.

Operating Procedures

The candidate for consultancy should indicate compliance with applicable ethical codes of performance either in printed promotional materials or in direct conversation with the organization seeking help (see Chapter Thirty). Sometimes a consultant's recommendations may need to be challenged or some of the consulting firm's employees may not meet the client's expectations. Recourse options in the event of disagreements should therefore be agreed on in advance. As in any commercial commitment, both parties to the contract need to know what steps to take to legally end a contract before its expiration.

Materials and Intellectual Property

Many consultants have developed formats, templates, specific language, and other materials over which they feel a certain proprietary domain. In other cases, such materials are developed by the consultant while working under contract to a particular organization. Often ownership of these products may become the subject of misunderstanding and conflict. Consequently, upon entering into a consulting relationship with an adviser of this type, an organization should clarify ownership issues with respect to materials that are brought to the project or developed during its progress. When such agreements are clearly in place, they can become the basis of a mutually satisfying long-term relationship involving the future use of those materials.

Deliverables and Fees

Finally, and most important, the conversation with a consultant should reveal the fee structure and should specify exactly what the client expects the consultant to deliver, including the approximate time frame.

Many consultants base their fees on the amount of time they expect to need to deliver the desired results and set the contract accordingly, often simply calculating a per diem amount. Others build that fee into the overall contract price but do not set a daily rate; they may then establish a schedule of payments for portions of that total, which may be weekly, monthly, quarterly, or on some less regular schedule.

From the organization's perspective and in its best interests, the "deliverables"—what the consultant is expected to provide—are the main factor and should be clearly specified in any written contract. Most codes of ethics (see Chapter Thirty) state that it is improper for fund raisers and consultants to work for a percentage of fund raising income. The reason is that such incentives, which encourage consultants to subvert donor interests to their own, can cause long-term harm to organizational relationships and to philanthropy in general. Organizations should insist on flat fees for all types of fund raising activities— for example, number of calls made, number of pieces mailed, or daily and hourly rates that are competitive with other consultants or firms. (The AFP code of ethics is presented in Exhibit 30.1 in Chapter Thirty.)

In some of the more specialized areas of consulting services, the deliverables may be stated in units (for example, so many mailings of so many addresses, so many events of such an expected attendance, or an executive search over a certain period of time and required number of members of the candidate pool). In the case of capital campaign consultancies, there will be additional deliverables to explore and specify, depending on whether the organization seeks overall campaign management consulting or a monitoring style of consulting assistance.

Sometimes unavoidable circumstances arise that prevent the achievement of the deliverables through no failure of either party in a consulting arrangement. As unfortunate and disappointing as that may be, that eventuality should be discussed in advance and plans made to resolve such a situation without rancor.

Because the lack of clarity or mutual understanding regarding the deliverables in a consulting contract is one of the main sources of later disputes and disappointments, spelling out the expected results to the agreement of both the consultant and the organization is one of the most crucial elements in working with consultants.

GOOD WORKING RELATIONSHIPS

Even the best-planned, best-executed, and best-intentioned relationships between consultants and organizations can go awry. However, with early attention to some fundamental human relationship concepts, mistakes can be avoided.

The working relationship between client and consultant is a true partnership, with mutually desirable results to be achieved. A consultant's long-term success depends on your success. In hiring consultants, stress that partnership, and emphasize the cooperative nature of the work on the project. Mutual respect and common understandings are the fabric of that relationship. Checklists and periodic and planned communications at mutually agreeable intervals are a part of those understandings. The involvement of a good mix of staff, volunteers, and consultant sometimes provides opportunities for bad "chemistries" to develop. Vigilance is needed so that these can be spotted and avoided and opportunities for good personality mixes can be enhanced and maximized. A good relationship results from a combination of mutually held philosophies, common interests and attitudes, and mutually expected styles of operation. But ultimately, the agreement on expected results, activities, deliverables, and fees is the key ingredient to a positive working relationship.

CONCLUSION

Consultants are often a key ingredient in an organization's success. They should be considered as potential members of the fund raising team. Choosing consultants and learning through them to expand potentials and projections are among the most satisfying aspects of working with a nonprofit cause with an inspirational mission. Making it work doesn't have to be a major challenge. Managing consultant relationships based on the ideas presented here can help us meet the expectations we set and the full potential consultants represent for us.

PART SEVEN

ETHICS, STEWARDSHIP, AND THE FUTURE OF THE FUND RAISING PROFESSION

This final part of the book covers the ethical and professional aspects of achieving excellence in fund raising. Hank Rosso was committed to ethical philanthropic fund raising and enhancing professionalism among those engaged in fund raising.

This part opens with Chapter Thirty, dedicated to values and ethics applied to fund raising, and closes with Chapter Thirty-Four, dedicated to the materials and resources available to practitioners today. Both are intended to prepare fund raising executives to conduct themselves in a professional way, founded on both ethical and technical information and standards.

The three chapters in the middle are new to this edition. Stewardship was a concept central to the Rosso philosophy of fund raising, and like ethics, it permeated all that he wrote and said about the field. Chapter Thirty-One, "Practicing Stewardship," makes explicit the role of stewardship and accountability in achieving excellence in fund raising. The Rosso principles have been adapted and taught around the globe, and The Fund Raising School has established partners in a number of other countries. Chapter Thirty-Two provides a look at fund raising in a number of other cultures. Chapter Thirty-Three is devoted to the development of fund raising as a profession built on ethical and technical standards and the pursuit of a career in fund raising.

According to INDEPENDENT SECTOR (2002, p. 11), "Those who serve the public good must assume the public trust." Those who assume the public trust must hold themselves to a higher standard. Part Seven is about holding ourselves as fund raisers to the highest standard possible.

CHAPTER THIRTY

Ethical Frameworks
for Fund Raising

Eugene R. Tempel

Why do the actions of a few individuals affect so many? This is one of the key questions that resulted from a study of fund raisers in the United States (Duronio and Tempel, 1997). The answer to this question lies in public expectations of the nonprofit sector. We in the nonprofit sector are held to a higher level of trust than our colleagues in the for-profit sector. And the Association for Fundraising Professionals (AFP) code of ethics (see Exhibit 30.1) challenges its members to accept responsibility, not only for their own behavior but for the behavior of their institutions as well, in areas such as stewardship, accountability, and confidentiality.

As fund raising practitioners work toward professional status, both technical and ethical standards are essential. Most of this volume deals with the rationale for, and technical aspects of, fund raising. This chapter deals with the ethical aspects. The ethical practice of philanthropic fund raising is essential to both the continued development of philanthropy through increased public confidence and trust and the professionalization of fund raising as a field of practice.

THE ISSUE OF TRUST

Americans were experiencing a crisis of trust as the twentieth century drew to a close. Only 57 percent of those surveyed in a national study indicated that they trusted private higher education—and that was the highest level of trust

Exhibit 30.1. AFP Code of Ethics and Standards.

Association of Fundraising Professionals (AFP)
Code of Ethical Principles and Standards of Professional Practice

CODE OF ETHICAL PRINCIPLES

Adopted 1964; amended October 1999

The Association of Fundraising Professionals (AFP) exists to foster the development and growth of fundraising professionals and the profession, to promote high ethical standards in the fundraising profession and to preserve and enhance philanthropy and volunteerism.

Members of AFP are motivated by an inner drive to improve the quality of life through the causes they serve. They serve the ideal of philanthropy; are committed to the preservation and enhancement of volunteerism; and hold stewardship of these concepts as the overriding principle of their professional life. They recognize their responsibility to ensure that needed resources are vigorously and ethically sought and that the intent of the donor is honestly fulfilled. To these ends, AFP members embrace certain values that they strive to uphold in performing their responsibilities for generating charitable support.

AFP members aspire to:

- Practice their profession with integrity, honesty, truthfulness and adherence to the absolute obligation to safeguard the public trust.
- Act according to the highest standards and visions of their organization, profession and conscience.
- Put philanthropic mission above personal gain.
- Inspire others through their own sense of dedication and high purpose.
- Improve their professional knowledge and skills, so that their performance will better serve others.
- Demonstrate concern for the interests and well-being of individuals affected by their actions.
- Value the privacy, freedom of choice and interests of all those affected by their actions.
- Foster cultural diversity and pluralistic values, and treat all people with dignity and respect.
- Affirm, through personal giving, a commitment to philanthropy and its role in society.
- Adhere to the spirit as well as the letter of all applicable laws and regulations.
- Advocate within their organizations, adherence to all applicable laws and regulations.
- Avoid even the appearance of any criminal offense or professional misconduct.
- Bring credit to the fundraising profession by their public demeanor.
- Encourage colleagues to embrace and practice these ethical principles and standards of professional practice.
- Be aware of the codes of ethics promulgated by other professional organizations that serve philanthropy.

Exhibit 30.1. AFP Code of Ethics and Standards, Cont'd.

STANDARDS OF PROFESSIONAL PRACTICE

Furthermore, while striving to act according to the above values, AFP members agree to abide by the AFP Standards of Professional Practice, which are adopted and incorporated into the AFP Code of Ethical Principles. Violation of the Standards may subject the member to disciplinary sanctions, including expulsion, as provided in the AFP Ethics Enforcement Procedures.

Professional Obligations

1. Members shall not engage in activities that harm the members' organization, clients, or profession.
2. Members shall not engage in activities that conflict with their fiduciary, ethical, and legal obligations to their organizations and their clients.
3. Members shall effectively disclose all potential and actual conflicts of interest; such disclosure does not preclude or imply ethical impropriety.
4. Members shall not exploit any relationship with a donor, prospect, volunteer, or employee to the benefit of the members or the members' organizations.
5. Members shall comply with all applicable local, state, provincial, and federal civil and criminal laws.
6. Members recognize their individual boundaries of competence and are forthcoming and truthful about their professional experience and qualifications.

Solicitation and Use of Charitable Funds

7. Members shall take care to ensure that all solicitation materials are accurate and correctly reflect their organization's mission and use of solicited funds.
8. Members shall take care to ensure that donors receive informed, accurate, and ethical advice about the value and tax implications of potential gifts.
9. Members shall take care to ensure that contributions are used in accordance with donors' intentions.
10. Members shall take care to ensure proper stewardship of charitable contributions, including timely reports on the use and management of funds.
11. Members shall obtain explicit consent by the donor before altering the conditions of a gift.

Presentation of Information

12. Members shall not disclose privileged or confidential information to unauthorized parties.
13. Members shall adhere to the principle that all donor and prospect information created by, or on behalf of, an organization is the property of that organization and shall not be transferred or utilized except on behalf of that organization.

Exhibit 30.1. AFP Code of Ethics and Standards, Cont'd.

14. Members shall give donors the opportunity to have their names removed from lists that are sold to, rented to, or exchanged with other organizations.
15. Members shall, when stating fundraising results, use accurate and consistent accounting methods that conform to the appropriate guidelines adopted by the American Institute of Certified Public Accountants (AICPA) for the type of organization involved. (In countries outside of the United States, comparable authority should be utilized.)

Compensation

16. Members shall not accept compensation that is based on a percentage of charitable contributions; nor shall they accept finder's fees.
17. Members may accept performance-based compensation, such as bonuses, provided such bonuses are in accord with prevailing practices within the members' own organizations, and are not based on a percentage of charitable contributions.
18. Members shall not pay finder's fees, commissions or percentage compensation based on charitable contributions and shall take care to discourage their organizations from making such payments.

Source: Copyright © 2002 Association of Fundraising Professionals (AFP), all rights reserved. Reprinted with permission.

reported for any American institution. The number for health care was 39 percent and for private and community foundations, 31.6 percent. Only 15.8 percent of Americans indicated they trusted Congress (INDEPENDENT SECTOR, 1996).

INDEPENDENT SECTOR challenges those who work in the nonprofit sector: "Those who presume to serve the public good must assume the public trust" (2002, p. 11). Interestingly, trust in government has risen since the events of September 11, 2001. A study of college students indicated that 60 percent trusted the federal government to "do the right thing," compared to 36 percent a year earlier (Harvard University Institute of Politics, 2001).

The events of September 11, 2001, illustrate the role and scope of the nonprofit sector as well. And those events heightened the notion of accountability and trust as the media and the public called for reports on how funds were being distributed, critiqued major nonprofit organizations for not distributing funds quickly enough, and challenged the American Red Cross on its use of the monies collected for victims of the terrorist attacks.

The events that catch our attention today are similar to those outlined in the first edition of *Achieving Excellence* (Fogal, 1991, p. 265):

1. Fund raising can be accomplished less and less on a "business as usual" basis.

2. The challenge to many fund raising habits comes from changes in nonprofit organizations themselves, from changes in the public's assumptions about nonprofits, and from technological shifts in how fund raising is done.

3. Being responsive to changing circumstances and conditions leads nonprofit leaders and managers to consider moral issues that pertain to their organizations.

ETHICS AND PROFESSIONALISM

Ethics is one of the key elements in making a group of practitioners a profession. Robert F. Carbone (1989) evaluated fund raising according to six criteria commonly accepted as essential to a profession: (1) autonomy, (2) systematic knowledge, (3) self-regulation, (4) commitment and identification, (5) altruism and dedication to service, and (6) ethics and sanctions. Fund raisers are moving toward a profession, having made significant progress on these six criteria. The majority of fund raisers are committed both to their organizations and to their careers. Fund raisers are more generous with their resources and time than other citizens. Fund raisers are concerned about the ethical behavior of other fund raisers. And the AFP has in place a process for sanctioning members who violate the code of ethics (Duronio and Tempel, 1997).

A profession is built on the notion of service to others and the trust that comes from a commitment to place the interest of clients above self-interest. As a profession, fund raising must focus on serving the public good rather than attempt to define itself in terms related to other professions (Pribbenow, 2000). Service to the public good ensures trust. Trust is built on the practitioner's performance with both technical and ethical proficiency.

There is a larger knowledge base to help us develop proficiency in both arenas. Scholars have attempted to assist fund raisers facing ethical problems and dilemmas. This chapter is an expansion of Chapter Four in *Principles and Techniques of Fund Raising* (The Fund Raising School, 2002). Presented here is a framework for dealing with the ethical questions faced by fund raisers and their nonprofit organizations.

As fund raising executives, leaders, and managers, each of us has a responsibility to be informed and to think carefully and critically about the ethical standards and ethical issues that are essential to the health of the nonprofit sector and philanthropy. We must be able to teach colleagues and donors about ethical issues. These issues are critical to the nonprofit organizations that carry out the work of the sector and to the fund raisers who help those organizations acquire their resources.

There are standards, covered later in the chapter, that can help guide us in ethical practice. But most ethical issues are not as simple as a series of dos and don'ts that can be memorized and uniformly applied. Ethical issues require us to develop broad frameworks, principles through which appropriate choices can be made. Robert Payton, former director of the Center on Philanthropy at Indiana University, has said, "There are no ethical answers; there are only ethical questions" (1988, p. 74). Therefore, as practicing fund raisers aspiring to be professional in our work to enhance the public trust, we need to educate ourselves about the ethical questions in our profession so that we can make the best choices when confronted with them.

Ethical standards can help us initially decide on a number of issues that are clearly unethical. The code of ethics of the Association of Fundraising Professionals (see Exhibit 30.1) provides such guidance. So do the codes of the Association of Healthcare Philanthropy (see Exhibit 30.2), CASE, and others. They provide excellent foundations for ethical practice. But they will not provide all the answers. Most decisions are not as simple as following rules. Therefore, we must prepare ourselves to function in an ethical context, where concern for meeting public and professional expectations as fully as possible is always our primary focus.

Some years ago, when Robert Payton was still an executive with the Exxon Education Foundation, he asked fund raisers, "Do we live for philanthropy, or do we live off philanthropy?" Professional fund raising executives must keep this question before them constantly. Personal gain is the first vulnerable point of public trust. Section 501(3)(c) of the Internal Revenue Code, which provides for the establishment of nonprofit organizations, defines criteria for those eligible for charitable contributions:

> Corporations, and any community chest, fund or foundation, organized and operated exclusively for religious, charitable, scientific, testing for public safety, literary, or educational purposes, or for the prevention of cruelty to children or animals, no part of the net earnings of which inures to the benefit of any private shareholder or individual, no substantial part of the activities of which is carrying on propaganda, or otherwise attempting, to influence legislation, and which does not participate in, or intervene in (including the publishing or distributing of statements), any political campaign on behalf of any candidate for public office.

As fund raising executives, we must be cognizant especially of the "nondistribution" clause: "no part of the net earnings of which inures to the benefit of any private shareholder or individual."

The nondistribution clause requires nonprofit organizations and those associated with them to commit themselves to the public good. It is the foundation

Exhibit 30.2. AHP Statement of Professional Standards and Conduct.

AHP Statement of Professional Standards and Conduct

All members shall comply with the Association's Statement of Professional Standards and Conduct.

Association for Healthcare Philanthropy members represent to the public, by personal example and conduct, both their employer and their profession. They have, therefore, a duty to faithfully adhere to the highest standards and conduct in:

- Their promotion of the merits of their institutions and of excellence in health care generally, providing community leadership in cooperation with health, educational, cultural, and other organizations;
- Their words and actions, embodying respect for truth, honesty, fairness, free inquiry, and the opinions of others, treating all with equality and dignity;
- Their respect for all individuals without regard to race, color, sex, creed, ethnic or national identity, handicap, or age;
- Their commitment to strive to increase professional and personal skills for improved service to their donors and institutions, to encourage and actively participate in career development for themselves and others whose roles include support for resource development functions, and to share freely their knowledge and experience with others as appropriate;
- Their continuing effort and energy to pursue new ideas and modifications to improve conditions for, and benefits to, donors and their institution;
- Their avoidance of activities that might damage the reputation of any donor, their institution, any other resource development professional or the profession as a whole, or themselves, and to give full credit for the ideas, words, or images originated by others;
- Their respect for the rights of privacy of others and the confidentiality of information gained in the pursuit of their professional duties;
- Their acceptance of a compensation method freely agreed upon and based on their institution's usual and customary compensation guidelines which have been established and approved for general institutional use while always remembering that: any compensation agreement should fully reflect the standards of professional conduct; and antitrust laws in the United States prohibit limitation on compensation methods.
- Their respect for the law and professional ethics as a standard of personal conduct, with full adherence to the policies and procedures of their institution;
- Their pledge to adhere to this Statement of Professional Standards and Conduct, and to encourage others to join them in observance of its guidelines.

for the establishment of trust between donors and organizations. As professional fund raising executives, we have a legal and ethical responsibility to make certain that we, and all others associated with our organizations, do not benefit personally from the funds that are contributed to the organization.

This does not mean we should not be paid fairly and equitably for our work. It does mean that we do not accept commissions on gifts. It does mean that we do not accept personal gifts from donors. It does mean that salaries must be commensurate with public expectations. It does mean that board members should not have competitive advantage in bidding for business with the organization. So important is the nondistribution clause to the issue of trust that associations representing professionals and organizations in the nonprofit sector worked together to pass legislation known as "intermediate sanctions" to aid the sector in its self-regulation and to provide the IRS with penalties it can impose for excessive benefit and inside dealing (INDEPENDENT SECTOR, 1998).

What distinguishes the professional from the technician may be trustworthiness. The professional is conscientious about putting the interests of the client first. Because we work on behalf of nonprofit organizations, we must be faithful to their missions. We must earn the trust of the organizations that employ us. Finally, we have an obligation to understand the larger mission of the nonprofit sector, to understand the role of philanthropy generally, not just our own organization, because the donor and the organization function in the larger environment of the nonprofit or philanthropic sector. Understanding the mission of the sector helps us view philanthropy from the donor's perspective. Increasingly, fund raisers will be called on to assist donors with philanthropy in ways other than to their own organizations (Tempel and Beem, 2002).

These issues of professionalism raise such broad questions as the following (The Fund Raising School, 2002):

- What is the role of trust in our development as fund raising professionals?
- What are the burdens placed on us as fund raising practitioners by the "nondistribution clause" in Section 501(c)(3) of the code?
- As fund raising practitioners, who is our client: the donor or the organization?
- In every transaction, what are the intents of the donor and what are the intents of the organization?
- How can we, as fund raising professionals, protect and maintain our integrity as "boundary spanners" between donors and organizations?
- How do we manage the tensions that arise as fund raisers working for organizations assist donors expand their philanthropy?

APPROACHES TO ETHICS

In some circumstances, these and other questions are easy to answer because there is a clear-cut best choice. But when there is conflict between two goods or the appearance of conflict between two goods, the questions become more difficult to answer, as in the typical tainted-money questions: If money obtained under less than honorable circumstances is offered for your worthy cause, should it be accepted? Does accepting it compromise your organization's integrity while it provides some public good? Does accepting it add legitimacy to the source of the money? Does denying it enhance your organization's integrity while denying fulfillment of some public need?

Payton's statement that there are only ethical questions echoes a number of other writers, including Josephson (2002), Anderson (1996), and Fischer (2000), who agree that ethics in fund raising is complex. Philosophers like Kant suggested that there were, in fact, right answers. But Kant's categorical imperative suggests that ethical theories and dilemmas are often difficult to assess at the level of practice.

Anderson (1996) refers to this approach as *formalism*. And formalism will take us a certain distance. In fact, some ethical matters can be decided based on minimum standards such as codes of ethics. But those situations in which there are competing goods require a more complex decision-making process. Both Josephson (2002) and Anderson (1996) refer to this as *consequentialism*. The question for fund raisers is, "What will be best for the greatest number of constituents in the long run?" The ethical conflicts we face as fund raisers can be reconciled through sets of values, beliefs, and commitments against which we can judge our actions.

What lies behind ethics? A set of values and beliefs that lead us to trust the decisions that are made, that lead us to form expectations about the actions of others. The Josephson Institute has surveyed more than ten thousand individuals to define the values that are important to an ethical or virtuous person. *Making Ethical Decisions* (Josephson, 2002) is grounded in the advocacy of ten major ethical values that form the basis for ethical decision making. Josephson's ten values are as follows:

1. Honesty
2. Integrity
3. Promise-keeping
4. Loyalty (fidelity)
5. Fairness

6. Concern for others

7. Respect for others

8. Law-abidingness and civic duty

9. Pursuit of excellence

10. Personal accountability

Anderson (1996) developed a similar list:

1. Respect
   - Individual autonomy
   - Personal privacy
   - Nonmaleficence

2. Beneficence
   - Public good
   - Charitable intent

3. Trust
   - Truth-telling
   - Promise-keeping
   - Accountability
   - Fairness
   - Fidelity of purpose

INDEPENDENT SECTOR (2002) outlined nine commitments that mirror the ethical values listed by Anderson and Josephson. These commitments are proposed as essential to those who are associated with the nonprofit and philanthropic sectors.

1. *Commitment beyond self* is at the core of a civil society.

2. *Obedience to the laws,* including those governing tax-exempt philanthropic and voluntary organizations, is a fundamental responsibility of stewardship.

3. *Commitment beyond the law,* to obedience to the unenforceable, is the higher obligation of leaders of philanthropic and voluntary organizations.

4. *Commitment to the public good* requires those who presume to serve the public good to assume a public trust.

5. *Respect for the worth and dignity of individuals* is a special leadership responsibility of philanthropic and voluntary organizations.

6. *Tolerance, diversity, and social justice* reflect the independent sector's rich heritage and the essential protections afforded it.

7. *Accountability to the public* is a fundamental responsibility of public benefit organizations.

8. *Openness and honesty* in reporting, fund raising, and relationships with all constituencies are essential behaviors for organizations that seek and use public or private funds and purport to serve public purposes.

9. *Responsible stewardship of resources* is a concomitant of public trust.

INDEPENDENT SECTOR (2002) proposes that all of us working in nonprofit, public benefit organizations must integrate these nine commitments directly into our work. This certainly holds true for fund raising.

These values and commitments apply to our behavior as fund raisers and to the various codes of ethics we include in the exhibits accompanying this chapter. In fact, when Peg Duronio asked participants in her study of fund raisers what they admired most about their ideal colleague, the overwhelming response was "integrity" (Duronio and Tempel, 1997).

We must be honest in our dealings with donors and organizations. Our behavior must be dependable. We must be true to our word. And to earn integrity, we must carry out our work in ways that represent our organizations and our colleagues best. We must keep the promises we make to donors when we accept gifts. We must be loyal to both the organization and the donor. Our negotiations must be fair to both the organization and the donor. We must demonstrate concern for the donor as an individual or entity and have genuine respect for donors rather than envy their resources or view them as objects to be manipulated for our gain.

We must not only abide by the laws but demonstrate our own civic and philanthropic responsibility as well. We have a responsibility to be the best that we can be as professionals in carrying out our work. And we must be personally accountable for our actions and the actions of our clients. Although we can agree to the set of obligations that Josephson's values promote, it is conflict among these values that requires complex decision making.

ETHICAL DILEMMAS

What does the professional fund raiser do (the matter of personal accountability) when the organization (loyalty-fidelity) decides to use funds given for one purpose by a donor (promise-keeping, integrity, honesty) for another purpose? Josephson (2002) recommends three steps for considering ethical conflicts:

1. All decisions must take into account and reflect a concern for the interests and well-being of all shareholders.

2. Ethical values and principles *always* take precedence over nonethical ones.

3. It is ethically proper to violate an ethical principle only when it is *clearly necessary to advance another true ethical principle, which according to the decision maker's conscience, will produce the greatest balance of good in the long run.*

Fischer (2000) has outlined a similar approach. She poses questions around three broad themes: organizational mission, relationships, and personal integrity.

INDEPENDENT SECTOR (2002) outlines three tiers of actions. First, some actions are clearly illegal. Our decisions about these are very clear. Second, some things are clearly unethical. Decisions about these actions are also fairly easy to make using codes of ethics. Third, there are what INDEPENDENT SECTOR calls *ethical dilemmas.* Decisions about ethical dilemmas resemble Josephson's model and Anderson's discussion where there are competing goods or conflicting values.

INDEPENDENT SECTOR (2002) recommends evaluating these choices in terms of the commitments beyond self. It provides examples of actions involving all three levels:

- *Example of an illegal act:* The organization's copying and fax machines are used routinely by a friendly candidate for public office. Why is this illegal?
- *Example of an unethical behavior:* In lieu of salary, the staff director prefers receiving a percentage of all funds raised. Why is this unethical?
- *Example of an ethical dilemma:* The all-volunteer organization recognizes that hiring its first executive director will absorb all the money on hand and in sight. Half of the board argues that all the time and money will go to support the position with nothing left for programs, and the other half says it's a necessary investment in future growth. What should the organization do?

Josephson's model provides a framework for getting to a best answer to the ethical dilemma. The problem posed is much like a choice that fund raising executives confront on an annual basis. On one hand, a new investment in fund raising leaves less money for programs. On the other hand, new investments in fund raising eventually produce additional dollars for programs. Under what circumstances does the future potential outweigh the current loss? What other ethical values come into play when this decision is made? Who are the key stakeholders?

APPLYING ETHICS IN FUND RAISING

Robert Payton designed an ethics cube to outline the categories of ethical dilemmas that fund raisers face. The top of the ethics cube bears the word "Individual" (here meaning the fund raiser), and the bottom is inscribed "Organization."

The four sides of the cube are labeled "Competence," "Language," "Relations," and "Mission."

The Individual and the Organization

The first ethical tension that fund raising executives must mediate is the potential conflict between themselves as individuals and the organization. Fund raising executives must examine their motives constantly to make certain that they are not acting in their own self-interest but rather in the interest of the organization.

At the same time, fund raising executives have a right to expect the organization to treat them as professionals. Issues of compensation, for example, arise from this tension. Fund raising executives have a right to expect fair and adequate compensation, in line with what others in the organization and in similar organizations are paid. But fund raising executives should not accept percentage compensation because it focuses their work on personal gain rather than on organizational benefit.

Another tension arises when fund raisers face the question "Who is the client?" Is the organization our client, or is the donor our client? We must protect the interests of both. This heightens the tension between the fund raiser as an individual and the organization that is the employer, a tension, as indicated earlier, that is likely to increase as time goes on.

The client question is a serious one. Mediating between the donor and the organization is the most difficult role the fund raising executive must play. Grounding oneself in ethical values and understanding the tensions that accompany this relationship are important steps in becoming a fund raising professional. We can best prepare ourselves by understanding that both the donor and the organization have rights and interests. We must first understand the boundaries, the parameters of the organization. We must also understand the boundaries of donors in general and the particular boundaries and interests of particular donors. Being honest with both the organization and the donor is the first step in mediating the interest of our organizations and our donors. Maintaining integrity and keeping promises are not possible without honesty about what is possible.

Competence

The concept of competence also applies to us as fund raising executives. If we are to be professionals, we must dedicate ourselves to being as competent as we can possibly be. What are the ethical and technical standards that we must learn and implement to become competent professionals? Training to develop technical standards and academic study to help us develop technical expertise are important. However, we must also understand ethical standards, develop ethical values, and apply standards and ethical values to decision making about ethical dilemmas in fund raising. The concept of competence relates to both Josephson's values and INDEPENDENT SECTOR's commitments. Josephson's values of law-abidingness and civic duty, pursuit of excellence, and personal accountability apply here. The INDEPENDENT SECTOR values of obedience of the law, commitment beyond the law, accountability to the public, commitment to the public good, and prudent application of resources apply here.

Language

Language is an important aspect of fund raising. The way we talk about our profession and the way we discuss the process of fund raising and philanthropy from individuals, corporations, foundations, and others are important to the dignity of our career processes. We do not refer to donors as "targets." We do not refer to the dignified process of inviting people to make gifts as "hitting them up." The materials we develop about our organization must also reflect the mission, intentions, and purposes of the organization. We do not use case materials to respond to donor interest with no intention of fulfilling donor interest once the gift is received. The Josephson Institute values of honesty and integrity are appropriate to the concept of language. The INDEPENDENT SECTOR commitment to openness and honesty applies to ethics in language.

Relationships

The fund raising process is about building relationships. One of the key questions for a fund raising executive is "Who owns the relationship?" We must remember that the relationship we have with the donor exists only because of the organization. The organization owns the relationship. We must ask ourselves constantly who benefits from the relationship. The benefits should accrue only to the organization. The role of trust is also important here. The donor must be able to trust that the fund raising executive will not benefit personally from the relationship. The organization must also be able to trust that the relationship will remain with the organization if the executive leaves.

The Josephson Institute values of promise-keeping, loyalty and fidelity, fairness, concern for others, and respect for others help us create an ethics of relationships. The INDEPENDENT SECTOR commitments of respect for the worth and dignity of individuals and a commitment to tolerance and diversity and social justice help us understand the ethics of relationships. The Rosso phrase often cited in this book, "Fund raising is the servant of philanthropy," applies here.

Mission

Fund raising begins with mission. Every organization has a responsibility to understand its rationale for existence as a nonprofit organization. We as fund raising executives must understand that mission and use mission as the means for bringing individuals, corporations, foundations, and others together with the organization based on mutual values and interests. Mission is directed to client needs. Mission is based on the public good. We have a responsibility to help organizations be true to their missions. All fund raising must be based on mission. The Josephson Institute values of honesty and integrity are applicable here. INDEPENDENT SECTOR's commitment beyond self is an excellent measure for mission. Mission must be directed externally beyond those who are employed by the organization. INDEPENDENT SECTOR's commitment to the public good is the foundation for the concept of mission and provides a basis for forming an ethical understanding of our actions related to mission.

These six concepts provide a framework for bringing together the various aspects of ethical values introduced earlier in this chapter and applying them to the area of greatest tension for fund raisers.

This chapter opened with the notion that there are no ethical answers, only ethical questions. As fund raising professionals, we must develop an ability to make ethical decisions to solve ethical dilemmas. However, there are some starting points. Every profession must have a set of ethical standards about which there are no questions. As fund raising executives, we might belong to several professional associations that provide guidance. General codes of ethics are included in the documents featured as exhibits in this chapter. A starting point for all fund raising executives is the code of ethics and the standards of practice developed by the AFP. All AFP members are asked to subscribe to both.

Another useful perspective for fund raising executives is the Donor Bill of Rights (see Exhibit 30.3). We must remember that the relationships between donors and organizations create certain expectations. If we are to develop the public trust necessary to function as professionals, we must have a minimum set of standards that protect donor rights. To remind ourselves of the importance of respecting donors and our responsibilities to them, the AFP, CASE, the AHP, the AAFRC, and a number of other organizations have signed a commitment to the Donor Bill of Rights. The sponsoring organizations encourage you to copy the Donor Bill of Rights or to order additional copies from the AFP to distribute to others in your organization.

CONCLUSION

A recent *U.S. News and World Report* article described fund raising as a "dance of deceit," where fund raisers and donors are less than honest with each other (Streisand, 2001). Elliot (1991) provided guidance on the concept of deception as applied to fund raising. Avoiding deception means telling the whole truth and not allowing either party to reach a conclusion because of something that has gone unsaid. The image of a "dance of deceit" calls for an ethical response by fund raisers and their organizations. It also calls for fund raisers to educate others about the values that motivate philanthropy.

Exhibit 30.3. Donor Bill of Rights.

Donor Bill of Rights

Philanthropy is based on voluntary action for the common good. It is a tradition of giving and sharing that is primary to the quality of life. To ensure that philanthropy merits the respect and trust of the general public, and that donors and prospective donors can have full confidence in the nonprofit organizations and causes they are asked to support, we declare that all donors have these rights: .

I. To be informed of the organization's mission, of the way the organization intends to use donated resources, and of its capacity to use donations effectively for their intended purposes.

II. To be informed of the identity of those serving on the organization's governing board, and to expect the board to exercise prudent judgment in its stewardship responsibilities.

III. To have access to the organization's most recent financial statements.

IV. To be assured their gifts will be used for the purposes for which they were given.

V. To receive appropriate acknowledgement and recognition.

VI. To be assured that information about their donation is handled with respect and with confidentiality to the extent provided by law.

VII. To expect that all relationships with individuals representing organizations of interest to the donor will be professional in nature.

VIII. To be informed whether those seeking donations are volunteers, employees of the organization or hired solicitors.

IX. To have the opportunity for their names to be deleted from mailing lists that an organization may intend to share.

X. To feel free to ask questions when making a donation and to receive prompt, truthful and forthright answers.

Transparency is the beginning of ethical behavior. Transparency means that organizations open their private organizational processes to public view because they serve the public good, and hence they must accept responsibility for the public trust. Transparency will create larger public involvement, better public understanding, and enhanced public trust.

CHAPTER THIRTY-ONE

Practicing Stewardship

Daniel Conway

Hank Rosso had a clear vision of what stewardship means and "where it fits" in the fund raising process. This chapter on stewardship is based largely on *Rosso on Fund Raising* (Rosso, 1996) and on an interview I conducted with Hank published in *New Directions for Philanthropic Fundraising* (Conway, 1997). Hank described stewardship as "a sacred trust" that voluntary organizations accept whenever they place themselves in positions of responsibility for the public good. "Organizations demonstrate that they are good stewards by being responsible for what they are doing, for their philanthropic mission" (p. 7).

Hank's personal understanding of stewardship was clearly present in his teaching (and in some of his writing), but for some reason it never made its way into the first edition of *Achieving Excellence in Fund Raising* or into The Fund Raising School's curriculum. I did have the privilege of interviewing Hank on stewardship and fund raising, as noted, and of teaching with him on more than two dozen occasions when he was invited to share his understanding of stewardship with representatives of Catholic parishes in Indiana and Kentucky. As a result, I believe that I have a good understanding of Hank Rosso's perspective on the role that stewardship plays in philanthropic fund raising. The following reflections on stewardship, gratitude, accountability, and "making a difference in our world" represent my sincere attempt to convey Hank's teaching in this critically important area of the practice of professional, ethical fund raising.

DEFINITIONS OF STEWARDSHIP

Merriam-Webster's Collegiate Dictionary defines *stewardship* as "the careful and responsible management of something entrusted to one's care." This definition is a good beginning. It identifies the two essential components of stewardship: the concept of being responsible for something of value (nurturing or caring for it) and the recognition that what is cared for actually belongs to someone other than the caretaker (the manager or steward). We can understand stewardship, then, as *being responsible for something valuable on behalf of someone who has entrusted it to our care.* This is not a bad way to begin thinking about the stewardship responsibility that voluntary organizations have for the resources entrusted to them.

Stewardship is not simply a series of management functions (gift acknowledgment, donor recognition, prudent investment, careful accounting, and many other activities related to the fund raising process). It is all of these things, of course, but also much more. Stewardship implies an even deeper burden of trust, responsibility, and accountability. It speaks to the heart of what philanthropy is, and hence it is a profound expression of the shared responsibility that individuals and organizations have to contribute to the common good. Trust and responsibility are essential components of good stewardship. They are also indispensable to the concept of ethical fund raising.

Deep in the soul of any organization that wishes to practice stewardship there must be a profound awareness that the gifts it receives are to be held in trust for the public good. This is what prompts ethical organizations to acknowledge gifts and to be accountable for their use. As agents of the public good, nonprofit organizations have a special obligation to use wisely and accountably all the resources entrusted to their care. Serious regard for this trust is the soul of stewardship.

THE SOUL OF STEWARDSHIP

If stewardship is the careful and responsible management of something entrusted to one's care by others, the "soul of stewardship" is found in the way this management for others is exercised.

Organizations that seek to demonstrate that they are good stewards should clearly reflect the understanding that they are servants of the public trust who must be responsible and accountable in carrying out this trust.

Organizations that demonstrate a profound respect for the public trust, as a constitutive element of their philanthropic mission, willingly demonstrate their good stewardship. They become good stewards because of the transparent and accountable ways that they carry out their missions and because of the prudent and responsible ways that they use the human, physical, and financial resources entrusted to their care.

No organization ever perfectly realizes its objectives, but more often than not, those organizations that have a keen sense of stewardship (or trusteeship) remain remarkably close to their carefully stated mission and goals.

Today, all nonprofit organizations are challenged to demonstrate that they are good stewards of the public trust by carefully identifying their mission and objectives and by developing policies, programs, and procedures that are transparent to all. As Hank pointed out, "If we accept the philosophy that stewardship flows from our common value system, then it is clear that ethical fundraising simply surfaces these values and illuminates them" (Conway, 1997, p. 13).

SAYING THANK YOU

A profound awareness of the "sacred trust" that nonprofits have accepted on behalf of the public good is what prompts organizations to acknowledge gifts. Saying thank you is not simply a reflection of good manners or a technique for renewing and upgrading gifts. It is a recognition that individuals, corporations, and foundations who invest in the mission and objectives of a nonprofit organization are contributing something important to the fabric of society. Gift acknowledgment goes far beyond being polite or cultivating relationships for future giving. It is a recognition of the solidarity that exists between the donor and the organization in carrying out a philanthropic mission that is also a public trust.

Most nonprofit organizations readily accept their responsibility for gift acknowledgment, but there is a danger in seeing this as merely an administrative function routinely carried out by an efficient development office. Saying thank you—even in simple ways—is often the most profound opportunity an organization has to communicate with people who have freely chosen to share in its philanthropic mission. Gratitude is a powerful and engaging emotion. When it is expressed genuinely, from the heart, it creates a strong bond between the organization and the donor being thanked.

Gratitude works wonders at tearing down the walls that separate people from one another. In fact, it is frequently contagious. Charles Dickens's classic story, *A Christmas Carol,* dramatically illustrates the power of gratitude. After Scrooge has been visited by ghosts on Christmas Eve and has had a change of heart, he encounters one of the fund raisers he rudely dismissed the day before.

Here is how Dickens portrays the relationship between gratitude and giving:

> "My dear sir," said Scrooge, quickening his pace, and taking the old gentleman by both his hands. . . .
> "Mr. Scrooge?"

> "Yes," said Scrooge. "That is my name, and I fear it may not be pleasant to you. Allow me to ask your pardon. And will you have the goodness"—here Scrooge whispered in his ear.
>
> "Lord bless me!" cried the gentleman as if his breath were taken away. "My dear Mr. Scrooge, are you serious?"
>
> "If you please," said Scrooge. "Not a farthing less. A great many back-payments are included in it, I assure you. Will you do me that favour?"
>
> "My dear sir," said the other, shaking hands with him. "I don't know what to say to such munifi—"
>
> "Don't say anything, please," retorted Scrooge. "Come and see me. Will you come and see me?"
>
> "I will!" cried the old gentleman. And it was clear he meant to do it.
>
> "Thank'ee," said Scrooge. "I am much obliged to you. I thank you fifty times. Bless you!"

Scrooge whispers into the gentleman's ear a pledge amount that is so staggering that the solicitor is barely able to express his thanks. Then Scrooge, who only the day before was a lonely and self-centered miser, further confounds the gentleman by expressing his own gratitude for the privilege of giving in this way!

A genuine word of thanks from a nonprofit organization often provokes an even stronger expression of gratitude on the part of the donor. As Dickens illustrated so beautifully, people who give from the heart are grateful for the opportunity.

Hank said, "This is true philanthropy, giving with joy in our hearts. Whenever we urge prospective donors to give from the heart, we are teaching the joy of giving and the true meaning of stewardship" (Conway, 1997, p. 15).

How do we urge people to give from the heart? A heartfelt expression of thanks is an excellent way to start.

A GENUINE WORD OF THANKS

Organizational policies on gift acknowledgment and donor recognition too often take on the character of quid pro quo commercial transactions. For a gift at x level, the donor receives y acknowledgment or recognition. This makes practical sense, of course, but it runs the risk of reducing gratitude to a set of bureaucratic formulas. It gives a donor an empty feeling to receive a two-paragraph letter with a strained expression of gratitude for a gift.

In keeping with the profound awareness of public trust, which is the soul of stewardship, it is important to find ways to complement our formal gift acknowledgment and recognition programs (which are essential elements of good stewardship) with additional expressions of gratitude that are as personal and spontaneous as possible.

In a very real way, there is no substitute for simply picking up the phone, writing a brief note, or stopping by just to say thanks. If this is impossible because of the sheer number of donors, then the organization needs to work that much harder to find various ways of expressing thanks that are genuine, appropriate, and communicated as personally as possible.

Who is responsible for saying thank you to donors? Everyone (including board members, staff, and volunteers) should accept some responsibility for expressing the organization's gratitude to those who share in its philanthropic mission.

As Hank said, "The role of steward and its corresponding obligation of stewardship is seen to apply to any person in a sensitive position, anyone who can preserve or shatter the integrity of the entity serving the public good" (Rosso, 1996, p. 64).

Gratitude is such a powerful emotion that its absence or abuse can be a serious breach of stewardship and accountability. An organization that fails to express its thanks in genuine and appropriate ways disrespects the donor and runs the risk of "shattering" the organization's integrity—at least for this particular donor, but perhaps for an entire constituency as well.

How does an organization decide what is appropriate for the acknowledgment and recognition of its donors? Who should be responsible for expressing the organization's thanks?

Guidelines are available, of course, through professional associations and the common practice of nonprofit organizations. But these decisions must be taken seriously by everyone who is in a position to manage or account for financial resources: members of the board of directors, the chief executive officer, the financial officer, the development officer, and other members of the fund raising staff.

The sacred trust that is accepted along with an organization's philanthropic mission demands that gratitude be taken seriously. But it also requires that grateful acknowledgment and recognition be shared generously (in appropriate ways) with those who freely choose to invest in the organization's mission—for the sake of the public good.

BEING ACCOUNTABLE

Accountability, like gratitude, springs from an awareness of the sacred trust that is a constitutive element of a nonprofit organization's philanthropic mission. When an organization qualifies for tax-exempt status under state and federal laws, the governing board assumes the responsibility for overseeing that organization's philanthropic mission. The board also becomes publicly accountable for stewardship of the organization's resources.

Standards for public accountability include legal, ethical, and fiscal considerations. They also increasingly involve awareness of "best practices" for nonprofit organizations that have distinguished themselves in the stewardship of human, physical, and financial resources.

A statement endorsed in 1995 by the Association of Fundraising Professionals (AFP), formerly known as the National Society of Fund Raising Executives (NSFRE), titled *The Accountable Nonprofit Organization* (1995), outlines some of these best practices, which include the following:

- Acknowledgment of "a public trust to improve the quality of life"
- A clear statement of mission and purpose along with a description of societal needs, programs and services provided, costs, and benefits
- Free and accurate sharing of information about governance, finances, and operations as well as openness and inclusivity in programs, processes, and procedures
- Accountability "to all those it exists to serve, to all those who support it, and to society"

In addition, the AFP statement outlines four basic areas of responsibility that demonstrate accountability on the part of nonprofit organizations: mission fulfillment, leadership on behalf of the public interest, stewardship, and quality. It will be helpful to our understanding of stewardship and accountability to look carefully at each of these indicators of nonprofit responsibility.

MISSION

"Mission fulfillment" commits the nonprofit organization to integrity in carrying out its philanthropic purpose.

As discussed in Chapter Six, Hank challenged nonprofit organizations to achieve a better understanding of the precise nature of their philanthropic missions and to communicate that clearly to others. Clarity of purpose is essential to the concept of serving as a public trust. In fact, if you don't have a firm grasp of what your vision and mission are, it's very difficult to demonstrate that you can be responsible or depended on when it comes to the use of gifts entrusted to your care.

The AFP statement makes it clear that nonprofit organizations that wish to be accountable to their constituents, and to society as a whole, need to have a sense of mission that is dynamic rather than static. The nature of an organization's mission is such that it should not be subjected to complete revision on an annual (or even five-year) basis, but the mission of a nonprofit organization should not be forever carved in stone. It must be capable of real and effective change as the needs of individuals and society change.

LEADERSHIP

"Leadership on behalf of the public interest" is another way of saying that non-profit organizations are truly making a difference in the communities they serve. The AFP statement mentions several indicators of this leadership on behalf of the public interest, including enhancing social well-being; promoting "inclu-siveness, pluralism, and diversity"; and appropriate forms of education and advocacy.

No organization is ever perfect in its achievement of a public leadership role. But the acknowledgment that *nonprofit organizations are expected to make a difference* says a lot about our philanthropic tradition and the high expectations that are placed on organizations seeking to occupy positions of public trust.

How easy or difficult is it to decide whether an individual nonprofit organi-zation truly makes a difference? These are essentially subjective judgments, of course, but Hank suggested that appropriate assessments can be made—by mea-suring the organization's performance against its stated mission and objectives and by asking whether the organization's leaders (board, executive manage-ment, volunteers, and development staff) truly reflect an awareness of the sacred trust that Hank considered the "soul of stewardship."

MANAGEMENT

Stewardship as defined by the AFP is a narrower concept than the view pro-posed in this chapter and is perhaps better understood as "effective manage-ment," but the AFP concept does include some vitally important components of the public trust that is a constitutive element of stewardship: effective gov-ernance and management; responsible development and use of human, physi-cal, and financial resources; and the avoidance of conflicts of interest or abuses of power. Giving, receiving, and managing human and financial resources responsibly are all aspects of stewardship. They should flow from the organi-zation's deeper philanthropic mission and therefore be governed not simply by generally accepted management practices but, again, by a profound awareness of the public trust that is a fundamental principle of good stewardship.

This understanding of the proper exercise of governance and management, and of the appropriate development and use of the organization's resources, flows directly from the broader understanding of stewardship as a sacred trust.

Hank made reference to Cotton Mather's "Essay to Rich Men," written in 1710 (Rosso, 1996, p. 146). Mather's thesis is that God had conferred on rich men an obligation to use their management skills (as well as their time and money) wisely and responsibly for causes that serve the public good. Hank argued that the concepts Mather articulated nearly three centuries ago still speak to people of our time—women and men, rich and poor—and to all organizations that have voluntarily accepted responsibility for the public good.

Whether or not the word *stewardship* is used, the idea of stewardship, which defines both motives for giving and responsibility for the way gifts are used, continues to have a profound influence on American philanthropy.

QUALITY

Quality is the fourth characteristic of good stewardship identified in the AFP statement. The two indicators suggested here are striving for and achieving excellence in all aspects of the organization and evaluating the total organization and its outcomes on an ongoing basis.

Quality and organizational effectiveness can be assured only if a nonprofit organization maintains a clear and consistent focus on its philanthropic mission and on its responsibility to make a difference in the lives of individuals and society as a whole.

Quality programming, like so many aspects of good stewardship, comes from the recognition that what the organization seeks to accomplish is the advancement of humanity itself, the public good. Hank said that more often than not, nonprofit organizations whose leaders reflect a profound awareness of this sacred trust demonstrate that they want to commit themselves (and their organizations) to the highest standards of excellence. They also show themselves to be eager to evaluate their policies, programs, and procedures in order to ensure that high standards of quality are being maintained.

DONORS' RIGHTS

Throughout Hank's teaching on stewardship, there is a consistent implied message that the stewardship of nonprofit organizations is a matter of justice. Those who contribute to an organization's philanthropic mission, those who are the primary beneficiaries of the organization's programs and activities, and society at large have rights that must be respected by organizations that serve the public good. These rights have been endorsed by various professional organizations, including the American Association of Fund Raising Counsel (AAFRC), the Association for Healthcare Philanthropy (AHP), the Association of Fundraising

Professions (AFP), and the Council for Advancement and Support of Education (CASE).

The Donor Bill of Rights developed by these organizations (see Exhibit 30.3 in Chapter Thirty) lists ten things that donors have a right to expect from responsible and accountable nonprofit organizations. A careful look reveals that all ten are based on the premise that a relationship of trust must exist between nonprofit organizations and the people who are invited to participate in the tradition of giving and sharing, which the sponsoring organizations believe is essential to American philanthropy.

The expectations contained in the Donor Bill of Rights can be summarized as follows:

- Donors have a right to expect complete, accurate, and pertinent information on mission, programs, personnel, and finances.

- Donors have a right to expect that their gifts will be used for the purposes for which they were given and that they will be acknowledged appropriately (with due respect for the donors' right to privacy and confidentiality).

- Donors have a right to expect that nonprofit organizations will be professional, truthful, and fully accountable in their dealings with donors and the public at large.

The statement containing these rights emphasizes that their purpose is to ensure that philanthropy merits the respect and trust of the general public and that donors and prospective donors can have full confidence in the nonprofit organizations and causes they are asked to support.

JUSTICE

Hank's perspective on donors' rights is fully consistent with the desire to ensure that philanthropy merits the public's respect and trust. Organizations that seek to demonstrate that they are good stewards should clearly reflect the understanding that they are servants of the public trust who must be responsible and accountable in carrying out that trust. Nonprofit organizations have no claim to voluntary support apart from the trust relationship that exists between the organization and those who have invested in its philanthropic mission.

This is a justice issue that concerns far more than the relationship between nonprofit organizations and their current or prospective donors. If this sacred trust relationship is shattered or weakened by poor stewardship of nonprofit organizations, the entire tradition of American philanthropy is at risk. Good stewardship is a sine qua non not just of effective nonprofit management but of philanthropy itself.

Confidentiality is indispensable to the trust relationship that must exist between a nonprofit organization and its constituents. At a time when increasingly sophisticated technology makes it possible for institutions (and governments) to learn nearly everything there is to know about individuals, including their resources and their living and giving habits, we must espouse a very strict code of ethics for gathering and maintaining donor files.

"Maintaining good information files does not constitute an invasion of privacy as long as the files never contain anything that would embarrass the person should he or she inadvertently comes across any of the text. A good test is to pretend that the person named in the file is standing behind you, reading your words as you write. Will this person be offended by or annoyed with the data being recorded? *If the observer would be disturbed, the wrong information has been gathered, and it should never be recorded anywhere at any time"* (Rosso, 1996, p. 65; emphasis added).

Stewardship as an expression of public trust includes the powerful notion that professional, ethical fund raising supports and enhances an organization's ability to exercise good stewardship.

People who truly understand what stewardship is all about welcome the opportunities that fund raising offers. Fund raising is educating, teaching, nurturing, advising, and counseling donors. It is encouraging and assisting donors in their philanthropic and stewardship objectives. Integrity—that is, stewardship at work—is a guiding principle in helping donors invest their money with the assurance that their gifts will be used judiciously in serving the public good.

Much of this book is based on Hank's belief that fund raising professionals have a special role to play in teaching stewardship both within and outside their organizations.

We who are professional fund raisers need to see ourselves as people who teach the joy of giving and who give witness to the meaning of stewardship. This means helping the organizations we work for and the people we serve recognize genuine needs in the human family and respond to those needs by sharing their gifts in generous and responsible ways.

GIVING BACK

Hank Rosso's teachings on stewardship reflected his firm belief that individuals and organizations are called to develop their gifts and talents and then use them for the betterment of society.

Stewardship reminds us that what we have is not entirely ours—including our time, our talent, and our energy as well as our financial resources—and it challenges us to share our gifts with others. This profound sense of responsibility for the public good is based on the conviction that nonprofit organizations can only truly be successful when they are making a difference in the lives of individuals and in the communities being served.

People sometimes complain that fund raising can be intrusive because it challenges them to think about needs or problems that they might otherwise overlook. This is not entirely bad. We need to be reminded occasionally that our gifts were meant to be shared with others and that we are all responsible for the world in which we live and for the broader needs of the human family.

CONCLUSION: THE SPIRITUALITY OF STEWARDSHIP

Like so many of the concepts embedded in the American philanthropic tradition, stewardship as understood, practiced, and taught by Hank Rosso is indelibly marked with the language and imagery of spirituality. His insistence that individuals and organizations are called to give and share their gifts—for the greater good of the community—is complemented by his equally strong conviction that self-giving and striving to make a difference in the world lead to authentic happiness and to the successful implementation of an organization's philanthropic mission.

Quoting the Puritan leader John Winthrop, who taught his congregation to "delight in each other and make each individual's concern our concern," Hank observed that stewardship is essentially a spiritual concept that challenges individuals and organizations to look beyond their own needs and interests to the welfare of others.

Hank called this profound understanding of stewardship "the heart of philanthropy." It represents so much more than the rather restrictive definitions sometimes used in fund raising literature. Certainly, stewardship concerns the processes nonprofit organizations use to acknowledge gifts and recognize donors. Equally important to good stewardship are the policies that govern investment practices, financial and personnel management, and the honoring of donor intent. And without transparency and integrity in financial reporting and accountability, no voluntary organization can be called a good steward of its human, physical, and financial resources.

But Hank Rosso's teachings challenge fund raising professionals and the leaders of nonprofit organizations to look beyond the administrative details (as important as these are) to the heart of the matter.

Through the practice of stewardship, we learn to care for others and to be responsible for the world in which we live. Through professional fund raising, we reach out to one another with an open invitation and a firm challenge to be better stewards by sharing our gifts and by making the best possible use of our resources in order to build a better world.

Building a better world by accepting, nurturing, and sharing a profound sense of responsibility for the public good—that was Hank Rosso's vision of stewardship, the heart of philanthropy.

CHAPTER THIRTY-TWO

International Perspectives on Fund Raising

Lilya Wagner
Marcella Orvañanos de Rovzar
Ben Imdieke

Awareness of philanthropic traditions and the practice of fund raising are growing globally. Factors that have contributed to this over the past decade or so include the disintegration of the Soviet Union, technology that has facilitated the spread of knowledge and communication, governments that have been unable to keep up with even basic services to their populations, the global justice movement, and increasing knowledge of philanthropy and its effects on society. All these have supported the rapid development of nongovernmental organizations (NGOs) and civil society organizations (CSOs). The result has been a new and energetic interest in organizations that can be service providers while also acting as advocates for reform. These shifts have created great opportunities as well as the necessity for citizens to become engaged in their political, social, and cultural lives.

The significance of NGOs, philanthropy, and volunteerism in other nations, and the comparison of ideals and practices among nations, is valuable for the U.S. professional fund raiser to understand. International fund raising practices inform our own methods and process, while at the same time U.S. models provide a base for establishing and improving fund raising in other countries and cultures. As fund raising practitioners, we have an obligation to understand international NGOs and CSOs. Not only does it give us entrance into the collegial community of fund raising professionals all over the world, but understanding international diversity also helps us comprehend what is happening in the culturally diverse world inside our own borders. Although we in the

United States have perfected many fund raising techniques and have much to offer in terms of sharing our expertise, we also have much to learn. International understanding enriches the global community of fund raising practitioners; we are part of a global system.

An international team coordinated by Lester Salamon and Helmut Anheier has undertaken the task of explaining, evaluating, publicizing, and indigenizing the global nonprofit sector in Johns Hopkins University's Comparative Nonprofit Sector Project. The multiphase work, as reported in *Global Civil Society: Dimensions of the Nonprofit Sector* (Salamon and others, 1999), compared twenty-eight different countries, collaborated with approximately 150 local analysts, and consulted with more than three hundred sector leaders in a series of advisory committees. The study resulted in five major findings. First, the nonprofit sector constitutes a major economic force. Second, the nonprofit sector varies greatly in size among different countries and regions. Generally, the formal nonprofit sector is larger in developed countries than in developing nations. A surprise to many, however, was that the United States was not the home of the relatively largest nonprofit sector. In fact, it ranks fifth in nonprofit share of total employment, following the Netherlands, Ireland, Belgium, and Israel. Third, welfare services dominate the nonprofit sector. Two-thirds of all nonprofit employment is in education, health, and social services. Fourth, fees for service and public sector money are the two primary sources of income for nonprofit organizations. Regional variations correlate strongly with the Western European countries being for the most part publicly funded and both the more developed and the less developed countries being more reliant on fees for service. Variations in subsectors reveal that professional, cultural, developmental, philanthropic, and environmental organizations are more fee-dominant and health, education, social service, and civic organizations are more publicly funded. Fifth, the ability of the nonprofit sector to generate employment growth is not assured. Growth of the nonprofit sector outpaced the level of increase in private philanthropy. This challenges nonprofit fund raisers to reassert the value of charitable giving over the growing dominance of fees for services and government funding as the key forces in nonprofit organizations.

The range of international NGO development is impressive. According to the Social Information Agency in Russia, forty thousand nonprofit groups have formed in Russia since the disintegration of the Soviet Union (Gessen, 1997, p. 123). Countries such as Croatia, which has a long-standing tradition of nonprofit activity, are seeing a reemergence of arts and cultural societies and other traditional NGOs and also an increase in organizations that meet needs engendered by war. Charitable efforts in Turkey range back several centuries, when foundations were formed to care for specific causes. Now the face of the Turkish nonprofit sector includes educational institutions, cultural organizations, hospitals, and homes and programs for street children. Yugoslavia, now consisting of the two republics of Serbia and Montenegro, has seen tremendous growth in refugee causes, but other interests, such as environmental concerns, are also in evidence. In Argentina, while well-known organizations including the Red Cross, Greenpeace, and SOS Children's Villages are prevalent and active, many nonprofit causes, such as museums of Jewish history and organizations benefiting the Pampas Indians, are part of an NGO movement that began in the early 1980s. China began moving toward NGO ideals in the late 1980s when organizations such as science foundations were established.

Philanthropy is present in every culture around the globe. It is not an American invention. Likewise, every country has developed structures for organized fund raising. Often what those who contact The Fund Raising School seek is the structure for integrating fund raising into the administrative structure of nonprofit organizations and for building a total development program. The Fund Raising School was adapted and offered in international settings. The first adaptations were in New Zealand and Australia, with special sessions also offered in Ireland. By now, The Fund Raising School has been offered on every continent except Antarctica. International enrollments in U.S.-based sessions of The Fund Raising School have often led to international adaptations and offerings.

Many philanthropic fund raising principles are universally adaptable while at the same time they must be culturally and situationally appropriate. Both differences and similarities between the United States and various international fund raising models must be noted. Some concepts and principles of fund raising are universal and can easily be adapted, for example:

- The need and art of making a strong, compelling case for funding and expressing this case in differing ways to different markets are concepts understood everywhere.

- Donor motivations, when discussed as part of both training and practice, are surprisingly universal. Some differences do exist, but the desire to help others is often a motivation that can be aroused or tapped.

- International fund raisers understand the need to research and know the potential markets, the application of the exchange relationship in determining why a donor might give, and diversity in funding sources.

However, there are differences in principles and practice:

- The matter of professional compensation, such as working for a commission, is without ethical challenge in many cultures.

- Prospect research becomes difficult in some places because of lack of research resources and prevailing attitudes toward privacy.

- Board responsibility is uneven in many countries, and the idea of board members seeking funds is often an unacceptable or unwelcome concept.

- Tax deductibility and the concept of planned gifts do not exist in many nations.

We are part of a growing professional scene. Fund raising, whether accomplished by professional staff or volunteers, is increasing daily on a global scale. Our international colleagues embrace the need for and value of fund raising even while dealing with issues that U.S. practitioners rarely face. And they are coming up with solutions from which we can learn. U.S. professionals can be more competent by understanding the global perspective.

Fund raising as a profession is enriched by its proliferation and adaptation across nations and cultures, awareness of cultural issues, sensitivity toward differences, and the expression of a genuine appreciation of our international fund raising professionals' efforts and achievements.

This chapter provides an introduction to the state of fund raising practiced in selected countries around the world, chosen to reflect the partnerships developed by the Center on Philanthropy that have helped us understand the structures and the adaptability of U.S. models.

MEXICO

Marcella Orvañanos de Rovzar, founder, PROCURA, Mexico

In Mexico, nonprofit organizations have become increasingly complex, and the professionalization of the nonprofit sector has become necessary. This is a multidimensional process in which each of the players—boards of directors, advisers, staff, volunteers, donors, beneficiaries—understands the appropriate role and performs adequately. PROCURA, founded to help adapt the training of The Fund Raising School to Mexico, has played a major role in the professionalization of nonprofits.

Philanthropy in Latin America cannot be explained without an understanding of the influence of the Catholic Church. For example, Hernán Cortés granted the first endowment in Mexico, in 1524, to the Hospital de Jesus, which is still functioning. Yet organized and corporate philanthropy has been hampered by an antagonism between church and state, where there is a domineering, strong, and active church and a powerful, paternalistic, and benefactor state. The participation of the state in social welfare began in 1861, when the liberal government nationalized the church's property and thus assumed the responsibility of providing for the causes of the needy. At that time, Mexico was a mostly rural country; modernization came slowly, and discrepancies in the distribution of income were prevalent. Private groups were permitted to work in traditional institutions like orphanages, clinics, and schools. The consequence of having first the church and then the state provide for philanthropic causes resulted in weak citizen participation that favored paternalism and a lack of participation by the business sector. Everything was in the hands of the government. People became subjects and not citizens.

Since 1960, citizen participation in areas of social responsibility has been growing. Residents are increasingly aware of issues of community development, protection of human rights, environmental preservation, education, and democracy. By the mid-1980s, and particularly during the 1985 earthquake that shook Mexico City and other parts of the country, citizen participation increased, as did the need to organize the assistance received. Society became aware of its capacity to participate, to provide creativity and innovation, and to share opportunities for involvement with everyone.

Research carried out by PROCURA tells us that the growth of such organizations may be attributed to the substandard economic and political situations of the country, as well as to the growth of nongovernmental organizations at an international level. It is now publicly acknowledged that the level of well-being of the population is not the exclusive responsibility of the state governments and that citizen participation and shared responsibility are necessary.

The growing visibility of nonprofit organizations and the increased capacity of citizens to respond called for a new level of professional fund raising as well. PROCURA was founded to strengthen the nonprofit sector through training. It has adapted The Fund Raising School's materials to Mexico and has helped people understand that philanthropy and marketing improve the capabilities of nonprofit organizations.

An example of the change an organization undergoes when it understands the importance of professional fund raising is that of the Saint Theresa Sisters order, which was founded over a century ago. From its inception, this order has been receiving donations and school tuition fees to pay for its services, provided in eight schools and twelve centers where some fifteen thousand people are currently served. But it wasn't until 1994 that one of the sisters came in contact with Hank Rosso's methodology through PROCURA. After many meetings with the sisters, laypersons, and consultants, three questions were considered and answered: Why do we exist? What do we want to do? How are we going to do it? As a result, in 1999, an NGO called Educación Teresiana was born to organize the order's social work in Mexico.

Today, Educación Teresiana has increased the donations received by 450 percent. It is publishing a brochure that informs the Saint Theresa family at a national level about what is happening, has undertaken direct mail campaigns with excellent results, and has started a campaign to extend social work to other states. Educación Teresiana can foresee new challenges—to expand its board and the number of volunteer leaders involved, to strengthen its strategic planning, and to support the increasing interests and needs of its donors.

CANADA

Bill Hallett, Ph.D., ACFRE, vice president and chief development officer, Hospital for Sick Children, Canada

The federal government issues charitable business numbers (sometimes referred to as the charitable registration number) to all charities in Canada. Each province develops its own legislation that has an impact on the charitable sector. Of note is that Alberta in 1995 enacted legislation that includes the Association of Fundraising Professionals (AFP) standards of practice, except for the standard relating to commission-based fund raising.

Estimates indicate that there are over two hundred thousand nonprofit organizations in Canada. In 2000, it was reported that within the nonprofit sector, there are eighty thousand registered charities in Canada, an increase of 2.6 percent (from seventy-eight thousand) in 1999. Most of these charities are relatively small; only 7 percent of them have gross revenues in excess of $1 million. Canadian charities are designated as public foundations, private foundations, or charitable organizations. The Canada Customs and Revenue Agency classifies charities by their purpose; categories include health, social services and welfare, education and research, religion, benefits to the community, and culture and the arts. Many Canadians volunteer their time and skills or make donations to these charities to better the lives of other Canadians and improve Canadian communities.

Coincident with the signing of the Canada Volunteerism Initiative accord in December 2001 was an announcement of a five-year, $50 million federal government program to strengthen volunteerism. The federal government will also permanently fund the National Survey of Giving, Volunteering and Participating (NSGVP), as well as a new Statistics Canada satellite account on nonprofit institutions and volunteering. In 1997, Michael Hall and Laura Macpherson presented a report on Canada's charities. They estimated that $91 billion in revenues flows through Canadian charities from all sources. Some of the highlights from the Hall and Macpherson report are as follows:

- 56 percent of revenues go to hospitals and teaching institutions, which together account for only 5 percent of charities.
- 60 percent of revenues come from government grants and payments, 26 percent from earned income, and 14 percent from private giving.
- Saskatchewan has the most charities per capita of any province and the third-highest charity revenues per capita.
- Ontario's charitable sector has the largest revenues per capita.

- Newfoundland charities are more dependent on government revenues than charities in other provinces.

- Prince Edward Island charities are the least dependent on government and the most dependent on earned income.

- Alberta charities receive a greater percentage of revenues from private giving than charities in other provinces.

Fund raising in Canada uses the entire range of fund raising techniques, and the public is paying increased attention to the practice. The number of non-governmental organizations is rising; contributing factors have included the changing role of government and its financing of the NGO sector as well as the need to address previously buried problems, such as child abuse. Philanthropy has received increasing attention and has included the creation of the Canadian Centre for Philanthropy as well as active Association of Fundraising Professionals chapters.

ARGENTINA

Daniel Yoffe, executive director, CEDES/The Fund Raising School, Argentina

From the time of the Spanish conquistadors to Argentina's Declaration of Independence in 1810, the Catholic Church was the main provider of social welfare. The concepts of charity and spreading the faith guided all of the church's actions. The religious orders of the church organized educational and cultural programs and carried out projects to help the poor, beggars, and outcasts. The Jesuits, whose schools and universities produced the first volunteer organizations in Argentina, were the most visible example of this early philanthropy.

Donations, wills, and trusts given by members of the community served as early vehicles for the transfer of funds. The religious orders used these funds to create lay organizations involved in education and health care, which were managed by the congregations.

Christian charity in colonial times, called *filantropía señorial* (seignorial philanthropy), was made possible through the donations and inheritances of distinguished citizens and was founded in a belief in the religious superiority of the rich over the poor.

During the early nineteenth century, philanthropy in Argentina was characterized by strong institutional growth, an increase in government support, and significant contributions by individuals. However, a comparable increase in private resources was notably absent.

The tension between government involvement and the activities of independent philanthropic organizations grew as the state assumed unprecedented responsibility in the area of social welfare under the presidency of Juan Perón in the 1940s and 1950s. With the creation of the Eva Perón Foundation in the mid-1940s, the charitable sector's responsibility for social welfare was further reduced.

During the 1970s and 1980s, Argentina suffered a profound economic and social crisis. In addition, the brutal military dictatorship that was in power from 1976 to 1983 carried out a systematic campaign of kidnapping, torture, and murder. Under the dictatorship, civil society organizations polarized the country.

In 1983, a new democratic government inherited a huge external debt—equivalent to 55 percent of gross domestic product—and an economic crisis marked by hyperinflation that reached 803 percent in 1985. In the early 1990s, the administration of President Carlos Menem initiated sweeping economic reforms highlighted by a massive privatization program. Beginning in 1996, renewed confidence in the Argentine economy stimulated local and foreign investment. Fueled by this surge in investment—27 percent more than in previous years—GDP grew by 8.4 percent and inflation fell to 0.5 percent, making the Argentine economy one of the most dynamic and arguably the most reliable in South America. Privatization resulted in a disproportionate concentration of wealth in the hands of a few, leading to an unprecedented gap between rich and poor. In addition, the traditionally high standard of living enjoyed by the middle class has dropped precipitously, giving rise to a generation of "new poor."

In December 2001, a four-year recession exploded into the worst economic and institutional crisis of Argentina's history. The crisis has had grave social consequences: 43 percent of the nation's 36 million people are now below the poverty line.

Professional fund raising is relatively new in Argentina. In 1998, The Fund Raising School was inaugurated through an arrangement between El Centro de Estudios de Estado y Sociedad (CEDES) and the Center on Philanthropy. This program drew from the experience of The Fund Raising School in the United States. It also applied a series of cultural and methodological adjustments, responding to the necessities of local professionals, while respecting the fundamental principles that led to the creation of the school. The most visible and fastest-growing fund raising strategy involves direct marketing. Due to the notorious inefficiency of Argentina's postal service, some organizations have turned to other means of communication, such as radio, television, newspapers, and magazines. The combined strategy of inbound and outbound telemarketing along with use of the credit card as a form of payment has led to the creation of programs that allow for fund raising while raising public awareness of this new form of giving. The Fundación Sales (cancer investigation), UNICEF Argentina, and Greenpeace were pioneers in these types of campaigns, and their methods were promptly imitated by other organizations.

In a nation with widening social inequalities, the time came for businesses to assume new responsibilities. Together with the growing movement called For Social Responsibility, which first appeared in 1998, many nonprofit organizations began to experience successful fund raising through e-businesses. This new form of communication has made the action of both private companies and NGOs more visible.

Major fund raising campaigns and large donations have received relatively little public recognition due to the cultural peculiarities of Argentina. Large donors in Argentina prefer to keep a low profile, even more so during the recent economic recession. Unfortunately, the lack of information on donations has a negative effect, creating the perception that few resources are available and discouraging professional development in the field.

NEW ZEALAND

Dwyllis Brown, consultant, New Zealand

Only recently has professional fund raising been recognized and embraced by the nonprofit sector in New Zealand. Until the 1980s, the country was a comprehensive welfare state, providing health care, education, employment, and a high standard of living. The number of community and voluntary sector organizations has exploded since then, and in the past decade, they have been joined by schools, universities, and arts organizations seeking professional fund raising. Historically, there were 8,700 nonprofit organizations registered in 1960; the population at that time was 2.4 million. By 1990, there were 25,000 nonprofit organizations and a population of 3.4 million. Today, New Zealand has about 4 million people in a country the size of Great Britain and an estimated 40,000 to 60,000 nonprofit organizations.

New Zealanders are willing to support the many community organizations, but there are few major philanthropists. With corporate change now focusing on social responsibility of businesses, a new role model sees philanthropic trusts being established by some business leaders to give a "hand up" rather than a "handout." The New Zealand Association of Philanthropic Trusts is the only organization that has attempted to research giving patterns in New Zealand, and recent philanthropic trends it has noted are the growth of statutory trusts and the development of community foundations.

Sponsorship is significant in the support of sports teams such as the All Blacks or the America's Cup yacht race, but it is difficult to access these funds for the welfare sector. New Zealand fund raising differs from some countries in that there is very little tax incentive for donors and none at all for planned giving or payroll giving. This may be seen as an advantage in that people give because they truly want to support the cause.

The Fundraising Institute of New Zealand is the professional organization that promotes training and development of excellence in fund raising. In 2001, the institute celebrated its tenth year of existence and looked back on the milestones that have shaped it to this point and set the foundations for future fund raising. Individual membership in the Fundraising Institute is available at three levels (full, associate, and affiliate) throughout the country. Membership requires adopting and following the institute's code of ethics and conduct; members are encouraged to share knowledge with peers, and regular evaluation of fund raising is promoted through the granting of annual awards for excellence. Fund raisers in New Zealand are proud of the profession and give generously of their voluntary time to work on fund raising committees and educate, mentor, and nurture new members. The mission of the Fundraising Institute is as valid as ever—to encourage people to be philanthropic and for fund raisers to foster this response through honest, responsible, and respectful fund raising practices. We still have much to do in developing this culture of generosity, but the members of our younger generation give us hope as they support and work for causes they believe make a difference in this world.

EAST ASIA AND THE PHILIPPINES

Marianne G. Quebral, executive director, Venture for Fund Raising, Philippines

The Asian nonprofit sector has a rich and dynamic history of philanthropy, owing to the region's strong religious and cultural influences. Home to four of the world's major religions—Islam, Buddhism, Hinduism and Christianity—Asia's long-established value system has revolved around the concepts of merit-making, almsgiving, and performing charitable acts.

The pervasive influence of religion in the lives of Asians helped establish the infrastructure necessary for organized philanthropy. In Islam, for example, it is mandated that Muslims observe the *zakat* (or *zakah*) tradition—the obligation to pay a social donation amounting to 2.5 percent of one's annual income. To help Muslims fulfill this responsibility, the governments of predominantly Muslim countries such as Indonesia and Pakistan have created agencies dedicated to *zakat* collection.

Giving in Christianity, although not as organized as in Islam, is just as vigorous. In a recent survey conducted by Venture for Fund Raising (2001), it was discovered that a clear majority (ranging from 60 to 88 percent) of respondents from six major Philippine provinces gave to churches and religious institutions over a twelve-month period. Much of this giving is done in places of religious worship, with some Christians practicing *tithing,* the custom of giving 10 percent of one's earnings to a church or religious organization.

In other religions, philanthropy is practiced by giving voluntary contributions to the needy (*datra datrva* and *daanam parmrarth* in Hinduism, *thamtaan* in Buddhism), or giving for religious merit-making (*thambun* in Buddhism).

Traditional societies in Indonesia, India, and Nepal also espouse voluntary service (*seva* among Hindus) and mutual aid (*gotong royong* among Indonesians) as forms of philanthropy. Moreover, the cohesive extended-family structure of most traditional Asian communities, coupled with the Confucian value of filial piety, made it customary for individuals to assist family members and neighbors in need. For the early Asians, therefore, philanthropy became an act of service to one's family, rather than a random charitable act to a complete stranger.

Although philanthropy for religious purposes has existed in Asia for centuries, it is only quite recently that the region has witnessed significant changes leading to the rapid development of the Asian nonprofit sector.

A recently concluded seven-country research project (Asia Pacific Philanthropy Consortium, 2002) suggests that philanthropy remains vigorous today, and this may be interpreted by nonprofit organizations as support for their causes. Although giving to nonprofit (or voluntary) organizations has a long way to go in the region, it is clear that a market for individual giving does exist. This means that there is a large potential for nonprofit organizations to seek the support of individual givers. Before they begin fund raising, however, nonprofits must reassure the communities they serve and the public from whom they seek support of their legitimacy, transparency, and accountability.

Individual fund raising in Asia is still in its infancy, but is supported by recent developments in the nonprofit sector, such as the decline in official development assistance and the need for nonprofit organizations to diversify their funding sources. The region's cultural and religious histories lend a strong case for fund raising, as Asians are by tradition philanthropic. Of course, much giving will continue to be directed to religious causes and organizations, but nonsectarian nonprofits are now learning how to draw some of this generosity to their own causes.

One mechanism for promoting individual giving and fund raising is the establishment of a self-regulatory board, which assures the legitimacy, transparency, and accountability of nonprofit organizations. The Philippine Council for NGO Certification (PCNC) is the first organization of its kind in the region, but it is paving the way for other countries to establish their own peer accreditation and certification systems.

Another factor leading to the advancement of Asian fund raising is the broadening experience of nonprofit organizations in different fund raising methods. A recently concluded research project managed by Venture for Fund Raising (Asia Pacific Philanthropy Consortium, 2002) provided the results of an analysis of over one hundred case studies on local resource mobilization, offering differing views on the effectiveness of the fund raising methods employed in the region.

GERMANY AND CENTRAL EUROPE

Jens-Uwe Boettcher, fund raising consultant and educator, Germany

In central Europe, raising funds for worthy causes has its roots in the religious rites of ancient civilizations, particularly in the Catholic religious tradition. Before the First World War, philanthropic giving was held in high esteem by the German upper and upper middle classes. The founding of Goethe University at Frankfurt is probably the finest example of the philanthropic spirit of the time: by merging several older scientific research foundations and similar private institutions, creating new foundations dedicated to the promotion of higher education, and conducting intensive canvassing among the citizens of Frankfurt, approximately 20 million marks was raised (with considerable funding coming from the wealthy and well-educated Frankfurt Jewish community), so that in 1914, Goethe University opened by royal charter.

After the First World War, a welfare state mentality took over in Germany and Austria. The policy of government for the people but not by the people was continued by the communists in East Germany right up to German reunification in 1990. In recent years, people have increasingly had to face the fact that social security is not an infinite commodity that can be subscribed to at fixed rates. Governments are so heavily indebted at the federal, state, and municipal levels that they can no longer adequately support many of the social and cultural programs hitherto regarded as more or less irrevocable and eternal.

Many charities are now having to look for other sources of income, whether this ties in with their welfare state political thinking or not. The tide of public opinion has begun to change, slowly but irreversibly. The empty wallet has always been the most powerful engine for precipitating necessary change and development. Opposition to change is still stiff, though, especially among those nonprofit officials who are afraid that government grants they feel entitled to would be reduced if they succeeded in fund raising.

In spite of this seemingly prevalent public sentiment toward philanthropic giving, the few statistics available suggest that philanthropy is as robust as the enthusiasm suggests. There are an estimated 240,000 to 280,000 acknowledged charitable organizations in Germany. About 20,000 of them raise funds actively, and of these, perhaps 250 to 300 are known nationally. The most successful fund raising organization in Germany, the Hermann-Gmeiner-Fonds (SOS Children's Villages Foster Families' Fund), collected slightly more than 100 million euros in 2001. The German UNICEF Committee came in second with roughly 77 million euros.

The income generated by the major charities has grown very little over the past decade. The seventy-nine major charities that account for 25 percent of the philanthropic revenue market report that their increase in income barely covered inflation during this period. An exceptional year was 1999, when spontaneous donations to the emergency relief programs for earthquake victims in Turkey and the Kosovo refugees drove the statistics up to new heights. That year, 41 percent of the population claimed to have donated to charity within the last twelve months. In 2000, the figure had dropped back to 37 percent, but the following year it rose again to 40 percent. It seems, however, that donations were less per capita, because the major charities reported that their income was still stagnant.

In Anglo-Saxon countries, where philanthropic giving is regarded as a much more normal part of life than in central Europe, corporate giving is not yet seen to yield a truly sizable proportion of philanthropic revenue. In Germany and Austria, the opposite is the case. Because, as noted, people prefer to point to their heavy tax load instead of donating when asked to do so, there is a tendency, especially among small fund raising nonprofits, to seek corporate support first. Soliciting a major gift from a corporation seems much easier than attempting to get the support of thousands, tens of thousands, or even hundreds of thousands of reluctant individuals. But the major charities in Germany go the tried-and-true way: they solicit mass support and major gifts from corporate donors whom they are by now able to identify and address in a professional manner.

CONCLUSION

An international survey by the Center on Philanthropy (Imdieke, 2002) revealed some interesting findings. Many respondents commented that the philanthropic climate in their country is weak due either to suspicion and corruption or to an ideology that historically relied on the government to provide for social goods instead of the private sector. A number of others commented that the economic climate was not strong and that the philanthropic climate would improve as the economy strengthened.

A second observation is that technologies that prove successful in the United States remain largely unsuccessful elsewhere. Although planned giving, major gifts, and corporate and foundation strategies appear to achieve neutral (neither successful nor unsuccessful) results, direct mail, telephone solicitation, e-mail, and Internet strategies seem mildly unsuccessful among international fund raisers.

Most respondents have not yet incorporated the newest technologies into their fund raising strategies, although a majority say they plan to do so in the future. This is most notable in the case of e-mail. Although only one respondent reported using e-mail for fund raising, 70 percent of respondents said they planned on integrating an e-mail strategy with their fund raising plans in the future. In the case of the Internet, 45 percent of respondents said they planned on setting up Web sites to accept donations, thereby augmenting the 30 percent who have begun using Web technology.

Using e-mail and the Internet could prove to be very effective, since many of these respondents have international donor constituencies. Forty percent describe their constituents as global, versus 29 percent who claim to have strictly national donors. Another 29 percent of respondents had either local or regional donors. The remaining 2 percent had no donors. NGOs, especially in underresourced areas, might effectively reach out to donors in stronger economic regions as a way to generate philanthropic revenue.

This would fit with our respondents' sentiments about the global fund raising climate in comparison with their own. Although fund raisers are unhappy with the philanthropic climate in their own countries, they are more optimistic about the global philanthropic climate. If this anecdotal evidence reflects at least a partial trend in international fund raising, we face a tremendous task of building fund raising capacity, sharing technological insights, and improving the perception of the NGO and the nonprofit community worldwide. Increasing professionalism among fund raisers helps legitimate their activity and minimize corruption. Staff must have access to training and technical assistance, and more resources must be made available to build institutional capacity on a global scale. Hank Rosso's work has not ended. The need to improve the practice of philanthropy remains as great as ever in much of the world.

The Fund Raising School's role in improving fund raising practice globally is to be responsive to requests from international NGOs. When invited to present workshops, personnel approach the event as thoroughly prepared as possible, having studied the philanthropic climate in the country extending the invitation, learned the status and statistics of the nonprofit sector, and adapted principles to the local culture. The U.S. fund raising practices serve as a model. Just as practitioners in the United States are helped by The Fund Raising School's workshops in applying the principles to their own organizations, cultures, and geographical settings, international participants are assisted in doing the same because philanthropy is culture-specific and rooted in traditions and values. Yet in spite of differences in philanthropic traditions, Hank's fund raising principles continue to apply to NGO work in countries such as Turkey, Yugoslavia, Brazil, Thailand, Australia, and Austria.

CHAPTER THIRTY-THREE

Fund Raising
as a Profession

Alice Green Burnette

T his book is about applying technical and ethical standards to the fund raising process. Hank Rosso's work was dedicated to helping practitioners
achieve professional status. This chapter deals with the issues involved in
professional fund raising. Working "in a profession" and working "in a professional way" create tensions and opportunities for fund raisers.

When an individual works "in a profession," the profession normally has
several distinguishing characteristics. Specialized knowledge is required. Intensive and lengthy preparations and comprehensive examinations are expected;
in Chapter One of this book, Gene Tempel noted that the number of formal
degree programs might increase to four hundred by 2005 ("Building Bridges,"
2001). A sufficient number of people are working in the field, creating a critical mass. Each professional is expected to conform to a predefined and enforce-
able set of technical and ethical standards. Given certain parameters, fund
raising outcomes can be reasonably predicted. The professional expects to be
employed throughout a lifelong career. Many who have examined "the profession of fund raising" have concluded that it has not yet reached these standards
of definition (Bloland and Bornstein, 1991; Carbone, 1989; Duronio and Tempel,
1997; Tempel and Beem, 2002).

Additional complications emerge when work "in the profession of fund raising" is defined in terms of the successful and timely completion of the countless chores, checklists, jobs, assignments, and tasks that are legitimately
associated with and supportive of the raising of money.

Finally, underlying these definitional and operational challenges is the intense, passionate, cause-oriented energy that drives most solicitors. Until very recently, ardent and zealous belief in and commitment to organizational mission (versus performance-based compensation) were essential and paramount to a fund raiser's sense of professional (and personal) satisfaction.

This chapter examines several topics with a view toward establishing fund raising as a profession. In order to attract increased numbers of competent and committed people to the profession, we should better understand the motivations of those who are successful in it. To recruit and retain fund raising professionals, a more candid assessment is needed in matching institutional needs with individual expertise. The tasks of fund raising must be better unified in order for the overall profession to be strengthened. New types of relationships with donors should be developed. An agenda for the future should be promulgated in the context of the profession's historical strengths as well as its contemporary opportunities and obligations.

FUND RAISERS: WHO THEY ARE AND WHAT THEY DO

Even the most casual observers can quickly learn that fund raising practitioners are in great demand. It appears that every nonprofit organization wants one (or more). We continue to see dramatic growth in the number of such organizations. We see that public financial support is diminishing for those organizations, even as they are being asked to "do more." These pressures on nonprofits result in, among other things, increased employment opportunities for fund raisers who are too often perceived as "the solution" or, even worse, "the salvation."

It would be wise for these prospective employers to clarify their needs. A scan of position announcements in the professional media reveals that the *very same job* is being advertised in multiple locations. The people who are writing and placing those ads are not taking the time to assess their needs and focus in on the type of expertise that they want and can afford.

Hank Rosso (1996) described the three phases of development through which nonprofit organizations pass as they increase their capacity to attract more and more money. I have adapted from Hank's work in forming my own observations about the three phases of professional acumen through which fund raisers pass as they become increasingly more competent in their work.

The Beginning Phase

In the *beginning phase* of a fund raising program, staff members are limited in number, in experience, and in expertise. They subscribe to two or three professional publications that highlight the fund raising successes of others. They attend one or two conferences or workshops each year and return to their home institutions dazzled (and sometimes depressed) by the panoply of keynote speakers and panelists who made it all sound so logical and easy.

These beginning phase staff members are very loyal, work long hours, and are unusually verbal about how important their work is to the institution. They have some (unstated) difficulties in understanding the importance of stewardship.

They have a cheerleading quality that is directed more toward "friend raising" than fund raising. They have a propensity to produce, without proper amounts of volunteer support, special events that result in a degree of goodwill and a much lesser degree of net funds raised.

Unfortunately, few people within their institutions pay much attention to them, with the possible exception of the chief financial officer, who considers their activities an unproductive and unnecessary drain on the budget.

Interactions between beginning phase fund raisers and their CEOs are characterized by fear and are almost always initiated by the CEO. The CEO is often overheard saying, "I don't know why I have a development office. I'm the only one around here raising any money."

Members of the governing board might notice this beginning phase development officer around the far reaches of the room at board meetings, but other than social chitchat, they have scant professional one-on-one contact because all interactions with board members are through and by the CEO. There is no board development committee, or else it exists in name only; board members do not consider fund raising among their duties, and they were not recruited with that purpose in mind.

In terms of budgeting for fund raising, the CEO and the board have no motivation to provide increased resources because the beginning phase fund raiser and his or her operation is perceived to contribute little toward achieving the goals and objectives of the institution. And of course, the chief financial officer would certainly not entertain the slightest notion of a budget increase.

The Developing Phase

In the *developing phase* of an institution's fund raising program, a more experienced fund raising professional is at the helm. This person understands the tested principles and practices of the profession and does not need to rely on "nuggets" gleaned at two-day workshops.

The developing phase fund raiser is usually a well-organized team builder who convenes regular staff meetings during which colleagues go on at length about how busy they are in the performance of their numerous and time-consuming tasks. There is little discussion of how everyone's activities contribute to a comprehensive strategy. As a result, the immediate and the urgent overtake and ultimately overwhelm the important.

This developing phase fund raiser can supervise others to implement a multifaceted program, usually consisting of annual giving (direct mail), alumni relations (activities, *not* fund raising), government relations, corporate and foundation fund raising, public relations, publications, and a modest effort at individual donor cultivation and solicitation that is usually grounded in an annual "friends of the organization" special event.

There is a modicum of interest in estate planned giving, but technical expertise in this area is minimal; the "right now" needs of the institution do not allow much time (or budget) to be allocated to estate planned giving.

The stewardship function is important to this developing phase fund raiser. However, the emphasis is more on getting acknowledgment letters mailed "in a timely fashion" than on focusing on personalization of those letters in ways that address the needs and interests of donors. Significant budgetary resources are expended to support computer-based prospect research, gift and grant administration, and report generation.

This fund raiser has a substantial understanding of the role and impact of a communication program, resulting in an aggressive tendency to seek placements of op-ed pieces and feature articles (in addition to photographs) in local media, as well as obtaining electronic media coverage of special events.

The developing phase fund raiser is acquainted personally with several government, corporate, and foundation program officers. As a result, the CEO will listen to his or her ideas about fund raising. However, confidence is still not high in terms of successful solicitation of major gifts from individual donor prospects.

The developing phase fund raising professional provides staff support to a development committee of the governing board, under the ever-watchful eye of the CEO. The committee meets a few times a year, and the fund raiser *reports* on his or her activities, as opposed to engaging board members about how they, individually and collectively, can further the institution's fund raising program.

Budget increases for a developing phase fund raising organization are modest and are usually responses to a few, documented fund raising successes, as opposed to budget increases provided for the long haul in terms of investment in the organization. However, those successes do build confidence in the individual and in the program he or she is managing.

The developing phase fund raiser has the potential either to take the institution to the next level or to manage an ongoing, will-never-really-change operation. These people have an intellectual grounding in the principles of good fund raising. They understand the interrelationships among the program components that they supervise. To get to the next level, what is required of the developing phase staff member is to do that one most important thing: demonstrate an ability to secure—using proper fund raising techniques and in concert with a board member, a volunteer, or the CEO—a "major gift" for a "major purpose." Nothing talks like the money.

The Maturing Phase

In the *maturing phase* of a development organization, the fund raiser becomes the orchestra conductor. The board members, the CEO, and the staff create the symphony, and all these people understand their roles and their interdependence. The fund raiser is a master strategist who is universally trusted to guide all participants (board members, CEO, staff, and donors) in meeting their objectives.

The CEO is very reliant on this fund raiser's opinions and asks for them constantly, often on matters that may seem to have little to do with fund raising. The fund raiser has easy, direct, and as-required access to the CEO and feels free to make a wide range of decisions without consultation.

The maturing phase fund raiser spends most of his or her time in the search for new major and principal gift donors. This fund raiser relies on a sophisticated prospect research function, as well as on his or her personal knowledge of corporate and foundation presidents (not program officers) to uncover these possibilities. This fund raiser will travel with the CEO and with board members for cultivation and solicitation purposes and often socializes with them away from the office.

In the maturing phase of a development program, meetings of the development committee of the board are light on reports and heavy on strategy. The fund raiser guides committee members toward realizing the organization's core values, mission, goals, and objectives by suggesting fund raising roles for them to play, consistent with their interests, abilities, and contacts, all of which the maturing phase fund raiser knows very well.

The maturing phase fund raiser is nationally recognized for creating fund raising success at the institution. He or she is called on for speaking engagements at professional meetings (no doubt dazzling the beginning phase fund raisers) and may even provide consulting services on an occasional basis. This person often donates fees received for such services to the home institution, being sure to copy the CEO on a gift transmittal note written on personal stationary.

This fund raiser is confident that the operation will run smoothly in his or her absence. The staff members are competent, well paid, and working toward universally understood goals and objectives, knowing that excellent results will receive not only commendations but performance bonuses as well.

Budget requests sought by the maturing phase fund raiser are relatively easy to obtain because fund raising outcomes can be reasonably predicted, based on the fund raiser's prior performance. The CEO feels that such budget requests are worthwhile "as investments in our future." Although the recurring level of budget support is usually substantial and heavily weighted toward personnel costs, budget requests normally do not seek large increases from year to year unless the institution is preparing for a campaign.

WHAT TO LOOK FOR IN SUCCESSFUL FUND RAISERS

Seldom, in real life, can an organization or its fund raising staff be neatly positioned in one of these three phases, with no overlap. However, identifying and being more honest about which phase it is in would go a long way toward assessing what an organization should expect from its fund raising staff. If prospective employers of fund raisers and fund raisers themselves would be more precise—and more candid—about where they stand on this continuum, recruiting would be more successful.

Recruiting staff members would also be more productive if institutions and individuals better understood the *personal* inclinations and motivations of people who are successful fund raising professionals. Scholars of our profession (Duronio and Tempel, 1997; Wagner, 2002) have provided some valuable investigations related to this subject. However, because their conclusions are not consistent, continued and expanded research appears to be an appropriate goal.

My own recent research (Burnette, 2001) into this matter has been decidedly qualitative in nature. I have been deeply interested in identifying the personal motivations that have resulted in commonality and consistency among African American fund raising professionals. My findings on motivation are different from those of others who have written on this topic (Holman and Sigler, 1998; Wagner, 2002). Following are some of my specific research findings, based on forty-seven one-on-one interviews that I conducted with *experienced* African American fund raising professionals. These particular findings focus on the basis for their persistence in this profession. These respondents reported consistency and commonality to me, in terms of the following:

- Although they were raised in challenging economic circumstances, the vast majority of these forty-seven people had both a mother and a father present in the homes where they grew up.

- The families of these respondents extolled a strong sense of community and the expectation that service should be provided to it. In Chapter One of this book, Gene Tempel cites Peter Drucker's research (1990) into the positive impact of philanthropy on community building. That research is consistent with my investigations, with the added dimension that the African American fund raisers I interviewed have a dual sense of "community"—the African American community that nurtured them and the larger community as well.

- Family influences were cited as the primary reason that these forty-seven respondents feel a deep sense of mission about their fund raising work.

- These fund raisers came from churchgoing families. The respondents vividly recalled their Sunday school experiences and the need to get Sunday dinner cooked on Saturday night. They still place a high value on church and faith and are very vocal in expressing its importance in sustaining their ability to persist in this profession. These fund raisers want to know more about the biblical and theological foundations of philanthropy in order to incorporate that information into their work.

- An overwhelming number of these particular fund raisers recalled the immense influence of a single person on their development—a non-family member, a minister, a teacher, a counselor, a coach. Someone who was more than a mentor. Someone who did not make suggestions but rather *told* them what they must do to get on a path toward productive, service-oriented lives.

- These respondents rely on a network of informal but sturdy support systems that they establish among their professional colleagues.

THE MOTIVATIONS OF FUND RAISERS

Based on my careerlong observations in organizations as diverse as the Smithsonian Institution, the United States Peace Corps, and colleges, universities, and medical schools, as well as on the research of others and my own research, I have identified what I believe to be personal motivations that are universal in the profession and that can create a useful barometer in predicting career success.

First, self-confidence is very important. How others see us, as individuals and as representatives of our institutions and organizations, can be a major determinant of our effectiveness.

Second, the best fund raisers are matchmakers. We close chasms by translating needs into opportunities for funding. We know how to help donors realize their dreams. We feel responsible for the perpetuation of the best traditions and for turning today's frontiers into tomorrow's opportunities.

Third, those who achieve excellence in fund raising are people who cherish their leadership roles. We *should* see ourselves as leaders, not as hustlers or apologists for the enterprise of philanthropy. Successful fund raisers also understand that their place is not at the top of a pyramid but at the center of a circle. They recognize the difference between being in charge ("having a title") and actually doing something ("being a leader"). Such leaders have resolved their own ego needs by committing themselves to institutions whose importance is enhanced by the receipt of excellent fund raising services, rather than vice versa. In other words, the case statement is more important than the résumé.

Finally, people in successful fund raising careers have been able to "ease the pain" of face-to-face solicitations for themselves and the volunteers with whom they work. I am convinced that true success in this profession is just not possible unless and until this hurdle can be overcome. It is well known and well documented that Americans are much more skilled at being consumers than they are at being philanthropists (Billitteri, 1999). One way to look at the fund raiser's role is that of helping prospective donors decide whether they will support a nonprofit organization or just spend their money. In pursuing that role, it is necessary to ask other people to give some of their money to your worthy cause.

We are seeing the emergence of the relatively new phenomenon of staff-driven solicitation that appears to be replacing traditional peer-to-peer solicitation of volunteers. A kind of "letterhead leadership" is resulting from a decline in the number of active and committed volunteers who lend their time, energy, and commitment to the nonprofit sector.

Successful fund raising would be more palatable to more people—volunteers and staff—if they considered it like a courtship. You will have to put in the time and be patient. You will have to listen. You must gain the other party's trust and respect. You will be required to discover what is important and what is repugnant. You will have to learn the life history, including the unpleasant parts. You will have to uncover the afterlife hopes.

Unlike a courtship, but very important, you must understand that while your organization will provide stewardship for a gift, *it is not a gift for you.* Therefore, *asking for money is not personal.* Gifts are vehicles whereby donors can fulfill *their* needs and dreams, *not* yours.

UNIFYING THE TASKS OF FUND RAISING

Most contemporary practitioners have become specialists in one of the many important microdimensions of the profession of fund raising. These, in turn, have expanded into volumes, conferences, workshops, software, and World Wide Web sites. This task orientation is heavily focused on how our work is done. These tasks can generally be categorized as follows:

- Organizational preparation for fund raising, which involves having such things as a strategic plan, a feasibility study, sufficient staff, adequate budgetary resources, committed leadership, and marketing and communication capacities

- Identifying sources of funds or having legitimate expectations about gifts that could be secured from board members, previous donors, and newly identified corporate, foundation, and individual donor prospects

- Assessing the most appropriate techniques for securing funds through individual major gift solicitations; annual gifts through the mail, by telephone, and via the Internet; estate planned gifts; foundation and corporate gifts and grants; and venture philanthropy investments

- Managing the process of fund raising, including producing reports, providing stewardship, controlling expenditures, and motivating and assessing staff performance

- Analyzing the results of fund raising in terms of which techniques produced the most money—in the shortest period of time—within budget—to meet stated goals

- Starting over

Performing these tasks constitutes the everyday work of fund raisers. Budgets are proposed and approved on the basis of the tools needed by staff in order to perform tasks. Compensation increases are granted on the basis of successfully completing tasks.

These tasks are the essentials of professional knowledge that *any* fund raiser must have to be productive. These can serve as the foundation stones on which a career can be developed, as a generalist or as a specialist. Even specialists must be cognizant of the big picture.

However, concentration on our tasks may be obscuring why most of us are working in the profession of fund raising. I believe that responsibility for this obfuscation lies primarily with the supervisors, specifically with the chief development officers. These supervisors know (or should know) that their goal is to consistently and successfully secure resources for the needs of their institutions and organizations by fulfilling the dreams and wishes of donors. These supervisors should also know that the most successful fund raisers focus their efforts on *building relationships* with prospects over time, sometimes greatly extended periods of time.

Successful fund raisers understand that the reason people give is not only because they are asked to give to meet organizational needs as illustrated in (beautiful and expensive) case statements. People give because they *want* to give and because the solicitor helps the donor do what he or she *wants* to do. This is true if the donor is a foundation or a corporation (both of which, helpfully, provide guidelines about their areas of funding interest) or if the donor is an individual, who does not provide written guidelines but does give us fund raisers the chance to try to find out. Elsewhere in this book, the research of Havens and Schervish (1999) has been cited in connection with the need for fund raisers to focus more intensely on the supply side of philanthropy (the donor) instead of the demand side (the needs of the nonprofit organization).

In short, once they have been asked properly, people give for the following reasons:

- They trust the institution, organization, or cause to handle their money properly.
- They think the institution will be a strong and capable partner.
- They think the institution has energy and direction.
- They have confidence in the institution as a result of having built a relationship with it.

Although we know the motivations and inclinations of donors, many of us do not translate or transmit this information very well to the subordinate staff members whom we hold responsible for performing the essential tasks of fund raising. Of course, chief development officers convene staff meetings, where the agenda focuses on the status of staff performance of tasks. And there are staff retreats, where improvements in staff working relationships and in sharing information are discussed in order to enhance the performance of tasks.

But do prospect researchers participate in oral debriefings after calls are made, or are they solely the recipients of written call reports? Do database administrators fully understand that reports on giving are essential to proper stewardship and cultivation, or are they simply working under deadline? Do corporate relations officers work in silos, separate from the silos occupied by major gift officers, thereby disabling both of them from focusing fully on a prospect who has a corporate relationship?

Because I have observed this "my turf" orientation in countless fund raising organizations, I have come to the conclusion that we are allowing a task-orientation segmentation to hinder our ability to "be a profession." Few of us are proactive enough in unifying the tasks that together constitute this profession. Such unification cannot be achieved solely through organization charts whose boxes are neatly connected with straight lines. Nor can such unification be achieved primarily through weekly senior staff meetings. Unifying the distinguishable components of fund raising activity is essential to give definition and strength to our profession.

NEW RELATIONSHIPS WITH DONORS

Among the many challenges associated with making fund raising a profession, few are more important than building new types of relationships with donors and prospective donors. We must continue to improve our understanding of the fact that the extent of donors' giving is usually a reflection of the extent of their involvement. In my view, success in establishing those new types of relationships will be the primary impetus toward achievement of "professionhood."

Historically, the nonprofit sector has been perceived as somewhat irrational and unpredictable due to its frequently less-than-businesslike ways. The unstated assumption has been that institutions and organizations in this sector could not—and need not—meet the rigid and rational protocols of the for-profit sector.

This degree of latitude is not granted to other professions. When one speaks about outcomes in other professions, there is an expectation of results (for example, if one's teeth hurt, the dentist *will* relieve the pain); such is not the case for the fund raising profession. In fact, few other professions have had such unpredictable outcomes.

However, as the twenty-first century unfolds, the latitude afforded in the past, which has discouraged external probes, challenges, and demands for accountability, is on the wane. Our constituents and our donors are leading this charge toward change. If we are to be successful in attracting their voluntary action for the public good, we must become much more responsive to their increasing insistence that we establish new ways of working with them, according to *their* wishes and in line with *their* benchmarks of accountability and responsiveness. The need for fund raisers to be much more alert to the interests of donors has been coupled with new Internal Revenue Service regulations intended to ensure more accountability (see Chapters One and Twenty-Eight).

We must not discard from our tool kits those trusty and tested techniques for building relationships with our constituents and donors, responding to their emotional needs and intellectual interests. But we must also become more familiar with new instruments that can be equally useful.

Our donors live in an information-rich world. This new boundless environment is creating a different (and perhaps more equal) relationship between them and organizations that have historically been the sole purveyors of organizational information. Barriers of distance have been virtually eliminated in terms of acquiring information. The sense of community that for so long supported and affirmed good fund raising is becoming increasingly global, and as a result, the very definition of *community* has changed. The antiquities under the Egyptian desert are now as worthy of our concern as the Anasazi cliff dwellings in the American Southwest. Relief for hurricane victims in Belize becomes as urgent as for those in coastal South Carolina. The education of children in Angola becomes as important as the education of children in Appalachia.

A network made possible and accessible by airplanes, cell phones, television satellites, fax machines, and the Internet seals this worldwide interconnectedness together. That network also brings worldwide needs—to be satisfied by fund raising—right into the everyday lives of our donors.

So donors must make choices. Making choices is usually driven by rational assessments and comparisons to answer a very basic question: What can I, as a donor, predict will work to solve this particular problem?

Toward the end of the twentieth century, an outpouring of interest in the cost of fund raising began to rear its head. Even with the understanding that it does "cost money to raise money," salary and benefit expenditures are usually significant at nonprofit organizations. In addition, the level of personal income persists as an extremely important barometer of professional "success."

I believe that donors will become increasingly interested in the levels of fund raisers' salaries. In our society, compensation is an important indicator of an individual's value to the organization where the individual works. As they make their choices about whether to support one nonprofit or another, donors will want assurances: Is a fund raiser's salary commensurate with his or her productivity? Can the fund raiser's productivity provide predictability in terms of whether an organization can and will actually solve a problem?

As we fund raisers come to terms with new relationships with donors, many of us will pass through new professional territories. Although we have engaged in strategic planning for some time, we are now beginning to see our plans directly linked to the number of prospect portfolios we are expected to manage. Many of us are surprised to learn that those strategic plans can actually be used to assess the productivity of our fund raising work.

Though we may be wizards at preparing budgets in our search for external support, many of us do not understand the details of how our organizations are financed, how their budgets are formulated and executed, or why our output (fund raising results) is essential to organizational financial health. A large number of us have poor or uninformed relationships with our organizations' chief financial officers. Although we aggressively seek funds to increase institutional endowments, too few of us understand the investment strategies that guide the management of endowed funds. Too many of us do not really understand the volatility of the stock market and its effect on our work.

Unfortunately, these information gaps are in subject areas that we should know very well. Even more unfortunately, our embarrassment about our dearth of knowledge in these areas results in sidestepping or silence. In our new donor relationships, we must talk about and master these matters. If we do not, we will not be able to contribute in significant ways to the establishment of fund raising as a profession.

AN AGENDA FOR THE FUTURE OF THE PROFESSION

Our profession is on the verge of what I believe will be its most exciting and difficult period. We have within our grasp and capability the opportunity to decide if we will pursue tasks, if we will pursue a career, or if we will function within the framework of a profession. The following trends will characterize the years to come:

- A massive transfer of wealth between generations
- An increase in the number of megagifts of transformative quality
- A heightened demand for accountability and predictability of outcomes
- A rise in the social investment expectations of many donors
- A continuation in the retreat by government from some of its former important roles, resulting in new pressures on the nonprofit sector
- An acceleration in the intrusion of the depersonalized World Wide Web into the traditionally personal ways to raise money
- Profound shifts in population and financial demographics

All of these changes will have an immediate and direct impact on us as fund raising professionals and on the institutions we serve. As we set our agenda for the future, there are some basic issues we must resolve in terms of deciding if we can work in new ways. Resolution of these issues must take place soon inasmuch as the nonprofit sector is under substantially increased public scrutiny and is consequently much more vulnerable than before.

First and foremost, in our efforts to be more contemporary, we must not walk away from the time-tested principles of our work. We must recommit not to skip steps in the identification, cultivation, solicitation, and stewardship of our donors. Passion is still pertinent. We must also add to the mix of those steps a fuller understanding that we must be more accountable and our work must be more predictable.

In our strivings toward being accountable, we should be sure that we are using new relationship-building tools in ways that will improve our ability to connect with our donors rather than to manipulate them. Some for-profit marketing devices are now highly developed predictors. However, we must remain loyal to the importance of establishing and maintaining personal connections with our donors, especially using volunteers.

We must insist on an increase in *tailored* training that is commensurate with our needs. One size will not fit all. Every profession provides encouragement and space for practitioners who are at widely varying stages in their professional development. In addition to the work of training for completion of tasks, more opportunities are needed in areas such as leadership development. Academic curricula should rely more heavily on the experiences of front-line practitioners. Meaningful exchange between practitioners and academics and involving academics and practitioners in teaching will strengthen the preparation of the next generation.

Mentoring, being mentored, and relying on peer networks all should become more legitimated as viable and valuable training experiences. I have long believed that every fund raising professional with less than five years' experience should have, as a *professional right,* a mentor with more than ten years' experience and that those ten-years-plus veterans should assume mentoring as a *professional obligation.* We must become much more assertive in terms of "growing our own."

There is a plethora of information about the impact of changing population and financial demographics in the United States and the influence these will have on the for-profit, government, and nonprofit sectors. The profession of fund raising will not be exempt from these influences. We must demand that our organizations become more inclusive in programming, staffing, and volunteer leadership. Without diversity reflected in all these ways, our institutions and organizations will be left by the wayside as demographic changes alter the fabric of the rest of our society.

Understanding how to raise money in communities of color cannot be relegated as a "task of trepidation" to be assumed only by fund raisers. *All* institutions and organizations should put a premium on understanding those communities. For centuries, ignoring those communities except as needy recipients of goods and services was highly institutionalized. Today, changing demographics are providing the impetus for the construction of a truly civil society. I believe that such a society must be achieved in the same way: by institutional inclusion.

Finally, we fund raisers must reject the implication that the goals we pursue are in fact merely "hopes." Fund raising has developed to the point that we have an understanding of what works and what will not work. What have not yet emerged are donor confidence and self-confidence in our ability to provide predictable outcomes.

CONCLUSION

When we reach a point in time that we have recruited and hired the most highly motivated people for fund raising positions, when we bring those people into organizations that keep strategic objectives at the forefront of all fund raising activity, and when our fund raising campaigns are characterized by providing donors with reasonable predictions about outcomes, only then will we be more confident that we are functioning as a profession.

We have a significant opportunity to contribute to the construction of our profession of fund raising in ways that will make our institutions and our donors proud.

CHAPTER THIRTY-FOUR

Resources for Strengthening Fund Raising Skills

Lilya Wagner

C ompetence is essential in fund raising, particularly in today's demanding competitive environment. Much has changed from the time fund raisers drifted into their jobs and learned by doing it as best they could or by following models of existing programs that worked. In the last couple of decades, much effort has been devoted to determining which appropriate skills, education, and training are needed and to improving the availability and quality of professional development.

Acquiring the requisite knowledge and developing special skills that are valued in the field can be done through academic programs, training programs such as workshops, and other means that will be discussed in this chapter. All of these efforts are designed to enhance the legitimacy of fund raising, to improve the quality of practice, and to ensure the highest possible level of success.

OVERVIEW OF PROFESSIONAL DEVELOPMENT OPPORTUNITIES

The following are the most prevalent and accessible forms of professional development. Some of these overlap in offerings and purposes. For example, some universities, in addition to degree programs, may also have continuing education in the form of certificate programs, nondegree courses, and centers and institutes. Some associations may offer conferences as well as courses and summer institutes.

- *Academic programs.* As the number of nonprofits have increased nationwide, so have the number and availability of courses of study in colleges and universities. This is true for both public and private institutions. Educational possibilities are available in most regions of the United States. Program offerings include the following:

Master's degree programs in philanthropic studies and other areas

Master's in public administration (M.P.A.), with a concentration on nonprofit management

Undergraduate coursework leading to minors

Graduate, undergraduate, and noncredit certificate programs

Fellowships

Doctoral programs that allow concentrations in nonprofit management and philanthropic studies

Interdisciplinary degree programs

- *Major associations.* There are several associations for fund raising professionals. The most prominent are the Association of Fundraising Professionals (AFP, formerly the National Society for Fundraising Executives), the Council for Advancement and Support of Education (CASE), the Association of Healthcare Philanthropy (AHP), the Association of Professional Researchers for Advancement (APRA), and the National Committee on Planned Giving (NCPG). These offer conferences, usually on a yearly basis, and courses, such as the AFP-sponsored First and Survey courses. Other offerings are institutes, certification programs, and training via the Internet.

Continuing education offered by major associations is generally credible and well planned and executed. The presenters of workshops and other offerings are usually well qualified, and for the most part their presentation skills are good. The emphasis is more often on practice; research and theory are limited and are usually relegated to academic programs.

- *Schools.* The most prominent institution in this category is The Fund Raising School (TFRS), part of the Center on Philanthropy at Indiana University. Continuing the work of Hank Rosso, it offers nine courses (in addition to customized training), covering all areas of fund raising practice. Acquiring training at TFRS has several advantages: it is the oldest recognized entity of its type, established in 1974; it has a curriculum based on the collective experience of its founders, faculty, and advisers; and it draws on research and theory. Other schools, such as The Grantsmanship Center in Los Angeles, offer courses in fund raising and nonprofit management locally or throughout the country.

• *Centers and institutes located at higher education institutions.* Many centers offer fund raising as part of their nonprofit study, although frequently such courses are electives. Among the most prominent centers are the Mandel Center at Case Western Reserve University, the Institute for Nonprofit Organizational Management at the University of San Francisco, and the Center on Philanthropy at Indiana University. A list of centers appears at the end of this chapter.

• *Affinity groups.* There are several associations that have specialized programs or are made up of similar types of nonprofits. Among these are the National Catholic Development Conference, various women in philanthropy groups, the Association of Lutheran Development Executives, the Christian Stewardship Association, and the American Association of Fundraising Counsel (AAFRC). Members of these association are similar in organizational type or mission (for example, fund raising for religious causes). These affinity groups also hold conferences and provide training opportunities and are generally highly credible.

• *Technical assistance and support centers.* Technical assistance centers were begun in the 1970s to assist nonprofits with a variety of services, such as nonprofit management, business skills, accounting, fund raising, volunteer management, fund raising research, and program evaluation. Most provide training programs, and some have consultation services. The Alliance for Nonprofit Management, based in Washington, D.C., is a membership association of technical assistance and support centers and a good place to start in seeking additional information, particularly local training through this type of continuing education.

• *Institutes.* A number of institutes are offered by associations, such as the CASE Summer Institutes (Independent School Advancement Professionals, Communications and Marketing, and Alumni Relations) and AFP's Executive Leadership Institute (ELI) and Executive Management Institutes (EMI). These are generally held either in the summer or during a compressed time period, such as two to three days, and focus on a specific level of professionalism and tenure in the profession. AFP's ELI is offered yearly to senior professionals who listen to experts on issues in fund raising and also engage in discussion and reflection. Another type of institute is the Learning Institute, which brings together speakers and professionals through the latest technology. It is a program of the Society for Nonprofit Organizations and collaborates with the University of Wisconsin Extension and Television Wisconsin, Inc.

• *Consulting firms or individual consultants.* As part of their efforts to create visibility and advertise their services, consultants offer workshops or seminars. Consultants are also frequent speakers at major conferences held by associations. Since there is no set of criteria to govern consultancies, the range and caliber of offerings vary greatly.

- *Continuing education programs at universities.* An increasing number of higher education institutions are offering fund raising courses through their continuing education departments, and several—including New York University, the University of Chicago, Indiana University–Purdue University Indianapolis, and the University of San Francisco—have certificate programs. Some colleges and universities combine centers, schools, and institutes in their offerings. For example, Indiana University offers The Fund Raising School courses through its Center on Philanthropy and a certificate in fund raising management (through The Fund Raising School). The distinct advantage of acquiring nondegree education and training through a university is the likelihood that research and theory will be included in the overall educational offering.

- *Fellowships and internships.* Specialized fellowships are available at various academic centers, such as the Hearst Minority Fellowship at the Center on Philanthropy at Indiana University. Internships are often arranged through academic programs but allow the student the added dimension of actual experience while enrolled in a master's degree program, for example. Internships can often lead to full-time work; at the least, they give credibility to a young professional's résumé.

- *In-house training.* Large and well-established nonprofits may have training programs that they offer to their employees only, not just providing training in fund raising and nonprofit management but actually tailoring it to the specific needs of their new employees. Some of the organizations that conduct such programs are the Girl Scouts, Boys and Girls Clubs, YMCA and YWCA, Junior Achievement, and the American Red Cross. This type of training differs somewhat from on-the-job training but may be combined with it.

- *Mentoring and on-the-job training.* Throughout most of the history of formalized fund raising, on-the-job training and mentoring were the primary or exclusive means of acquiring fund raising knowledge and skills. Although alternative options have expanded considerably, these are still significant methods of professional development, either singly or as part of an overall plan for acquiring skills and experience. Mentoring and on-the-job training aren't only for entry-level personnel. Experienced professionals can enhance their career development through these avenues also.

- *Self-study.* By reading, using videos and audiotapes, and taking advantage of resources on the Internet, a fund raiser can undertake a personalized professional development program. Resources are plentiful, and most academic programs offer bibliographies and other lists of resources.

The opportunities for training and education are numerous, and in today's learning climate, a professional, whether highly experience or new to the field, can put together a learning plan that is both personalized and of the highest quality.

ACADEMIC PROGRAMS

Prior to the availability of formal educational offerings in nonprofit management and fund raising, most persons acquired a bachelor's degree before embarking on a fund raising career. The most likely disciplines leading to fund raising were communication, management, public relations, and to some extent, social work and psychology. Certainly courses from these areas are worthwhile for success in fund raising, but most career seekers lacked specific training in nonprofit management, budgeting, fund raising, and philanthropy. In order to meet these needs, some major areas of study, such as social work and health care administration, offered some management education in the specialty areas. In some cases, students were urged to take business courses on the assumption that the nonprofit organization should be, or could be, managed like a business.

As demands for accountability and professionalism in the nonprofit sector have increased, organizations have had to become more businesslike. This means expertise in marketing, personnel management, strategic planning, budgeting, and other components of a credible organization.

Currently, institutions seeking to hire fund raising personnel generally indicate a bachelor's degree as a minimum requirement for employment, and some prefer a master's or even a doctorate. This is particularly true, of course, among higher education institutions. What has changed, however, is the availability of specialized degrees, certificates, and courses that offer a professional the opportunity to focus on the eventual career and not put together his or her educational experience bit by bit, attending a course here and a workshop there.

Most specialized academic programs, those focusing on nonprofit sector studies and philanthropy, are at the graduate level. Undergraduate work is somewhat lacking. Some introductory courses to the nonprofit sector and nonprofit management are available, and a few institutions have been innovative enough to actually offer a major or at least a program of study. Most of these would be interdisciplinary in nature. American Humanics, which is a national alliance of colleges, universities, and nonprofit organizations, prepares undergraduates for careers with youth and human service agencies. Summer institutes that allow undergrads to concentrate on the nonprofit sector, such as the Summer Institute on Philanthropy and Volunteerism at the Center on Philanthropy at Indiana University, are available as well. Certificate programs are available for academic credit. Some specialize in nonprofit management in general, while others focus on subspecialties such as fund raising. Fellowships attract exceptional students and allow them to study specific issues and areas of nonprofit organizations.

Some master's degree programs, usually for the M.P.A. or M.B.A. degree, allow concentrations in nonprofit management. Some master's degree programs are attractive because they are offered through an executive track, allowing professionals to acquire a degree without discontinuing their careers. There are additional master's degree programs, such as the master of arts in philanthropic studies offered by Indiana University and the master of arts in policy studies at Johns Hopkins University.

Doctoral programs are few, but several that are offered allow students to focus on nonprofit management. These may be housed in departments such as management, history, economics, or social work. There are also executive doctoral programs that allow the student to continue a career while pursuing a degree. Doctoral programs focusing specifically on philanthropy and the nonprofit sector are not plentiful, but some are available, such as personalized degrees offered through the Union Institute, and others are currently being planned. A Ph.D. in philanthropic studies is offered through the Center on Philanthropy at Indiana University.

A Web site (http://pirate.shu.edu/ ~ mirabero/Kellogg.html) lists all the offerings in nonprofit management education at university-based programs. It includes courses through continuing education, undergraduate programs, and graduate courses or degrees.

What courses might a student expect to take if enrolling in a certificate or degree program? The most likely curriculum for a program of study would include most or all of the following courses:

- Management of nonprofit organizations
- Accounting and financial management
- Marketing
- Volunteer and personnel management
- Legal issues
- Economics
- Overview of the sector
- Some history and philosophy of the sector
- Research

Some curricula may include tax policies, government and the nonprofit sector, and issues of the sector and its organizations.

Most programs include an internship and possibly directed study of a special area of interest. This allows the student to gain experience, work in an organization that interests him or her, and build a résumé.

Oddly enough, not all programs require fund raising courses or similar "hands on" education, but often these are available as electives. This is due to another ongoing debate in academe—how much practical experience should be included in higher education and whether such experience should be acquired elsewhere. Case studies, however, are a popular method of study in graduate courses and do allow for experiential learning.

In spite of the availability of degree and certificate programs in nonprofit management and the fact that students from these areas of study have done well, some hiring organizations still prefer candidates from traditional areas of study, such as public or business administration, or a degree in the field on which the student chooses to focus and build a career, such as health care. However, academic programs specializing in nonprofit management and philanthropy have achieved credibility and a growing demand in the marketplace.

CONTINUING EDUCATION

In contrast to formal education of the sort just described, continuing education and professional development programs offer short-term, quick, compressed, streamlined training and are guided by the needs of employers and students, as well as the opinions and suggestions of seasoned practitioners. For the most part, they are practitioner-driven. However, to simply achieve competence without understanding the principles behind the competence, to ignore the theory on which ethical and successful philanthropic practice is based, is a serious error. A scholarly approach and a research base are vital criteria for excellence in fund raising education, and these elements should not be excluded from continuing education and training. This is perhaps the foremost criterion for selection of the best training possible.

Organizations that offer continuing education include the following, which have already been described in greater detail earlier in this chapter:

- Professional associations
- Educational institutions and schools
- Centers and institutes
- Affinity groups
- Technical assistance centers
- Consulting firms or individual consultants
- Continuing education programs at universities

Evaluating the credibility and benefits of fund raising training can be challenging, given the wide variety of selections available. In planning for continuing education, the professional or novice seeking training should do a personal assessment and determine the special areas of interest, short- and long-term professional goals, type of work preferred, and personal job satisfaction factors. The fund raiser should also determine the credibility of the professional development offering and assess the respectability of the organization offering the training. Peers and mentors or teachers can be reliable sources for suggestions.

PRINTED MATERIAL, VIDEOS, AUDIOTAPES, AND AUDIOCONFERENCING

Another excellent way to engage in professional development is to read. Currently, there are many relevant journals and other publications on the market, and books are added continually. Bibliographies and recommended reading lists are often available through the organizations or entities that offer the training. The credibility of the reading lists is often reflective of the credibility of the training program. A bibliography of the best books and journals is updated yearly by The Fund Raising School at the Center on Philanthropy at Indiana University, and information on this resource can be found on the center's Web page (http://www.philanthropy.iupui.edu).

Videotapes and audiotapes are also available, as is training through teleconferencing. Tapes can often be acquired through any of the professional development methods and organizations described in this chapter. For example, most major conferences provide audiotapes of their sessions and make these available to individuals who were unable to attend the conference itself. The Association of Fundraising Professionals, for example, advertises tapes from its annual conferences in issues of *Advancing Philanthropy*, the association's official journal.

Videos are less commonly available but can be found in the catalogues of major publishers such as Jossey-Bass, in libraries that have a selection of nonprofit resources, or through interlibrary loan. Support centers and continuing education programs, as well as the staff or faculty for these, can often recommend useful materials in this category.

Teleconferencing makes it possible for the learning to be interactive. Professional associations often offer specific topics delivered by experts through this medium. Fund raisers at various sites can connect to such a conference; the possibility of on-the-spot two-way communication, usually in the form of questions and answers, is an attractive feature of this method.

USE OF THE INTERNET

The increasing use of the Internet has expanded learning possibilities greatly. Options range from academic programs that are available on-line to short newsletters sent by e-mail. In the academic or continuing education arenas, for example, the Center on Philanthropy at Indiana University now offers a certificate in nonprofit management entirely via the Internet, and the Foundation Center has on its Web site a proposal writing course that is self-directed.

Web sites of trainers, consultants, and nonprofit assistance centers provide information on courses available through traditional means, but they often also include practical suggestions, tips, and resources. On-line newsletters provide a vast range of information, from how to write a direct mail letter to in-depth discussions of giving trends. Although the quality may be uneven, these sources should not be discounted because they make instant education available. Many sites are free of charge.

Networking for professional collegiality and learning is also enhanced by use of the Internet, e-mail, chat rooms, forums, and other forms of cyber-exchange that turn up, develop, change, improve, or go out of business daily. These provide an exciting array of possibilities for meeting colleagues and kindred spirits without the expense of travel, lodging, and formal conference fees.

CERTIFICATION

Today there is a definite trend toward recognition of competence in many areas, from government to professional associations. A "seal of approval" for fund raisers guarantees that persons entering a field can demonstrate an ability to perform tasks at an acceptable level, have a body of knowledge on which to base practice, and have already been of service to the profession. Credentialing also enhances the reputation of the profession and allows for the screening out of individuals who behave in ways that discredit the profession.

The Certified Fundraising Executive (CFRE) Professional Certification Board offers the CFRE credential in cooperation with nine leading philanthropic organizations. It is a credential that is achieving more respect, although it isn't yet a criterion for employment. The CFRE implies that members can demonstrate a certain level of knowledge, have a certain amount of experience, and subscribe to a code of ethics and best practices. Both the Association of Healthcare Philanthropy (AHP) and the Association of Fundraising Professionals (AFP) offer advanced certification. The goals of certification are to support professional development in fund raising and to provide guidelines and professional standards for employing organizations. The CFRE requires that the applicant pass a test and document work experience (minimum of five years in the profession), fund raising success, service to the profession, and professional development.

At present, the CFRE is not a significant criterion for being hired in a fund raising position. Certification doesn't translate into competent behavior. However, many practitioners claim that certification does lead to job opportunities, greater professionalism, better salaries, more impressive titles, and additional perks. The best outcome of certification may well be that the process of achieving certification causes a fund raiser to think seriously about what he or she knows and how this knowledge is applied in practice. In this sense, certification does contribute to the professionalism of fund raisers.

ON-THE-JOB TRAINING AND MENTORING

On-the-job training is a time-honored way of learning. Sometimes it's simply a matter of being in the right place at the right time, but more often the fund raiser must take the initiative. On-the-job training, of course, occurs regularly and often along with formal training such as conferences or workshops, but sometimes it is the primary or only way a professional will acquire knowledge and expertise. At times, on-the-job training is part of an employment agreement; at other times, the professional must develop a plan for obtaining such training. There are a number of reasons why on-the-job training is still prevalent and preferred. Some people learn best by doing, observing, and experimenting. Some work in organizations that can't afford to send personnel for training, even to conferences. Some simply don't see the necessity of any other type of learning.

Mentoring is an important part of professional development, whether on-the-job training or more formal education is involved. Mentoring is a major key to success under any circumstances, particularly if learning experiences are limited for a novice or entry-level professional. At the most ideal, a mentor will be available for advice, will help a deserving professional by paving the way to advancement or acquisition of knowledge, and will be that person's advocate. At the least, a mentor can be someone who listens, shares experiences, boosts the confidence of the mentee, and passes on information about the profession. At any level, a fund raising professional can learn from someone who takes an interest in him or her, will help in learning the ropes and provide some knowledge of the community and its donors, and will be the key in making friends among professionals. The wise professional will seek out two or three close mentors and thereby benefit from a variety of connections, advice, and viewpoints.

Most people are willing, if not eager, to share of their background and experiences and to provide information on best practices. A mentor can have a positive influence on a fledgling professional, and such a relationship can turn into a lifelong friendship. Mentors could come from the ranks of teachers and trainers, senior professionals with years of successful experience, senior colleagues, consultants, and people outside of the field who can provide counsel and express objective viewpoints.

SETTING YOUR PROFESSIONAL DEVELOPMENT GOALS AND DESIGNING YOUR CUSTOMIZED PROGRAM

The most ideal professional development plan, of course, involves education, training opportunities, on-the-job training, and mentoring.

How can a fund raising professional evaluate credibility and benefits of fund raising education and training? The following suggestions may be used as possible criteria for determining what and where the best investment in professional development can be.

First, the professional or novice should do a personal assessment. Determine the special areas of interest, short- and long-term professional goals, type of work that is preferred, and personal job satisfaction factors. For example, are you interested in the annual fund, proposal writing, or planned giving? Where do you want to be in three years? In ten years? What type of organization interests you most, human services or health care? Higher education or child care? What types of working conditions are most satisfying for you? For example, do you prefer autonomy or working in a team? Do you prefer to work alone or with volunteers?

Second, determine the credibility of the professional development offering. Assess the respectability of the organization offering the training. Ask your peers and mentors or teachers for suggestions.

Third, assess your professional development needs and goals. Do you want to study for a formal degree or a certificate program? What do you want your professional development to accomplish for you and your work? Are you seeking improvement in your performance or advancement in your career? How much time is required by the program you select, and how much time can you devote to it? What does your employer wish to have you accomplish through professional development? Who will pay for the training, and what are your obligations if your employer covers the costs?

Finally, put the pieces together and create a plan. Your plan will differ from others' because of the flexibility of continued education or professional development, unlike the formal structure of a higher education program. Your plan should be rational, logical, and personalized.

The availability of professional development resources is infinite. The wise professional will keep abreast of changes, discover what is timeless and credible, and develop a personal plan that will be flexible, because fund raising is a dynamic and developing profession.

RESOURCES

Selected Journals and Newspapers

Advancing Philanthropy. Arlington, Va.: Association of Fundraising Professionals (published quarterly). How-to articles and reports on successful fund raising practices.

Chronicle of Philanthropy. Washington, D.C. (published biweekly). The latest issues in philanthropy, from case histories and people in the profession to statistical data on major contributions. Sections of this newspaper can include fund raising, giving, foundations, corporations, marketing, management, volunteering, grants, international fund raising activities, and many other areas of philanthropy. Continuing education and job opportunities are listed in the last section.

Currents. Washington, D.C.: Council for Advancement and Support of Education (published monthly). Publication of the major association for education institutions. Includes articles on fund raising, public relations, and alumni administration.

Fundraising Management. Garden City, N.Y.: Hoke Communications, Inc. (published monthly). Current topics and strategies in fund raising. Special feature articles provide helpful management and practical information for the fund raising executive. Conference reports keep readers up-to-date on issues and trends. Every issue includes a development section, calendar of events, club news, newsmakers, marketplace, cassettes, fund raising directory, and a classified section.

Grantsmanship Center News. Los Angeles, Calif.: Grantsmanship Center (published bimonthly). Lists continuing education courses in fund raising, particularly proposal writing. Contains advice on writing grant proposals and articles related to foundation giving. Also lists sources for assistance and helpful advertising.

Grassroots Fundraising Journal. Oakland, Calif.: Chardon Press (published bimonthly). Articles on alternative sources of funding, book reviews, and bibliographies. Geared toward the low-budget organization.

New Directions for Philanthropic Fundraising. San Francisco: Jossey-Bass (published quarterly). Created to strengthen voluntary giving by addressing how the concepts of philanthropy pertain to fund raising practice. In each quarterly paperback, authors address themes related to fund raising management and techniques, always keeping in mind the values of volunteerism and public benefit that characterize philanthropic organizations. The journal is sponsored by the Indiana University Center on Philanthropy and the Association of Fundraising Professionals.

Nonprofit and Voluntary Sector Quarterly. Thousand Oaks, Calif.: Sage (published quarterly). The journal of the Association for Research on Nonprofit Organizations and Voluntary Action (ARNOVA). An international, interdisciplinary journal that reports on research and programs related to volunteerism, citizen participation, philanthropy, and nonprofit organizations.

Nonprofit Management and Leadership. San Francisco: Jossey-Bass (published quarterly). Latest developments in nonprofit management theory and practice; includes articles, features, book reviews, research reports, and updates on professional conferences.

NonProfit Times. Skillman, N.J. (published monthly). Focuses on nonprofit management and fund raising techniques. Sections may include news and features, computer software, technology, management and finance, commentary on current issues, and other areas of interest. Job-related continuing education opportunities are also listed. Free to subscribers who meet certain qualifications.

Nonprofit World. Madison, Wis.: Society for Nonprofit Organizations (published bimonthly). Articles on all aspects of running an effective nonprofit organization, including fund raising, income generation, legal advice, and professional development.

Philanthropy Matters. Indianapolis, Ind.: Center on Philanthropy (published semiannually). Articles cover a wide range of issues concerning the nonprofit sector and professional development of the field. Issues also include book reviews.

Books

Association of Fundraising Professionals. *Profile of AFP Members.* Alexandria, Va.: Association of Fundraising Professionals (published every two to three years). Comprehensive career survey covering background, employer, professional activities, compensation, use of technology, and opinions on professional issues. The results represent a sample of the AFP's members and provide useful information about the profession and individuals involved in raising philanthropic dollars.

Duronio, Margaret A., and Eugene R. Tempel. *Fund Raisers: Their Careers, Stories, Concerns, and Accomplishments.* San Francisco: Jossey-Bass, 1997. An overview of fund raisers—their educational and career backgrounds, their values and concerns, and the challenges and rewards they experience in their work.

Kelly, Kathleen S. *Effective Fund-Raising Management.* Mahwah, N.J.: Erlbaum, 1998. Explores fund raising management, which can be the key to success or the door to demise. An organization that does not understand and effectively manage its fund raising programs will soon be suffering. This work explores what it takes to run an effective fund raising program.

Tempel, Eugene R., Sara B. Cobb, and Warren E. Ilchman (eds.). *The Professionalization of Fundraising: Implications for Education, Practice, and Accountability.* New Directions for Philanthropic Fundraising, no. 15. San Francisco: Jossey-Bass, Spring 1997. A collection of readings regarding the development of professionalization in fund raising, ranging from considerations of how to acquire the appropriate training and education to issues of public trust.

Wagner, Lilya. *Careers in Fundraising.* New York: Wiley, 2001. A comprehensive volume on fund raising as a career, including the context and traditions of fund raising, preparation for a career, how to find a job, how to work professionally and manage various challenges in the field, and the future of fund raising. A particularly thorough resource covering all aspects of the profession.

Professional Associations and Technical Assistance Providers

The Alliance for Nonprofit Management
1899 L Street, N.W., Suite 600
Washington, DC 20036
Phone: (202) 955-8406
Fax: (202) 955-8419
Internet: http://www.allianceonline.org

American Association of Fund-Raising Counsel & AAFRC Trust for Philanthropy
10293 North Meridian Street, Suite 175
Indianapolis, IN 46290
Phone: (800) 462-2372; (317) 816-1613
Fax: (317) 816-1633
Internet: http://www.aafrc.org

Association for Research on Nonprofit Organizations and Voluntary Action
(ARNOVA)
Center on Philanthropy at Indiana University
550 West North Street, Suite 301
Indianapolis, IN 46202
Phone: (317) 684-2120
Fax: (317) 684-2128
Internet: http://www.arnova.org

Association of Fundraising Professionals (AFP)
1101 King Street, Suite 700
Alexandria, VA 22314
Phone: (703) 684-0410
Fax: (703) 684-0540
Internet: http://www.afpnet.org

Association of Healthcare Philanthropy (AHP)
313 Park Avenue, Suite 400
Falls Church, VA 22046
Phone: (703) 532-6243
Fax: (703) 532-7170
Internet: http://www.go-ahp.org

Association of Professional Researchers for Advancement (APRA)
414 Plaza Drive, Suite 209
Westmont, IL 60559
Phone: (630) 655-0177
Fax: (630) 655-0391
Internet: http://www.aprahome.org

CFRE Professional Certification Board
1101 King Street, Suite 700
Alexandria, VA 22314
Phone: (703) 519-8483
Fax: (703) 684-1950

Council for Advancement and Support of Education (CASE)
1307 New York Avenue, N.W., Suite 1000
Washington, DC 20005
Phone: (202) 328-5900
Fax: (202) 387-4973
Internet: http://www.case.org

Council on Foundations
1828 L Street, N.W., Suite 300
Washington, DC 20036
Phone: (202) 466-6512
Fax: (202) 785-3926
Internet: http://www.cof.org

Foundation Center
79 Fifth Avenue, 8th Floor
New York, NY 10003
Phone: (212) 620-4230
Fax: (212) 691-1828
Internet: http://www.fdncenter.org

INDEPENDENT SECTOR (IS)
1200 Eighteenth Street, N.W., Suite 200
Washington, DC 20036
Phone: (202) 467-6100
Fax: (202) 467-6101
Internet: http://www.independentsector.org

National Center for Nonprofit Boards (NCNB)
1828 L Street, N.W., Suite 900
Washington, DC 20036
Phone: (202) 452-6262
Fax: (202) 452-6299
Internet: http://www.ncnb.org

National Committee on Planned Giving (NCPG)
233 McCrea Street, Suite 400
Indianapolis, IN 46225
Phone: (317) 269-6274
Fax: (317) 269-6276
Internet: http://www.ncpg.org

National Council of Nonprofit Associations (NCNA)
1900 L Street, N.W., Suite 605
Washington, DC 20036
Phone: (202) 467-6262
Fax: (202) 467-6261
Internet: http://www.ncna.org

Members of the Nonprofit Academic Centers Council

Arizona State University
Robert F. Ashcraft, Director
Center for Nonprofit Leadership and Management
Arizona State University
P.O. Box 874905
Tempe, AZ 85287
Phone: (480) 965-0607
Fax: (480) 727-8878
E-mail: ashcraft@asu.edu
Internet: http://www.asu.edu/copp/nonprofit

Boston College
Paul G. Schervish, Director
Social Welfare Research Institute
Boston College
515 McGuinn Hall
Chestnut Hill, MA 02467
Phone: (617) 552-4070
Fax: (617) 552-3903
E-mail: Paul.Schervish@bc.edu
Internet: http://www.bc.edu/swri

Case Western Reserve University
Susan Lajoie Eagan, Executive Director
Mandel Center for Nonprofit Organizations
Case Western Reserve University
10900 Euclid Avenue
Cleveland, OH 44106
Phone: (800) 760-2275; (216) 386-2275
Fax: (216) 386-8592
E-mail: SLE7@po.cwru.edu
Internet: http://www.cwru.edu/mandelcenter/

City University of New York
Kathleen D. McCarthy, Director
Center for the Study of Philanthropy
Graduate School and University Center, CUNY
365 Fifth Avenue
New York, NY 10016
Phone: (212) 817-2010
Fax: (212) 817-1572
E-mail: emiller@gc.cuny.edu
Internet: http://www.philanthropy.org

Duke University
Charles Clotfelter, Director
Center for the Study of Philanthropy and Voluntarism
Terry Sanford Institute of Public Policy, Duke University
P.O. Box 90245
Durham, NC 27708
Phone: (919) 684-2672
Fax: (919) 681-8288
E-mail: cltfltr@pps.duke.edu
Internet: http://www.pubpol.duke.edu/

George Mason University
Patricia F. Lewis, Nonprofit Professional-in-Residence
Nonprofit Management Studies
George Mason University, Arlington Campus
Old Building, Room 318
3401 North Fairfax Drive, MS 5A7
Arlington, VA 22201
Phone: (703) 799-4279
Fax: (703) 799-3896
E-mail: Plewis1@gmu.edu

Georgetown University
Virginia Hodgkinson, Director
Center for the Study of Voluntary Organizations and Service
Georgetown Public Policy Institute
3240 Prospect Street, N.W., LL
Washington, DC 20007
Phone: (202) 687-0514
Fax: (202) 687-0517
E-mail: hodgkinv@georgetown.edu
Internet: http://www.georgetown.edu/grad/gppi/welcome.htm

Grand Valley State University
Donna Van Iwaarden, Director
Dorothy A. Johnson Center for Philanthropy and Nonprofit Leadership
Grand Valley State University
232C DeVos Center
401 West Fulton Street
Grand Rapids, MI 49405
Phone: (616) 336-7587
Fax: (616) 336-7592
E-mail: vaniwaad@gvsu.edu
Internet: http://www.gvsu.edu/philanthropy

Harvard University
Mark Moore, Director
Hauser Center for Nonprofit Organizations
Harvard University
79 John F. Kennedy Street
Cambridge, MA 02138
Phone: (617) 495-1113
Fax: (617) 495-0996
E-mail: mark_moore@harvard.edu
Internet: http://www.ksghauser.harvard.edu/

Indiana University
Eugene R. Tempel, Executive Director
The Center on Philanthropy at Indiana University
550 West North Street, Suite 301
Indianapolis, IN 46202
Phone: (317) 684-8904
Fax: (317) 684-8968
E-mail: etempel@iupui.edu
Internet: http://www.philanthropy.iupui.edu/

Johns Hopkins University
Lester M. Salamon, Director
Center for Civil Society Studies
Johns Hopkins University
Wyman Park Building
Baltimore, MD 21218
Phone: (410) 516-5463
Fax: (410) 516-7818
E-mail: lsalamon@jhunix.hcf.jhu.edu
Internet: http://www.jhu.edu/ ~ ccss/

Louisiana State University in Shreveport
Dr. Norman A. Dolch, Director, Institute for Human Services and Public Policy
Louisiana State University in Shreveport
One University Place
Shreveport, LA 71115-2399

New School University
Aida Rodriguez, Chair, Nonprofit Management Program
Milano Graduate School of Management and Urban Policy
New School University
72 Fifth Avenue, 4th Floor
New York, NY 10011

Phone: (212) 229-5311, ext 1216
Fax: (212) 229-5904
E-mail: arodrigu@newschool.edu
Internet: http://www.newshcool.edu/splash.html

New York University
Kathy O'Regan, Director
Robert F. Wagner Graduate School of Public Service
Public and Nonprofit Management and Policy Program
4 Washington Square North
New York, NY 10003
Phone: (212) 998-7498
Fax: (212) 995-3890
E-mail: Katherine.oregan@nyu.edu
Internet: http://www.nyu.edu/wagner/

New York University Law School
Jill S. Manny, Executive Director
National Center on Philanthropy and the Law
New York University School of Law
110 West Third Street, 2nd Floor
New York, NY 10012
Phone: (212) 998-6272
Fax: (212) 995-3149
E-mail: Jill.many@nyu.edu
Internet: http://www.law.nyu.edu/ncpl/

Northwestern University
Donald Haider, Director
Center for Nonprofit Management
Kellogg School of Management
Northwestern University
Evanston, IL 60208
Phone: (847) 491-3415
Fax: (847) 491-8525
E-mail: d-haider@nwu.edu
Internet: http://www.kellogg.nwu.edu/

Portland State University
Suzanne C. Feeney, Director
Institute for Nonprofit Management, Division of Public Administration
Hatfield School of Government
P.O. Box 751
Portland, OR 97207

Phone: (503) 725-8217
Fax: (503) 725-8250
E-mail: feeneys@pdx.edu
Internet: http://www.upa.pdx.edu/PA/INPM/

Regis University
Ramon Del Castillo, Chair
Center for Nonprofit Leadership
Regis University
Mail Code L-16
333 Regis University
Denver, CO 80221
Phone: (303) 964-5271
Fax: (303) 964-5538
E-mail: rdelcast@regis.edu
Internet: http://www.regis.edu/spsgrad/

Rockefeller University
Darwin H. Stapleton, Executive Director
Rockefeller Archive Center
15 Dayton Avenue
Sleepy Hollow, NY 10591
Phone: (914) 631-4505
Fax: (914) 631-6017
E-mail: stapled@mail.rockefeller.edu

Seattle University
Michael Bisesi, Professor and Director
Center for Nonprofit and Social Enterprise Management
Seattle University
900 Broadway
Seattle, WA 98122
Phone: (206) 296-5435
Fax: (206) 296-5402
E-mail: bisesim@seattleu.edu
Internet: http://www.seattleu.edu/artsci/npl

Seton Hall University
Naomi Wish, Director
Center for Public Service
Seton Hall University
Kozlowski Hall, 5th Floor
South Orange, NJ 07079

Phone: (973) 761-9501
Fax: (973) 275-2463
E-mail: wishnaom@shu.edu
Internet: http://www.artsci.shu.edu/cps/

State University of New York at Albany
Judith R. Saidel, Director
Center for Women in Government and Civil Society
Rockefeller College of Public Affairs and Policy
State University of New York at Albany (SUNY)
135 Western Avenue
Albany, NY 12222
Phone: (518) 442-3896
Fax: (518) 442-3877
E-mail: Saidel@albany.edu
Internet: http://www.cwig.albany.edu

University of California, Berkeley
M. Frances Van Loo, Associate Professor
Haas School of Business
545 Student Services #1900
University of California
Berkeley, CA 94720
Phone: (510) 642-4722
Fax: (510) 642-4700
E-mail: vanloo@haas.berkeley.edu
Internet: http://www.haas.berkeley.edu

University of Delaware
Pamela Leland, Interim Director
Center for Community Development and Family Policy
University of Delaware
Newark, DE 19716
Phone: (302) 831-1682
Fax: (302) 831-4225
E-mail: pleland@udel.edu
Internet: http://www.udel.edu/ccdfp

University of Maryland University College
Ralph Ted Field, Director,
Not-for-Profit Management Graduate School
University of Maryland University College

3501 University Boulevard East
Adelphi, MD 20783
Phone: (301) 985-7200
Fax: (301) 985-4611
E-mail: rfield@umuc.edu
Internet: http://www.umuc.edu/

University of Michigan
Diane Kaplan Vinokur, Director
Janet Weiss, Codirector
Program on Nonprofit and Public Management
School of Social Work
University of Michigan
1080 South University Avenue
Ann Arbor, MI 48109
Phone: (734) 647-2553
Fax: (734) 763-3372
E-mail: dkv@umich.edu

University of Minnesota
Director
Program on Public Policy, Philanthropy and the Nonprofit Sector
Humphrey Institute of Public Affairs
301 19th Avenue South
Minneapolis, MN 55455
Phone: (612) 626-0340
Fax: (612) 625-3513
E-mail: wdiaz@hhh.umn.edu
Internet: http://www.hhh.umn.edu/

University of Missouri—Kansas City
David Renz, Director
Midwest Center for Nonprofit Leadership, Cookingham Institute
Program on Nonprofit and Public Service Leadership
University of Missouri
310 Bloch, 5110 Cherry
Kansas City, MO 64110
Phone: (816) 235-2342
Fax: (816) 235-1169
E-mail: renzd@umkc.edu
Internet: http://www.mcnl.org

University of Missouri—St. Louis
John McClusky, Director
Nonprofit Management and Leadership Program
University of Missouri
8001 Natural Bridge Road
St. Louis, MO 63121
Phone: (314) 516-6713
Fax: (314) 516-4245
E-mail: mcclusky@umsl.edu
Internet: http://www.umsl.edu/

University of Pennsylvania
Ira Harkavy, Director
Center for Community Partnerships
Penn Program for Public Service
University of Pennsylvania
133 South 36th Street, Suite 519
Philadelphia, PA 19104
Phone: (215) 898-5351
Fax: (215) 573-2799
E-mail: harkavy@pobox.upenn.edu
Internet: http://www.upenn.edu/ccp/

University of San Francisco
Michael Cortés, Director
Institute for Nonprofit Organization Management
University of San Francisco
2130 Fulton Street, LM-222
San Francisco, CA 94117
Phone: (415) 422-6867
Fax: (415) 422-5881
E-mail: cortesm@usfca.edu
Internet: http://www.inom.org/

University of Southern California
James M. Ferris, Director
Center on Philanthropy and Public Policy
University of Southern California
Lewis Hall 210
Los Angeles, CA 90089
Phone: (213) 740-0388
Fax: (213) 740-0001
E-mail: jferris@usc.edu
Internet: http://www.usc.edu/philanthropy

University of St. Thomas
Patricia Wilder, Director
Center for Nonprofit Management, Graduate School of Business
University of St. Thomas, TMH153
1000 LaSalle Avenue
Minneapolis, MN 55403
Phone: (651) 962-4292
Fax: (651) 962-4125
E-mail: pswilder@stthomas.edu
Internet: http://www.gsb.stthomas.edu/non.htm

University of Texas at Austin
Curtis Meadows Jr., Executive Director
RGK Center for Philanthropy and Community Service
LBJ School of Public Affairs
P.O. Box Y
Austin, TX 78705
Phone: (512) 232-7061
Fax: (512) 232-7063
E-mail: meadowscw@cs.com
Internet: http://www.rgkcenter.org

University of Washington
Steven Rathgeb Smith, Professor
University of Washington
Graduate School of Public Affairs
P.O. Box 353055
Seattle, WA 98195
Phone: (206) 616-1674
Fax: (206) 685-9044
E-mail: smithsr@u.washington.edu
Internet: http://www.evans.washington.edu/

University of Wisconsin—Milwaukee
John Palmer Smith, Executive Director
Helen Bader Institute for Nonprofit Management
University of Wisconsin—Milwaukee
P.O. Box 413
Milwaukee, WI 53201
Phone: (414) 229-3176
Fax: (414) 229-4477
E-mail: jpsmith@uwm.edu
Internet: http://www.helenbaderinstitute.uwm.edu

Virginia Commonwealth University
Russell A. Cargo, Director, Nonprofit Studies
Virginia Commonwealth University
P.O. Box 842028
Richmond, VA 23284
Phone: (804) 828-8096
Fax: (804) 828-7463
E-mail: racargo@vcu.edu
Internet: http://www.vcu.edu

Yale University
Lisa Berlinger, Director
Program on Nonprofit Organizations
Yale University
409 Prospect Street
New Haven, CT 06511
Phone: (203) 432-9574
Fax: (203) 432-6591
E-mail: lisa.berlinger@yale.edu
Internet: http://www.yale.edu/ponpo/

York University
Brenda Gainer, Director
Nonprofit Management and Leadership Program
Schulich School of Business
York University
4700 Keele Street
Toronto, Canada M3J 1P3
Phone: (416) 736-5092
Fax: (416) 650-8071
E-mail: bgainer@schulich.yorku.ca
Internet: http://www.schulich.yorku.ca/ssb

GLOSSARY OF
FUND RAISING TERMS

Accountability The responsibility of the donee organization to keep a donor informed about the use that is made of the donor's gift as well as the cost of raising it.

Account P.O.D. See *Totten trust.*

Acknowledgment A written expression of gratitude for a gift or service.

Acknowledgment letter A letter sent by a donee, or on behalf of a donee, to the donor expressing appreciation for a gift and identifying the use that will be made of the gift. An acknowledgment letter may be a form letter but is usually personalized.

Acquisition mailing A mailing to prospects to acquire new members or donors; also known as a *prospect mailing.*

Advance gift A gift given or pledged in advance of a public announcement of a campaign. Advance gifts are solicited before a campaign is announced because the success or failure of a campaign may depend on the size of advance gifts.

Advisory board A group of influential and prominent individuals whose association with a development program is calculated to lend luster and implied endorsement of the program's goals and objectives.

Analysis The part of a study that deals with the factors essential to success in a fund raising program, principally the case for support, leadership potential, and fields of support.

This glossary is drawn from *Principles and Techniques of Fund Raising* (Indianapolis, Ind.: The Fund Raising School, 2002b) and *Glossary of Fundraising Terms* (Alexandria, Va.: Association of Fundraising Professionals, 1996).

Annual giving A program seeking repeated gifts on an annual or recurring basis from same constituency; the income is generally used for operating budget support.

Annual report A yearly report of financial and organizational conditions prepared by the management of an organization.

Anonymous gift A gift that, by specific wish of the donor, can be announced only by amount; the name of the donor is withheld.

Appreciated real property and securities gift Real estate or securities held for a long period before being donated to a charity. Such gifts are deductible for federal income tax purposes at the full fair market value on the day of the gift, with no capital gains tax on the appreciation.

Associate Any individual or group supporting an institution through contributions at a prescribed level, serving in a special advisory capacity, or sponsoring special institutional events.

Audit An internal evaluation of development procedures as practiced by a nonprofit institution or agency; normally conducted by professional fund raising counsel.

Bargain sale The sale of property at less than its fair market value. Frequently, a person will sell property to a 501(c)(3) organization or institution at a "bargain" price (often the individual's cost as opposed to its market value). The transaction is thus partly a gift and partly a sale.

Benefactor A contributor who makes a major gift to an institution or agency; also, an arbitrary classification of contributors whose gifts are above a certain level, which is calculated to single them out as a group and to stimulate similar giving by others.

Benefit event A form of fund raising that involves the organization and staging of a special event for charitable purposes; all proceeds above expenses are designated as a contribution to the charitable institution concerned.

Benevolence A disposition to do good; an act of kindness; a generous gift.

Bequest A transfer, by will, of personal property such as cash, securities, or other tangible property.

Big gift A gift in the upper ranges, the precise levels of which vary from one institution to another. The importance of big gifts is emphasized in all fund raising campaigns.

Board of directors Individuals selected (as by other directors or members) in accordance with law (usually reflected in bylaws) to establish policy and oversee the management of an organization or institution.

Book value The amount of an asset stated in a company's records, not necessarily the amount it could bring on the open market.

Bricks-and-mortar campaign A campaign designed to secure the funds needed to build, maintain, and operate an institution's physical premises.

Budget A detailed breakdown of estimated income and expenses for a development program, prepared in advance. Budgets show various cost categories, including personnel, printed materials, purchase and rental of equipment, office expense, headquarters, mailing charges, and costs of events.

Campaign An organized effort to raise funds for a nonprofit organization.

Campaign costs Expenditures that are deemed essential to the planning and operation of a campaign and that are directly related to campaign budget projections.

Campaign leadership Top volunteers who are an essential ingredient of any campaign organization and one of the three major pedestals on which fund raising success must rest, the others being the case and sources of support. Campaign leaders provide and maintain the momentum and enthusiasm that are essential to the motivation of the entire organization of volunteers.

Campaign materials Forms and other documents required for use by campaign workers, such as fact sheets, prospect lists, and other items essential to the effective functioning of a campaign; printed materials such as brochures used to advance a campaign.

Capital campaign A carefully organized, highly structured fund raising program using volunteers supported by staff and consultants to raise funds for specific needs, to be met in a specific time frame, with a specific dollar goal. A capital campaign allows donors to pledge gifts to be paid over a period of years.

Case for support Carefully prepared reasons why a charitable institution merits financial support, including its resources, its potential for greater service, its needs, and its future plans. Often called simply the *case*.

Cash flow Predictable cash income to sustain operations, in capital campaigns or whenever pledges are secured; anticipated annual cash receipts resulting from payments on pledges.

Cash gift The simple transfer of cash, check, or currency (other than special collections) to a gift-supported organization or institution.

Cause-related marketing An arrangement that links a product or service with a social cause to provide the cause with a portion of the profits received by the corporation.

Certified Fundraising Executive (CFRE) A credential granted to a fund raiser by the Association of Fundraising Professionals, based on performance as a fund raising executive, knowledge of the fund raising field, tenure as a fund raiser (minimum of five years), education, and service to the profession.

Challenge gift A substantial gift that is made on condition that other gifts must be secured, either on a matching basis or according to some other prescribed formula, usually within a specified period, with the objective of stimulating fund raising activity generally.

Charitable contribution A donation of something of value to a gift-supported charitable organization; such contributions are usually tax-deductible.

Charitable deduction The value of money or property transferred to a 501(c)(3) organization, which is deductible for income, gift, and estate tax purposes. In most cases, *charitable deduction* refers to the portion of a gift that can be deducted from the donor's income subject to federal income tax. A donor's charitable deduction should not be confused or equated with the value of a gift; for example, gifts for purposes of life income agreements are not federally deductible at full value.

Charitable deferred gifts Gifts made currently with benefits to be paid in the future. Can take the form of wills, revocable and irrevocable trusts, charitable gift annuities, gifts of home or farm retaining a life estate, and Totten trusts.

Charitable gift annuity A transfer of cash or other property to a charitable organization, in exchange for which regular payments are made to the donor of a specified amount determined by age during the donor's lifetime. The rates paid are the most recent ones adopted by the Committee on Gift Annuities as agreed to by most major charities. There is an immediate income deduction for the present value of the amount ultimately to pass to the charity; part of the income received by the donor is also tax-free.

Charitable remainder annuity trust A trust that pays (annually to the donor or another beneficiary) a fixed amount equal to not less than 5 percent of the initial fair market value of the property placed in trust. The income is paid for the donor or beneficiary's life or for a fixed term not exceeding twenty years. The ultimate recipient of the trust, after the death of the donor or beneficiary, is a nonprofit charitable organization or institution.

Charitable remainder unitrust A separately invested trust that pays the beneficiary a designated percentage (not less than 5 percent) of the market value of the trust's assets as valued each year by the managers of the trust. The unitrust differs from standard trust arrangements by abolishing the distinction between income and principal. The whole fund is treated as a unit, and the interests of the beneficiaries, immediate or deferred, are related to the whole fund.

Commemorative gift A gift given in honor or memory of someone in appreciation of the person's activities.

Community foundation A philanthropic foundation that is specifically committed to the support of institutions in its own community, often receiving bequests from persons whose legacy is modest.

Company-sponsored foundation A private foundation whose corpus is derived from a profit-making corporation or company and whose primary purpose is the making of grants. The company-sponsored foundation may maintain close ties with the donor company, but it is an independent organization, most often with its own rules and regulations (like those of other private foundations). Companies form foundations to enable them to invest in philanthropy with funds that would otherwise be subject to capital gains taxes or income taxes and to make maximum use of the corporate charitable deduction.

Constituency All people who have in some way been involved with the institution seeking support; consists of members, contributors, participants (past or present), clients, and relatives of clients.

Consultant A specialist in one or more areas of fund raising who is hired by an organization for the purpose of recommending solutions to problems and generally providing advice and guidance related to fund raising efforts.

Corporate foundation The philanthropic arm created by a corporation to deal with requests for contributions from various agencies—locally, regionally, or nationally.

Corporate giving program A grantmaking program established and controlled by a profit-making corporation or company. The program does not necessarily include a separate endowment, and the annual grant total my be directly related to the previous year's profits. Giving directly from corporate profits is not subject to the same reporting restrictions as giving from private foundations. Some companies may make charitable contributions from corporate profits, operating budgets, or company-sponsored foundations.

Corporate philanthropy Support through gifts, equipment, supplies, or other contributions by business firms to charitable institutions, sometimes through organized programs that may include corporate foundations.

Corpus The principal of a fund or endowment, as distinguished from interest or income.

Cultivation The process of promoting and encouraging interest or involvement on the part of a potential donor or volunteer leader; an educative process to inform about an institution and the reasons why it merits support.

Deferred gift See *planned gift*.

Designated gift A restricted or commemorative gift made for a specific purpose and designated for a specific use.

Development All aspects of an ongoing fund raising program (annual giving, special gifts, planned gifts, public relations, and so on).

Direct mail The solicitation of gifts or volunteer services and distribution of information pieces by mass mailing.

Director of development The individual who heads an organization's development program, either with this or some other title, such as vice president for development or vice president for external affairs and development.

Dollar objective. See *goal*.

Donor The individual, organization, or institution that makes a gift.

Donor acquisition The process of identifying and attracting donors.

Donor-directed gift A gift or bequest to a foundation, organization, or institution for which the donor specifies to whom the money should be distributed.

Donor list A list of contributors prepared for a particular purpose or in conjunction with list building.

Donor recognition The policy and practice of showing appreciation for gifts, first through immediate acknowledgment by card or letter and subsequently through personalized notes, personal expressions of appreciation directly to donors, published lists of contributors, and other appropriate ways.

Donor relations A planned program of maintaining donor interest through acknowledgments, information, personal involvement, and other actions.

Drop date The date on which direct mail letters must be delivered to a post office for mailing.

Electronic funds transfer (EFT) A method whereby donors instruct their banks to make monthly deductions from their accounts, designated for the charitable organization of their choice.

Employee matching gift A contribution made by an employee to a 501(c)(3) organization that is matched by a similar contribution from the employer.

Endowment Principal or corpus maintained in a permanent fund to provide income for general or restricted use of an agency, institution, or program. Also known as a *pure endowment;* compare *quasi-endowment.*

Enlistment Agreement by an individual to serve an agency, organization, or institution in some voluntary capacity.

Estate The total assets of a person in life or at the time of death; also, the rights of ownership of those assets.

Ethics The morality of the activities of a philanthropic organization. Also, standards of conduct and methods of doing business by organizations of fund raising counsel that provide assurances of professionalism in client relationships.

Face-to-face solicitation Soliciting a prospective contributor in person at the prospect's home, office, or other location.

Family foundation A foundation whose funds are derived from members of a single family. Generally, family members serve as officers or board members of the foundation and play an influential role in grantmaking decisions.

Feasibility study An in-depth examination and assessment of the fund raising potential of an institution or agency, conducted by fund raising counsel and presented in the form of a written report setting forth various conclusions, recommendations, and proposed plans.

Foundation See *philanthropic foundation.*

Fund raiser A person who makes his or her living working as a member of an organization's or institution's development department, as an independent fund raising consultant, or as a member of a fund raising counseling firm; also, a volunteer who raises funds for a cause or an event held to raise funds for a cause.

Fund raising counsel An individual or firm that provides guidance and advice to charitable institutions on all aspects of fund raising.

Fund raising executive An individual employed by an institution or organization to provide direction, counsel, and management of its fund raising operations.

Fund raising plan All elements of an organization's procedure for attaining a campaign goal; a fund raising program including objectives, case, leadership requirements, timetable, personnel requirements, and budget; overall strategy or grand design for successful implementation of a campaign.

Fund raising program An organization's or institution's strategy, tactics, objectives, case, and needs, in their entirety; a campaign that is loosely defined in terms of time frame and specific funding opportunities; a campaign; a timetable for a campaign.

GAAP An acronym for *generally accepted accounting principles.*

General gift Any of the final 5 to 20 percent of funds collected in a campaign.

Gift A voluntary, irrevocable transfer of something of value without consideration (that is, without receiving anything tangible in return) at the time of transfer or at any time in the future. If the individual making the gift entertains any idea of reclaiming it, the transfer is not a gift. See also *advance gift, big gift, general gift,* and *major gift.*

Gift annuity A contract between the donor and the charity wherein the donor transfers property to the charity in exchange for the charity's promise to pay the donor a fixed annual income for life or some other mutually agreed period. The donor's right to income may be deferred for a period of years. The annuity may be in joint and survivor form.

Gift in kind A contribution of equipment or other property on which the donor may place a monetary value and claim a deduction for income tax purposes.

Gift of home or farm retaining a life estate The gift of a homestead with the proviso that the donor retains use thereof until death. The federal income tax deduction is based on the present value, figured on the prospective years of using the property before it goes to the charity.

Gift range chart A table of gift amounts that enables campaign leaders to know, in advance of a campaign, the size and number of gifts that are likely to be needed at each level of giving in order to achieve the campaign goal.

Gift receipt A form that is sent to donors (with copies to appropriate officials of the campaign and the organization or institution), either separately or as an enclosure with an acknowledgment, officially and explicitly recognizing their contributions.

Giving club Any of various categories, established by the recipient organization or institution, grouping donors who give gifts at a similar level.

Goal An all-embracing focus of accomplishment, supported by specific objectives, that an organization seeks to achieve; also, the amount of money to be achieved by a fund raising campaign, also known as the *dollar objective.*

Governance Oversight by the governing authority of an organization or institution.

Grant An allocation of funds from a foundation, corporation, or government agency.

Grassroots fund raising Raising modest amounts of money from individuals or groups from the local community on a broad basis. Usually done within a specific constituency or among people who live in the neighborhood served or who are clients. Common grassroots fund raising activities include membership drives, raffles, bake sales, auctions, benefits, and dances.

House file The names and addresses of active and recently lapsed donors and members of an organization.

Independent sector A term used to describe all nonprofit organizations, as distinct from government and corporations formed to make a profit; also known as the *third sector;* not to be confused with the organization INDEPENDENT SECTOR.

Identification The process of ascertaining, through investigation, research, and analysis, which of various candidates appear to be most promising as prospective leaders, workers, and donors.

Indicia Markings on an envelope indicating that a nonprofit mailing permit for reduced-rate bulk mailing has been obtained; used in place of stamps or meters.

Involvement The calculated effort, perennially undertaken by development offices, to stimulate interest and enthusiasm on the part of prospective donors and candidates for volunteer leadership through active participation in institutional affairs; an extension of cultivation.

Intestate Without a will.

Irrevocable trust Either a charitable remainder unitrust or a charitable remainder annuity trust (which see). Although the principal of these trusts cannot be withdrawn, there are additional benefits to the donor through immediate income tax deductions and fund management. The donor will receive yearly income from the trust as well as an immediate partial federal income tax deduction for the interest that ultimately passes to the charity.

LAI principle The fund raising axiom of qualifying prospects on the basis of *linkage, ability,* and *interest.*

Leadership The individuals within an institution, agency, program, or fund raising campaign that stimulate others to act or give.

Leadership gift Normally, the second tier of gifts to a campaign that will inspire extraordinary giving by subsequent donors.

Legacy A disposition in a will of personal property. A *demonstrative legacy* is a legacy payable primarily out of a specific fund. A *specific legacy* is a legacy of a particular article or a specified part of the estate.

Letter of inquiry A letter sent by an organization to a foundation or corporation presenting a project for which funding is being sought and asking the foundation or corporation to consider funding the project or receiving a full proposal.

Letter of intent A pledge form stated in more informal, nonlegalistic terms for use by potential donors who view the pledge card as a contract and refuse to commit themselves to multiple-year gift payments because of this contractual aspect.

LIA principle The fund raising axiom of separating advocate-askers from donors on the basis of *linkage, involvement,* and *advocacy.*

Life income gift An irrevocable gift of cash, securities, or real estate to a gift-supported organization, with the donor (or other beneficiaries) receiving income from the donated assets for a period of time through an annuity or trust arrangement.

Life income pooled trust A charitable remainder trust that holds the commingled irrevocable gifts of donors who receive income annually based on the earnings of the trust and their individual entitlement as participants. Upon termination of an income interest, the underlying property is transferred to a charitable organization or institution.

Life insurance gift The irrevocable assignment of a life insurance policy for charitable disposition for which the present value is fully tax-deductible, as are the premiums paid by the donor.

Life interest An interest or claim that does not amount to ownership and that is held only for the duration of the life of the person to whom the interest is given or for the duration of the life of another person; an interest in property for life.

Lybunts Term derived from the acronym for donors who gave "last year but not this" year.

Major gift A gift of a significant amount of money (the size may vary according to the organization's needs and goals); may be repeated periodically. Also a program designation.

Market The pool of potential sources of funds, members, or clients (individuals and organizations).

Matching gift A gift that is made on condition that it be matched by another donor's gift within a certain period, either on a one-to-one basis or in accordance with some other formula; also, a gift made by a corporation in the same amount as a gift made by one of its employees.

Memorial A gift made to perpetuate the memory of an individual. (The term is *not* used to refer to a gift to honor a living person.)

Mission A philosophical or value statement expressing the reason the organization exists. Do not confuse *mission statements* with statements of goals or objectives.

Needs In fund raising terms, *needs* refers specifically to the institution's dollar requirements that can constitute objectives for an intensive campaign or for a continuing fund development program.

Capital needs are building or property needs, in the form of new construction, additions, expansion, or remodeling or acquisition of property. They are sometimes related to equipment purchases or to raising funds for an addition to endowment capital. *Endowment needs* are funds required to add to the invested principal or corpus with only income used for sustaining funds, special project support, and other purposes. *Program needs* are annual support for the operational budget, funds required to supplement income through revenues to sustain operation of the agency or institution. *Project needs* are for program activity or small equipment acquisition. *Validated needs* are needs that have been identified, analyzed, and approved by management and by the governing body and other volunteers as being legitimate and appropriate to the functioning of the institution.

Nonprofit organization An establishment operated by members or volunteers (or both) that is classified by the Internal Revenue Service as providing a public benefit without purpose of generating a profit for its members. Also called a *not-for-profit organization.*

Operating foundation A fund or endowment designated by the Internal Revenue Service as a private foundation, yet which differs from a typical private foundation in that its primary purpose is to conduct research, promote social welfare, or engage in other programs determined by its governing body or establishment charter. It may make some grants, but the sum is generally small relative to the funds used for the foundation's own programs.

Outright gift The simple transfer of cash or an asset to the recipient without any conditions or terms of trust.

Philanthropic foundation A corporation or trust established with funds contributed by an individual, family, corporation, or community for the support of nonprofit organizations and to which such organizations may appeal for grants in support of their programs and projects.

Philanthropist Broadly speaking, anyone who makes a gift; usually used to describe a wealthy individual known for exceptional generosity in support of charitable causes.

Philanthropy As used at the Center on Philanthropy, voluntary action for the public good, including voluntary service, voluntary association, and voluntary giving.

Planned gift A gift provided for legally during the donor's lifetime but the principal benefits of which do not accrue to the institution until some future time, usually at the death of the donor or other income beneficiary.

Planned giving The application of sound personal, financial, and estate planning concepts to the individual donor's plans for lifetime and testamentary giving.

Pledge A signed and dated commitment to make a gift over a specified period, generally two or more years, payable according to terms set by the donor in a series of scheduled monthly, quarterly, semiannual, or annual payments.

Private foundation Broadly, a 501(c)(3) organization that is originally funded from one source, derives revenue from earnings on its investments, and makes grants to other charitable organizations as opposed to administering its own programs. (The definition used by the Internal Revenue Service is more technical.)

Proposal A written request or application for a gift or grant that states why the project or program is needed, who will carry it out, and how much it will cost.

Prospective donor Any logical source of support, be it an individual, corporation, organization, government, or foundation.

Prospect mailing See *acquisition mailing.*

Public charity A 501(c)(3) organization that is not a private foundation, either because it is "publicly supported" (that is, it normally derives at least one-third of its support from gifts and other qualified sources) or it functions as a "supporting organization" to other public charities. Some public charities engage in grantmaking activities, but most engage in direct service activities. Public charities are eligible for maximum tax-deductible contributions from the public and are not subject to the same rules and regulations as private foundations.

Quasi-endowment A fund whose principal can be invaded by a board to meet its operating costs. Such endowments include gifts for which donors specify their use; they may also include gifts that are given for no specific purpose and that a board treats as an endowment.

Rating An estimate of a prospective contributor's ability to contribute. The rating becomes an asking figure for the solicitor to suggest in requesting a contribution or pledge.

Real estate gift The transfer of property to a 501(c)(3) organization or institution, the value of which is determined by the fair market value of the property at the time of transfer.

Recognition Formal or informal acknowledgment of a gift or contributed services; an event, communication, or significant item honoring a gift or service.

Renewal mailing A mailing to donors or members requesting renewed support.

Restricted fund A fund in which the principal and earnings are bound by donor guidelines as they relate to investment or expenditure (or both).

Restricted gift A gift for a specified purpose clearly stated by the donor.

Revocable trust A trust that allows the grantor to withdraw any or all assets during his or her lifetime while at the same time having full enjoyment of the property. At death, the assets flow efficiently to the beneficiaries, saving probate and administrative costs. A charity can be named as one of the beneficiaries.

Screening The process of assigning prospects to broad categories of potential giving ranges preliminary to conducting more refined evaluations through the process of prospect rating.

Seed money A substantial gift, generally by a foundation or an affluent individual, to launch a program or project.

Sequential giving A cardinal principle of fund raising counsel that gifts in a campaign should be sought "from the top down," that is, that the largest gifts in a gift range chart should be sought at the outset of a campaign, followed sequentially by a search for lesser gifts.

Solicitors Volunteers and institutional staff who ask for contributions to a campaign or development program. Professional solicitors are paid to solicit for programs or causes.

Special event A fund raising function designed to attract and involve large numbers of people for the purpose of raising money or cultivating future donors.

Special gift Any of the gifts that fall within the fourth tier of giving to a campaign; gifts that require special attention by the recipient organization in order to attract donor participation.

Standard of giving An arbitrary but generally realistic assignment of giving potential to groups or categories of prospects based on past performances and other criteria.

Stewardship The philosophy and means by which an institution exercises ethical accountability in the use of contributed resources and the philosophy and means by which a donor exercises responsibility in the voluntary use of resources; the guiding principle in philanthropic fund raising.

Strategic plan A program incorporating a strategy for achieving organizational goals and objectives within a specific time frame and with substantive support in the form of methods, priorities, and resources.

Support services The full range of activities required to support a fund raising effort: office management; word processing; gift receiving, posting, and acknowledging; budget management and control; and so on.

Tax benefits Savings in income, gift, and estate taxes brought about by giving to charitable institutions.

Telemarketing Raising funds or selling products or services by telephone.

Telephone-mail campaign A fund raising technique, often referred to as "phone mail," that combines mail and telephone solicitation in a sophisticated manner through the use of paid solicitors and management of the program; a telephone solicitation supported by a mail component for confirmation of verbal pledges.

Third sector See *independent sector.*

Timing Determination of the most favorable times to complete certain fund raising objectives in order to achieve maximum results.

Totten trust A bank account, bond, or other security for which a charity is named as a beneficiary, as permitted by state law; also known as an *account P.O.D. (payable on death)*.

Trust A fiduciary relationship with respect to property, subjecting the person by whom the title to property is held to equitable duties to deal with the property for the benefit of another person. For example, A gives property in trust, with A as trustee, to pay income to B for life and then to give the property to C free and clear.

Trustee A person or agent of a trust, such as a bank, holding legal title to property in order to administer it for a beneficiary; a member of a governing board; in a corporate trust, any of the directors of the trust.

Trust funds Money, securities, and property held in trust by an agent of wealth (bank, estate manager, or attorney) or managed by an institution under a trust agreement to produce income for the beneficiary.

Unrestricted gift A gift to an institution or agency for whatever purposes the officers or trustees choose.

Vehicle The particular form in which a fund raising program is organized and executed (for example annual giving, capital campaign, direct mail).

Volunteerism The willingness of private citizens to voluntarily provide their services to a wide variety of programs and causes, both in fund raising programs and in other capacities.

Will A legally executed written instrument by which a person sets forth the disposition of his or her property to take effect after death. A *holographic will* is entirely written and signed by the testator (maker) in his or her own hand. A *nuncupative will* is an oral will made by a person in his or her last illness or extremity before witnesses, often not honored in a court of law. Under a *pour-over will*, assets controlled by the will are directed to be "poured over" into a trust. A *reciprocal will* is made by two persons in which each leaves everything to the other. A charity may be named a beneficiary under a will in many ways, receiving gifts of specific real or personal property, a stated amount of money, or a percentage of the remaining estate after other specific bequests have been made.

REFERENCES

AAFRC Trust for Philanthropy. *Giving USA, 2002: The Annual Report on Philanthropy for the Year 2001*. Indianapolis, Ind.: American Association of Fundraising Counsel, 2002.

Adizes, I. "Organizational Passages: Diagnosing and Treating Lifecycle Problems of Organizations." *Organizational Dynamics,* Summer 1979, pp. 3–25.

Allen, P. A. *How to Research and Analyze Individual Donors.* San Francisco: Jossey-Bass, 1991.

Anderson, A. *Ethics for Fundraisers.* Indianapolis: Indiana University Press, 1996.

Anft, M. "Raising Money with Sense and Sensibility," *Chronicle of Philanthropy,* Oct. 18, 2001, pp. 21–22.

Anft, M. "Tapping Ethnic Wealth." *Chronicle of Philanthropy,* Jan. 10, 2002, pp. 4–6.

Asia Pacific Philanthropy Consortium. *Investing in Ourselves: Giving and Fund Raising in Asia.* Manila, Philippines: Venture for Fund Raising, 2002.

Association of Fundraising Professionals. *The Accountable Nonprofit Organization.* 1995. [http://www.afpnet.org/tier3_cd.cfm?folder_id = 897&content_item_id = 1072].

Austin, J. "The E-Philanthropy Revolution Is Here to Stay." *Chronicle of Philanthropy,* Mar. 8, 2001, pp. 72–73.

Beyel, J. S. "Ethics and Major Gifts." In D. F. Burlingame and J. M. Hodge (eds.), *Developing Major Gifts.* New Directions for Philanthropic Fundraising, no. 16. San Francisco: Jossey-Bass, 1997.

Billitteri, T. J. "Moving Giving off the Dime." *Chronicle of Philanthropy,* Oct. 21, 1999, pp. 1, 10.

507

Billitteri, T. J. "Endowment Assets Nationwide Climb to Nearly $600 Billion, New Study Finds." *Chronicle of Philanthropy,* June 15, 2000, p. 45.

Billitteri, T. J. "Survey Finds Rapid Rise in Assets and Grants of Donor-Advised Funds." *Chronicle of Philanthropy,* May 31, 2001, pp. 10–11.

Black, S. S. "Native American Philanthropy." In P. C. Rogers (ed.), *Philanthropy in Communities of Color: Traditions and Challenges.* Indianapolis, Ind.: Association for Research on Nonprofit Organizations and Voluntary Action, 2001.

Bloland, H. G. "No Longer Emerging, Fund Raising Is a Profession." *CASE International Journal of Educational Advancement,* 2002, *3*(1), 7–19.

Bloland, H. G., and Bornstein, R. "Fund Raising in Transition: Strategies for Professionalization." In D. F. Burlingame and L. J. Hulse (eds.), *Taking Fund Raising Seriously: Advancing the Profession and Practice of Raising Money.* San Francisco: Jossey-Bass, 1991.

Blum, D. E. "Making a Place for Arab-Americans." *Chronicle of Philanthropy,* Jan. 10, 2002, pp. 26–27.

Bolman, L. G., and Deal, T. E. *Leading with Soul: An Uncommon Journey of Spirit.* San Francisco: Jossey-Bass, 1995.

Bremmer, R. *American Philanthropy.* (2nd ed.) Chicago: University of Chicago Press, 1988.

Buber, M. *I and Thou* (R. G. Smith, trans.). (2nd ed.) New York: Scribner, 1958.

"Building Bridges Between Practice and Knowledge in Nonprofit Management Education: An Initiative That Is Unleashing Resources for the Common Good." Report to the W. K. Kellogg Foundation Board, Mar. 2001. [http://centerpointinstitute.org/bridges/Papers&Reports/papers.htm].

Bundles, A. *On Her Own Ground: The Life and Times of Madam C. J. Walker.* New York: Scribner, 2001.

Burlingame, D. F. "Corporate Fund Raising." In J. M. Greenfield (ed.), *The Nonprofit Handbook: Fund Raising.* (3rd ed.) New York: Wiley, 2001.

Burlingame, D. F., and Young, D. R. (eds.). *Corporate Philanthropy at the Crossroads.* Bloomington: Indiana University Press, 1996.

Burnette, A. G. *The Privilege to Ask.* Palm Coast, Fla.: Advancement Solutions, 2001.

Campobasso, L., and Davis, D. *Reflections on Capacity-Building.* Woodland Hills, Calif.: California Wellness Foundation, 2001.

Carbone, R. F. *Fund Raising as a Profession.* College Park, Md.: Clearing House for Research on Fund Raising, 1989.

Carson, E. D. "On Race, Gender, Culture, and Research on the Voluntary Sector." *Nonprofit Management and Leadership,* 1993, *3,* 327–335.

Carson, E. D. "The New Rules for Engaging Donors of Color: Giving in the Twenty-First Century." In E. R. Tempel and D. F. Burlingame (eds.), *Understanding the Needs of Donors: The Supply Side of Charitable Giving.* New Directions for Philanthropic Fundraising, no. 29. San Francisco: Jossey-Bass, 2000.

Carver, J. *Boards That Make a Difference.* San Francisco: Jossey-Bass, 1990.

Castle, A. "Analyzing Your Institution's Readiness for a Women's Philanthropy Initiative." Paper presented at the Council for Advancement and Support of Education (CASE) conference, Cambridge, Mass., June 21, 1999.

"Celebrating 25 Years of Service." Seventh Generation Fund, 2002. [http://www.7genfund.org].

Center on Philanthropy at Indiana University. "Indiana Gives 2000: Hoosier Hospitality to Charitable Organizations." 2001. [http://www.philanthropy.iupui.edu/IndianaGives2000.pdf].

Chaitt, R. "The New Work of Nonprofit Boards." *Harvard Business Review,* Sept.-Oct. 1996, pp. 36–46.

Christensen, J. "Tools for the Aftermath: Relief Agencies Retool to Handle Online Food." *New York Times,* Sept. 26, 2001, p. H1.

Cone/Roper Cause Trends Report: The Evolution of Cause Branding. Boston: Cone Inc., 1999.

Connell, J. E. "Budgeting for Fund Raising." In J. M. Greenfield (ed.), *The Nonprofit Handbook: Fund Raising.* (3rd ed.) New York: Wiley, 2001.

Conway, D. "Interview with Henry Rosso on Stewardship and Fundraising." In D. Conway and C. H. Price (eds.), *The Practice of Stewardship in Religious Fundraising.* New Directions for Philanthropic Fundraising, no. 17. San Francisco: Jossey-Bass, 1997.

Cortes, M. "Fostering Philanthropy and Service in U.S. Latino Communities." In P. C. Rogers (ed.), *Philanthropy in Communities of Color: Traditions and Challenges.* Indianapolis, Ind.: Association for Research on Nonprofit Organizations and Voluntary Action, 2001.

Dees, J. G., Emerson, J., and Economy, P. *Enterprising Nonprofits: A Toolkit for Social Entrepreneurs.* New York: Wiley, 2001.

Dees, J. G., Emerson, J., and Economy, P. *Strategic Tools for Social Entrepreneurs: Enhancing the Performance of Your Enterprising Nonprofit.* New York: Wiley, 2002.

Deloitte & Touche. *She Said: A Study of Affluent Women and Personal Finances.* Washington, D.C.: Deloitte & Touche, 1998.

Dennis, M. *Emerging Philanthropy in Communities of Color: A Report on Current Trends.* Battle Creek, Mich.: W. K. Kellogg Foundation, 1999.

Drucker, P. F. *Managing the Nonprofit Organization.* New York: HarperCollins, 1990.

Drucker, P. F. "It Profits Us to Strengthen Nonprofits." *Wall Street Journal,* Dec. 19, 1991, p. A14.

Duffy, M. "What Do Nonprofits Use Databases For?" TechSoup.org, Sept. 29, 2000. [http://www.techsoup.org/articlepage.cfm?ArticleId = 215&topicId = 6].

Dunlop, D. R. "Fundraising for the Largest Gift of a Lifetime: From Inspiring the Commitment to Receiving the Gift." Workshop at the Council for Advancement and Support of Education (CASE) conference, Charleston, S.C., May 22–24, 2000.

Duronio, M. A., and Tempel, E. R. *Fund Raisers: Their Careers, Stories, Concerns, and Accomplishments.* San Francisco: Jossey-Bass, 1997.

Elliot, D. "What Counts as Deception in Higher Education Development." In D. F. Burlingame and L. J. Hulse (eds.), *Taking Fund Raising Seriously: Advancing the Profession and Practice of Raising Money.* San Francisco: Jossey-Bass, 1991.

Ellis, S. J., and Noyes, K. H. *By the People: A History of Americans as Volunteers.* (rev. ed.) San Francisco: Jossey-Bass, 1990.

Emerson, J. "A Commitment to Accountability: The Coming Challenge to Venture Philanthropy." In M. Morino, *Venture Philanthropy, 2001: The Changing Landscape.* Washington, D.C.: Morino Institute and Venture Philanthropy Partners, 2001.

Emerson, R. W. "Circles." *Essays: First Series,* 1841.

Fischer, M. *Ethical Decision Making in Fund Raising.* New York: Wiley, 2000.

Fisher, J. L., and Quehl, G. H. (eds.). *The President and Fund Raising.* Washington, D.C.: American Council on Education, 1989.

Fisher, J. M. "Celebrating the Heroines of Philanthropy." In A. I. Thompson and A. R. Kaminski (eds.), *Women and Philanthropy: A National Agenda.* Madison: Center for Women and Philanthropy, University of Wisconsin, 1993.

Fogal, R. E. "Standards and Ethics in Fund Raising." In H. A. Rosso and Associates, *Achieving Excellence in Fund Raising: A Comprehensive Guide to the Principles, Strategies, and Methods.* San Francisco: Jossey-Bass, 1991.

Foundation Center. *Foundation Growth and Giving Estimates.* New York: Foundation Center, 2001.

Frantzreb, A. C. "Seeking the Big Gift." In H. A. Rosso and Associates, *Achieving Excellence in Fund Raising: A Comprehensive Guide to Principles, Strategies, and Methods.* San Francisco: Jossey-Bass, 1991.

Friedan, B. *The Feminine Mystique.* New York: Dell, 1984.

"Fundraising and the New Wealth: A Reality Check. *Advancing Philanthropy,* Mar.-Apr. 2001, pp. 14–18, 42–43.

Garber, S. "The Fund Raising Professional: An Agent for Change." Paper presented at the International Conference for the Association of Healthcare Philanthropy, Chicago, Oct. 4, 1993.

Gardner, J. W. *On Leadership.* New York: Free Press, 1990.

Gessen, M. "The Rebirth of Russian Charity." *American Benefactor,* Spring 1997, pp. 123–124.

Gilbert, M. C. "The Gilbert Email Manifesto (GEM)." *Nonprofit Online News,* Apr. 10, 2001. [http://news.gilbert.org/gem].

Gilligan, C. *In a Different Voice: Psychological Theory and Women's Development.* Cambridge, Mass.: Harvard University Press, 1993.

Goss, K. A. "Volunteering and the Long Civic Generation." *Nonprofit and Voluntary Sector Quarterly,* 1999, *28,* 378–415.

Gow Pettey, J. *Cultivating Diversity in Fundraising.* New York: Wiley, 2001.

Grace, K. S. "Managing for Results." In H. A. Rosso and Associates, *Achieving Excellence in Fund Raising: A Comprehensive Guide to the Principles, Strategies, and Methods.* San Francisco: Jossey-Bass, 1991.

Grace, K. S. *Beyond Fund Raising: New Strategies for Nonprofit Innovation and Investment.* New York: Wiley, 1997.

Grace, K. S., and Wendroff, A. L. *High Impact Philanthropy: How Donors, Boards, and Nonprofit Organizations Can Transform Communities.* New York: Wiley, 2000.

Greenberg, J. M. "Forms of Bias." In *Building Bridges with Reliable Information: A Guide to Our Community's People.* Washington, D.C.: National Conference for Community and Justice of the National Capital Area Region, 2002.

Greenfeld, K. T. "A New Way of Giving," *Time,* July 24, 2000, pp. 49–51.

Greenfield, J. M. *Fund-Raising Cost Effectiveness: A Self-Assessment Workbook.* New York: Wiley, 1996.

Greenfield, J. M. *Fund Raising: Evaluating and Managing the Fund Development Process.* (2nd ed.) New York: Wiley, 1999.

Greenfield, J. M. "Accountability: Delivering Community Benefits." In J. M. Greenfield (ed.), *The Nonprofit Handbook: Fund Raising.* (3rd ed.) New York: Wiley, 2001.

Greenfield, J. M., and Dreves, J. P. "Fund-Raising Assessment." In J. M. Greenfield (ed.), *The Nonprofit Handbook: Fund Raising.* (3rd ed.) New York: Wiley, 2001.

Hall, M., and Macpherson, L. G. "A Provincial Portrait of Canada's Charities." *Research Bulletin, Canadian Centre for Philanthropy,* Sept. 16, 1997.

Hall-Russell, C., and Kasberg, R. H. *African American Traditions of Giving and Serving: A Midwest Perspective.* Indianapolis: Center on Philanthropy at Indiana University, 1997.

Harrah-Conforth, J., and Borsos, J. "The Evolution of Professional Fund Raising, 1890–1990." In D. F. Burlingame and L. J. Hulse (eds.), *Taking Fund Raising Seriously: Advancing the Profession and Practice of Raising Money.* San Francisco: Jossey-Bass, 1991.

Harvard University Institute of Politics. "Attitudes Toward Politics and Public Service: A National Survey of College Undergraduates." 2001. [http://www.iop.harvard.edu/projects-survey.html].

Havens, J. J., and Schervish, P. G. *Millionaires and the Millennium: The Forthcoming Transfer of Wealth and the Prospects for a Golden Age of Philanthropy.* Boston: Social Welfare Research Institute, Boston College, 1999.

Hero, P. de C. "Giving Back the Silicon Valley Way: Emerging Patterns of a New Philanthropy." In E. R. Tempel (ed.), *Understanding Donor Dynamics: The Organizational Side of Charitable Giving.* New Directions for Philanthropic Fundraising, no. 32. San Francisco: Jossey-Bass, 2001a.

Hero, P. de C. "Language Matters: It Is Time to Change Our Name." *AFP Newsletter,* Association of Fundraising Professionals, Silicon Valley (Calif.) Chapter, Oct. 2001b.

Hispanic Federation. *Hispanic New Yorkers on Nueva York.* New York: Hispanic Federation, 1999. [http://www.hispanicfederation.org/sv99-p.htm].

"Historical Prices: Dow Jones Industrial Average." Yahoo! Finance, 2002. [http://table.finance.yahoo.com/t?a = 01&b = 01&c = 91&d = 12&e = 31&f = 00&g = m&s = %5Edji&y = 0&z = %5Edji].

Holman, M. M., and Sigler, J. *The Complete Guide to Careers in Fund Raising.* Dubuque, Ia.: Kendall/Hunt, 1998.

Imdieke, B. J. "Internet-Based Testing of the Philanthropic Giving Index Questionnaire Among a Nonrandom Sample of International NGO Leaders." Report prepared for the Center on Philanthropy, Indianapolis, Ind., May 2002.

INDEPENDENT SECTOR. *Ethics and the Nation's Voluntary and Philanthropic Community: Obedience to the Unenforceable.* Washington, D.C.: INDEPENDENT SECTOR, 1991.

INDEPENDENT SECTOR. *Giving and Volunteering in the United States.* Washington, D.C.: INDEPENDENT SECTOR, 1996.

INDEPENDENT SECTOR. "Public Policy Update: Special Report." July 30, 1998. [http://www.independentsector.org/programs/OldPPU/ppu_specialsanctions.pdf].

INDEPENDENT SECTOR. *Public Trust and Accountability Report, 2000.* Washington, D.C.: INDEPENDENT SECTOR, 2000.

INDEPENDENT SECTOR. "Giving and Volunteering in the United States: Findings from a National Survey." 2001a. [http://www.independentsector.org/programs/research/gandv.html].

INDEPENDENT SECTOR. "Sources and Disposition of Annual Funds by Subsector, 1977, 1982, 1987, 1992, and 1996." 2001b. [http://www.independentsector.org/programs/research/table4_2.html].

INDEPENDENT SECTOR. *The New Nonprofit Almanac and Desk Reference.* Washington, D.C.: INDEPENDENT SECTOR, 2002.

Internal Revenue Service. *Survey of Income Bulletin* (Vol. 19, no. 4). Washington, D.C.: Government Printing Office, 1999.

Johnston, M. "Regulating Online Fundraising." In M. Warwick, T. Hart, and N. Allen (eds.), *Fundraising on the Internet: The ePhilanthropyFoundation.Org Guide to Success Online.* (2nd ed.) San Francisco: Jossey-Bass, 2002.

Josephson, M. *Making Ethical Decisions.* (2nd ed.) Marina Del Ray, Calif.: Josephson Institute on Ethics, 2002.

Joslyn, H. "Foundations Report Increase in Number of Paid Staff Members." *Chronicle on Philanthropy,* Oct. 4, 2001, p. 68.

Katz, D., and Kahn, R. L. *The Social Psychology of Organizations.* (2nd ed.) New York: Wiley, 1978.

Kearns, K. P. *Managing for Accountability: Preserving the Public Trust in Public and Nonprofit Organizations.* San Francisco: Jossey-Bass, 1996.

Kelly, K. S. *Effective Fund-Raising Management.* Mahwah, N.J.: Erlbaum, 1998.

Klinger, D. "Tale of Two Rides: Preliminary Results of the 2000 NACUBO Endowment Study." *NACUBO Business Officer,* Apr. 2001, pp. 24–31.

Knowledge Works on e-Philanthropy. "e-Philanthropy v2.001: From Entrepreneurial Adventure to an Online Community." 2001. [http://www.actknowledgeworks.net/ephil].

Kotler, P., and Andreasen, A. R. *Strategic Marketing for Nonprofit Organizations.* (3rd ed.) Upper Saddle River, N.J.: Prentice Hall, 1987.

Kramer, M. R. "Venture Capital and Philanthropy: A Bad Fit." *Chronicle of Philanthropy,* Apr. 22, 1999, pp. 72–73.

Kübler-Ross, E. *On Death and Dying.* Old Tappan, N.J.: Macmillan, 1969.

Larose, M. D. "Assets of Donor Advised Funds Totaled $12.36 Billion Last Year, Survey Finds." *Chronicle of Philanthropy,* May 30, 2002, p. 11.

Letts, C. W., Ryan, W., and Grossman, A. "Virtuous Capital: What Foundations Can Learn from Venture Capitalists." *Harvard Business Review,* Mar.-Apr. 1997, pp. 2–7.

Levy, B. R. *The NSFRE Fund-Raising Dictionary.* New York: Wiley, 1996.

Manetta, D. J. "College Endowments Enjoyed Healthy Returns in Fiscal Year Prior to Market Collapse." Press release, National Association of College and University Business Officers, Apr. 5, 2001. [http://www.nacubo.org/accounting_finance/endowment_study/].

Marcello, M., Van Dien, G., and Vehrs, K. *Women's Philanthropy at Research Universities, 1998–1999.* Madison: Survey Research Center, University of Wisconsin, 2000.

Marchetti, D. "Magazine Publisher's Charity Begins—but Doesn't End—at the Office." *Chronicle of Philanthropy,* Jan. 13, 2000, p. 22.

Marx, J. "Women and Human Services Giving." *Social Work,* 2000, 45(1), 27–39.

Mixer, J. R. *Principles of Professional Fund Raising: Useful Foundations for Successful Practice.* San Francisco: Jossey-Bass, 1993.

Morino, M. *Venture Philanthropy, 2001: The Changing Landscape.* Washington, D.C.: Morino Institute and Venture Philanthropy Partners, 2001.

Morris, T. *If Aristotle Ran General Motors.* New York: Henry Holt, 1997.

Muirhead, S. *Corporate Contributions: The Views from 50 Years.* New York: Conference Board, 1999.

Mullen, R. "The Evolution of Charitable Giving." In C. Walker and C. Pharoah (eds.), *A Lot of Give: Trends in Charitable Giving for the 21st Century.* London: Hodder & Stoughton/Charities Aid Foundation, 2002.

National Committee on Planned Giving. *Planned Giving in the United States, 2000: A Survey of Donors.* Indianapolis, Ind.: National Committee on Planned Giving, 2001.

National Endowment for Financial Education. "Frozen in the Headlights: The Dynamics of Women and Money." Feb. 2000. [http://www.nefe.org/pages/innovative.html].

National Foundation for Women Business Owners. *Styles of Success: The Thinking and Management Styles of Women and Men Business Owners.* Washington, D.C.: National Foundation for Women Business Owners, 1994.

National Foundation for Women Business Owners. *Philanthropy Among Business Women of Achievement.* Washington, D.C.: National Foundation for Women Business Owners, 1999.

National Foundation for Women Business Owners. *Leaders in Business and Community: The Philanthropic Contributions of Women and Men Business Owners.* Washington, D.C.: National Foundation for Women Business Owners, 2000.

National Foundation for Women Business Owners. "Key Facts." 2001. [www.nfwbo.org/key.html].

Newton, H. *Newton's Telecom Dictionary: The Authoritative Resource for Telecommunications, Networking, the Internet, and Information Technology.* (18th ed.) Jericho, N.Y.: CMP Books, 2002.

Newman, D. *Opening Doors: Pathways to Diverse Donors.* Washington, D.C.: Council on Foundations, 2002.

Nichols, J. *Changing Demographics: Fund Raising in the 1990s.* Chicago: Precept Press, 1990.

O'Neill, M. "Fund Raising as an Ethical Act," *Advancing Philanthropy*, 1993, *1*, 30–35.

Payton, R. L. *Philanthropy: Voluntary Action for the Public Good.* New York: American Council on Education/Macmillan, 1988.

Peter D. Hart Research Associates. "Toward 2000 and Beyond: Charitable and Social Change Giving in the New Millennium, Part 2. A Craver, Mathews, Smith & Company Donor Study." *Fund Raising Management*, June 1999, pp. 24–28.

Pribbenow, P. P. "Love and Work: Rethinking Our Models of Profession." In P. P. Pribbenow (ed.), *Serving the Public Trust: Insights into Fundraising Research and Practice.* New Directions for Philanthropic Fundraising, no. 26. San Francisco: Jossey-Bass, 2000.

Pribbenow, P. P. "Pursuing Accountability: Organizational Integrity, the Advancement Profession, and Public Service." *CASE International Journal of Educational Advancement*, 2001, *1*, 197–208.

Prince, R. A., and File, K. M. *The Seven Faces of Philanthropy: A New Approach to Cultivating Major Donors.* San Francisco: Jossey-Bass, 1994.

Public Management Institute. *How to Build a Big Endowment.* San Francisco: Public Management Institute, 1980.

Reis, T. K., and Clohesy, S. J. "Unleashing New Resources and Entrepreneurship for the Common Good: A Philanthropic Renaissance." In E. R. Tempel (ed.), *Understanding Donor Dynamics: The Organizational Side of Charitable Giving.* New Directions for Philanthropic Fundraising, no. 32. San Francisco: Jossey-Bass, 2001.

Rooney, P. M., and Tempel, E. R. "Repeal of the Estate Tax and Its Impact on Philanthropy." *Nonprofit Management and Leadership*, 2001, *12*, 193–211.

Rosso, H. A. "A Philosophy of Fund Raising." In H. A. Rosso and Associates, *Achieving Excellence in Fund Raising: A Comprehensive Guide to the Principles, Strategies, and Methods.* San Francisco: Jossey-Bass, 1991a.

Rosso, H. A. "The Trustee's Role in Fund Raising." In H. A. Rosso and Associates, *Achieving Excellence in Fund Raising: A Comprehensive Guide to the Principles, Strategies, and Methods.* San Francisco: Jossey-Bass, 1991b.

Rosso, H. A. *Rosso on Fund Raising: Lessons from a Master's Lifetime Experience.* San Francisco: Jossey-Bass, 1996.

Rosso, H. A., and Associates. *Achieving Excellence in Fund Raising: A Comprehensive Guide to the Principles, Strategies, and Methods.* San Francisco: Jossey-Bass, 1991.

Salamon, L. M., Anheier, H. K., List, R., Toepler, S., Sokolowski, S. W., and Associates, *Global Civil Society: Dimensions of the Nonprofit Sector.* Baltimore: Center for Civil Society Studies, Johns Hopkins University, 1999.

Schervish, P. G. "Inclination, Obligation, and Association: What We Know and What We Need to Learn About Donor Motivation." In D. F. Burlingame (ed.), *Critical Issues in Fund Raising* (New York: Wiley, 1997).

Schervish, P. G. "The New Philanthropy: Investing in Tomorrow." *Success,* July-Aug. 2000a, pp. 32–35.

Schervish, P. G. "The Spiritual Horizons of Philanthropy: New Directions for Money and Motives." In E. R. Tempel and D. F. Burlingame (eds.), *Understanding the Needs of Donors: The Supply Side of Charitable Giving.* New Directions for Philanthropic Fundraising, no. 29. San Francisco: Jossey-Bass, 2000b.

Schervish, P. G., and O'Herlihy, M.A. *The Spiritual Secret of Wealth: The Inner Dynamics by Which Fortune Engenders Care.* Boston: Boston College, 2001.

Schwarzwalder, K. "Focus on the Future: A Partnership of Women in the Campaign to Renovate the YWCA of Columbus, Ohio." In J. C. Conry (ed.), *Women as Fundraisers: Their Experience in and Influence on an Emerging Profession.* New Directions for Philanthropic Fundraising, no. 19. San Francisco: Jossey-Bass, 1998.

Schwinn, E., and Sommerfield, M. "Revolving-Door Dilemma." *Chronicle of Philanthropy,* Apr. 18, 2002, pp. 39–42.

Seiler, T. L. *Developing Your Case for Support.* San Francisco: Jossey-Bass, 2001.

Sharpe, R. F., Sr. *Planned Giving Simplified: The Gift, the Giver, and the Gift Planner.* Alexandria, Va.: Association of Fundraising Professionals, 1999.

Shaw, S. C., and Taylor, M. A. *Reinventing Fundraising: Realizing the Potential of Women's Philanthropy.* San Francisco: Jossey-Bass, 1995.

Shaw-Hardy, S. C. *Creating a Women's Giving Circle.* Rochester, Mich.: Women's Philanthropy Institute, 2000.

Smith, B. S., Shue, S., Vest, J. L., and Villarreal, J. *Philanthropy in Communities of Color.* Bloomington: Indiana University Press, 1999.

Smith, C. "The New Corporate Philanthropy." *Harvard Business Review,* May-June 1994, pp. 105–116.

Smith, H. W. "If Not Corporate Philanthropy, Then What?" *New York Law School Law Review,* 1997, *41,* 757–770.

Stein, M., and Osten, M. "72 Reasons Why E-Mail Is Still the Killer App!" *DotOrg Newsletter #4,* Aug. 9, 2001. [http://www.dotorgmedia.org/Publications/Publications.cfm?ID = 52&c = 18].

Sterling, C. "Gender Differences in Planned Giving: The Way Women Give." *Planned Giving Today,* Dec. 2000, p. 1.

Streisand, B. "The New Philanthropy." *U.S. News & World Report,* June 11, 2001, pp. 40–42.

Sturtevant, W. T. *The Artful Journey: Cultivating and Soliciting the Major Gift.* Chicago: Bonus Books, 1997.

Taylor, M. A. *Study on Women's Philanthropy for Health Care: St. Luke's Medical Center, Milwaukee.* Madison, Wis.: Women's Philanthropy Institute, 1995.

Tempel, E. R. "Donor Interests: Time for New Approaches." *NonProfit Times,* July 2001, pp. 1–2.

Tempel, E. R., and Beem, M. J. "The State of the Profession." In M. Worth (ed.), *New Strategies for Educational Fund Raising.* Washington, D.C.: American Council on Education/Greenwood, 2002.

The Fund Raising School. *Developing Leadership for Major Gifts Workbook,* Indianapolis, Ind.: The Fund Raising School, 2000.

The Fund Raising School. *Principles and Techniques of Fund Raising.* 2002b edition. Indianapolis, Ind.: The Center on Philanthropy at Indiana University, 2002.

Thompson, A. I., and Kaminski, A. R. *Women and Philanthropy: A National Agenda.* Madison: Center for Women and Philanthropy, University of Wisconsin, 1993.

Tocqueville, A. de. *Democracy in America* (R. D. Heffner, ed.). New York: New American Library, 1956. (Originally published 1835.)

UCLA Foundation. *The UCLA Women and Philanthropy Focus Groups.* Los Angeles: UCLA Foundation, 1992.

United Way of America. *Measuring Program Outcomes: A Practical Approach.* Alexandria, Va.: United Way of America, 1996.

United Way of America. *Community Leaders Conference Workbook.* Alexandria, Va.: United Way of America, 2001.

United Way of the Bay Area. "Frequently Asked Questions." Dec. 2001. [http://www.theunitedway.org/faqs.html#Aramony].

Venture for Fund Raising. *Survey on Giving, 2001.* Manila, Philippines: Venture for Fund Raising, 2001.

Wagner, L. "The Road Least Traveled: Board Roles in Fundraising." In T. L. Seiler and K. S. Grace (eds.), *Achieving Trustee Involvement in Fundraising.* New Directions for Philanthropic Fundraising, no. 4. San Francisco: Jossey-Bass, 1994.

Wagner, L. *Careers in Fundraising.* New York: Wiley, 2001.

Wagner, L., and Hall-Russell, C. "The Effectiveness of Fundraising Training in Hispanic Religious Organizations. In L. Wagner and A. F. Deck (eds.), *Hispanic Philanthropy: Exploring the Factors That Influence Giving and Asking.* New Directions for Philanthropic Fundraising, no. 24. San Francisco: Jossey-Bass, 1999.

Warwick, M. *The Five Strategies for Fundraising Success.* San Francisco: Jossey-Bass, 2000.

Warwick, M. *How to Write Successful Fundraising Letters.* (rev. ed.) San Francisco: Jossey-Bass, 2001.

Waterman, R. *The Renewal Factor: How the Best Get and Keep the Competitive Edge.* New York: Bantam Books, 1985.

Weeden, C. *Corporate Social Investing.* San Francisco: Berrett-Koehler, 1998.

Weisbrod, B. A. *The Nonprofit Economy.* Cambridge, Mass.: Harvard University Press, 1988.

Wilson, M. S., Hoppe, M. H., and Sayles, L. R. *Managing Across Cultures: A Learning Framework.* Greensboro, N.C.: Center for Creative Leadership, 1996.

Wisdom, P. E. "Another Look at Costs." In J. L. Fisher and G. H. Quehl (eds.), *The President and Fund Raising.* Washington, D.C.: American Council on Education, 1989.

Women's Funding Network. *Annual Report, 2000.* San Francisco: Women's Funding Network, 2001.

Women's Philanthropy Institute. *Rutgers University: Women in Philanthropy: Analysis of Focus Groups.* Rochester, Mich.: Women's Philanthropy Institute, 2001a.

Women's Philanthropy Institute. *Women and Philanthropy: Model Programs in Higher Education.* Rochester, Mich.: Women's Philanthropy Institute, 2001b.

INDEX

A

A. P. Smith Mfg. Co. v. Barlow, 178

AAFRC Trust for Philanthropy, xxi, xxii, xxiii, 12, 13, 31, 72, 139, 159, 178, 189, 482. *See also* American Association of Fund Raising Counsel (AAFRC)

Ability, 45, 164. *See also* LAI (linkage, ability, interest) principle

Academic programs, 10, 59, 471, 474–476

Accountability, 380–399; AFP on practices for, 436–438; broad, 8; and budgeting, 384–389; circle of, 397–398; comprehensive approach to, 398–399; to constituents, 33; demanded of nonprofit sector, 7–8, 39, 380; determining how to demonstrate, 381–384; and fulfillment of community needs, 395–397; gift reports for, 389–393; measuring performance results for, 393–395, 396; narrow, 8; "new" philanthropists demand for, 219–220; as stewardship, 435–436

Acknowledgment of gifts: in fund raising cycle, 24, 29; standard procedure for, 316; as stewardship, 433–435. *See also* Recognition

Active donors, direct mail to, 246

Addams, J., 201, 203

Adizes, I., 328

Advocacy: e-philanthropy for, 271–272; by governing board members, 343–344

Affinity groups, 472

African Americans: income and poverty status of, 230; involved in United Way of Central Indiana, 173; and philanthropy, 233–234; research findings on, as professional fund raisers, 461–462

Alliance for Nonprofit Management, 408, 472, 482

Altruistic model of corporate giving, 180

American Association of Fund Raising Counsel (AAFRC), 408, 438, 472, 482. *See also* AAFRC Trust for Philanthropy

Anderson, A., 423, 424

Andreasen, A. R., 32, 33

Anft, M., 227, 230

Anheier, H., 443

Annual fund, 71–88; calendar of activities for, 85; committee for, 86; consultants for, 401; effectiveness of solicitation methods for, 81–84; as element of integrated development plan, 67; gift range charts for, 74, 76–79; importance of, 72; integrating planned giving with, 152–153, 156; objectives of, 73; profiling and analyzing donor base in planning for, 79–81; summary of, 86–87; as type of fund raising program, 61, 62

Application service providers (ASPs), 281, 376–377